Debating the Middle Ages

Debating the Middle Ages:
Issues and Readings

Edited and introduced
by

Lester K. Little and Barbara H. Rosenwein

Blackwell
Publishing

350 Main Street, Malden, MA 02148-5020, USA
108 Cowley Road, Oxford OX4 1JF, UK
550 Swanston Street, Carlton, Victoria 3053, Australia

First published 1998 by Blackwell Publishing Ltd
Reprinted 2004

Library of Congress Cataloging-in-Publication Data

Debating the Middle Ages : issues and readings / edited and introduced
    by Lester K. Little and Barbara H. Rosenwein.
        p. cm.
    Includes bibliographical references and index.
    ISBN 1–57718–007–0. — ISBN 1–57718–008–9 (pbk.)
1. Middle Ages — History. I. Rosenwein, Barbara H. II. Little, Lester K.
D117.D43   1998
909´.1—dc21   97-32706
                                                         CIP

A catalogue record for this title is available from the British Library.

Set in 10 on 11.5 pt Ehrhardt
by Best-set Typesetter Ltd, Hong Kong
Printed and bound in the United Kingdom
by Athenaeum Press Ltd, Gateshead, Tyne & Wear

For further information on
Blackwell Publishing, visit our website:
http://www.blackwellpublishing.com

Contents

Editors' Acknowledgments

The editors wish to acknowledge with gratitude the many scholars, students, and editors who have helped to bring this book into being.

We thank the readers who commented on various versions of our introductions and choices of articles: Stuart Airlie, Allen Frantzen, Patrick Geary, Walter P. Simons, Mary Warnement, Max Withers, Chris Wickham, and a few who were anonymous.

We are beholden to the translators of articles from German, French, and Italian: Warren Brown, Louisa Burnham, Lella Gardini, and Valerie Ramseyer. If we changed some of their renderings, it is they who were the pioneers in sometimes dense verbal thickets. Our gratitude goes also to Cécile Treffort of Poitiers for supplying information about the capital that is shown in the cover illustration, as well as to John W. Baldwin of Johns Hopkins University and to Richard Lim of Smith College for their helpful responses to our queries.

Lastly we thank Tessa Harvey, who had the initial idea for this book. She has nourished its metamorphoses and tempered its exuberance.

Acknowledgments to Sources

The editors and publishers wish to thank the following for permission to use copyright material: *Archaeologia Polona* and the author for Walter Pohl, "Conceptions of Ethnicity in Early Medieval Studies," *Archaeologia Polona* 29 (1991): 39–49; Pierre Bonnassie for extracts from Pierre Bonnassie, *La Catalogne du milieu du Xe à la fin du XIe siècle*, vol. II (1975), pp. 575–99, 609–10; Monique Bourin for an extract from Monique Bourin and Robert Durand, *Vivre au village au moyen age: les solidarités paysannes du 11e au 13e siècles* (Messidor/Temps Actuel) (1984), pp. 139–53; Cambridge University Press for R. I. Moore, "Literacy and the Making of Heresy, *c.*1000–1150," in P. Biller and A. Hudson, eds, *Heresy and Literacy 1000–1530* (1994), pp. 19–37; Fredric Cheyette for Fredric Cheyette, "Suum cuique tribuere," *French Historical Studies* 6 (1969/70): 287–99; Gerald Duckworth & Co. Ltd with Cornell University Press for extracts from Richard Hodges and David Whitehouse, *Mohammed, Charlemagne, and the Origins of Europe: Archaeology and the Pirenne Thesis* (1983), pp. 14–15, 23–53. Copyright © 1983 by Richard Hodges and David Whitehouse; the Ecclesiastical History Society for Janet Nelson, "Queens as Jezebels: the Careers of Brunhild and Balthild in Merovingian History," originally published in *Medieval Women: Essays Dedicated and Presented to Professor Rosalin M.T. Hill*, Studies in Church History, Subsidia, vol. 1 (Oxford: Blackwell, 1978), pp. 31–77. Copyright © The Ecclesiastical History Society 1978; the Ecole française de Rome for Sofia Boesch Gajano, "Uso e abuso del miracolo nella cultura altomedioevale," in *Les fonctions des saints dans le monde occidental* (1991), pp. 105–22; Librairie Arthème Fayard for extracts from Dominique Bathélemy, *La société dans le comté de Vendôme de l'an Mil au XIVe siècle* (1993), pp. 333–4, 349–61, 363–4. Copyright © Librairie Arthème Fayard 1993; Oxford University Press for Alexander Murray, "Missionaries and Magic in Dark-Age Europe," *Past and Present* 139 (1992): 186–205; Princeton University Press for an extract from Walter Goffart, *Barbarians and Romans, AD 418–584: The Techniques of Accommodation* (1980), pp. 3–39. Copyright © 1980 by Princeton University Press; *Revue Belge de Philologie et d'Histoire* for Ian Wood, "Gregory of Tours and Clovis," *Revue Belge de Philologie et d'Histoire* 63 (1985): 249–72; the Royal Historical Society for Pauline Stafford, "Women and the Norman Conquest," *Transactions of the Royal Historical Society*, 6th ser. 4 (1994): 221–49; the University of California Press for an extract from Caroline W. Bynum, *Holy Feast and Holy Fast: The Religious Significance of Food to Medieval Women* (1987), pp. 282–94. Copyright © 1987 The Regents of the University of California; the University of Chicago Press for Marie-Dominique Chenu, "The Evangelical Awakening," in *Nature, Man and Society in the Twelfth Century: Essays on New Theological Perspectives in the Latin West*, trans. Jerome Taylor and Lester K. Little (1968), pp. 239–69; and Christiane Klapisch-Zuber, "The 'Cruel Mother': Maternity, Widowhood, and Dowry in Florence in the Four-teenth and Fifteenth Centuries," in *Women, Family, and Ritual in Renaissance Italy*, trans.

Lydia Cochrane (1985), pp. 117–31; the University of Minnesota Press for Susan Mosher Stuard, "Burdens of Matrimony: Husbanding and Gender in Medieval Italy," in *Medieval Masculinities: Regarding Men in the Middle Ages*, Medieval Cultures Series, vol. 7 (1994), pp. 61–72; Chris Wickham for "La chute de Rome n'aura pas lieu," *Le Moyen Age* 99 (1983): 107–26; Wissenschaftliche Buchgesellschaft for an extract from Gerd Althoff, *Verwandte, Freunde und Getreue: Zum politischen Stellenwert der Gruppenbindungen im früheren Mittelalter* (1990), pp. 88–119. Copyright © 1990 Wissenschaftliche Buchgesellschaft, Darmstadt.

Every effort has been made to trace the copyright holders, but if any have been inadvertently overlooked the publishers will be pleased to make the necessary arrangement at the first opportunity.

A Note on Format

Some of the materials published here are excerpted from longer articles or books, and so their original note numbers make little sense. This problem has been handled in the following way.

In the text the footnotes or endnotes have been renumbered, beginning with 1. However, the original note number has been retained, following a full point, in the notes. Thus, for example, in chapter 14, "Women and the Norman Conquest," the first note is[1] in the text but[1.20] in the notes because it was originally note[20]. This may be especially useful to readers when it comes to translated materials, as they may find the original passage more easily by tracing it through the original note number.

Other changes have also been made, even (often) in cases where complete articles have been used. Indeed, nearly all the studies republished required some interventions by the editors, either to explain terms that students might not ordinarily be familiar with, or to translate passages that have been left in their original language (very often, Latin). In most cases, such passages in the original have been followed by English translations in brackets. In some instances, however, where the passages are extensive, they have been moved to the notes, and English has been substituted for them in the text.

Abbreviations

AASS	*Acta Sanctorum quotquot toto orbe coluntur*, ed. Joannus Bollandus et al., 66 vols (Venice, 1734–70 and in later editions)
AAWL	*Abhandlungen der Akademie der Wissenschaften und der Literatur*
AJ	*Ampleforth Journal*
BS	*Biblioteca Sanctorum*, 12 vols (Rome, 1961–9)
CCM	*Cahiers de Civilisation Médiévale*
CCSL	*Corpus Christianorum, Series Latina*
CV	C. Métais, *Chartes vendômoises* (Vendôme, 1905)
GAbt	*Germanistische Abteilung*
HZ	*Historische Zeitschrift*
JRS	*Journal of Roman Studies*
MB	C. Métais, *Marmoutier. Cartulaire blésois* (Blois, 1889–91)
MD	E. Mabille, *Cartulaire de Marmoutier pour le Dunois* (Châteaudun, 1874)
MGH	*Monumenta Germaniae Historica*
	AA *Auctores antiquissimi*
	DD *Diplomata*
	Epp. *Epistolae*
	SS *Scriptores*
	SSrG *Scriptores rerum Germanicarum*
	SSrL *Scriptores rerum Langobardicarum*
	SSrM/SRM *Scriptores rerum Merovingicarum*
MStn	*Mittelalterliche Studien*
MV	A. de Trémault, *Cartulaire vendômois de Marmoutier* (Vendôme, 1893)
NA	*Neues Archiv*
PL	*Patrologiae Cursus Completus, Series Latina, ed. J.-P. Migne, 161 vols (Paris, 1841–66)*
PP	*Past and Present*
RH	*Revue historique*
SC	Sources chrétiennes
SM	A. Salmon, *Le livre des serfs de Marmoutier* (Tours, 1864)
Spoleto	*Settimane di Studio sull'alto medioevo*, Centro sull'alto medioevo, Spoleto
TRHS	*Transactions of the Royal Historical Society*
TV	C. Métais, *Cartulaire . . . de la Trinité de Vendôme* (Paris, 1893–5)
ZRG	*Zeitschrift der Savigny-Stiftung für Rechtsgeschichte*

Introduction

The Middle Ages aren't what they used to be. When the term was coined in the sixteenth century, it was not only in Latin but also in the singular (*medium aevum*), and it referred to a thousand-year-long period, the Middle Age, largely undifferentiated, separating Classical Antiquity from the Renaissance. Moreover, this period bore the stigma of a value-judgment so negative that its adjectival form "medieval" came to be used by some as a synonym for "dark," "ignorant," "barbaric," or the like.

Knowledge of this field and awareness of the vast differences it embraced so advanced in the late nineteenth and early twentieth centuries that a convention arose, at least among American specialists, by which it was divided into three parts: the Early, the High, and the Late Middle Ages. Actually they picked up this clumsy mixture of metaphors, along with their preferred method of studying this time-period, from German scholars, who divided the period into the *Früh*-(Early), *Hoch*-(High), and *Spätmittelalter* (Late Middle Ages). In the Romance languages, a variant of this convention arose, for there the subdivisions are only two instead of three, and the terms employed, while corresponding roughly to what the Germans and Americans mean by "early" and "late," are expressed in those languages, respectively, by the words for "high" and "low." The notion behind this is that when one goes back in time, one goes up into the past, and on the return trip comes down toward the present. Thus in French and Italian and so on, the Early Middle Ages are called *le haut moyen-âge*, *l'altomedioevo*, etc.; the Late Middle Ages, *le bas moyen-âge*, *il basso medioevo*, etc. As these languages lack a specific term for the middle of the Middle Ages, writers who use them occasionally resort to the general term "Middle Ages" to denote just that middle part.

Whatever the language or the convention, all such terms serve as far more than mere subdivisions, for they are, or at least for many persons once were, laden with values. The most obviously value-laden expression among them is "High Middle Ages." While historians have set many different chronological boundaries for this period, they have almost uniformly included in it the twelfth and thirteenth centuries. And what made these centuries "high" were the many experiences and developments that took place during them that historians both looked upon favorably and considered to be quintessentially "medieval." Those two centuries mark the age of the Gothic cathedral, the Crusades, the origins of universities and parliamentary institutions, the heyday of the papacy, the emergence of vernacular literature, the integration of Aristotelian philosophy into Christian theology, the very beginnings of scientific investigation, the travels of Marco Polo, and so on; the list could be many times longer. Perhaps it will suffice to point out that one noted historian, Charles Homer Haskins, in reacting to the barrage of claims about important cultural beginnings that took place during the Renaissance, published a book in 1927 entitled *The Renaissance of the*

Twelfth Century, and that back in 1907 a Jesuit historian, James Joseph Walsh, published *The Thirteenth, Greatest of Centuries*.

The time-period designated as the "Late Middle Ages" is problematic because one of the centuries it embraces, the fifteenth, is invariably also claimed by surveyors staking out the boundaries of the Renaissance; these have also on occasion been known to dispute part or all of the fourteenth century. Specialists in these centuries have long denied this problem by fixing in their minds that certain things and phenomena are "medieval" while others belong to the "Renaissance," without permitting these categories to get in each other's way, or allowing this coexistence to alter their preconceived notions of either the "Middle Ages" or the "Renaissance." The main criterion for placement in either category was age; that which seemed old and decadent belonged in the "Late Medieval" bin, while the new and innovative belonged in that of the Renaissance. The papacy, scholastic theology, feudal warfare, and flagellation were placed in the former, while classicizing taste, tyrannical princely government, and geometric perspective went in the latter. Two noted books that deal with precisely this period, the fourteenth and fifteenth centuries, Johann Huizinga's *The Waning of the Middle Age* (1919) and Edward P. Cheney's *The Dawn of a New Era* (1936), are every bit as different in both subject matter and approach as their titles suggest.

The "Early Middle Ages" as a historical period is problematic in ways quite different from these other two. The poor cousin in this historiographical family, it is very long, stretching roughly from 500 to 1100, and rarely has anyone tried to lay claim to some part of it for another period. It lacks a clear identity of its own, having become a sort of "Middle Age" itself, stuck between the Roman imperial period and the "High Middle Ages," and clearly not up to the standards of either. The paradigm of decline from previously held heights became fixed in the western imagination at the latest by Edward Gibbon in his *Decline and Fall of the Roman Empire* (1776–88). Gibbon and countless others accepted and perpetuated Roman notions of civilization and barbarism, and as civilization was for them equated with Roman culture, the Early Middle Ages could not fail to be seen as witnessing the collapse of civilization. Such a view is encapsulated in the title of a survey of the period from 476 to 918, *The Dark Ages*, by Charles Oman (first published in 1895 and with a sixth edition in 1923). The phrase "Dark Ages," however, while it has some currency in common speech, is rarely used by historians outside the British Isles.

As medieval history became an academic discipline in the late nineteenth century, and as the historian's craft became organized at about the same time as a profession, individual practitioners were encouraged to become specialists. Furthermore, the cult of science and the faith in scientific method then so strong obliged them to be rigorous in citing written evidence for all their assertions and conclusions. Just as they had to place chronological and geographical limits upon their research, they also came to specialize in certain subjects: constitutional history, political history, institutional history, economic history, and so on. Besides, the demands of doing research in these various subjects were such that they felt compelled to specialize in the study of particular kinds of sources: chronicles, charters, coroners' reports, papal letters, and so on. Over the course of a century, these new-style professionals, with their specialized areas and methods of expertise, have produced extraordinary results.

Yet however specialized and rigorously scientific these historians were, the premises and prejudices of their respective cultures nonetheless permeated much of their work. For example, most of these historians firmly believed in progress in human history, with regard not only to science and technology but also to morals and ethics. This belief was in turn bolstered by evolutionary theory, which encouraged people to see history in terms of ever greater improvement and refinement. Thus in some cases history itself became the story of the progress of liberty, a view associated especially with the Italian philosopher–statesman Benedetto Croce (1866–1952). Other historians were motivated by nationalism, which in one European country after another supplied the driving force behind the quest for origins, especially in the Middle Ages, by means of a powerful mix of political ideology with state funds for the support of research institutes and publications. The case of Belgium is instructive. The fact that it was a political expedient created by diplomats in 1815 after the Napoleonic wars did not deter, quite the contrary, the Belgian historian Henri Pirenne from producing a seven-volume *Histoire de Belgique*, published between 1899 and 1932, much of it devoted to the medieval period.

The same tendency was present in the history of modern institutions, which historians projected into the remote past in their continuing search for origins. Much of value came from this type of investigation, to mention only the vast store of political and constitutional history that was uncovered by research into the origins of parliamentary institutions. Or take the case, a favorite of academics, of universities. We learned that schools and universities as we know them go back to the twelfth century, and that the whole organization of faculties, courses, lectures, examinations, and degrees dates from that time, just as the student subculture most of us have experienced does. And the educational system itself, a system based on the raising of critical questions about what we think we know, and on the belief that by doing so we can go further and learn more, even more than the very teachers who guided us to the edge of the unknown know, also dates from that time. One could say much the same concerning banks and systems of credit, courts and legal procedures, and many other fundamental institutional features of modern society.

When our predecessors looked further back than the twelfth century for universities, they found none. Neither did they find banks or credit mechanisms, nor institutional safekeeping of wealth or institutional investment. In fact, they found very little money in circulation. So historians in the early decades of this century could identify well with what they thought of as the High Middle Ages, but not with the Early Middle Ages. They assumed that the earlier period, found lacking in universities, must have had no higher learning; as it was lacking in banks and currency, it had no rational economy; and as it was lacking well-functioning courts backed up by powerful states, it was thought to be lawless or chaotic. It is little wonder that these centuries appeared to them to constitute a dark age.

Despite the radically different approaches taken by some historians as early as the 1920s, most notably Marc Bloch, who with Lucien Febvre founded the *Annales d'histoire économique et sociale* in 1929, with the stated goal of integrating the theories and methods of the social sciences into historical studies, the historiographical situation described in the preceding paragraphs was still very much the case until the 1960s, when it began to change dramatically. By approaching early medieval society in the manner of an ethnographic observer, a historian would not look for banks or letters of credit (and, when not finding them, declare this a society without economic organization), but rather take note of how the people survived, of how they made their living, and declare that to be their economy. Perhaps the latter will be seen as operating at subsistence level, and involving the exchange of gifts more than the circulation of coins, but whatever the investigator observed of these matters constitutes, for us, their economic organization. Similarly, the historian should not set out to look for recognizable educational institutions, but instead observe without prejudice how the young are brought up, socialized, and prepared to take their places as adults; or not to look for courts and lawyers, but to observe how people resolved disputes; finally, and most important, not to treat these areas of human endeavor as separate entities, but as parts of an integrated cultural whole. One major result of these developments has been to make the Early Middle Ages understandable and accessible in ways that they were not before. Indeed, there has been a notable shift of interest on the part of historians to this previously impenetrable period.

In yet another shift, one even more recent, some medieval historians (especially in the United States) have taken seriously the concerns represented by postmodern critical theory. They have problematized medieval texts, pointing to the ways in which literary productions and archival documents alike portray not "reality" but constructed and self-interested representations of the world, its actors, and its meaning. Thus Gabrielle M. Spiegel, for example, suggests that history is a "reading" of the structures, language uses, metaphors, and other discursive practices of texts.[1]

There have been, in short, many sorts of changes in medieval historiography, far more than we were able to include in this volume. Rather than offer a brief sampling of each new tendency we could identify, we agreed that historical debate is interesting only if explored in some depth, and so we sought to define a few areas (in the end we settled on four) marked in the past quarter-century by intense investigation and discussion, and to reproduce in the limited space available a few outstanding examples from each. We considered including sections on the strategies and tools of early medieval governance, on the nobility and peasantry in the later Middle Ages, on minorities and others "on the margin," on regional studies, and on the history of literacy, perception, and "mental tools."

The four we chose: the fate of Rome's western provinces, feudalism and its alternatives, gender, and religion and society, seemed to us the best combination for maximizing the inclusion of seminal work and intense debate. For instance, the chapter on feudalism does touch on some of the issues of early medieval governance; it includes translations from two regional studies; and it has a selection on the peasantry, though not in the later Middle Ages. The history of minorities is to some extent represented by one essay looking at the meaning of ethnicity and by another on the idea of heresy. This latter essay also deals with the history of literacy and perception. We wanted our choices to reflect, also, the international character of the field, for example, by avoiding any topic dominated by one national historiography. As it turns out, though, gender studies have by and large been dominated by English-speaking scholars. Yet it would be unthinkable to issue just now a book on current debates in medieval history without a section devoted to gender, which engages the commitments of researchers and readers as few other topics can. One last criterion we thought critical: that none of the issues we selected be regarded as settled; indeed, all four display a most promising vitality.

Thus the history of the European Middle Ages is no longer what it used to be. The purpose of this book is to demonstrate in detail some of the more significant ways in which it has recently changed and why – since history will always be a debate – it will continue to do so.

---

[1] Gabrielle M. Spiegel, *The Past as Text: The Theory and Practice of Medieval Historiography* (Baltimore: Johns Hopkins University Press, 1997).

Part I The Fate of Rome's Western Provinces

Part I The Fate of Rome's Western Provinces

By his own account, rendered in two meticulously crafted versions, Edward Gibbon conceived the plan for his grandiose historical work, *The Decline and Fall of the Roman Empire*, as he sat amid ancient ruins in Rome in 1764. With Gibbon's wit and powers of analysis, the collapse of one of history's greatest political and military structures made for an exciting tale of change, with a full quota of battles and other events, as well as of colorful military and political figures. And yet when a group of scholars met at the University of California at Los Angeles in 1964 to reflect on "Gibbon's problem after two centuries," the role given to events and personalities was considerably reduced and the publication that emerged from their colloquium was called *The Transformation of the Roman World*, a title equally suggestive of continuity as of change. Lynn White, the group's convener, observed that modern western scholars were less parochial and less class-bound than Gibbon, less inclined to identify with the ancient Romans than Gibbon, and less persuaded than he that Antiquity came to an abrupt end.[1]

This tendency toward a greater appreciation of historical continuity fostered a breakthrough in 1971 by Peter Brown, who encouraged readers of his book, *The World of Late Antiquity, AD 150–750*, to think of the period embraced by the later Roman Empire and the Early Middle Ages in an entirely new way. "It is only too easy to write about the Late Antique world as if it were merely a melancholy tale of 'Decline and Fall.'" Instead, Brown argued, it is an age that should be approached for its astounding new beginnings, for discovering why Europe became Christian and why the Near East became Muslim. Freed from the historiographical restraints of seeing only decline from past heights, we are better able to appreciate "the 'contemporary' quality of the new, abstract art of the age," as well as the modern sensibilities of some of its writers.[2]

In recent decades, historians have moved far beyond the "melancholy tale." Their work has blurred some of the sharp and confidently defended boundaries of the past, boundaries between Romans and barbarians, between one tribe and another, between pagans and Christians and, indeed, between late Roman history and early medieval history. Here we will look at four areas of debate concerning Rome's western provinces that have emerged in the recent work of historians: ethnogenesis of the new peoples, accommodation between Romans and the new peoples, archaeology and history, and conversion of the new peoples to Christianity.

[1] *The Transformation of the Roman World: Gibbon's Problem after Two Centuries*, ed. Lynn White, Jr (Berkeley: University of California Press, 1966), pp. 295–301.
[2] Peter Brown, *The World of Late Antiquity, AD 150–750* (London: Thames & Hudson, 1971), p. 7.

Ethnogenesis of the New Peoples

"Many books and historical atlases contain a map purporting to show the tracks of the barbarian invaders, typically from Scandinavia to Spain and North Africa or from Central Asia to the centre of Gaul." Here the Canadian historian Walter Goffart evoked the common experience of everyone who has read of the coming of the Germanic tribes into Roman territory, whether in terms of invasion or migration, with those familiar maps that reduce this complex phenomenon to an immediately comprehensible graphic representation. Goffart analyzed the risks of such reduction:

> In most instances, as many as five hundred years of migration, real and supposed, are plotted on a single geographical background. By a mere glance at the arrows boldly sweeping from every direction through the Roman frontiers and provinces, the impression is gained that no empire could withstand such pressure.

Besides the maps, the accompanying narratives, with their rhetoric of waves, tides, and floods, came under Goffart's scrutiny.

> The maps and metaphors reflect the desire of modern historians to look upon the barbarian invasions as a purposive movement of upwardly mobile Teutons or as an irresistible force of nature – or both. Hardly anything has been done more to obscure the barbarian question than the talk and images of wandering peoples tirelessly battering down the Roman frontiers and flooding into the empire.[3]

The first fault in such maps concerns the very integrity of those tribes through time. Once a Lombard, always a Lombard? And only a Lombard? What makes a Frank a Frank? And are the Vandals at the head of the arrow on the map of Africa in the year 500 truly descendants of those Vandals at the tail of the arrow near the Baltic Sea four centuries before? The argument that the peoples of the Germanic successor-kingdoms in the western parts of the old Roman Empire were not the heirs of an unbroken genetic line reaching back through the centuries to their pre-migration days was made by a German scholar, Reinhard Wenskus, in a book on tribal formation in 1961.[4] In the view of Wenskus, they were instead heirs of loose and shifting amalgams of peoples gathered in varying circumstances at various times.

The major study of one tribal formation in this vein is a history of the Goths published by an Austrian historian, Herwig Wolfram, in 1979.[5] Through a painstaking examination and assessment of literary, linguistic, archaeological, and other kinds of evidence, Wolfram reconstructed the ethnogenesis of the Goths. "Ethnogenesis," he wrote, "is not a matter of 'blood' even though the Anglo–Saxons (in England) said of the Old Saxons (back in Germany): 'We are of the same bones and blood,' but rather a matter of situational historical occurrences."[6] In his study of the Goths, he found ethnic definitions especially fluid in times of migration, for any capable fighting men who could bring benefit to the army gained acceptance and status, regardless of ethnic or social background. And once they were within

[3] Walter Goffart, "Rome, Constantinople, and the Barbarians," *American Historical Review* 86 (1981): 275–306, the passage quoted at 283–4.
[4] Reinhard Wenskus, *Stammesbildung und Verfassung. Das Werden der frühmittelalterlichen Gentes* (Cologne: Böhlau, 1961).
[5] Herwig Wolfram, *History of the Goths*, trans. Thomas J. Dunlop (Berkeley: University of California Press, 1988).
[6] *Typen der Ethnogenese unter besonderer Berücksichtigung der Bayern*, 2 vols (Vienna, 1990); vol. 1, ed. Herwig Wolfram and Walter Pohl, from the introduction by Wolfram, p. 30.

the Roman Empire, "the polyethnic structure of the Gothic peoples remained intact." This was equally true of the Gothic army that settled in southern Gaul in 418 and of the Gothic kingdom of Italy under Theodoric the Great.[7] It should be added that this book does contain maps, and these have arrows; but the maps are six in number, and each serves carefully restricted geographical and chronological purposes.

Wolfram's book has served as a model for other scholars, not least his disciple Walter Pohl, a specialist on the Avars and Bulgars. In 1990 Wolfram and Pohl edited a large collection of essays that includes studies on the Lombards, the Burgundians, and the Basques.[8] In 1991, Pohl published a brief article that synthesizes many of the main findings of Wolfram and others on ethnogenesis (chapter 1).[9] Both Wolfram and Pohl have since turned to the genre known as *origo gentis*, literally, "origins of the people," referring to those mythical accounts set down for each of the major tribes, beginning with the Goths in the sixth century, i.e. well after they had settled in the West.[10] These accounts took elements of oral tradition, but purified them of the disturbing complications of polyethnicity, so as to give the tribe or people the illusion of a divine origin and its current leaders that of a royal genealogy stretching back to remote times. In the light of such studies, Ian Wood has re-examined the seventh-century fabrication of a Trojan origin for the Franks.[11] It is a testimony to the success and staying-power of these *origines gentium* that it has taken scholars such long, intensive investigation to reconstruct plausible ethnogeneses of the "peoples." Even today, most parts of the world have an abundant supply of ethnic myths, which serve strongly felt needs for group identity but which in many cases, as in the former Yugoslavia, also fuel murderous rivalries.

Accommodation Between Rome and the New Peoples

Gibbon left no doubt that the "decline and fall" was a tale in which barbarians were pitted against the civilized, and that the triumph of the former over the latter was a catastrophe. His view still had adherents in the 1940s, as shown by the terse assertion of the French historian André Piganiol in 1947: "Roman civilization did not die a natural death. It was murdered."[12] This assertion and others like it engendered much criticism, stimulating scholars to examine not just the identities and ethnic coherence of the new peoples, but also the conditions under which they entered Roman territory. Here we again encounter Walter Goffart, who in 1980 published an influential study of relations between Romans and barbarians in the fifth and sixth centuries, a study that bears the noteworthy subtitle *The Techniques of Accommodation*. Goffart set out to pursue the question of why the settlements of the Goths, Burgundians,

[7] *History of the Goths*, pp. 7–8.
[8] Cited above, n. 6.
[9] Chapter 1: Walter Pohl, "Conceptions of Ethnicity in Early Medieval Studies," *Archaeologia Polona* 29 (1991): 39–49.
[10] Herwig Wolfram, *"Origo et religio*. Ethnic Traditions and Literature in Early Medieval Texts," *Early Medieval Europe* 3 (1994): 19–38; Walter Pohl, "Tradition, Ethnogenese und literarische Gestaltung: eine Zwischenbilanz," in *Ethnogenese und Überlieferung: Angewandte Methoden der Frühmittelalterforschung*, ed. Karl Brunner and Brigitte Merta (Vienna: Oldenbourg, 1994), pp. 9–26.
[11] Ian N. Wood, "Defining the Franks: Frankish Origins in Early Medieval History," in *Concepts of National Identity in the Middle Ages*, ed. Simon Forde, Leslie Johnson, and Alan Murray (Leeds: Leeds University Press, 1995), pp. 47–57. For an excellent sketch of the main characteristics of works in this genre and a discussion of their political functions, see Susan Reynolds, "Medieval *Origines gentium* and the Community of the Realm," *History* 68 (1983): 375–90.
[12] André Piganiol, *L'Empire chrétien* (Paris: Presses Universitaires de France, 1947), p. 422.

and Lombards in Gaul and Italy were so uncontested. His study focused on the traditional practice of *hospitalitas*, an obligation imposed by the Roman state upon its citizens to billet soldiers. What Goffart argued was not that these Germanic newcomers were housed with Romans but that they were allowed, usually by explicit agreement with the imperial government, to settle in certain areas where they took responsibility for defense and the collection of taxes. In his view, this was for the most part a mutually satisfactory arrangement at the time, as well as one with long-term consequences, such as establishing a process whereby the new tax collectors became the new rulers. Goffart came to the conclusion that "the fall of the Western Roman Empire was an imaginative experiment that got a little out of hand." His statement of the problem and of the main lines of his argument are set out in his book's opening chapter: "The Barbarians in Late Antiquity and How They Were Accommodated in the West" (chapter 2).[13]

A French scholar, Jean Durliat, expressed high praise for Goffart's "revolutionary book" in a long article in 1988. He sought to extend the argument beyond the limits set and observed by Goffart. By making a parallel study of the Vandals, Durliat was able to argue that the kind of peaceful balance established by amicable agreement in the cases studied by Goffart was established, both in Spain and subsequently in Africa, under the utterly different circumstances of out-and-out conquest.[14] Durliat took the continuity theme to its furthest lengths (so far) in his study of public finances from the time of Diocletian to the generations after Charlemagne (284–888). Here he argued that no fundamental change in institutions–fiscal, administrative, military–took place over that 600-year period. This work drew fire from an English specialist on early medieval Italy, Chris Wickham, who published a review of it under the ironic title "The Fall of Rome Will Not Take Place" (chapter 3). Wickham contends that Durliat's readings of Frankish material in particular are mistaken, taking little account of changed circumstances and meanings, and so concludes that the book represents an enormous error of judgment.[15] Clearly, even the main questions surrounding the accommodation of the Germanic peoples within the Roman Empire remain open.

Archaeology and History

Only very rarely now do new written sources for the age of Late Antiquity come to light. "New" sources are more likely to be the material remains found by archaeologists. Their discipline, to be sure, was developed to investigate societies that left few or no written records. While the application of archaeology to the Middle Ages cannot be called a recent invention, by comparison with the 200-year-old tradition of classical archaeology its medieval counterpart has been a modest enterprise indeed. And yet a new interest is signaled by

[13] Chapter 2: Walter Goffart, *Barbarians and Romans, A.D. 418–584: The Techniques of Accommodation* (Princeton: Princeton University Press, 1980), pp. 3–39. In a review in *Speculum* 57 (1982): 885–6, Edward James, an English specialist on the Franks, expressed the worry that "the details, resting as they do on scanty and intransigent evidence, are extremely hypothetical and often established only by analogy with equally hypothetical conditions elsewhere."
[14] Jean Durliat, "Le salaire de la paix sociale dans les royaumes barbares (Ve-VIe siècles)," in *Anerkennung und Integration. Zu den wirtschaftlichen Grundlagen der Völkerwanderungszeit, 400–600*, ed. Herwig Wolfram and Andreas Schwarcz, Österreichische Akademie der Wissenschaften, Philosophisch-Historische Klasse, Denkschriften, 193 (Vienna, 1988), pp. 21–72.
[15] Chapter 3: Chris Wickham, "La chute de Rome n'aura pas lieu," *Le Moyen Age* 99 (1993): 107–26; cf. his "The Other Transition: From the Ancient World to Feudalism," *PP* 103 (1984): 3–36.

the founding of journals dedicated to medieval archaeology in the following languages: English (1957), French (1971), German (1973), and Italian (1974).[16]

A challenging thesis propounded by the Belgian economic historian Henri Pirenne in the 1920s and 1930s held that the Roman world survived the Germanic incursions in all its essentials, only to collapse under the pressure of the Arab conquests in the seventh century.[17] Although historians had refuted several of Pirenne's particular points in subsequent decades, in 1983 two English archaeologists, Richard Hodges and David Whitehouse, subjected them to a series of archaeological findings that almost all contradicted Pirenne's hypotheses. This they were able to do, they explained, because some archaeologists had been turning away not just from Antiquity but from art history, with its emphasis on unique, precious, and aesthetically refined artifacts.

> In the 1960s a number of archaeologists were greatly influenced by theoretical and methodological developments in anthropology, biology, geography and mathematics. The so-called "New Archaeologists" tried to introduce concepts from allied fields and then set out to discover the means of testing these hypotheses in the field. Their chief purpose was to turn archaeology into a science and in particular to search for patterns in human behaviour in the past.

Computers were essential for allowing them to analyze large quantities of data quickly, but what really separated them from their predecessors was "their premise that archaeology is the past tense of anthropology." In their chapter on "The Decline of the Western Empire" (chapter 4), Hodges and Whitehouse show what can be deduced from analysis of potsherds (pieces of broken pottery), coins, and glass objects.[18]

The move of the Franks and the Alemanni into Roman territory was far more gradual than that of some of the peoples mentioned earlier. Neither an invasion nor a migration, this move might be better thought of as an infiltration (although it was not done secretly) or a tricklein. It is barely perceptible in the written sources, and thus makes a fine case for turning to material evidence. Archaeologists have long concentrated on Frankish graves, finding not just their contents interesting but also the way they were arrayed in clearly defined rows. The graves do not reveal the carry-over through time and distance of old traditions, but rather Frankish adoption of Gallo-Roman traditions, and hence assimilation.[19] The archaeology of funerary practices has also been central to the history of the eventual takeover of much of Gaul by the Franks in the late fifth and the sixth centuries.[20] But it is settlement archaeology that deals principally with the landscape and the human presence within it at particular

---

[16] The journals are: *Medieval Archaeology, Archéologie médiévale, Zeitschrift für Archäologie des Mittelalters,* and *Archeologia medievale.*

[17] Henri Pirenne, *Medieval Cities,* trans. Frank D. Halsey (Princeton: Princeton University Press, 1925), pp. 3–26; and *Mohammed and Charlemagne,* trans. Bernard Miall (London: Allen & Unwin, 1939).

[18] Chapter 4: Richard Hodges and David Whitehouse, *Mohammed, Charlemagne and the Origins of Europe: Archaeology and the Pirenne Thesis* (Ithaca, NY: Cornell University Press, 1983), pp. 20, 23–53; passage cited from pp. 14–15.

[19] Bailey Young, "The Barbarian Funerary Tradition in Gaul in Light of the Archaeological Record: Considerations and Reconsiderations," in *Minorities and Barbarians in Medieval Life and Thought,* ed. Susan J. Ridyard and Robert G. Benson, Sewanee Mediaeval Studies, 7 (Sewanee, 1996), pp. 197–222.

[20] Patrick Périn and Laure-Charlotte Feffer, *Les Francs,* 2 vols (Paris: A. Colin, 1987), 1: 187–8, 192–201.

periods. By making use of aerial photography in concert with excavations, its practitioners have been able to delineate astonishing numbers of Roman villas and of the villages and houses of the Germanic settlers who subsequently occupied the land.[21]

Most archaeological investigations, in the new style or the old, are carried out on the basis of carefully developed hypotheses and plans. Yet the discipline has also been known to experience fortuitous discoveries, such as the bodies that occasionally emerge from northern European peat bogs. Some of these bodies have been found in northern Germany and Scandinavia, where some of the arrows on those maps of the Germanic migrations originate, and not a few date from roughly two millennia ago, around the time that Tacitus wrote the *Germania*. This Roman report on the Germans from the end of the first century AD, regarded by many as more reliable for what it reveals about Roman attitudes, has received corroboration on a few points from the discoveries of bog bodies. As archaeology necessarily deals with durable materials, we expect human remains to consist of skeletons, or at least bones. One exception discovered in the early 1990s is the body of a prehistoric man found preserved in ice in an Alpine pass. The bodies found in peat bogs are also exceptions, for such bogs have acidic qualities ideal for preserving flesh, in effect, by tanning. While the skeleton of a body placed in a bog will disintegrate, the skin and organs (and remains of the person's final meal) are preserved. The first recorded discovery of a bog body was in Ireland in 1781, while the first discovery that permitted modern on-site and laboratory investigation came in Denmark in 1952. These and other finds, mainly in Denmark, Germany, and the British Isles, were written about by Peter V. Glob in *The Bog People: Iron-Age Man Preserved*, first in Danish in 1965 and then in English translation in 1969. One such body has its hair tied in just such a Swabian knot as the one described by Tacitus, while other bodies have been found pinned down by forked branches with sharpened ends, just as Tacitus described the treatment meted out to certain criminals.[22] Here, it appears, is an ideal joining of material-history with text-history.

Conversion of the New Peoples to Christianity

As they had done with the migrations, scholars and teachers in presenting conversion have, over the years, resorted to maps, and with similar problems. Shading in a piece of territory with the color appropriate for Christianity raises at least as many problems as it clarifies. Which variety of Christianity? Did acceptance of Christianity necessarily mean a total renunciation of pagan beliefs and practices? And when we read that a king converted, are we to understand that all his followers also converted? Such questions are in line with a recent trend among historians of religion in the Middle Ages, who (and this will be spelled out below in Part IV, "Religion and Society") have shown far greater interest in what people of all sorts believed and how they practiced their religion than in the institutional history of the Church or the comings and goings of its hierarchy.

In 1978 Patrick Wormald called into question an exclusive and uncritical reliance upon Bede's *Ecclesiastical History of the English Nation* for understanding the conversion of the

---

[21]   For an excellent survey, see Jean Chapelot and Robert Fossier, *The Village and House in the Middle Ages*, trans. Henry Cleere (London: Batsford, 1985), pp. 12–13 for a glossary and pp. 15–128 on the early medieval period. For Ireland, i.e. territory with neither Roman nor Germanic settlements, see Nancy Edwards, *The Archaeology of Early Medieval Ireland* (Philadelphia: University of Pennsylvania Press, 1990).

[22]   Peter V. Glob, *The Bog People: Iron-Age Man Preserved*, trans. Rupert Bruce-Mitford (Ithaca, NY: Cornell University Press, 1969).

Anglo-Saxons to Christianity. Bede was writing in the 730s, more than a century and a quarter after the start of a long, complicated process, which, however, he presented in a tidy, triumphant narrative. Wormald's suggestion for gaining a more balanced appreciation of the religious outlook of the dominant class was for one to fold in with Bede a reading of the ideals of traditional warrior society from Anglo-Saxon poetry, particularly the *Beowulf* epic.[23] Similar doubts have been raised about over-reliance upon the account given by Gregory of Tours of the conversion of the Frankish king, Clovis. This indisputably important conversion is a foundation-stone of Frankish, not to say French, history. In the view of Gregory of Tours, writing a century after the fact, Clovis, a pagan king, departed from the practice of virtually all other Germanic leaders, who had embraced Arian Christianity, to become a Catholic instead; Clovis thereby sealed the Catholic destiny of France. Yet there are problems here, arrestingly stated by an American historian, Patrick Geary: "From what Clovis converted is not certain. ... To what he was converted is equally problematic."[24] Two scholars, Friedrich Prinz in Germany and Ian Wood in England, raised these doubts in 1985. Wood's article, "Gregory of Tours and Clovis" (chapter 5), untangles the polemical purposes of Gregory's historical writings from the more reliable sources from the time of Clovis. The result is a conversion account far less neat than Gregory would have had us believe.[25]

Turning now from the case of a lone, albeit immensely powerful, individual to the masses of people who inhabited the former western provinces of the Roman Empire, the Christianity that these people eventually professed was significantly different from both that of the Apostles and that of later generations, in the thirteenth century and beyond. In an attempt to characterize this early medieval form of Christianity and the process by which it came about, an Australian historian, Valerie Flint, published a large, synthetic study, *The Rise of Magic in Early Medieval Europe* (1991). Flint argues that the generally agreed-upon nature of the religion of the age did not result from mere pagan survival but came about by design. The Roman clergy, in her view, moved from an initial rejection of magic to tolerance, and from there to active rescue, preservation, and encouragement, for the express purpose of appealing to and gaining the adherence of the peoples newly settled in the West. Such a bold thesis has provoked considerable discussion, not least from Richard Kieckhefer, an American expert on medieval magic, who in a substantial review article finds fault with Flint's understanding of magic itself. In another such article, the Oxford historian Alexander Murray gives a sympathetic reading to Flint's thesis; he explores intriguing examples of the mutual borrowing of Christianity and pre-Christian magic; and he uses Flint's work as a base for suggesting a number of further explorations (chapter 6). "What is undeniable," says Murray,

---

[23] Patrick Wormald, "Bede, 'Beowulf' and the Conversion of the Anglo-Saxon Aristocracy," *British Archaeological Reports* 46 (1978): 32–95.
[24] Patrick J. Geary, *Before France and Germany: The Creation and Transformation of the Merovingian World* (New York: Oxford University Press, 1988), pp. 84–5.
[25] Friedrich Prinz, *Grundlagen und Anfänge: Deutschland bis 1056*, Neue Deutsche Geschichte, 1 (Munich: Beck, 1985), pp. 63–4. Chapter 5: Ian N. Wood, "Gregory of Tours and Clovis," *Revue belge de philologie et d'histoire* 63 (1985): 249–72. Cf. William M. Daly, "Clovis: How Barbaric, How Pagan?," *Speculum* 69 (1994): 619–64. The celebration of what was alleged to be the 1,500th anniversary of the baptism of Clovis in the fall of 1996 was the occasion for intense political debate in France, reported, for example, by Adam Gopnik in the *New Yorker* of October 7, 1996, pp. 44–53. The scholarly discussion is found in *Clovis: histoire et mémoire*, ed. Michel Rouche (Paris: Presses de l'Université de Paris, 1997).

whether we accept the present thesis in full or only in part, is that it remains a challenge, obliging the student of Dark-Age culture to confront baffling themes he might otherwise have brushed aside in all directions as "barbarous", "superstitious", or "credulous" – if not ignored altogether.[26]

The religious history of Late Antiquity, like the same age's political and ethnosocial history, remains open to explorers.

[26] Valerie I. J. Flint, *The Rise of Magic in Early Medieval Europe* (Princeton: Princeton University Press, 1991). Richard Kieckhefer, "The Specific Rationality of Medieval Magic," *American Historical Review* 99 (1994): 813–36; and chapter 6: Alexander Murray, "Missionaries and Magic in Dark-Age Europe," *PP* 136 (1992): 186–205.

1 Conceptions of Ethnicity in Early Medieval Studies

Walter Pohl

Recently, the problem of ethnicity has been one of the most widely discussed topics in early medieval studies. From the historian's perspective, the discussion on ethnicity owes its decisive impulse to Reinhard Wenskus (1961; his approach was elaborated in the monographs by Herwig Wolfram in 1979 and Walter Pohl in 1988). Traditional research has taken the meaning of the terms "people" or "tribe" for granted. In this view, a "people" is a racially and culturally highly homogeneous group sharing a common descendance and destiny, speaking the same language and living within one state. Peoples (and not individuals or social groups) were often seen as factors of continuity in a changing world, as the real subjects of history – almost immutable in its course, indeed more a natural than a historical phenomenon. Their fate was described using biological metaphors: birth, growth, flowering, and decay. This historical conception was rooted in the national movements of the nineteenth and twentieth centuries, and it had its share in encouraging all kinds of chauvinist ideologies. The idea that anything apart from one people living in one state was an anomaly (and should be corrected by all means) was, tacitly or explicitly, supported by many historians. Even today, after centuries of modern nationhood, the identity of people and state is the exception and not the rule, as the examples of Switzerland, Austria, the Germans, the Jews, the Arabs, the United States, or the Soviet Union show. Today's nationalist movements in many eastern European countries have rediscovered the nineteenth-century ideal of the homogeneous nation-state; it is sad to see that after so many tragedies it has brought about, some more seem to follow, and often in the name of history.

This situation explains the crucial importance of early medieval studies for the conceptions and preconceptions of ethnicity. Nations that for some reasons felt that they fell short of the "one people, one state" doctrine looked to those sombre times for a justification of their claims. The existence of Romans, Germans or Slavs in the fifth or seventh centuries became important arguments in an endless series of national struggles, culminating in the bizarre revival of the fair and reckless Germanic hero that lured an entire people into the Nazi Holocaust.

That the peoples in the Migration Period had little to do with those heroic (or sometimes brutish) clichés is now generally accepted among historians. But still, ethnic terms carry their load of emotions and preconceptions and tend to evoke misleading ideas. Even if we try to substitute "people" or "tribe" with the contemporary terms *ethnos* or *gens* for scientific use, we do not escape this methodological problem. It is remarkable enough that we still seem to rely upon biological metaphors – for instance, when we speak of "ethnogenesis."

Even the Marxist ethnologist Bromley (1974: 69) has coined the term "ethnosocial organism (ESO)" to describe the interdependence of ethnicity with the social and political sphere. This type of imagery can help to express the complexity of ethnic structures; but it should not be misunderstood as placing them in the realm of nature, far beyond the reach of history.

It has become clear enough now that ethnic units are the result of history. It may be discussed if ethnicity, in a very general sense, has been a basic organizing principle from times of old, a position that the English sociologist Anthony D. Smith (1986: 6ff) has labelled "primordialist," vs the "modernist" view that sees the nation as a relatively new phenomenon. But single peoples (or *ethne*, to use the technical term – I do not dwell on the problem if *ethnos* and "people" – *Volk* – *narod* cover the same range of phenomena) can have a beginning and an end; their composition changes; and their development is not the result of inherent "national" characteristics, but is influenced by a variety of political, economic, and cultural factors. Of course, ethnic changes are mostly a question of the *longue durée* ["long haul", a phrase often used by the French historian Fernand Braudel]; they scarcely even become obvious to contemporaries. In this respect, the Avars mark an exception – it was noted how quickly they disappeared without leaving a trace (in a well-known passage of Nestor's chronicle, but also in a lesser-known letter of Nikolaos Mystikos – cf. Pohl 1988: 323). But this "relatively persistent character of ethnic features" (Bromley 1974: 61) should not obscure its historical dimension.

Secondly, early medieval peoples were far less homogeneous than often thought. They themselves shared the fundamental belief to be of common origin; and modern historians, for a long time, found no reason to think otherwise. They could cite Isidore of Seville's seventh-century definition: "*Gens est multitudo ab uno principio orta*" ("a people is a multitude stemming from one origin"); it has often been ignored that Isidore continues: "*sive ab alia natione secundum propriam collectionem distincta*" ("or distinguished from another people by its proper ties" – Isidore, *Etymologies*, IX, 2, 1). *Natio*, in those days, was a near-equivalent to the term *gens*, whereas *populus* carried a connotation of a political body or a Christian community (cf. Lošek 1990). It is hard to render the meaning of *propria collectio*; but I think it is as good as any modern definition trying to pin down the elusive characteristics of ethnicity. It was Reinhard Wenskus in his comparative study of German ethnogeneses who worked out some of the mechanisms of *collectio*, of collecting and holding together a *gens*, an early medieval people; and he made it clear that the idea of common origin was a myth. This myth, however, was an essential part of a tradition that shaped the particularity of the *gens*, its beliefs and institutions. A relatively small group guarded and handed on this tradition and set it up as a standard for much larger units; Wenskus calls this group *Traditionskern* (the term "kernel of tradition" had already been used in a similar sense by H. M. Chadwick in 1912, as my collegue Andreas Schwarcz in Vienna observed). This conception fits very well with recent sociological theories that see the ties within a given group based on a common interpretation of symbols (Girtler 1982; Smith 1986 calls this a *mythomoteur*). These broader units were often of various origin; the Lombards in Italy, for instance, incorporated Gepids, Suevians and Alamans, Bulgarians, Saxons, Goths, Romans, and others. This "polyethnic" composition was generally observed; Alcuin, for instance, congratulated Charlemagne on having subdued "*gentes populique Hunorum*," the peoples of the Huns (i.e. the Avars); and his contemporary, Paul the Deacon, could list the components of the *gens Langobardorum* (Pohl 1988: 215; Paulus Diaconus, *Historia Langobardorum* 2, 26).

The third important discovery is the dynamic and often contradictory character of ethnic affiliations. The Russian ethnologist Shirokogoroff (1935) had already written in the 1930s that we can describe *ethnos* as a process rather than a unit (cf. Daim 1982: 65). Ethnic boundaries are not static, and even less so in a period of migrations. It is possible to change one's ethnicity (otherwise the Indians would still be the only Americans we know). Even more frequently, in the Early Middle Ages, people lived under circumstances of ethnic ambiguity. We may cite Edica and his son Odoacer as striking examples; at different stages of their career they were taken to be Huns, *Sciri, Turcilingi* (or Thuringians), Rugians, Eruls, and even Goths, while Odoacer made his career as a Roman officer and eventually became king of Italy. We do not have to sort out the "errors" from this list to arrive at an "authentic" ethnic background; presumably, the two princes used a polyethnic background for wide-spread and flexible claims to the political loyalty of their partners and followers. However, they belonged to a social class in which ethnicity mattered. We have scarcely any proof that the lower strata of society felt part of any large-scale ethnic group (Geary 1983 remarks that our sources only put members of the upper classes – including the armies – into ethnic categories); it is more likely that their identity was rooted in smaller local groups, like clans or villages. To advance socially thus meant to grow into a dominating group with high prestige, to copy its lifestyle. Processes of assimilation produced a variety of transitional stages (Mühlmann 1985; 26f; Pohl 1988: 219). Also, there were individuals who were Avars or Lombards in a fuller sense than others who claimed to be so; and one could easily be Lombard *and* Gepid, or Avar *and* Slav, at the same time. Usually one of these names denoted the higher, constitutional unit, the other one a subgroup that had stuck to the reminders of another ethnic tradition. Which of these affiliations prevailed often depended on the situation: this is why Geary (1983) has called ethnic identity a "situational construct."

Consequently, we cannot expect to classify peoples in the same way that Linnaeus classified his plants. In the language of philosophy, ethnic terms are not classificational but operational terms; ethnic groups cannot be deliminated from each other clearly, and their reality has to be constantly reproduced by human activity (Oeser 1985; Girtler 1982; Pohl 1988: 14f). Therefore, we do not have to look for ethnicity as an inborn characteristic, but as an "ethnic practice" that reproduces the ties that hold a group together. In the political sphere, this means political actions and strategies that we can partly reconstruct from literary sources; on a cultural level, it denotes a rich variety of objects and habits that serve as expressions of ethnic identity. Later on, I shall return to the methodological implications for historical and archaeological research; now I want to give a few examples for the role – and the contradictions – of ethnicity in early medieval central and eastern Europe.

Avars, Bulgarians, Slavs, Romans: Types of Ethnicity

Maps of Europe in the early Middle Ages usually show clear ethnic boundaries; only in some cases do they allow for areas of overlapping populations. Coloured arrows denote routes of migration; although these sometimes become quite intricate (as in the case of the Goths) they nonetheless establish an equation between the bearers of identical names in different periods and areas. This picture may help the general orientation, but at the same time it obscures the variety of ethnic groups, the different forms of cohesion and their interdependence.

A map of Europe east of the Elbe, Enns and Adria rivers in the seventh century would show Avars, Bulgarians, Slavs, and Byzantines. In a certain sense we could call these four the dominant peoples of the period. A closer look, however, makes it clear that none of them was a "people" in the modern sense of the word; that ethnicity meant something different for each of them; and that they all were tied to each other in a complicated pattern of interdependence that shaped the very form of their ethnic existence.

The world they all lived in had developed in the course of Antiquity; indeed, it was the creation of the *Imperium Romanum*. Perhaps it seems paradoxical to see the "mass of Slavs," as the Byzantines disdainfully called them, as an offspring of the Roman world; even more of a paradox is Patrick Geary's brilliant statement: "The Germanic world was perhaps the greatest and most enduring creation of Roman political and military genius" (1988: vi). But the very bipolarity between civilization and the barbarians, between the imperium and the *gentes*, was a result of the Roman system. It attracted generations of barbarian warriors and profoundly changed barbarian societies; Roman gold, goods and symbols became inevitable factors of prestige among barbarians, social inequalities and tensions grew, and many a rural population was militarized by the enticing new possibilities to fight for – or against – the Romans who had accumulated such incredible wealth. Late Antiquity saw a veritable explosion of this "pull to the centre"; the dramatic confrontation between the Empire and the barbarians spread all over its provinces. But the first victim was not the Empire itself but its Germanic periphery that virtually collapsed in the course of the sixth century. German *gentes* either followed the lure of the Empire and managed to gain control of a part of its tax system – paying the price of a certain assimilation (or, for many, subjection by a half-romanized warrior class). Or they lost their independence (with the exception of Scandinavia, and, partly, the continental Saxons and Frisians).

By the end of the sixth century, the old bipolarity had been reestablished on a "lower" level. New peoples had taken the role of the Germans in the vast areas outside – and increasingly inside – the ancient Danube frontier. On the one hand, Slavic populations proved rather impenetrable to Roman influence. On the other hand, there were those who took the place of the "outer" Germanic (and Hunnic) warrior aristocracies, living outside of the provincial framework of the Empire but inside its system of balancing power. The emperor had to keep the balance (Theophylaktos even polemically compares him to a referee in sports), financing a number of various armies and bands of more or less barbarian warriors and furnishing them with Roman titles and honours, playing them off against each other and thereby securing a kind of deadlock among them. Technically, Goths, Vandals, Franks, even Huns were not enemies of the Roman Empire – they were its (initially external) members and federates, and their attacks were more of an upheaval than an invasion by foreigners (Wolfram 1990). None of their kings could have kept his position without the revenues from the Roman tax system, whether he took them by force or by treaty, whether he was charged with guarding part of it (again, usually by treaty), or was paid off directly.

The heirs of the Germans in this system were the Avars and the Bulgars. Their ethnogeneses in Europe would not have been possible without the Empire. It is characteristic that the first thing the Avars did when they came near the Caucasus on their flight from Central Asia was to send an embassy to the aging emperor Justinian. That took place sometime in winter 558/59, and they struck the usual deal: the Avars were to fight for the Empire against unruly *gentes* and in turn would receive annual payments and other benefits. Indeed, for 20 years to come the Avars, under their Khagan Baian, fought Utigurs and Antes, Gepids and Slavs, whereas their policy towards the Empire relied more on negotiation than on war. Toward 580, Baian had established his supremacy over practically all groups of barbarian warriors along the Balkan frontier. This gave him a monopoly only Attila had enjoyed before him for a few years. Despite growing difficulties with unruly groups of Slavs, his sons managed to preserve his position until the failure of the siege of Constantinople in 626. They used it to increase the pressure on the emperor – and the payments in gold and kind reached the record sum of 200,000 *solidi* shortly before 626. These treasures allowed the Khagans to win the loyalty of their growing army; nowhere could a barbarian warrior hope to gain more prestige than by following the Khagan with his legendary victories and his dazzling wealth (see Pohl 1988).

The ethnogenesis of the Avars followed the pattern laid out by this strategy. Their "kernel" had crossed a considerable part of Central Asia to escape from the Turks, who had just destroyed the two leading steppe empires, the Juan-juan and the Hephtalites. It is pointless to ask who exactly the forefathers of the European Avars were (see the detailed attempts of Haussig 1953 and Czeglèdy 1983 and the methodological objections by Pohl 1990 and 1988: 27ff). We only know that they carried an ancient, very prestigious name (our first hints to it date back to the times of Herodotus); and we may assume that they were a very mixed group of warriors who wanted to escape domination by the Turks. The charismatic tradition that they made their own proved a very powerful unifying factor, indeed a self-fulfilling prophecy. This tradition was indissolubly linked to the Khaganate. It maintained an absolute monopoly on the name "Avar" right until the end; it is remarkable that our sources do not call anyone else an Avar. Secessionists breaking out of the Khagan's dominion were known as Bulgarians; even in the case of the renegade Kuver around 680, whose following was initially composed of Roman provincials, Avars, and Bulgarians. After the fall of the Avar Empire around 800 the name disappeared within one generation. This did not mean that the Avars had all disappeared; a contemporary source around 870 calls the population of Pannonia "the people that have remained from Huns (Avars) and Slavs in these parts" (*Conversio Bagoariorum et Carantanorum*, c. 6; Pohl 1988: 325). It simply proved impossible to keep up an Avar identity after Avar institutions and the high claims of their tradition had failed.

The Bulgarians had roughly the same political and cultural background as the Avars: the world of the steppe with its specific forms of organization. And yet Bulgarian ethnogeneses took a very different path. From the end of the fifth century, Bulgarian groups (and other groups following a similar model of organization, usually carrying names ending "-*gur*," like Utigurs or Onogurs) appear in the sources. They are characterized by a marked discontinuity; Khan Kuvrat managed to unify the majority of Bulgarian groups under his rule north of the Black Sea only for a brief period in the middle of the seventh century. While Asparuch and his successors built up the Bulgarian state in the Balkans, Bulgarians stayed behind under Khazar domination, others lived in the Avar Khaganate, and many had joined the Byzantines. Kuver and Mavros failed in their attempt to erect a Khaganate of the *Sermesianoi* Bulgarians around Thessalonika, and the Alzeco-Bulgarians enjoyed an autonomous existence in the Lombard duchy of Benevento; later on, another Bulgarian ethnogenesis took place in the Volga region. Usually, these groups can be distinguished by their leaders. Whereas the Avar Khagans are usually only presented in the sources by their title (we have only a single name, Baian), we know all the important Bulgarian leaders by name; and they bear very different titles. Bulgarians often did not mind living under non-Bulgarian rule; but even in this case, they usually managed to preserve their ethnic identity for a long time.

In the world of the steppe warriors, Avars and Bulgarians represent complementary principles of organization. It is pointless to postulate any homogeneous ethnic substrate as a basis for these differences, for both *gentes* were the heirs of the polyethnic barbarian environment of the sixth century that had split up into so many bands and petty kingdoms. Of course, organizing a large group of warriors and their following always meant setting off an ethnogenesis; only ethnic bonds, supported by traditional myths and rites, could be strong enough to hold such a group together, to give it a structure that could resist failure. But even so, it was by no means invulnerable. Misfortune led to erosion; after 626 many "Avars" turned to the new Slavic regional powers at the periphery of the Khaganate, or they became Bulgarians. Only in exceptional cases can these phenomena of migration and change of ethnic identity be traced in our sources as in the famous Kuver story in the *Miracula Sancti Demetri* (c. 2, 5; cf. Pohl 1988: 278ff).

If Avars and Bulgarians were, in a certain sense, the heirs of the Germanic military aristocracies between the Alps and the Black Sea, the Slavs took up another line. Traditional Germanic societies had virtually split up into an active, aggressive part that stimulated – and fulfilled – the Roman demand for military manpower on the one hand; and those staying behind as deprived peasants, unable to cling to the ancient rural traditions that gave their existence a name and a meaning. This gap was filled by the Slavs. They reestablished the old bipolarity between a more or less self-sufficient "barbarian" periphery and the Roman world. It has often been argued that their apparent "primitiveness" made them a victim to any foreign intervention. In reality, it was exactly the refusal to build up stable concentrations of power and to tolerate the establishment of a durable military kingship that, in the long run, secured the success of the Slavs. Avars and Bulgarians conformed to the rules of the game established by the Romans. They built up a concentration of military power that was paid, in the last resort, from Roman tax revenues. Therefore they paradoxically depended on the functioning of the Byzantine state. The Slavs managed to keep up their agriculture (and a rather efficient kind of agriculture, by the standards of the time), even in times when they took their part in plundering Roman provinces. The booty they won apparently did not create a new military class with the greed for more and a contempt for peasant's work, as it did with the Germans. Thus the Slavic model proved an attractive alternative for the lower classes on both sides of the old Danube frontier. What's more, it proved practically indestructible, in spite of all its defeats. It is characteristic that the final breakdown of the Danube *limes*, which had been kept against Goths, Huns, Gepids, Bulgarians, and Avars, took place after a series of Byzantine campaigns against Slavs. Emperor Maurikios wanted to continue the purge, but the army had learned its lesson well enough: the exasperated soldiers mutinied, marched on Constantinople, and overthrew the emperor. The war that could not be won was given up (Pohl 1988: 121ff, 159ff). Of course this does not mean that the early Slavs lived in a purely egalitarian society. In some regions (for instance, north of the Danube in the second half of the sixth century), tendencies towards the formation of a military kingdom appear; but these kings could never compare with the power of an Avar or Bulgarian leader, and they were systematically attacked by Byzantines and Avars alike.

The Slav way of life again represents a model complementary to that of the Avars and Bulgarians. Slav traditions, language, and culture shaped, or at least influenced, innumerable local and regional communities: a surprising similarity that developed without any central institution to promote it. For the theory of ethnicity this constitutes an important example: should we speak of one Slav *ethnos* (and we have reason to believe that a certain conscience of Slavic identity existed)? Apparently ethnicity operated on at least two levels: the "common Slavic" identity, and the identity of single Slavic groups, tribes, or peoples of different sizes that gradually developed, very often taking their name from the territory they lived in. These regional ethnogeneses inspired by Slavic tradition incorporated considerable remnants of Roman or Germanic population ready enough to give up ethnic identities that had lost their cohesion.

Even so, "Romans" survived as an important ethnic factor in eastern Europe. It is perhaps the most contradictory form of ethnic identity we know from the Early Middle Ages. In the first place, "Roman" was the Empire, an empire that had established itself as a singular form of ruling "the world," of supremacy among the kings and princes. For more than a millennium to come, one could not be an emperor without being a Roman emperor. This political principle, that, to its defenders, belonged more to the realm of the history of salvation than to that of human history, had some astonishing effects: a Roman empire of the Franks and Germans, a "Third Rome" in Moscow, Seljuk princes named after the Romans whose neighbours they were; and, of course, the Roman Empire of the Greeks (which we call Byzantine by a modern name). For indeed, the Byzantines called themselves *Romaioi*, Romans, although they mostly spoke Greek, which they soon came to call the "Roman" language, and their capital was the "New Rome," Constantinople (Koder 1990). To them, being Roman gave them a special position among the *gentes*, the *ethne*: Roman identity meant belonging to an empire both earthly and heavenly, an example of civility and salvation. Even in the fifth century contemporaries believed it had forever brought ethnic conflicts to an end. This *Romanitas* already posed severe problems of delimitation to contemporaries; for us, it is almost impossible to define, as great numbers of barbarians lived inside the Empire, became Christians, and could even become highest Roman officials. In a certain sense Theodoric the Ostrogoth, who grew up as hostage in Constantinople and went through a splendid career as a *magister militum*, consul, and patrician, was a Roman; in another respect, he remained a barbarian. Large areas of ambiguity surrounded the notion of *Romanitas*.

On the other hand, even outside the Empire the Roman-Christian tradition in a variety of forms proved an important factor of ethnic aggregation. Again, the Kuver story can serve as a proof of how Roman provincials in a barbarian environment (in this case, as prisoners and slaves of the Avars) preserved their Roman identity. Roman enclaves in the Alps reached different stages of a local "Roman" ethnogenesis, as did the Aquitainians (Rouche 1990). The most striking example, of course, are the Romanians; centuries after the fall of the Balkan provinces, a pastoral Latin-Roman tradition served as the point of departure for a Valachian-Roman ethnogenesis. This kind of virtuality – ethnicity as hidden potential that comes to the fore under certain historical circumstances – is indicative of our new understanding of ethnic processes. In this light, the passionate discussion for or against Roman-Romanian continuity has been misled by a conception of ethnicity that is far too inflexible.

Some Methodological Conclusions

Many of the problems of early medieval ethnicity are, of course, unsolved. Still, it is possible to propose a few methodological principles.

1. "Ethnicity was not an objective phenomenon . . . but it was likewise not entirely arbitrary" (Geary 1983). Therefore, we cannot expect to find direct and objective proofs of ethnic identity. The subjective ethnic consciousness of an individual or a group of people was the decisive factor; but usually we do not know what group they felt they belonged to. Yet the specific form of ethnic consciousness gave objects an ethnic dimension. Archaeological objects or data can allow hypotheses about the "ethnic practice" that once gave them their context and meaning.

2. Many of the objects found by archaeologists may be direct or indirect expressions or symbols of ethnic identity – especially if they were left behind in ceremonial form (e.g. in burials) – but there is no object or group of objects that is ethnically unequivocal. As far as the many attempts to list distinctive and ethnically typical features have shown, almost anything can take or lose ethnic significance. Only an ensemble of objects and habits can serve as a basis for ethnic interpretation.

3. The written sources have preserved a great number of ethnic names that become concrete when political events or cultural expressions are recorded in connection with one of them. Many of these names are, of course, topical (like "Scythians" for the Huns). Others are names given and used by foreigners (as *Venidi* for the Slavs). It is possible that one and the same group is recorded under different names; but also that two groups are – justly or not – subsumed under the same name. The complexity of the relation between peoples and ethnic names should not be reduced too easily. Likewise, we should be very cautious in identifying *gentes* bearing the same name in different contexts. As long as there is no apparent link between the two groups of the same or similar name, no direct connections should be postulated – far less an identity, direct origin, or common ethnic substance.
4. Archaeological cultures and ethnic groups often coincide, but they cannot always be expected to be fully identifiable. Even more so, political boundaries, ethnic territories, linguistic groups, and areas of a certain material culture should not be mixed up, for they do not necessarily have the same extension.
5. Different types of ethnicity should be kept in mind. They pose different problems of interpretation. As has been shown, we may assume that Avar and Slav ethnicity was based on radically different socioeconomic models; but ethnogenetic processes sometimes tend to obscure such distinctions. Thus, we cannot be sure if some Avar-style warriors would not have called themselves Slavs, or vice versa; if we want to be precise, we could speak of an individual following this or that model. However, we can reach relatively high statistical probability in such cases.

In the case of the Avars, a great number of grave finds may rather easily be attributed to the leading strata of warriors following the Avar Khagan. Quite characteristically, the discussion in this case has paid much attention to the ethnic composition of this group. To contemporaries, this question apparently was much less significant – they were usually content to call Khagan's warriors Avars, even if they were of Cutrigur or Slav origin. To a certain extent, we may adopt a similar view. In spite of many attempts, no clear ethnic or socioethnic divisions within the Avar Empire have yet been proved; we may assume a very dynamic situation, showing all stages of acculturation.

In the case of the Slavs, it is much harder to trace groups mentioned in the sources in archaeological finds. Whereas the Avar warriors sought to display their splendor even after death, Slavs were often more modest; in other cases, they copied Avar or Byzantine apparel. Cremation also contributed to obscuring what they left behind. Thus, only areas of compact and stable Slavic culture can easily be identified, like north of the Carpathians; in other regions, for instance the Eastern Alps, sixth- to eighth-century Slavic culture remains quite unknown; and Slav components in mixed populations still are very hard to sort out. In those cases where clearly Slavic elements appear in conjunction with Avar features, as in the plains north of the Danube and east of the Morava, this should not be interpreted politically (Pohl 1988: 290f); again, this should be seen as a sign of dynamic processes of acculturation.

Bulgarians have long been a favourite for the attribution of warrior-type finds throughout eastern Europe. Not in all cases is this methodologically acceptable. We cannot always be sure what kind of material culture corresponded to the Bulgarian tradition and type of organization. Especially within the Avar Empire, this is not yet sufficiently clear. Hungarian archaeologists have tried to prove that middle and/or late Avar culture had been introduced by a Bulgarian invasion; historical arguments for this hypothesis have turned out to be rather untenable (Pohl 1987, 1988; 282ff; to support the hypothesis, among many others, Bona 1988), and the cultural changes discovered so far cannot prove *per se* the appearance of a new people.

   The most difficult problem is posed by finds of late Roman or Byzantine style. It is almost impossible to prove that the person who wore or used these objects really was and felt Roman. Byzantine culture and its various provincial and barbarized derivatives penetrated all early medieval cultures; barbarian leaders especially used all kinds of Byzantine objects as symbols of prestige and luxury goods. But again, archaeology and literary history both mirror one of the fundamental conditions of early medieval ethnicity: the *gentes* could only define themselves vs the overwhelming reality of a polyethnic, late Roman state and civilization. The degree of dependence on or refusal of Roman models shaped early medieval Europe; it laid the basis for success or failure of a great number of ethnogeneses. It was not any ethnic quality (force, number, talent) that decided their fate; it was their ability to adapt to an environment going through rapid changes, and to give this adaptation a credible meaning rooted in tradition and ritual. Slavs or Bulgars succeeded because their form of organization proved as stable and as flexible as necessary; the Avars failed in the end because their model could not respond to new conditions. The medieval peoples and their cultural characteristics were the result, not the condition, of this complex historical process.

References

Bona, I. 1988: Die Geschichte der Awaren im Lichte der archäologischen Quellen. *Settimane di Studio del Centro Italiano* 35: 437ff.

Bromley, J. 1974: *Soviet Ethnology and Anthropology Today*. The Hague and Paris.

Chadwick, H. M. 1912: *The Heroic Age*. Cambridge.

Czeglèdy, K. 1983: From East to West. *Archivum Eurasiae Medii Aevi* 3: 25–126.

Daim, F. 1982: Gedanken zum Ethnosbegriff. *Mitteilungen der Anthropologischen Gesellschaft in Wien* 112: 58–71.

Geary, P. 1983: Ethnic identity as a situational construct in the Early Middle Ages. *Mitteilungen der Anthropologischen Gesellschaft in Wien* 113: 15–26.

– 1988: *Before France and Germany. The Creation and Transformation of the Merovingian World*. New York and Oxford.

Girtler, R. 1982: "Ethnos," "Volk" und andere soziale Gruppen. *Mitteilungen der Anthropologischen Gesellschaft in Wien* 112: 42–57.

Haussig, H. W. 1953: Theophylakts Exkurs über die skythischen Völker. *Byzantion* 23: 275–436.

Koder, J. 1990: Byzanz, die Grechen und die Romaiosyne – eine "Ethnogenese" der "Römer"? In *Typen der Ethnogenese*, ed. H. Wolfram and W. Pohl, vol. I, pp. 103–11. Vienna.

Lošek, F. 1990: Ethnische und politische Terminologie bei Jordanes und Einhard. In *Typen der Ethnogenese*, ed. H. Wolfram and W. Pohl, vol. I, pp. 147–52. Vienna.

Mühlmann, W. 1985: Ethnogonie und Ethnogenese. *Abhandlungen der Rheinisch-Westfälischen Akademie der Wissenschaften* 72: 9–38.

Oeser, H. 1985: Methodologische Bemerkungen zur interdisciplinaren Problematik der Ethno- und Glottogenese. In *Entstehung von Sprachen und Voxikern*, ed. P. Sture Ureland, pp. 1–6. Tübingen.

Pohl, W. 1987: Das awarische Khaganat und die anderen Gentes im Karpatenbecken (6.–8. Jh.). *Südosteuropa Jahrbuch* 17: 41–52.

– 1988: *Die Awaren*. Munich.

– 1990: Verlaufsformen der Ethnogenese – Awaren und Bulgaren. In *Typen der Ethnogenese*, ed. H. Wolfram and W. Pohl, vol. I, pp. 113–24. Vienna.

24   *Walter Pohl*

Rouche, M. 1990: Peut-on parler d'une ethnogenèse des Aquitans? In *Typen der Ethnogenese*, ed. H. Wolfram and W. Pohl, vol. I, pp. 45–51. Vienna.

Shirokogoroff, S. M. 1935: *Psychomental Complex of the Tungus*. London.

Smith, A. D. 1986: *The Ethnic Origins of Nations*. Oxford.

Wenskus, R. 1961: *Stammesbildung und Verfassung*. Cologne and Graz.

Wolfram, H. 1979: *Die Goten*. Munich.

– 1990 *Das Reich und die Germanen*. Berlin.

2 The Barbarians in Late Antiquity and How They Were Accommodated in the West

Walter Goffart

This study is concerned with an ostensibly peaceful and smooth process: how the paraphernalia of Roman government, both military and civil, was used and adapted when, in the fifth century, several barbarian peoples were accorded an establishment on provincial soil. The details of these arrangements are worth investigating because they tell us something about the prolongation of sophisticated state institutions into the early Middle Ages and about the conditions of property ownership in the earliest barbarian kingdoms. Although one may doubt that the transfer of rule from Roman to barbarian hands took place without violence and disruption, there is no disputing the survival of a body of evidence that documents a lawful adaptation of Roman governmental practices to the novel requirements of Goths and Burgundians. Almost all the evidence is concerned, not with the moment of transition, but with the status quo many decades after barbarian rule had begun; despite the passage of time and the crystallization of alien regimes, the documented situation continues to betray its descent from Roman public law. We are able to reconstruct how the barbarians fitted into the society of certain western Roman provinces, as well as to establish what had become of the once pervasive mechanisms of taxation under new management.

The barbarian invasions form the background to the circumstances that the chapters [i.e. of Goffart's book] to come will study. But how are we to imagine these invasions? Many modern narratives are available, telling approximately the same story. None of them prepares us adequately for the undramatic adjustments between barbarians and Romans that we shall meet.

The invasions, as currently presented, are an awesome spectacle, running parallel with Roman history itself for many centuries before the barbarians made permanent inroads into the Empire. "It is essential . . . ," we are told, "to bear constantly in mind that the phenomenon we are observing is a migration of peoples, not merely an invasion of 'barbarians.'"[1] According to this traditional schema, the Germanic peoples had been in motion since the third or first century BC, engaging in periodic mass migrations that pressed northern tribes down upon earlier emigrants to the south with such increasingly disruptive force that the Roman frontier, which had impeded the migrants' progress for several centuries, was torn down around AD 400. The moving Germanic masses then surged forward and halted in

---

[1] Joseph Vogt, *The Decline of Rome*, trans. Janet Sondheimer (London, 1967), p. 183.

imperial territory.[2] Yet this final step turns out to be remarkably modest: those involved in it were a mere handful of peoples, each group numbering at the most in the low tens of thousands, and many of them – not all – were accommodated within the Roman provinces without dispossessing or overturning indigenous society. In other words, the barbarians whom we actually find coming to grips with the Roman Empire in the fourth to sixth centuries, and leading the earliest successor kingdoms of the West, are remarkably deficient in numbers, cohesion, assertiveness, and skills – altogether a disappointment when juxtaposed with the long and massive migrations that are thought to characterize their past.[3]

The dimensions of this problem are better grasped by considering specific instances. The chapters [i.e. of Goffart's book] to come will be concerned with the time when the Visigoths, Burgundians, and Ostrogoths obtained stable establishments on Roman soil. If the backdrop to each of these events were to be sketched, where should the story begin? Two very distinct courses are available to us, depending on the quality of evidence and the scale of conjecture and combination we are willing to tolerate. Those very strict in the selection and handling of sources will refuse to go farther afield than to the lands bordering the Roman Empire in the fourth century AD. Those, however, who welcome a wider range of documentation and liberally resort to hypothesis and speculation, will find it possible and even desirable to reach as far out in space as Scandinavia and as far back in time as before the Christian era. This major difference of approach to the period of the barbarian invasions deserves to be spelled out and elaborated, because little is said about it outside the German academic scene.[4]

[2] A vocabulary of floods, waves, and other vivid images suggestive of forces of nature has long been standard in accounts of the invasions. See, e.g., Lucien Musset, *Les Invasions*, vol. 1, *Les vagues germaniques*, Nouvelle Clio 12 (Paris, 1965), pp. 50–74. Musset is now available in a translation by E. and C. James (University Park, 1975), which I have not used. For a representative passage in which this imagery takes on a life of its own, see Geoffrey Barraclough, *The Medieval Papacy* (London, 1968), p. 28: "Fifteen years after Leo [the Great]'s death [461], the barbarian flood, whose beginnings he had seen, engulfed the West." This seems to refer to aliens pouring in, but the West was not invaded by anyone between 461 and 476. As explained by Ludwig Schmidt, "Die Ursachen der Völkerwanderung," *Neue Jahrbücher für das klassische Altertum, Geschichte und deutsche Literatur* 11 (1903): 340, the migrations can be thought to begin long before the Christian era (cf. below, at n. 44) or only with the Hunnic attack on the Goths in the 370s, which, even according to contemporaries like Ammianus Marcellinus (*Rerum gestarum libri*, 31. 2ff), set in motion a chain of disasters. Dating from the Huns: Hans-Joachim Diesner, *Die Völkerwanderung* (Leipzig, 1976), pp. 70–2, 86. The two starting points are often treated as complementary; e.g. Pierre Courcelle, *Histoire littéraire des grandes invasions germaniques*, 3rd ed. (Paris, 1964), pp. 14–20.

[3] Numbers: Schmidt, "Ursachen," p. 347, agreeing with Hans Delbrück, *Geschichte der Kriegskunst*, 3rd ed. (Berlin, 1921), vol. 3, pp. 300–14. Cohesion: the many instances of barbarians fighting for Rome against their fellow tribesmen (Frankish generals in the fourth century; Sarus the Goth in the times of Alaric; the circumstances of the dissolution of the Vandal and Ostrogothic kingdoms; repeated Lombard defections to the Byzantines; etc.). Assertiveness: below, n. 54. Skills: E. A. Thompson, "Early Germanic Warfare," *PP* 14 (1958): 2–29.

[4] A selective, but profound, account of the vagaries of recent German *Altertumskunde* [ancient studies] is given by Rolf Hachmann, *Die Goten und Skandinavien*, Quellen und Forschungen zur Sprach- und Kulturgeschichte der germanischen Völker N.F. 34 (Berlin, 1970), pp. 145–220; cf. the review of T. M. Andersson in *Speculum* 46 (1971): 373–5. Equally revealing is the defense of traditional methods and tales by Ernst Schwarz, *Germanische Stammeskunde zwischen den Wissenschaften* (Constance and Stuttgart, 1967), pp. 7–53, and *Zur germanischen Stammeskunde. Aufsätze zum neuen Forschungsstand*, Wege der Forschung 249 (Darmstadt, 1972), pp. vii–xxx, 287–308 (the latter specifically against Hachmann). Malcolm Todd, *The Northern Barbarians, 100 B.C.–A.D. 300* (London, 1975), pp. 19–29, 55, and *passim*, provides an up-to-date summary of these difficulties from the archaeological standpoint.

If one takes a conservative course, the chain of events that ended in 418 with the settlement in Roman Aquitaine of the Visigoths led by Wallia should be traced back no earlier than the rebellion of Alaric in 395. The Goths whom Alaric led were then based in the Balkans, within the territories governed by the emperor of East Rome. It would not be amiss, however, to indicate the more remote background to the uprising. Earlier in the fourth century, the Goths had lived north and east of the Danube frontier of the Roman Empire (we would say in Romania and south Russia), in lands that they had occupied for as long as anyone could remember. (By identifying them directly with the Scythians who had anciently inhabited these lands, Roman observers expressed the belief that the Goths were a new name, not a new population.) Direct neighbors of the Empire, they were a normal part of the barbarian landscape, neither relentless enemies nor trustworthy friends. From the last third of the fourth century, the course of Gothic history was highly discontinuous; every major step taken by the (Visi)goths away from Romania and south Russia implied à break in cohesion, the start of a new sequence of events whose relations to the immediate past seem tenuous and disconnected: an internal crisis in the 370s exacerbated by the apparently irresistible onset of the Huns; a partial and disorganized, though peaceful, migration onto Roman territory (376); an uprising marked by a great victory (378) but also entailing severe losses before the acquisition of a regulated status in the Empire (382); and two major campaigns to the West as Roman auxiliaries with great loss of life (388, 394). Only after these incidents does one come to Alaric's rebellion of 395, which itself initiated two decades of campaigning punctuated by defeats as well as successes. No smooth line of historical narrative can connect the Goths in south Russia to the heterogeneous peoples led by Alaric and his successors in Italy, Spain, and Gaul during the first two decades of the fifth century. However Gothic in name, their following was no lineal prolongation of the nation that Athanaric had ruled in the 370s; it is more evocative of the great company of successive condottieri than of a phenomenon of popular migration.[5]

The exclusion from the preceding account of any earlier past for the Goths than their residence alongside the Roman frontier is not meant to depreciate them by comparison with peoples who have longer histories, or to preclude the possibility that they had an ancient culture, identity, or past. The point is simply that a strictly controlled historical narrative presupposes a certain minimum of evidence, rather than a string of hypotheses and combinations; much as one might wish to write the ancient history of the Goths, the documentary basis for doing so is lacking. Tales of the early Goths were eventually told; the main ones that have reached us were set down in sixth-century Constantinople, and, not surprisingly, they

---

[5] Ludwig Schmidt, *Geschichte der deutschen Stämme bis zum Ausgang der Völkerwanderung. Die Ostgermanen*, 2nd ed. (Munich, 1941), pp. 195–249 (to the Hunnic attack), 400–26 (to the establishment of the kingdom of Toulouse); Musset, *Vagues germaniques*, pp. 83–6; Ernst Stein, *Histoire du Bas-Empire*, vol. 1, trans. J. R. Palanque (Brussels, 1959), pp. 207, 216–17; André Piganiol, *L'Empire chrétien (325–395)* (Paris, 1947), pp. 211–14, 222–3, 247–8, 251–5, 260–1, 266–8. Bloodshed in the suppression of Maximus: Jerome, *Epistolae*, 60. 15, without specific reference to Goths. On the identification of recent peoples with older ones (Goths as Scythians), see the valuable, but unsympathetic, comments of J. Otto Maenchen-Helfen, *The World of the Huns*, ed. Max Knight (Berkeley, 1973), pp. 5–9. (The name Visigoth, which we associate with Alaric's people, is not attested until the sixth century.) Fustel de Coulanges, *L'invasion germanique et la fin de l'Empire*, 3rd ed. (Paris, 1911), pp. 430–1, stressed discontinuity; Musset, *Vagues germaniques*, pp. 84–5, states that, after 25 years in the Balkans and 11 in Italy, the Visigothic people "n'est toujours qu'une armée errante" ["is nothing but a wandering army"]; to the contrary, Schmidt, *Ostgermanen*, p. 426 (chiefly on the basis of Isidore of Seville!). Socrates, *Historia ecclesiastica*, 4. 8 conveys the Constantinopolitan idea that, after doing much damage, the Goths in the Balkans were wiped out.

have nothing in common with our standards of credible history. We can repeat these stories in their proper chronological and cultural context as testifying to a highly civilized desire to reconstruct the *origo gentis* [story of the origins of a people]. But, since such tales lay in the future, their contents would be out of place in a background to the Goths in fifth-century Aquitaine.[6] What is at stake in all this is not one's sympathy or antipathy toward barbarians, Germans, or Goths but rather a conception of how history in the modern manner may legitimately be assembled and written.

Equally conservative accounts may be given of the Burgundians and Ostrogoths. The Burgundians whom we shall be concerned with were the survivors of two devastating defeats, one by Roman troops, the other by Huns. The disasters of 435 and 436 wiped out a Burgundian kingdom in the Roman province of Germania II that had lasted a little over two decades and may have been about to expand its space.[7] The Burgundians in Germania II had not arrived from far away. In the second half of the fourth century, a Roman historian situates them at some distance east of the Rhine, settled to the north of the Alamanni and cooperating with the Roman army against this common enemy. The same author tells us that the Burgundians knew themselves to be descended from Romans, and another, a little later, specifies that the generals of Augustus had established them in camps as advance guards in the interior of Germany. Whatever these stories are worth, they imply that the fourth-century Burgundians were thoroughly rooted to the districts they inhabited.[8] Their roots were not so deep, however, that they stood their ground in the tumult of the early fifth century. How much did the Burgundians of the late 430s remember even of a homeland east of the Rhine? It was a severely chastened and diminished remnant that the West Roman government relocated southward from the Rhineland in 443, to a district where, in the century to come, the Burgundians never grew into a great or dangerous people.[9]

The Ostrogoths had an even more abbreviated past. For close to eight decades after the 370s, they had lived as subjects of the Huns, eventually under the overlordship of Attila. When Attila's empire disintegrated (454) and the Gepids emerged as the direct heirs to the Hunnic position, the Goths led by Valamer sought the patronage of the East Roman emperor and obtained lands in the abandoned frontier province of Pannonia. The subsequent history of these Goths is comparatively well known, as might be expected of a tribe living continuously within the territory of the old Empire. After Valamer died, his younger brother led a part of his people westward to eventual absorption by the Goths of Toulouse. The remainder came under the rule of Valamer's nephew Theodoric, who long served the Emperor Zeno

---

[6] The work containing these tales of the early Goths is, of course, Jordanes, *De origine actibusque Getarum* (commonly *Getica*), ed. Theodore Mommsen, *MGH, AA*, V about which more below. Although Jordanes wrote in Latin, he was a proper Byzantine, as is made obvious by his chronicle of Roman history (*Romana*, ed. Theodore Mommsen, *MGH, AA*, V). On origin stories, Elias Bickerman, "Origines gentium," *Classical Philology* 47 (1952): 65–81. Ammianus, 15. 9, on the Gallo-Romans, clearly illustrates how such an account departs from our standards and expectations.

[7] Schmidt, *Ostgermanen*, pp. 136–7; Musset, *Vagues germaniques*, pp. 111–12; K. F. Stroheker, *Germanentum und Spätantike* (Zurich and Stuttgart, 1965), pp. 257–8. Hydatius, *Chronicum*, 108, 110, ed. Alain Tranoy, SC, 218–19 (Paris, 1974), vol. 1, p. 134, vol. 2, pp. 72–3 (commentary).

[8] Ammianus, 28. 5. 9–11; Orosius, *Historia adversus paganos*, 7. 32. 12. Eduard Norden, *Alt-Germanien Völker- und Namengeschichtliche Untersuchungen* (Leipzig, 1934), pp. 62–4, explained the Roman inspiration of these stories. Such inventions would have been worthless, however, if an alternative origin legend had been firmly entrenched among the Burgundians of the time.

[9] Schmidt, *Ostgermanen*, pp. 191–4; Musset, *Vagues germaniques*, pp. 112–15; Alfred Coville, *Recherches sur l'histoire de Lyon du Ve au IXe siècle (450–800)* (Paris, 1928), pp. 153–8, studied the evidence on Burgundian numbers; cf. Schmidt, *Ostermanen*, p. 168.

but then found it advantageous to move his followers against Odoacer, the "tyrant" of Italy (488). Ostrogothic settlement that will later interest us occurred after Theodoric's people succeeded in wresting Italy from Odoacer's control.[10]

In part, these short Gothic and Burgundian backgrounds embody an admission of ignorance. The past of these tribes may have contained much more that was relevant to what they would become in the Roman provinces, but we simply are not informed. Deficient sources, however, are not the main justification for excluding references to earlier centuries. We have no reason to think that the distant past weighted more heavily upon barbarians than it did upon literate Romans. Fourth-century events in the Empire took place with notable unconcern for historical precedent; the most ambitious histories written in the fifth century looked back only to Constantine.[11] Modern authors do not find it indispensable to evoke Augustus, Trajan, or Gallienus as relevant to the battle of Adrianople and its aftermath, and neither does an account of the growth of the Roman Empire obligatorily accompany one of its decline. According to students of the oral traditions surviving in twentieth-century Africa, the memory of a tribe reaches to the districts inhabited prior to the last migration, but not any further back.[12] If this finding is valid for all nonliterate peoples, our information about the Goths and Burgundians, which stems from Roman writings, is considerably fuller than what was available to them from their own resources. The memory of the Visigoths in Aquitaine after 418 could have reached only to their Balkan homes before 395; that of the Burgundians in eastern Gaul after 443, to the Rhenish kingdom before 436; and that of the Ostrogoths in Italy, to their settlements in Pannonia and the Balkans between 454 and 488. Forgetfulness – the interruption and loss of oral memories – is probably an inevitable accompaniment of migrations.[13] For all these reasons, the fourth century may be thought to afford an adequate perspective for barbarian enterprises from 395 onward. But this is by no means the more widely held view of the matter.

The longer perspective on the barbarian past can be expressed in generalizations as well as in the narrower form of individual tribal histories. To begin with generalization, one hears

[10] Jordanes, *Getica*, 268–96, offers an intelligible consecutive account; cf. Musset, *Vagues germaniques*, pp. 92–3.

[11] The Chronicles of Eusebius and Jerome, as well as the *Breviaria* of Eutropius and Festus, suggest how much Roman history the fourth century was able to dispense with. Constantine as beginning: the church histories of Philostorgius, Socrates, Sozomen, and Theodoret (before 450); the Roman law gathered into the Code of Theodosius II (published in 438); introductory chapters to the lost History of Malchus of Philadelphia (late 5th century) and the last book of the lost Chronicle of Hesychius of Miletus (*c*.518). For Malchus and Hesychius, see Wilhelm Christ, Wilhelm Schmid, and Otto Stählin, *Geschichte der griechischen Litteratur*, 6th ed., pt 2, 2nd half (Munich, 1924), pp. 1036, 1039.

[12] Yves Person, "Chronology and Oral Tradition" (1962), trans. Susan Sherwin, in Martin Klein and G. Wesley Johnson, ed., *Perspectives on the African Past* (Boston, 1972), p. 8: "A visual element . . . is almost always necessary to sustain [the] memory [of oral traditions]. Everything earlier fades within a man's lifetime." See also Ruth Finnegan, "A Note on Oral Tradition and Historical Evidence," *History and Theory* 9 (1970): 195–201, including important observations on the rarity of epics and other historical narratives in Africa, the unreliability of their transmission, and the special distortion of migration stories (pp. 196–8).

[13] Historical forgetfulness seems common in literate societies; e.g. the famous line of Ammianus about *antiquitatum ignari* ["those ignorant of ancient times"] (31. 5. 11). For a notable illustration, see Evagrius, *Hist. ecclesiastica*, 3. 41 (*c*.593): one proof of the superiority of Christian to pagan times was that the Roman emperors since Constantine had been more secure on their thrones than their pagan predecessors. The argument could work only if all the overthrown western emperors from Constantine II to Romulus Augustulus were forgotten, as they obviously were.

that "the pressure of the northern peoples upon settled German tribes . . . continued until the [Roman] frontier was permanently breached."[14] A popular expansion of this thought involves the idea of a prolonged contest between Germans and the Mediterranean world that lasted from the expedition of the Cimbri and Teutones *c.*102 BC until the fall of the Western Empire. In this version, it seems to be presupposed that the northerners had a set goal that they kept moving toward – such as "the old objective of the wandering Indo-Germanic peoples" – and that, for a long time, the Romans stood in the way of their attaining it.[15] Even without reference to a goal, a connection is assumed to have existed between all the barbarian tribes speaking Germanic dialects, and the acts of any of them are held to be significant for all. Thus, after the disaster of Varus in AD 9,

> free Germany became for the Roman Empire a lasting danger that one sought to avert by securing the frontier. . . . The recruitment of Germans into the Roman army only temporarily filled gaps and could not prevent it from happening that, from the beginning of the fifth century, Germanic tribes strove to erect states of their own on the soil of the Roman Empire.[16]

Such lines hint at a dangerous anachronism. United Germany is a phenomenon whose past extends no earlier than the ninth century; even though Tacitus wrote about Germania (*c.* AD 98), he never imagined that the peoples whom he described formed anything more sophisticated than disunited tribes;[17] yet the talk in our books about Germans confronting and striving against the Roman Empire often implies that a single coherent entity lay beyond the Roman border and that it had united ambitions and aspirations vis-à-vis the Empire. For this reason, a recent author who assembled Roman observations of the barbarian invasions was chided by a reviewer for providing only a "partial" picture, and future historians were invited to "try to build up a comprehensive picture of the German invasions from both sides."[18] By the terms of such reasoning, the Roman state looked outward toward a coherent "other side," rather too reminiscent of the Germany to come.

In narrative, migratory movements are what impart community to this "other side." The history assigned to every tribe consists primarily of a travel diary; Lucien Musset writes:

> The Burgundians . . . appear in the first century [AD] in the Baltic region as an element of the *Vindili* group; then they plunge into the interior, on the middle

---

[14] Edward Peters, *Europe: The World of the Middle Ages* (Englewood Cliffs, 1977), p. 43 (this textbook is chosen only for its recent data; many others might supply similar quotations).

[15] Hermann Aubin in *Neue Propyläen-Weltgeschichte*, ed. Willy Andrea, vol. 2 (Berlin, 1940), p. 78. Here, as elsewhere, I have translated the quotation. Aubin's narrative (pp. 52–78) is a notably colorful portrayal of the *Völkerwanderung* [wandering of the peoples]. For persistent ideas of a goal, or of the unavoidable attractions of the Mediterranean sun, Diesner, *Völkerwanderung*, p. 70.

[16] Schwarz, *Zur germ. Stammesk.*, p. xviii. Stories of the same kind are familiar outside Germany; e.g. Daniel D. McGarry, *Medieval History and Civilization* (New York, 1976), pp. 69–70.

[17] Heinz Löwe in Bruno Gebhardt, *Handbuch der deutschen Geschichte*, 8th ed. (Stuttgart, 1954), p. 79, envisaged a caesura between the Germanic peoples, including the East Germans of the invasion period, and the beginnings of the German (*deutsche*) people in the ninth century – quite a novel organization of material by comparison with the 7th ed. of Gebhardt's *Handbuch* in 1930. Tacitus, *Germania*, 33 is the *locus classicus* on disunity; the sketch of 210 years of war between Rome and the Germans (*Germania*, 37), which lies behind such modern narratives as cited above nn. 15–16, derives its unity from being written from the Roman standpoint. On the questionable continuity of tribes, see below, n. 30.

[18] Gerald Bonner, review of Courcelle, *Hist. litt.*, in *JRS* 56 (1966): 247.

Vistula. But their language and traditions no doubt allow them to be derived from Scandinavia. Their east German dialect was close to Gothic, and their traditions, gathered at a late date, lead to "the island called Scandinavia." In fact, several Scandinavian lands bear names analogous to theirs: the land of Borgund, on the Sognefjord in Norway, and especially the Baltic island of Bornholm (Borgundarholm in the thirteenth century).

From their Polish habitat, the Burgundians began in the course of the third century to slide toward the West. After 260, they are alongside the Alamanni.[19]

The account may end here, for the sequel, related above, takes up the story from the point when the Burgundians were neighbors to the Alamanni. The longer background is highlighted by verbs of action. Emerging from Scandinavia, plunging to the middle Vistula, then sliding west, the Burgundians expressed the kind of *Wanderlust* [restlessness] that, by anticipation, explains their future advances to Roman soil.

The Goths play an extraordinarily important part in the extended scheme of barbarian history. A recent summary of their movements reads:

> The best known of these migrating peoples were the Goths, who settled upon the banks of the Vistula at the beginning of the first century, and in Poland somewhat later. The Goths had come originally from the Baltic region. Further migrations from that region had begun to press upon them, and in turn they began to migrate south and east. To the south, they encountered the Vandals and Burgundians, the periphery of the "neighborhood" settled tightly around the Roman frontier. The Goths continued to move south and east toward the Ukraine, but their movements and the pressures of the Gepid people following them disturbed the territorial settlements of other peoples and precipitated the progressive mass movements of still other tribes into territories ever closer to the Roman frontier.[20]

One pattern visible here is a chronological sequence: Vandals and Burgundians first, then Goths, finally Gepids. The Goths provided the push that, in our previous quotation, precipitated the westward "slide" of the Burgundians; in turn, the onset of the Gepids forced the Goths southeastward. The latter movement so disturbed the frontier peoples of the Roman Empire, one learns elsewhere, that they launched a great attack across the border; the then emperor, Marcus Aurelius, took years to subdue these attackers and to reestablish the northern frontier. According to modern historians of the Empire, the reign of Marcus [161–180] was the turning point from moderate to difficult imperial defense, and the Gothic movement indirectly occasioned this crucial change.[21] The chronological sequence in which

[19]   Musset, *Vagues germaniques*, p. 111. Cf. Norden, *Alt-Germanien*, pp. 17–23, where the succession of (highly disparate) evidence is clearly visible. Norden, a classicist by training, was particularly impressed by the affirmation of Germanists that the Burgundians were East Germanic and therefore totally alien from their neighbors, the Alamanni (pp. 18 n. 1, 20–1). It would have been useful to add that nothing in the written sources tends to confirm this idea.

[20]   Peters, *Europe*, p. 42; cf. Musset, *Vagues germaniques*, pp. 80–2.

[21]   Gothic movement indirectly causing the attack on the Empire: Schmidt, "Ursachen," p. 341; Aubin in *Propyläen-Weltgeschichte*, vol. 2, pp. 56–7; Musset, *Vagues germaniques*, p. 52. For a more reticent account, George Kossack in Fergus Millar, *The Roman Empire and Its Neighbours* (London, 1967), pp. 317–18. The turning point coinciding with Marcus Aurelius, typically, M. I. Finley, "Manpower and the Fall of Rome," in C. M. Cipolla, ed., *The Economic Decline of Empires* (London, 1970), p. 86. Todd, *Northern Barbarians*, p. 210, endorses this common opinion without stating whether there is any archaeological evidence substantiating it.

the Goths are thought to have been involved turns easily into a pattern of causation influenced by ideas of panic rippling through a mob.[22] The Goths are also prominent because they were the subject of the earliest "barbarian history." This narrative locates their primitive home in Scandinavia and explicitly tells of migrations that took them to Scythia – south Russia northeast of the lower Danube; that it also dates these migrations to the second millennium BC is rarely taken to detract from their authenticity.[23]

This Gothic history was written at Constantinople in the middle of the sixth century, after the Goths had traveled very far indeed from where they had still lived in the 370s. Since its author completely disagrees with modern historians over the time when early migrations in eastern Europe took place, there is hardly any basis for charting the movements of East Germans (Vandals, Burgundians, Goths, and so forth) before the third century AD, let alone for expressing them as a simple dramatic narrative.[24] Contemporary Roman observers were unaware that tides and waves of human beings were menacingly lapping at the barbarians residing just beyond the imperial borders. Their ignorance of such phenomena is so notorious that modern commentators sometimes point to it with annoyance: "Claudian's contemporaries [*c.* AD 400] did not understand why it was that fresh barbarian hordes kept battering at the frontiers of the empire."[25] The idea of migratory pressure is also somewhat strange in view of the well-documented events known to us. The onset of the Huns in the 370s did impel some Goths to abandon their lands and seek admission into the Roman Empire, but hardly another movement of the invasion period fits into this pattern of one people being pressed onward by another. (Even here, it is improbable that the Huns attacked because they needed or coveted the lands of the Goths for themselves.) The Vandals were not driven to North Africa, nor the Saxons to Britain, nor the Ostrogoths to Italy; no one has ever shown that the descent of Radagaisus upon Italy in 405, or the great Rhine crossing of 406/7, was carried out by tribesmen forced out of their lands by strangers whom they could not resist.[26] Since the Slavs subsequently filled the lands that the East Germans abandoned, it seems obvious that the fourth and fifth-century movements into the Roman Empire could not have

---

[22] Ferdinand Lot, *Les invasions germaniques* (Paris, 1935), p. 322: the foremost tribes "were driven forward by the pressure exerted by the tribes advancing behind them," with the result that any people invading the Roman world was itself "pressed forward in the manner of a man who, drawn into the surge of a maddened crowd, is thrown upon a neighbor and exerts upon it a pressure all the more irresistible for being involuntary."

[23] Jordanes, *Getica*, 9, 16–29. For arbitrary modern emendations of his dating, e.g. Kossack as above, n. 21, p. 318: the Goths "who, according to their migration myth, had landed in the Vistula estuary around the time of Jesus' birth, coming from Scandinavia." Mommsen's annotation sets out Jordanes's own choice of date.

[24] For an example whose special value is to spell out the limits of our knowledge, Christian Courtois, *Les Vandales et l'Afrique* (Paris, 1955), pp. 11–32.

[25] Alan Cameron, *Claudian: Poetry and Propaganda at the Court of Honorius* (Oxford, 1970), p. 74.

[26] According to E. A. Thompson, *A History of Attila and the Huns* (Oxford, 1948), p. 28, "it is agreed" that the Huns impelled the crossing of 406 (citing Gibbon); similarly, Diesner, *Völkerwanderung*, pp. 126–7. For explicit counter-arguments, Schmidt, "Ursachen," pp. 349–50 and Maenchen-Helfen, *World of the Huns*, pp. 60–1 (Radagaisus), 71–2. For a Roman text on pressure, see *Historia Augusta* (hereafter *HA*), *Marcus Aurelius*, 14. 1: "Victualis et Marcomannis cuncta turbantibus, aliis etiam gentibus, quae pulsae a superioribus barbaris fugerant, nisi reciperentur, bellum inferentibus" ["Both the Victuali and Marcomanni were throwing everything into disorder, and other peoples as well, who had fled under pressure from more distant barbarians, were threatening to make war unless they were allowed in"]; but when these lines were written, the Huns had already bumped the Goths.

been occasioned by a continual pressure of Germanic immigration from the north, least of all if that immigration occurred far in the past. The image of a crowded *barbaricum*, full of people being driven frantic by newcomers continually shoving in upon them, is entertaining but, at least to a conservative historian, is not borne out by the facts.

The examples cited of the Burgundians and Goths are also noteworthy for the manner in which the track of each tribe has been traced by modern scholarship. First, there is the composite and conjectural nature of the tale. In Musset's version, the Burgundians are said to be traceable to Scandinavia because "their traditions," gathered in an eighth-century hagiography, say so; because "their east German dialect" – unattested except for personal and place names presumed Burgundian by modern philologists – "was close to Gothic"; and because certain toponyms in Scandinavia, first attested in the Late Middle Ages, have affinities to the Burgundian name. The Burgundians are also said to have lived near the Baltic or in Poland because the tribal name occurs in a list of Germanic tribes in Pliny's *Natural History*. The location of these tribes has occasioned much modern discussion. What is any of this worth? The contemporary information about what the Burgundians thought of their origins in the fourth century has been cited above: they were neither Scandinavian, nor Polish, nor otherwise exotic. The very late hagiography enshrines a literary borrowing from Frankish history, not a tribal memory or "saga."[27] Even if there were credible remnants of Burgundian dialect, its affinity to Gothic would be irrelevant to a history of migration.[28] As for Scandinavian toponyms, the precise value of such delicate data would first have to be ascertained; a name like Borgundarholm is surely explicable by other assumptions than that a nation called the Burgundians once lived there or passed by.[29] Much the same problem is raised by the mention in Pliny: what's in a tribal name? In Pliny at least, the name Burgundian – *Burgodiones*, to be precise – antedates the fourth century. But a recognizable people bearing that name, a people whom we may meaningfully connect with fifth-century

[27] The seventh-century Frankish chronicler whom we call Fredegar (3. 65, in *MGH*, *SSrM*, II) tells a story of Lombard origins akin to that of the *Origo gentis Langobardorum* (in *MGH*, *SSrL*); in writing about the early Burgundians, the eighth-century *Passio s. Sigismundi* (in *MGH*, *SSrM*, II) plagiarized Fredegar. All this is learned work, not the pious collection of "popular traditions." Besides, the *Passio* is rightly said to be "durchaus fränkisch orientierte" ["thoroughly Frankish in orientation"]; Erich Zöllner, *Die politische Stellung der Völker im Frankenreich*, Veröffentlichungen des Instituts für österreichische Geschichtsforschung, ed. L. Santifaller, 13 (Vienna, 1950), p. 112.
[28] Similarly Diesner, *Völkerwanderung*, p. 130, drew ethnographic inferences from the Burgundians' long retention of nasalization. Yet Burgundian is extinct: Musset, *Vagues germaniques*, p. 48. On the surviving evidence for it, Schmidt, *Ostgermanen*, p. 191; Schwarz, *Zur germ. Stammesk.*, p. 301; and, especially, Hachmann, *Goten*, p. 148, on its inadequacy. The writing of history out of linguistic evidence is basic to recent accounts of the migrations: Ernst Wahle in Bruno Gebhardt, *Handbuch*, 9th ed. (Stuttgart, 1970), vol. 1, pp. 41–3; to Schmidt, "Ursachen," p. 340, Germanic history began with the departure from the "indo-germanische Urheimat" ["original Indo-Germanic homeland"]. For further illustration, Felix Dahn, "Die Ursachen der Völkerwanderung," in E. von Wietersheim, *Geschichte der Völkerwanderung*, 2nd ed. (Leipzig, 1888), vol. 1. pp. 3–10. Such endeavors have very doubtful standing in a strictly linguistic perspective; see Calvert Watkins, "Language and Its History," in *Language as a Human Problem*, ed. Morton Bloomfield and Einar Haugen (New York, 1974), pp. 85–97.
[29] Cf. the cautious treatment of comparable data about the Vandals by Courtois, *Vandales*, pp. 15–17 (endless disagreements since, after all, there is no way to prove any hypothesis; besides, "nothing allows us to establish the antiquity of these toponyms"). Similarly, Schmidt, *Ostgermanen*, pp. 551–2, on toponyms abusively associated with the Heruli. On the devastating weakness of such proof, Hachmann, *Goten*, pp. 150–3, 156–63; see also ibid., p. 34 n. 75, for interesting evidence on the change of historians' attitudes toward these toponyms between 1878 and 1939.

events, does not occur until long after Pliny and, then, far from the Baltic.[30] It is pointless to deny early Burgundian migrations; the questionable practice is to combine appallingly tenuous evidence in order to affirm them. What possible gain to our knowledge of the barbarians is there in doing so?

Much ink has flowed over the history of the Goths before they reached the south Russian districts where they were in contact with the Roman Empire. A question of surpassing concern to students of Jordanes, the Byzantinized Goth who wrote the first Gothic history, is the credibility of his early chapters: most of all, the assertion of Scandinavian origins.[31] Only one answer seems tolerable. For taking a different approach, the author of a recent, moderately critical book on the subject was stiffly rebuked by a leading spokesman for Germanic tribal studies (*Stammeskunde*):

> Hachmann gives himself great trouble . . . to establish how Germanists, histori-
> ans, and prehistorians developed a "Scandinavia-topos" – Scandinavia as home-
> land of the Germanic tribes. . . . [But] one must not pursue secondary sources
> when primary ones are available. The report of Jordanes on the journey of the
> Goths over the Baltic is known and easy to consult in the *Getica*. The issue is only:
> does one believe it or not? is significance to be attributed to the three ships? how
> wide does one make the Swedish district of origin? are one large emigration or
> many small ones to be assumed?[32]

The orthodoxy called for here is of religious intensity. Jordanes himself was more relaxed. The verisimilitude he attributed to the migration tales is best measured by his dating them from 1490 to 1324 BC; for over a millennium and a half before the advent of the Huns, the Goths he wrote about occupied the lands where the Huns would find them. Modern scholars who make Jordanes's legend their own not only emend its date drastically but also look hard for linguistic, ethnographic, and archaeological elaborations, fitting together bits and pieces of the same type as were met in the Burgundian case. We hear, for instance, that "the true history of the Goths" – true, that is, as distinct from legendary "but not inadmissible" – "begins with Pliny, who, toward AD 75, cited the *Gutones*, and Tacitus, who, towards 98,

---

[30]   Again, cf. Courtois, *Vandales*, pp. 21–8, with the great merit of opening with an exposition of the evidence; also, timely comments on the nature of peoples and tribes (pp. 26–7). The continuity of *Stämme* [tribes] is one of the most tender points in Germanic *Altertumskunde*; note the confidence of Schmidt, *Ostgermanen*, p. 85; Schwarz, *Germ. Stammesk.*, opens by mentioning the fundamental criticism by Franz Steinbach in 1926 (p. 7), but goes on, in the traditional way, to treat each tribe as a fixed entity from prehistory onward. Further about this, Gerold Walser, review in *Historia* 7 (1958): 122–4. Ancient "tribal traditions" could hardly be passed along to very late writers like Jordanes and Paul the Deacon unless the tribes were continuous entities; hence the recent stress upon an enduring *Traditionskern* [kernel of tradition] (Schwarz, *Zur germ. Stammesk.*, p. viii), against which see the apt criticism of František Graus in *Historica* 7 (1963): 188–91.

[31]   At a time when, for example, it generally goes unnoticed that Jordanes and Procopius lived at the same time and place, whole books fasten on the few chapters about Gothic origins: Curt Weibull, *Die Auswanderung der Goten aus Schweden* (Gothenburg, 1958), healthily negative; Josef Svennung, *Jordanes und Scandia. Kritisch-exegetische Studien* (Stockholm, 1967) – more by Svennung on the same subject listed by Hachmann, *Goten*, p. 529; Norbert Wagner, *Getica. Untersuchungen zum Leben des Jordanes und zur frühen Geschichte der Goten*, Quellen und Forschungen zur Sprach- und Kulturgeschichte der germanischen Völker N.F. 22 (Berlin, 1967); Hachmann, *Goten*, pp. 15–143; Gilbert Dagron, "Discours utopique et récit des origines, 1: Une lecture de Cassiodore-Jordanès", *Annales: Économies, sociétés, civilisations* 26 (1971): 290–305.

[32]   Schwarz, *Zur germ. Stammesk.*, pp. 299–300.

knows the *Gothones*."[33] Prodigies of ingenuity are performed in creating arguments that sometimes are wholly circular.[34] By normal standards of source analysis, the early Gothic migrations in Jordanes are about as historical as the tales of Genesis and Exodus; to champion their simple equivalence to history is a task for religious fundamentalists.

The wellspring of such piety is not difficult to discern. A whole program, the collective endeavor of generations since the sixteenth century, appears to be at stake:

> As regards history in the narrow sense, it is to be said that a great intellectual impetus was needed to roll away the enormous burden of biblical–classical convention in historical conceptualization and to find an independent point of departure for German history outside the *orbis universus* ["ecumenical" world of classical and Christian Antiquity]. Yet German historical research set about this liberation from [the time of] Beatus Rhenanus [1485–1547] and Wimpfeling [1450–1528] onward and has achieved it.[35]

Another commentator is less confident but stresses the importance of somehow providing nonliterate Germania not just with a past, but with a history:

> the reports of the Roman writers must be regarded as one-sided and, since written sources are lacking, one must utilize other [sources] and thus endeavor to fill the gaps of ancient reports. To a historian of antiquity this may seem dangerous and unacceptable, since he knows only his sources from which he himself attempts to take as much believable matter as possible. But did only that happen which entered the Roman field of vision? Is it not self-evident that right in the centuries around Christ's birth much went on within the Germanic world?
>
> Greek and Latin authors . . . portrayed relations to the Germans from their own standpoint. Consequently it is the responsibility of Germanic *Stammeskunde* [tribal studies] to liberate itself as much as possible from the one-sidedness of these sources. Understandably, this is not easy.[36]

---

[33] Musset, *Vagues germaniques*, pp. 81, 80. "Not inadmissible" legends remind one of the verdict of the second Dreyfus trial: guilty of high treason but with "extenuating circumstances." Equally strange, the conclusion of Courtois, *Vandales*, p. 18: after immense effort, German erudition has only piled up hypotheses from which no certitudes may be extracted; but once this is said, "il ne me semble pas qu'il soit interdit à l'historien d'imaginer" ["it does not seem to me that the historian is forbidden to imagine"]. Does the "true history" of tribes listed by Pliny and Tacitus begin even if the names never occur again?

[34] It would be invidious to cite examples. Some idea of the problem is suggested by Herwig Wolfram, "Athanaric the Visigoth: Monarchy or Judgeship. A Study in Comparative History," *Journal of Medieval History* 1 (1975): 261: although conceding that the premises of the proposed comparison are dubious and that a chronological leap of 350 years is involved, he concludes, nevertheless, that "a functional comparison . . . seems justified and may well be methodologically heuristic." For a valuable characterization of such writings, E. G. Stanley, *The Search for Anglo-Saxon Paganism* (Cambridge, 1975), p. 122: "In [the last 150 years] the unknown (as I think, the unknowable unknown) was so firmly used to explain the known that scholars felt no doubt in their methods or results."

[35] Hermann Aubin, "Zur Frage der historischen Kontinuität im Allgemein," in his *Vom Altertum zum Mittelalter* (Munich, 1949), p. 70. Can history begin independently of the classical–biblical mainstream of historical technique? For example, will there now or eventually be African history that begins independently of European history? Aubin's statement has the value of forcing us to choose whether to endorse such a notion or not.

[36] Schwarz, *Germ. Stammesk.*, pp. 24, 7. The first part of the quotation is in criticism of Gerold Walser, *Caesar und die Germanen*, *Historia*, Einzelschriften, H. 1 (Wiesbaden, 1956).

It follows from this view that the scholars of today continue to have weighty obligations. The conviction that a great deal happened in the "Germanic world" should inspire them to portray from miscellaneous gleanings what no early narrator ever depicted. Moreover, they ought to rectify the one-sidedness of whatever narratives there are. Something very odd happens, however, when the bias of ancient authors in talking about early Germans is actually detected:

> It is of course necessary to test the character of these important sources, to investigate the intentions of ancient authors, to discover their methods of work, to study how their conception of historical truth differs from that of today, to make out their relationship to their sources. But is one justified in considering only this standpoint? Should they not be trusted to have also acquired information from elsewhere or to have made use of personal information? . . . It would be wrong to think about [Caesar's] literary sources and his political intentions and to overlook his personal experiences with the Germans. The same questions will arise with Tacitus and Cassiodorus [-Jordanes].[37]

In other words, criticism cannot be carried to such a point that it impugns the data that reconstructed "Germanic history" depends upon. At one moment, the Mediterranean observers may be qualified as one-sided and, at another, as sincerely committed to trustworthy and disinterested reporting about the early Germans.

This chapter began with the observation that general histories of the barbarian invasions are too theatrical to jibe with the known incidents of Roman–barbarian encounter in the fourth to sixth centuries such as those that are to be studied in the pages to come [i.e. in Goffart's book]. It was also pointed out that two rather different historical backgrounds – short or long – could be given to such fifth-century peoples as the Goths and Burgundians. What ought now to be apparent is that the long background assigned to these peoples is intimately related to general histories of the barbarian invasions; it is, in effect, a large fragment of the other. Great efforts have been applied in the recent past to creating an "early German history" from which medieval and modern Germany would seem to derive, and very few positive steps have been taken, least of all by those writing in English or French, to counteract this enterprise.[38] The problem has been eloquently defined:

---

[37] Schwarz, *Germ. Stammesk.*, p. 8, cf. *Zur germ. Stammesk.*, pp. xiv–xv. To show that an author could have obtained accurate information gets us little closer to proving that he did; obviously any ancient author stood nearer to the early Germans than we do even if he never wrote about them. Though paradoxical, the attitude expressed by Schwarz has a distinguished precedent: as Weibull, *Auswanderung*, p. 15, pointed out, the scholar who brilliantly established the bookish character of Tacitus's information (Eduard Norden, *Die Germanische Urgeschichte in Tacitus Germania* [Leipzig and Berlin, 1920]) did not think his findings limited the value of the *Germania* as a source on the early Germans.

[38] The outstanding French exception is Fustel de Coulanges, *Invasion germanique*. The heirs to this approach were Alfons Dopsch (in part) and Henri Pirenne (who circumvented the invasions); in France itself, notable medievalists like Lot, Marc Bloch, and Louis Halphen tended to take their barbarian history from Germany rather than from Fustel, whose promising aperçus were left undeveloped.

In beginning a new history of Germany, Josef Fleckenstein omits the usual account of the *Völkerwanderung* and opens instead with a chapter of apparently timeless historical sociology ("Die sozialen Grundlagen"): *Grundlagen und Beginn der deutschen Geschichte*, Joachim Lenscher, ed., *Deutsche Geschichte*, vol. 1 (Göttingen, 1974), pp. 17–32. Although the exposition is of high quality, an opening chapter of this kind seems nevertheless to replace the traditional Exodus with something only

the concept "Germanic" is completely vague and stems from a purely learned construct of [the modern science of Germanic philology]. Whoever collates the sources of the individual Germanic areas – regardless of whether these sources are charters, chronicles, inscriptions, works of art, archaeological finds, etc. – is invariably struck by the great variety and differences that prevent one from yet speaking of a "Germanity" (*Germanentum*) at this time. . . . The notion of a united "Germanity," which was lovingly nurtured by historiography in conjunction with the Romantic [movement], still haunts historical writing, even though the postulates of this construct have long been shattered. . . . The specter of "Germanity" persists, unfortunately, in haunting the heads of individual scholars and political demagogues – those places outside which it has never existed.[39]

An affirmation is implicit in these lines of criticism, namely that if the anachronistic and untenable concept of *Germanentum* is to be rooted out, the history we write should explicitly reflect the diversity and disunity of the peoples that the Roman Empire faced across its borders.[40] This implies, more precisely, a reevaluation and deemphasis of the phenomenon of migration.

A major rhetorical point in defense of "early German history" in the traditional manner is the question "Were there really no Germanic wanderings?," with the inevitable reply, "the fact of such movements of peoples is established."[41] The flaw in such contentions is that, as social anthropologists remind us, movements of peoples are not specific to any period of time or to any ethnic group: "Of migrations there is no end, for man is always on the move."[42]

---

slightly less mythical – a sort of Germanic garden of Eden. The questionable postulate expressed by Aubin (n. 35), "an independent point of departure for German history outside the *orbis universus*," continues to be affirmed.

[39] František Graus, *Volk, Herrscher und Heiliger im Reich der Merowinger* (Prague, 1965), pp. 23–4. Cf. Stanley, *Search*, p. 91: "Grimm and those who followed him [regarded] Germanic antiquity as a common civilization of those who spoke the Germanic languages, and a civilization to which they clung tenaciously through the centuries."

[40] Perhaps the most valuable portrayal of this diversity is afforded by the early fourth-century *Laterculus Veronensis*, whose catalogue of "gentes barbarae quae pullulaverunt sub imperatoribus" [barbarian peoples who sprouted up under the emperors] not only reminds us of the many non-Germanic peoples along the frontier (e.g., Scoti, Sarmatae, Persae, Mauri), but also reflects official recognition of the presence of barbarians within the borders (Isauri in Asia Minor, Cantabri in Spain). Text in Alexander Riese, *Geographi Latini minores* (Heilbronn, 1878), pp. 128–9. The unique copy of the *Laterculus* is appended to the Christian-influenced B version of the *Cosmographia* of Julius Honorius in an early seventh-century codex (Riese, *Geographi*, pp. xxxii–xxxiii, xxxvii). As argued by T. D. Barnes, "The Unity of the Verona List," *Zeitschrift für Papyrologie und Epigraphik* 16 (1975): 275–8, one internal contradiction in the list of provinces suggests that the document may not be homogeneous, but it remains to be shown whether its date differs markedly from that arrived at by A. H. M. Jones, "The Date and Value of the Verona List," *JRS* 44 (1954), 21–9. Cf. Stein, *Bas-Empire*, vol. 1, pp. 437–8 n. 22.

[41] Schwarz, *Germ. Stammesk.*, p. 24; *Zur germ. Stammesk.*, pp. xvi–xvii. For the indispensability of migrations as the integrative element in narratives of early German history, Schmidt, "Ursachen," p. 340.

[42] A. M. Hocart, quoted by Rodney Needham, introduction to A. M. Hocart, *Kings and Councillors*, ed. R. Needham (Chicago, 1970), pp. lv–lvi; further, the paraphrase of S. Ratzel on p. lxxiii: " 'Restless movement' is the characteristic of man . . . it can lead only to confusion to seek points of origin and routes of migration." Historians of the Middle Ages have too casually invoked migrations as a basis for periodization. E.g. Marc Bloch, *Feudal Society*, trans. L. A. Manyon (Chicago, 1961), p. 56, "Till [the eleventh century] . . . these great movements of peoples have in truth formed the main fabric of history

What matters is not whether demonstrable migrations exist – as, of course, they do – but what function they are called on to play in modern narratives. As must be apparent simply from the items that have been reviewed thus far, migrations have served as the factual underpinnings for the theory of early Germanic unity; if retraced with orthodox piety, they even lead back to prehistoric Scandinavia as the common motherland, the single womb that poured its progeny upon an expectant Europe.[43] By fastening upon and giving greatest prominence to the migrations that are common to many periods and peoples, historians have called into being a thematic entity that begins at latest with the Cimbri and Teutones wandering southward a century before Christ and closes with the Lombards invading Italy in AD 568. This is the famous "age of the migrations of peoples, by which is to be understood not only the period after the Hunnic invasion in AD 375 but already the period from the first century BC onward."[44] The mental landscape can only with great difficulty be cleared of such heavily beaten tracks, but, until it is, there can be no hope of improving our understanding of how, in late Antiquity, several barbarian peoples came to establish kingdoms in western provinces of the Roman Empire.

One word more about migrations, even at the risk of belaboring the point. Spectacular incidents like the invasions of the Cimbri and Teutones, the attack of the Marcomanni and their confederates in the late second century AD and even the Rhine crossing of the Vandals, Sueves, and others in 406/7 are those that we most long to grasp from the standpoint of the invaders. The Greco-Roman accounts that we have are not so much one-sided as inadequate, raising more questions than they answer. That is regrettable, but beyond remedy. Neither archaeology nor the other disciplines of prehistory have the resources needed to satisfy our curiosity.

What archaeology does confirm is that the Germanic peoples practiced settled modes of life, not nomadism of even a limited kind:

> The overriding impression conveyed by the excavated sites is of stable and endur-
> ing communities, some occupying the same sites for many decades or even centu-

---

in the West as in the rest of the world. Thenceforward the West would almost alone be free of them." Yet Europe has hardly been freer of "great movements" after that time than it was before; it exported 80 million people in the nineteenth century alone. Cf. Musset, *Vagues germaniques*, p. 43: the stability of west European population is normally taken for granted, as is that of the Roman Empire, with the period of the "great invasions" as a parenthesis of troubles between two eras of normality; "Il serait plus sage d'adopter une attitude inverse" ["it would be wiser to see just the reverse"]. Musset appears to identify stable government with stable population. They do not, in fact, necessarily coincide. The relative prevalence or absence of migrations seems as tenuous a basis for periodization as the prevalence or absence of wars. It is also doubtful that migrations, or any other feature of the "longue durée" ["long haul"] for that matter, may correctly be said to constitute (in Bloch's words) "the main fabric of history."

[43] Diesner, *Völkerwanderung*, p. 87, because written in [the former] East Germany, suggests that this idea is no less acceptable to "socialist" than to "bourgeois" historians. Montesquieu's version of the same thought (ultimately derived from Jordanes) is quoted by Marc Bloch, "Sur les grandes invasions. Quelques positions de problèmes," in Bloch, *Mélanges historiques* (Paris, 1963), vol. 1, pp. 91–103, in a valuable historiographical survey. In addition to the derivation of individual peoples from Scandinavia by Jordanes, Fredegar, the *Passio Sigismundi*, etc., certain early ninth-century authors already expressed the thought that the Northmen were the common ancestors of all Germans: Zöllner, *Politische Stellung*, pp. 46–7, 52. It remained for modern authors to implement such an idea in historical narrative.

[44] Schwarz, *Zur germ. Stammesk.*, p. viii. Cf. n. 2 above. On the other hand, Rolf Hachmann, *The Germanic Peoples*, trans. James Hogarth (London, 1971), pp. 69–71, drew attention to a marked discontinuity between late BC and early AD in the archaeological evidence.

ries, others shifting their dwellings without moving far beyond their original confines. . . . It is clear . . . that the early German economy . . . was probably essentially similar to peasant agriculture within the Western Roman provinces.[45]

Moreover, archaeologists have now abandoned the correspondence between, on the one hand, the cultural provinces inferred from material remains and, on the other hand, the approximate localization of tribes indicated by Greco-Roman writings. For the better part of this century, these two categories of information were believed to correspond.[46] As long as they were, a partnership of rare intensity could exist between archaeology, toponymy, and history; the dynamic syntheses of "early German history" that have been touched on in the preceding pages were all affected by the certitudes that seemed possible when cultural provinces were thought to coincide with (as well as to circumscribe) tribal territories. This postulate can no longer be entertained. Once it is accepted that Greco-Roman ethnography is not directly mirrored in the material remains of Germania, unwritten evidence loses most of its voice; it can be called on only in minor ways to amplify the testimony of literate observers. Any historical narrative of ours will be based almost exclusively on these observers and will consequently be bound to address itself, not to the Germanic tribesmen as they knew themselves or as archaeologists can know them, but merely to the neighbors of the Roman Empire – a collection of peoples who need have had no more in common than the Mediterranean perspective in which they were seen. The chronology and unifying theme of such a narrative derives necessarily from Roman history.

It was Rome that, by its expansion and high standards of security for the provinces, set a conspicuous frontier between itself and the varied aliens beyond. The fate of that border – hardly less of a burden for the Empire to maintain than for the barbarians to endure – may well be the dynamic focus of the story. The emphasis on Rome ought not to be confused with the problematic idea of a "continuity" from Roman into medieval history.[47] On the contrary, the theme of Roman security gives prominence to the disruptive activities of Alamans, Franks, Goths, Vandals, and others in Late Antiquity and hardly denies their capacity for turning the course of events in novel directions. The only denial applies to the conspicuous

[45] Todd, *Northern Barbarians*, pp. 116–17, 131, explicitly correcting an historian of antiquity (M. I. Finley). Marc Bloch, "Une mise au point: les invasions," in Bloch, *Mélanges historiques*, vol. 1, pp. 116–18, gave a subtle and highly developed description of supposed Germanic nomadism, which he connected directly to the *Völkerwanderung*. Also, Robert Folz and others, *De l'Antiquité au monde médiéval*, Peuples et civilisations, vol. 5, 2nd ed. (Paris, 1972), p. 36. Confirming Todd, Johannes Haller and Heinrich Dannenbauer, *Der Eintritt der Germanen in die Geschichte*, 4th ed., Sammlung Goschen 1117 (Berlin, 1970), pp. 20–1: the notion that the Germans were half-nomads is a major error.

The fact of stability has nothing in common with the allegation of a Germanic agriculture more progressive than that of the Roman Empire set out by William H. McNeill, *The Shape of European History* (New York, 1974), pp. 65–8. McNeill's contention, although presented as if it embodied a learned consensus, has no parallel in the literature known to me. It is patently incorrect. Cf. the long abandoned belief that the Germans' attaining the "stage" of settled agriculture created population pressure, which was thus the initial cause of their migrations: Dahn, "Ursachen der Völkerwanderung," pp. 5–6, 8–9.

[46] Todd, *Northern Barbarians*, pp. 20–1, 55. For a different perspective, Schwarz, *Zur germ. Stammesk.*, pp. x–xiii, 301–3.

[47] Graus, *Volk, Herrscher*, pp. 19–21, 24. Graus's criticism, which stresses contemporary Roman statements suggestive of discontinuity, may make too little allowance for what Ammianus talked of when he said "falluntur malorum recentium stupore confixi" ["they are led astray by the horror they feel over the latest misfortunes"] (31. 5. 11) – transitory misfortunes puffed up into unprecedented calamities by observers lacking historical perspective, a common enough phenomenon in our own experience.

fallacies earlier defined: that a coherent "other," or Germanic, side faced the Empire and that this side had an inborn disposition – the accumulated steam of continual migrations – to break into Roman space. The Greco-Roman observers who will be relied on were well aware of the variety and disunity of the peoples facing them (even if all were called barbarians), and they had no illusions about migratory tides. A study based principally on their reports will be imperfect and, to some extent, one-sided, but all sources have shortcomings: our conviction that the barbarians had thoughts does not authorize us to imagine what they were. It is enough that the authentic experience of some contemporary observers should be reflected, rather than modern reconstructions, however well intentioned. Further clarity will result from recognizing that all writings emanate from the literate Mediterranean even when authored by a Goth, an Anglo-Saxon, or a Frank.[48] It was as converts to the religion of the Empire that certain barbarians stopped being mere nuisances and threats to the imperial borders and became instead peoples with a past and, perhaps, even a future. The Empire was as unifying a center for their emergence into history as it was for the expansion of Christianity.[49]

The essential point for the chapters [i.e., of Goffart's book] to come is that the Goths and Burgundians in the provinces of the Empire, as well as the Romans who dealt with them, should not be set in an unduly long perspective. Except for the Alans and Huns, the barbarians who participated in the invasions were all neighbors of the Empire; those with whom we shall be concerned had been on imperial soil, and in frequent contact with the private and public levels of Roman life, for several decades prior to the agreements and transactions that will presently be studied. If these facts deserve to be stressed, it is not in order to intimate that the barbarians had been "Romanized" either by proximity to the frontier or by almost a generation of exposure to Roman provincials. As recent authors remind us, the notion of higher and lower civilizations making contact with each other – unequally filled vessels being connected up and thus finding a common level – is an oversimplification that human experience tends to contradict: " 'Civilisation' does not contact 'barbarism.' . . . What happens is, that men make contact with other men. Or, with other kinds of women."[50] If people meet at all, they do so as individuals, not collectivities. What they communicate to each other has less to do with the social and historical background that any individual may bring to the encounter than with elementary traits of personality and character. The most that may be said on a collective plane is that, for all the parties involved, living together modifies the quality of existence, the more so when the association is permanent.

The circumstances that brought barbarians onto Roman territory in sufficient numbers and with enough power to make a difference were not all the same. At the two extremities of Roman Europe, the island of Britain and the Balkan peninsula, the aliens who immigrated were so numerous that, by the close of the sixth century, the space inhabited by barbarians

---

[48] Cf. the sentiments of Aubin quoted above, at n. 35. The Gothic blood in Jordanes no more makes his *Getica* Germanic than the Vandal blood in Stilicho altered his loyalty to the empire he served. Our most realistic image of a barbarian kingdom comes from a Gallo-Roman, Gregory of Tours.

[49] Contrast to the deeply rooted presupposition that medieval history proceeds from an equilateral trinity of Roman, Christian, and Germanic elements, or involves an "encounter of Germanity with Christianity and the inheritance of Antiquity" (H. Löwe) [n. 17]. A history of Christianity apart from the Roman Empire would be as distorted as Aubin's "independent point of departure for German history" (n. 35). Besides, the notion of triune beginnings tacitly assumes an antecedent catastrophe, after which it was necessary to rebuild from distinct heaps of materials.

[50] A. P. Thornton, "Jekyll and Hyde in the Colonies," *International Journal* 20 (1965): 226–7.

had expanded across the North Sea and the Danube, apparently dislodging and displacing the Roman provincials. Over the long stretch extending between Britain and the Balkans, the similar, but much more limited, retreat of the Empire from its former bounds is delineated, rather roughly, by the modern frontier between Romance and Germanic dialects.[51] These two forms of retreat, in turn, bore little resemblance to the more spectacular, but also more precarious, circumstances with which we shall be concerned. The fifth-century settlements in imperial territory that the present study considers were made in one piece by single bands of barbarians wholly cut off from *barbaricum*. The aliens in these instances penetrated far from the old frontier, then halted in a sea of Romans and took charge, usually by explicit agreement with the imperial government, which accepted them as military auxiliaries.[52] Their numbers are very difficult to establish; the one documented figure that modern historians have been ready to trust [80,000 Vandals and others whom Geiseric led from Spain to Africa in 429] is easier to interpret as fiction than as a head count. Nevertheless, tens of thousands may have been involved in each group – enough to matter. Besides, these were armed bands under military leadership moving into open space populated by unarmed, untrained civilians. They could inspire fear and respect even if they risked being culturally swallowed up by the population amid which they lived.

The prototype for these settlements was the immigration of Gothic refugees authorized by the emperor Valens in 376, or, more precisely, the pacification of these Goths in 382. They had rebelled in 377 and won a great victory at Adrianople (378), but then had been gradually worn down by Roman arms and diplomacy to the point at which their leaders accepted an advantageous treaty. By necessity or by choice, Theodosius I and his descendants were willing to tolerate, rather than to expel or annihilate, those barbarians who rebelled within the imperial borders (like the Goths of 377 and 395) or broke across them in a massive raid (like the Vandals, Alans, and Sueves in 406/7).[53] The Roman government had long cultivated certain of its neighbors as a precious military asset usable for the benefit of the Empire and had thus convinced many barbarian leaders, such as the Goth Athaulf, that the most advantageous course for them and their followers was to serve and protect Romania.[54]

[51] Cf. the second zone described by Löwe in Gebhardt, *Handbuch*, 9th ed., vol. 1, p. 92 (the three-zone scheme was proposed by Aubin). The division I suggest proceeds from what the Empire did: evacuation of Britain; limited withdrawal from the Rhine and upper Danube border districts; inadequate defense of the Balkans (where the Slavs settled). Barbarian immigration into these lands was gradual and complex; e.g. the process that sent Irish and Saxons to Britain and Britons to Armorica. Löwe stressed the distinctiveness of the Germanic tribes involved, but this does not work for the Franks (see next note) and makes no allowance for the Slavs in the Balkans – an important reminder that the "fall" of the Empire was not an exclusively western phenomenon.
[52] Nicely characterized by Musset, *Vagues germaniques*, p. 69 n. 1. The Merovingian kingdom resembled this type of settlement to the extent that Clovis and his successors established their capitals very far from the limits of concentrated Frankish population.
[53] The third-century Empire experienced incursions that were at least as severe as those faced by Theodosius and his sons, but all the invaders were then cleared out, at the cost of a little territory: why did this not happen again? Many Roman historians currently maintain that barbarian "pressure" was too great: Piganiol, *Empire chrétien*, p. 422; A. H. M. Jones, *The Later Roman Empire, 284–602* (Oxford, 1964), pp. 1027–31; J. F. Matthews, review, in *JRS* 56 (1966): 245. An alternative worth exploring is that, to the Roman government, concessions to barbarians were safer than the domestic risks of efficient defense (the third-century emperors Aurelian, Probus, etc., had paid a heavy personal price).
[54] Military use of barbarians: Jones, *Later Roman Empire*, pp. 619–23, 199–200; Stroheker, *Germanentum u. Spätantik*, pp. 9–29, 30–53; Manfred Waas, *Germanen im römischen Dienst im 4. Jahrhundert n.C.* (Bonn, 1965). The famous story of Athaulf, in Orosius, *Historia adversus paganos*, 7.

These were fragile ideas with limited life spans; Roman philo-barbarism was no sturdier or widespread than barbarian devotion to the public interests of the Roman state. Historians of Late Antiquity have not fully explained why the emperors since Constantine placed markedly greater confidence in foreign troops and generals than their predecessors had, and it is worth noting as well the change that official opinion at Constantinople underwent in the second half of the fifth century: its mounting hostility towards free barbarians laid the ideological basis for Justinian's campaigns.[55] Nevertheless, the attractive power of the Empire, typified by the government's welcome to foreign military elites, had a more certain role than any impulse from the barbarian side in establishing exotic dominations on provincial soil. When set in a fourth-century perspective, what we call the fall of the Western Roman Empire was an imaginative experiment that got a little out of hand.

The present [i.e., Goffart's] book, to whose specific subject matter we now turn, is directly concerned with one aspect of this experiment: on what legal terms did barbarian soldiers and their dependants take root in the empire? The question must go unanswered in several regions for lack of evidence; in others, there is enough to permit at least an approximate reply. We begin with a Roman countryside whose most novel feature, instituted since the reign of Diocletian, was a high level of bureaucratic regimentation with a view to the levying of taxes and the performance of essential tasks. At the chronological close of the inquiry, the fiscal organization had shrunk and withdrawn to managing the financial interests of barbarian kings, but the countryside continued to be characterized, on the one hand, by a high level of large, absentee landownership and, on the other hand, by the presence of a servile working force whose bondage stemmed in large part from tax law. As for the barbarian settlers, some of them had been suppressed or displaced by hostile armies, whereas others endured. In either eventuality, their installation had had a real but limited effect upon the organization of landownership in the districts of settlement: much of the regimentation peculiar to late Roman life evaporated, whereas other dimensions of the age became, if anything, more deeply entrenched than ever before. It remains to be seen who the barbarians in question were and what were the technicalities of their installation in the western provinces.

In 418, the Visigoths of King Wallia accepted the settlement in Aquitaine offered them by the Roman government; in 443, the "remnants" of the Burgundians were settled by Aëtius in a part of eastern Gaul; in 476, the army of Italy, composed of various small barbarian peoples, forced the deposition of the last western emperor and the accession of Odoacer as their king in order that they might obtain landed allotments; in the 490s, after Theodoric

43. 3–6, deserves to be combined, on the one hand, with the report of an Alamannic king who was promoted to command of a unit in the Roman army of Britain (Ammianus, 29. 4. 7), and, on the other, with Jordanes's *Getica*, portraying service to the Empire as the historic raison d'être of the Goths. Gerhard Wirth, "Zur Frage der foederirten Staaten in der späteren römischen Kaiserzeit," *Historia* 16 (1967): 240, cf. 236, spoke of "the customary attacks whose object was [for the attackers] to be taken into the Empire and then give up their own political existence in favor of the advantages offered by service to the Empire."

55 Alexander Schenk von Stauffenberg, "Die Germanen im römischen Reich," *Die Welt als Geschichte* 1 (1935): 72–100, 2 (1936): 117–68, attempted an interpretation. The idea of an economic weakening or decline of the Empire is often substituted for an explanation. The distinction made by Musset, *Vagues germaniques*, pp. 224–6, between "infiltrations" (such as military recruitment) and the invasions proper is misleading. For hostility prior to Justinian: the historians Victor Vitensis, Zosimus, and Count Marcellinus (also the Gallic Chronicler of 452?); the reign of Leo I, with its campaign against the Vandals (469) and downfall of the Aspar military dynasty (471), seems important; perhaps the Vandal seizure of Carthage (439) was the turning point.

overthrew Odoacer, the Ostrogoths were assigned lots in Italy; and two groups of Alans accepted similar settlements in the course of the fifth century. These were all regulated operations, presupposing the cooperation of barbarian leaders with the Roman authorities, conducted according to law and intended to maintain at least relative harmony between the barbarian people being settled and the indigenous population. They were different from the arbitrary expropriations by which Geiseric provided for the Vandals in North Africa or from the prolonged depredations of the Sueves in northwest Spain. At the heart of each regulated settlement was the provision of an allotment for each qualified Goth, Burgundian, or whatever. Whether these awards were distributed as soon as the treaties with the West Roman government came into force is not known and perhaps unlikely; sooner or later, however – and almost immediately in Italy – allotments were made: barbarian warriors acquired a stake in the countryside alongside Roman landowners. Both for the beneficiaries and for the Romans who paid the bill, it was a memorable moment.

However momentous at the time, these settlements have left a very poor record, which fails to answer essential questions and leaves much to the imagination. Several chronicles devote single lines to the subject; the Burgundian laws provide intriguing but obscure evidence, which is paralleled rather than developed in the Visigothic Code; Procopius alone attests to the first settlement in Italy, and he, along with the *Variae* of Cassiodorus, offers what glimpses may be had of the scheme instituted by Theodoric.[56] Hardly any of this is descriptive or portrays human beings actually installing barbarian settlers in the Roman provinces; most of the information is inferential, and it bears on the legal or institutional technicalities of land assignment. Altogether, the relevant lines of source material would fit onto five pages or less.

This scanty evidence has been known for many decades. Gaupp's book on the subject, published in 1844, is still judged to be the indispensable point of departure, and many commentaries have followed, down to Ferdinand Lot's long article, "Du régime de l'hospitalité" ["On the Regimen of Hospitality"], published in 1928.[57] Since then, certain aspects of barbarian settlement have aroused lively discussion, but these have not included the land assignment itself, a subject that is regarded either as having been exhausted by Lot and his predecessors, or as being too poorly documented to be knowable.[58] Neither of these views is altogether correct. Earlier commentators have left many questions unsettled, and, though the thrust of Lot's investigation was admirable, the conclusions he reached were

[56] *Chronica minora*, ed. T. Mommsen, *MGH, AA*, vols 9, 11; *Leges Burgundionum*, ed. Ludwig Rudolf de Salis, *MGH, Leges*, vol. 2, pt 1; *Leges Visigothorum*, ed. K. Zeumer, *MGH, Leges*, vol. 1; for Procopius, below, ch. III [in Goffart's book]; Cassiodorus *Variae*, ed. A. J. Fridh, *CCSL* ch. 96 (Turnhout, 1973), also ed. T. Mommsen, *MGH, AA*, vol. 12.

[57] Ernst Theodor Gaupp, *Die germanischen Ansiedlungen und Landtheilungen in den Provinzen des römischen Westreiches* (Breslau, 1844); Ferdinand Lot, "Du régime de l'hospitalité," *Revue belge de philologie et d'histoire* 7 (1928): 975–1011.

[58] E. A. Thompson, "The Settlement of the Barbarians in Southern Gaul," *JRS* 46 (1956): 65–75; J. M. Wallace-Hadrill, "Gothia and Romania," in his *The Long-Haired Kings and Other Studies in Frankish History* (New York, 1962), pp. 25–48, esp. 30–3. Thompson depended essentially on Lot, "Hospitalité," without reconsidering the evidence; so also Thompson, "The Barbarian Kingdoms in Spain and Gaul," *Nottingham Medieval Studies* 7 (1963): 3–33. Wallace-Hadrill, "Gothia and Romania," p. 30 n. 2, "we know almost nothing of [the Visigothic] settlement" (a correct appraisal of the evidence). The main expositions since Lot are: Schmidt, *Ostgermanen*, pp. 171–3, 316–17, 327–9, 362–3, 505–6 (little influenced by Lot); Wilhelm Ensslin, *Theodorich der Grosse* (Munich, 1947), pp. 94–7, 193–6, 203–5 (Italy only); and, especially, Musset, *Vagues germaniques*, pp.284–8, ibid., trans. James, pp. 214–17.

disappointing and uneven. As for the documentation, no new texts can be introduced, but the ones there are – most of all those bearing upon Italian conditions – can be better interpreted than they have been.

The present study [i.e., Goffart's book] reexamines this old subject and introduces three novelties into the discussion. To begin with, a critical appraisal will be made of the assumption that the allotments to barbarians followed Roman practices for quartering soldiers, known to moderns as "the hospitalitas system." Some historians have been less wedded to this notion than others, but none has established what basis there was in Roman law for assigning land, not just shelter, to barbarian soldiers. Next, the Italian evidence will be set at the forefront of the discussion, as constituting, in effect, the only body of source material that is extensive enough to illustrate the technicalities of a barbarian settlement. The other texts are late and fragmentary and should not be interpreted without the assistance of the Italian example. Finally, it will be argued that the "land" given to barbarians was not ordinary property but a special mode of ownership made possible by late Roman tax law. The allotment that a barbarian initially received consisted of tax assessment and its proceeds – a "superior" ownership that did not extinguish or supersede the private proprietary rights of the Romans owning assessed land and paying its taxes. This peculiarity helps to explain why the settlements occasioned hardly a ripple of protest from the Roman provincials and why the few protests they aroused assumed the form they did.

3 The Fall of Rome Will Not Take Place

Chris Wickham

Jean Durliat has published, with the *imprimatur* of the German Historical Institute in Paris, one of the most iconoclastic books on early medieval history in recent years, in a field already prone to iconoclasm.[1] His argument runs, briefly, like this. The Germanic invasions had no effect on the fiscal structures of the Roman Empire. These structures had, since Diocletian at least, been heavily decentralized, with *possessores*, tax-farmers, charged with the responsibility of exacting taxes from their own *possessiones*; in fact, every late Roman reference to *possessiones* or to *fundi* is to such fiscal districts. This practice continued into Frankish Gaul and the other Romano–Germanic kingdoms; *villae* were not estates but fiscal units, and *coloni* were not tenants but landowning peasants who owed their taxes, through these *villa* units, to the state. Carolingian polyptychs were simply tax-registers for these units; the Carolingian state until its collapse maintained all the fiscal structures of the so-called Late Empire. So: large landowning, the early medieval politics of land, and weak early medieval political systems all are to vanish from our mental maps of the past; the surviving Roman Empire is to take their place, at least up to 888.

Such a program will recall to mind Guy Bois's equally bold attempt to extend "antique" socioeconomic patterns up to the year 1000, even if Bois's project is very different both in form and content.[2] Bois is, however, a loner; Durliat, by contrast, has already convinced a number of well-known associates who are engaged in parallel research or who are keen to support his views, such as Elisabeth Magnou-Nortier, Martin Heinzelmann, and Karl Ferdinand Werner. He links himself, furthermore, to a matrix of important revisionist studies on late Rome, notably by Walter Goffart and Jean Gascou, whom to some extent he is simply extending into the early medieval West. It would not, as a result, be possible to dismiss his work with the abuse to which Bois was subjected (abuse which Bois amply returned; the whole debate has become a paradigm of how not to conduct historical discussion). Anyway, Durliat's book is substantial, and it deserves a substantial reply.[3] On the other

---

[1] *Les finances publiques de Dioclétian aux Carolingiens (284–888)*, Beihefte der Francia xxi (Sigmaringen, 1990), x + 368 pp. Page references in the text will be to this book. The title says "889"; an erratum slip corrects it to 888. I am grateful to John Haldon and Ian Wood for commenting on the text; they are not responsible for its inadequacies.

[2] G. Bois, *La mutation de l'an mil* (Paris, 1989).

[3] See, already, Jean-Pierre Devroey's critique of his earlier articles on the Carolingians, "Polyptyques et fiscalité à l'époque carolingienne: une nouvelle approche?", *Revue belge de philologie et d'histoire* 63 (1985): 783–94.

hand, it is not as fully argued as it could be, which is a pity. The book has a tendency to make bald statements substantiated by a couple of references, even when it is making points that diametrically contradict previous opinion; counter-arguments are too seldom considered. This does not seem to me an adequate way of presenting arguments that would, if accepted, destroy most historians' entire image of the Early Middle Ages. They contrast notably with the careful presentations by Goffart in his *Barbarians and Romans*, which aimed to overturn the standard views of the Germanic settlements; Goffart's book has not convinced everybody, but his views have been accepted in some of the most powerful recent discussions of the Romano-Germanic kingdoms.[4] Durliat often seems content to state, not to try to convince. Nonetheless, his book is no less of a challenge; if he is right, we are wrong. Since he has not convinced me, then, my task will have to be to try to disprove him; the reader must recognize at the outset that this is the aim of this essay. I hope to disprove Durliat while at the same time respecting the interest of his problematic.

I shall first discuss Durliat's view of the Late Empire, where he is most at ease; then some of the difficulties of his post-Roman and Carolingian theories. I will spend more time on the Roman than on the post-Roman period, in fact: partly because Durliat's main arguments themselves have their roots there; partly because I expect that other critics will concentrate on the Carolingian period, and they might assume that, given Durliat's greater expertise in late Rome, his arguments do indeed fully work there – which, as I shall argue, they do not. Finally, I will make some brief comments on the implications of his theories for the Early Middle Ages as a whole, the aspect of his book which is in many ways the most problematic of all.

Jean Durliat is a late Romanist and early Byzantinist by training, with a thesis on Byzantine Africa behind him and, among other works, a large book on the food supply of Mediterranean towns in the third to the seventh centuries that has appeared virtually simultaneously with the book under review. (Since I will be consistently critical of the latter, it is fair to state that his book on towns seems to me entirely admirable; I learnt a huge amount from reading it, and would accept nearly all his arguments – the exceptions mostly being the sections where he comes closest to *Les finances publiques*.)[5] He convinces us without difficulty that he has at his fingertips the appalling complexities of late Roman fiscality. This is a good thing, for it makes it less necessary to unpick all his arguments on the topic; here, I will simply

---

[4] W. Goffart, *Barbarians and Romans, A.D. 418–584: The Techniques of Accommodation* (Princeton, 1980). For the unconvinced, see, e.g., the detailed critiques of M. Cesa, "Hospitalitas o altre 'techniques of accommodation'?," *Archivio storico italiano* 140 (1982): 539–52; S. J. B. Barnish, "Taxation, land and barbarian settlement in the western empire," *Papers of the British School at Rome* 54 (1986): 170–95; I count myself among this number for similar reasons. For good examples of how Goffart's arguments can be used positively, see H. Wolfram, *History of the Goths* (English ed., Berkeley, 1988), pp. 295–300; M. F. Hendy, "From public to private," *Viator* 19 (1988): 29–78. Some of Durliat's most convincing arguments actually help to back up parts of Goffart's thesis (see their contributions to H. Wolfram and A. Schwarcz, eds, *Anerkennung und Integration* [Vienna 1988]); it may also be observed that Durliat's book will help to make Goffart's arguments seem positively mainstream.

[5] *De la ville antique à la ville byzantine. Le problème des subsistances* (Rome, 1990). I would argue that, in this book, Durliat understresses the role of private beneficence in urban building (cf. also *Finances publiques*, pp. 45, 61–2), and that archaeological evidence supports the presence of private commerce more than he allows. His discussion of the seventh-century crisis also needs more thought. But these are details. The book is, above all, about urban grain supply; on that subject, it is the best discussion in print.

summarize them, and focus on those that are most important for his vision of the Early Middle Ages.

Durliat intends to modify our picture of late Roman land taxation. It was heavy, but stable, and lower than has been previously thought, at around 20 percent of harvested crop (pp. 16–19, 296–9; it is curious here that he does not criticize, or even cite, the standard calculations by A. H. M. Jones, which are somewhat higher). It was exacted essentially from abstract land units, *iuga*; the capitation tax was separate but relatively low. More importantly, it was not only collected by city councillors, *curiales*, but also largely administered by them: the expenses of the cities themselves, which amounted to a third of imperial revenues, were managed by the *curiales*, without any more central intervention (pp. 38–45), and so was much of the imperial revenue reserved for the army (pp. 46–9).[6] Durliat's other book amply backs up his picture of local public expenditure. The *curiales* become less of an object of pity, as they flee from their public burdens; it becomes easier to see why people also *wanted* city office (e.g. pp. 75–7), for handling taxation is always going to be a profitable process. This basic point is indeed extremely persuasive. Durliat is more controversial when he discusses the Church (pp. 52–63), which, he argues, was simply seen as part of the state administration, with no autonomy from the emperor at all. This seems to me an unsafe conclusion to draw from the undoubted facts that the Church was dominated by imperial policy-making, or that bishops had certain secular political powers and rights. But this point of his theory cannot be discarded; his whole Carolingian section depends on it.

The real problem, however, comes with Durliat's theories about the detail of how tax is collected. He is worried about the fact that fourth- and fifth-century laws tend to assume that *possessores* are responsible for tax collection along with *curiales* and other officials. The traditional view is that *possessores* were landowners, and paid the taxes (including, at least after c.370, those of their *coloni*, their tenants) to the *curiales*; but why, then, do the laws put both together as responsible for taxation in the same way? Durliat's solution is to see *possessores* as tax-farmers, local collectors rather than landowning taxpayers (pp. 65–74). He sees the Empire as divided up between property-owners, who have *propriété utile* [property one can make full use of], and *possessores*/farmers, who have *propriété éminente* [property whose tax revenues one controls]. Property thus in a sense exists on two levels, that of direct exploitation and that of fiscal rights. The idea is interesting, and has some similarities with the *pronoia* of Middle Byzantium, for example, or with the Arab *iqṭāʿ*. It could certainly explain why the *Codex Theodosianus* [*Theodosian Code*, 438] emphasizes the *possessores* so strongly. It is at least conceivable that the Romans of the Late Empire combined their ideas of land tenure with those concerning fiscal obligations.[7] After all, the classic historiography on the subject of the *coloni* says nothing very different from this. It is particularly easy to imagine how the Roman legislators of the fourth century could have adopted land terms like *possessio* and *possessor* in order to give them a new technical, fiscal meaning. But Durliat tends to reason like a legal historian: if fiscal laws give *possessio* and *possessor* a fiscal meaning, then no other meaning is possible. The same is true for the word *fundus*: "the technical term to designate tax assessment . . . which can have no other meaning" (p. 68). It is also the same with the term *colonus* (pp. 85–93): a passage from the *Codex Theodosianus* (5.19.1) that

---

[6] For tax figures, refs in A. H. M. Jones, *Later Roman Empire* (Oxford, 1964), pp. 819–23, 1340. For the army, see also Durliat in Wolfram and Schwarcz, eds, *Anerkennung*, pp. 30–6 and *passim*.

[7] An important argument along these lines is J. Gascou, "Les grands domaines, la cité et l'état en Egypte byzantine," *Travaux et mémoires* 9 (1985): 1–90, esp. 6–35; I would more easily accept his arguments for Egypt than his generalizations from Egypt to the rest of the Empire.

mentions the fact that the *coloni* could possess their own *peculium et propria* [private property] proves that "*the colonus* is thus a proprietor" (p. 85n.: the italics are mine): not just some *coloni*, but all of them. These passages dominate the entire book, and must be discussed in some detail. In my opinion, they raise many more problems than they solve.

Take the word *fundus*. This is a word common throughout Antiquity. It means "base" – of a vase, of a mountain, as well as in a particular sense, "land" or "estate." In the first century, for example, Columella consistently uses it in its specifically agrarian meaning. Even Isidore of Seville, who was certainly making use of early sources, but was himself contemporary to the period studied by Durliat, wrote: "*fundus dictus quod eo fundatur vel stabilisatur patrimonium*" ["an estate is called *fundus* because it is that on which a patrimony is founded and made stable"], in a chapter devoted to agriculture. In everyday language, it was quite simply a word that meant "land," and despite the best efforts and intentions of legislators, they were not capable, then or now, of forcing people to use words only in the ways they wanted, especially if these ways were new ones. But for Durliat, *fundus* after *c*.300 only means tax unit, in every kind of source; indeed, it already did in the Early Empire (p. 68, n. 24) – something that would have surprised Columella.[8] In particular, all our records of *fundi* in late Roman documents are to *assiettes fiscales* [fiscal territories], and not to property. He justifies this by an appeal to agrarian logic: sixth-century Ravenna papyri show extremely low prices for *fundi*, which would make them absurdly small as the basis of "great estates" if they were land (pp. 153, 166, 302–3); much better to see them as the buying and selling of fiscal rights, which were cheaper. Furthermore, sales and gifts regularly show the division of *fundi* into *unciae* (twelfths), and even half-*unciae*, which makes no sense if a *fundus* is an estate, for this would need "a certain structure to render it exploitable" (p. 72n.).[9] This argument is developed later when Durliat discusses the Merovingian and Carolingian *villa*, which is to be another fiscal territory (pp. 153–8, 193, 253–4); Magnou-Nortier has made similar points also.[10] Whole estates cannot, they say, be partitioned and sold off with the insouciance implied in our sixth- and seventh-century documentation; how could one split a village into portions (pp. 154–5), or (Magnou-Nortier) a bipartite estate, which requires an undivided structure to work at all? Finally, how is it that people buy and sell property *in* a *fundus* (or, later, a *villa*), if the latter is an agrarian unit? "One sells a part of a property, but not a good that is found on a property without being part of it" (p. 66). Once again, much better to see *fundi* and *villae* as fiscal units; these can be split up into as many parts as one

---

[8]   Columella, *De re rustica*, 1.4.8 and *passim*; Isidore, *Etymologiae*, ed. W. M. Lindsay (Oxford, 1911), 15.13.4. On the *fundus* in the Early Empire, the basic survey is P. W. de Neeve, 'Fundus as economic unit,' *Tijdschrift voor rechtsgeschiedenis* 52 (1984); 3–19. And, for the late Roman law of *possessio*, see the fundamental E. Levy, *West Roman Vulgar Law. The Law of Property* (Philadelphia, 1951), mysteriously uncited by Durliat; there is a lot of material here on *possessio* as meaning, in effect, "*propriété utile*" that would be very difficult to controvert. (One must note that much later in the book – p. 256n. – Durliat admits that *possessio* has various meanings; if he really means this, much of his early argument, e.g. p. 69, falls immediately.)

[9]   See also J. Durliat, "Qu'est ce que le Bas-Empire? A propos de trois ouvrages récents," *Francia* 16/1 (1989): 137–54, at 144–50 (p. 144 for *fundi* as "grandes domaines").

10. E. Magnou-Nortier, "La terre, la rente et le pouvoir dans les pays de Languedoc pendant le haut moyen âge," *Francia* 9 (1981): 79–115; 10 (1982): 21–66; 12 (1984): 53–118, at 9: 93–6, 10: 28–64; E. Magnou-Nortier, "Le grand domaine: des maîtres, des doctrines, des questions," *Francia* 15 (1987): 659–700, at 679–88; E. Magnou-Nortier, "La gestion publique en Neustrie," in H. Atsma, ed., *La Neustrie* i (Sigmaringen, 1989), pp. 271–320, at 273–85. Magnou-Nortier's work is not under review here, so I will not consider it in detail; it fits very closely with Durliat's work, however, and I would make a similar critique of it.

likes, and, in that case, property in a *fundus* is simply located inside someone else's fiscal territory.

These arguments, in my opinion, betray a profound ignorance of how land was exploited in our period, and do not even fit the documents. To take the latter first: of course, if *fundus* or *villa* – and the same is argued for *possessio*, and indeed in some contexts every other possible agrarian term – must have a fiscal meaning, then most documents are just about tax rights, and not about land tenure. Direct landowning thus becomes oddly difficult to document at all (I will return to the point), but then, as Durliat remarks, so was the organization of tax collection in the traditional theories of the late Roman fiscal system. For this argument to work, however, there cannot be any reference to *fundi* as directly exploited property in our sources. I do not think this is true. Let us look at some examples in the Italian papyri in order to pursue the point.[11] *P. Ital.* 8 (a. 564) describes the inheritance of a certain Collictus, which is to be sold and divided between his heirs. It lists his movables, and those of his dead freedman Guderit; it then moves onto urban houses, and then, without a break, portions of *fundi* (and a *casa* and a *casale*) in the territories of Ravenna and Bologna. How can we conclude that these properties are of two distinct types, *utile* and *éminente*? There is no change in the formularies; one just follows on from the other. This is normal, indeed; charters frequently move smoothly from listing *fundi* to naming other property (e.g. a garden and a vineyard in *P. Ital.* 17, early sec. VII); and *fundi* in one text are described with identical formularies to *iugera* of land, *propriété utile* without doubt, in another text (cf. *P. Ital.* 30, 31; Durliat, pp. 153–4, 166). And in *P. Ital.* 44 (mid sec. VII), the church of Ravenna leases part of an urban house with a very detailed description of its appurtenances alongside a rural *massa cum fundis*; the aristocratic tenant is held both to restore the house and to improve the crops (probably the vines) on the *massa* [estate] – hardly a sign of the latter being an *assiette fiscale*. There are not that many Italian papyri, and not all of them force us to make a clear choice between the two readings of the word *fundus*, but not one of them must necessarily be read in the way that Durliat proposes. Even *P. Ital.* 10–11 (for the year 489), a transfer made by Odoacer of *fundi* in Sicily to the *vir illustris* Pierius, which certainly and explicitly has a fiscal context (p. 168),[12] can admit both readings as it stands. One could also observe that it would perhaps have been unnecessary for the municipal functionaries of Syracuse to ride on horseback around the limits of the *fundi*, interrogating the *inquilini* [tenants] and the *servi* [slaves], if they had merely been registering a change in their fiscal status.

The conclusions drawn by Durliat about agrarian matters allow us to develop these remarks further. What exactly was the *fundus* according to traditional historiography? Certainly not a "great estate"; the word is much too vague in classical Latin. Ulpien wrote: "*non enim magnitudo locum a fundo separat, sed nostra affectio*" ["it is not size that separates a place from a *fundus*, but our disposition"]; if we wish to cultivate any land whatsoever as a separate unit, whether it be small or large, it can be called a *fundus*.[13] The second-century table of Velleia lists hundreds of *fundi*, which often could have been small, or, quite plausibly, fragmented. In the countryside around Rome from the ninth to the eleventh centuries, where agrarian units were still called *fundi*, their size varied from a few fields to an entire estate. They, too, could be fragmented, and were often divided: sections of *fundi* could be

---

[11] J.-O. Tjäder, ed., *Die nichtliterarischen lateinischen Papyri Italiens aus der Zeit 445–700* (Stockholm, 1955–82), cited in the text as *P. Ital.*
[12] See further W. Goffart, *Rome's Fall and After* (London, 1989), pp. 199–200, from a reprint of a 1972 article, for a fiscal context for *P. Ital.* 10–11. The text needs more analysis.
[13] De Neeve, "Fundus", p. 6.

sold or given away in the form of parcels that were regularly described as *in* or *ex fundo*. There was no difference between the *fundi* of the eleventh century and those of Columella or of Pliny as to the way in which they appear in the documentation; they were and remained parcels of land, provided with names (*fundus calvisianus*, or the like – one could add that it might seem curious to give a tax unit a name). They had very little relationship to the pattern of settlement, unlike *villae* or *vici* [both terms for village]. They were simply units of property, which did not necessarily involve a fixed system of agricultural exploitation. The vast properties in the Roman countryside in the tenth and eleventh centuries were commonly built up of many *fundi*, perhaps, for all we know, each with different agrarian functions.[14] It is because of all this that there are serious problems with Durliat's argument when he states that the fact that late Roman *fundi* should have had low or varying prices, or should have been regularly divided, makes it implausible that they were economic units. Indeed, all landowning in Italy, from the first century to the present day, has usually been so heavily fragmented that division (a normal feature, after all, of both Roman and Germanic inheritance law) would make very little difference to it.

This argument can be extended to Lombard–Carolingian Italy, which tended to have more articulated tenurial structures, including bipartite estates. These estates (*curtes*) could be divided with the utmost detachment, sometimes into dozens of pieces. (So could villages – indeed, there were scarcely any villages in Italy that were not divided among many landowners – and tenures.) At the very least, if a bipartite estate was divided, one could postulate that the item that was really divided was its produce; but great estates could be physically fragmented as well, and Carolingian documents for Italy include numerous examples of the holders of single tenures (*casae massariciae*, or *mansi*) owing labour services on fragments of demesnes, often many kilometers away.[15] Here, too, the possibility that bipartite tenurial patterns can be pretty loose contradicts the assumption that Durliat and Magnou-Nortier have, that *villae* (whether villages or integrated estates) cannot be divided up and sold without losing their coherence. And it is easy to supply Italian examples for these processes from every century of the Middle Ages.[16] There is indeed an unbroken continuity in the way land is described in north-central Italy, from the Lombard period right into the thirteenth century and beyond, which sits ill with any theory of *assiettes fiscales*, if we suppose that the latter ever broke down. It looks as if, despite the hostility that Durliat and Magnou-Nortier have for classical polyptych theory, that they have absorbed one of its weakest elements, the idea that estate management needed to be (or could ever be) organized through rigid and unchanging structures. In the end, all that estate-owners need is produce from their agricultural workers, and this can be obtained by a variety of different procedures, sometimes inside the same estate or even the same tenure. It might be argued, since these arguments are drawn exclusively from Italian examples, that they are an incomplete answer to a book whose post-Roman arguments are focused on Francia. But Durliat does hold that

[14] See, for example, C. J. Wickham, "Historical and topographical notes on early medieval South Etruria," *Papers of the British School at Rome* 46 (1978): 132–79, e.g. 142–3, 174–6. For similar patterns in the Romagna, A. Castagnetti, *L'organizzazione del territorio rurale nel medioevo* (Turin, 1979), pp. 169–88; G. F. Pasquali, "Gli insediamenti rurali minori," in A. Vasina et al., *Ricerche e studi sul "Breviarium ecclesiae Ravennatis"* (Rome, 1985), pp. 125–44. In practice, I expect, early medieval *fundi* were simply collections of (one or more) rent-paying tenures, with no fixed internal structures.

[15] For surveys, see B. Andreolli and M. Montanari, *L'azienda curtense in Italia* (Bologna, 1983); P. Toubert, "Il sistema curtense," *Storia d'Italia. Annali* 6 (1983): 5–63; C. J. Wickham, *The Mountains and the City* (Oxford, 1988), pp. 68–84.

[16] E.g. Wickham, *The Mountains and the City*, pp. 221–35.

Italy after 550 would fit his model (e.g. pp. 153, 290); anyway, if his arguments do not work for Italy as well as Francia, then, as they are presently constituted, they fall. Above all, the illustrations I have given are intended to show that Durliat's general agrarian objections do not hold; his texts describe a perfectly coherent rural economy if they are seen as describing property-holding rather than fiscal territories.

Even if Durliat were right about late Roman *fundi*, there would be two other problems about his picture. The first is what happens to landownership. Durliat's *coloni* are, he says, not tenants; they are taxpaying landowners. He also thinks rural slavery was relatively unimportant in the Late Empire (pp. 20, 176: in this, which is another currently heated debate, I entirely agree with him, at least insofar as he is talking about slave plantations). Who is left to cultivate the properties of those who were not peasants? Large landowning does not just become ill documented; it vanishes. This revolution from the world of Columella and Pliny has gone unnoticed by our sources; ought not someone to have mentioned it, in the years around 300? The picture also takes no account of, for example, Palladius, whose fifth-century estate manual would make no sense if interpreted in this way.[17] I cannot see how we can avoid the conclusion that *coloni* could at least sometimes, and perhaps even normally, be tenants (as they were also for Columella and Pliny). But then Durliat's position unravels at the other end: if some *coloni* could be tenants, then some of the *domini*, *patroni* and *possessores* of the *Codex Theodosianus* reappear as landlords. I do not think that Durliat's theory of the *assiette fiscale* can survive these observations, at least in the global version presented in the book under review.

The second problem is this. The word *possessio* can mean many things at the same time, then as now. It is possible that one of these meanings could be territory with a fiscal element: I would not dismiss this possibility *a priori*. But if this is the case, it is striking to note that the Roman state of the Late Empire (or its predecessors) chose to use all the classical words concerning landowning that were available at that time to designate these *assiettes fiscales*. At the very least, the Romans cannot have had a very clear idea of the differences between "*propriété utile*" and "*propriété éminente*." Why did the *possessores* not try to tighten their grip on the latter kind of property, which was generally revocable, by turning it into the former? Why were landowning *coloni* not reduced (or brought back) to the status of tenants? We can certainly propose that Salvian was lamenting precisely this phenomenon in the middle of the fifth century in Gaul; and the Ostrogoths in sixth-century Italy included individuals who very much wanted to establish themselves as proprietors, with or without the permission of the law.[18] The reluctance of the Germans to pay taxes on their land is well known (cf. pp. 109–10). But who would be willing to pay taxes on any kind of property if the state (or the city) was unable to enforce such a demand? After all, resistance to taxation is well documented in our sources, especially in sixth- and seventh-century Gaul. Why did the whole procedure not collapse in the confusion of the fifth to seventh centuries, as Goffart has argued?[19] The two versions of "property" could in these situations very easily slip together into one; *possessio* as tax-farming would soon become indistinguishable from any other kind of possession in a situation where its revocability – and still more, the actual paying of taxes

[17] R. Martin, ed., Palladius, *Traité d'agriculture* i (Paris, 1976), e.g. 1.6. The best guide to land tenure in this period is D. Vera, "Forme e funzioni della rendita fondiaria nella tarda antichità," in A. Giardina, ed., *Società romana e impero tardoantico* i (Rome, 1986), pp. 367–447.
[18] See, e.g., G. Lagarrigue, ed., Salvian, *De gubernatione dei* (Paris, 1975), vol. 5, pp. 17–45; Goffart, *Barbarians and Romans*, pp. 89–100, for the Goths.
[19] Goffart, *Barbarians and Romans*, pp. 228–30, and Goffart, *Rome's Fall*, pp. 213–31 (from an article published in 1982).

– could not be enforced. Every student of central medieval military feudalism knows this; and it is hard to imagine that in, for example, the decentralized environment of late seventh-century Gaul, the checks and balances were strong enough to prevent it. This all makes the picture far more complex than Durliat allows.[20] It is, of course, possible that states, when they reestablished their power after periods of weakness, resumed the tax burden on the land, or converted *de facto* landowning back into tax-farming, as happened often enough in the Islamic world.[21] I do not in fact know of any early medieval western examples of such recentralization; but anyway, Durliat does not discuss the issue. There is no politics in Durliat's picture; only administration.[22] But, whatever we think of the transformations that took place in the West in the fifth century and onwards, we cannot argue that it was short of politics.

Here, however, we are moving into the period of the Germanic invasions and the Romano-Germanic kingdoms that followed them. Durliat's picture of the Late Empire has serious problems, but at least it is coherent, and has a certain elegance. What follows is more seriously unconvincing, for the reasons already set out and for some new ones. We know, after all, that the late Romans did tax; and no one has contested some fiscal continuity, at however low a level, in the successor states until at least the early seventh century. Durliat does not produce any unambiguous evidence for the land tax after that date except a few specific references that have been widely recognized, and analysed as exceptions, such as the Ardin document from 721 (pp. 97–114; actually, he spends less time on Ardin – e.g. p. 173 – than I would have expected, and says surprisingly little about the seventh-century Tours documents, even though they ought to be the major supports for arguments that would prolong the organization of the land tax past its traditional end-point as a general exaction in *c.*650).[23] For the Carolingians, he restricts himself to listing references to *census* in the capitularies in a fairly casual way (pp. 192, 199, 247).[24] Nor is he very convincing on the expenses of the state, the major scale of which in both the Romano-Germanic and the Carolingian periods is invoked to justify his hypotheses about taxation (pp. 122ff, 221ff). He admits that secular city spending declined (pp. 128–9, 134–6), and, somehow, vanished (pp.

---

[20] Durliat only discusses issues of this kind in the context of the Carolingian period, e.g. pp. 260–1; earlier on, ordinary administration continued, little changed (pp. 159–62).

[21] See, in general, C. Cahen, "L'évolution de l'iqtā' du IXe au XIIIe siècle," *Annales ESC* 8 (1953): 25–52.

[22] Durliat consciously wishes to abolish political crisis: "Alaric, Clovis, Théodoric et les autres n'ont pas 'conquis' la Gaule; ils ont imposé à l'empereur de les reconnaître comme ses délégués" ["Alaric, Clovis, Theodoric, and the others did not 'conquer' Gaul; they forced the emperor to recognize them as his delegates"] (p. 186). A bit like the situation of the Germans in France during the Vichy period, I suppose.

[23] For Ardin, see further, Goffart, *Rome's Fall*, pp. 243–6 (241–52 for Tours); Magnou-Nortier, "Gestion publique", pp. 300–5; for Tours, see Durliat's own more detailed survey, "Qu'est-ce qu'un polyptyque?," in *Media in Francia, Recueil de mélanges offerts à K. F. Werner* (Paris, 1989), pp. 129–38. Note that Durliat concentrates on the Franks from now on. This is wholly understandable; but he then should not arbitrarily introduce Ostrogothic or Vandal material, all necessarily very early, to fill in his Frankish arguments, as, e.g., on p. 111, n. 117, or p. 148, n. 198.

[24] Some Carolingians did organize some form of land taxation, of course, notably Charles the Bald in his attempts to buy off the Vikings (pp. 199, 219, 268–9). See, in general, A. Dopsch, *Die Wirtschaftsentwicklung der Karolingerzeit* (Cologne, 1962), pp. 335–7, a reference often cited by Durliat, for a collection of examples. These examples need to be analysed in greater detail, and more carefully, than Durliat does. His remarks on the edict of Pîtres (pp. 277–8) do not convince: see below.

235–8); but he claims that the army continued to be a major expense throughout, and, at least in the Carolingian period, so did the civil administration. If the Merovingians and the Carolingians continued to have a large salaried standing army, then one would indeed have to recognize a financial scale for the post-Roman state that has hitherto been denied. But Durliat does not produce any serious evidence for it in the Merovingian period (pp. 126–8), and the major secondary source he cites here, Bachrach, shows clearly that standing-army units were of only minor importance.[25] In the Carolingian period, the army can only be argued to be salaried because the *mansi* that the capitularies use as the basic units by which army service is calculated are by definition fiscal revenues rather than landed properties (pp. 222–9); Durliat provides no other proof for the claim that the Carolingian army was salaried, and here runs close to a circular argument. That the Carolingians had a more imposing civil administration than has often hitherto been assumed has been convincingly argued by Werner,[26] and Durliat takes the point up in a relatively uncontroversial section (pp. 230–9) – even if he tends to assume, a little idealistically, that every institution referred to in the capitularies functioned regularly and consistently. This is clearly one of the reasons why Werner gives his *imprimatur* to the book on pp. ix–x; still, it does not seem to me that the latter's arguments require as much modification to the standard picture of the public responsibilities of major landowners as either of them think.

Durliat does not, in short, succeed in showing that the large-scale enterprise of the late Roman state and its tax network so obviously survived beyond 600 or so that the burden of proof lies on opponents of his arguments about post-Roman taxation; one thus, logically, should question all his major statements in the second two-thirds of the book. Durliat claims, among other things, that the Church continued to be simply an administrative arm of the state, and that therefore every piece of evidence for the financial activities of any church is direct evidence for the functioning of public power (pp. 146–51, 211–12, 239–51); that the word *servus* can mean "free landowner" (pp. 176–9, 181–3, 280–4); and that Carolingian *mansi* are always fiscal units, at least in the capitularies (pp. 195–203, 253–9, 315–21; elsewhere, they can be real smallholdings, with a completely different size, about a quarter of that of fiscal *mansi*: pp. 201–9).[27] These are not just casual claims; if Durliat is wrong about any of them, his whole theory falls, for church documents, i.e. the polyptychs, are his major source for how the Carolingian land-tax worked on the ground, and for him to have any evidence for it at all, then the *coloni* and *servi* on the *mansi* of the polyptychs have to be landowning taxpayers.

It is not possible to go through every one of these arguments – not to speak of the others – at the length necessary to show up all their inherent problems; I will illustrate some of them as examples only. For Durliat to be able to claim that the Church was simply an arm of the state, one of the things he has to show is that its lands were interchangeable with fiscal lands. He can easily show that kings gave much land to churches, that they protected church lands, and even that they sometimes had to be consulted when a church alienated land (p. 142 – not that this consultation is usually very evident in the huge numbers of ecclesiastical transac-

---

[25] B. S. Bachrach, *Merovingian Military Organization 481–751* (Minneapolis, 1972), e.g. pp. 65–73, 87–90, 110–11.

[26] K. F. Werner, "Missus-Marchio-Comes," in W. Paravicini and K. F. Werner, eds, *Histoire comparée de l'administration (IVe–XVIIIe siècle)* (Munich, 1980), pp. 191–239.

[27] It is hard, even for Durliat, to be sure which sort of *mansus* is being discussed in which source (p. 254 n.). For more on *mansi*, see, among several previous articles, J. Durliat, "Le manse dans le polyptyque d'Irminon," in Atsma (ed.), *La Neustrie*, pp. 467–504; and Devroey, "Polyptyques et fiscalité".

tions documented in the ninth century). But he cannot so easily show that kings could legally transfer land *out* of church control. For the period before 750 or so, he thinks he can show it (pp. 148–9), but his argument here is simply that, despite Lesne's long lists of confiscations of church lands under Charles Martel and his predecessors, there are no extant court cases in which churches make recourse to the courts to get them back before 700, and no documented protests against Charles Martel in his lifetime. "*Thus* the law is respected right up to the beginning of the eighth century. When a king takes the property of churches, one must *therefore* consider that he is acting in conformity with legal principles" (p. 149, my italics). Given the extent of seventh-century documentation of any sort, this is naive. So is the slip from the "normal" behaviour of rulers to their legal powers. That the latter used church lands when they could get away with it does not mean that the Church *belonged* to them. Carloman, in 744, needed the Church's consent when he wished to use church lands for the army, and these cessions were not of full property, but of *precaria* [land held temporarily], and for rent (pp. 149, 242–3). One may remark that Chilperic I's famous complaint, "*ecce pauper remansit fiscus noster, ecce divitiae nostrae ad ecclesias sunt translatae*" ["behold our treasury remains a pauper, our riches have been carried off to churches"], cited several times by Durliat, would make no sense if the *ecclesiae* were simply his own government departments. But if they were not, then ecclesiastical polyptychs were not government documents either.

The theory that *servi* can be free landowners has as many problems. The point here is that not only *coloni* owed dues on the Church's *villae* and *mansi* in Carolingian polyptychs; *servi* did too, whether on *mansi ingenuiles* [free] or *mansi serviles* [servile]. If the latter were really slaves, then they could not be taxpayers, and the dues listed in the polyptychs could not easily be argued to be tax. Durliat here develops Magnou–Nortier's argument that *servi* could be people who had alienated part of their social status away and would in future owe services (*servitia*) of different kinds (pp. 176–9);[28] and, later, adds they might also just be an ill-defined subtype of *coloni* (p. 283: "a *servus* is one who has been allocated by the state to serve an institution and who frees himself from his fiscal debt by working for his own profit"). Exactly why such small owners should be referred to by the same word as that used for slaves, in a period when slaves still existed as a legal category (one very much feared by the free, as numerous ninth-century court cases attest), is not explained. Still less is it explained how Durliat knows that the particular *servi* of the polyptychs, and the *servi* and *mancipia* of numerous diplomas and private documents, are not such slaves (cf. p. 178). In one of Marculf's formularies, a man who commends himself to a *dominus* [lord] agrees that he can be treated like other *servi*, even including being sold; Durliat glosses this last penalty as only operative in the case of serious misconduct or "total insolvency" (p. 183), but the reading is unconvincing – Marculf shows that a person in this situation has become, in effect, "servile" in the most traditional medieval sense.[29] (One must anyway ask, among other things, why, if such people can alienate away even their status, they cannot also alienate their land, thus immediately becoming tenants! Durliat occasionally mentions the possibility of tenanted land, e.g. p. 182, but never develops it.)

---

[28]   Magnou-Nortier, "Gestion publique", pp. 297–9.

[29]   *Marculfi Formulae*, 2.28, in K. Zeumer, ed., *Formulae merowingici et karolini aevi* (Hanover, 1886), p. 93. The formulary says that if the dependant does not do his lord's will, or if he tries to get out of the latter's *servitium*, then he can be disciplined in any way whatsoever, including being sold. It gives no indication that the dependant keeps any land, and states flatly that he is devoid of *res*. I cannot understand the basis of Durliat's reading.

In fact, however, the whole discussion of *coloni* and *servi* in the polyptychs (pp. 274–84) is inadequate. Durliat has divided his book into three sections, late Roman, Romano-Germanic, and Carolingian, each with the same subheadings and very similar arguments. By the time he reaches the Carolingians, he has a tendency to assume that he has already proved that *mansi* and *villae*, like *fundi* and *possessiones* before them, were *assiettes fiscales*, and *coloni* landowners; his Carolingian sections thus often add little to his documentation except hypotheses about how the administration of the capitularies and polyptychs might have functioned in the light of his theories (e.g. pp. 203–9). That these texts, although lengthy and detailed, do not add any extra unambiguous evidence for his interpretations does not seem to him a problem. Nor does he see it necessary to extend his database, either to ninth-century narratives (which, to be sure, say little about taxation, but surely they might be expected to have said more? After all, Gregory of Tours did), or to the enormous range of private land transactions. At the most, he uses the Lorsch cartulary in a rather desultory way: he claims that it shows small owners in areas where the Lorsch polyptych lists only *coloni*, but without giving any details (pp. 274–5), and he argues that *mancipia* alienated with *suis possessionibus* [their possessions] in the cartulary must be landowners, whose tax *assiettes* are alienated by *propriétaires éminentes*, for otherwise the *possessiones* would not be "theirs" (p. 276; see also p. 275 for other statements that *suus* and *eorum* have to mean "belonging to people in full property," not just "associated with them"). If one uses private documents in a more systematic manner, however, then a number of his claims become much more questionable. I have already cited Italian documents for the general issue of the concept of property-owning; I will end this section by returning to them in order to look at a few examples of land tenure.

Take the inventories of the cathedral of Lucca, dating to the late ninth century. The first of these is in a fairly typical (if relatively abbreviated) polyptych form, listing properties estate by estate, sometimes with a style reminiscent of Charlemagne's *Brevium exempla* ("*Invenimus in villa Veccliano: curte indominicata, case I*"), sometimes more simply ("*De Sugrominio: terra indominicata ad seminandum sistariorum XII*") ["we find in the *villa* of Vecchiano: a demesne centre and one house. . . . concerning Sugromigno: demesne land sufficient to sow twelve *sistarii* (of grain)"]. Each estate includes *manentes* with differentiated burdens, usually counted up at the end of the paragraph. The second inventory lists lands handed out to aristocratic dependants of the bishop in benefice, and the paragraphs here are subdivided first by benefice and then by locality. Again, the dependants in each place are usually called *manentes*, which is one of the standard ninth-century Italian equivalents of the Frankish term *coloni*. Agrarian organization in Italy was, as already noted, much less tight than on the estates of St-Germain-des-Prés, but estate structures could at least be analogous; Lucchese tenants owed *angaria* [labor service] on their lords' demesnes (*indominicatae* and variants), for instance. Durliat would have no difficulty in seeing these documents as describing the same world as that in one of the looser northern polyptychs. But this is Italy, and we have more documents for Lucca than just inventories. In particular, we have over two hundred ninth-century leases to cultivators. Some of these are to cultivators mentioned in the inventories; the entries match up. In 867, the bishop of Lucca leased land (*res*) in Cascio to one Leoprando for rent in wine, money, labor-service, and *exenia* (yearly gifts, a sheep and cloth); in the second inventory the same rent (minus the *exenia*) is listed for the same man. In 893, the bishop leased a *casa et res* (an equivaient of the Frankish *mansus*: Durliat, p. 193) in Segromigno to the successor of a certain Liusprando, named in the first inventory; the lease mentions rent in wine, oil, and labor-service, and the inventory lists the same rent, though this time adding some extra dues as well. The point is that these leases are quite clearly to cultivators: they are leased (the phrase is *livellario nomine dare*) property *ad laborandum et gubernandum et meliorandum* [to work, run, and improve]; they are often put into that property by the bishop, if their predecessor has died without heirs; they owe rent for the property (*census* or *pensio* or *iustitia*), and so on. They are not landowners. And yet they also appear in the inventories in just the same way as *coloni* do in Frankish polyptychs.[30] Now Durliat has an instance of *coloni* selling land, in the Edict of Pîtres in 864 (pp. 277–8). He uses this as proof that *coloni* are owners. It is the only proof for this that he develops in his Carolingian section. I do not in fact read the text in this way, for free tenants can sell their tenures in many areas of early medieval Europe as long as the rent is still paid by someone, and I do not accept that the phrase *censum ad partem dominicam* in Pîtres has to mean tax rather than rent. But even if we let it stand, all it would show is that *some coloni* are owners, and pay tax. Almost anything was possible, after all, in the confusion of contrasting local realities that was the Early Middle Ages. But Durliat's theory depends on the claim that they *all* are; and this, in my Lucca examples, is evidently not the case. Durliat might reply that my examples are ecclesiastical, and therefore public, and that dependants on fiscal land are different from those on private land. There are, of course, no private lay polyptychs; but there are at least a few Italian leases by laymen to laymen, and these look much the same as those I have just cited for Lucca.[31] I do not believe that even Durliat could look coldly at the evidence for Italy as "un honnête historien ayant conduit une enquête systématique" ["an honest historian having carried out a systematic inquiry"] (p. 148 n.) and conclude that his fiscal theories work there. But, to reiterate; if they fail in Italy, his Frankish arguments are in ruins too.

It would be inappropriate to go on; further detailed discussion would tire the convinced, and would not necessarily persuade the unconvinced. I do not think that Durliat has established any of his principal arguments. I cannot see the Carolingians making more than fragmentary and occasional exactions on the lands of free landowners, until Charles the Bald's short-lived collections to pay the Vikings. I cannot accept that all our references to great landowners in the sources are to tax-farmers, and that large-scale landowning thus disappears in the ninth century just as, supposedly, in the fourth. Still less can I imagine that these tax-farmers, if they existed, never subjected the peasant owners under them to a more systematic servitude (perhaps as in the Marculf formulary cited above). Like Durliat, I do not subscribe to the theory that the Carolingians were dependent entirely on pillage (pp. 264, 286–7); landownership was a more stable and systematic recourse than some more romantic historians have supposed. But Roman emperors is what Durliat wants the Carolingians to be, and he has not proved his case.

In conclusion, I want to make a few more general points. Durliat is interested in continuity. When he cannot prove something has changed (the decline of city councils and circumscriptions, for instance), he assumes it has not. The whole period thus becomes flattened out;

---

[30] For the inventory citations, see A. Castagnetti et al., eds, *Inventari altomedievali di terre, coloni e redditi* (Rome, 1979), respectively pp. 219, 214, 231 (Leoprando), 215 (Liusprando). For the charters, D. Barsocchini, ed., *Memorie e documenti per service all'istoria del ducato di Lucca* vol. 2 (Lucca, 1837), nn. 800, 988; and, for general commentary, B. Andreolli, "Contratti agrari e patti colonici nella Lucchesia dei secoli VIII e IX," *Studi medievali* 19 (1978): 69–158.

[31] E.g. L. Schiaparelli, ed., *Codice diplomatico longobardo* i–ii (Rome, 1929–33), nn. 263–4 (a. 772). It should be added that Durliat's concern to show that peasant owners existed in large numbers in the Early Middle Ages, which he argues many times, seems to me entirely persuasive; it is just that they existed *beside grandes domaines*, rather than on them.

differences both in time and in place disappear. Nothing, in its essentials, really alters for him, until an obscurely characterized and maybe only partial involution of the state after 888 (pp. 8, 261, 289). This vision is already unconvincing; but it is only possible at all because Durliat concentrates so vigorously on administrative regulations. It is fair to note that this area of enquiry has been neglected (pp. 285–6); but it is not the only issue in history. The *rest* of history gives the lie to his theories. Why, for example, if the German occupation was just an administrative detail, does the level of documentation for the early medieval period collapse? (Roman papyri existed in their millions, as any Egyptologist knows; no one, however, claims that eighth-century parchments ever did. Parchment survives better than papyrus, one must also remember.) And, perhaps above all, if the Merovingians and Carolingians had the resources of Diocletian or Theodosius, at least on a slightly more localized level, why does this have so little reflection in the material culture of the Early Middle Ages? The Roman Empire was full of goods, made by artisans and moved about; large quantities of Roman pottery are found on every imperial-period excavation, much of it produced centrally and often a long way away, in Africa or Spain. Not so in the Early Middle Ages; technologies decayed (and in some areas collapsed); the geographical distribution of archaeological objects becomes much more localized, and their quantities decline dramatically. Building technology suffered even more drastic changes; no one has ever found early medieval buildings that match the standard arrays of Roman villas, for example. Even Aachen, the central focus of Charlemagne's state organization, was not impressive by the standards of Roman cities like Ravenna or Milan, or for that matter Trier. Why ever was all this so, except as the result of some crisis at the level of a whole social system?

I am held to be a continuitist by many archaeologists. I agree with Durliat, for example, that this material decline is quite different from total abandonment (p. 196), just as I agree with him that the rebuilding of aqueducts shows that technological skills did not have to vanish everywhere in the Early Middle Ages (pp. 236–7).[32] But I would still say that it is nonsense to put the Early Middle Ages on the same level as the Roman Empire in any material sense. It cannot be that a period so little documented and so badly evidenced materially should be seen as the unchanging successor of one whose remains still stand throughout Europe. The whole material and documentary framework of the Early Middle Ages is senseless in Durliat's vision. In this world, not only politics, but history itself is effaced.

At this point, I am reduced to the sort of rhetorical statements I rejected at the start of this article. But why Durliat should have wanted to produce such a disorientating theory, and on such meagre bases, is genuinely incomprehensible to me. His considerable intellectual effort (this at least must be conceded him, for he is remarkably coherent, and is taking on a near-universal historiographical tradition) has been wasted. Durliat is a serious and careful historian, as many of his works attest;[33] but this book is a huge misjudgment.

---

[32] It may be fair here to mention articles of my own that set out an alternative image of the Early Middle Ages, for it is from their presuppositions that, ultimately, I am arguing: "The other transition," *PP* 103 (1984): 3–36; "L'Italia e l'alto medioevo," *Archeologia medievale* 15 (1988): 105–24; "Mutations et révolutions aux environs de l'an mil," *Médiévales* 21 (1991): 27–38; "Problems of comparing rural societies in early medieval western Europe," *Transactions of the Royal Historical Society* 6 ser., ii (1992). The first, second, and fourth of these are now collected in Wickham, *Land and Power* (London, 1994).

[33] See, for example, n. 5 above; of his tax articles, I would mention "Les attributions civiles des évêques mérovingiens: l'exemple de Didier, évêque de Cahors (630–655)," *Annales du Midi* 91 (1979): 233–54, which retains its value whether one accepts his underlying theories or not.

4 The Decline of the Western Empire

Richard Hodges and David Whitehouse

Pirenne drew two sweeping conclusions:

1. The Germanic invasions destroyed neither the Mediterranean unity of the ancient world, nor what may be regarded as the truly essential features of Roman culture as it still existed in the fifth century.
2. The cause of the break with the tradition of Antiquity was the rapid and unexpected advance of Islam.[1]

The purpose of this chapter and the next [i.e., in Hodges's and Whitehouse's book] is to examine these conclusions, which summarize the first part of Pirenne's book.

Long-distance Trade

A cornerstone of Pirenne's first conclusion – that the Mediterranean world was essentially the same in 600 as it had been in 400 – was the continuation of trade. In the fourth century, as in earlier periods, trade was intense and commodities were moved in bulk across the length and breadth of the Mediterranean. Was this still happening in 600? As a historian, Pirenne based his case almost exclusively on written evidence, using two categories of information: on traders, and on the articles they traded.

First, the traders. Salvian (d. *c.*484) wrote of the Syrian merchants of Marseille, and Caesarius, bishop of Arles (d.542), composed hymns not only in Latin (for the local population), but in Greek (for the foreign community, presumably merchants). We hear of merchants in Spain in about 570 and of Jews, Greeks, and Syrians at Narbonne in 589. As far as the merchandise is concerned, we have numerous references to goods from the eastern Mediterranean in the western provinces in the sixth century and after. Gregory of Tours (*c.*539–94), for example, mentions a bequest of wine from Gaza to a church in Lyon for use in the Eucharist.[2] These snippets of information, which confirm the continuation of trade, are useful – but only up to a point. They tell us nothing about the *volume* of trade; indeed, the very fact that they mention traders and trade goods implies that we are dealing with the exception rather than the rule.

Fortunately, archaeological evidence is beginning to compensate for this deficiency. Imported objects found in excavations can be quantified and used to estimate the volume of trade, while their distribution can suggest the extent of commercial networks. Let us

---

[1] Henri Pirenne, *Mohammed and Charlemagne* (London, 1939), p. 284.
[2,3] Gregory of Tours, *A History of the Franks*, ed. Lewis Thorpe (Harmondsworth, 1974), p. 411.

consider three recent excavations – in Rome, Carthage, and the small north Italian port of Luni – which tell us much about the economy of the fifth and sixth centuries.

Rome

The so-called Schola Praeconum (the name is modern) stands at the foot of the Palatine, overlooking the Circus Maximus. In 1978–80 excavation revealed that part of the building had been deliberately filled with earth and rubble. The fill consists of rubble from the demolition of a well-appointed building and of domestic (and possibly warehouse) rubbish. Thirty-eight legible coins show that the filling dates from the second quarter of the fifth century, perhaps from *c*.430–40.[3]

The filling in the Schola Praeconum contained a large amount of broken pottery: 22,315 fragments, weighing 423 kg. A significant proportion of the pottery (44.6 percent of the sherds, or 60 percent of the total weight) consists of amphorae, used for the transportation and storage of perishable commodities, such as olive oil, wine, and *garum* (a kind of fish sauce, which the Romans consumed in great quantities). We know enough about the characteristics of Roman amphorae and the clays from which they were made to suggest where many of the fragments originated. [We give below] two analyses of the pottery from the Schola Praeconum, with particular reference to the amphorae.

Class of pottery	% fragments	% weight
Domestic	10.6	8.5
Amphorae	44.6	60.0
Not classified	44.8	31.5
Total	100.0	100.0

Type of amphora	% fragments	% weight
North African	42.5	63.0
Biv	20.5	6.9
Bii	19.2	14.7
Others	17.8	15.4
Total	100.0	100.0

The three most common types of amphora – North African, Biv, and Bii – come from three different parts of the Mediterranean. The North African amphorae, which have a distinctive brick-red fabric, sometimes with a white surface, were imported from Tunisia. It has always been assumed that they contained olive oil, and recent analyses of lipid residues embedded in the fabric of sherds from the Schola Praeconum have shown this assumption to be correct.[4] Biv amphorae also have a distinctive fabric: they are deep brown in colour,

[3,4] D. Whitehouse, G. Barker, R. Reece, and D. Reese, "The Schola Praeconum 1. The coins, pottery and fauna," *Papers of the British School at Rome* 50 (1982).
[4,5] S. Passi, M. C. Rothschild-Boros, P. Fasella, M. Nazzaro-Porro, and D. Whitehouse, "An application of high performance liquid chromatography to analysis of lipids in archaeological samples," *Journal of Lipid Research* 22 (1981): 778–84.

with abundant mica and a "soapy" texture. The characteristics of the clay suggest that they were made in western Turkey, perhaps in the Meander valley. Bii amphorae also come from the East, possibly from Antioch in Syria. The amphorae from the Schola Praeconum, therefore, indicate the continuing existence of large-scale seaborne trade between Rome, North Africa, and the eastern Mediterranean, in about 430–40. They also provide our first illustration of the importance of pottery when discussing commerce.

Carthage

The Schola Praeconum provides an insight into the long-distance trade of Rome in the fifth century; Carthage widens the discussion. The leading Punic and Roman port of the Maghreb, Carthage was the capital of the imperial province of Africa until it fell to the Vandals in 438. Before this most of the vast crop of North African corn destined for Italy passed through Carthage, as did huge quantities of olive oil. Historians have argued that Gaiseric's seizure of Carthage curtailed Rome's access to her traditional granary and that alternative supplies were needed until Belisarius recaptured the city for Justinian in 534. Massive excavations sponsored by UNESCO have made it possible to examine the traditional picture. The American and British teams, in particular, have concentrated on the latest phases of occupation. In the process both teams have been forced to handle vast amounts of pottery, including hundreds of thousands of amphora sherds and African Red Slip (ARS) tablewares. The preliminary analyses of these many different types of pottery, in conjunction with parallel studies of the coins, have induced M. J. Fulford and John Riley to offer alternative interpretations for Carthage's final centuries.[5]

Fulford writes as follows:

> In the early fifth century (*c.*400–425), only about 10 percent of the amphorae can be assigned to East Mediterranean sources. This percentage is doubled by *c.*AD. 475–500 and, in the groups deposited at about the time of Belisarius' invasion . . . , 25–30 percent of all the amphorae can certainly be attributed to sources in the East Mediterranean.

Riley arrived at the same conclusion. But surprisingly, both have shown that after 534 the proportion of imported to local amphorae in Carthage dropped dramatically, and that by about 600 the incidence of eastern Mediterranean amphorae is in fact negligible. The impression that Carthage enjoyed a buoyant economy in the late fifth and early sixth centuries is to some extent confirmed by the large numbers of high-quality tablewares (African Red Slip wares) found in the excavations. Finally, Fulford points out that Vandal coinage issued in Carthage was widely circulated around the Mediterranean. By contrast, after Justinian reestablished an imperial mint at Carthage, coins from other mints in the eastern Mediterranean found in the city amount to a tiny fraction of the numismatic collection as a whole. "Out of more than 325 Byzantine coins catalogued from the American excavations," writes Fulford, "only eight are from eastern mints, two from Sicily and two from Constantine in Numidia," and he shows that the Carthaginian issues minted after 533 are rare around the Mediterranean.[6]

[5,6] M. J. Fulford, "Carthage: overseas trade and the political economy, *c.* AD 400–700," *Reading Medieval Studies* 6 (1980): 68–80; J. A. Riley, "The pottery from the cisterns 1977. 1, 1977. 2 and 1977. 3," in J. H. Humphrey, ed., *Excavations at Carthage 1977 Conducted by the University of Michigan* (Ann Arbor, 1981), pp. 85–124.
[6,7] Fulford, "Carthage," pp. 71, 74.

Fulford interprets this new archaeological evidence in an imaginative way. He argues that once the province was released from its obligation to Rome, it was possible to sustain a lively trading relationship with various parts of the Mediterranean. Although in practice agricultural production within the province may have fallen, great emphasis was still placed on commerce, because the surplus was no longer exported as tax or invested in monumental buildings. There is certainly some evidence of a decline of estates in the fifth century. However, once Justinian reconquered the city and it was again burdened with taxes, commercial life diminished and the corn sold for private luxuries under the Vandals was requisitioned to meet the needs of the state.

The last phases of occupation in several buildings near the city wall betray the pitiful condition of Carthage in the seventh century.[7] The British excavators uncovered a comparatively well-preserved mud-brick building, L-shaped in form, dating from the late sixth or early seventh century. After its abandonment the zone was used as a burial ground. Henry Hurst, the excavator, writes that

> late burials occur commonly within the former urban area of Carthage, as in other sites of Byzantine Africa, and are conventionally interpreted as representing a late stage of decline, economically and in terms of population, when large areas of the city were redundant and the traditional regulations requiring burial areas to be outside the city walls were relaxed.

A further building over this graveyard has been interpreted as the home of refugees from the Arabs, who arrived in the province in 695–98. By then, the city was only a shadow of its former self and must have resembled the decaying industrial towns with which, today, we in the West are beginning to become familiar.

Luni

The later history of Luni, a small Roman town near La Spezia, is strikingly similar to that of Carthage. Careful excavations by Bryan Ward-Perkins in the forum at the centre of the walled town have revealed its post-classical history.[8] Until about 400 Luni's wealth was principally derived from the export of Luna (Carrara) marble, quarried nearby. The decline of the marble trade must have had a devastating effect on the town, but nevertheless it survived in Byzantine hands until 640, when eventually it fell to the Lombards. Under Lombard rule it remained a diocesan centre until 1201–4, when the bishopric was moved to Sarzana. The recent excavations have uncovered the vestigial remains of wooden structures, probably dwellings, spanning the period between the fifth and the ninth centuries or later, associated with deep rubbish pits and wells.

The archaeology of the latest Roman phases at Luni is particularly interesting because the excavations have been so meticulous, and suggest what might be found at other classical sites in the Mediterranean. The interim reports show that the post-built dwellings bear a striking resemblance to the homes of the barbarians best known, at this period, in West Germany.

[7.8] Henry Hurst, "Excavations at Carthage 1977–8. Fourth interim report", *Antiquaries Journal* 59 (1979): 19–49, esp. 44–6.
[8.9] Bryan Ward-Perkins, "Luni – the decline of a Roman town," in H. McK. Blake, T. W. Potter, and D. B. Whitehouse, eds, *Papers in Italian Archaeology* 1, BAR supplementary series 41, (Oxford, 1978), pp. 313–21; "Luni: the prosperity of the town and its territory," in G. Barker and R. Hodges, eds, *Archaeology and Italian Society*, BAR International Series 102, (Oxford, 1981), pp. 179–90; "Two Byzantine houses at Luni," *Papers of the British School at Rome* 49 (1981): 91–8.

Yet the material trampled into the thin floor surfaces and dropped in activity areas indicates that "Byzantine" copper coinage continued in use until about 600. In addition, eastern Mediterranean amphorae and Syrian glass were being imported. After about 600, on the other hand, the material standard of life appears to have suffered a further decline – imports from other parts of the Mediterranean are rare, although analysis of the refuse implies that there was no significant alteration in the diet.

Bryan Ward-Perkins contends that the town's impoverishment after the collapse of the marble trade was due in large measure to the decay of the classical drainage systems in the food-growing *territorium*. Gradually much of this territory reverted to marshland. It is clear that Luni was barely operating as a port when the Lombards ousted the last Byzantine governor in 640. The town was never abandoned, though there was no more than a cluster of Byzantine households within its walls, and these were remote from their classical predecessors in almost every respect. The excavations have aroused considerable interest, mainly because archaeologists are beginning to wonder whether the decay of Luni can be used as a model for the decay of classical towns generally in Italy. Bryan Ward-Perkins opposes this view and points to the documentary evidence for the survival of centres like nearby Lucca. Nevertheless, the evidence from Luni itself is incontrovertible. Whatever happened elsewhere, the port collapsed.

These glimpses of late Roman trade suggest two working hypotheses. First, the arrival of the "barbarians" in the late fourth and fifth centuries damaged, but did not destroy, the commerce of the central and western Mediterranean: Rome continued to import oil and wine (and many other things) after the Gothic invasion; under the Vandals, Carthage may actually have experienced a boom in trade with the East; Luni was still receiving foreign goods in the sixth century. As we shall see [later in this book] the spinoff from Mediterranean trade in the time of Theodoric arrived (in the form of coins and metal vessels) as far north as Sweden. Secondly, however, the situation had changed completely by about 600: Carthage had virtually ceased trading with the East and at Luni imported luxuries disappeared.

Admittedly these are large hypotheses built on flimsy evidence. The excavation of a tiny fraction of Carthage and an even smaller fraction of Rome, one might object, is hardly significant. And what of Luni, a minor town dependent on a single product – marble? Well, the decline of the marble trade itself speaks volumes and, as we shall see [also further on in this book], the pattern we suggest in the central Mediterranean is not dissimilar from the pattern emerging in the East. In any case, the hypothesis that intensive long-distance trade and the market economy collapsed in the sixth century can be tested by a study of rural settlement in Dark-Age Italy.

Rural Settlement in Italy

The acid test of major social and economic change is its detection on a regional scale. Individual centres such as Rome, Carthage, or Luni might survive or decline for highly individual reasons, but the fortunes of villas and peasant holdings should reflect economic trends of a more general kind. We must ask, therefore: when was the classical pattern of settlement and land-use succeeded by the medieval pattern?

The dating of rural settlement, especially smallholdings, is notoriously difficult because of the rarity of the closely datable objects that occur much more commonly in urban contexts. Coins, in particular, are scarce on rural sites, since they were used less frequently than in towns. This being so, the principal means of dating late Roman farms and villas is the pottery. In practice this means that we use the well-studied fine wares, which are found in urban contexts with coins and are therefore datable. In the Mediterranean we have come to use North African Red Slip ware (ARS) to date the remains of the last two centuries of classical settlement. In 1972 J. W. Hayes published an invaluable analysis of all the varieties of ARS, together with the evidence for their distribution and date.[9] Hayes's catalogue makes it possible to date sherds of ARS to relatively short periods, sometimes of less than a century. Indeed, ARS often provides a better means of dating archaeological deposits than the minute bronze coins that were minted in Italy, Greece, and Byzantium after about 400. Two other types of pottery also throw light on the chronology of rural sites. The first is a glazed ware, known as Forum ware, which is now thought to have been produced in Rome in about 600; the most frequent forms are spouted pitchers, which often have applied scales on the body and handle. The second is a south Italian product, made in one form or another from the fifth century to about 1,000 or later. This is the so-called "Broadline" red-painted pottery, which occurs on the sites of late Roman villas, in early Christian cemeteries, and at early medieval settlements. These three classes of pottery ARS, Forum ware and Broadline painted ware – are essential to understanding the changing pattern of rural settlement.[10]

The central and south Italian classical landscape contained a "dispersed settlement pattern," in contrast with the pattern of nucleated hilltop settlements of the medieval period. There are, of course, variations within both the classical and medieval patterns, and any generalization should be treated with caution. Nonetheless, the shift from a settlement pattern consisting of villas and smallholdings in open or exposed areas to one highly concentrated on naturally defensible hilltops was very widespread indeed, and is a subject eminently suited to archaeological analysis. Several archaeological surveys in Italy have focused on this particular problem. Two are relevant to our concern with the process of socioeconomic change in the world of Late Antiquity.

The first was in the area immediately north of Rome known as South Etruria. This ambitious project was planned and directed by John Ward-Perkins, the Director of the British School at Rome from 1946 to 1974. The idea of the survey of South Etruria was deceptively simple. In the 1950s suburban expansion, and in particular mechanized agriculture, began to change the face of the Roman Campagna, revealing – and destroying – archaeological sites at an unprecedented rate. Ward-Perkins's response was a massive campaign of fieldworking, designed to record the sites before they were lost forever. At the end of the campaign, well over two thousand sites had been recorded, ranging in size from isolated farms to entire settlements, and in date from the Bronze Age to the Renaissance. They key to interpreting a survey consists of the datable objects – usually pottery – picked up on the surface: if there is first-century pottery, the site was occupied in the first century, and so on. The earliest parts of the South Etruria survey were completed before the publication of Hayes's catalogue of African Red Slip wares, and so the initial survey reports have to be used with caution. Five areas of South Etruria were investigated, however, using Hayes's chronology: these are Eretum, the Ager Veientanus, the Via Gabina, the Cassia-Clodia area, and the Ager Faliscus.[11]

[9.10] J. W. Hayes, *Late Roman Pottery* (London, 1972); *Supplement to Late Roman Pottery* (London, 1980).

[10.11] D. B. Whitehouse, "Forum ware," *Medieval Archaeology* 9 (1965): 55–63; "Medieval painted pottery in South and Central Italy," *Medieval Archaeology* 10 (1966): 30–44; "The medieval pottery of Rome," in Blake et al., eds, *Papers in Italian Archaeology* 1, (Oxford, 1978), pp. 475–93; "Forum ware again," *Medieval Ceramics* 4 (1980): 13–16.

[11.12] The most convenient overview of the many detailed papers is T. W. Potter, *The Changing Landscape of South Etruria* (London, 1979). For the detailed studies see *Papers of the British School in*

Hayes divided the history of ARS into three main periods on the basis of fabric. The dates of the periods are:

ARS I   *c*.80–320
ARS II   *c*.350–450
ARS III   *c*.450–625

The finds from Eretum, Ager Veientanus, Via Gabina, and the Cassia-Clodia area have been published by reference to Hayes's divisions. The numbers of sites with ARS I, II and III are given below.

	Number of sites		
Area	ARS I	ARS II	ARS III
Eretum	47	20	7
Ager Veientanus	307	92	46
Via Gabina	27	9	6
Cassia-Clodia	57	10	6
Total	438	131	65

The standard interpretation of the data is that the Roman Campagna supported a large dispersed population until the third century, when a dramatic change began. In 1968, John Ward-Perkins summed up the situation in the Ager Veientanus as follows:

> Of the 310 [*sic*] sites known to have been in occupation at the end of the second century, three-quarters had vanished a century later . . . ; in certain marginal areas . . . the proportion of sites that disappear from the record is so high that one may reasonably suggest that many of the steeper slopes were allowed to revert to pasture or woodland.[12]

Today there are three good reasons for asking whether the third century was indeed a period of dramatic change and, if so, whether there were others. First, such scrappy data as we possess from Rome suggest the possibility of a rapid decline in population after about 367. Secondly, the chronology of ARS has been revised since the publication of the Ager Veientanus. Thirdly – and most important of all – the dramatic contrast between the numbers of sites with ARS I and ARS II is accentuated, and the contrast between sites with ARS II and ARS III is diminished by the fact that ARS I was in use for about 240 years, ARS III for about 175 years, and ARS II for only 100 years.

The survey of the Ager Faliscus, if typical, answers our first objection.[13] T. W. Potter classified the ARS by forms rather than fabrics and therefore obtained a tighter chronology, with the result [given below]:

Rome 23 (1955); 25 (1957); 29 (1961); 30 (1962); 31 (1963); 33 (1965); 36 (1968); 40 (1972); 41 (1973); 43 (1975); 45 (1977).

[12.13] A. Kahane, L. Murray-Thriepland, and J. B. Ward-Perkins, "The Ager Veientanus north and east of Veii," *Papers of the British School at Rome* 36 (1968): 1–218, at 152.

[13.14] Potter, *Changing Landscape*, p. 140.

Date	2nd C.	3rd C.	4th C.	5–6th C.
Number of sites	95	67	31	22

The figures indicate a reduction of 29 percent in the number of sites with ARS between the second and third centuries and a reduction of 54 percent between the third and fourth centuries. Although this is a less dramatic picture than the reduction of 75 percent in 100 years proposed for the Ager Veientanus, it is striking nonetheless; sometime between the third and fourth centuries the rate of reduction in the number of sites on which ARS has been found almost doubled, from 29 percent per 100 years to 54 percent per 100 years.

Was this the only period of rapid decline? Let us return to the Eretum, Ager Veientanus, Via Gabina, and Cassia-Clodia surveys and consider only those sites which have both *terra sigillata* [bright red, polished ware made of clay impressed with designs] and ARS I (and therefore were occupied when ARS I came into use in about AD 80), both ARS I and ARS II (occupied *c*.350), or both ARS II and ARS III (occupied *c*.450).

Area	No. of sites		
	c.80	*c*.350	*c*.450
Eretum	42	20	5
Ager Veientanus	268	91	39
Via Gabina	22	9	6
Cassia-Clodia	45	9	3
Total	377	129	53

We are dealing now with numbers of sites known to have been occupied at given dates. Between *c*.80 and *c*.350, the numbers of known sites were reduced by between 52 percent and 80 percent (the average is 66 percent) in 270 years, and the data from the Ager Faliscus suggest that the figures conceal one relatively slow and one relatively rapid period of reduction. Between *c*.350 and *c*.450, the rates of reduction were between 33 percent and 75 percent (the average being 41 percent). The overall reduction between *c*.80 and *c*.450 was 86 percent.

In round figures, therefore, the total number of smallholdings and villas known to have been occupied in the Roman Campagna seems to have fallen by well over 80 percent between the late first century and the mid-fifth century. The decline began in the second and third centuries and for a while ran at just under 30 percent per 100 years. It accelerated to more than 50 percent for every hundred years between the third and fourth centuries and thereafter continued, but at a slower pace.

How can we explain the phenomenon? The possibilities are: (1) quite simply, a decline in the use of ARS (our evidence, remember, consists entirely of the distribution of potsherds); (2) a change in the pattern of settlement involving the replacement of many small sites by fewer large ones; (3) migration from the countryside to the country towns; (4) migration to Rome; (5) a decline in the population of the countryside and the country towns and of Rome itself.

None of the first three possibilities satisfactorily explains what happened. Excavations in Rome show that ARS was still common in *c*.430–40, and a massive decline in its importation seems improbable for most of the period in question, though the Vandal invasion of Africa may have reduced the supply and so distorted our estimate of the number of sites in *c*.450; indeed fifth- or sixth-century ARS has turned up on at least three excavated sites in northern Lazio. On the second possibility: while the proportion of villas to smallholdings rose, the actual number of villas declined. The change was in any case far too small to absorb all the inhabitants of the abandoned smallholdings. On the third possibility: the scarcity of ARS III and of late inscriptions at the sites of the country towns seems to imply that they, too, declined.

We are left with: (4) migration to Rome and (5) an overall reduction of population. The present evidence suggests that these were the important factors. All the information from the South Etruria survey tells the same story: an uneven, but continuous decline in the number of rural sites known to have been occupied which, if we are correct in rejecting explanations (1) to (3), represents an uneven, but continuous, decline in the rural population. Rome, on the other hand, if the figures for the dole (discussed below) are even remotely indicative, also experienced an overall decline, but with periods of growth in the fourth century and the second quarter of the fifth. These observations are consistent with the view that an overall reduction in the size of the population may have taken place between the second or third centuries and the mid-fifth century (and after), but that on two occasions the population of Rome was "topped up" by immigrants from the Roman Campagna. This reduction in the total population may well have been smaller than the reduction in the number of identified sites implies, but we find it difficult to believe that *no* reduction took place.

Indeed, the decline of more than 80 percent in the number of known sites in the Roman Campagna was not an isolated phenomenon. The Theodosian Code tells us that in Campania alone 528,042 *iugera* (1332 square kilometers) were no longer taxable and so presumably had gone out of cultivation by 395. The Visigoth invasion exacerbated the problem, and in 413 taxes on cultivated land were reduced in Campania, Tuscany, Picenum, Samnium, Bruttium, Calabria, and Lucania. In 418 they were reduced again (to one-ninth of the original figure) in Campania, Picenum, and Tuscany. We find a similar state of affairs in Africa. In 422 the area of taxable (i.e. cultivated) land was reduced from 7,425 to 3,768 square kilometers in Byzacena: an overall decline of 49 percent. Although C. R. Whittaker reminds us that the sources are "atrocious" and we cannot know precisely what reductions in the amount of taxable land imply for the size of the population, we find it difficult to escape the conclusion that the classical pattern of dispersed settlement was transformed in the late imperial period.[14]

The temptation at this point is to become suspicious of the archaeological evidence for a substantial decline in population. After all, might not the disappearance of the diagnostic later sixth-century African Red Slip wares simply reflect the economic changes in the western Mediterranean? In other words, is it not possible that smaller farms that could not obtain, or simply could not afford, ARS continued to exist? Chris Wickham, reviewing the survey data from South Etruria, went so far as to state that "generalised demographic collapse is a difficult enough process even to imagine, let alone . . . locate in the evidence." He goes on: "What historical sources we have in the eighth century; primarily the *Liber Pontificalis*, give no impression that the countryside had been abandoned."[15]

[14,15] C. R. Whittaker, "Agri deserti," in Moses I. Finley, ed., *Studies in Roman Property* (Cambridge, 1976), pp. 137–65. For Africa see Denys Pringle, *The Defence of Byzantine Africa from Justinian to the Arab Conquest*, BAR International Series 99 (Oxford, 1981), pp. 109–20.

[15,16] C. J. Wickham, "Historical and topographical notes on early medieval South Etruria: part II," *Papers of the British School at Rome* 47 (1979): 66–95, esp. 86.

What kinds of settlement were in existence as the classical pattern dissolved and, we suggest (despite Whittaker, Wickham, and others), the actual size of the population declined? And when, precisely, was there a shift towards occupying hilltops, thereby breaking with the tradition of a thousand years?

The form of the latest Roman farms in South Etruria remains something of a mystery, since the only site of the period for which we have even interim reports, at Anguillara Sabazia, is something of a freak. An imposing tower-like structure, built in the second century, perhaps as the country retreat of a wealthy resident of Rome, was made defensible some time in the period 450–550. Immediately outside the walls, soil and rock were removed to create, on one side at least, a shallow ditch 5 meters wide. Windows on the ground floor may have been blocked; they are blocked today, but we cannot determine when this was done. Evidently bandits or a specific military threat – the Gothic invasion, perhaps – persuaded the fifth- or sixth-century inhabitants of the area to create a refuge.[16] More conventional establishments may have resembled the fifth-century complex at S. Giovanni di Ruoti in Basilicata, now being excavated by Professor Alistair Small. Rebuilt on an impressive scale in about 460, Ruoti consisted of a well-appointed residential unit, farmyard, and ancillary buildings, which remained in use until about 525.[17]

The transformation of the classical pattern of dispersed settlement has proved a lively topic of debate in the case of South Etruria. Several years ago the historian T. S. Brown boldly proposed that the beginnings of change lay in the later sixth or seventh centuries when Alboin's Lombard invasion overran Italy.[18] He encouraged archaeologists to examine hilltops overlooking the roads which may have been used first as refuges and later became permanent settlements. Archaeological evidence for precisely this type of hilltop settlement in the late sixth or seventh centuries has now been found on the northern edge of the South Etruria survey area. The identification of the earliest hilltop settlements was made possible by the redating of Forum ware to the period around 600. It has been suggested recently that a zone of hilltop sites, some 40 kilometers north of Rome, dates from precisely the time of the Lombard invasion, when they served as parts of a system of defence in depth: a series of "strategic hamlets," blocking the approaches to the city, one of which (at Ponte Nepesino) has just been discovered. At the same time it is clear that many of the "lowland" settlements behind this protective screen remained in use throughout the period in question.[19]

The South Etruria survey brings us tantalizingly close to observing the transition between the "classical" and "medieval" landscapes. Even so, the transition from classical to medieval building types is still a closed book. Similarly, at present the shift from open dispersed sites to fortified upland settlements is only explained as a defence against Lombardic invaders; this may be a satisfactory explanation for the change on the edge of the Roman Campagna, but its wider implications have to be assessed. The recent survey and related excavations in Molise, classical Samnium, in east-central Italy, have begun to provide the answers. Extensive work has been carried out in two parts of Molise by teams from the University of

[16.17] David Whitehouse, "Le Mura di S. Stefano, Anguillara Sabazia (Roma). Ultima relazione provvisoria," *Archaeologia Medievale* 9 (1982).

[17.18] Alistair Small, "San Giovanni di Ruoti: some problems in the interpretation of the structures," in K. Painter, ed., *Roman Villas in Italy*, British Museum occasional paper 24 (London, 1980), pp. 91–109.

[18.19] T. S. Brown, "Settlement and military policy in Byzantine Italy," in Blake et al., eds, *Papers in Italian Archaeology* 1, pp. 323–38.

[19.20] David Whitehouse and Timothy Potter, "The Byzantine frontier in South Etruria," *Antiquity* 55 (1981): 206–10.

Sheffield. One survey area is centred on the Biferno valley, which runs from the Apennines to the Adriatic. The other zone lies in the upper Volturno valley, in the foothills of the Apennines, where the early medieval monastery of San Vincenzo al Volturno held its estates. Several points relating to the late Roman and early medieval settlement patterns can be made in advance of the final publications.[20] First, a sharp decline in the number of villas (larger farms) occurred in both zones after about 400 (a date based on ARS). After this date, only a few nucleated sites existed in the Biferno valley, together with a few tiny farmsteads nearer the Adriatic; in the Volturno region, on the other hand, only widely spaced nucleated sites have been identified so far. At San Vincenzo itself a large nucleated complex of the fifth to sixth centuries has been found beneath the eighth-century monastery. It appears, however, unless here, too, we are being misled by the absence of ARS, that in the sixth or possibly the seventh centuries all – or virtually all – the open "classical" sites were abandoned in favour of hilltop locations. Moreover, here too there are signs of a dramatic decline in the population, consistent with the evidence from South Etruria, with comparatively few inhabitants occupying the tops of the hills.

The reasons for this shift are many and may never be accurately determined. Increased taxation by the Byzantine government after Justinian's reconquest of Italy might account for a phase of rural depopulation in the sixth century. Similarly, we cannot ignore the impact of the Great Plague of 542 which ravaged Byzantium and Europe.[21] If the Black Death carried off a third of the population of Europe in the fourteenth century, who knows what effect it had in the sixth? A smaller population may have felt more vulnerable and perhaps sought security on hilltops, where their homes would be more easily defensible against marauding bands. In addition, there may have been a certain amount of movement within each region to select land more suitable for producing subsistence foodstuffs than cash crops, for the decline of cities and rural markets must have had a direct impact on peasant farming generally. The replacement of the bureaucratic Roman political system by Germanic tribal elites must have led to a massive diminution of local taxes, as in the case of Carthage under the Vandals. The markets and the apparatus of government diminished, farmers were compelled to provide not only basic necessities but also manufactured goods which previously had been acquired by purchase or barter, and long-distance trade collapsed.

What did the new hilltop settlements look like? Excavations in the Biferno valley provide an answer. Santa Maria in Città is a prominent hilltop overlooking the river Biferno at a point where it can be forded or bridged.[22] A survey of the hill followed by small-scale excavations in 1978 revealed two small clusters of buildings inside a circuit of fortifications enclosing the summit. At the highest point was a modest church. The excavations suggest that the dwellings were built up against the defences in a typical medieval form, with storage pits behind the buildings in the zone 10 to 20 meters from the defenses. The excavations showed that the inhabitants had access to a very limited range of manufactured goods but were able to acquire them in large quantities, while their diet was of a high standard with a mixture of livestock, cereals, and legumes. It is evident, however, that the population of this settlement was by no means tightly packed into the defended area, as in the case of villages

[20,21] Richard Hodges, "Excavations and survey at San Vincenzo al Volturno, Molise: 1981," *Archaeologia Medievale* 9 (1982).

[21,22] J.-N. Biraben and J. Le Goff, "The plague in the Early Middle Ages," in R. Forster and O. Ranum, eds, *The Biology of Man in History* (Baltimore, 1975), pp. 48–80.

[22,23] Richard Hodges, Graeme Barker, and Keith Wade, "Excavations at D85 (Santa Maria in Città): an early medieval hilltop settlement in Molise," *Papers of the British School at Rome* 48 (1980): 70–124.

of the tenth century and later. Instead, the evidence suggests that there were no more than about fifty inhabitants to defend the timber and stone ramparts, which in reality would have required about six hundred. Indeed the investigation at Santa Maria in Città seems to show that the site was transitional between the classical villa complexes, where several households were loosely nucleated, and the hilltop villages of the Middle Ages. Eventually Santa Maria in Città was abandoned in favour of a site that still exists on the other side of the river, Guardialfiera. The latter was defended and had ready access to a larger area of good soil, now required to meet the demands of a population far in excess of fifty. Thus, while in two areas we can trace the origins of medieval vernacular architecture and the idea of hilltop villages to the sixth or seventh centuries, in practice it was not until the economic revival of the tenth century that these phenomena became almost universal in central and southern Italy, as a result of the process known as *incastellamento* [the regrouping of the rural population into fortified villages].

Rome

And what of Rome, once the capital of the Empire? Cassiodorus, writing as Praetorian Prefect in 523–27, looked back to the time when it was a teeming metropolis:

> The great size of the population of the city of Rome in former times is clear from the fact that it required the provision of foodstuffs from distant regions to supply its needs. While the food requirements of foreign cities were met from the adjacent provinces, Rome depended on imported yields. The great extent of the walls, the seating capacity of the places of entertainment, the remarkable size of the public baths and the number of mills . . . bear witness to the hordes of citizens.[23]

The corn supply apart, Cassiodorus was thinking of the Aurelianic wall (length: 18.1 kilometers), the Colosseum and the Circus Maximus (estimated capacities: 73,000 and 300,000 respectively) and baths like those of Caracalla (area: 11 hectares) and Diocletian (area: 14 hectares). He might have added the aqueducts, for the Anio Vetus, Marcia, Claudia, and Anio Novus alone delivered some 600,000 cubic meters of water per day.[24]

Estimates of the maximum size of the population vary enormously. Geoffrey Rickman offers a figure "near to 1,000,000," based on Augustus's claim (in *Res Gestae*, 15.2) that he distributed food to 320,000 urban *plebes* – by definition, adult males – in 5 BC. Peter Brunt calculates that adult males accounted for some 35 percent of the free population in the time of Augustus; R. P. Duncan-Jones prefers two-sevenths (28.6 percent). Brunt's figure would give us a populace of 914,000; Duncan-Jones's figure would give us 1,220,000. To arrive at the total population, we must add slaves, who did not qualify for the dole. Thus in 5 BC the population of Rome cannot have been far short of one million, and was perhaps greater.[25]

Although the population probably declined in the interval, Mazzarino suggests a figure for the late fourth century which is roughly the same as our estimate for 5 BC. The figure is based on the compensation paid to pork suppliers for losses in transit. Legislation of 367 states that

[23.24] Cassiodorus, *Variae*, 11. 39.
[24.25] D. R. Blackman, "The volume of water delivered by the four great aqueducts of Rome," *Papers of the British School at Rome* 46 (1978): 52–72.
[25.26] P. Brunt, *Italian Manpower, 225 BC–AD 14* (Oxford, 1971), p. 117; R. P. Duncan-Jones, *The Economy of the Roman Empire* (Cambridge, 1974), 264n. 4; G. Hermansen, "The population of Imperial Rome: the Regionaries," *Historia* 27 (1978): 129–68; S. Mazzarino, *Aspetti sociali del IV secolo* (Rome, 1951), pp. 230–8; Geoffrey Rickman, *The Corn Supply of Ancient Rome* (Oxford, 1980).

losses were calculated at 15 percent and compensated in kind by the payment of 17,000 amphorae of wine, one amphora being the equivalent of 70 *librae* of meat. If 15 percent of the pork supply was (70 × 17,000) *librae*, the total was (70 × 17,000 × 100/15), or 7,933,333 *librae*. If a single ration was 25 *librae* per year, as in 419 (see below), the number of recipients was 7,933,333/25, or 317,333; it was 320,000 under Augustus.

Mazzarino converts the number of recipients into the total populace by following Beloch and assuming that every 1,000 adult males imply 796 women and 137 children (i.e. that adult males made up 51.7 percent of the total). (317,333 × 100/51.7) is 613,405. After allowing for slaves and temporary residents, Mazzarino arrives at a total population of between 800,000 and one million. If we use the formulae of Brunt or Duncan-Jones, the figure rises. In 367, therefore, the dole size suggests that once again the population was almost one million.

Cassiodorus makes it clear that the population had fallen by his day, and 500 years later it was negligible, by Augustan standards; J. C. Russell guesses 30,000 in the tenth century.[26] Regular importation of grain ceased in the seventh century, and Lazio itself probably supplied most of the city's food. Towards the end of the eighth century the *Liber Pontificalis* records that the papal estate at Capracorum, only 15 kilometers from the town, supplied staples that imperial Rome had obtained from all over the Mediterranean: grain, wine, and olive oil.

Where, then, we may ask, between the poles of a large population dependent on imported food (as in 367) and a small population supplied locally (as in the eighth century), did Rome stand in Late Antiquity?

Our main source of information on Rome itself is the Theodosian Code, which includes legislation governing the supply of free bread and meat. Two rescripts concern the period in question; one was issued in 419, the other in 452. The first established that householders were entitled to a monthly ration of pork five times a year and that 4,000 rations were to be distributed daily. The official number of recipients in 419, therefore, was (4,000 × 30), or 120,000. The second rescript established that Rome should be provided with 3,628,000 *librae* of pork a year, of which 3,528,000 *librae* were to be distributed free at the rate of 5 *librae* per month, five times a year. The official number of recipients in 452, therefore, was 3,528,000/25, or 141,120.[27]

The following estimates emerge if we calculate the size of the populace by equating householders with adult males and using the ratios proposed (admittedly for other periods) by Brunt, Duncan-Jones and Mazzarino.

Date	Recipients	Populace according to % of recipients		
		28.6%	35%	51.7%
419	120,000	419,568	342,857	232,108
452	141,120	493,427	403,200	272,959

If we assume that the populace amounted to roughly 80 percent of the population (as apparently under Augustus), we can reach the following estimates for the number of inhabitants of Rome.

[26,27] J. C. Russell, "Late Ancient and Medieval Population", *Transactions of the American Philosophical Society*, New Series 48/3 (Philadelphia, 1958): 73; 93.
[27,28] C. Pharr, *The Theodosian Code and Novels and the Sirmondian Constitution* (Princeton, 1952).

Date	Population if recipients = × % populace		
	28.6%	35%	51.7%
419	524,460	428,571	290,135
452	616,783	504,000	341,198

It is not unreasonable, therefore, to guess that the population of Rome was 400,000 ± 25 percent in 452. In 523–7, Cassiodorus implied that it was considerably smaller, and between the sixth and the ninth centuries the population was whittled down to a few tens of thousands. All these estimates, however, depend on fragmentary (and uncheckable) information. It would be foolish to take any of the figures as "accurate." Nevertheless, they do give us the strong impression that Rome at its greatest extent contained more than a million people; that the population was half, or less than half, that figure in the mid-fifth century; and that after this date it declined very sharply indeed. The process, although erratic – Procopius 7.22.9 claims that Rome was abandoned at one stage of the Gothic war – was inexorable.

Summary

We have investigated the decline of the classical world in the heart of the Western Empire and stand by the two hypotheses advanced above. Archaeological evidence confirms Pirenne's belief that Alaric's assault on Rome in 410 was simply one incident in a long and complex process. Excavations in Carthage, Rome, Luni, and elsewhere in Italy have demonstrated the persistence of commercial life (albeit on a diminishing scale) within the Mediterranean until the sixth century. But the growing evidence from both urban and rural excavations compels us to look for the final degradation of Rome in the sixth century and to see the Arab advance after 630 as the consequence rather than the cause of the catastrophe.

Archaeology supports the historical impression that, after a brief resurgence in the mid- to late fifth century, an irreversible decline set in. The size of towns and standard of urban housing fell in a way that would have been inconceivable to the administrators of the early Empire; the economic basis of Justinian's reunified Empire was short-lived and soon seen to be hollow. The metamorphosis from the classical to the medieval system had begun. The Byzantines levied heavy taxes to pay for the army and central government in a time of almost continuous warfare, while agricultural and industrial production declined and social unrest, mass-movements and perhaps also plague led to a sizable depopulation of the countryside. Urban life resisted a little longer, propped up, we suspect, as much by individual commercial activity as by the local bureaucracy. But this, too, was doomed by Justinian's taxes. The system gradually wound down. The instability of the countryside, now revealed by regional surveys, such as those in South Etruria and Molise, provided the opportunity for kings and tribal chiefs from north of the Alps to carve out new territories in the Mediterranean and allowed them to establish their own social and economic systems. These systems were described by late classical writers as less innovative than perhaps they were, and Pirenne too laid heavy emphasis on the survival of Roman institutions. We beg to differ. By the end of the sixth century, conditions in the western Mediterranean bore little resemblance to those in the second century. Before the Arabs arrived, the transformation was virtually complete.

Historians – rightly – are skeptical about the idea of a "generalized demographic decline" that lasted for centuries. After all, though the Black Death slaughtered one European in three, the population was restored to its former level within two or three generations. The Black Death, however, destroyed only people. An alternative analogy for the Mediterranean in Late Antiquity is South America in the sixteenth century, where the conquistadors not only slaughtered on a massive scale, but also destroyed the traditional social and economic systems. The result was indeed generalized demographic collapse. In the Mediterranean, the structure of Roman society and its economy were undermined, and its wealth was absorbed by two centuries of intermittent warfare. Depopulation, therefore, is not impossible; the ruined towns and wasted countryside suggest that it happened in the Mediterranean at the end of the Roman period – and the burden of proof rests with those who maintain that it didn't.

5   Gregory of Tours and Clovis

Ian N. Wood

For over a century the chronology of the reign of Clovis has been the subject of debate. The onslaughts on Gregory of Tours's account, especially those directed by Krusch and van de Vyver, exposed the weaknesses of the chapters associated with the king's conversion in Book Two of the *Libri Historiarum* [*Books of Histories*], but a host of major scholars continued to defend the traditional outline of Clovis's reign, and prevented any alternative interpretation from securing unanimous support.[1] Indeed the arguments over Clovis's baptism were so indecisive that Tessier proposed a truce, insisting that the exact date did not matter.[2] Nevertheless, historians have continued to argue about the chronology, with Weiss upholding the attitude of acute skepticism towards Gregory's account,[3] while Reydellet has asserted his acceptance of the bishop of Tours's narrative.[4] The continuity of the debate is in itself an indication that, *pace* Tessier, the chronology of Clovis's reign is an issue of significance. Indeed the chronology affects, or is affected by, one's interpretation of the career of the Frankish monarch. At the same time the account of Clovis in Gregory of Tours is intimately linked to that historian's purpose and his view of history. It is, in fact, unfortunate that the historiographical issues raised by the *Decem Libri Historiarum* [*Ten Books of Histories*] are usually kept separate from the historical problem of Clovis's chronology. Much of the best work on Gregory has preferred not to discuss the precise factual problems created by his reconstruction of events.[5] Meanwhile the defenders of Gregory's account of Clovis have

---

[1] See especially B. Krusch, "Zwei Heiligenleben des Jonas von Susa; II. Die ältere Vita Vedastis und die Taufe Chlodovechs," *Mitteilungen des Instituts für österreichische Geschichtsforschung* 14 (1893): 427–48; A. van de Vyver, "La victoire contre les Alamans et la conversion de Clovis," *Revue Belge de Philologie et d'Histoire* 15 (1936): 859–914, 16 (1937): 35–94; A. van de Vyver, "L'unique victoire contre les Alamans et la conversion de Clovis en 506," *Revue Belge de Philologie et d'Histoire* 17 (1938): 793–813. For a recent overview of the debate, R. Weiss, *Chlodwigs Taufe: Rheims 508* (Berne and Frankfurt, 1971), pp. 9–14.
[2] G. Tessier, *Le Baptême de Clovis* (Paris, 1964), pp. 124–5; G. Tessier, "La conversion de Clovis et la christianisation des Francs," in *Spoleto, 14, La conversione al cristianesimo nell'Europa dell'alto medioevo* (Spoleto, 1967), pp. 166–9.
[3] Weiss, *Chlodwigs Taufe*, pp. 15–19.
[4] M. Reydellet, *La royauté dans la littérature latine de Sidoine Apollinaire à Isidore de Séville* (Rome, 1981), pp. 95–113.
[5] One regrets the decision of J. M. Wallace-Hadrill not to embroil himself in these factual problems; see *The Long-haired Kings* (London, 1962), pp. 49–70, 163–85. It is perhaps symptomatic of this state of affairs that Reydellet discusses the problem of Clovis's chronology in a chapter on Avitus of Vienne and not in his more perceptive chapter on Gregory of Tours.

tended to treat it as a primary source, although Books One and Two of the *Libri Historiarum* are secondary narratives written a considerable time after the events concerned. My purpose in this paper is to discuss Gregory's Clovis and the real Clovis as aspects of a single problem. It is impossible to come to any firm conclusions about the reign of the great Merovingian without examining the sources and historical methods which underlie Gregory's account. By so doing I hope to clarify the problems involved, even if I fail to offer unquestionable solutions.

In the second half of Book Two of the *Libri Historiarum* Gregory is not dependent on narrative or chronicle sources as he had been for the opening chapters, but he still had access to written evidence. On two occasions the reader is referred explicitly to saints' lives; to a *Vita Remigii* [*Life of St Remegius*] for an account of the bishop of Rheims raising a dead man to life[6] and to a *Vita Maxentii* [*Life of St Maxentius*] for miracles additional to that performed by Maxentius before the battle of Vouillé.[7] As well as these texts cited by Gregory, the inclusion of a miracle associated with St Hilary's basilica at Poitiers might suggest access to Venantius Fortunatus's *Liber de Virtutibus sancti Hilarii* [*Book on the Virtues of St Hilary*], where the same story appears, but the details in the two versions differ enough to cast doubts on such a conclusion.[8] There are also, however, problems with the two *Vitae* explicitly cited by Gregory. The *Vita Maxentii* no longer exists, and although the hagiographical corpus of works sometimes attributed to Venantius Fortunatus contains a *Vita Remedii* [*Life of St Remedius*] which includes the miracle to which Gregory refers,[9] there are other aspects to the hagiography of Remigius which give pause for thought. Both in Fredegar's history and Hincmar's *Vita Remigii*, but not in that ascribed to Venantius Fortunatus, the famous vase of Soissons is said to have belonged to the bishop of Rheims.[10] Hincmar's testimony is, of course, suspect, but that of Fredegar might suggest that even in the sixth century the story was associated with Remigius. More suggestive still is Gregory's comparison of Remigius and Silvester.[11] This image is absent from the earliest "Life of Remigius"; traditionally it has been assumed that Gregory himself drew the parallel on the grounds of his reading of the *Vita Silvestris* [*Life of St Silvester*], but we do not know that he had read that work, and there are considerable objections to assigning the comparison to the imagination of the bishop of Tours, since Gregory has little time for Constantine. In Book One, when relating the reign of the first Christian emperor, he refers to the restoration of peace to the churches, but otherwise contents himself with a statement on the murder of Fausta and Crispus, together with references to the invention of the True Cross and the commissioning of Juvencus's metrical version of the Gospels.[12] The reason for this astonishing silence is not difficult to detect. Gregory's chief source at this moment is Jerome's chronicle, which not only deals with the murder of Fausta and Crispus, but also asserts that Constantine was baptised as an

---

[6] Gregory of Tours, *Libri Historiarum*, ed. B. Krusch and W. Levison, *MGH, SRM*, I, 1 (Hanover, 1951), II, 31.

[7] Gregory, *Liber Historiarum*, II, 37.

[8] Ibid.; Venantius, *Liber de Virtutibus sancti Hilarii*, ed. B. Krusch, *MGH, AA*, IV, 2 (Berlin, 1885), 7.

[9] *Vita Remedii*, ed. B. Krusch, *MGH, AA*, IV, 2, 8.

[10] Fredegar, ed. B. Krusch, *MGH, SRM*, II (Hanover, 1888), III, 16; Hincmar, *Vita Remigii*, ed. B. Krusch, *MGH, SRM*, III (Hanover, 1896), 11. See also G. Kurth, *Histoire poétique des Mérovingiens* (Paris, 1893), pp. 218–23.

[11] Gregory, *Liber Historiarum*, II, 31.

[12] Gregory, *Liber Historiarum*, I, 36.

Arian.[13] If we turn to Orosius, another of Gregory's sources, we find an allusion to the restoration of peace to the churches, but no detail on the emperor's conversion or baptism.[14] Despite his knowledge of the Christian historiography of the fourth and fifth centuries, Gregory could not conclude from it that Constantine was a model to be upheld.[15] This being so, the images of Clovis as a new Constantine and Remigius as a new Silvester can hardly have been Gregory's. They may belong to the *Vita Remigii* to which Gregory had access; more likely than not the parallel between Remigius and Silvester belongs to a Rheims tradition, while the Constantine–Clovis comparison could have been suggested in a sermon preached by Remigius himself at the baptism of the king.

Gregory certainly did have access to one work written by Remigius, his letter to Clovis on the death of Albofledis, which has survived in the *Epistulae Austrasiacae* [*Austrasian Letters*].[16] It is not impossible that there was a collection of letters and sermons from Remigius's pen in the sixth century. The letters of Avitus of Vienne circulated together with his sermons composed for specific occasions,[17] and these formed another of Gregory's sources from which he reconstructed the religious history of the Burgundian kingdom in the time of Clovis.[18] For the previous decades Gregory had recourse to a further letter-collection – that of Sidonius Apollinaris – together with the bishop of Clermont's mass book.[19] Although these sources provide vital information, it is information that needs using with care. Modern scholarship has provided a plausible chronology for Sidonius's correspondence;[20] for Gregory, however, the letters would have been dateless. The works of Avitus, for the most part, remain undated, and while the bishop of Tours probably had access to more of them than now survive, he is unlikely to have had any better information on the precise context of individual letters.

The other major source for Gregory's account of Clovis's reign was doubtless oral history. For the modern historian this is the hardest material to access. There are no clear criteria to help identify oral traditions and there is no criterion, except common sense, on which to assess their validity as evidence. Nevertheless some points stand out. First an oral tradition can easily take on a somewhat epic colour – and this not only among the Germans but also among the Gallo-Romans. Sidonius's account of how his brother-in-law Ecdicius and a force of "scarcely eighteen men" rode through the Gothic army with impunity strains credulity, even though the incident is being recounted to Ecdicius himself.[21] Gregory of Tours remembers the tale as describing the repulse of the Gothic army by ten men![22] Doubtless the story

---

[13] Jerome, *Chronicon*, ed. R. Helm, *Eusebius Werke*, VII (Berlin, 1956), pp. 228–34.

[14] Orosius, *Historiarum adversum paganos Libri*, ed. C. Zangemeister, *Corpus Scriptorum Ecclesiasticorum Latinorum*, V (Vienna, 1882), VII, 28, 1 and 15.

[15] Even his knowledge of Eusebius/Rufinus – see *Liber Historiarum*, IX, 15 and *Liber Vitae Patrum*, ed. W. Arndt and B. Krusch, *MGH, SRM*, I, 2 (Hanover, 1885), VI, 1 and *Liber in Gloria Martyrum (ibid.)*, 20 – does not appear to have helped here. For Rufinus's translation see *Eusebius Werke*, II (Leipzig, 1908–9), ed. E. Schwartz and T. Mommsen.

[16] Gregory, *Liber Historiarum*, II, 31; *Epistulae Austrasiacae*, ed. W. Gundlach, *MGH, Epp.*, III (Berlin, 1892), 1.

[17] I. N. Wood, "The audience of architecture in post-Roman Gaul," in L. A. S. Butler and R. Morris, eds, *The Anglo-Saxon Church: Papers on History, Architecture and Archaeology in honour of Dr H. M. Taylor* [Council for British Archaeology, Research Report 60 (London, 1986), pp. 74–9].

[18] Gregory, *Liber Historiarum*, II, 34.

[19] Gregory, *Liber Historiarum*, II, 22, 24–5.

[20] See the edition by A. Loyen (Paris, 1960–70).

[21] Sidonius, *ep.*, III, 3.

[22] Gregory, *Liber Historiarum*, II, 24.

of how Aridius outwitted Clovis by his cunning and persuaded the Frankish king to make terms with Gundobad is another Gallo-Roman tale.[23] How much of it is legendary, and how much reliable is impossible to determine.[24] To establish the reliability of a tradition, it is not sufficient to attribute its origins to a named individual; the individual may have exaggerated or have had a faulty memory. Some historians have reasonably inferred that information was passed from Chrotechildis to the church at Tours,[25] but even in stories which might have originated with the queen there are suspicious features which demand cautious treatment. The tale of Chilperic's death, Chrotechildis's exile, her discovery by Clovis's envoys and Gundobad's pusillanimous agreement to her marriage has reasonably been described as an epic.[26] The murder of Chrotechildis's father – which looks remarkably like a doublet for the later killing of Sigismund[27] – is hard to reconcile with Avitus's comment addressed to Gundobad, the supposed murderer, "*flebatis quondam pietate ineffabili funera germanorum*" ["in the past, with ineffable tenderheartedness, you mourned the deaths of your brothers"].[28] The princess's exile apparently involved no more than living in Geneva, if one accepts Fredegar's information,[29] but this detail raises further doubts, since, although Gundobad appears to have been sole ruler of the Burgundian kingdom,[30] his brother Godegisil had his household in Geneva – at least in 494.[31] It is not easy to see why Gundobad should have sent a niece, whose father he had murdered, to a city dominated by his brother. Nor is the subsequent account of Chrotechildis's vengeance against Gundobad's family entirely plausible. It is odd that she should wait some thirty years, until 523, to raise the issue.[32] Gregory makes no attempt to depict Clovis's attack on the Burgundian kingdom in 500 as part of a bloodfeud[33] and the truce which ended the war does not appear to be the composition of a vendetta. Admittedly Gregory attributed to Clovis, as to Chrotechildis, a capacity to nurse a grievance over several decades; when at the end of his reign – and the incidental details of tonsuring and ordination do suggest a date after his conversion – Clovis murders Chararic, he does so because the latter had not helped him against Syagrius, apparently in 486.[34] As with Chrotechildis's prosecution of the bloodfeud, it seems legitimate to wonder whether the notion of revenge has not been introduced in order to explain an apparently unjustifiable

[23] Gregory, *Liber Historiarum*, II, 32.

[24] There is a possible reference to Aridius saving the Burgundian kingdom in Avitus, *ep.*, 50. On the identity of Aridius/Arigius see A. Jahn. *Die Geschichte der Burgundionen und Burgundiens bis zum Ende der I. Dynastie* (Halle, 1874), II, pp. 205, 452 n. 3.

[25] Tessier, *Le Baptême de Clovis*, p. 74.

[26] Gregory, *Liber Historiarum*, II, 28; Kurth, *Histoire poétique*, p. 237.

[27] Gregory, *Liber Historiarum*, II, 28; III, 6; Kurth, *Histoire poétique*, pp. 245–7.

[28] Avitus, ed. R. Peiper, *MGH, AA*, VI, 2 (Berlin, 1883), *ep.*, 5; Kurth, *Histoire poétique*, pp. 241–2. [The translations of passages by Avitus here and throughout this essay are by Danuta Shanzer who, with Ian Wood, is preparing a translation of Avitus's letters for the Translated Texts for Historians series.]

[29] Fredegar, III, 18. *Exilium* in Gregory does not appear to entail much; compare Hermenigild's *exilium*, *Libri Historiarum*, V, 38; VI, 43.

[30] I. N. Wood, "Kings, kingdoms and consent," in P. H. Sawyer and I. N. Wood, eds, *Early Medieval Kingship* (Leeds, 1977), pp. 21–2.

[31] Ennodius, *Vita Epifani*, ed. F. Vogel, *MGH, AA*, VII (Berlin, 1885), 174.

[32] Gregory, *Liber Historiarum*, III, 6; for the date, Marius of Avenches, Chronicle, ed. T. Mommsen, *MGH, AA*, XI (Berlin, 1894). The chronology leads me to take a more skeptical view of the story than that of Wallace-Hadrill, *The Long-haired Kings*, p. 131.

[33] Gregory, *Liber Historiarum*, II, 32; for the date, Marius of Avenches. I find Kurth's attempt to explain this away (*Histoire poétique*, pp. 247–8) unconvincing.

[34] Gregory, *Liber Historiarum*, II, 27, 41.

action. Certainly the chronology suggested by Gregory seems to cast doubt on his interpretation of events.

Oral tradition, if it supplied Gregory with his account of the relations between the Merovingians and the Gibichungs, can hardly be accepted as reliable, regardless of the identity of the supposed author of the information. Without comparative material it is impossible for the modern historian to detach the facts from their epic casing. For Gregory oral tradition would have been as unreliable and intractable as the hagiography and letters at his disposal. From none of this information could he have deduced a reliable chronology, and it is not easy to assess how far he could have dovetailed the stories culled from widely differing sources into a narrative where each episode was in order. That Gregory himself was faced with an absence of trustworthy dates in his sources can be seen clearly in his attempts to compute the date of Clovis's death. Clovis, we are told, died five years after Vouillé, that is, in 512; 11 years after Licinius became bishop of Tours, which apparently gives a date of 517 or later; and 112 years after the death of Martin, which comes to 509.[35] Gregory's later computations on the deaths of Theudebert and Chlothar,[36] however, and the regnal dating for the fifth Council of Orleans,[37] seem to require an obit for Clovis of 511–12. Nevertheless, before accepting this, it is worth recalling the fact that the king was clearly alive at the time of the first Council of Orléans, which consular and indictional dates place firmly in 511.[38] Moreover the *Liber Pontificalis* [*Book of Pontiffs*] records Clovis's gift of a votive crown to the shrine of St Peter in the pontificate of Hormisdas, in other words between 514 and 523.[39] Although the weight of the evidence does suggest that Clovis died in late 511 or 512 the chronological confusion in Gregory's attempts to calculate this can only imply that the bishop did not have reliable evidence on which to base his computations. This coincides with the conclusions suggested above, that Gregory's known sources would have provided him with no dates, and it means that even the most general chronological indications in the second half of Book Two of the *Libri Historiarum*, with the possible exceptions of the quinquennial dates for the defeat of Syagrius and the Thuringian war,[40] are invalid as historical evidence.

Despite the weakness of Gregory's chronology, it is still possible that his overall interpretation of Clovis's reign may stand. The vengeance motifs, albeit questionable, are not central to the account, which revolves largely around the depiction of the king as an agent of Providence, especially in his role as the champion of Catholicism.[41] Fortunately one aspect of this theme, that of the conflict between Catholics and Arians, can be investigated in some detail. Essentially the narration of the religious events of Clovis's reign begins with the

[35] Gregory, *Liber Historiarum*, II, 43. Licinius's predecessor was still alive at the time of the Council of Agde in 506, to which he sent a representative; see *Concilia Galliae, A 314–A 506*, ed. C. Munier, *Corpus Christianorum Series Latinorum*, 148 (Turnhout, 1963), pp. 214, 219. For further problems on Licinius's chronology see Weiss, *Chlodwigs Taufe*, p. 17.
[36] Gregory, *Liber Historiarum*, III, 37; IV; 21. W. Levison, *Zur Geschichte des Frankenkönigs Chlodowech*, in his *Aus rheinischer und fränkischer Frühzeit* (Dusseldorf, 1948), p. 208.
[37] Orléans, V (549), *Concilia Galliae A 511–A 695*, ed. C. de Clercq, *Corpus Christianorum Series Latinorum*, 148 A (Turnhout, 1963), p. 157. Levison, *Zur Geschichte des Frankenkönigs Chlodowech*, p. 208.
[38] Orléans, I, pp. 13–15; Levison, *Zur Geschichte des Frankenkönigs Chlodowech*, p. 208.
[39] *Liber Pontificalis*, ed. L. Duchesne (Paris, 1955), 54.
[40] Gregory, *Liber Historiarum*, II, 27. Two further quinquennial dates appear in some manuscripts only; *Liber Historiarum*, II, 30, 37. The authenticity of these dates was defended by Levison, *Zur Geschichte des Frankenkönigs Chlodowech*, pp. 205–7 and denied by Weiss, *Chlodwigs Taufe*, p. 16.
[41] Reydellet, *La royauté*, pp. 402–8.

persecution instigated by Euric against the Catholics. For this Gregory had the evidence of a letter written by Sidonius to Bishop Basilius, and his account faithfully mirrors that of the bishop of Clermont.[42] At the same time, considerable distortion is involved. Sidonius's outburst against Euric's ecclesiastical policies is a rhetorical *tour de force*. It relates to a specific moment in time, and is not an accurate representation of the state of affairs once the Visigoths had established control over the Auvergne. Gregory, in fact, generalized from a single instance and in so doing created a thoroughly misleading impression.[43] It is possible that the deception was not deliberate – only Stroheker's painstaking scholarship provided an accurate account of Euric's policies before the publication of an annotated edition of Sidonius's letters. However Gregory would have had no desire to portray the Visigothic king in a favorable light. It suited his purposes admirably to caricature Euric as a persecutor and portray his death (here incorrectly and without the support of Sidonius) as the speedy vengeance of God.

The portrayal of Arian monarchs continues in the same rather exaggerated way with the assertion that Gundioc, king of the Burgundians, was a relative of Athanaric, the fourth-century Gothic ruler with a reputation as a persecutor.[44] In fact no historian has ever satisfactorily established a connection between the two men and it may be that Gregory's assertion is no more than a slur on the Gibichung dynasty. If so, the point can be placed alongside his misleading reference to the deaths of Godegisil, Gundobad, and Godomar, who are said to have lost their kingdoms and their souls at the same time;[45] certainly Godegisil was an Arian and died trying to overthrow Gundobad;[46] the latter, however, appears to have died peacefully and as a crypto-Catholic, even if he had not publicly entered the Church;[47] Godomar's end is unknown, but there is no reason to regard him as a heretic.[48]

The centre of Gregory's description of Arian–Catholic conflict in this period, however, is his description of Clovis's decision to attack Alaric, because he found the occupation of part of Gaul by heretics objectionable.[49] This statement is preceded by an account of the flight of Quintianus, bishop of Rodez, from the Arians.[50] Doubtless the two issues are meant to be considered together, with the story of Quintianus illustrating the background to Clovis's intense hatred of the Goths. There are, however, reasons for believing not only that the Rodez anecdote involves a misrepresentation of the facts, but also that Gregory could have provided an accurate account if it had suited his purpose. In the *Libri Historiarum* we are told that Quintianus fell foul of the Goths and the people of Rodez because he was regarded as being one of the many people who wished to be under Frankish rule; he therefore fled to Clermont where he was received by bishop Eufrasius. All this is assigned to the period before the battle of Vouillé.[51] The events and the chronology, however, are in conflict. Rodez is too

---

[42] Gregory, *Liber Historiarum*, II, 25; Sidonius, *ep.*, VII, 6.

[43] For the exposure of Gregory's error see K. F. Stroheker, *Eurich, König der Westgoten* (Stuttgart, 1937), pp. 40–4.

[44] Gregory, *Liber Historiarum*, II, 28; cf. II, 4.

[45] Gregory, *Liber Historiarum*, III, *praef.*

[46] Gregory, *Liber Historiarum*, II, 33.

[47] Gregory, *Liber Historiarum*, II, 34; by 512 Gundobad was commissioning theological works from Avitus, e.g. the *Contra Eutychianam Haeresim*.

[48] Gregory, *Liber Historiarum*, III, 11.

[49] Gregory, *Liber Historiarum*, II, 37.

[50] Gregory, *Liber Historiarum*, II, 36.

[51] Gregory, *Liber Historiarum*, II, 35–7.

far south to have been within the range of the Franks before 508; and if treason against the Goths was Quintianus's intention it is difficult to see why he should flee to Clermont, another Gothic town. Moreover when Quintianus was later appointed bishop of Clermont, it was, according to Gregory, because the saint had been exiled from Rodez on account of his love for Theuderic,[52] seemingly after the latter had become king. This dating fits perfectly well with the arrival of Quintianus in Clermont during the episcopate of Eufrasius, who died *c*.515, nor is it contradicted by the appearance of the former at the Council of Orléans in 511.[53] Between 508 and Clovis's death Rodez was almost certainly subject to the Franks.[54] Quintianus fled to Clermont, therefore, after Rodez was recaptured by the Goths and according to Gregory's *Liber Vitae Patrum* [*Book of the Lives of the Fathers*] not primarily because of his Frankish sympathies, but because of his interference in the cult of the local saint Amantius.[55] The implications of this are clarified by the will of Quintianus's successor, Dalmatius, which stated that no alien should be consecrated bishop of Rodez.[56] Since Quintianus was an African,[57] it appears more than likely that as an outsider he had paid no attention to the sensitivities of the Rutenois and had hence fallen foul of them. The chief illustration, therefore, of Catholics in an Arian kingdom acting as a fifth column for the Franks, proves to be a figment of Gregory's imagination. More worrying, the misinterpretation of Quintianus's history is exposed by Gregory's own evidence. Not only is the bishop of Tours's account wrong, it is deliberately fraudulent.

Once Gregory's interpretation of the Arian–Catholic conflict is discarded, the evidence tells a very much more complicated tale than that offered in the *Libri Historiarum*. There were complaints directed against bishops; Aprunculus of Langres fled from Dijon to Clermont, perhaps because of Burgundian hatred, but that hatred can scarcely be associated with fear of the Franks, since at the time of Aprunculus's flight they were still ruled by a pagan king – and the bishop in any case fled west to the Gothic kingdom and not north.[58] Further light is shed on treason accusations by those directed against Caesarius of Arles at this time. In these instances the bishop's chief opponents were not Goths, but Gallo-Roman Christians and Jews who played on the suspicions of their masters in order to oust a bishop they did not like.[59] Granted that Caesarius himself had come from Chalon-sur-Saône in the Burgundian kingdom, it was not difficult to present the saint as a potential traitor. In comparison with Caesarius's accusers, however, the Goths behaved with considerable restraint. The conflict was clearly not between Arian and Catholic, but the outcome of local tension within the *civitas* [city] of Arles. This provides a much more plausible general model for the interpretation of treason accusations levelled against bishops than that offered by Gregory, although it is possible that the exiles of Volusianus and of Verus, both bishops of the frontier town of Tours, resulted from suspicions of treachery.[60]

[52] Gregory, *Liber Historiarum*, III, 2.
[53] Orléans, I, pp. 13–19.
[54] Gregory, *Liber Historiarum*, II, 37.
[55] Gregory, *Liber Vitae Patrum*, IV, 1.
[56] Gregory, *Liber Historiarum*, V, 46.
[57] Gregory, *Liber Vitae Patrum*, IV, 1.
[58] Gregory, *Liber Historiarum*, II, 23. For a full discussion of this and other treason accusations, I. N. Wood, "Avitus of Vienne: religion and culture in the Auvergne and the Rhône valley, 470–530" (unpublished D.Phil. thesis; University of Oxford, 1979), pp. 172–6. For a traditional interpretation, M. Rouche, *L'Aquitaine des Wisigoths aux Arabes* (Paris, 1979), pp. 46–8.
[59] *Vita Caesarii*, ed. B. Krusch, *MGH, SRM*, III (Hanover, 1896), I, 21, 29f, 36.
[60] Gregory, *Liber Historiarum*, II, 26; X, 31.

Despite a single, unexplained reference to *persecutio* [persecution] in the writings of Avitus of Vienne,[61] the contemporary evidence suggests cooperation between Arian monarchs and their Catholic subjects. Avitus's detailed information on Gundobad's Burgundian kingdom presents a picture of harmony, although it is possible to detect some traces of irritation relating to the establishment and endowment of Arian churches.[62] Apart from the period of crisis surrounding the deaths of Boethius and Symmachus,[63] there is little evidence for conflict in the kingdom of Theodoric in Italy. Alaric II's Visigothic realm may seem to be an exception with its treason accusations and cases of flight and exile, but neither the case of Quintianus nor that of Caesarius supports Gregory of Tours's interpretation. The supposed disaffection of the senator Apollinaris may illuminate the atmosphere of suspicion engendered by Clovis's expansion, but it does not associate the uneasiness with religion.[64] The chronological coincidence of the summoning of the Council of Agde and the compilation of the Breviary of Alaric in 506 with the outbreak of war in 507 has sometimes led to the suggestion that the Visigoths were making dramatic concessions to a disaffected people in the former year. Agde, however, is best viewed as the achievement of Caesarius and of Gallo-Romans at court; hence the presence of bishop Peter *de palatio* [of the palace] and the inclusion of prayers for the king. Moreover the expectations of another council to be held in Toulouse in 507 suggests that Agde was intended to initiate a period of conciliar activity and was not a temporary sop to the Catholics.[65] The Breviary of Alaric, which did not affect the legal status of the Gallo-Romans, can hardly be seen as a concession by the king. It can only have been compiled by the Roman population, presumably for the convenience of administrators, and its publication is likely to have enhanced Alaric's prestige.[66] The flurry of activity in Visigothic Gaul in 506 looks more like an assertion of confidence in the government than anything else. Meanwhile at court, an orthodox Catholic minister was prepared to order the destruction of the upper storey of a Catholic church to improve the view from the palace.[67]

Gregory's view of the age of Clovis is thus in serious need of revision. The reasons for his interpretation, however, are relatively clear. A causal link between Clovis's Catholicism and his success would have seemed obvious enough to anyone who expected to see divine intervention in human affairs, and Gregory, both as an accomplished hagiographer and as a historian who had read Eusebius and Orosius, would have taken such causation for

[61]   Avitus, *ep.*, 8.

[62]   Avitus, *ep.*, 7.

[63]   H. Chadwick, *Boethius* (Oxford, 1981), pp. 46–68.

[64]   Avitus, *epp.*, 24, 51–2; Gregory, *Liber Historiarum*, II, 37.

[65]   Agde, ed. C. Munier, pp. 192, 213–19; Caesarius to Ruricius, *Fausti aliorumque epistulae*, ed. G. Luetjohann, *MGH, AA*, VIII (Berlin, 1887), 12. The traditional case is stated by Rouche, *L'Aquitaine*, p. 48. For a detailed discussion of the context of the council, K. Schäferdiek, *Die Kirche in den Reichen der Westgoten und Suewen bis zur Errichtung der westgotischen Staatskirche* (Berlin, 1967), pp. 54–5, 57–8.

[66]   P. Wormald, "*Let scripta* and *verbum Regis*: Legislation and Germanic kingship from Euric to Cnut," in Sawyer and Wood, eds, *Early Medieval Kingship*, pp. 133–4. The opposite view is held by P. D. King, *Law and Society in the Visigothic Kingdom* (Cambridge, 1972), pp. 10–11 and Rouche, *L'Aquitaine*, p. 48.

[67]   Gregory, *Liber in Gloria Martyrum*, 91. It should be noted that Roman legislation tried to prevent new buildings from depriving older ones of light; *Lex Romana Burgundionum*, ed. L. R. de Salis, *MGH, Leges*, II, 1 (Hanover, 1892), xvii, 6.

granted.[68] The association between Clovis's baptism and his victories had, in any case, already been made by Nicetius of Trier, the subject of one of Gregory's biographies, in his letter to Chlodoswintha, queen of the Lombards.[69] Indeed Nicetius, in his attempt to provide the queen with arguments to convert her husband Alboin, went further than Gregory in interpreting Clovis's Burgundian war, which he placed after Vouillé, in a religious light. The idea that Frankish success was related to divine support was not, however, dependent on the king being Catholic. At the very beginning of Clovis's reign, Remigius could associate the success of the Merovingian, who was still pagan, with the judgment of God.[70] Gregory's view of Clovis as the agent of Providence is thus the natural extension of contemporary assumptions about successful monarchs. At the same time his understanding of the behaviour and fate of Arian rulers was influenced by the knowledge that Arius himself had been struck by divine judgment in a privy[71] and by traditions concerning the Vandalic persecutions, originally circulated, no doubt, by African Catholics in exile.[72]

The way in which Gregory's assumptions about Arianism colored his reading of events is more clearly seen in his account of the rebellion of Hermenigild. According to the bishop of Tours the Visigothic prince was converted to Catholicism by his Frankish wife Ingundis, who had been maltreated by Hermenigild's Arian stepmother Goiswintha. On hearing of the conversion, the king, Leovigild, decided to destroy his son. Deserted by his Byzantine allies, Hermenigild was captured and exiled.[73] Still in Spain, however, he gained the support of Miro the Catholic king of the Suevi of Galicia. Leovigild mounted a second expedition and captured, imprisoned, exiled, and finally killed the prince.[74] Gregory was more or less writing up his account of these events at the time of their occurrence and yet every point of his version of events is apparently inaccurate.[75] Hermenigild converted after he had rebelled against his father and probably under the influence of Leander of Seville rather than Ingundis;[76] his stepmother, who was also the grandmother of Ingundis, far from being hostile to the prince, seems to have encouraged him in his act of rebellion.[77] Despite the description of his defeat and exile, he appears to have retained his independence until his final overthrow, when Miro was probably fighting for Leovigild, not against him.[78] It is

---

[68] Gregory, *Liber Historiarum*, I, *praef.*, 6, 36, 41; II, *praef.*, 9; V, *praef.*, IX, 15; *Liber in Gloria Martyrum*, 20; *Liber de Virtutibus Sancti Juliani*, ed. W. Arndt and B. Krusch, *MGH, SRM*, I, 2, 7; *Liber Vitae Patrum*, VI, 1; *Liber in Gloria Confessorum*, ed. W. Arndt and B. Krusch, *ibid.*, I; *De cursu stellarum*, ed. W. Arndt and B. Krusch, *ibid.*, 3.
[69] Gregory, *Liber Vitae Patrum*, XVII; *Epistulae Austrasiacae*, 8.
[70] *Epistulae Austrasiacae*, 2.
[71] Gregory, *Liber Historiarum*, II, 23.
[72] Gregory, *Liber Historiarum*, II, 2–3.
[73] Gregory, *Liber Historiarum*, V, 38; VI, 18, 40.
[74] Gregory, *Liber Historiarum*, VI, 43; VIII, 28.
[75] For a reconstruction of Hermenigild's rebellion, R. Collins, "Mérida and Toledo: 550–585," in E. James, ed., *Visigothic Spain* (Oxford, 1980), pp. 215–17, with modifications in E. James, *Early Medieval Spain* (London, 1983), pp. 46–9.
[76] This is suggested by the fact that although Gregory I had met Leander, the supposed agent of Hermenigild's conversion, in 579, he did not know of the conversion until *c.*585; Gregory I, *Dialogues*, ed. A. de Vogüé, SC, 251, 260, 265 (Paris, 1978–80), III, 31. On the date of the conversion see Collins, "Mérida and Toledo," pp. 215–17, with the criticisms of I. N. Wood, *History* 215 (1980): 460, and Collins, *Early Medieval Spain*, p. 47.
[77] John of Biclarum, ed. T. Mommsen, *MGH, AA*, XI, *sub anno* 579.
[78] John of Biclarum, *sub anno* 583. For this interpretation of the obscure Latin, Collins, "Mérida and Toledo," p. 216.

difficult to believe that Gregory was inaccurately informed about all these events; there were numerous legations between Spain and Gaul at this time, some of which passed through Tours.[79] All that one can say is that Gregory's assumptions about Arians and Catholics prevented him from presenting an accurate picture of events. Thus in his mind Goiswintha as an Arian stepmother-in-law must have been opposed to the Catholic Ingundis; the latter must have persuaded her husband to become Catholic; Leovigild's reaction must have forced Hermenigild to revolt; the Catholic king Miro was involved, therefore he must have supported Hermenigild. Oddly the bishop of Tours does not depict the prince as a martyr, although Gregory the Great does,[80] but then the former had strong views on rebellious sons.[81] Again it is bias which determines interpretation.

In various ways Gregory's account of Hermenigild is linked to his description of Clovis's conversion. At a simple level there is the role of the Catholic wife, on the one hand Chrotechildis, on the other Ingundis (who plays the part assigned elsewhere to Leander). More thought-provoking is the fact that despite his agitation about Arianism in the Prefaces to Books One and Three of the Histories, the majority of anti-Arian remarks concern the reigns of Clovis and Leovigild.[82] The only exceptions in the Histories are an excursus on Vandal Arianism,[83] a reference to the Burgundians as heretics,[84] mention of Amalaric's maltreatment of Chrotechildis,[85] a blatantly untrue tale about the death of Audofleda, widow of Theodoric and sister of Clovis,[86] allusions to the heretical upbringing of Brunichildis and her sister,[87] and an account of the conversion of Leovigild's younger son, Reccared.[88] The Miracula [Miracles] add little to this total.[89] It is difficult to know whether there is any connection between Gregory's interpretations of Clovis and of Hermenigild deeper than the simple fact that both stories afforded opportunities for anti-Arian diatribe. Probably Book Two of the Histories had been completed before Hermenigild's conversion – its date of composition is usually held to be by the end of the mid-570s,[90] but the only firm terminus post quem non [latest possible date] is the completion of the second book on the Virtutes of St Martin, which can be placed between 577 and 581.[91] Nevertheless Gregory's only contact with a living Arian tradition was through Visigothic envoys.[92] If his understanding of Arianism depended on Leovigild's legates, this might account for the relationship between the religious problems of Clovis and of Hermenigild, as they appear in the Libri Historiarum.

---

[79] Gregory, Libri Historiarum, V, 37, 43; VI, 18, 29, 33, 34, 40; VIII, 28, 35, 38, 45; IX, 1, 16, 25, 28.

[80] Gregory I, Dialogues, III, 31, 3 and 8.

[81] Gregory, Liber Historiarum, VI, 43; cf. IV, 16, 20 and V, praef. See Collins, Early Medieval Spain, pp. 48–9.

[82] Clovis's reign, Liber Historiarum, II, 28, 31–4, 37; Leovigild's reign, Libri Historiarum, V, 17 (cf. Liber in Gloria Martyrum, 23), 38, 43; VI, 18, 40; see also Liber in Gloria Martyrum, 80, 81.

[83] Gregory, Liber Historiarum, II, 2–3.

[84] Gregory, Liber Historiarum, II, 9.

[85] Gregory, Liber Historiarum, III, 10; cf. V, 38 on the treatment of Ingundis.

[86] Gregory, Liber Historiarum, III, 31; on Theodoric see Liber in Gloria Martyrum, 39.

[87] Gregory, Liber Historiarum, IV, 27–8.

[88] Gregory, Liber Historiarum, IX, 15.

[89] Gregory, Liber in Martyrum, 12, 24, 25, 39, 78, 79, 80, 81, 90; Liber in Gloria Confessorum, 47; see also Liber de Virtutibus sancti Martini, ed. W. Arndt and B. Krusch, MGH, SRM, I, 2, I, 11.

[90] G. Monod, Etudes critiques sur les sources de l'histoire mérovingienne, Bibliothèque de l'Ecole des Hautes Etudes, VIII (Paris, 1872), p. 45; R. Buchner, Gregor von Tours, Zehn Bücher Geschichte (Darmstadt, 1955), p. xxi.

[91] Monod, Etudes critiques, p. 42.

[92] Gregory, Libri Historiarum, V, 43; VI, 40, cf. Liber in Gloria Martyrum, 80.

At the same time Chilperic's dabbling in doctrinal matters may have made Leovigild's religious experiments seem particularly threatening.[93] The amount of identifiable error and bias in Gregory's depiction of Arian–Catholic relations and the poverty of his sources for the late fifth and early sixth centuries, mean that we are entitled to reject or view with suspicion any fact supplied by the bishop of Tours, unless it can be shown to have some support from earlier, reliable material. Effectively we are forced back to reconstruct the reign of Clovis from contemporary evidence, which relates in the main to four separate issues; the king's accession, his wars, his church policy, and his baptism.

The exact date of Clovis's accession is unknown; we are dependent on Gregory's computations.[94] There is, however, the letter from Remigius of Rheims to the young king, congratulating him on taking over the administration of *Belgica Secunda* [a Roman province corresponding to parts of northeastern France and western Benelux].[95] Because that province included Soissons, which was held according to Gregory by Syagrius until the fifth year of Clovis's reign,[96] historians have been at a loss to know whether Remigius is referring to the king's accession or to his defeat of Syagrius. The letter, however, makes no allusion to a conquest, but rather stresses the fact that Clovis now holds the position of his ancestors. An early date, if accepted, has profound implications for our interpretation of Syagrius's kingdom. There is no evidence to suggest that Soissons had remained a Roman stronghold throughout Childeric's reign; it is perfectly possible that Syagrius established himself in a position of power after Clovis's accession; the latter must have been a young man – even if we ignore Gregory's claim that he became king at the age of 15.[97] He was still active enough to lead his troops in 507 and therefore may have been no more than a youth 25 years earlier. A momentary collapse of Frankish power at Clovis's accession is quite likely. After his death his sons undoubtedly lost substantial areas of land,[98] despite the maturity of Theuderic. The second decade of the sixth century is remarkably void of Merovingian activity, which suggests that not all was well. Similar problems may have existed after Childeric's death.

Clovis's emergence as a figure of importance is most probably the result of his success as a war leader, nevertheless there is precious little to illustrate this outside the *Libri Historiarum*. For Clovis's first campaigns against the Visigoths[99] and for the Burgundian war of 500[100] we only have later sources, with the possible exception, in the latter case, of discreet allusions in the letters of Avitus of Vienne.[101] We are better informed on the Alaman wars, because their outcome was of interest to the government of Italy. A major Frankish victory over the Alamans can be dated to *c*.506, from the writings of Cassiodorius,[102] but although this may have been the final battle between the two peoples it can scarcely have been the

---

[93] Gregory, *Liber Historiarum*, V, 44, which follows directly after Gregory's debate with Agilan. For Leovigild's religious policy, Collins, "Mérida and Toledo," pp. 211, 213, 217.

[94] Gregory, *Liber Historiarum*, II, 43.

[95] *Epistulae Austrasiacae*, 2. For its date see Wallace-Hadrill, *The Long-haired Kings*, p. 166.

[96] Gregory, *Liber Historiarum*, II, 27.

[97] Gregory, *Liber Historiarum*, II, 43.

[98] See above on the evidence from Rodez. Weiss, *Chlodwigs Taufe*, p. 53 stresses the coincidence of the youth of Clovis's sons and Frankish inactivity in this period.

[99] *Continuatio Havniensis Prosperi*, ed. T. Mommsen, *MGH, AA*, IX (Berlin, 1892), *sub anno* 498.

[100] Marius of Avenches, *sub anno* 500.

[101] Avitus, *ep.*, 50; *De spiritalis historiae gestis, ep. ad Apollinarem episcopum*

[102] Cassiodorus, *Variae*, ed. T. Mommsen, *MGH, AA*, XII (Berlin, 1894), II, 41. On the date and on protection subsequently offered by the Ostrogoths to the Alamans, see van de Vyver, "La victoire contre les Alamans," pp. 45–64 and Weiss, *Chlodwigs Taufe*, pp. 23–36.

only one.[103] While his sole testimony cannot be regarded as unimpeachable, Gregory of Tours apparently knew of two periods of conflict between Alamans and Franks; he refers not only to Clovis's victory,[104] which is given no geographical setting, but also to an apparently different encounter between the Ripuarian Franks and the Alamans at Tolbiac.[105] Even more central to Ostrogothic interests were the relations between Clovis and Alaric II, which are the subject of a number of the *Variae* [letters of Cassiodorus].[106] In the opinion of Theodoric, or Cassiodorus, the causes of the outbreak of war in 507 were trivial;[107] a point of view which scarcely supports Gregory's reading of events.[108] Avitus of Vienne apparently offers more detail on this point; *"quam nuperrime rex Getarum secuturae praesagam ruinae monetis publicis adulterium firmantem mandaverat"* ["that very recently, the king of the Visigoths had commanded to the public mints (as) confirming adulteration (of the coinage)"].[109] Debasement of the Visigothic coinage is only too clear from surviving specimens[110] and in some way it was associated with Clovis's invasion of Aquitaine. Finance and tribute bulk large in Gregory's account of the Burgundian war;[111] money appears to have played a part in 507. A religious reading of events is further undermined by Gundobad's intervention against the Visigothic kingdom in 508;[112] a fact significantly overlooked by Gregory. An Arian would scarcely fight with the Catholics in an anti-Arian crusade. Gundobad's campaign also undermines the bishop of Tours's claim that the Burgundian king reneged on the payment of tribute to Clovis.[113] Apparently the two monarchs were still cooperating after Vouillé; presumably tribute was still forthcoming at that time, if not until Clovis's death.

There is no need to invoke religion or hereditary enmity between Franks and Goths to explain the outbreak of war in 507.[114] The causes of the conflict seem to have been specific, minor, and economic, although Clovis may also have felt constrained by political pressure at home to provide his eldest son Theuderic with an opportunity for military exploits, and he was doubtless aware, as Theodoric was, that years of peace had weakened Visigothic military competence.[115] After Vouillé Theodoric's intervention put a temporary stop to Frankish

[103] F. Lot, "La victoire sur les Alamans et la conversion de Clovis," *Revue Belge de Philologie et d'Histoire* 17 (1938): 64.
[104] Gregory, *Liber Historiarum*, II, 30.
[105] Gregory, *Liber Historiarum*, II, 37. There is no reason to elide these two battles. Tolbiac/Zülpich is so far north as to suggest Alaman aggression, not a last stand against the Franks. Weiss, *Chlodwigs Taufe*, p. 29, quite unjustifiably assumes that Vedast met Clovis on the road from Tolbiac/Zülpich to Toul. Jonas, however, does not name the place of victory, *Vita Vedastis*, ed. B. Krusch, *MGH, SRM*, III, 2. We do not know that Clovis ever went to Tolbiac/Zülpich.
[106] Cassiodorus, *Variae*, III, 1–4.
[107] Cassiodorus, *Variae*, III, 4, *"causis mediocribus."*
[108] Gregory, *Liber Historiarum*, II, 37.
[109] Avitus, *ep.*, 87.
[110] J. P. C. Kent, "Un monnayage irrégulier du début du Ve siècle de notre ère," *Cercle d'Études Numismatiques* 11 (1974): 23–9. See also *Lex Gundobada*, ed. F. Beyerle, *Gesetze der Burgunden* (Weimar, 1936), *constitutio extravagans*, XXI, 7.
[111] Gregory, *Liber Historiarum*, II, 32, 33.
[112] *Chronicle of 511*, ed. T. Mommsen, *MGH, AA*, IX, 689–90; Isidore, *Historia Gothorum, Wandalorum Sueborum*, ed. T. Mommsen, *MGH, AA*, XI, 37. On the insignificance of religion see also Wallace-Hadrill, *The Long-haired Kings*, pp. 173–4.
[113] Gregory, *Liber Historiarum*, II, 33.
[114] But see Wallace-Hadrill, *The Long-haired Kings*, p. 173.
[115] Cassiodorus, *Variae*, III, 1. On Theuderic's role in the campaigns against the Visigoths, Gregory, *Liber Historiarum*, II, 37; on his position at the end of Clovis's reign, Wood, "Kings, Kingdoms and Consent," p. 26.

expansion southwards, although the Burgundians suffered more from this policy than did the Franks.[116] Clovis ceases to appear in the Italian records at this time; it may be significant that it is the period to which Gregory assigned the extermination of his hero's northern rivals.[117] Blocked in the south after 508, Clovis may have turned his mind towards enhancing his prestige in the Rhineland and perhaps across the English Channel.[118]

To these last years also belong the few contemporary pieces of evidence on Clovis's church policy, leaving aside the hortatory advice offered by Remigius to the still pagan ruler on his assumption of the government of *Belgica Secunda*.[119] The earliest piece of Merovingian ecclesiastical legislation was in many ways the manifestation of the ideals of Remigius; in a letter written after Vouillé, Clovis announced to his bishops that *en route* for the battle he had promulgated an edict protecting widows, clerics, and those whom the Church wished to defend.[120] More complex are the canons of the first Council of Orléans, which reflect, in part, some *tituli* [edicts] presented by the king.[121] Most probably royal concern was centered on matters of jurisdiction and rights,[122] but it is notable that the Catholic bishops at Orléans were more willing to offer concessions towards the Arian Church than their Burgundian colleagues at Epaon (517), led by bishop Avitus.[123] Where Clovis's Church appears least impressive is in a letter of Remigius, in which the bishop justifies the ordination of an unsuitable priest, because the man had been recommended by the king, *"qui erat non solum praedicator fidei catholicae, sed defensor"* ["who was not only a preacher but the defender of the Catholic faith"].[124] Gregory's account of the forcible ordination of Charatic and his son is perhaps an accurate record of the way Clovis abused the Church.[125]

There remains the question of Clovis's conversion and baptism. It is important to be precise about the issue. As we have seen there is no need to associate the success of the Franks with the religious beliefs of their leader.[126] The notion that the Catholics of Gaul longed to be ruled by a Catholic monarch does not stand up to scrutiny. Moreover, because the subject of Clovis's Catholicism is absolutely central to Gregory of Tours's theme at the end of Book Two of his Histories, it is necessary to be especially skeptical of his treatment of the king's conversion. Indeed nothing in this account, not even the number of children

[116] K. Binding, *Das burgundisch-romanische Königreich* (Leipzig, 1868), pp. 200–14, is still among the best discussions of Theodoric's counter-attack.
[117] Gregory, *Liber Historiarum*, II, 40–2. For arguments in favour of the late dating of these events, Wood, "Kings, kingdoms and consent," p. 28.
[118] For Clovis's interest in Anglo-Saxon England, see I. N. Wood, *The Merovingian North Sea* (Alingsås, 1983), pp. 12–13.
[119] *Epistulae Austrasiacae*, 2.
[120] *Chlodowici regis ad episcopos epistula, Capitularia Merowingica*, ed. A. Boretius, *MGH, Capitularia Regum Francorum*, I (Hanover, 1883), 1.
[121] Orléans, I (511), *epistola ad regum*; see Wallace-Hadrill, *The Long-haired Kings*, p. 177.
[122] Orléans, I (511), 1–6; see Wallace-Hadrill, *The Long-haired Kings*, p. 177, and C. de Clercq, *La législation religieuse franque de Clovis à Charlemagne (507–814)* (Louvain and Paris, 1936), pp. 8–13.
[123] Cf. Orléans, I (511) 10 with Epaon (517), 15, 16, 29, 33 and with Avitus, ep., 7.
[124] *Epistulae Austrasiacae*, 3.
[125] Gregory, *Liber Historiarum*, II, 41. In general I take a less favorable view of Clovis's church than does Wallace-Hadrill, *The Long-haired Kings*, pp. 177–9, although I am deeply indebted to the insights expressed there.
[126] Wallace-Hadrill, *The Long-haired Kings*, pp. 173–4. From this point of view Tessier's view of the insignificance of the date of the baptism is correct; *La conversion de Clovis*, pp. 168–9.

born to Chrotechildis before her husband's baptism,[127] can be taken on trust. The unreliability of Gregory's sources and the bishop's own bias demand that in the first instance we work only from the contemporary evidence, that is from the writings of Avitus of Vienne.

The chief document relating to the king's baptism is the letter of congratulation addressed by Avitus to Clovis.[128] It is a complex, rhetorical work,[129] the understanding of which is made more difficult by the state of the text.[130] Another work which would doubtless have clarified the context of the baptism is the now lost homily of the bishop of Vienne *De conversione Lenteildis Chlodovaei sororis* [*On the Conversion of Clovis' sister Lenteildis*].[131] The very fact that Avitus preached on the occasion of Lenteildis's abjuration of Arianism may imply that he had been expected to attend Clovis's baptism.[132] A third document presents many more difficulties. In a letter sent apparently to the pope, Avitus announces the conversion of a king; "*adhuc de regibus solus est quem in bonum transisse non pudeat*" ["he is still the only one of the kings who has not been ashamed to come over to the good (side)"].[133] The convert in question had certainly been an Arian and he is usually identified as Gundobad's son, Sigismund. If this identification is accepted, it then becomes necessary to decide whether Avitus regarded him as the first of all the barbarian kings or only as the first Burgundian king to become a Catholic,[134] since in the former case the letter would provide a *terminus ante quem non* [earliest possible date] for Clovis's baptism. There are, however, problems in accepting the identification of the king in question as Sigismund. First, although Sigismund was undoubtedly a Catholic by 515, when he founded the monastery of Agaune,[135] he was not elevated to the kingship until the following year.[136] Second, Avitus refers to the newly converted prince building a basilica in *regni sui caput* [the capital of his kingdom] and asks the pope for relics for the church. Although there is a case for thinking that Sigismund built a church dedicated to St Peter, in Geneva,[137] it is not clear that the city was regarded as his

---

[127] I therefore regard the argument about the age of Clovis's children as irrelevant to the issue of the king's baptism, but see Weiss, *Chlodwigs Taufe*, pp. 50–8, and E. Ewig, "Studien zur merovingischen Dynastie," *Frühmittelalterliche Studien*, 8 (1974): 36–8, which undermines the case for a late date for Chrotechildis's marriage upheld by Weiss, *Chlodwigs Taufe*, p. 40.

[128] Avitus, *ep.*, 46.

[129] Reydellet, *La royauté*, pp. 99–122, offers interesting comments on the letter, but fails to appreciate the amount of rhetoric associated with traditional panegyric in Avitus's language.

[130] Reydellet, *La royauté*, pp. 111 n. 91, 112 n. 94, but the author fails to draw attention to another set of variants; compare van de Vyver's translation, as quoted p. 109 n. 86 with the Latin as cited in the same note.

[131] Avitus, *hom.*, 31; cf. Gregory, *Liber Historiarum*, II, 31.

[132] This would undermine Reydellet's interpretation: Reydellet, *La royauté*, p. 97.

[133] Avitus, *ep.*, 8.

[134] Van de Vyver, "La victoire contre les Alamans," pp. 888–98; Weiss, *Chlodwigs Taufe*, pp. 47–8.

[135] Avitus, *hom.*, 25; Marius of Avenches, *sub anno*, 515. For the chronological problems of Sigismund's conversion, Wood, *Avitus*, pp. 208–16, although the arguments should be modified in view of the case set out here.

[136] Marius of Avenches, *sub anno*, 516; Fredegar, III, 33. Van de Vyver argued that Sigismund was already *rex* before that date, "La victoire contre les Alamans," p. 893 n. 2. I accepted this interpretation in "Kings, Kingdoms and Consent," p. 22, but now take a more skeptical view. Certainly, in view of the manuscript variants, the references to Sigismund as *rex* in the headings of Avitus's letters cannot be used as evidence; see M. Burckhardt, *Die Briefsammlung des Bischofs Avitus von Vienne* (Berlin, 1938), p. 22.

[137] K. H. Krüger, *Königsgrabkirchen* (Munich, 1971), p. 62. Like the subject of Avitus, *ep.*, 8, Sigismund wanted Petrine relics; Avitus, *ep.*, 29.

capital.[138] Since it is difficult to identify Sigismund as the *rex* in question, it is worth looking seriously at Clovis as the possible subject of Avitus's letter. Clovis was undoubtedly a king at the time of his conversion, and he built a church dedicated to St Peter in Paris, his *cathedra regni* [the seat of his kingdom].[139] The one objection to this identification is that Clovis is thought never to have been an Arian, therefore he cannot have converted *in catholicam vestram de pristino errore* [to your catholicism from an earlier error]. The view that Clovis's conversion was from paganism directly to Catholicism, however, is that propounded by Gregory of Tours; while Avitus, in his letter to Clovis, contradicts this; *"vestrae subtilitatis acrimoniam quorumcumque scismatum sectatores sententiis suis variis opinione, diversis multitudine, vacuis veritate Christiani nominis visi sunt obumbratione velare;"* "the adherents of all sorts of schismatic sects have been seen to blind with obfuscation the sharpness of your intelligence through their opinions, which are various in conjecture, diverse in number and empty of the truth of Christ's name".[140] This looks like a very polite way of saying that Clovis had been converted to heresy before his decision to be baptized as a Catholic. Here it is significant that one of his sisters, Lenteildis, had received Arian baptism, although she apparently lived among the Franks;[141] and this fact is all the more striking when it is realized that not a single woman of the Burgundian royal house is known to have been an Arian, although many of them were certainly Catholics.[142] That Gregory does not mention the heretical aspect of Clovis's original conversion is not surprising; the Catholic Church would surely have wished to ignore the king's flirtation with heresy which preceded his baptism into the True Faith.

Clovis's baptism was not just a decision to abjure the paganism of his ancestors and hence the religious aura attached to his own family,[143] it was also a rejection of heresy into which he and his family had fallen. The opening lines of Avitus's letter thus introduce us to a set of issues left untouched by Gregory of Tours. The centre of the letter takes us further from Gregory's interpretation. Unfortunately, the manuscripts provide variant readings at a crucial moment of the text. The clearest and most logical reading runs, *"Gaudeat equidem Graecia habere se principem legis nostrae; sed non iam quae tanti muneris donum sola mereatur"* ["Let Greece, to be sure, rejoice in having an orthodox ruler, but she is no longer the only one to deserve so great a gift"]. The alternative version emphasizes the political association of Clovis and Byzantium, with no apparent reference to religion; *"Gaudeat equidem Graecia principem legisse nostrum"* ["As far as I am concerned, let Greece rejoice in having chosen our ruler"]. In either case, however, Avitus appears to be placing the king's baptism against a

---

[138] Avitus, *ep.*, 77 may imply that Sigismund usually accompanied his father, but the *pius pater* could be Maximus of Geneva; see *ep.*, 74. If Geneva was a capital under Gundobad, it was not the centre of an independent kingdom; see Wood, "Kings, kingdoms and consent," pp. 21–2.

[139] Gregory, *Liber Historiarum*, II, 38.

[140] Avitus, *ep.*, 46.

[141] Avitus, *hom.*, 31; Gregory, *Liber Historiarum*, II, 31. The use of the noun *conversio* in Avitus and of the verb *crismare* in Gregory imply an earlier Arian baptism.

[142] As well as Chrotechildis and her sister Sedeleuba – see Fredegar, III, 17–18, IV, 22 – there is the wife of Chilperic I, Sidonius, ep., IV, 12, 3; Caretene, wife of Gundobad, G. Kirner, "Due vite inedite di S. Marcello Vescovo di Die," *Studi Storici*, 9 (1900): 323; *MGH*, *AA*, VI, 2, p. 185; Gregory, *Liber de Virtutibus Sancti Juliani*, 8; and perhaps Theudelinda, wife of Godegisil, see Wood, *Avitus*, p. 151.

[143] Despite Reydellet's attack on the notion that Avitus refers to sacral kingship, *La royauté*, p. 106, it seems to me that H. Moisl, "Anglo-Saxon royal geneaologies and Germanic oral tradition," *Journal of Medieval History* 7 (1981): 223–6, has established beyond doubt that both Avitus and Gregory of Tours were aware of sacral traditions within the Merovingian family.

background of Byzantine interest.[144] This imperial context strikingly recalls the comparison between Clovis and Constantine drawn in the *Libri Historiarum*.[145] As we have seen this comparison can scarcely be the invention of Gregory himself; it might even have originated with Remigius. In addition, Clovis's decision to build a church of the Holy Apostles[146] may imply a deliberate attempt by the king himself to ape Constantine, especially since he chose as the site of his foundation a city which had been an imperial capital in the fourth century.[147]

Having established the context of Clovis's decision to be baptized as a Catholic, Avitus provides an imaginative reconstruction of the baptism itself, before offering some words of advice to the king. Within this exhortation is a reference to the *"misericordia"* ["mercy"] recently extolled by a *"solutus a vobis adhuc nuper populus captivus"* ["recent freeing by you of a hitherto captive people"]. Since the significance of this allusion can only be determined by arriving at a date for Avitus's letter, it is necessary to approach that thorny question. According to van de Vyver, during the siege of Vienne by Gundobad in 501, all Avitus's writings were lost and therefore no surviving work, except his biblical epic, can be dated earlier than the following year.[148] The survival of the *De spiritalis historiae gestis* [*On the Events of Religious History*], which probably dates from the 490s, does not help van de Vyver's case, but it should be acknowledged that no letter of Avitus can be securely dated to the years before 502. Clovis's Burgundian campaign, however, may provide a more serious reason for accepting a date later than 501 for Clovis's baptism. The bishop of Vienne could scarcely have written to the Frankish monarch, praising his acceptance of Catholicism and encouraging him to evangelize the pagans, without incurring some suspicion of treason, if the relations between Gundobad and Clovis had been anything but the most cordial. Since Avitus went on to preach at Lenteildis's public abjuration of Arianism,[149] Gundobad must have knowingly acquiesced in the public condemnation of his own beliefs and the public approval of the doctrinal position of the Merovingians. This state of affairs would not be easy to imagine before 500, but as a result of Clovis's invasion of Burgundy in that year Gundobad seems to have become tributary to the Franks.[150] As I have argued above, he may not have changed his status before the death of Clovis. The early years of the sixth century therefore provide a more plausible background for Avitus's letter than any time in the previous decade.

The imperial context of Clovis's baptism supports this picture. The degeneration of relations between Theodoric and the Emperor Anastasius, leading to open hostility in 508,[151] coincides suggestively with Gregory's record of the conferment of some notable office on Clovis at Tours in that year.[152] Indeed the chronological coincidence of Clovis's consulship and a Byzantine attack on Italy serves both to inspire confidence in the "consulship" and to provide a clue as to its meaning; with his new Byzantine office, the king of the Franks was

---

[144]   Avitus, *ep.*, 46.
[145]   Gregory, *Liber Historiarum*, II, 31.
[146]   Gregory, *Liber Historiarum*, II, 38. Krüger, *Königsgrabkirchen*, pp. 40–54.
[147]   Wallace-Hadrill, *The Long-haired Kings*, p. 181; Weiss, *Chlodwigs Taufe*, pp. 120–1.
[148]   Van de Vyver, "La victoire contre les Alamans," pp. 882–7.
[149]   Avitus, *hom.*, 31; Gregory, *Liber Historiarum*, II, 31.
[150]   Gregory, *Liber Historiarum*, II, 32.
[151]   Marcellinus comes, *Chronicle*, ed. T. Mommsen, *MGH*, *AA*, XI.
[152]   Gregory, *Liber Historiarum*, II, 38.

doubtless to be reckoned as having a status superior to Theodoric[153] in the eyes of the emperor. Were one to accept *"Gaudeat equidem Graecia principem legisse nostrum"* as the correct reading in Avitus's letter to Clovis, it would be difficult to interpret this more neatly than as a reference to the "consulship" of 508. Granted the absence of any other indication of close links between Clovis and Anastasius, the diplomatic relations between the two rulers at this time provide the most satisfactory context for Avitus's imperial references, whichever manuscript reading is preferred.

One possible objection to this is the fact that Anastasius was regarded by the papacy as schismatic. Curiously, however, Avitus was not aware of this until he came to write his hopelessly misinformed *Libri contra Eutychianam Haeresim* [*Books Against the Eutychian Heresy*] in 512–13.[154] It is possible that the papacy had never informed the Gallic bishops about the outbreak of the Acacian schism and it is most unlikely that news of the relations between the pope and the emperor reached Gaul in the first decade of the sixth century; the disputed election of Symmachus and Laurentius appears to have led to a break in papal correspondence with the Empire,[155] while communication between Symmachus and the bishops of Gaul was not particularly frequent.[156] Comparison between the doctrine of Clovis and that of Anastasius would have been perfectly possible in 508.

The same date also provides a remarkably simple solution to the identity of the *"populus captivus"* to which Avitus refers. The defeat of Alaric II had freed the Aquitanians from the tyranny of an Arian ruler.[157] Naturally this description of events is somewhat exaggerated, but it is appropriate for a letter on Clovis's baptism. Having fought at Vouillé, the king is said to have wintered at Bordeaux;[158] Christmas 508 is, therefore, the earliest date subsequent to the "liberation" of the Aquitanians for the baptism. The Tours "consulship," which provides an admirable context for Avitus's references to the emperor, fits neatly between these two events.

Against this it might be argued that Clovis must have been converted before he set out on his campaign against Alaric II in 507, because it was *en route* for Vouillé that he issued his edict protecting widows, clerics, and those whom the Church wished to defend.[159] While accepting this edict as an indication that Clovis had been converted, it is does not necessarily follow that the king had been baptized by then, and Avitus's letter does no more than date

---

[153] A. H. M. Jones, "The constitutional position of Odovacer and Theodoric," *Journal of Roman Studies*, 52 (1962): 126–30. For Clovis's consulship, see the penetrating remarks of Wallace-Hadrill, *The Long-haired Kings*, pp. 175–6, and, for the meaning of the passage, Reydellet, *La royauté*, pp. 406–8. See also Weiss, *Chlodwigs Taufe*, pp. 110–19.

[154] The extent of Avitus's ignorance is apparent from the opening section of each book of the *Contra Eutychianam Haeresim*. See Wood, *Avitus*, pp. 184–207, on the evidence for Gallic knowledge of the Acacian schism. Reydellet, *La royauté*, pp. 131–2 oversimplifies the complexity of the theological situation.

[155] There is only one surviving letter from Pope Symmachus to Emperor Anastasius; A. Thiel, *Epistolae Romanorum Pontificum Genuinae* (Brunsberg, 1867), Symmachus, *ep.*, 10; but see also *ep.*, 13.

[156] Avitus, *epp.*, 8, 20, 29; see also *ep.*, 34; Symmachus, ed. Thiel, *epp.*, 2–3, 14–15 (*ep.*, 4 is a forgery).

[157] I am not convinced by the alternative interpretation of the passage offered by G. Reverdy, "Note sur l'interprétation d'un passage d'Avitus," *Le Moyen Age*, 26 (1913): 274–7. If *misericordia*, however, does mean "good works," as Reverdy argues, it might reasonably be thought to refer to Clovis's edict, *MGH, Capitularia*, I.

[158] Gregory, *Liber Historiarum*, II, 37.

[159] *MGH, Capitularia*, I.

the baptism. Moreover, the 507 edict is the first datable indication of a collaboration with the Catholic Church, and it was promulgated to the army apparently without the knowledge of the clergy; the king only informed his bishops of the legislation subsequently. It is the letter of information that survives. Against this background the edict seems more like an attempt to curry favour with the Church than the action of a king proceeding on the advice of bishops.

That Clovis was deliberately going out of his way to appease the God of the Catholics as he marched against Alaric II seems likely, especially when his edict is compared with Gregory of Tours's account of the advance to Vouillé. In particular the record of the king's offerings to the shrine of St Martin[160] adds to the impression of a deliberate commitment to the Catholics and their saints. Although, as we have seen, there is no reason to believe that the Visigoths suffered from a Catholic fifth column in Aquitaine, it is possible that Clovis hoped to win over the support of the Gallo-Romans and their God as he went to war in 507. If this were so, the seed of Gregory of Tours's interpretation was sown by Clovis himself. Open alignment with the Catholics at the start of the Vouillé campaign and baptism undergone in the context of Franco-Byzantine relations may imply that Clovis's entry into the Catholic Church was the result of opportunism rather than belief. This is not impossible. Other conversions in this period have been associated with Byzantine support.[161] Nevertheless Clovis's decision to become a Catholic was not uninformed; Avitus talks of the king's acuity.[162] The capacity of barbarian monarchs to enquire into doctrinal matters should not be underestimated; Gundobad was no theological fool.[163] Ultimately, however, such questions cannot be answered with any degree of certainty.

The contemporary evidence for Clovis and his reign rarely illuminates specific points, particularly points of motive, although it allows us to study, often in surprising detail, the problems encountered by barbarian monarchs as they entered a world dominated by an ecclesiastical hierarchy. It is extraordinary, for instance, that both Clovis and Gundobad were reprimanded by their bishops for being overcome with grief as a result of the deaths of relatives. Kings should not show excessive emotion.[164] Alongside this encounter with the Church, contemporary sources highlight the continuing influence of the emperor and imperial tradition in sub-Roman politics. From this material it is possible to build up a context against which to interpret Clovis's reign. The context also provides the only possibility for establishing a chronology for Clovis's baptism. Leaving Gregory of Tours's information on one side, it is remarkable how neatly the evidence fits into place. In order to disprove the 508 dating it would be necessary to find another context which fitted all the contemporary evidence more clearly.

By comparison with what we find in the documentation from Clovis's own lifetime, Gregory's account appears remarkably unsatisfactory, and in many ways it is. Yet just because Avitus makes no mention of Chrotechildis in his letter to Clovis, that does not mean that she played no part in the king's conversion. Nor should we reject the possibility that war provided the background to Clovis's decision to become a Christian. Gregory's known sources pass over the battle at the Milvian Bridge as a model context for conversion;[165] the

[160] Gregory, *Liber Historiarum*, II, 37.
[161] See, e.g., the interpretation of Hermenigild's conversion offered by Collins, *Early Medieval Spain*, p. 48.
[162] Avitus, *ep.*, 46.
[163] Avitus, *Contra arrianos*, 30; *Contra Eutychianam Haeresim*, 1, 2; *Epp.*, 4, 6 (?), 22, 30.
[164] Avitus, *ep.*, 5; *Epistulae Austrasiacae*, 1.
[165] See above on Gregory's knowledge of Constantine.

military setting of Clovis's appeal to the God of the Christians may not be just a literary *topos*. Avitus's letter leaves room for the possibility that the queen and war had roles to play in the king's conversion, if not in his baptism, but along with the other evidence from the early sixth century it makes it difficult to accept both Gregory's overall interpretation and also many of the specific details relating to the first Christian ruler of the Franks. The reign of Clovis, however, is the period for which one should least expect accuracy from the bishop of Tours. The sources available to him were unsatisfactory; he could rely neither on narrative or chronicle accounts nor on accurate oral tradition. Moreover the events themselves were too closely related to issues which affected the Catholic Church for Gregory to write about them without bias. The extraordinary scholarly approach apparent in his discussion of the use of the word *rex* in early Frankish history[166] was unlikely to manifest itself in Gregory's account of Clovis. Besides there are virtues in the picture of the great Merovingian offered by the *Libri Historiarum*.[167] Even the attempt to present the multi-faceted nature of an individual's decision to become a Christian is worthy of attention. Bede managed to do no better when it came to describing the conversion of Edwin of Northumbria,[168] and his approach to the problem is so similar to that of Gregory that it is tempting to see the one as dependent on the other. It would be unreasonable to expect a "scientific" approach to history in the sixth century; allowance must be made for the moralizing aspects of Catholic historiography. Once that is done, Gregory's achievement in drawing together material of very different kinds – sometimes admittedly with comic results[169] – stands out as a formidable one, even if his interpretation of Clovis lacks credibility.

[166] Gregory, *Liber Historiarum*, II, 9.
[167] See Wallace-Hadrill, *The Long-haired Kings*, pp. 163–85.
[168] Bede, *Historia Ecclesiastica*, ed. C. Plummer (Oxford, 1896), II, 9–14.
[169] C. N. L. Brooke reviewing J. M. Wallace-Hadrill, *Early Medieval History* (Oxford, 1975), *English Historical Review*, 92 (1977): 358 n. 1. It seems to me that the comic effect is largely related to the juxtaposition of widely different sources.

Additional note. Two recent publications have dealt at some length with the letter of Avitus to Clovis, and although neither is concerned specifically with the date of the king's baptism, both raise points of interest for the foregoing arguments. N. Staubach, "Germanisches Königtum und lateinische Literatur vom fünften bis zum siebten Jahrhundert," *Frühmittelalterliche Studien* 17 (1983), pp. 34–6, and A. Angenendt, *Kaiserherrschaft und Königstaufe* (Berlin, 1984), p. 171, both stress Avitus's concern with Arianism in the letter. Moreover Angenendt also has much to say about relations between Clovis and the Byzantine Empire, especially in the light of the 508 consulship (pp. 171–3), but he makes no specific connection between that and the king's baptism. The interest of both scholars, however, is focused on religious matters; Staubach's chief concern being an elucidation of the Epiphany imagery used by Avitus, and Angenendt's being that of baptism and more especially the role of godfather. As such they have considerable insights to offer on aspects of the Avitus letter not dealt with above.

6 Missionaries and Magic in Dark-Age Europe

Alexander Murray

Homo sapiens is chronically at odds with his environment. It leaves undone things he thinks it ought to have done, and does things he thinks it ought not to have done. Reason, which saves him from most of the plagues that defeat animals, makes his own plight irremediable; for with it he can foresee all the awful things that are going to happen, notably death. Because this condition is common to all men, and they talk about it and pass things on, it engenders cultural strategies, and three in particular: religion, science, and magic – the three interwoven "threads" of Sir James Frazer's *The Golden Bough*,[1] and still the ruling trinity in our study of culture.

Like all divisions of reality the trinity is partly subjective, its distinctions imperfect. The histories of magic and science, with their common interest in the "properties of things," are for long periods almost inextricable.[2] The priesthoods and persecutions of science, meanwhile, as chronicled for instance in T. S. Kuhn's *The Structure of Scientific Revolutions*, show, if nothing else does, how science can assume religious qualities.[3] Religion has returned the compliment when – as in some eighteenth-century currents – it claims to be no more than rational. As for the last of the frontiers, between magic and religion, it is notoriously the most open of all: trampled, backwards and forwards, by all manner of feet.

This third frontier is the subject of Valerie Flint's *The Rise of Magic in Early Medieval Europe*. The centuries it covers, roughly the six from AD 500 to 1100, were formative for modern western culture. We inherit the core of that culture from the "Roman Empire" – to use a simplifying label. The core was then thoroughly reshaped by those six following centuries, beginning with the "barbarian invasions" – to use another. In those centuries two cultural worlds interacted, destroying and creating on both sides, in ways only the smallest fragment of which was recorded in writing. The survival of *Romanitas* was threatened. What survived of it did so round a kernel of Christianity which now represented, old quarrels forgotten, all that the Romans had had which the barbarians did not. Since this included

[This article is an extended review of] Valerie I. J. Flint, *The Rise of Magic in Early Medieval Europe* (Oxford, Clarendon Press, 1991), xii + 452 pp. I would like to thank John Blair and C. E. Stancliffe for help with this review.

[1] Sir James Frazer, *The Golden Bough*, abridged ed. (London, 1922), pp. 711–14.
[2] Hence their fusion in L. Thorndike, *A History of Magic and Experimental Science*, 8 vols (New York, 1923–58).
[3] T. S. Kuhn, *The Structure of Scientific Revolutions*, 2nd ed. (Chicago, 1970).

writing, now reduced to levels which made successors despair of the period as a "dark age," historians who wish to study it must do so from a small platform of texts, nearly all ecclesiastical, and nearly all in genres reflecting the peculiar conditions – battle-conditions – under which Christian *Romanitas* endured. It is from this small platform, mostly but not all in printed editions, that Flint has constructed her reading of Dark-Age culture.

Her story touches the conversion of the Germanic kingdoms. Despite tidy legends, she argues, the conversion amounted to little more than the establishment of protected missionary stations. Christianity stood as David to Goliath. St Boniface of Mainz, in the eighth century, complained to Egbert of York about the paucity of priests at his disposal. Hagiography confirms his picture, portraying its Dark-Age holy men as alone among people at times hostile, at best stolid, and in general culturally inert. It is among these people, peering into the darkness from her small platform of evidence, that the author sees a "powerful presence . . . hard fully to recover and harder still exactly to describe."[4]

It is that of the "witch-doctor." Gathered passages from hagiography, law, sermons, and polemic attest the presence of witch-doctors, or magicians, at every level of society. In sixth-century Francia a villager who fell sick would resort first, and as if it were the normal thing to do, to a figure with a title like *hariolus* [diviner] or *incantator* [enchanter]. Such practitioners were to be found even in monasteries or at courts. In the early ninth century Paschasius Radbertus, for instance, spoke of magicians when denouncing the bad company prevailing at the court of Louis the Pious after his unpopular marriage with Judith.[5]

That protest by Paschasius uses a long list of terms. They are grouped with contemptuous indifference to their precise meaning. Comparable lists, with the same indifference to distinctions, are common in both legislation and polemic. Pairs of words are even commoner, like *medici* [physicians] *et incantatores* or *harioli et incantatores*. The vocabulary extends to well over a dozen terms, including *sortilegi, auruspices, tempestarii, caragii, divini, [h]arioli, vaticinatores, strigae, phitonissae (quae et ventriloquae), malefici* and *venefici*, together with some quasi-synonymous couples like *divinas, id est pitonissas*, or *veneficos necne idolorum cultores* [soothsayers, augurs, diviners, prophets, witches, wizards, worshipers of idols, etc.].

The precise translation of any one of these terms would call for an article in itself. But a few terms do suggest on their own what acts were involved. The *sortilegus*, for instance, cast lots (*sors*) – probably with dice or knucklebones, or perhaps blocks marked with letters to form prophetic words. But even that has to be "perhaps": the medieval authors here may have used, as Flint certainly has, classical authors whose bearing on medieval practice invites separate verification. One independent index of what the various professions did is the lists of objects confiscated from them. A sixth-century *maleficus* [magician], for instance, had on him "a large bag full of the roots of various herbs; there were also in it moles' teeth, bones of mice, and the claws and grease of bears"; while ninth-century witches, according to Archbishop Hincmar of Rheims, employed as *medicamenta* [cures] bones, ashes, coals, hair, bits of colored thread, herbs, snail-shells, and snakes.[6] A few of these objects themselves suggest the use they were put to: for example, bowls of water, mirrors, and even crystal balls, which had shiny surfaces appropriate for divination. As well as these names of objects, just occasionally there survive direct descriptions of magical practice, especially in penitentials [handbooks to aid the priest-confessor in the administration of private penance], like

[4] Flint, *Rise of Magic*, p. 59; for Boniface, see ibid., p. 79 n. 58.
[5] Ibid., pp. 60–1, 63.
[6] Ibid., pp. 248, 64.

"Theodore's Penitential" and Burchard's *Corrector*, or in Anglo-Saxon medical books. One penitential, for example, tells how, to cure a child's fever, he might be placed on a roof or in an oven, or drawn through an aperture dug in the earth.[7]

There is more of this; for the period before 1100, immeasurably more, for example, than is to be found in the well-known histories of medieval magic and witchcraft by Josef Hansen (1900), J. B. Russell (1972), Edward Peters (1978), and (the admirable) Richard Kieckhefer (1990).[8] The expert may wish more quotations had been given in Latin rather than suspect English ("vampire" is a Hungarian word for a mainly Slavonic creature, and enters European languages only in the eighteenth century[9]). But, in Latin or English, the surviving evidence is here, and in quantity.

This quantity is relative. As an observation platform for a whole continent for six centuries the evidence remains meagre, and its meaning must be coaxed out. Another device the author employs for the purpose – besides classical sources – is modern anthropology, in the form of consultation with Mary Douglas and others in print and in speech. The medievalist is rightly wary of twentieth-century analogues. But they are right in this case. For the reason why Dark-Age magic was little recorded in writing makes it at the same time part of *l'histoire de la longue durée* [history over the "long haul", as distinguished from a history made up of events]. Contrary to the optimism of some people who have written things down, and long-lasting though the results can sometimes be, some unwritten cultural patterns last as long or longer: an eye-opening example, recently discovered, are the post-mortem rites associated with *hypogea* (caves) in southwestern France, basically unchanged from pre-Roman times to the seventeenth century.[10] This endurance reflects the nature of the forces that create these customs: not literary influence, but the age-old emotional geometry of social situations, involving love, death, jealousy, and so on. Down on these levels anthropologists *are* a guide, and bring the medievalist an extra bonus: they approach folk culture by different routes – sight, speech, indeed everything *but* writing – so that, with different patterns of inclusion and exclusion, the two disciplines can sharpen each others' eyes to elusive signs in the others' evidence.

The Rise of Magic illustrates these advantages. One illustration is the filling-out of Dark-Age allusions to rural medicine by a detailed close-up of a New Guinea witch-doctor, sitting alone outside his hut, muttering spells in the form of "songs he sings to himself for hours on end."[11] *Aficionados* of E. E. Evans-Pritchard, the pathbreaking student of magic in East

---

[7] Ibid., pp. 40–1, 214, 250–1.

[8] Josef Hansen, *Zauberwahn, Inquisition und Hexenprozess im Mittelalter und die Entstehung der grossen Hexenverfolgung*, Historische Bibliothek xii (Munich, 1900; repr. Aalen, 1964); followed by Josef Hansen, *Quellen und Untersuchungen zur Geschichte des Hexenwahns und der Hexenverfolgung im Mittelalter* (Bonn, 1901; repr. Hildesheim, 1963); J. B. Russell, *Witchcraft in the Middle Ages* (Ithaca, NY, 1972); Edward Peters, *The Magician, the Witch and the Law* (Philadelphia, 1978); Richard Kieckhefer, *Magic in the Middle Ages* (Cambridge, 1990).

[9] Used by Flint, *Rise of Magic*, p. 64; see G. Klaniczay, "The Decline of Witches and the Rise of Vampires under the Eighteenth-Century Habsburg Monarchy," in his *The Uses of Supernatural Power: The Transformation of Popular Religion in Medieval and Early-Modern Europe* (Cambridge, 1990). The allusion to vampires quoted translates "quidam autem a lamiis sive genicialibus feminis debilitati" ["some are drained by witches or female servants"]: Hincmar, *De divortio Lotharii et Tetbergae*, in *PL* 125, col. 717D.

[10] J. Bordenave and M. Vialelle, *Aux racines du mouvement cathare: la mentalité religieuse des paysans de l'Albigeois médiéval* (Toulouse, 1973).

[11] Flint, *Rise of Magic*, pp. 64–5, quoting M. Stephen, "Master of Souls: A Mekeo Sorcerer," in M. Stephen, ed., *Sorcerer and Witch in Melanesia* (Melbourne, 1987), p. 55.

Africa,[12] will find other such resonances. One is the description by Hincmar of Rheims of the antics of those magicians at the court of Lothar II. They would, he says, dress up in many-colored garments and drive themselves mad by consuming special foods and drinks, allowing themselves to be hypnotized by *strigae* or "sucked dry by vampires (*lamiis*)," or changed into members of the opposite sex.[13] The allusions to hallucinogens, trances, and transvestism have unmistakable parallels in ethnologists' findings. Those searching for such parallels will also alight on references to the "profits" of *harioli* (like one in the Fourth Council of Toledo) as echoes of the payments apparently normal for magic, rarely done *gratis*; and also Maximus of Turin's reference to orgiastic self-wounding by a *Dianaticus*, in the fifth century.[14] Each comparison must of course be assessed on its own. But together they refine our picture of Dark-Age magical practice, and affect its aetiology.

Flint has brought to the light, then, by a blend of industry and interpretation, much that has lurked in shadow, showing what lay under the floorboards of a culture we thought in some way Christian. In this her book makes a first impact reminiscent of that of Keith Thomas's *Religion and the Decline of Magic* for early modern England, or R. J. W. Evans's *The Making of the Habsburg Monarchy* for Catholic Austria-Hungary, not to mention the various studies of magic in the Roman Empire.[15] Was there really all *that*, we ask, behind the familiar structures?

Apparently there was; and this fact, now proven for so many different periods, invites the historian, whose subject is change, to pose his central question. What peculiarities did Dark-Age magic absorb from the conditions of its own period, and what forces shaped it? The author's picture has been summarized here as if it were static. In fact it is dynamic: her magic *rose*. Her theory of how it did so is simply stated. Dark-Age churchmen were essentially missionaries, she argues, front-line troops on a cultural boundary. Tactically, two paths were open to them. The first, once the kings were won over (occasionally before), was to attack paganism head-on. A score or more stories from Dark-Age Gaul and Germany tell of the cutting-down of sacred trees, the demolition of temples and statues, and so on (how far all these represented magic is a question I shall touch on later).[16] Conciliar acts and penitentials meanwhile bombarded forbidden usages on a wider front. But this purist approach had flaws. Not least, it could be counter-productive: attack could provoke counter-attack. The protection afforded by kindly kings or (according to the sources) miracles was not enough. At all events a second approach was possible, and ended by being preferred. It was that recommended in Pope Gregory the Great's famous letter to Abbot Mellitus, *en route* for England in 597, preserved in Bede's *History*. Gregory recommends not the destruction, but the adaptation of pagan shrines and celebrations, for "it is impossible to cut out everything at once from their stubborn minds."[17]

---

[12] I refer especially to E. E. Evans-Pritchard, *Witchcraft, Oracles and Magic Among the Azande*, abridged ed., intro. Eva Gillies (Oxford, 1976).

[13] See above, pp. 93–4.

[14] Flint, *Rise of Magic*, pp. 66–7, 65–6 n. 22.

[15] Keith Thomas, *Religion and the Decline of Magic* (London, 1971; repr. Harmondsworth, 1973); R. J. W. Evans, *The Making of the Habsburg Monarchy, 1550–1700* (Oxford, 1979), pp. 346–418; for the Roman Empire, see the bibliography to P. Brown, "Sorcery, Demons and the Rise of Christianity: From Late Antiquity into the Middle Ages," in his *Religion and Society in the Age of Saint Augustine* (London, 1972), pp. 143–6.

[16] See below, p. 102.

[17] Quoted in Flint, *Rise of Magic*, p. 77.

The entire history of medieval religion is a commentary on Gregory's letter. In its field so is this book, whose burden is that churchmen both adapted and adopted their converts' magic. Since adaptation involves selection, chapters here appropriately distinguish "Forbidden Magic" from "Encouraged Magic," "The Discredited Practitioner" from "The Figure of Esteem" (the priest; the Gospel *magi*; St Benedict; the bishop; the sacral king). Magic, that is, was split into good and bad, along the diaphanous boundary of defined orthodoxy. This selective adoption, the argument goes, entailed a paradoxical *increase* in the sum-total of magic as Christianity took over command of the high places.

That is the thesis. It is not all new; good theses seldom are.[18] It is also strictly undemonstrable. The vast bulk of the author's original magic, after all, is admittedly a mere "presence" behind the sources, itself irrecoverable and certainly not to be measured. Astrology, it is true, may be an exception. Carolingian manuscripts show it was studied earlier than M. L. W. Laistner and others taught; and Flint thinks this may show a monkish stratagem to impress magic-minded peasants.[19] Even so, it would suggest rather than demonstrate. From one angle, then, the title promises more than it can deliver, and may even suggest to connoisseurs that it was chosen as counterpoint to Thomas's "decline" of magic. That is all debatable. What is undebatable, whether we accept the present thesis in full or only in part, is that it remains a challenge, obliging the student of Dark-Age culture to confront baffling themes he might otherwise have brushed aside in all directions as "barbarous," "superstitious," or "credulous" – if not ignored altogether.

Of the baffling themes two are hardier than the rest. In one, the *accidentia* [non-essentials] of pre-Christian magic have been absorbed into Christianity; in the other, vice versa. The most obvious case of the first is the healing miracle done by a saint, a type of miracle which was daily bread for hagiographers. Strictly a miracle was done *through* a saint, *by* God – so not magic at all. But narrators could underplay God's role, almost to nothing, so that the saint then does appear as a kind of magician, only more effective for being of the right party. That is all the more so in stories in which the patient has previously sought a cure from a *hariolus*, and been disappointed. The magical background to miracle stories is similarly evinced in poetry and art. A carving on the Ruthwell Cross, for instance, puts a wand in Christ's hand as he heals the eyes of a blind man, healed in the Gospel only by his fingers.[20]

That was one kind of absorption. The other, going the other way, brought Christian objects into pre-Christian magical ritual, and Christian words into spells. The use of the consecrated host for magic was repeatedly condemned, Flint shows, but less sternly when used for healing than when, as in one case mentioned here, it was used for an uncharitable purpose, of killing someone.[21] Mere "charms" were more problematic. The hanging of an amulet or herb round one's neck was called a *ligatura*. It was age-old magic, and condemned with the rest. But what if it was a saint's relic or holy text? That too was condemned, but apparently done. For illiterates, writing in particular had a mysterious power of its own, rendering sacred texts irresistible to magicians, despite the canons. I shall come back to it.

Looking at both effects it is sometimes hard to know which side has absorbed which. One example is the *sors biblica* or *liturgica*, the picking of a text at random as an oracle. The casting

---

[18] See F. Graus, *Volk, Herrscher und Heiliger im Reich der Merowinger: Studien zur Hagiographie der Merowingerzeit*, Tschechoslowakische Akad. der Wissenschaften (Prague, 1965), pp. 527 ("Magie"), 534 ("Zauberer").

[19] Flint, *Rise of Magic*, pp. 93, 145.

[20] Ibid., p. 260.

[21] Ibid., p. 364 n. 18; for spells involving the host more generally, see ibid., p. 298.

of lots was an ancient divinatory practice. But it had been baptized in Acts 1:26, when *sors* was used to elect the apostle Matthew. Yet was the practice really Christian, or not? St Augustine himself had two views. He condemned even the *sors* with a holy text, but the whole world knew from his *Confessions* how he had himself used the procedure at a turning point in his own life. Such was the ambivalence of divination. Aquinas was still debating its use in the thirteenth century (he said it was either superstitious or "vain").[22]

Flint's dynamic treatment of Dark-Age magic, then, offers an illustration, vividly documented, of a theme familiar in most periods of religion. To win converts missionaries lower their demands in matters they deem peripheral. The converts are duly won, happy to know that by dropping some of their old ways they can keep the rest. As a result, all things considered, the world is a better place. But there is one flaw, not there before. The old ways that remain, modified though they may be, and peripheral though they may once have been judged, now have the sanction of religion. So their effects are deeper. They are harder to budge, and more misunderstanding is likely to occur if anyone tries to budge them. The history of Christianity and war, public justice, and a host of other issues illustrates this theme. So does *The Rise of Magic*. Among its particular examples one starts with Caesarius of Arles in the sixth century. He recommended the recitation of the Creed as a cure for sickness. In 1597 that would be taken as the mark of a witch, and people were burned for it.[23] Necessary compromise had come to look like backsliding.

No history book can exhaust its subject, and it remains to suggest areas where the questions raised by this one can be taken further. I have three suggestions, all extending the author's dynamic approach. Let me first explain that adjective. The generation of Frazer, Henry Charles Lea, and Josef Hansen sought to describe and classify magical beliefs. But their labor had its natural limit since magical beliefs turn out to be unsystematic. That was the clearest single lesson of Evans-Pritchard's study of the Azande,[24] and in Dark-Age Europe it is indirectly witnessed by, among other things, those undifferentiated lists. But system can be found in the beliefs if they are read in their social situations. That was demonstrated by Alan Macfarlane's *Witchcraft in Tudor and Stuart England*,[25] which related its data to the village jealousies of Essex; another example, in a smaller format and more remote period, was Peter Brown's correlation of late Roman sorcery with status-rivalries in and near the imperial court.[26]

The three areas into which Flint's approach can be extended are in this class. The first concerns magic within the local, face-to-face society. There is of course nothing like enough evidence to furnish a Dark-Age Macfarlane. In Flint's period the only face-to-face groupings which do yield evidence of magic are courts, like the Merovingian, or that of the wife-hating Carolingian Lothar II. But even among magnates there is no Dark-Age magical dossier to rival those compiled in the early fourteenth century against Bishop Guichard of Troyes or Dame Alice Kyteler.[27] However, the assembly of scraps of data from many places does allow the construction of certain generic pictures, of a *type*, that is, of such a small society. Brown, after all, did this for the Merovingian bishops and their milieu in his *The Cult of the*

[22] Augustine, *Confessions*, viii. 12; Thomas Aquinas, *Opuscula theologica*, ed. R. A. Verardo, 2 vols (Rome, 1954), I: 165–7.
[23] Flint, *Rise of Magic*, p. 83 n. 71.
[24] Evans-Pritchard, *Witchcraft, Oracles and Magic*, pp. xviii, 4, 48, 56, 63, 146–50, 198–9, 200–2, 221.
[25] A. D. J. Macfarlane, *Witchcraft in Tudor and Stuart England* (London, 1970).
[26] See above, n. 15.
[27] See Norman Cohn, *Europe's Inner Demons* (London, 1975), pp. 182–92, 198–204.

Saints,[28] though there on the whole he was only able to handle the supernatural in the form of miracles. What Flint offers now is material for a generic picture of the smaller ecclesiastical unit, the one in due course to be called the parish.

The picture can be presented in the form of a threefold scheme.[29] I call it a "scheme" advisedly, since it is meant to show only how the main elements relate to each other and not to trace their exact contours on the ground, like the London Underground map. Its first phase can be called "missionary." In it the Church was confined mainly to cities and quasi-urban settlements, such as some big monasteries. In respect of most of the land surface of Europe the pastoral duty of clergy, where aspired to at all, was focused largely on preaching; supernatural power was meanwhile represented by the *hariolus*, the "powerful presence" hidden behind all those miracle stories (part of the preaching).

The second phase came with attempts by the authorities to cover that land surface with a territorial "grid" of pastoral responsibilities, each with its priests or group of priests. It was during this phase that the word *parochia* lost its original meaning of "diocese" and came to denote the local circumscription later familiar. The dating of this phase, region by region, is still not clear, but its most obvious single initiative was that taken in Francia in the late eighth century, perhaps with a corresponding one in England. Evidence for the initiative comes largely from new laws, which sought to train and appoint clergy for this pastoral service. But here is the problem. What precisely are they evidence for: accomplished facts or good intentions? Probably the latter, at least in large part and at least if we follow *The Rise of Magic*. That means that these good intentions – mainly Carolingian – were doing for the clergy what Constantine's had once done for Christianity: overstretching it. There were not enough holy men to go round. The result was that the new parish priest remained in part the old *hariolus*, but with sacerdotal status. Flint reads Alcuin's rules for priests as a tacit prohibition of magical practices, and adds examples of the kind of priest he may have had in mind (and others will cross our path in a moment).[30]

The third, mature phase is that of Gregory VII's reform. It made efforts on a new scale to generalize the view of priesthood backed by the Carolingian ideologists. A priest's supernatural involvement was to be concentrated into the sacraments (especially the Eucharist) to the exclusion of all else. Students of the reform will surely find illustrations of their own for

---

[28]   Peter Brown, *The Cult of the Saints* (Chicago, 1981).

[29]   The following schematic summary of the genesis of the parish is based on G. W. O. Addleshaw, *The Beginnings of the Parochial System*, 3rd ed. (Ecclesiol. Soc., London, 1982; 1st pub. 1970); G. W. O. Addleshaw, *The Development of the Parochial System from Charlemagne (768–814) to Urban II (1088–1099)*, St Anthony's Hall Pubns vi (York, 1954); with exceptions and debate in papers contained in D. Baker, ed., *The Church in Town and Countryside*, Studies in Church Hist. xvi (Oxford, 1979), esp. the articles by C. E. Stancliffe, I. N. Wood, Paul Fouracre, Rosamund McKitterick, and Janet L. Nelson; J. Blair, *Minsters and Parish Churches*, Oxford Univ. Committee for Archaeol. Monographs xvii (Oxford, 1988); J. Blair and R. Sharpe, eds, *Pastoral Care before the Parish* (Leicester, 1992). An emphasis on preaching among a priest's pastoral duties is found in writers of the "first phase" by A. Thacker, "Bede's Ideal of Reform," in P. Wormald, D. Bullough, and R. Collins, eds, *Ideal and Reality in Frankish and Anglo-Saxon Society: Studies Presented to J. M. Wallace-Hadrill* (Oxford, 1983), pp. 99–129; P. Wormald, "Monks, Preaching and Pastoral Care in Early Anglo-Saxon England," in Blair and Sharpe, eds, *Pastoral Care before the Parish* (see also Addleshaw, *Beginnings of the Parochial System*, p. 10). For a possible synchronism of English and Frankish developments, see C. Cubitt, "Pastoral Care and Conciliar Canons: The Provisions of the 747 Council of *Clofesho*," in Blair and Sharpe, eds, *Pastoral Care before the Parish*. For the development of the modern use of *parochia* from the ninth century, see Addleshaw, *Beginnings of the Parochial System*, p. 7.

[30]   Flint, *Rise of Magic*, pp. 359–60, 363–4.

this phase of the scheme. R. I. Moore, for instance, has told us how Gregory's reform, just at the moment when urban growth was making the priest's life difficult anyway, shone a "dazzling light" on his moral obligations – as if no one had noticed them before.[31] It is no accident, again, that it should be in the decades after 1066 that English monasteries, whose earlier compendia of folk medicine form such an important source for magic, turned to the scientific medicine of Galen and Constantinus Africanus – as if science, like religion, was snatching *its* half-share in succession to the obsolescent culture.[32] Doubters of this anti-magical aspect of the reform might reread Gregory's threat to the king of Denmark in 1077 that God will punish the *king* if he does not stop a practice (clearly long-established) by which priests were "savagely punished," together with female witches, after storm-damage to crops. The pope's words remind us among other things that it was not just what priests, still less their pious superiors, thought, that moulded priestly status, but what was thought of priests by their flocks.[33]

That threefold scheme is brutally simple, and Flint is too careful a historian to expound it outright. But its ghost is there in her book, ready, with its straight-line model, to help guide all of us who explore the early history of parish clergy.

The second direction in which Flint's questions can be taken further is not, now, down-wards to the village, but outwards, to political society. Among Evans-Pritchard's Azande one of the two most important functions of magic, together with the medical, was the judicial: it was used both to detect crime and curb it with sanctions.[34] Fresh from *The Rise of Magic*, European medievalists will be readier to see the same magical element in two of their own judicial institutions.

The earliest evidence of the judicial ordeal comes from a time when secular and ecclesiastical justice were scarcely distinct. It reflected a peculiar fusion of the natural and the supernatural – natural crime and supernatural detection – and grew extinct in proportion as that fusion was ended. The declaration of independence by canon law, which had its own views of the supernatural, culminated in this case in 1215, when priests were told to take no further part in ordeals. Literature on ordeals has accepted their "superstitious" character without fully exploring the latter's rationale, a rationale only thinly disguised by the Christian formulae which witness to it. Before theologians finally scrapped the disguise the "judgements of fire and water" were said to be done *by* God *through* those elements. But the core-belief was surely animistic. Those two elements, being pure, could detect impurity. These, and a dozen other kinds of ordeal, invite new consideration in the context of Flint's magic.[35]

We could say also, in the context of her magician; or rather her priest–*hariolus* hybrid, who had blessed the iron and water that told the truth. It was the Christian purists who had

[31] R. I. Moore, *The Origins of European Dissent* (London, 1977), p. 278; R. I. Moore, "Family, Community and Cult on the Eve of the Gregorian Reform," *Transactions of the Royal Historical Society*, 5th ser., xxx (1980): 49–69.

[32] A. Dawtry, "The *Modus Medendi* and the Benedictine Order in Anglo-Norman England," in W. J. Sheils, ed., *The Church and Healing*, Studies in Church Hist., xix (Oxford, 1982), pp. 25–38.

[33] Gregory VII, *Registrum*, ed. E. Caspar *MGH*, Epistolae selectae, II, 2 vols, Berlin, 1920–3; repr, 1955), p. 498, ll. 13–26 (letter vii.21). Note especially "hanc pestiferam *consuetudinem* . . . funditus extirpare" (ll. 22–3) ["abolish this pestilent *custom* absolutely"], and "quascunque molestias *corporum*" (l. 16; emphasis added) ["certain ills of the *body*"]. Cf. Hansen, *Zauberwahn*, pp. 36–121.

[34] Evans-Pritchard, *Witchcraft, Oracles and Magic*, pp. 50–1, 162–3, 184–9, 195; for the corresponding endorsement of magic by political superiors, see ibid., pp. 41, 61, 162.

[35] H. C. Lea, *Superstition and Force* (Philadelphia, 1892), pp. 249–428 ("The Ordeal").

condemned magic who also condemned the ordeal, and even from the same period (as Robert Bartlett has shown, criticism of the ordeal is as old as our evidence of it, and starts in the eighth century).[36] But it was only after the Gregorian reform, appropriately, that this opposition mustered the strength that bore legislative fruit in the fourth Lateran Council. Again, the fruit was legislative rather than in all cases actual. In practice the ordeal died only gradually, lingering in some places – Hungary, for instance – until the fifteenth century.[37] Its endurance confirms its archaic character, and that of the priest who blessed it. It was the Dark-Age, magical priest who had operated the ordeal; the new, sacramental priest who respected the canons. Why should the old sort do likewise? The rules he obeyed were older and unwritten.

If the magic of the ordeal detected crime, another quasimagical practice punished it: excommunication. The post-Gregorian church inherited this practice, too, from an age when ecclesiastical and secular jurisdiction were ill distinguished. This time it was ecclesiastical judges that hung on to it; naturally, for it was a sanction to their own canon law, whose growing autonomy left them with no other (they could not shed blood). It was Lester K. Little, developing the work of Lea, who best exposed the character of early medieval excommunication as a quasi-magical "curse," affecting to bring disaster and damnation to its victim. Here too Christian priests were the heirs of their pre-Christian predecessors, notably of druids (whose curses are reported by Caesar); and here too serious divines were embarrassed by non-Christian aspects of the ritual, as flouting the command to love enemies. Although their misgivings were understandably slower to mature, excommunication would by the middle of the thirteenth century be firmly redefined as "medicinal," with, once more, imperfect effect among the unenlightened (plenty of evidence of maledictory excommunications survives even from the fifteenth century).[38]

Public justice, then, provides a second area into which the thesis of *The Rise of Magic* can throw light. There is a third, more problematic. It draws our attention not downwards, now, to village society, nor outwards to the political; but upwards, towards the gods themselves. Flint's thesis derives its dynamic character from her distinction between two configurations, pagan and Christian, whose contest engendered the "rise" of magic. Now she tells us, more than once, that magic was "not a pagan survival."[39] That does of course need saying: the name "magic" came from the *magi* of a Persian religion which Christianity had superseded back in the first and second centuries AD. But students of the diaphanous frontier between Christian and non-Christian thought must remember a golden rule. All written historical evidence, terminology included, distorts the truth it reveals: because it was written for

---

[36] R. Bartlett, *Trial by Fire and Water: The Medieval Judicial Ordeal* (Oxford, 1986), pp. 70–5. On the role of political superiors, critical to Bartlett's thesis, his findings should be compared with those of Evans-Pritchard: see above, n. 34.

[37] R. C. Van Caenegem, "La preuve dans le droit du moyen âge occidental," *Recueils de la Société Jean Bodin* xvii (1965): 691–753.

[38] H. C. Lea, "Excommunication," in his *Studies in Church History* (Philadelphia and London, 1869), pp. 223–487; L. K. Little, "Formules monastiques de malédiction aux ixe et xe siècles," *Revue Mabillon* lviii (1970–5): 377–99; L. K. Little, "La morphologie des malédictions monastiques", *Annales ESC* xxxiii (1979): 43–60. For the new theology, see L. Hödl, *Die Geschichte der scholastischen Literatur und der Theologie der Schlüsselgewalt*, pt 1, Beiträge zur Geschichte der Philosophie und Theologie des Mittelalters xxxviii.4, pt 1 (Münster-in-Westphalen, 1960). The change is summarized in A. Murray, *Excommunication and Conscience in the Middle Ages* (John Coffin Memorial Lecture, London, 1991), pp. 15–16. On canonical aspects, see E. Vodola, *Excommunication in the Middle Ages* (Berkeley, 1986).

[39] Flint, *Rise of Magic*, pp. 69, 310.

contemporary purposes, not ours, and purposes color the language that serves them. In its missionary phase the purpose of Christian language was to win hearts from both paganism *and* magic, so it lumped them together, charging us, much later, with the task of their separation.

Magic was not, then, a pagan survival. That leaves the question of what it and paganism were; and more particularly, what the relation of each was to Christianity. Students of religion can, I am sure, be too evolutionist. But they need be only moderately so to see that some pagan thought-forms approached those of Christianity, and indeed that conversion could not have occurred otherwise. By that "conversion" the religious core of paganism – or those kinds of paganism; and by "core" I mean the part whose aspirations approximated most closely to those of Christianity – was simply swallowed up. Thus there *was* no pagan survival, as magic or as anything else. The core had gone, except perhaps as a suggestive shape inside its devourer. The old religions knew what was coming better than we do, and trembled, responding to the conqueror's approach by a reaction analogous to the "adaptation" described by Flint on the Christian side. Whether this was really a stratagem, a pagan "pious fraud" like that she attributes to the Christians, or whether both reactions were not rather, at bottom, expressions of religious intuitions common to an age, pagan religions can be seen growing more like Christianity as conversion approached. Thus in 274, as Roman religion felt the end near, it rallied round the quasi-monotheistic cult of *Sol invictus*; a shift whose only permanent result, after the Christian victory a generation later, was that the sun-god's feast, December 25, was absorbed with everything else, the defiant symbolism of "the Unconquered Sun" consummated in the Christmas Gospel: "The light shineth in the darkness."[40] The same happended later in the North. As the monotheistic devourer drew near, Thor edged ahead to supremacy in the Nordic pantheon, runes were "consecrated" to (or by) him, and images of his hammer grew more like a cross. Then that "paganism" too was swallowed up. Christianity – that of *The Dream of the Rood* – became a bit more "heroic." The Virgin Mary inherited a prayer or two from old beliefs in fertility, of which her giving birth to God himself and without human aid made her the *ne plus ultra*. But the vital assets of pagan religion as such had been taken over and reshaped.[41]

The religious core of paganism, then, could not survive – or rather could only survive within a new living body. What was left behind was debris, a bric-a-brac of words, names and language. Bric-a-brac is not useless. But it usually serves in humbler stations than those for which its elements were intended. The very name "magic" is a case in point. The religion it recalled was one from which, by way of post-exilic Judaism, Christianity had in fact swallowed the useful core in the form of doctrines thenceforward essential to itself (for instance, bodily resurrection).[42] Much the same had happened with Roman religion. The name "Jupiter" is cognate, for instance, through Indo-European roots older than Latin, with the latter's *Deus pater* [God the Father]. But by the Middle Ages the one-time "father in the sky"

[40] M. P. Nilsson, "Studien zur Vorgeschichte des Weihnachtsfestes," *Archiv für Religionswissenschaft* xix (1918): 50–150, is still indispensable for the pagan background; the origin and development of the Christian feast are summarized by C. W. Smith, "Christmas and its Cycle", in *New Catholic Encyclopaedia*, 15 vols (New York, 1967), iii, pp. 655–60 (with bibliography).
[41] E. O. G. Turville-Petre, *The Myth and Religion of the North* (London, 1964), esp. ch. 3; E. Marold, "Thor weihe diese Runen," *Frühmittelalterliche Studien* viii (1974): 195–222. For Mary, see Nilsson, "Studien zur Vorgeschichte des Weihnachtsfestes," 148–9; cf. ibid., 131 n. 1.
[42] R. C. Zaehner, *The Dawn and Twilight of Zoroastrianism* (London, 1961), pp. 60–1, 183 (qualified dualism), 317 (resurrection of the body).

had become one demon among others, at best a planet with a soul.[43] Even Judaism was not spared. Hebrew, once God's own language, would become by the late Middle Ages a quarry for spells.[44] None of these old religions could of course have complained at their treatment. Persian Zoroastrianism had meted out much the same to the polytheism *it* had replaced, in the sixth century BC;[45] while seven centuries earlier the Jews' plunder of the wicked Egyptians had included – the bit *not* in the Old Testament account – palpable religious borrowings.[46]

The name of magic, then, was part of the bric-a-brac. Was the same true of magic itself? It suited Christianity to say so, coupling it and paganism in double condemnation. But it was not just that magic and paganism were different after the conversion. They always had been. If Flint had brought Scandinavian religion into the reckoning this difference would have been more obvious than she makes it. For some Scandinavian gods, notably Loki, actually *practiced* magic, as a distinct enterprise within the religion they embodied. For the old religion, too, had its renegades and unofficial undercurrents. Magic was one, and it was this undercurrent, *with* the bric-a-brac, that survived into the Christian period.

"With" it: the relation of magic to the bric-a-brac was that of workman to materials. Magic used the appurtenances of religion for its own purposes, much as Stonehenge is used today by rootless youth. *Inter alia* this meant it could take material from the new religion, Christianity, as well as the old; indeed, since the new religion was clearly more powerful, it took more. Hence its use of those consecrated hosts and relics, and more particularly, of sacred writing.

The eclecticism of magic is nowhere better illustrated than in this last case. "Magic is a force closely linked with writing," writes Kieckhefer, in the best introduction to medieval magic.[47] But it is clear that most of Flint's early village witch-doctors had never been within ten miles of any writing. How, then, can a learned author make this mistake? It is because he is concentrating on *later* medieval evidence; from a time when even the most ignorant were aware of, without understanding, the power inherent in the arts of "clergie". Hence, *pari passu* with the growth of schools, the magicians' adaptation of writing to a "cargo-cult" – a cult, that is, which manipulates the externals of a superior culture without grasping its principles. Christianity, true to Flint's portrait, had not been above using such "book-magic" on its own account. Its early medieval ascendancy partly relied on its mastery of the mysterious medium, a mastery used to good effect, for instance, when Gospels were bound with jewels, or parchment *auctentica* [documents attesting to authenticity] attached to relics. The difference was that Christian divines, right from the start, had known just why "Scripture" mattered, having – *inter alia*, and long before they got a virtual monopoly of writing in the Dark Ages – actively developed the use of the codex and other writing techniques.[48] The

---

[43]   G. Dumézil, *La religion romaine archaïque* (Paris, 1966), pp. 181–2; J. Seznec, *La survivance des dieux antiques*, Warburg Inst. Studies xi (London, 1940); trans. by B. F. Sessions as *The Survival of the Pagan Gods* (New York, 1961).
[44]   Kieckhefer, *Magic in the Middle Ages*, pp. 148, 159.
[45]   Zaehner, *Dawn and Twilight of Zoroastrianism*, pp. 15–57.
[46]   H. Ringgren, *Israelite Religion*, trans. D. Green, 2nd ed. (London, 1969), pp. 108–9, 377. The above paragraph takes into account also the remarks on conversion from Roman "pagan" culture in R. Markus, *The End of Ancient Christianity* (Cambridge, 1990), pp. 1–17, 223–4, 48–50; the last of which, on St Augustine's conversion, is a reminder that much the same story could be told of Neoplatonism.
[47]   Kieckhefer, *Magic in the Middle Ages*, p. 53; cf. ibid., pp. 77, 112, 141–2.
[48]   L. D. Reynolds and N. G. Wilson, *Scribes and Scholars* (Oxford, 1974), p. 31. For *auctentica*, see N. Herrmann-Mascard, *Les reliques des saints*, Société d'histoire du droit, Collection d'histoire

book that Shakespeare's Prospero would drown, in a word, was indirectly a Christian product.

Just as Christianity adapted to meet its rivals, then, they show a corresponding "adaptation," if only (in the case of magic) in a borrowing of externals. This double-sided magnetism raises, finally, the question where the exact boundary lay across which it was exercised – the diaphanous boundary between orthodoxy and superstition. There are two difficulties here. The first is that the boundary was inconstant. A well-known case will illustrate this. In 643 a clause in the Lombard king Rothari's Edict (cap. 376) sought to stop blood-vengeance against a woman on the grounds that she was a witch (*strigam, quem dicunt mascam*): "for Christian minds must not believe a woman could eat a living man from inside him."[49] Influential Christians for centuries after that can be shown to have shared the pious king's scepticism (if it was his). But none of them would have got away with it in front of the late fifteenth-century authors of the *Malleus maleficarum*, who not only believed such things, but said it was heresy to deny them. Now the fact was, and can be seen by shining the right light on earlier evidence, that some *less* influential Christians had gone on believing these things ever since Rothari had tried to stop them. It only needed special social conditions, peculiar to the Renaissance period, to magnify and arm the previously recessive doctrine.

The full history of that inconstancy cannot, however, be written; and that is because the boundary presents a second difficulty: it was also uncertain. The condemnations do not always make clear whether their authors believed in the magic they were forbidding: whether, that is, they were condemning effective practice or mistaken belief. I do not mean only that it is unclear to us, now. One reason it is, is that it was often unclear to the authorities themselves, then. Between what they believed possible or impossible in nature, lay a no man's land where no one was quite sure. "Who, in his heart of hearts, knows what is and is not possible [in nature]?," as one of the most perceptive of all medieval intellectuals would put it in the twelfth century.[50] In medieval "supernatural" narratives – to use an adjective only invented in this regard in the thirteenth century – there is much to endorse his observation, not least their common qualification by phrases like *seu vera seu falsa* ("whether true or false").[51]

The discovery of this uncertainty entails a modification in Flint's thesis. Perhaps she, too, has simplified her material for the sake of clarity. The resulting scheme is at all events simple. On one side she has pure Christians, on the other the magic-minded; and the former make concessions to the latter to win their allegiance – as if disingenuously, sacrificing candour to proselytism. Now there is much to support that reading. Not only does Gregory's letter to Mellitus do so. Gregory's whole *oeuvre* supports it, with its baffling contrast between the miraculous *Dialogues* and everything else. So, for that matter, does the well-known contemporary *penchant* for "pious fraud," on which there are now whole books.[52] But another view is possible, all the more so because it can be combined with the first. It is that everyone, intellectual or rustic, actually accepted both modes of thinking, magical and non-

institutionelle et sociale, vi (Paris, 1975), pp. 120–4: *auctentica* were labels written to identify relics.

[49] *Edictus Rothari*, cap. 376 (ed. G. H. Pertz, *MGH*, Leges, 5 vols, Hanover, 1835–89, iv, 87).

[50] John of Salisbury, *Metalogicon*, 871a (ed. C. C. J. Webb, Oxford, 1929, p. 85, ll. 29–30): "Quis enim novit penitus quid esse possit aut non possit?"

[51] For the word *supernaturalis*, see H. de Lubac, *Surnaturel* (Paris, 1946), pp. 325–428.

[52] H. Fuhrmann, *Einfluss und Verbreitung der pseudo-Isidorischen Fälschungen*, 3 vols (*MGH*, Schriften, xxiv, Stuttgart, 1972–4), esp. i, 65–136. For orientation and bibliography, see P. J. Geary, *Furta sacra* (Princeton, 1978; revd. ed. 1990).

magical, but in ratios widely differing, and, in each person, with a boundary of uncertainty between what they did and did not believe. Of inconstancy, too: even in one person the ratios may have changed with time, as apparently in St Augustine with his *sors biblica*.

A modification on these lines would in the first place make Flint's picture of early medieval religion less socially two-sided. For it would "internalize" whatever tension there is between magical and Christian belief. But by doing so it would also soften the harsh portrait of magic in the sources; and that, in turn, would open our eyes to a characteristic in magic which Flint does not identify, but which her sources allow us to detect: its religious aspirations. These may be more obvious in sub-Saharan African magic than in Dark-Age European.[53] That is to be expected, for in Europe religion had been self-conscious, and a fortress of a specialist caste, since long before Christianity; and that meant that magic, too, was left more "specialized," skimmed, that is, of moral and devotional elements that might have marked it for higher things. But their vestiges are still to be seen for all that. They are there in the self-laceration of St Maximus's proto-flagellant *Dianaticus*; in the more sober demands for pre-ritual abstinence in some Anglo-Saxon magic manuals; in the widespread use of Christian holy objects; and even – the signs survive only from the late Middle Ages – in some "deprecative" magical formulae (formulae that ask rather than command).[54]

In nature a small organism can live on a large, drawing on the same food. Magical belief stood in this relation to the religions that housed it, including, and most visibly, Christianity. It may have misused their bric-a-brac, and for its private purposes. But these purposes had just enough in common with those of real religion to allow the mutual attraction which [Flint's] book attests. How much *was* that, in the last resort? Was it enough to challenge the generic distinction between magic and religion, with which we started? Let us look again at one feature of magic. Its beliefs have been found unsystematic, only making sense when replaced in the social circumstances that give rise to them – as if they were the intellectual surface of an emotional solid, a polyhedron of human relationships out of whose context the beliefs are incoherent. Whatever the mutual adaptations between magic and religion, that surely puts a chasm between the two cultural forms. Or so one might think. But does it, really? There is food for reflection, here too.

[53] Evans-Pritchard, *Witchcraft, Oracles and Magic*, pp. 131–3 (taboos and abstinence), 44, 177 (importance of inner disposition). A comparison between this book and E. E. Evans-Pritchard, *Nuer Religion* (Oxford, 1951), poses the question why the author found "magic" in one culture and "religion" among its neighbours. There were reasons, not least the mysterious flecks of Judaistic belief among the Nuer. But the difference remains one of degree, and was not uninfluenced by the author's personal development between 1937 and 1951: M. Douglas, *Evans-Pritchard* (London, 1980), pp. 87–106.
[54] Flint, *Rise of Magic*, pp. 65–6, 323 ("holy wisdom, as God Almighty dictated"). For a deprecative formula, see Kieckhefer, *Magic in the Middle Ages*, p. 161.

Part II Feudalism and Its Alternatives

Part II Feudalism and Its Alternatives

There is today lively debate regarding feudalism. One subject of discussion concerns definitions: what does "feudalism" mean? what period does it describe? and is it even an appropriate term? Another subject of discussion (see "Alternatives", below) concerns alternative institutions which, some historians think, may better describe the essential elements of medieval culture.

Models

The year 1940 is a convenient starting point for viewing today's debate regarding feudalism's definitions; in that year the French historian Marc Bloch circulated his *La Société féodale (Feudal Society)*[1] among his friends. Here the word "feudal" was considered in such broad terms as even to lose its connection to the word "fief," whence it had been derived. Instead, Bloch's book embraced a "total history," a picture of an entire society. For Bloch the key element of this feudal society (by contrast with ancient slave societies and modern democracies) was its system of graded dependencies in which men were subordinated one to another.

Because of the elasticity of the term for Bloch, he could speak of two feudal ages. The first began as the Carolingian world waned and the assault of the Hungarians, Scandinavians, and Muslims left Europe poor, depopulated, and rural; the second began in the mid-eleventh century with the growth of cities and a money economy.

Bloch's study ranged over all of Europe, though it rested most often on places within the contours of the former Carolingian Empire. The next, post-war generation of French historians abandoned this panoramic view. The young Georges Duby, at the forefront of this movement, took on Bloch's subject, feudal society, but (following the lead of economic historians) did so via a detailed study of one region, in his case the Mâconnais (in Burgundy), which measured all of about 315 square miles.[2]

---

[1] Trans. L. A. Manyon (Chicago: University of Chicago Press, 1961).

[2] It would be only fair to say that this sort of regional research already had a long history in Germany, where *Landesgeschichte* (regional history) had already begun in the mid-nineteenth century. At that time "Germany" consisted not of a unified state but of *Länder*, regions with a variety of political organizations. *Landesgeschichte* was suited to this context, for it focused on each region's economy and culture. Yet in the eyes of many historians at German universities, historians of the *Land* did less glamorous and important work than those who wrote about the state and glorified the nation. With the unification of Germany in the 1870s, *Landesgeschichte* lost even more prestige. Only in the wake of Germany's defeat in the First World War did regional history gain new lustre. Thus in post-war Germany, historians such as Alfons Dopsch and Otto Brunner were creating a newly revitalized *Landesgeschichte* – one which welcomed the findings of other disciplines regarding geography, settle-

Duby's methods, which included careful mining of archival sources, were much imitated; thus began the great spate of regional histories in France, with consequences far wider than the question of "feudalism" *per se*. But with regard to feudalism, the results were revolutionary enough. In a seminal study, "The Evolution of Judicial Institutions," based on documents from the Mâconnais, and published only a few years after Bloch's book, Duby proposed a key modification of Bloch's schema.[3] First, he argued from the regional evidence that Carolingian institutions persisted deep into the tenth century; in this way, he essentially eliminated Bloch's "first" feudal age. Second, he signaled the exceptional importance of the "first thirty years of the eleventh century" as the time when "the simple and coherent Carolingian system gave way to a confused conception of the judicial function entirely at the mercy of personal relations and domestic considerations."[4] This marked the period of transition to "the classic feudal period [i.e. the 12th century]." It was the "part of the early middle ages when feudal society was establishing itself." The two parts of the divide were clearly marked in Duby's mind: before 1000 there had been "public" institutions, afterwards they were "private" and "almost familial'; before 1000 the count, surrounded by the great men of the region, had had real "territorial jurisdiction" and sat in court as "judge" with the power to enforce his decisions; afterwards he was the center of personal relations, and sat as "an arbiter and conciliator," with no more power than those inherent in curses, anathemas, and expressions of good intentions; and he drew to his court only a lesser group of men, the armed *milites* ("knights"), while the great magnates, protected by their castles, maintained their own courts and jurisdictions.

There were hints in this article of other changes as well: "About the year 1000 there appeared the first complaints against the imposition of unjust customs upon the lands of others."[5] Here Duby was referring to a change in the nature of taxation. He argued that taxes (in Latin, often *exactiones*) had previous to this time been public, imposed by kings or their agents. Now, around the year 1000, the vocabulary shifted: taxes were beginning to be called "customs" (*consuetudines*) and often "bad" or "unjust" customs. Duby connected this change in vocabulary and attitude to social and political developments: private lords such as castellans – men ruling from their fortifications – imposed their own taxes on the surrounding population, whether on independent peasants who owned their own property (i.e., allodists who held allods) or on people who lived on church lands that the lord considered part of his "banal seigneury." Indeed, the seigneury became the central political node of the new order: its lord imposed his "ban" (in Latin, *bannum*) – that is, his right to command, coerce, judge, and impose fines – on the men and women who lived not only on his estates but beyond them and in their interstices. The banal seigneury, then, was not the same as "land lordship'; it was lordship over people.

A few years later, Jean-François Lemarignier wrote an influential article that called this fragmentation of authority within the old territorial jurisdictions the "dislocation" of the *pagus*, the *pagus* representing the ancient Roman subdivisions on which public power had

---

ment patterns, and economic and cultural conditions – precisely at the same time as Marc Bloch and other French historians, well aware of what was happening across the Rhine, were working out their conception of "total" history. Regional histories in France began only in the twentieth century; the pioneers included Robert Latouche and André Déléage.

[3] Now in English in *The Chivalrous Society*, trans. Cynthia Postan (Berkeley: University of California Press, 1977), 15–58, but originally published in *Le Moyen Age* 52 (1946): 149–94; 53 (1947): 15–38.
[4] *Chivalrous Society*, p. 23.
[5] Ibid., p. 20.

been based.[6] In 1953, Duby published his *thèse* (somewhat like a Ph.D. dissertation, but often much more extensive), *La société aux XIe et XIIe siècles dans la région mâconnaise (Eleventh- and Twelfth-century Society in the Region of Mâcon)*, where "pouvoir banal" (banal power) and "féodalité" (feudalism) were paired together and contrasted with "l'alleu" (the allod).

Duby traced the process by which small and middling allodists in the Mâconnais were gradually absorbed into the great lordships, the poorer ones sinking to the level of dependent serfs, the richer and more powerful ones becoming vassals:

> most [of the well-off allodists] broke off all relations with the count and placed themselves under the protection of the castellan or of the closest religious institu- tion; but they did so by their own free decision and in the very flexible way afforded by the contract of vassalage. (149)

The date of the transformation to this "organisation féodale" was 980–1030.

The numerous regional studies that followed in the wake of Duby's *thèse* largely con- firmed his general scheme, while noting, of course, local variations.[7] In chapter 7, Pierre Bonnassie discusses a social and political transformation in Catalonia, today a region of Spain.[8] He finds (just as Duby had found in the Mâconnais) that around the end of the first millennium there was a marked decline in the number of independent allodists. At the same time, institutions of public justice, which in Catalonia were based on the administrative unit called the *vicaria*, gave way to the private justice of seigneurial lords. Catalan castellans imposed their ban (though in Catalonia the word *mandamentum* was normally used instead of *bannum*). One important difference between Catalonia and the Mâconnais was the exist- ence of a frontier (against the Muslims) in the former; by 1000, however, that source of new land had largely dried up.

The changes that Duby, Bonnassie, and many others traced in various regions of the medieval West were mirrored at the top, in the view of Jean-Francois Lemarignier.[9] Lemarignier argued that the Capetian monarchy experienced the same sort of privatization and truncation of power at the level of the monarchy as Duby and others had found at the level of the count. The king had become a "banal lord" within his own seigneury; beyond that, he had very little power or influence.

In 1980, in a book that served as a synthesis of the preceding studies, Jean-Pierre Poly's and Eric Bournazel's *La mutation féodale, Xe-XIIe siècles (The Feudal Transformation, 10th– 12th Centuries)* proclaimed by its very title the persistent use of the word "feudal" as a portmanteau term for politics, society, and culture after the turning point of the millen-

[6] Jean-François Lemarignier, "La dislocation du *pagus* et le problème des 'consuetudines' (Xe-XI siècles)," in *Mélanges d'histoire du Moyen Age dédiés à la mémoire de Louis Halphen* (Paris: Presses Universitaires de France, 1951), pp. 401–10.
[7] Of a huge bibliography, the following may be singled out as notable examples of French regional studies: Guy Devailly, *Le Berry du Xe siècle au milieu du XIIIe. Etude politique, religieuse, sociale et économique* (Paris: Mouton, 1973); Robert Fossier, *La terre et les hommes en Picardie jusqu'à la fin du XIIIe siècle* (Paris: B. Nauwelaerts, 1968); and (applying the method to Italy), Pierre Toubert, *Les structures du Latium médiéval. Le Latium méridional et la Sabine du IXe à la fin du XII siècle* (Rome: Ecole française de Rome, 1973). To these should be added, of course, the studies by Bonnassie (excerpted in chapter 7) and Barthélemy (chapter 8).
[8] Chapter 7: Pierre Bonnassie, *La Catalogne du milieu de Xe à la fin du XIe siècle. Croissance et mutations d'une société*, 2 vols (Toulouse, Association des Publications de l'Université de Toulouse-Le Mirail, 1975), vol. 2, pp. 575–99, 609–10.
[9] Jean-François Lemarignier, *Le gouvernement royal aux premiers temps capétiens (987–1108)* (Paris: Picard, 1965).

nium.[10] This book marked a high tide of a consensus about "feudalism," at least among French historians and many in the United States as well. The consensus held that the feudal world, created in the decades around the year 1000, was a society in which all phenomena were powerfully touched by the relations of dependency and lordship implicit in the term.

Yet only a decade later a former student of Georges Duby, Dominique Barthélemy, challenged the prevailing view. He did so in two very different ways and venues. In a review of the second edition of Poly's and Bournazel's book, he roundly criticized those whom he called the "mutationists" – historians who thought there had been a near-revolution around the millennium.[11] At about the same time, in his *thèse* focused on the region of Vendôme in France (from which chapter 8 is an excerpt), Barthélemy emphasized the essential continuity within the whole period from the ninth to the early twelfth centuries as well as the extremely gradual nature of the changes that took place in those 300 years.[12] He argued that "bad customs" were nothing new, and that the men imposing them were not always castellans. He insisted that the word "allod," which historians have taken to mean "land held outright," was not always distinguished from the word "fief" or "benefice," which historians take to mean land held from a lord; and therefore, in Barthélemy's view, it is hard to know what to make of an alleged devolution from the "allod" to the "fief." In short, he challenged the consensus.

While this debate about the nature and timing of feudalism continued, another debate challenged the very use of the term. The opening salvo to rid the medievalist's vocabulary of the word "feudalism" was Elizabeth A. R. Brown, "The Tyranny of a Construct; Feudalism and Historians of Medieval Europe," published in the *American Historical Review* in 1974 (chapter 9).[13] Brown's approach grew out of Anglo-American empiricism: "feudalism" was a term created in the mid-nineteenth century, based at best on legal terms from the eighteenth century; it represented a mental "construct," according to Brown, that never did (and never could have) existed anywhere at any time.

Anglo-American scholars generally reacted favorably to Brown's point, with only a tiny note of dissent sounded by Thomas Bisson, who wondered whether feudalism wasn't too "congenial" a tyrant to be dispensed with.[14] More recently, an entire book by Susan Reynolds on the subject was dedicated "to Peggy Brown, Homage and fidelity." Pointedly entitled *Fiefs and Vassals: The Medieval Evidence Reinterpreted*, Reynolds's book traces the creation of the idea of "feudalism," with its tidy linkage of vassals to fiefs, to late twelfth-

---

[10] Translated into English as Jean-Pierre Poly and Eric Bournazel, *The Feudal Transformation 900–1200*, trans. Caroline Higgitt (New York: Holmes & Meier, 1991).

[11] Dominique Barthélemy, "La mutation féodale a-t-elle eu lieu? (Note critique)," *Annales: économies, sociétés, civilisations* 3 (1992): 767–77. Poly and Bournazel replied in "Que faut-il préférer au 'mutationnisme'? ou le problème du changement social," *Revue Historique de Droit français et étranger* 72 (1994): 401–12. This was followed in turn by a response from Barthélemy, "Encore de débat sur l'an mil!," in the same journal, 73 (1995): 349–60 and, this time responding to an article by Bisson (see n. 20 below), an essay, "Debate: the 'Feudal Revolution,' Comment 1," *PP* 152 (1996): 196–205. Undoubtedly this is not the final volley, as demonstrated by the new collection of Barthélemy's articles in *La Mutation de l'An Mil – A-t-elle Eu Lieu? Servage et Chevalerie dans la France des Xe et XIe siècles* (Paris:. Fayard, 1997).

[12] Chapter 8: Dominique Barthélemy, *La société dans le comté de Vendôme de l'an Mil au XIVe siècle* (Paris: Fayard, 1993), pp. 333–4, 349–61, 363–4.

[13] Chapter 9: Elizabeth A. R. Brown, "The Tyranny of a Construct: Feudalism and Historians of Medieval Europe," *American Historical Review* 79 (1974): 1063–88.

[14] Thomas Bisson, "The Problem of Feudal Monarchy: Aragon, Catalonia and France," *Speculum* 53 (1978): 461.

century lawyers who were serving new-style bureaucratic governments. That is, the concept was created precisely at the moment when the society it proposed to describe was being superseded by the power of the state.

Alternatives

In a review of Reynolds's book, Patrick Wormald dwelled on the unsettling effects of the anti-feudalism movement: "It will never again be possible to write of government and society in the medieval West as if 'feudalism' were its dominant trait. What more can one ask? The answer, if it is not ungrateful to say so, is clearer guidance to where we go from here."[15] Yet already some historians had begun to question the very assumptions that had lain behind the interest in (indeed attachment to) feudalism. For the whole issue of feudalism was "modern" not only because moderns liked to reify and conceptualize but also because they knew about and measured all against the non-feudal state. Hence the oppositional terms of Duby: public, jurisdictional, and coherent (the justice of the state) vs private, personal, and chaotic (feudal justice). In a book of collected essays tellingly entitled *Lordship and Community in Medieval Europe: Selected Readings*,[16] the editor, Fredric Cheyette, demonstrated that one way not to talk about feudalism was to talk instead about medieval institutions and cultural forms that mediated relations among people of approximately the same social strata. Communities were held together not only by vertical relations but by horizontal ones; historians needed to explore the "rules of the game" on these more level playing fields.

In his article "Suum Cuique Tribuere" ("Giving Each His Due"), published in 1970, and here reprinted in its entirety (chapter 10)),[17] Cheyette looked at the way that disputes among property owners in southern France were handled. There were no regular courts with institutional, official standing; rather, the courts functioned as pressure groups. They did not "decide" cases; they made it possible, desirable, or even unavoidable for litigants to negotiate a settlement.

Cheyette's work was soon followed by a series of articles by Stephen White (looking at northern France), William Miller (studying the Icelandic world), and Patrick Geary (again, for France).[18] Their studies, which were inspired in part by their personal friendships and contiguity (White and Miller, for example, taught together at Wesleyan; Cheyette was not far away at Amherst), was nevertheless part of wider currents. A new generation of historians, largely educated at Oxford under the tutelage of J. M. Wallace-Hadrill, combined his interest in anthropology with a new materialism that took charter (rather than normative) evidence with utmost seriousness. They used these charters not, as previously, by and large to establish dates, definitions, and authenticity, but to discuss "law in action." In their exploration of legal cases, they made use, in particular, of accounts of *placita*, meetings

---

[15] Patrick Wormald, "Farewell to the Fief," *Times Literary Supplement* 4,797 (March 10, 1995): 12.

[16] New York: Holt, Rinehart, & Winston, 1968.

[17] Chapter 10: Fredric L. Cheyette, "Suum cuique tribuere," *French Historical Studies* 6 (1969/70): 287–99.

[18] A few examples: Stephen D. White, "Pactum . . . Legem Vincit et Amor Judicium: The Settlement of Disputes by Compromise in Eleventh-Century Western France," *American Journal of Legal History* 22 (1978): 281–308; William Ian Miller, *Bloodtaking and Peacemaking: Feud, Law, and Society in Saga Iceland* (Chicago: University of Chicago Press, 1990); Patrick J. Geary, "Living with Conflicts in Stateless France: A Typology of Conflict Management Mechanisms, 1050–1200," in his *Living with the Dead in the Middle Ages* (Ithaca, NY: Cornell University Press, 1994), pp. 125–62.

(sometimes formal, sometimes less so) at which disputes were handled. Their work resulted in the collective enterprise *Settlement of Disputes in Early Medieval Europe*, edited by Wendy Davies and Paul Fouracre.[19]

The question of settlement of disputes could only with difficulty be kept separate from the issue of violence. When medieval people of the upper classes had disputes, they often did not go to court; they went to war. Already Cheyette's article had explored the norms that legitimized informal systems of litigation by looking at *chansons de geste*, epic poems that dealt with honor, fealty, and fighting. To the anthropological eye, both litigation and war were part of "dispute processing." Stephen White was (and remains) particularly active in exploring the "game" – admittedly a sometimes dangerous and deadly game – that was played through feuds that spilled onto the battlefield. The view that the Middle Ages was violent was recently vigorously restated by Thomas Bisson in an issue of *Past and Present*.[20] But the meanings, uses, and limits of that violence in the context of the cultural norms of medieval society as a whole were equally vigorously asserted by Stephen White in a rejoin-der.[21] Although the two scholars might not be happy to see themselves cast as ideal types, they may here stand for the ongoing debate between those who (like Bisson) see the hierarchy and domination of feudalism as the defining elements of the Middle Ages, and those who (like White) stress the importance of non-hierarchical cultural norms that lead to conflict as well as solidarity.

Horizontal relationships were similarly emphasized in new studies of peasant society. While peasants and agricultural life figured importantly in the work of Bloch, Duby, Poly, and Bournazel, these scholars (as may be seen in chapter 7) were above all interested in peasant subjugation, status, taxation, and other burdens imposed by the seigneurial system. In the 1980s some historians began to shift the emphasis as they explored issues of local community identify.[22] As Susan Reynolds put it, speaking of the effect of the upper classes on rural communities:

> It is certainly true that as government became more systematic and as rulers got more control of legislation and law-enforcement, so lords found ways of exacting their dues more consistently. The parcelling out of the countryside into defined jurisdictions . . . helped . . . to define the communities within which peasants acted. Nevertheless, defining the boundaries of actual communities is not the same as creating the sense of community in the first place.[23]

[19] Cambridge: Cambridge University Press, 1986. The same group more recently published *Property and Power in the Early Middle Ages* (Cambridge: Cambridge University Press, 1995).

[20] Thomas N. Bisson, "The 'Feudal Revolution,'" *PP* 142 (1994): 6–42.

[21] "Debate: The 'Feudal Revolution,' Comment 2," *PP* 152 (1996): 205–23.

[22] As, for example, Robert Fossier, "Les communautés villageoises en France du nord au moyen âge," *Flaran* 4 (1982): 29–53; Susan Reynolds, *Kingdoms and Communities in Western Europe, 900–1300* (Oxford: Clarendon Press, 1984), pp. 101–54; Monique Bourin, *Villages médiévaux en bas-Languedoc: genèse d'une sociabilité (Xe–XIVe siècles)*, 2 vols (Paris: L'Harmattan, 1987); Léopold Génicot, *Rural Communities in the Medieval West* (Baltimore: Johns Hopkins University Press, 1990), comprising the author's James S. Schouler lectures for 1986–7, and preparatory to his study of rural communities of the Namurois. There is an important discussion of the historiography of work on rural communities as well as a detailed study of the formation of some Tuscan rural communes in Chris Wickham, *Comunità e clientele nella Toscana del XII secolo: Le origini del comune rurale nella Piana di Lucca* (Rome: Viella, 1995).

[23] Susan Reynolds, *Kingdoms and Communities in Western Europe, 900–1300* (Oxford: Clarendon Press, 1984), p. 109.

The many elements of that sense of community were described in the synthetic work, *Vivre au village au moyen âge: les solidarités paysannes du 11e au 13e siècles (Living in the Medieval Village: Peasant Solidarity from the Eleventh to the Thirteenth Centuries)*, in which Monique Bourin and Robert Durand took up one by one the solidarities both created and expressed by the village family, parish, cycle of religious festivals, charitable organizations, agricultural activities, and sense of being neighbors, from which section comes chapter 11.[24]

Finally, particularly among German historians, for whom the question of feudalism was always secondary, given the particular history of the Empire, other institutions of social solidarity, particularly among elite groups, came into the forefront of research after the Second World War. This focus was especially important in the work of Gerd Tellenbach and the members of his *Arbeitskreis* (team) at Freiburg, whose many studies illuminated the numerous mechanisms that existed in the Middle Ages to create and cement "personal relations," not so much among individuals (itself a modern construct) as between groups: families, *Sippen* (clans), and *Gemeinschaften*, communities so closely bonded as to constitute virtually artificial families. Much of this work focused on monastic confraternities, spiritual communities that bound together lay and religious groups.[25] This work had enormous implications for the analysis of medieval social, cultural, and political life, removing it far from the vocabulary of statism or feudalism. Thus Hagen Keller wrote about personal alliances as the "foundations" of Ottonian kingship,[26] Gerhard Oexle considered the group behavior of medieval guilds,[27] while Gerd Althoff, as in the book excerpted in chapter 12, wrote about the medieval institution of "friendship."[28]

---

[24] Chapter 11: Monique Bourin and Robert Durand, *Vivre au village au moyen âge: les solidarités paysannes du 11e au 13e siècles* (Paris: Messidor/Temps Actuels, 1984), ch. 8.

[25] As, for example, in the classic article by Karl Schmid and Joachim Wollasch, "Die Gemeinschaft der Lebenden und Verstorbenen in Zeugnissen des Mittelalters," *Frühmittelalterliche Studien* 1 (1967): 365–405. For further context for this article, see Part IV of this volume.

[26] Hagen Keller, "Grundlagen ottonischer Königsherrschaft," in *Reich und Kirche vor dem Investiturstreit*, ed. Karl Schmid (Sigmaringen: Jan Thorbecke Verlag, 1985), pp. 17–34. On this topic, see also Karl J. Leyser, *Rule and Conflict in an Early Medieval Society: Ottonian Saxony* (Bloomington: Indiana University Press, 1976).

[27] Otto Gerhard Oexle, "Gruppenbindung und Gruppenverhalten bei Menschen und Tieren: Beobachtungen zur Geschichte der mittelalterlichen Gilden," *Saeculum* 36 (1985): 28–45.

[28] Chapter 12: Gerd Althoff, *Verwandte, Freunde und Getreue: Zum politischen Stellenwert der Gruppenbindungen im früheren Mittelalter* (Darmstadt: Wissenschaftliche Buchgesellschaft, 1990), pp. 88–119.

7 The Banal Seigneury and the "Reconditioning" of the Free Peasantry

Pierre Bonnassie

[A charter reads:]

This is a brief reminder of what the bishop ought to have in his castellany of Sanahuja, by use and by right.

In the first place, half of the revenue of the courts without deceit. From the market, half of what comes to the lords, by justice and by right, that is to say of the fines, with the exception of rights on the udders of the cows, which belong to the castle. Of the oven, half. Of rights on minting, half.

And the bishop agrees with the lords of Sanahuja that they should bring before him the men (of the castellany), and that he should levy on them, every year, the *queste* [a tax] of bread and meat. The bailiff of the lord should go with the bailiff of the bishop to the cellars of Sanahuja, and they should judge the barrels together for levying the *compra* [a tax] of the bishop. And that the bailiffs of the lords should assess the service of those who owe army service with donkeys and other equipment, that it should be estimated under oath, and when it has been estimated, the revenue should be shared by the lord and the *castlà* [the head of the garrison that guards the castle, i.e. *castlan*], and the *castlà* should give the bishop his part. . . .

In the houses of Sanahuja, the bishop has the use of the wood, cabbages, chard, cheese, ewes, except in the houses of the priests, the *cabalers* [mounted soldiers; "knights"] and the bailiffs of the lords; and all this he may use in all the other houses of Sanahuja. . . . And the peasants of Sanahuja who work with a team should give the bishop a *sextarius* [a unit of measure] of oats and a sheaf; those who share a team with several others should give a *hemina* [another unit of measure] of oats, and a sheaf.

And if an animal enters into the bishop's *dominicatura* [demesne – the land belonging to the lord] in Sanahuja, and is retaken there, his master should buy him back for as many pennies as the animal has feet. And the bishop's woods enjoy a franchise [a privilege] such that no man may hunt within a stone's throw of it . . . and a man of Sanahuja who catches a rabbit in the woods must give an ox, a pig, and nine pairs of live rabbits to the bishop in reparation.

And all the men of Sanahuja must work for the bishop on the construction of his houses and owe him transport services on the back of their beasts, with the exception of priests, *cabalers*, the lords' bailiffs, and merchants.

And no lord may award any franchise at Sanahuja without the consent of the bishop.

And the men of Sanahuja must carry the bishop's bulls and messages at his command, to any place he may desire. . . .

And in all the mills in the territory of Sanahuja already constructed, or those to be constructed, the bishop should have the quarter (of the revenues?), and in all the use of *destre mugar* [free use of the mill for his grain], under compulsion. . . .

This was enacted by Guillem Guifred, bishop.[1]

If I have decided to quote so extensively from this document, drawn up between 1041 and 1075 at the dictation of the bishop of Urgel, it is because it provides a remarkably precise repertory of the burdens and new fees which fell upon the Catalan peasantry toward the middle of the eleventh century. In addition, this document does not simply describe them, but allows us to see their origins, tells us how they were collected, and shows how social relations in the heart of the castellany were organized, first of all between the masters of the ban (the bishop and his *fideles* [loyal men], the lords of Sanahuja), but also those between these and their agents (the *castlà*, the *cabalers*, the bailiffs of the bishop, and those of the lords), and finally between these latter and the peasants. In this sense, this document constitutes without a doubt the best possible introduction to the study of the regime of the banal seigneury in Catalonia. But before we analyse this document, it is appropriate to define the conditions under which it was able to be created.

Birth of the Seigneury

The Weakening of the Free Peasantry

In the tenth century, and even at the beginning of the eleventh, Catalan peasants were for the most part entirely free men. They knew no other authority besides the count's: either directly, on free lands, or elsewhere through the intermediary of the *vicarii* [regional representatives of the count]. At the judicial level, they were subject only to the public tribunals, and thus escaped all sorts of arbitrary [judgments and authorities]. There were two principal reasons for this privileged situation: allodists for the most part, [these peasants] were economically independent; and as soldiers, they had the means to defend themselves against any threat of oppression. The count himself needed them as much to ensure the protection of his frontiers as to establish his own power over the countryside.[2]

The first blow against the peasantry came from its own landed patrimony. The phenomenon of land concentration, which appeared at the beginning of the tenth century, if not before,[3] did nothing but increase during the first half of the eleventh century. The means did not change, but the small property was increasingly unable to resist the appetite of the land

---

[1] Archivo Capitular Urgel, Cart. I, no. 525. Fragments of this text have been published by J. Miret i Sans, "Aplech de documents dels segles XI i XII per a l'estudi de la llengua catalana," *Boletín de la Real Academia de Buenas Letras de Barcelona*, vol. VI (1911–12): 383.

[2] [See Pierre Bonnassie, *La Catalogne du milieu du Xe à la fin du XIe siècle. Croissance et mutations d'une société*, 2 vols (Association des Publications de l'Université de Toulouse – Le Mirail, 1975),] vol. 1, ch. IV, pp. 311–19.

[3] Ibid., ch. III, pp. 236–42.

consolidators. The disintegration of the judicial system facilitated confiscations: it was no longer necessary to take the path of slow public trials, nor to produce probative titles in order to deprive a peasant of his property. The castellan (or the abbot or the bishop) had merely to invite the proprietor of the desired allod to prove his right to his property himself, by plunging his arm into boiling water, for instance.[4] In a pinch, one could convict the poor peasant of some crime: his house and his fields would be the amount of his fine.[5]

In order to avoid such annoyances, many allodists took precautions. Alms became a preventive remedy not merely against the torments of the afterlife, but also against those more earthly, but just as menacing. Churches, which were seeing the liberalities of the great diminish somewhat, continued therefore to benefit from the gifts of lesser folk. But the castellans also profited from these land transfers. As early as 1016, a widow and her children gave their allod to the *vicarius* of Gaià – "*per nostrum salvisientem*" ["for our safety"], they said – only to receive it back from him on condition that the *tasca* [rent based on a share of the crop] be perpetual.[6] Later, many other barons (among whom was Bonfill Guillem de Castellví)[7] received such "gifts," whose spontaneity we may well hold suspect.

Nevertheless, the magnates did have the means to pay, and some of them had the elegance at least to make a gesture. In approximately fifteen transactions between 1029 and 1053, Brocard de Castelltallat and his wife Legards bought houses, gardens, dovecotes, fields, and vineyards in the heart of their castellany, each time for a few *solidi* [monetary accounting units; shillings].[8] They were not alone: Guifred Sendred and his wife Maria acted similarly at Espadamala, near Torelló,[9] as did Ricard Guillem[10] or Bonuz Vivas[11] in the region of Barcelona. As in the past, the acts of acquisitions thus continued to testify to the process by which land became concentrated [in fewer hands].

However, such acts became rarer and rarer. Throughout the tenth century, they represented approximately 70 percent of the original documents (and as much as 80 percent during the decade from 990 to 1000). After the year 1000, the percentage did nothing but shrink: 65 percent towards 1025, 55 percent towards 1050, 35 percent in 1075, 25 percent around 1100.[12] How can we interpret this phenomenon? Certainly, new types of acts [e.g.] (*convenientiae* [agreements], oaths of fidelity) begin to appear in the archives, which tend to make the proportion of charters of sale lower than before. Nevertheless, it is surprising to see the number of sale transactions diminish spectacularly at the very moment when the renewal of exchanges intensifies. We need to look at the evidence: if sales of allods were less and less frequent, it must be because there were fewer and fewer allods to sell. Integrated, shred by shred, into the great lay and ecclesiastical estates, peasant micro-property was slowly dying.

---

[4] Archivo de la Corona de Aragón, perg. [parchment] R. Ber. I, no. 305 (1064); Archivo Capitular Urgel, Cart. I, no. 210 (1081).
[5] Archivo de la Corona de Aragón, perg. R. Ber. I, no. 355 (1066).
[6] Archivo Capitular Vich, perg. no. 1347.
[7] Archivo de la Corona de Aragón, perg. R. Ber. I, no. 437.
[8] Arch. Montserrat, perg. Bages, nos 1333, 1339, 1352, 1362 A, 1362 B, 1373, 1401, 1402, 1410, 1411, 1414 B, 1436, 1444; Archivo de la Corona de Aragón, Monacales, perg. S. Benet, nos 185, 260.
[9] Archivo Capitular Vich, perg. nos 288, 1028, 1034, 1035, 1415, 1425, 1426, 1427, 1431, 1435, 1436, 1439.
[10] Archivo de la Corona de Aragón, perg. R. Ber. I, nos 323, 334, 335, 341, 344, 346, 347, 348, 349, 356, 394, 399, 440, 452, 456, 468, 471, 473.
[11] The son of Vivas de Provençals. On his acquisitions, see P. Bonnassie, "Une famille de la campagne barcelonaise et ses activités économiques aux alentours de l'An Mil," *Annales du Midi* LXXVI (1964): 266, 301–3.
[12] [Bonnassie, *La Catalogne*,] Annexe VI, p. 893.

In any case, by 1050, it had lost the dominant position that it had still occupied at the end of the tenth century in the land structures of Catalonia.

This evolution is easily explained. In the ninth and tenth centuries, the peasant allod was already being continually eroded by the mass of alienations of which it was the object; but it was continually being re-created by means of assarts [land clearance and drainage] in pioneer areas. After about 950, however, while these losses continued at the same rate, they could no longer be replaced because the frontier had stabilized. The rare conquests of land still realized in the western regions could no longer balance the losses suffered by peasant property back home.

Can we indeed still speak of peasant property? Even in uncultivated areas, the allodist could use what was his only under the control of the heads of the *quadras* [organized groups of pioneer peasants].[13] Elsewhere, charters tell of the limits imposed on the right to dispose of the allod, particularly, a prohibition against alienating it without the consent of the castellan.[14] Alamany Hug of Cervelló and his wife Sicards even gave themselves the right of preemption on all peasant lands sold in their castellany.[15] This was the *retrait seigneurial*.[16]

Many allodists therefore found themselves reduced to the state of tenants: either because their allod was no longer any different from a servile holding (because of the various labor and fiscal duties that encumbered it), or because they had been constrained to alienate it (in whole or in part), and to go and beg for land to work from a magnate or from a church. Indeed the burdens that weighed down properties subject to rent were increasing. Since vacant lands were becoming rare, land rents rose. On tenures in the cleared lands, old or new, the *tasca* was no longer the only rent demanded: added to it was the *braçatge* (*braciaticum*), another charge based on a share of the crop (one-sixteenth of the harvest) which appeared between 1030 and 1050, and which became increasingly frequent after the latter date.[17] On

---

[13] [Ibid.,] vol. I, ch. VII, pp. 439–40.

[14] This type of limit is not unique to Catalonia: we can find examples in almost any region of the West during this period. Nevertheless, there is a problem to which it is impossible to provide a clear solution: if the castellans were able to forbid the sales of peasant allods, they could also – it goes without saying – authorize them. In this case, the deposit which the master of the donjon brought to the transaction could no doubt constitute a sufficient guarantee for the buyer: he, therefore, backed by the lord's word, would be less likely to demand the preparation of a written contract. This could be another way to explain the lowering of the percentage of acts of land acquisition in the documentation. This, however, hardly changes the heart of the question: if the peasant allod continued to exist under seigneurial domination, it was only in a very mutilated form, very far indeed from that of the classic property. Many examples of prohibitions against alienation are to be found in the archives: Archivo Capitular Vich, perg. no. 1386 (1030); Arch. Montserrat, perg. Bages, nos 1380 (1038), 1386 (1040); Archivo de la Corona de Aragón, perg. R. Ber. I, no. 196 (1056).

[15] Archivo Capitular Barcelona, Divers C-c, perg. 473 (1045/1046).

[16] This expression is based on the "*retrait censuel*," which applies to tenure, and the feudal "*retrait*" which applies to fiefs (or, rather, it will apply to them at a later period). On both of these customs, see R. Boutruche, *Seigneurie et féodalité* (Paris, 1968–70), vol. II, pp. 115–16, 218–19.

[17] Archivo Capitular Barcelona, Divers C-b, perg. no. 224: in this document dated 1063, two witnesses declared that the *braçatge* had been levied, over and above the *tasca*, for at least thirty years on the lands which the abbey of Sant Pol de Mar possessed in the parish of Arenys. See also J. Serra Vilaro, *Baronies de Pinós i Mataplana. Investigació als seus arxius* (Barcelona, 1950), vol. III, p. 101 (which publishes a document from approximately 1050 where there is mention of *braccage*) and J. Rius Serra, ed., *Cartulario de Sant Cugat del Vallés* (Barcelona, 1946), vol. II, no. 656 (1067). E. de Hinojosa (*El regimen señorial y la cuestión agraria en Cataluña durante la Edad media* [(Madrid, 1905)], pp. 175–6) declares, without giving any references, that *braçatge* represented one-twentieth of the harvest; an assessment contract of 1105 stipulates quite clearly, however, that it is equal to one-sixteenth (Arch. Monserrat, perg. Bages, no. 1628).

good lands, it was in vain that a peasant might seek to acquire a property to rent without engaging to turn back a quarter or a third of all the grain harvested and half of the wine; and furthermore, he had to pay dearly for the right to settle on it – up to ten pieces of gold to the master of the arable.[18]

The peasants, whether allodists or tenants, thus found themselves in a considerably weakened economic position. The same was true of their military situation. Methods of combat had evolved to their disadvantage. Miniatures from the beginning of the eleventh century still show battle scenes with foot soldiers dressed in their everyday workclothes, and equipped with merely a javelin or a sword.[19] They cut a poor figure next to the heavily armored knights protected by their shields, helms, and hauberks. While the peasant soldiers cut each other up with javelin blows, or even simply by throwing rocks, the troop of *milites* passed by indifferently, without even a glance at the obscure mêlée below, saving themselves for more distinguished assaults. In fact, jousts on horseback increasingly determined the results of warfare.[20]

Host service therefore ceased to be demanded of all free men, even in the frontier land of Catalonia: it was converted into a replacement tax.[21] For the most part, peasants were sent back to their hoes and their spades. Only a few of them, richer or more skilled, were employed in the *mesnies* [households] which maintained the fortresses. But once these had become professional warriors, they ceased to belong to the peasantry and became parasites on them, alongside the nobility by birth.

Thus impoverished and deserted by its most warlike members, the peasant class found itself in a weak position to defend the fruits of its labour.

From the Vicaria to the Seigneury

These peasants found themselves even more powerless in that they were at the same time largely deprived of the protection the counts had given them. The only authority they knew was that exercised – almost entirely without control – by their immediate superiors, the masters of the castles.

Formerly known as *vicarii*, public officials, these individuals had held the command that they exercised over the core of their respective castellanies from the count.[22] Now, they no longer held their power from anyone but themselves, and they sought to forget the origins of their function. The very word "*vicarius*" fell into discredit: while in 1026, for example, Guillem de Castelví appeared with that title,[23] his son Bonfill Guillem ceased to use it. After

---

[18] Archivo de la Corona de Aragón, Monacales, perg. Bagà, no. 292 (1063): See also ibid., no. 190 (1035); Archivo Capitular Vich, perg. no. 1401 (1040); Rius Serra, ed., *Cart. S. Cugat*, vol. II, nos 543 (1036), 672 (1071), 691 (1077), etc.

[19] The Roda Bible (Paris Bibliothèque Nationale Latin ms. 6), vol. III, fos 134, 144. [Reproduced in Bonnassie, *La Catalogne*,] p. 576.

[20] The Roda Bible miniatures also provide illustrations of this new type of horse-combat. See, for example, vol. III, fo. 144 (illustration reproduced [in Bonnassie, *La Catalogne*,] vol. I, p. 304).

[21] Archivo Capitular Urgel, Cart. I, no. 525 (text translated in the original, pp. 575–6). On this problem, see also [Bonnassie, *La Catalogne*,] pp. 586–8.

[22] [Ibid.,] vol. I, ch. II, pp. 173–7.

[23] Archivo de la Corona de Aragón, perg. Ber. Ram. I, no. 56: "*quidam vir nomine nobilis Vuilelmus vicarius scilicet de Castro Vetulo*" ["a certain noble man named William, vicarius of Castro Vetulo"].

1050, this title, which had lost much of its value, was very rarely used to describe castellan barons:[24] on the contrary, some of them used it at times to describe their own *castlans*.[25]

They called themselves simply *seniores*, and were known as such to all.[26] The transformation of the title *vicarius* into *senior* seems to have happened gradually, through an imperceptible confusion: "this vineyard," reads an act of 1032, "is from dom Guillem, lord of Mediona (*senior Midione*) and it is vicarial (*vecheraria*)."[27] In the course of this gradual evolution, which we can fix around the year 1050, the *vicaria* became no less definitively a 'seigneury.'

This moment is of capital importance in the social history of medieval Catalonia. Since it had escaped the constraints of the domanial system, the region had never really known the lordship exercised by right of landlordship.[28] It was instead from the castle, and from the castle alone, that the subjection snaring both allodists and free tenants had its origin.

Castellan lordship thus led to the banal seigneury.[29] The foundation of the lord's authority rested upon the *mandamentum* (more rarely, *bannum*), which his ancestors had received by delegation from the count.[30] It was the power to command all the men and all the women

---

[24] One of the last (if not the last) examples of this use is in an act of 1055: Archivo de la Corona de Aragón, Monacales, perg. Bagà, no. 261.

[25] Archivo Capitular Barcelona, Divers. A, perg. no. 258 (1055): the *vicarius* mentioned in an act of 1055 is a *castlà*. See also Archivo Capitular Vich, perg. no. 2155 (1049).

[26] Archivo de la Corona de Aragón, perg. Ber. Ram. I, no. 107 (1033), perg. R. Ber. I, no. 196 (1056); J. M. Font Rius, ed., *Cartas de población y franquicia de Cataluña*, vol. I (Barcelona, 1969), no. 18 (1036); etc. See also the document above relating to Sanahuja.

[27] Archivo de la Corona de Aragón, Monacales, perg. S. Benet, no. 218: "*in vinea de domino Guilelmus, senior Medione, que es vecheraria*".

[28] On this subject, see [Bonnassie, *La Catalogne*,] ch. III, pp. 242ff.

[29] It would be pointless to enter into all the quarrels over vocabulary which disunite (or rather which have disunited) historians considering the correct word to describe this kind of lordship: "castellan," because centered around fortresses, "high," because dominated by magnates, "political," because of its public origin, but above all "banal" because it was founded on the lord's right of *ban*, whence were derived all the various burdens imposed on the inhabitants. Discussions that focus on the problem of the origins of this kind of lordship are more fertile: some (though fewer and fewer) base it on the demesne; others (in which camp I place myself without hesitation), consider that it was born from a delegation or a usurpation of powers and public rights. Actually, the two positions are not mutually exclusive: for Picardy, R. Fossier has written: "the ban was certainly the determining factor for success, but it could never have been accorded or usurped without the territorial base on which rests the authority of the master" (*La terre et les hommes en Picardie jusqu'à la fin du XIIIe siècle* [Paris and Louvain, 1968], vol. II, p. 518). In Catalonia, where the network of fortresses was considerably tighter than elsewhere in the West, this "territorial base" had always been simply, at the beginning, possession of a castle. Afterwards (see [Bonnassie, *La Catalogne*,] ch. XV), certain rich landowners were able to profit from the opening created by the castellans and were able in turn to impose banal burdens on their tenants. But this was at a late stage of this evolution (the end of the eleventh and the beginning of the twelfth centuries). At its heart, the conflict between partisans of the "public origin" and partisans of the "demesnial origin" could very well simply be resolved in chronological terms. The penury of documentation for the eleventh century has helped to obscure the debate – Catalonia is a happy exception. On this subject, the basic references are: G. Duby, *La société aux XIe et XIIe siècles dans la région mâconnaise* (Paris, 1953), pp. 205–29, 319–30; *L'économie rurale et la vie des campagnes* (Paris, 1962), p. 401–14, 452–61 [*Rural Economy and Country Life in the Medieval West*, trans. Cynthia Postan (Columbia, SC, 1968)]; Boutruche, *Seigneurie et féodalité*, vol. I, pp. 114–17, vol. II, pp. 125–40; Fossier, *La terre et les hommes en Picardie*, vol. II, pp. 510–34.

[30] The term *mandamentum* (in Catalan, *manament*) is by far the more frequent of the two. The word *bannum* has a less precise meaning: sometimes it designates the authority of the count, sometimes that of the lords, or even the penalities inflicted for infractions of the public order (see M. Bassols de

(*homines utriusque sexus*)[31] living within the limits of the castellany, with the single exception – but this reserve was entirely theoretical – of those among them who depended on immune churches [churches granted their own jurisdiction], or who benefited from a privileged status. It also meant the right to muster the army, or as became more and more frequent, that of claiming the fees and the services that replaced it. Finally, it was the capacity to receive the oaths of fidelity which free men formerly swore either to the count or to his representative in the *vicaria*.

However, as the independence of the castellans grew, the notion of *mandamentum* expanded and came to mean whatever the lords wanted it to mean. At the same time, the ties which attached the inhabitants of the castellany to the master of the castle grew tighter, their nature changed, and they became more personal. The old oath of allegiance of free men lost its public character, and to it was added *hommage*. "*Omines de nostro ominatico*," declared Alamany Hug de Cervelló and his wife Sicards in 1045–46, describing the inhabitants of their castellany who had become *their* men.[32]

In these conditions, the castellans became the ungoverned heads of peasant communities. Since these communities no longer had any recourse to the count's tribunal, they found themselves defenseless before their very judges. In particular, they could no longer protect communal lands which certain lords appropriated by virtue of their *mandamentum*: "*afrontat ipsa terra in alaude comunis de te*" ["this land borders on the allod that is your 'commons'"], one group declared to the castellan of Oló in 1066.[33] Generally, rights of easement and of passage (*ademparamentum, empriu*) that village collectivities had always freely enjoyed now depended on the seigneurial ban.[34]

Without any obstacles in its way, this ban therefore came to include all aspects of the public and private life of peasants, whatever their condition. If it happened this way, it is because, along with the *mandamentum*, came another power, even more formidable: the *districtum* (*destret*), that is to say, the right to judge, or, more precisely, to punish.[35] Its origin is no different: the authority over pleas was one part of the vicarial function. But the justice of the *vicarii* was no different in its nature or in its functioning from that of the counts: it was rendered with the agreement of judges, and according to the prescribed forms of Gothic law. Once it became seigneurial justice, how did it evolve?

A quick comparison between the only two trials which castellan courts have left us is very instructive. The first presents a plea presided over by Alamany de Cervelló and his mother Adalez under the porch of their castral chapel on May 30, 1032: to be sure, classic procedure there was somewhat mismanaged, and an oath of purgation replaced the written proof; but the judge, Pons Bonfill March, provided surety by his presence, and he himself wrote up the act dropping the claim.[36] On July 12, 1066, the same scene [took place] before the church of

---

Clement and J. Bastardas Parera, *Glossarium mediae latinitatis Cataloniae (Voces latinas y romances documentadas en fuentes catalanes del año 800 al 1100)* (Barcelona, 1962), pp. 234–5).

[31]   Archivo de la Corona de Aragón, perg. R. Ber. I, no. 383 (1067).

[32]   Archivo Capitular Barcelona, Divers C-c, perg. no. 473.

[33]   Biblioteca Central de la Diputación Provincial de Barcelona, perg. no. 2134. See also ibid., no. 2078: "*in alaude comunis de nos*" (1072).

[34]   E.g. Archivo de la Corona de Aragón, perg. R. Ber. I, no. 438: "*dono tibi adempracionem de ipsos omines*" ["I give you the right of easement of these men"] (infeudation, in 1071, of the castle of Barbera).

[35]   The two terms *mandamentum* and *districtum* (*manament et destret*) are always associated. References are to be found in nearly all the *convenientiae*.

[36]   Archivo de la Corona de Aragón, perg. Ber. Ram. I, no. 101.

the castle of Castellví, but this time there was no judge: it was the lords of the castle alone who determined the debates and pronounced the sentence; and if Gothic law was still evoked, it was only the better to be violated: the sum owed by the condemned did not go to the family of the victim, but was instead confiscated by the castellans *"ut quicquid exinde facere vel iudicare voluerint in eorum proprio consistat arbitrio"* ["so that whatever they wanted to do or judge consisted of their own will"].[37]

"Let them decide according to their free will": a tremendously apt description of the discretionary power which the lords had acquired in judicial matters. *Iustitia* (justice) became *districtum*, and *districtum* was their personal property. They could guard it for themselves, or grant it to someone else; exercise it themselves, or confide its management to the *castlà*; divide it among their heirs, just like any of their allods; give fragments of it to their friends as a tokens of their gratitude, or to their *fideles* in return for services rendered.[38]

Such gifts were always appreciated, for the *districtum* was the source of juicy profits. In practice, it could provide almost unlimited revenue. With might taking the place of right, all one had to do was to impose sufficiently on the peasants in order to multiply indefinitely the number of fines, cash in on pecuniary compositions, and sovereignly decree confiscations of allods or reductions to servitude.[39] A delightful institution, seigneurial justice, which offered to those who held it both considerable material satisfaction and the more troubling pleasures of repression.

Banal Charges and Exactions

For the lord, justice was only one instrument of coercion among many, and the ways in which he could put pressure on the peasants were extremely diverse. It is indeed quite difficult to classify satisfactorily the numerous new burdens that were imposed on free men by means of the castellan ban. It is best, perhaps, to go by the letter of the documents, which generally distinguish between the rights – real or pretended – that the lord had inherited from public power, and the usages which he instituted without the slightest juridical foundation, and which we can consider – and which his contemporaries did consider – to be exactions.

Charges of Public Origin

The *vicarius* represented the public power in his district. As such, he levied the dues owed to the *potestas* [e.g. the king or count]. The castellan continued this tradition, but entirely arbitrarily, and by keeping the profits raised for himself, his family and his *fideles*.

Alberga *[Rights of Lodging] and Similar Charges*
The first duty of any free man was to offer hospitality under his own roof to the count or to his agents when the necessities of public service obliged them to move about.[40] This obligation remained occasional, and as long as "public personages" likely to use it remained few,

---

[37] Archivo de la Corona de Aragón, perg. R. Ber. I, no. 355.

[38] There are many examples of this parcelling out of seigneurial justice: Archivo de la Corona de Aragón, perg. R. Ber. I, nos 105 (1049), 204 (1057), 383 (1067), 405 (1068), etc. See also the text relating to Sanahuja, and [Bonnassie, *La Catalogne*,] pp. 600–5.

[39] Archivo de la Corona de Aragón, perg. R. Ber. I, no. 355 (confiscation of allods and reduction to servitude). Also see [Bonnassie, *La Catalogne*,] pp. 588–90.

[40] See [Bonnassie, *La Catalogne*,] vol. I, ch. II, pp. 159–60.

it was not too harsh on those who were so obliged. Everything changed when the beneficiary became the lord next door. He could invite himself at any moment, and he never came alone: his entire troop of parasites was also invited to the feast. On this diet, the food reserves of peasant homes were quickly depleted, and if they repeated their visits too often, the revellers were likely to find an empty table. The service of *albergum* thus became regulated: all homes in the perimeter of a castle were subjected by turns. To compensate, it was now only an annual reception (*receptio, receptum, recet*).[41] On this occasion, the peasant was obliged, during one day and one night, to provide bread and meat to the *cabalers* who came down from the castle, to let them drink their fill, to lodge them (in winter, heating his home with a big fire),[42] to feed their *servientes* [servants], and to give oats to their horses.

But it could seem a bother to the lord and his *fideles* to consume their peasants' production on site. It was much simpler to have it delivered to the castle. The *receptum* thus also became a rent in kind. Sometimes it was without limits, as at Sanahuja, where the bishop could demand at any moment, from every head of family, wood, vegetables, cheeses, and sheep (ewes); more often it was fixed, as in the exterior hamlets of the same *castrum*:

> At Masco, the bishop has a *receptum* of two pigs worth 6 *solidi* of good money, and five *quarteres* of good oats, and fifty loaves of bread, and six *sextarii* of nice wine. And in the valley of Murrias, a pig worth three *solidi* of good money, twenty loaves of bread, and three sacs (skins) of good wine and a half-muid of good oats. From Pujol, the same thing. From Paladol, a pig worth three *solidi* of good money, a *sextarius* of grain to make bread, three *sextarii* of good wine, and between the *receptum* and the *civades* [a tribute of oats], a muid and two *sextarii* of good oats. From Upper Fiter and from Lower Fiter, a pig worth two *mancusos* for the *receptum*. From the allod of Mal Duran, a pig worth two *mancusos*.[43]

Did the *receptum* thus conceived become confused with other annual rents, also collected in kind, and practically in the same form, that were levied in other castellanies? At Vallvert, in 1039, the peasants owed the lord a *perna* of 12 pennies (or 12 pennies in cash);[44] those of Vilaseca, in 1057, owed *porcos annuales*, and those of Orpinell delivered *annuales* to the castle of Mediona;[45] in 1067, the inhabitants of Aramprunyà were subjected to "offerings of pigs and sheep."[46] These charges of pigs or in quarters of meat, which became increasingly general in the middle of the eleventh century,[47] may well have been derived from the right

---

[41] Among the earliest mentions of *receptiones* or of *recepta* is F. Monsalvatje y Fossas, *Noticias históricas del condado de Besalú* (Olot, 1908), vol. II, p. 233 (1029); F. Miquel Rosell, ed., *Liber Feudorum Maior* (Barcelona, 1945), vol. I, no. 118 (around 1044). The word *receptum* is found in a document from 927, but this act has had material interpolated, and the reference is contained in the interpolated section (F. Udina Martorell, *El archivo condal de Barcelona en los siglos IX y X* [Barcelona, 1951], no. 92). On the other hand, the term *alberga* already designates a reception of annual character in 1024, in Rius Serra, ed., *Cart. S. Cugat*, vol. II, no. 495: "*donent anuatim ad ipssum abbatem alberga cum duos socios et unum armigerum*" ["they give *alberga* annually to this abbot and his two companions and one squire"].
[42] For a precise description of a *receptio* of this kind, see J. Soler, ed., "Cartulario de Tabernoles", *Boletín de la Sociedad castellonense de cultura* XXXVI, XXXVII, XXXVIII (Castellón de la Plana, 1960–62), no. 55 (1049).
[43] Archivo Capitular Urgel, Cart. I, no. 525 (1041/1075).
[44] Archivo de la Corona de Aragón, perg. R. Ber. I, no. 30.
[45] Ibid., no. 204.
[46] Ibid., no. 383.
[47] In 1068, for example, the inhabitants of the castellany of Barberà were likewise assigned charges in *quarters*: quarters of pigs? (ibid., no. 405).

of lodging. It is nevertheless possible that they represented a vestige of the ancient *censum* [tax], received directly by the public power, and collected from everyone by the *vicarii*.

Levies of a Paramilitary Character

If peasants were required less and less to take up arms in warring expeditions, host service continued no less to weigh on them in less noble forms. They began to be burdened by the *conductum* (*conduit*), that is, the transportation of the supplies and baggage that followed the knights.[48] The *convenientiae* written for the preparation of military campaigns always prescribed the services of donkey-drivers.[49] But these services, in turn, were converted into ordinary dues. The peasant host, "with donkeys owed or otherwise," was thus "appreciated" at Sanahuja and, once the estimation was made, the lords could collect its counterpart in kind or in cash. If in this case we are not entirely certain that the conversion had been turned into cash, it becomes certain sometime later, at Fontanet, where the peasants had to give, according to their means, between two and twelve *argencios de oste* ["army money"].[50]

But the host was not all: there were also *guaitas*, or guard services. Of vital importance during a period when settlers themselves assured the protection of the frontiers, they became obsolete from the moment that garrisons of professional warriors took their place in the castles. As early as 1040, in a castellany as exposed as Albinyana, the *guayta* was no longer anything more than a fee imposed by the castellan,[51] and later the word designated nothing other than an ordinary tax.[52]

Fogaces (loaves of bread) and *civades* (oats) complete this collection of impositions linked to military service. The first, in principle destined for the consumption of warriors on campaign, had long been collected as a tax by both counts and bishops: the barons of the eleventh century did little more than to generalize their collection.[53] The second, however, is an innovation linked to the growth of the cavalry's needs. Its diffusion was extremely quick: almost everywhere, peasants were constrained to cultivate a piece of land with oats for the castle.[54] The word *civada* itself came to designate a unit of taxation (a *sextarius*, two

[48] On the meaning of *conductum* in Catalonia, see E. Rodón Binué, *El lenguaje técnico del feudalismo en el siglo XI en Cataluña* (Contribución al estudio del latín medieval) (Barcelona, 1957), pp. 64–5. See also *Gloss. mediae lat. Cataloniae*, cols 632–3. In all cases inventoried, the word means "food, victuals, campaign provisions."

[49] E.g. Archivo de la Corona de Aragón, perg, R. Ber. I, no. 105: "*et Bernardus donet ad hoc asinos et asinarios qui portent cibaria et conred predicto Reimundo et eius cavalariis atque cavallis*" ["and Bernard gives for this purpose his donkeys and their drivers, who carry food and provisions to Reimundo and his knights and their horses"] (1049).

[50] An undated document (from the end of the eleventh century), published by J. Miret i Sans, "Documents en langue catalane (haute vallée du Sègre, XIe–XIIe siècles)," *Revue hispanique* 19 (1908): 13–15.

[51] Rius Serra, ed., *Cart. S. Cugat*, vol. II, no. 553.

[52] Archivo de la Corona de Aragón, perg. nos 204 (1057), 405 (1068); Miquel Rosell, ed., *Liber Feudorum*, vol. I, no. 232 (1067). See also Rodón Binué, *El lenguaje técnico*, p. 127.

[53] As early as 839, the parishioners of the diocese of Urgel were subjected to dues in loaves of bread (Archivo Capitular Urgel, Cart. I, no. 15). For a typical example of how *fogaces* became ordinary rents in the eleventh century, see Archivo de la Corona de Aragón, perg. R. Ber. I, no. 30 (1039).

[54] Ibid. (1039); Soler, ed., *Cart. Tabernoles*, no. 55 (1049); Archivo Capitular Urgel, Cart. I, no. 101 (1062); Miquel Rosell, ed., *Liber Feudorum*, vol. I, no. 111 (1066); Archivo de la Corona de Aragón, perg. R. Ber. I, nos 383 (1067), 405 (1068), 438 (1071), etc., but see also the act relative to Sanahuja, pp. 575–6.

sextarii, a muid, according to the region) of almost universal character: "I commend to you this castle, and I give to you one *civada* from every man."[55]

But obligations of a military kind also imply, naturally, labor services. Men who lived in the castle's shadow had always been obliged to participate in the maintenance of its defenses, in their rebuilding, or in the construction of new protective fortifications. Within the framework of the seigneury, this duty remained just as imperious, but new constraints were added. If peasants were accustomed to working on the keep or on the ramparts, why should the castellan deprive himself of their labour in constructing the *solarios* [houses] that he installed at the foot of the walls, and similarly, why shouldn't he have them maintain (for free) all the other buildings he possessed in the castellany? "The men of Sanahuja must work for the bishop in constructing his houses," decreed Guillem Guifred.[56]

But the lord did not stop on such a pleasant route. While he was making the rustics work, it was also profitable to use them in the fields: "and do 'castle-guard' there with one man and a pair of oxen," Berenguer d'Almenara enjoined on the settlers of Vallvert in 1039.[57] Thus the peasant *estage* – service of the watch or of guard formerly owed by soldier–settlers – was transformed into labor services. Continually extended, cleverly manipulated by the masters of the ban, the military service of free men led eventually to the corvée [see below, p. 128].

Levies of a Judicial Nature

Placitos, iusticias: these words, from now on almost always used in the plural, were charged with new meanings. As early as 1040, they designated the revenues which the lord received on account of his *districtum*.[58] Were the two terms synonymous? It is difficult to be sure: understood by all, they never merited explanations on the part of scribes, who simply included them without commentary in the lists of various rights linked to the possession of fortresses. Since *placitos* constituted, without any doubt, the direct profits gained from trials, we can perhaps see in *iusticias* the fees of less occasional character which the castellan levied on the inhabitants of his jurisdiction as payment for his judicial functions.

However we look at it, one of the lord's principal privileges was to receive in his hand the *estacaments*, that is to say the deposits paid by litigants at the opening of litigation. This was truly a monopoly, sometimes given the first place in the list of seigneurial powers: "we give you the castle of Taiad . . . with its *estacaments* and its *mandamenta* and *districtum* and *seniorivum*."[59]

We can understand the lords' considerable attachment to this right: it placed the castellan in a position of strength *vis-à-vis* the peasants whom he called, often against their will, before his tribunal. Once he had received their deposits, he was able to determine in complete tranquillity the sum total of the *placitos* he would impose.

These varied according to the cases being judged. Very early on, it became customary to distinguish between *placitos minores* and *placitos maximos*. The former were simple fines,

[55] "*commendo tibi ipsum castrum et dono tibi de unoquoque ominem I civada.*" Archivo de la Corona de Aragón, perg. R. Ber. I, no. 438 (1071).
[56] See above, p. 115.
[57] "*et faciatis statica inde de I omo cum I parelio de bovis.*" Archivo de la Corona de Aragón, perg. R. Ber. I, no. 30.
[58] Rius Serra, ed., *Cart. S. Cugat*, vol. II, no. 30.
[59] "*donamus vobis ipso puig de Taiad . . . , cum ipsis estachamentis et mandamentum et districtum et seniorivum.*" Archivo Histórico Nacional (Madrid), Clero, perg. Poblet, carp. 1993, no. 11 (original), nos 9, 10 (copies): 1079.

inflicted by the lord on those whom he judged guilty of "bad conduct," either toward the lord himself or in their relations among themselves.[60] They were based on the right of correction: it is thus that we can understand the expression *"placitos et rexiones"* which sometimes designates them.[61]

"Major pleas" were, on the contrary, those which involved the confiscation of the property of the condemned. The high profits which these promised placed them in a particular category (later known as "high justice")[62] and called for special clauses in the contracts of the castle guardian. From the beginning of the eleventh century, these documents classify these pleas under three rubrics: *omicidios, cugacias,* and *arsinas.* The first term [homicide] requires no commentary. The second indicates adultery by a wife, or more precisely, the cuckolding of a husband. The sums resulting from these crimes figure prominently among the revenues of castellans from before 1060.[63] The word *arsina,* however, does not appear in the written documentation until 1071, but as of this date, it appears constantly, always linked with the two other terms.[64] Thus, like these two others, it designates a major crime, and consequently, the profits to be realized by the lord by its repression. *Arsina* (etymology: *ardere/arsus,* to burn) must have been, at its beginning, voluntary arson, but from its earliest appearance, the term indicates any kind of fire whatsoever. What is remarkable is that the indemnification due by the arsonist was immediately charged to the victim: the peasant who allowed his house to be burned was punished for his negligence and for the disturbance of public order which it had caused – and no doubt so that the lord could avoid the trouble of any further inquiry.[65]

The line between the arbitary levy of public rents and pure and simple exaction was extremely fine. It was thus all the more easily crossed by the masters of the ban.

Seigneurial Piracy

Usus, exactiones: from 1010 on these terms appear occasionally in Catalan acts.[66] By 1040–50, they have entered into everyday language to designate the body of new rents that began to fall upon the peasant class in this period. Towards the middle of the century, these two

---

[60] Archivo de la Corona de Aragón, perg. R. Ber. I, no. 204: *"terciam partem de placitis que per directum abuerit de vilanis de malas facturas que fecerint inter* se" ["the third part of the *placitos* which he had by right from the villeins because of the bad things that they did among themselves"] (1057).

[61] Archivo de la Corona de Aragón, perg. R. Ber. I, no. 438 (1071); Archivo Histórico Nacional, Clero, perg. Poblet, carp. 1993, no. 11 (1079).

[62] High justice, and not blood justice: the guilty man was not condemned to death, but constrained – which was much more profitable – to work the rest of his life in the lord's service for free, or, if the lord consented, in the service of the family of the victim.

[63] In the act of infeudation of the castle of Forès, erroneously dated to 1038, in reality from 1058 (Miquel Rosell, ed., *Liber Feudorum,* vol. I, no. 257 and Font Rius, ed., *Cartas de población,* vol. I, no. 20). See also Archivo de la Corona de Aragón, perg. R. Ber. I, no. 405 (1068) and B. Alart, *Cartulaire roussillonnais* (Perpignan, 1880), pp. 28–9 (forged act dated 976, but in all likelihood written in the middle of the eleventh century).

[64] E. Baluze, ed., *Marca hispanica* (Paris, 1688), app. 281 (1071); Miquel Rosell, ed., *Liber Feudorum,* vol. I, nos 73 (1079), 75 (1080). The mention of *arsinas* in a document of 968, published by B. Alart, *Cartulaire roussillonnais,* p. 22, is the result of an interpolation.

[65] On *arsina* as one of the "bad customs," see [Bonnassie, *La Catalogne,*] ch. XV, p. 826. See also Hinojosa, *El regimen señorial,* pp. 240–1 and W. Piskorski, *El problema de la significación y del origen de los seis "malos usos" en Cataluña* (Barcelona, 1929), pp. 36ff.

[66] Archivo Capitular Urgel, Cart. I, no. 613 (1010).

[words] tended to disappear behind another word with the same meaning, but rather more concrete: *forcias*.[67] *Forçar* (*forcare*) means to extort by violence, and *forcias* were the gains thus acquired. [68] They were of multiple nature.

Toltes, Questes, Tailles

Toltes and *questes* represent the levies made directly by the master of the keep and his agents on the food reserves of the castellany's inhabitants. The percentages seem to have been more or less proportional to the resources of each head of family. Thus, in Mediona in 1057, the lord assessed each peasant one *hemina* of wine for each *modiata* of vineyard;[69] in Sanahuja, before taking the *compra* (another name for the *tolte*) of the bishop, the bailiffs estimated the barrels in all the cellars of the village.[70] The nature of the requisitioned products varied according to the region, and very probably according to the needs and the humor of the master: here, wine and meat (that is to say, dried quarters of pork and of mutton), there only wine, elsewhere again, wheat and straw.[71] As to the frequency of the levies: in the beginning, they obeyed only the lord's whim, which was moved to demand requisitions (*appellationes*, *acclaments*) every time the situation allowed it.[72] It appears, however, that fairly quickly such *toltes* and *questes* became annual: in any case, such was the case at Mediona and Sanahuja.

The *taille* was in part similar to these exactions, even though the word (*talla* or *taig*) – always used in Catalonia in its most precise sense – designated rather the right of the lord or his agents to cut wood on peasant lands as they saw fit.[73] Thus understood, the *talla* is normally associated with the *erbaticum*, which gave the lord the power to pasture his horses and his livestock on all the fields located within his castellany, or to demand fees in hay.[74]

---

[67] Archivo Capitular Gerona, Llibre verd, fo. 182 vo (1062); Archivo de la Corona de Aragón, perg. R. Ber. I, no. 278 (1062); Miquel Rosell, ed., *Liber Feudorum*, vol. II, no. 499 (1073–8). All these documents, which are acts of restitution, refer to a period prior to their actual composition. See also Rodón Binué, *El lenguaje técnico*, pp. 121–2.

[68.67bis] *Exactiones, toltas, forcias*: what is the origin of these very pejorative words which appear in themselves to reprove the very practices to which they refer? We encounter them in three kinds of documents: in plea notices (or arbitration), quitclaims, and *convenientiae*. In the first case, they were used by clerics who thus denounced the abuses committed by castellans against peasants on ecclesiastical estates. In the second case, we find them in the mouths of lay lords who accused themselves of violence against tenants of church properties, and who renounced the claims that they had attempted to make against them. Finally, in the *convenientiae* (but the case is much less frequent), they were used, not without cynicism, by the masters of the ban themselves to describe their own demands. *Exactio* was a learned term, and therefore not very significant. *Forcias* and *toltas*, on the other hand, were popular terms: they prove that peasants were fully aware of the unfair, or more precisely, illegal (might over right), character of these new customs which were imposed upon them. As they passed into everyday language (as the only words able to describe these new realities), they were adopted, seemingly with little reticence, by clerics and lay lords (see especially Archivo de la Corona de Aragón, perg. R. Ber. I, no. 278: example discussed [in Bonnassie, *La Catalogne*,] pp. 598–9).

[69.68] Archivo de la Corona de Aragón, perg. R. Ber. I, no. 204.

[70.69] See [Bonnassie, *La Catalogne*,] p. 575.

[71.70] Archivo Capitular Barcelona, Divers C-b, perg. no. 332 (1058); Archivo de la Corona de Aragón, perg. R. Ber. I, no. 204 (1057); and see also [Bonnassie, *La Catalogne*,] pp. 575–6.

[72.70bis] Archivo Capitular Gerona, Llibre verd, fo. 182–vo 183 (1062).

[73.71] Archivo Capitular Barcelona, Divers C-b, perg. no. 332 (1058); Archivo Histórico Nacional, Clero, perg. Poblet, carp. 1996, no. 7 (1121).

[74.72] Archivo Capitular Barcelona, Divers C-b, perg. no. 332 (1058).

Acaptes *and Other Usages*

To these regular revenues for the holder of the *mandamentum* were added casual profits, generally designated by the name *acaptes*. The meaning of the word (*acaptum, acaptos, acaptes*, from the verb *accaptare*: to take, obtain) is very large and was applied to many different objects.[75] In the specific sense of "seigneurial tribute," it is usually associated with the words *tolta* and *forcia*, which it complemented.[76]

We are far from knowing all the pretexts which could give rise to a levy of *acaptes*: the arrival of new inhabitants to the castellany is one example,[77] and it even seems that the families of immigrants remained subject to this tax long after they were settled.[78] But more than exceptional cases were involved: all of the peasants dependent on the fortress had, on various occasions, to give *acaptes*. In certain cases, *acaptes* – known also as usages (*usaticos*) – took particular forms, which it is important to note carefully, since they became widely diffused later in medieval Catalonia.

Most important were the rights which the castellans gave themselves over marriages contracted between peasant men and women in their seigneury. This could be the power to choose a husband or a wife; it certainly included the power of "presenting" the future spouses to each other, and this right of presentation gave rise to the levying of a fee. This custom (*presentalias de ipsos aut ipsas qui duxerint maritos aut uxores* [presenting to one another those who take husbands or wives]) was already solidly established at Aramprunyà in 1067.[79]

Death also aroused the greed of the great. Despite legal proscriptions, the lords gave to themselves a certain share in the inheritances of their subjects. In which cases it is unfortunately impossible to know, and doubtless in the middle of the eleventh century there was as yet no clear rule established. But the profits gathered from *causas lexivas* appeared before 1060, seized by powerful masters; such profits would only grow in the future.[80]

Finally, the last of the *acaptes* which it is possible to identify: *trobas*. Theoretically, this referred to shipwrecks. But we find this usage in 1068 in the castellany of Barberà, located considerably inland.[81] Therefore, it must refer to whatever has been found, or more exactly, considered to have been "found", and which the lord saw fit to appropriate by virtue of the power of the ban.

Banal Corvées

The peasants living on the territory of a *castrum* also owed services. Many of these were derived clearly from the ancient public obligations that weighed upon free men. There was,

---

[75.73] On the different meanings of *acapte* in Catalonia, see Bassols de Clement and Bastardas Perera, *Gloss. mediae lat. Cataloniae*, cols 11–15.

[76.74] Archivo Capitular Gerona, Llibre verd, fo. 182–vo 183: "*acaptes et adempraments et toltas*" (1062); Monsalvatje y Fossas, *Noticias históricas*, vol. XI, no. 326: "*acaptes et toltes*" (1066); Archivo Capitular Barcelona, Lib. Ant. III, no. 222: "*neque forcia neque tolta, neque acapte*" (1068); Miquel Rosell, ed., *Liber Feudorum*, vol. II, no. 499: "*acaptes et usadges et toltes et forcias*" (1073/1078).

[77.75] Archivo de la Corona de Aragón, perg. R. Ber. I, no. 30 (1039).

[78.76] Archivo Histórico Nacional, Clero, perg. Poblet, carp. 1993, no. 5: donation of the *acapte* of two men in the castellany of Talladell: "*donamus vobis II sortes de vinea . . . asi com la acapte de Geral de Graiena, en Gombal l'acapta den Selvan*" ["we give to you two shares of vineyard . . . along with the *acapte* of Geral de Graiena and at Gombal the *acapte* of Selvan"] (1063).

[79.77] Archivo de la Corona de Aragón, perg. R. Ber. I, no. 383.

[80.78] Rius Serra, ed., *Cart. S. Cugat*, nos 599 (before 1053), 612 (1058); Archivo de la Corona de Aragón, perg. R. Ber. I, no. 383 (1067). For later references, see [Bonnassie, *La Catalogne*,] ch. XV, p. 826.

[81.79] Archivo de la Corona de Aragón, perg. R. Ber. I, no. 405.

for example, the duty to carry the messages of the castellan wherever he might require.[82] The same was true of the *tragins*, transport services, which any owner of a donkey or a mule owed to the lord on his request.[83]

The corvée posed other problems. While it was almost entirely unknown in Catalonia in the Early Middle Ages, it was introduced in the eleventh century under the castellans. The first reference to it appears in 1039: the allodists of Vallvert were obliged to provide a *iova* – one day of labour per year, for each one of them – on the *dominicatura* of the castle.[84] Thirty years later (in 1068), the custom appears to have been in common use, at least in western Catalonia: in the act of infeudation of the donjon of Barberà, the *iovas* appear naturally in the list of rights that the castellan possessed over the inhabitants.[85] Thereafter, for the next few centuries, they continued to appear regularly among the burdens weighing on the Catalan peasantry.[86] The origin of these corvées is complex. It is clear that they were in some way a replacement for the peasant host, as in many other areas of the West.[87] The simple fact that they were always mentioned beside the *tragins*, the *guaitas*, the *civadas*, and other paramilitary burdens is a very clear indication. But they were not only that: in Vallvert, for example, there was a distinction made between the *iova* and the *statica*, also a corvée of labour, but one issued more directly from a warring obligation. We need to keep looking for a complementary explanation.

The word *iova* (from *iou*, yoke) provides one clue. These new banal corvées were owed only by peasants who owned teams. Therefore, we are dealing with burdens that struck at the organization of labor. It appears that the lords, ever attentive to perfecting agricultural techniques, modified their demands depending on the technical equipment that their various subjects possessed. In Sanahuja, for example, the bishop imposed higher *toltes* on the *iuvers* (those who possessed a team) than on the *coniunters* (those who shared a team with others), and these were taxed more highly than the *exaders* (those who worked only with a hoe). What was true for taxes in kind was also true for fees paid in labor. The castellan was indifferent to those mediocre services which those who worked with their hands could provide, but was rather more interested in the regular and heavy labor he could extract from those peasants who had their own draft animals. In this sense, banal corvées appear as a product of technical progress, and as one of the ways in which the masters of power seized its benefits.[88]

Banalités

We must look at the *banalités* properly speaking from the same point of view, since their principal object was to ensure the lord's control over the transformation (and therefore the worth) of agricultural production. They imply a direct seizure on his part of the technical infrastructures of the castellany.

[82.80] See [Bonnassie, *La Catalogne*,] p. 576.
[83.81] Archivo de la Corona de Aragón, perg. R. Ber. I, nos 405, 438; Soler, ed., *Cart. Tabernoles*, no. 40.
[84.82] Archivo de la Corona de Aragón, perg. R. Ber. I, no. 30.
[85.83] Archivo de la Corona de Aragón, perg. R. Ber. I, no. 405.
[86.84] On the history of the *iova* in Catalonia, see Hinojosa, *El regimen señorial*, pp. 188ff.; J. A. Brutails, *Etude sur la condition des populations rurales du Roussillon au Moyen âge* (Paris, 1891), pp. 165–7. These two authors provide references primarily from the thirteenth century.
[87.85] See [Bonnassie, *La Catalogne*,] pp. 587–8. For a look at the wider picture, see Duby, *L'économie rurale*, vol. II, pp. 427–8, 452–3.
[88.86] This idea was a hypothesis of Duby, *L'économie rurale*, vol. II, p. 428, which has been abundantly confirmed for Catalonia.

Their appearance seems to have been slightly later than that of the other banal exactions. It is in 1067 and 1068 that we find the first dated references: since these refer to an already existing situation, we can imagine that the first *banalités* were imposed toward the middle of the century.

In 1067, mention was made of a castral grain barn in Aramprunyà, with the fees associated with its use.[89] If we can believe this single witness, the lords had perhaps tried to impose their control over the storage of all the grain produced in the castellany. The experiment failed, perhaps because of the organizational difficulties involved, but also doubtless because the peasants resisted giving up their sacks of grain.

Whether stored on the farm or in the castle, however, the barley and the wheat were obliged eventually to pass through the mill: hence, the lords were determined to establish their monopolies on milling. The moment was propitious: the now very old *molinos* or *molendinos* [mills] which had been built by the settler communities were beginning to fall into ruin; also, many of the shares (that is to say, days and nights of milling) which had belonged to former co-proprietors had already fallen into the hands of the powerful. Finally and most especially, these old mills were outdated establishments which could no longer fulfill the needs of the community and could hardly compete with the *mulnares* [mills] that the lords began to build.

In spite of all this, if we read the Sanahuja inventory carefully, we realize that the lords still had to use force to compel the peasants, and they were only able to impose their monopolies step by step. The first step was doubtless to grant themselves the privilege of milling their own grain for free in all the mills of the castellany (it is thus that we must in all likelihood understand the right to mill, or *dextre mugar*). The second step was to establish a general fee on the milling of grain, whether it was done in their own mills or (and here is where the privilege passes ordinary limits) in the mills which did not belong to them. This stage of the evolution was reached in approximately 1040–75. The rest is easy to foresee: the "allodial mills," which were subjected to the same fees as the seigneurial *mulnares*, but which were technologically inferior, could not possibly compete. Eventually, this situation turned into a monopoly by right.

A similar path was taken concerning ovens and forges. At Aramprunyà, Mir Géribert established a *ferreria* (forge) near the parish church, and Bishop Guillem Guifred owned a *furnum* (oven) in Sanahuja. Already between 1050 and 1070, these were bringing in appreciable profits.[90] In order to increase these profits further, it sufficed for the lords to impose a general fee on the fabrication and maintenance of iron instruments and on the baking of bread: the first mention of *loced* or *locidum* (*llosar*: to sharpen/grind) is from 1074; that of *furnaticum* follows shortly.[91]

The Seigneurial Regime

The revenues which the lord was able to extract from his power of command were therefore numerous and varied. New names for them abound, covering a vast array of rights and usages, sometimes dissimilar, sometimes closer in meaning, always entangled. Not all were

[89.87] Archivo de la Corona de Aragón, perg. R. Ber. I, no. 383.
[90.88] Because they were the object of a precise sharing-out between the castellans and their *castlans* (ibid., and see [Bonnassie, *La Catalogne*,] pp. 602, 605).
[91.89] On these two levies, see the interesting observations of J. Balari Jovany, *Orígens históricos de Cataluña*, 2nd ed. (Sant Cugat del Vallès, 1964), vol. II, pp. 551–3.

equally profitable. We must recognize in particular that the labor services demanded of the [Catalonian] peasants were never particularly heavy: a few days of work per year, some transport services. Nothing there could possibly compare with the exhausting corvées to which many of the peasants of northern France had been subject for centuries. All together, however, the banal seigneury assured its holders a rather considerable sum of benefits, entirely out of measure with the mediocre profits that the powerful men of the tenth or eleventh centuries were able to extract from their land alone.

The riches that they appropriated also allowed the castellans to maintain a numerous and efficient staff in their territory, whose sole function was to maintain and to increase the volume of rents demanded of the peasants. Certainly at first, around 1030 or 1040, the demands appear to have been made in a rather anarchic fashion by poorly organized bands. But from 1060 on, the banal seigneury came to be a well-structured institution, nicely adapted to its goals (the confiscation of all the surplus derived from working the land), and perfectly functional.[92]

Agents and Methods of Seigneurial Oppression

Most lords did not govern their castellanies directly. They only commanded the garrisons lodged in their fortresses in person when the hazards of war, or other grave circumstances, required them. Generally, they were satisfied to come to live for a few days or a few weeks at a time in the keep, or more often, in the residences that they had had constructed in the neighborhood. This gave them a simple opportunity to survey the management of their agents. Outside of these brief periods, it was these agents, the bailiffs and the castlans, who were the true masters of power within the seigneury.

Exploitation of the Seigneury: the Bailiffs
The institution of *baylies* [bailiffs' districts] was an ancient one. Around the year 1000 – and without a doubt, long before – certain very great landowners confided the administration of a part of their patrimony to bailiffs. In this sense, the *baiulus* appears primarily to have been an agent for the estate, charged with watching over the regular payment of the taxes owed by the tenants. On fiscal lands, he might also collect fees of a public character. But these bailiffs were few, and were seen only on the immense estates of counts and churches.[93]

[92.89bis] These remarks should not be construed as an *a priori* indictment of the seigneurial regime: they are, in fact, directly inspired by reading the charters. The strongest impression (and doubtless also the most moving) that one has after perusing the thousands of documents that survive from the ninth, tenth, and the beginning of the eleventh centuries, is that of continuous, unremitting peasant labor, frequently accomplished under inhumane material conditions. The labor of these pioneers was orderly, that is to say, it operated within the framework of rules that village communities established themselves, under the strict surveillance of comital power. But at the very moment when the most difficult work had been accomplished, and when their labor began to bear fruit (and when exterior dangers had disappeared), that is to say, at the very moment when the peasant class might have hoped for a certain security of existence, it was then that they began to fall into the snares of the seigneurial system and were condemned to lose, not only the fruits of their labor, but also their freedom. We might say that the existence of a free and dynamic peasantry was an anachronism in the year 1000, and that its survival after 1050 was an absurdity; we can even state that the seigneurial regime was necessary so that growth could get its second wind. But isn't this exactly the *a priori* position that it would be best to avoid?

[93.90] There is a reference to this kind of bailiff in the testament of Ermengol I of Urgel in 1010: "*de baiulia de Isarno sunt porcos centum*" (Baluze, ed., *Marca hispanica*, app. 162).

In the eleventh century, the diversification of sources of revenue, along with the increasingly frequent absenteeism of the castellans, meant that bailiffs were instituted on even the most modest of seigneuries. The process of infeudation [granting out as fiefs] of the fortresses multiplied them even further across the heart of each castellany, since each holder of the ban believed it necessary to be represented on site by someone in whom he had confidence. In Sanahuja, the bishop had his bailiff, while his *fideles* – the *seniores* of the castle – had theirs.

These men retained their domainal administrative functions. It was particularly their job to direct the cultivation of the *dominicaturas* which the castellan had reserved for himself on the ancient *terras de feo* which surrounded his fortress, to make the prebendaries [tenants] and the *boves dominicos* [the lord's oxen] of the castle[94] work on them, and to watch over the corvées owed by the neighboring allodists. It was also their job to make sure the tenants didn't cheat their masters in paying the *tasque*, the *braçatge*, and other taxes based on a share of the crop.

But the bailiffs were now also very closely associated with the exploitation of the ban: they were the ones who set the level of fees that might be imposed on each of the heads of household in the castellany, they fixed limits which might not be passed in portioning out exactions, they kept the accounts of the *questes*, the *toltes*, and the *acaptes*, they sought out the services of laborers or of donkey-drivers. In short, they were both the controllers and the receivers of all the new impositions.[95]

Frequently, they also dispensed justice. Paradoxically, it was high justice which fell to their lot most frequently. This can be easily explained: they had to judge the cases which the castellans had reserved for themselves in the contracts of fortress-guard, that is to say, all the cases which involved paying the *placitos maximos* by those judged. Thus, during the long absences of the master, homicides, *cugucias*, and *arsinas* were judged by the bailiff.[96] The bailiff was thus both the personal representative of the lord and also the individual responsible for the economic exploitation of the seigneury. In this last function, he harvested the fruits sown by the *castlans* and the *cabalers*.

Agents of Repression: Castlans *and* Cabalers

Banal profits were the product of constraint: they would have been negligible were this constraint not exercised in a systematic and permanent fashion. This obvious fact (and there are some obvious facts which bear reemphasizing) brings us to reexamine, from a different perspective, the role allotted to the fortress garrisons.

It was the *castlans'* and the *cabalers'* job to defend the keep in which they were lodged and the territory which depended on it.[97] But this important mission only occupied them occasionally, when the enemy threatened. Was it truly their primary function? Let us listen to Geribert de Gelida dictate his instructions to his *castlà* Mir Onofred in 1062: "and on his estate Mir should not exact *tolta* or *forcia* except those which a *castlà* ought to do in his *kastlania*."[98]

[94.90bis] Rius Serra, ed., *Cart. S. Cugat*, vol. II, no. 553 (1040).

[95.91] Besides the text relating to Sanahuja, see Rius Serra, ed., *Cart. S. Cugat*, vol. II, no. 612, "*Baiulos autem prefati abbatis*" (1058), and Archivo de la Corona de Aragón, perg. R. Ber. I, no. 405 (1068).

[96.92] Miquel Rosell, ed., *Liber Feudorum*, vol. I, no. 232 (1067); Archivo de la Corona de Aragón, perg. R. Ber. I, no. 405 (1068).

[97.93] On this function, see [Bonnassie, *La Catalogne*,] ch. IX, pp. 571–3.

[98.94] *et que Miro in ipsa honore non facieat tolta nec forcia nisi talem qualem debet facere kastla in sua kastlania.*" Archivo de la Corona de Aragón, perg. R. Ber. I, no. 278 (1062).

Before anything else, the *castlà's* job was to force (*forcare*) peasants, that is to say, to prepare them to submit to banal exactions by subjecting them to a regime of measured terror. Judiciously conditioned, they would pose no further resistance to the requisitions which the bailiffs might seek from them in complete contempt of their status as free men. And if they did resist, repression rained down. The documents are actually very discreet about the means of this repression, and mention physical violence used against the rustics only when this violence mistook its target, that is to say, when the *castlans* and the *cabalers* set on men who did not belong to the castle which they were guarding. Thus we learn by accident that in 1057, the *milites* of the keep of Figols "seriously wounded without cause" two peasants who worked for the abbey of Bagà, or that in 1062, Guillem Bernard of Odena cut off the foot of a man of Sant Cugat: these affairs had judiciary consequences only because the two monasteries [involved] considered themselves wronged in their own patrimony, and through the voice of their abbots, sought reparation.[99] But when the victims were indeed subject to the castle, there was only silence.

Seigneurial terrorism did have its limits, which even the *castlans* knew not to pass. Excessively weakening the peasantry would have been absurd; the peasantry was the productive force on which the riches of the great were founded. It was sufficient to keep it in fear and submission. For that, actual force was not always needed; hence the importance of the "cavalcade," the almost daily rounds imposed on the castle garrison.[100] These continual rounds through the fields and the scrublands of the castellany commanded respect from the peasants, who knew they were permanently watched by the knights of the donjon. Were additional means of intimidation necessary? The right of *albergum* provided all possible reasons to bring a recalcitrant allodist to his senses: he would hasten to deliver his "gifts" to the castle himself, rather than run the risk of whatever reprisals the unruly soldiers might inflict upon his home.

Castlans and *cabalers* were indeed the worker bees of the banal seigneury. It made sense that they should see their share of its profits.

[. . .]

Conclusion

In the ninth and tenth centuries, the Catalan peasants had suffered greatly: fear and misery were their most faithful companions. But at least they were free. At the very moment when danger retreated and when economic progress began to bear its fruits, they lost that freedom. And the subjections to which they were increasingly constrained brought them neither peace nor ease.

In fact, we cannot look on banal lordship in Catalonia as an institution of peace without laughing. Before it began, order reigned: the authority of the counts, respect for Gothic law, the prestige of public tribunals, and the self-discipline which village communities imposed upon themselves were the pillars of public order. Certainly, after 1020–30, violence was unleashed, but it was the work of the very ones who fully intended to be rewarded for supposedly fighting against it. Disorder came from on high, and repression fell on those who were its victims.

[99.95] Archivo de la Corona de Aragón, Monacales, perg. Bagà, no. 265, and Rius Serra, ed., *Cart. S. Cugat*, vol. II, no. 627.
[100.96] See [Bonnassie, *La Catalogne*,] ch. IX, p. 573.

Additionally, the imposition of banal obligations dealt the death blow to the process of the betterment of the peasant condition which had been so clearly visible at the end of the tenth and at the beginning of the eleventh centuries (in particular, in the increasingly frequent sales of agricultural products in which small and mid-sized allodists were engaging). Growth of production no longer profited the peasants, who, after countless exactions, *toltes*, and other *acaptes*, were left only the bare minimum for survival. That part of the surplus which was not swallowed up by demographic expansion – in particular, by the consumption of the towns – was confiscated by those in authority. It took only a single year of bad harvests (such as, apparently, the year 1053), and the peasants once again knew the pangs of famine.[101]

On the other hand, the banal requisitions assured the prosperity of an idle class, which grew rapidly. The old noble lineages were not the only ones to live off peasant labour: to exploit their seigneuries, they surrounded themselves with a crowd of auxiliaries – *castlans*, *cabalers*, bailiffs – whose healthy appetites they had to satisfy with a share in the banal booty. As the weight of this parasitical corps grew, both the requisitions and their necessary constraints became heavier. At the same time, the solidarity which tied those who profited from the ban to each other was reinforced, and gave birth to a tight network of relations between one man and another.

The rapid and precocious development of the Catalan economy shook power relations at the heart of society, even before 1060. It also menaced the political balance of the country-side. Faced with an aristocracy grown rich, numerically powerful, and which had succeeded in placing the free peasantry under its yoke, the power of the counts weakened.

[101.115] In 1060, the woman Blanca, inhabitant of Copóns, acknowledged in her own name and in that of her children that she had received ten sacks of barley, five *quarteres* of wheat, and seven *quartes* of wine for the sale of half of a mill, a vineyard, some gardens, and a field of flax: "*et hoc totum fuit donatum in ipso anno quando fuit grande necessitas fame per totam nostram regionem*" ["and this was all given in that year when there was great famine throughout the whole region"] (Archivo de la Corona de Aragón, perg. R. Ber. I, no. 246). The year referred to might be the year 1053, or possibly 1054, in the course of which the monasteries of Sant Pol de Mar and of Ripoll complained about bad harvests (Archivo, Capitular Barcelona, Divers A, perg. no. 368f, Divers C-b, perg. no. 187).

8 The Year 1000 Without Abrupt or Radical Transformation

Dominique Barthélemy

What will decide the question of whether or not there was such a thing as "the transformation of the year 1000" is not the history of events, but an examination of the fundamental structures of the society of the time. Were the taxes of the eleventh century and the numerous *milites* [knights] the sign of a new world, or did they simply bring "the early Middle Ages" into the second millennium? Let us consider these two points.

1. Was there a "castellan crisis"[1] in the first half of the eleventh century, which provoked a dislocation of the *pagus*, and the multiplication of "bad customs"?[2]
2. Was there a corollary "social tempest"[3] which swallowed up an entire class of allod-holding peasants, and which gave rise to a lesser knightly class, composed of the servants of "seigneurial terrorism"?

[. . .]

[The following summarizes my findings: Several new castles sprang up on the periphery of the *pagus* of Vendôme in the tenth and eleventh centuries: Montoire, Lavardin, Freteval, Château-Renault. But the areas that they controlled were not very extensive and covered mainly forested areas. Thus it is incorrect to say that the castellanies dislocated the *pagus*. As for the customs (*consuetudines*) that their lords collected: they were of the same sort as those due to the count of Vendôme.]

Bad Customs: Polemic and Revelation

The file on "unjust customs" in the Vendômois is not very large. This is because the great monasteries whose archives we possess had only just been founded in the middle of the eleventh century [or had just developed their property-holdings at this time], and they had

The editors wish to thank Professor Barthélemy for reading and correcting this translation and for supplying them with some fresh material.

[1].395 We remained too attached to this expression in *L'Ordre seigneurial* (Paris, 1990), ch. 1.
[2].396 J.-F. Lemarignier tried to link these two phenomena in the regions of the Seine and the Loire: "La dislocation du *pagus* et le problème des *consuetudines* (Xe–XIe siècle)," in *Mélanges Louis Halphen* (Paris, 1951), pp. 401–10 [the *pagus* was a Roman administrative district which, Lemarignier argued, survived intact until the late tenth century].
[3].397 A. Guerreau expresses doubt in his "Lournand au Xe siècle: histoire et fiction," *Le Moyen Age* 96, 5e série, 4 (1990): 519–37.

not yet had to defend or restore their immunities[4] as St-Denis near Paris, Fleury in the Orléanais, and many others [had to do]. We have, nevertheless, just mentioned [*Vendôme* (see below, n.5), p. 327] a possible right of *vicaria* [i.e. jurisdiction and the fees that went with it] in the case of [the monastery of] St-Laumer of Blois, and we have Fulbert's letter to count Renaud,[5] as well as [Renaud's] renunciation, in 1005, of his right to shelter, and that of his huntsmen at Vauboin in the lands of [the monastery of] St-Julien of Tours in Beaumont-sur-Dême: "customs which justly or injustly he or his predecessors held in the lands in the power of St-Julien."[6] In this latter case, we need to note the relative gentleness of the tone, the reference to precedent, and finally, the absence of any ties between the comital pretension and any nearby castle (at least, any "major" castle). The problem was exactly the same for [the monastery of] La Trinité, not very far away (in the Gâtine), between 1060 and 1064: Fulk l'Oison finally did away with the "bad customs which he had earlier introduced,"[7] and took his huntsmen to task. We have also just mentioned, also nearby, the struggles of La Trinité and Marmoutier with the lords of Château-Renault: in this case they had to distinguish between "legitimate custom"[8] and "unjust attacks."[9] In reality, the mentions of bad customs are linked to the appearance of sources of a denser nature. Let us examine two obvious facts.

1. The very word and the practice of customary taxation were not new: *consuetudinaria functio* [customary exaction] was constantly mentioned in Merovingian times.[10] Even those preambles which follow the very oldest of styles – as we have seen[11] – all invoke the *lex* and the *consuetudo*, the law and custom, together, as had been done since the [ninth] century.[12] Marc Bloch's elegant pages on the role of collective memory within the seigneury[13] can be applied both before and after the year 1000. There was no upheaval of the "rules of law," even if certain periods (the second [half of the] tenth century?) may have been more favorable to "bad customs."

2. That these taxations were bad and unjust was obviously a value-judgment brought by the monks who sought to abolish them, in the purest ecclesiastical tradition: what church had not fought them, from as early as Merovingian times?[14] As A. Dumas noted as early as 1933,

---

[4.512] J.-F. Lemarignier, "De l'immunité à la seigneurie ecclésiastique. Les 'territoires coutumiers' des églises en Ile de France et dans les régions voisines d'après les diplômes des premiers Capétiens (987–1107)," in *Études d'histoire et de droit canonique dédiées à Gabriel Le Bras*, vol. I (Paris, 1965), pp. 619–30: evolution according to him, revelation according to us.

[5.513] See the *leges atriorum*, discussed [in Barthélemy, *La société dans le comté de Vendôme de l'an Mil au XIVe siècle* (Paris: Fayard, 1993),] on p. 327.

[6.514] "*consuetudines quas juste vel injuste ipse suique antecessores in terra potestatis sancti Juliani habuerant.*" *CV* 415.

[7.515] "*Malas consuetudines quas nuper induxerat.*" *TV* 174.

[8.516] "*consuetudo legitima.*" *MV* 37.

[9.517] "*injuste invasiones.*" *TV* 293 (1080).

[10.518] W. Goffart, "Old and New in Merovingian Taxation," *PP* 96 (1982): 3–21.

[11.519] J. Flach, "Le droit romain dans les chartes du IXe au XIe siècle," in *Mélanges H. Fitting* (Montpellier, 1907), vol. I, p. 403.

[12.520] On this subject, see the fundamental (but too often forgotten) article of A. Dumas, "Quelques observations sur la grande et la petite propriété à l'époque carolingienne," *Revue d'Histoire de Droit français et étranger* 4e série, 5 (1926): 213–79, 613–72 (esp. 637–41).

[13.521] *La société féodale* (Paris, 1949), p. 172 [English translation: *Feudal Society*, trans. L. A. Manyon (Chicago, 1961), pp. 113ff.].

[14.522] Thus the *exactiones publice* [public requisitions] were reputed to be "a very bad and wicked custom" ("*pessima et impia consuetudo*") due to "*ex antiqua consuetudine mala*" ["an ancient and bad

"because there is no one to give the opposing position, the picture of the feudal regime tends to be black."[15] When we read the letters of Geoffrey of Vendôme[16] carefully, as with many other acts devoted to lay seizure of church goods at the end of the century, we must be careful to give the word *violentia* its technical meaning:[17] "wrong, against the law." Use of the word was not equivalent to a denunciation of "class terrorism."[18]

We are not trying to deny violence in and of itself. The entire seigneurial order was grounded in relationships of force. However, the eleventh century should not, *a priori*, be dramatized any more than the rest of the "early Middle Ages." In reality, most of our documentation provides the negative image [stressed by] the monks: in this sense, the struggle against bad customs signifies the establishment of their privileges!

The polemic which tended in the opposite direction [. . .] certainly existed: M. Garaud cites a capitulary of 815 which denounced the way in which the counts passed off as "legal customs" taxes which they obtained by force![19]

In the Loire, [complaints] appeared in the texts of the end of the tenth century as soon as the reformed monasteries (St-Florent of Saumur, Marmoutier) began to keep their archives. They protested, demanded, and informed us about their daily problems.[20]

Did these taxes, partly ancient, and partly new, and of unequal legitimacy (as the monks sometimes describe them), have any specific ties with the castles?

Engebaud the Breton demanded a *vicaria* at Mousseau (in the Lancé)[21] and the rights of justice for major cases at Chauvigny;[22] but these claims were as tied to the local seigneury in the immediate neighborhood as to the eminent rank of this particular individual in the *curia* [court] of the Vendôme. The *commendise* of Baigneaux [its protection and the taxes for it] was created [and given to the count] because the count of Blois was a personage of the first rank, whose anger impressed the troublemakers [there]; later, it was enfeoffed [given in fief] by him to men from the aristocracy of Blois.[23]

Helgaud "the Ax" placed a *saisimentum* [requisition] on *Villa malardi* and on a wood close to Pinoche (in the Crucheray) between 1075 and 1085, and then gave it up.[24] Just because he could be found at court pleas at Château-Renault, ought we to conclude that he derived his authority from belonging to the garrison? Pinoche was awfully far away.

---

custom"] (*Vita Balthildis*, cited by B. Guérard, *Polyptyque de l'abbé Irminon*, vol. I, "Prolégomènes," p. 691).

[15.523] "Etude sur le classement des formes des actes," *Le Moyen Age* 3e série, 4 (1933): 259. Dumas also notes that neither *depredatio* nor *exactio* (a normal requisition by public power) has a pejorative connotation.

[16.524] *PL* 157, cols 37, 102, 121.

[17.525] See *SM* 116.

[18.526] Thus we can share the doubts of A. Guerreau on the so-called "social tempest" of the beginning of the eleventh century: "Lournand au Xe siècle", p. 536. The monks of the eleventh century tended to call any legality competing with their own *violentia*: whence the myths of feudal anarchy.

[19.527] [M. Garaud,] *Les Châtelains de Poitou et l'avènement du régime féodal. XIe et XIIe siècle* (Poitiers, 1967), p. 153 n. 230.

[20.528] See also [ibid.,] pp. 113–14: there is continuity from the Carolingian *functiones publice* [public taxes] to the "bad customs."

[21.529] *MV* 75.

[22.530] *MV* 129.

[23.531] *TV* 318.

[24.532] *MV* 174 (this was certainly a tax, "*quamdam consuetudinem*" ["a certain custom"], and not a confiscation).

In other cases, how was the *taxamentum* [a protection tax] of Villeberfol, which we know was held in 1061 by Robert de Moncontour and Foucher de la Tour from the count of the Vendôme,[25] established, or that of Rhodon, so close by,[26] or of Le Sentier, held by Leubert the Bastard of Château-Renault?[27] In all these cases, the tie with fortresses is neither affirmed nor denied by our sources. Nevertheless, it is tempting to think of the localized authority held by individuals like Guichard de Chazelle or Bernard de la Chapelle de Bragny, [who appear] in G. Duby's Mâconnais.[28]

In other words, the Vendômois and the neighboring regions do not bear the signs either of a dislocation of the *pagus* nor of an unprecedented proliferation of taxes. The seigneurial order continued to adjust, as it created new castles, which were neither more "private" nor less "public" than the older ones. It was brought up to date by developing new taxes to replace the old. Thus, a new generation of *consuetudines* appeared at the beginning of the twelfth century[29] and, like those of the eleventh, made some people unhappy.

Allods and the Seigneury

But how, then, can we account for the shrinking number of allods? In the first chapter [i.e., of *Vendôme*], we linked this essentially to an evolution in the "style" of the acts. Here we will develop this idea and distinguish between possible peasant allods, which would be countered by "feudalism," and incontestable knightly allods, which would be transformed into fiefs.

It is important to study the vocabulary carefully, and especially to distinguish between two "styles" of documentation. A privileged link exists between the use of the word *alodium* and what we have called the "old style": when a man or a woman wished to alienate his or her land by gift or by sale to a church, the appropriate formula (which had its root in the early Middle Ages, as we know), used the term *alodium in pago*. This "style" is extremely terse: it economizes in reporting both the concrete description of the land, as well as the title of the noble donor. This is why many historians have been able to make mistakes.[30] In the "new style," however, which is arrived at through narration and concrete detail, though the function of the act itself has not changed, the allod or allods become less frequent, more concrete, and relatively more specific.

All in all, these word-oppositions, synonyms, and their connotations are complex enough to warrant us spending a little time on them.

Allod and Fief

First of all, let us note: [allod] is not the opposite of "fief" (*"feodum"*) or "benefice" (*"beneficium"*). An example is the knight Hugh and his wife in the *Cartularium Vindocinense* of Marmoutier: they donate "from their benefices, that is to say from their lands and

---

[25.533] *MD* 126.

[26.534] *MB* 43.

[27.535] *MV* 80.

[28.536] [G. Duby,] *La Société aux XIe et XIIe siècles dans la région mâconnaise* (Paris, 1971), pp. 178–9.

[29.537] See [Barthélemy, *Vendôme*,] pp. 738–40.

[30.538] See, however, the remarkable study of C. Duhamel-Amado, "L'alleu paysan a-t-il existé en France méridionale autour de l'an Mil?," in R. Delort, dir., *La France de l'an Mil* (Paris, 1990), pp. 142–61.

churches and allods,"[31] an expression which would seem to imply an agreement to give up the lands, churches, and allods held from them in benefice. We are here talking about the most important family of the Vendômois, the Fulcherides,[32] and it was quite normal for the monasteries to require the agreement of important lords, in general and often in advance, for the gifts made by their vassals "*de suo feodo*" or "*de suo casamento*."[33] This explains why so many of the allods in this cartulary were given away without mentioning a feudal lord, since all the donors appear to have been clients of the Fulcherides. In any case, the text shows the compatibility between allod and "benefice" (a term used in the "old style" for "fief," as well as secondarily with other meanings).

In the *Grand Cartulaire* from La Trinité, we find Leudonius: at the request of Archembaud, his '*fidelis*" (in the "old style", "old words"), he authorizes [Archembaud] to sell "the allods which up to now he has held in benefice from me."[34] Then there is the noblewoman Hersende: after she had given all of her part of the allod of Montrieux, near Vendôme, she ceded "the allod which Herbert holds from her in fief in the village of Gombergean [within the boundaries of the Blésois]" and then "also an allod in Villegomblain [in the Oucques] which Tetbaldus son of Fridonis holds in fief."[35] In 1067, there are two charters (*cartule*) of acquisitions by La Trinité at Villarceau: the first states that Thierri de Faye gave "all his allods," with his wife's consent as holder of the dowry;[36] the second adds the agreement of Engebaud the Breton and his wife, "since it was held by them in benefice."[37]

Consequently, we are at once obliged to recognize the very important presence of 'feudalism," but not to oppose to it knightly allods in the way that G. Duby understands it in the Mâconnais: our eleventh century is therefore more feudal than his!

Nevertheless, the idea of the allod was not uncommonly brandished as a sign of independence [or even of feudal lordship] among the nobility. When he intervened in certain situations in the Vendômois, Lancelin II of Beaugency affirmed his right of allod: thus, at Villarceau in 1067, in addition to Engebaud's consent, Thierri de Faye needed Lancelin's as well, "whose allod this land is."[38] And in 1080, the gift of Robert de Moncontour to Coulommier was also made with the ritual participation of Lancelin: "and he has given and authorized this land just as his own allod," and his son Raoul was also present, since the land was "of the benefice of both of them."[39] Let us return to the *Cartularium Vindocinense* of Marmoutier to examine a *cartula* (series NDS). [Documents from 1060 and after begin "Nosse debebitis si," NDS, for short.] It relates that Foucois de *Banasta* sold "a certain land

---

31.539 "*de suis beneficiis videlicet terras et ecclesias atque alodos.*" *MV* 100.

32.540 See [Barthélemy, *Vendôme,*] pp. 309–11.

33.541 [Both phrases translate to "from his fief."] E.g.: *TV* 418, 485; *MV* 4, 12B, *TV* 123, 383.

34.542 "*alodos quos in beneficium de me hactenus tenere videbatur.*" [Reference missing].

35.543 "*ad villam Gomberge alodium quod tenebat ab ea in fevum Herbertus*" and "*item alodia de Villa comblen que habebat in fevum Tetbaldus filius fridonis.*" *TV* 111: these lands were dependent on a central locus of the fief near Vendôme, and were 15 to 20 kilometers away, thus at the limit of the *pagus*.

36.544 "*omnia alodia sua.*" *TV* 181.

37.545 "*de quorum beneficio.*" *TV* 185. We could also mention *TV* 383, entitled "*de medietate alodiorum Hatonis*" ["Concerning half of the allods of Hato"], and in which there is the agreement of Salomon de Freteval "*de cuius casamento ipsa terre erat*" ["of whose fief this land was"]. See also the acts of Ronceray of Angers (ed. P. Marchegay, *Archives d'Anjou* [Angers, 1854], III): the purchases of the count and the countess in about 1028 are alternately called "fiefs" (no. 1), and "allods" (no. 47).

38.546 *TV* 185 (*sic*).

39.547 "*terramque ipsam sicut alodium suum tam donavit quam auctorizavit,*" and "*de quorum utroque beneficio.*" *TV* 299.

of his allod"; thus "since, as we said, it was his allod, there was no need to seek the authorization of anyone for it except for that of his wife . . . and sons."[40] Finally, we know the importance of the monastery of La Trinité's status as "*alodium beati Petri*" ["the allod of Saint Peter"].

These statements may seem contradictory, or rather, paradoxically, it is in the "new style," after 1060, that the opposition between fief and allod seems to regain a vigor lost in the artifices of the old! It seems to us, however, that the contradiction, which is real enough to give rise to the debate, is primarily fueled by the fact that the idea of the allod is principally that of family patrimony; its rights belong to the kin. We can see this in the remarkable document from La Trinité relating to the allods of Freducia:[41] unable to be maintained by her wealthy cousin, she nevertheless had to leave her a part of her allods.[42] Therefore, if certain "allods" were really fiefs, it is because the fief was itself clearly patrimonialized; at the furthest extreme, the NDS document about Foucois de Banasta would be the echo of the position of a vassal attempting to erase the rights of his lord. It is this benefit of the feudal allod that Odo II of Blois claimed for the county of Troyes in a famous letter to King Robert;[43] and even so, we must be clear that in our body of documents [for the Vendôme] the county and castles are called *honores*,[44] never allods.

Moreover, vassalage involved a paradox to which we shall return: the vassal was simultaneously dependent and yet free, therefore noble,[45] a contradiction which required elaboration through symbolism. It is not surprising, therefore, that the same ambiguity found in the status of men should be found in land, that the allod should be a "tenure," and yet free land, indeed noble land. Feudalism was not a pure institution, but a system of tensions nicely revealed by the concretization of vocabulary.

The Allod and the Local Seigneury

Like any fief, the allod in the Vendôme could also be a seigneury over peasants: a land lordship (*seigneurie foncière*) and, as we shall see, even banal! But it was never a fiscal right conceived independently of the concrete situation.

Alodium was the synonym of *villa*, of *curtis*, and of *terra*. Very often, the allods mentioned were called "*de Villa x*" and it is possible that "*Villa x*" was the name of the land being given up. In the Gombergean, the "*alodium nomine Mansus*" is today Mézé.[46] The allod ceded to St-Laumer by Corbonita was certainly an allod before the year 1000, "with cultivated and uncultivated lands, with fields and with all the things which I have there."[47] The same formula was used for the allods of Archembaud, the *fidelis* of Leudonius: they were sold "*cum*

[40.548] "*quoniam eius, ut premisimus, erat allodium, auctoramentum alicuius super hoc queri non opus fuit, preter uxoris sue . . . ac filiorum suorum.*" *MV* 106.

[41.549] *TV* 233.

[42.550] The part which came from the ancestor in common with this cousin, the wife of Gervais, son of Lancelin.

[43.551] A letter cited by L. Halphen, "La lettre d'Eude II de Blois au roi Robert," in his *A travers l'histoire du Moyen Age* (Paris, 1950), pp. 241–50. [See *The Letters and Poems of Fulbert of Chartres*, ed. and trans. Frederick Behrends, Oxford: Clarendon Press, 1976, no. 86, pp. 152–4.]

[44.552] See [Barthélemy, *Vendôme,*] pp. 559–60.

[45.553] [Ibid.,] p. 508.

[46.554] *MV* 112.

[47.555] "*cum terris cultis et incultis, cum pratis et cum omni re que ibi visus (sic,* though it is a woman) *sum habere.*" Loire-et-Cher Archives départementales, 11 H 128, p. 7.22.

omni justa et legitima integritate" ["wholly and justly"], and "*cum adjacentiis sibi terris atque debitis*"[48] ("adjacent tenures and rents"). The proximity of the words *ecclesia* and *alodium*[49] reminds us strongly of "*ecclesia et curtis*"; we know that a church was often the center of an estate, and that its parish rights strongly resembled bans!

We must therefore envisage the allod as a "reserve" in the context of an authentic land lordship, and we must describe its functioning by referring to the "demesne" of the early Middle Ages. We must remember, with R. Boutruche, that the demesne was the "seat of power,"[50] and we must therefore recognize that the most important allods had all the prerogatives of the "local seigneury" whose picture we must paint in the long eleventh century [*c.*980–1160] in order to contrast it with the period of the "new lords" (of the thirteenth century).

When the *Cartularium Vindocinense* passes to the NDS series, there is a veritable revelation. On one hand there are the laconic *cartule* of the old style; such-and-such a donor, for a certain allod, in a particular *villa*: this is the case for the allod in the *villa* of Claireau, in St-Amand.[51] On the other hand, in the same parish, there is the allod of Rigny, documented by an NDS *cartula*.[52] We learn considerably more here. First, we learn that it was divided between the donor Renard and Germain de Lavardin, who held part of it "*in fevum*" [in fief]; this recalls the lands of Villarceau (1067),[53] and reminds us that the donor of "his own allod" cedes only his own rights over it, without prejudice to any possible infeudations or sharings-out. Then, we learn what the borders are, and that he owes no customs except the tithe. Finally come the privileges. The first is judicial: even for causes that require the duel or the ordeal, the only judge of the inhabitants is the "lord and owner of the allod" ("*dominus et possessor alodii*"); he is recognized as "himself the authority and judge of wrongdoing, of whatever kind it may be, and demands the compensation required by law": in other words, we have here what the thirteenth century would call "*grosse voyrie*," and the only hesitation is over the posssibility that some justice was held back[54] (it would have been comital) since the donor, the seneschal of Chalonnes in the Anjou, was such an important person. Implicitly, this formulation reveals that in other allods there were commonly rights of justice for [cases worth] less than 60 *solidi*, or without the duel or ordeal (these being the most serious *leges*), that is to say, even including the oath! The second privilege belonged to the inhabitants themselves (*incole*), and concerned a neighboring forest (Champars, in the Ambloy): they had the right to take wood "for their own uses" ("*in usus proprios*") and even to construct dwellings with the consent of the foresters. This is a "franchise," a "usage from Gâtine" mentioned in the list of *Hommages* of 1311[55] – including assarts [rights to clear land], which were still permitted in the eleventh century. One such local seigneury, Rigny, bears comparison with others seen in the twelfth century ("assart" co-seigneuries in the Perche) and even in the fourteenth (fiefs described in 1355).

It is the paradigm of the "two ages of the banal seigneurie" – where the first was castellan until it gave way to that of the village *c.*1200 – that the acts from the Vendôme are beginning to undermine!

48.556 *TV* 8.
49.557 See *MV* 100 and also, in the Dunois, *MD* 121.
50.558 [R. Boutruche,] *Seigneurie et féodalité* (Paris, 1968), vol. II, p. 125.
51.559 *MV* 110.
52.560 *MV* 122.
53.561 *TV* 185 [see above, p. 138].
54.562 "*per se ipsum districtor et judex forisfacti, cujuscumque generis sit et legis emendationem exigit.*" See [Barthélemy, *Vendôme,*] pp. 325–7.
55.563 Nos 77, 92, 96, 100.

The expression "small estate" that G. Bois borrowed from Ganshof[56] is not, therefore, the worst possible way to describe the situation, so long as we understand there was not only a land lordship (and therefore a cultivated entity to be described and clarified), but also a judicial seigneury. In such a seigneury, there were customary taxes; we have just seen them at Rigny,[57] where the donor concluded an agreement with Marmoutier identical to that made for the allods at *Villa malardi* with Rosthon: "while he should live, he should have one part of the customs of the *villa* and St Martin the other part."[58] As J.-F. Lemarignier has noted, the *consuetudines* existed in the context of the *villa* (here, "allod"[59]). The *vicaria* was understood to be included in the rights which a *possessor* had in a place like Rigny; others explicitly ceded a piece of land "with the whole vicaria, and all of its customary charges," like Frodon of Vendôme at *Osmoys*.[60]

The allod was thus just one of the names given to a basic seigneurial unit, like *villa, terra, mansura terre*, or even *carruca*: both the possession of the land and its rent were liable to be shared, but always within indivisible systems. In this sense, we can think of it as an atom of the seigneury.

Relativity of the Idea of the Allod

Nevertheless, in several of the examples already cited, and in many other cases, we are dealing not with *an* allod but with *several* allods. This introduces us to the concrete description of the seigneurial unit: it was composed of a series of peasant farms compelled to pay rent, the very same *consuetudines* that we have just mentioned. This is the origin of the *mansuras* or *arpenta* [units of acreage][61] "of allods" ("*alodiorum*"). "His allods" ("*alodia sua*") is meant from the lord's point of view,[62] as we saw when Lancelin of Beaugency intervened [in the Vendômois],[63] and as in the expression "*de suo casamento*" ["regarding his fief"]; it is only in this sense that the meaning of "allod" comes close to "simple fiscal right," but this is not the true meaning of the word. The allodist receives a rent from the individual who is actually working his land.[64]

The allod-holder was thus the chief lord, so long as we are not thinking of noble or feudal service, but only of rent, the levy on work. In 1084, the knight Roger gave a small piece of land thus, "very good [land], and even more important, free, like an allod."[65] The knightly

56.564 G. Bois, *La mutation de l'an mil. Lournand, village mâconnais de l'Antiquité au féodalisme* (Paris, 1989), p. 98 and *passim* [English translation: *The Transformation of the Year One Thousand: the Village of Lournand from Antiquity to Feudalism* (Manchester, 1992), p. 57].

57.565 *MV* 122, and also 123 (Renard kept half "*de consuetudinibus terre*" for his lifetime).

58.566 "*Quamdiu ipse vixerit, habeat de consuetudinibus villanorum partem unam et sanctus Martinus alteram.*" *MV* 116 bis.

59.567 "La dislocation du *pagus*," p. 408.

60.568 "*cum tota vicaria et omnibus consuetudinibus.*" *MV* 72.

61.569 *MV* 88 (two arpents of allods, held by a chaplain from his secular master), *TV* 138.

62.570 For example, *MV* 33: the knight Guimand gives "*sua alodia omnia apud villam que Curtisozii dicitur, vel etiam ubicumque sita*" ["all his allods in the village called *Curtisozii*, or which are situated elsewhere"]. See also *MV* 16, *TV* 335.

63.571 See above, p. 138, and also *TV* 340, 1092.

64.572 Otbert gave to La Trinité "*alodum de villa benigni, illum quem tenebat Fulcoenus ad censum duos solidos reddentem*" ["an allod in the *villa benigni*, which Fulcoenus holds from him for a rent of two *solidi*"].

65.573 "*valde bona et prorsus, sicut alodium, libera.*" *TV* 316. Consider also this arpent of vineyard at Angers, "allodially immune, that is free from paying any rent or vicaria" ("*alodialiter immunem, hoc est ab omni census et vicaria redibitione liberum*"). *TV* 72.

allod clearly had to be distinguished from the *manufirma*, [land][66] held in return for rent:[67] the takers of *manufirma* land were often either knights or clerics.

From now on, a change in the exploitation of the land or in the division of rights over it would modify its status as an allod. In the Dunois, in 1074, Osanne gave two acres of field free of rent (thus, allodial acres), and two others *"de quadam manufirma"* [from a certain *manufirma*] which owed a rent of twelve *denarii*, "when, in the past, it was cultivated" (*"dum priscis coleretur temporibus"*) but at present, "because they are deserted, they owe no rent, but are allodial."[68] On the contrary, the creation of a rent on sales (by a common practice [in which the buyer paid the seller an annual rent], as we have seen)[69] could turn an allod into a rent-paying property. The case of Otbert, son of Sevin, is a curious example: he gave an oven as a fief to his vassal Gautier Chanard, who then sold it without rent to a third party; later, however, Otbert bought it back from the third party, at the price of a rent to be paid to Gautier![70] This was not an "allod," but the incident does illustrate the complex status of many lands.

There is a sense of hesitation in the formulas. Foucher the Rich gave the allod of Pinoche to Marmoutier "absolutely free from any claims and all customs or any exactions, just as he had held it himself."[71] However, a token rent was needed, so they established one,[72] along with a clause characteristic of the *manufirma* (namely, that late payment of the rent merely entailed a fine, and not the loss of the land), and with many stylistic precautions: the charter repeated that this was an allod, owing neither service nor customary fees. To sum up, the fact of owing merely a rent could be dangerous to allodial status, just like paying tithes, but it was not fatal!

In these conditions, the rights of the allod and of the fief, two noble kinds of land, were not far from each other: in fact, this is exactly what we will see when we deal with *parage* [land held by kinsmen].[73]

At the same time, however, the word could be immobilized, as a "geographical" expression. In the Dunois between 1060 and 1064, we find the opposition of a *"commendisiam de alodio"* ["protection tax from an allod"] and a *"censum de exertio"* ["tax on an assart, i.e. newly cleared land"] – and all of this *"in eisdem alodiis"* ["in the same allods"]![74] An allod within other allods, this text is similar to those which so struck E. Magnou-Nortier. But things here are hardly as complicated as her system! Such a lexicographical incident is perfectly conceivable, as soon as we recognize the relativity (and thus the virtual interlocking) of the idea of

---

66.574 On this, see [Barthélemy, *Vendôme*,] pp. 44–50. See *MV* 17: *"ut hec non manufirma sed alodus deinceps existat Majoris Monasterii monachorum"* ["that this may exist henceforth not as *manufirma* but as an allod of the monks of Marmoutier"] (in donating the land, the donor, Archembaud the Provost, merely abandoned the rent which one of the lay brothers, no doubt Mainard, owed him).

67.575 See *TV* 231 (1072): deathbed gift by Gautier the Devil of all his lands, "both the allods and those owing rent" (*"tam alodiorum quam censivarum"*).

68.576 *"quia vasta est, nil census reddit, sed est alodium."* *TV* 244.

69.577 See [Barthélemy, *Vendôme*,] pp. 51–3. See the details for the acquisitions of brother Thibert: a sale and a gift *"sine ullo censu"* ["without any rent"]. *TV* 139, 148; we must understand that a *cens* might be established at the very time of a sale or even of a donation.

70.578 *TV* 160.

71.579 *"ab omni calumnia omnique consuetudine seu alicuius redditus exactione liberum atque absolutum, sicut ipse eatenus tenuerat."* *MV* 105.

72.580 The same thing occurred at Coudray, after the gift of Guibert: *TV* 25, before 1040.

73.581 See [Barthélemy, *Vendôme*,] pp. 530–1.

74.582 *MD* 121.

the allod: in a group of lands called by its lord "the allods", there existed an internal zone which had a different status from the external zone: older land versus the assarts.

In the Vendômois, the "allods" of Bezay were the very heart of the hamlet. The same was true at *Villa arventi* and at *Viveris*.[75] This reminds us of the *corpus ville*, as it was understood in the twelfth century by the agreements on the co-seigneuries in the Perche, that is to say, those zones defined by the ancient roads on the cadastral maps of the nineteenth century. But we must be careful: none of these "allodial" sites was destined to become the center of a parish; they were all secondary centers (including Allets in the Danzé, known only by name).[76] We cannot necessarily read "villager" for "allodist." But were there no "authentic" peasants among them? Let us examine this issue carefully.

"The Allods" of Bezay and of "Villa Arventi"

These two cases push us in the direction of essentially knightly allods.

After 1040, Marmoutier acquired several lands in Bezay (the name was written *Burzeium* or *Buziacum*[77]). The great abbey did not enumerate them specifically, but eight acts of its *Cartularium Vindocinense*[78] report gifts or purchases at Bezay or later claims that followed. We can distinguish different levels by the rank of their lay partners as well as by the size of the stakes.

1. The seigneurial lineage of St-Amand participated three times. The noblewoman Aremburga gave a carrucate of land [a carrucate was a unit of plowland].[79] Her sons renounced their *dominium* over "the allods of Bezay" (and there followed an enumeration of domainal practice to which we will return), except for the *fevis militum* [fiefs of the knights].[80] Finally, their successor, Renard the seneschal (himself a vassal of the viscount Raoul I of the Lude), was the lord of Herluin, a knight who sold some land *"de Manso,"*[81] that is to say, one of the fiefs that Marmoutier had not yet acquired [in the earlier transactions].

The other great neighboring lineage (based in Crucheray) was represented by the noble-woman Adèle, daughter of Foucher I of Vendôme, and by her husband Hugh: here, too, were given up all or some of the "allods of Bezay."[82] In this case it was a matter of effective possession, since Adèle, at least, kept for her lifetime half of the lands – and we must understand, above all, their revenue.[83] But like the St-Amands, the Fulcherides [members of Foucher's family] had settled their vassals here, and their property was not involved in the initial gift. Thus Marmoutier had to put up with Robert Brachet, an otherwise notorious vassal of the Fulcherides,[84] "on certain property belonging to him and located between our

75.583 See [Barthélemy, *Vendôme*,] p. 447.
76.584 *TV* 512.
77.585 *Burzeium*: *MV* 42, 58, 60, 61. *Burziacum*: *MV* 60, 62, 64, 90. *Beziacum*: *MV* 94. An intermediary form: *Burziacum* in *MV* 59, 97. Despite the formula of *MV* 60 (taken up in the rubric) which speaks of parcels *"apud Buziacum sitis"* ["located at Bezay"] and of *"alia itidem terra unicus carruce apud Burzeium consistente"* ["other land there of one carrucate located at Bezay"], there is no reason to think of two different locations; this is clearly the present-day Bezay (in the Nourray).
78.586 Cited in the previous note.
79.587 *MV* 42.
80.588 *MV* 58.
81.589 *MV* 90. Herluin was also presented as a vassal of Renard the seneschal in *TV* 64.
82.590 *MV* 59, 61, 62.
83.591 By analogy with gifts such as those of Otbert at Fontenail: *MV* 73; or that of Rosthon at *Villamalardi*; *MV* 116 bis.
84.592 See [Barthélemy, *Vendôme*,] pp. 536–7.

own and Bezay," and also on a carrucate.[85] We can note the importance of feudal structure on allodial sites: the initial gift of the lords of the first rank opened the way for (difficult) negotiations with vassals whom they could not force to imitate their generosity.[86]

2. There were also gifts and sales of more modest size at Bezay. Hugh Cordella sold a "two-ox" piece of land plus an arpent of field;[87] before him, a certain Brehard gave five arpents of allod, in fields and arable land "located in Bezay in the *villa* which is called *Mansilis* [Manse] or *Alodus* [Allod],"[88] the very same place where the knight Herluin gave a "four-ox" piece of land, subject only to rent. Are we descending the social scale with Hugh and Brehard? Hugh is otherwise unknown to us, but Brehard is striking because he appears in connection with several villages.[89] The size of their lands brings these donors close to the knights of second rank (approximately equal, for example, to the carrucate of Robert Brachet). We do not know if they farmed it themselves,[90] nor if they paid anything for it besides this rent, about which it was said when Herluin made his gift: "a four-ox piece of land, free from all customs and charges, except for 6 *solidi* in rent which is owed on it on the feast of the beheading of Saint John the Baptist."[91] Implicitly, other lands must have paid heavier charges.

3. Marmoutier did not acquire all the land in Bezay. In 1060, there was a *terra sancti Georgii* which belonged to the collegial church in the *castrum* [castle] of Vendôme; when he became a monk at La Trinité, canon Hubert donated the property he had [at the *terra sancti Georgii* at Bezay]: a vineyard, house, and field – and also, a "two-ox" piece of land owing a rent, another house, and yet another piece of land.[92] This allows us to confirm the distinction between residential and specialized arpents, and arable and rent-paying land.

Thus, there were at one and the same time composite patrimonies of knights of various ranks, and common patrimonies, both put together any which way! It makes perfect sense that the fiefs of the two great neighborhood lineages should have become entangled, since we are between Nourray and Saint-Amand. Between the knights and the others, there was no particularly notable social discontinuity. Several traits appear to bring Bezay close to *Viveris*, which we will look at shortly, including the existence nearby of a *manufirma*: that of Otbert son of Sevin at Fontenail, enlarged by a piece of land closer to Nourray,[93] was included in the same *calumnia* [dispute] as the Manse or Allod at Bezay.[94]

[. . .]

85.593 *"super quibusdam terre particulis inter ceteras nostras apud Burziacum sitis."* MV 61.
86.594 See, a little while later, formulas of advance authorization.
87.595 MV 64 [land was classified by the number of oxen need to plough it in a day].
88.596 *"sitos in Burziaco apud villam que Mansilis vel Alodus appellatur."* MV 97.
89.597 Brehard was also said to be "of Gombergean" (MV 68); elsewhere, he appears at *Tridiacus* (MV 97, doubtless Villethierry) and at Claireau (MV 68).
90.598 Remember that the eleventh-century acts ascribe the cultivation of the land to its possessor even if the work is done by his *servi* or *colliberti* [unfree peasants].
91.599 *"terram ad IV^or boves, liberam totius consuetudinis et reditus, preter VI solidos censum qui ex ea solvitur ad festum decollationis sancti Baptiste Johannis."* MV 90. The term used is reminiscent of a rent for a *manufirma*, but at a rather high price.
92.600 TV 137.
93.601 MV 73.
94.602 MV 94. Trémault's identification, *Grand Mât*, is false: this term replaced Haut Mât, itself taken for *Osmoys* (1355), *Ulmeta* (eleventh century). It is thus not derived from "Grand Manse." We can more likely find the Manse in the territory of les Mannes.

Villa arventi is a place-name that has now disappeared, but which is easily located: "our land of Villarvent . . . which is in Gombergean," says an act of the twelfth century.[95] In 1061, La Trinité of Vendôme possessed a cell[96] in Gombergean, which was the kernel of the place. It was in this period (1060–63) that the lay brother Thibert, also known as Thibaud, who lived there, left records of five acquisitions by purchase or by gift.[97]

The number of arpents acquired ranged from a *demi-quarte* (that is, thirty arpents)[98] to a mere three, passing through thirteen and six[99] – and also a "one-ox" piece of land, joined to two arpents of field.[100] The word "allod" was used each time that the land acquired did not owe any rent; however, [the recorders of these deeds] seemed to think it necessary to reinforce this by adding *"sine ullo censu"* ["without any rent"][101] – as if this didn't go without saying. As for the land bought from Gaudri de Lavardin, it was "from the allods" of his wife, but owed a rent . . . to him! Thus the use of the word "allod" was essentially correlated to the right of the person in question: there was no such thing as an allod in the absolute.

In any case, the sellers/donors of allods were not *rustici* [peasants]: Arnaud Russel was a knight of Château-Renault,[102] Helgaud Securis (elsewhere Cuneata, "the Ax")[103] was also at the court of Château-Renault in 1060 and *c.*1068,[104] and Dodon *"de Meso"* (father of Foucolin, the co-donor of three arpents of field)[105] could well have been the husband of one of Helgaud's nieces.[106] *Mesum* must be Mézé, on the present border between Gombergean and St-Cyr-du-Gault. The third seller was Gaudri de Lavardin, a knight well known in that castle;[107] the fourth is unknown. The only true commoner in the bunch was Foucolin's co-donor, *Heraldus faber*,[108] Harold the Smith – and this livelihood was hardly a poor one.

Three of the sales represented in reality the liquidation of an inheritance or of the dowry of a mother or a wife.[109] This is to say that we are only dealing with secondary elements of the knights' patrimony;[110] the limited size of these lands thus tells us nothing about their

---

95.603 *"terram nostram de Villarvent . . . que est apud Gomberjam."* *TV* 580: it is thus a *villa* within the *villa* of Gombergean. In fact, *TV* 147 (1061) mentions an allod at St-Cyr (du-Gault) *"iuxta Villam arventi."* In *MV* 86, too, a *"terra"* consists of two *ville.*

96.604 *TV* 147.

97.605 *TV* 138 (purchase), 139 (purchase and gift-purchase), 147 (purchase), 148 (gift in return for *societas*), 167 (all we have is the rubric).

98.606 *TV* 167: see *TV* 156.

99.607 Respectively, *TV* 148, 136, 139.

100.608 *TV* 147.

101.609 *TV* 139, 148.

102.610 Seller in *TV* 138, *calumniator* in *TV* 139.

103.611 Seller-donor in *TV* 139; see *MV* 54, 1065: "Securi, or as he is commonly called, the Ax" (*"Securi sive, ut loquitur vulgus, Cuneata cognominato"*). He is certainly (as in *TV* 139) the brother of Eude Landan, *miles* (*Landelinus* or *Landanus*: from the *landes* [wasteland] around Blois?).

104.612 *MV* 172.

105.613 *TV* 148.

106.614 Helgaud pleaded in favor of Marmoutier against Dodon, husband of his niece Hildeburge: *MV* 172. The name Foucolin is also found at Chaillon, right next to Mézé (*MV* 108), but somewhat earlier, and in a different lineage (son of Foucois).

107.615 *TV* 147.

108.616 *TV* 148. We cannot trace him at Vendôme; possibly at Blois, or at Gombergean itself (where there was indeed a *pretor* [high official]).

109.617 *TV* 138, 139, 147.

110.618 The motives for these sales are missing. A desire to manage better by eliminating outlying holdings? Poverty or need for money?

wealth or lack of it. On the other hand, the case of Gaudri de Lavardin is exemplary, because it shows how rent-paying could work. The precision of documents from the 1060s, reinforced with a touch of prosopography [study of personal names and family links], allows us to refute here the impression of a first quick reading about the not very feudal character of all these sites.

It is only at *Viveris*[111] that we will see peasant "allodists," though here in fact this meant tenants and sometimes serfs; here the relativity of the notion of the allod was played out to the full.

Let us sum up. The allod was no obstacle to the chains of subordination that are sometimes talked about. Indeed, the allod could be a fief or another kind of tenure. It assuredly meant full ownership, but in a society where full ownership did not exist! It also had a logical tie to some tax exemptions, inasmuch as an allod – according to the opinion dear to L. Génicot – must indeed first of all indicate nobility rather than peasantry.[112] Only the relativity of these concepts can allow us to encounter peasant allodists. In any case, it would be illegitimate for us to concoct the idea of an "allodial class" simply from the allod itself.

The allod in the Vendômois in the eleventh century, especially before 1060, was above all a local seigneury, one part of the local seigneury whose organization we can discern thanks to gifts to monasteries. The series of these donations (1030–60) does not indicate the death of a class but the establishment of habitual ties between the local nobility and new or reinvigorated monasteries, such as the early Middle Ages had always known. The later decline of the word signifies only the updating of the formulary and vocabulary: the "fief" succeeded to the "allod" as the patrimonial land *par excellence*, and after all, even today, common sense is not far from the truth in the use it makes of this term! The stars of the National Assembly are well known to possess, here and there, electoral "allods." [In France, an "electoral fief" is a district from which a legislator is invariably elected – hence, his or her "allod."]

[. . .]

Conclusion

This chapter has brought together the evidence from before the year 1060 and the arguments which, after considerable reflection, have made us reject the model of the "transformation of the year 1000" for the Vendômois and the Loire valley. In fact, those historians who pledge allegiance to that model afterwards see nothing but signs of crisis in all the documentation for the eleventh century: degraded forms of justice, knights on the rampage, peasants adrift. They take ["the powerful and true harmony"] of the feudal world, which Michelet called on us to decipher,[113] for a series of accidents. The moment that we free ourselves from the tyranny of this model, however, we leave our eyes and our pens free to see other perspectives, other intrigues. We can follow, where it is possible, the suggestions of anthropology.

And if we are asked where to place the origins of feudal society, we can answer that it doesn't matter, since it is out of the range of our vision, but that the concept of an already feudal Carolingian society does not seem so bad. In his admirable book of 1939–40, Marc Bloch finessed a little the classic question of whether "the vassalic principle" undermined the

[111].619   See [Barthélemy, *Vendôme*,] pp. 441–50.
[112]   [See L. Génicot, *L'Economie rurale namuroise au bas Moyen Age* (Louvain, 1960), vol. 1, ch. 1.]
[113]   [Jules Michelet, *Le Moyen Age* (Paris, 1981), p. 182.]

Carolingian empire,[114] and he was wrong to privilege the cataclysmic genesis [of feudalism] with the Viking invasions at the end of the ninth century. For the "mutationists," there were troubles linked to the multiplication of castles a century later. But weren't both these crises exaggerated by the monks [who reported them]? And was the construction of peripheral castles really a catastrophe? No more so than the Scandinavian raids. Like those, [castles] certainly brought about a rise in social tensions, but here it would not be inopportune to link this to the new expansion of the black monks, because of whom we see the feudal revelation. But we will certainly be discussing this in the years to come!

[114.628] *La société féodale* (see n. 13.521). The force of his writing comes from his initial decision to paint a picture, rather than to tell a story, but this is also his book's limitation: the Carolingians do not appear until long after (pp. 224–9) the later invasions (p. 23).

The Tyranny of a Construct: Feudalism and Historians of Medieval Europe

9

Elizabeth A. R. Brown

At a recent conference Thomas N. Bisson introduced his paper "Institutional Structures of the Medieval Peace" by cautioning his audience that in his discussion of peace movements, peace associations, and peace institutions in southern France and Spain he would not attempt to relate his findings to "feudalism."[1] His approach was descriptive – and thoroughly enlightening – and no further reference to any ism occurred until the question period. Then, bestowing the double-edged praise that is his hallmark, Professor John F. Benton asked how historians could have managed to overlook for so long such abundant evidence that would necessitate the revision of numerous lectures on medieval society. Responding to this remark, Professor Bisson again alluded to the eventual necessity of evaluating his conclusions with reference to the general topic of feudalism, but time prevented him from elaborating. It occurred to me as this interchange was taking place that the failure of historians to take account of the data used by Bisson may well have resulted from their concentration on feudalism – as model or Ideal Type – and their consequent tendency to disregard or dismiss documents not easily assimilable into that frame of reference.

Whatever their relevance to the subject of Professor Bisson's paper, feelings of uneasiness concerning the term "feudalism" are not uniquely mine. Historians have for years harbored doubts about the term "feudalism" and the phrase "feudal system," which has often been used as a synonym for it. One of the first, and certainly one of the wittiest and most eloquent, to comment on the problem was Frederic William Maitland. In lectures on English constitutional history prepared in 1887 and 1888 he wrote:

An earlier version of this article was presented to a meeting of the Columbia University Seminar on Medieval Studies on May 8, 1973. I am grateful to the members of the seminar for their questions and suggestions. For their advice and counsel I would also like to express my thanks to Professor Fredric Cheyette of Amherst College, Professor John Bell Henneman of the University of Iowa, Professor Joshua Prawer of the Israel Academy of Sciences and Humanities, Professor Thomas N. Bisson of the University of California at Berkeley, Professor John F. Benton of the California Institute of Technology, Professors Edwin Burrows, Philip Dawson, Charlton Lewis, and Hyman Sardy of Brooklyn College of the City University of New York, Barbara W. Tuchman, and finally the members of the History Club and my students at Brooklyn College.
[1] Thomas N. Bisson, "Institutional Structures of the Medieval Peace," a paper presented to a colloquium held at Princeton University on March 31, 1973.

Now were an examiner to ask who introduced the feudal system into England? one very good answer, if properly explained, would be Henry Spelman, and if there followed the question, what was the feudal system? a good answer to that would be, an early essay in comparative jurisprudence.... If my examiner went on with his questions and asked me, when did the feudal system attain its most perfect development? I should answer, about the middle of the last century.[2]

Thanks to J. G. A. Pocock, it is now known that Henry Spelman, a learned English antiquarian of the seventeenth century, used neither the term "feudal system" nor the word "feudalism," but this does not detract from the validity or the importance of Maitland's observations. Following in the steps of the Scottish legal scholar Sir Thomas Craig, Spelman held that the social and political relationships of medieval England had been uniform and systematic enough to be described adequately as regulated by a "'feudal law' [which] was an hierarchical system imposed from above as a matter of state policy." The work of Craig and Spelman had its virtues, for they were the first British historians to attempt to relate British institutions to continental developments. Both, however, relied for their knowledge of continental institutions on Cujas's and Hotman's sixteenth-century editions of the twelfth-century Lombard *Libri Feudorum*, which gave, to paraphrase Pocock, a precise and detailed "definition of the *feudum* whereby it could be recognized in any part of Europe," or, as he says, "a systematic exposition of the principles of tenure, forfeiture and inheritance." These criteria Craig and Spelman employed to classify the evidence from Scottish and English sources, and their simplification and regimentation of phenomena notably offset the advantages to historical thought of their demonstration that the development of England and Scotland could be understood only in the context of the European experience.[3]

Given these beginnings, it is no wonder that eighteenth-century British writers began to accept the concept of a uniform feudal government and to concentrate on the system, the construct, instead of investigating the various social and political relationships found in medieval Europe. "They were," Pocock observes, "making an 'ism' of [feudalism]; they were reflecting on its essence and nature and endeavoring to fit it into a pattern of general ideas."[4] In so doing they resembled Boulainvilliers and Montesquieu, who wrote of *féodalité* and *lois féodales* as distinguishing a state of society, thus, incidentally, expanding the concept to include a far wider range of phenomena than it had for legal scholars.[5] The writers of the eighteenth century, like those of later times, assigned different meanings to the term *féodalité*, or, in English, "feodality." Some used it to designate a system of government, some to refer to conditions that developed as public power disappeared. By 1800 the construct had been launched and the expression "feudal system" devised; by the mid-nineteenth century

---

[2] Frederic William Maitland, *The Constitutional History of England*, ed. H. A. L. Fisher (Cambridge, 1908), p. 142. See also Fisher's introduction to this edition, p. v.

[3] J. G. A. Pocock, *The Ancient Constitution and the Feudal Law: English Historical Thought in the Seventeenth Century* (Cambridge, 1957), pp. 70 n. 2, 93–4, 249, 79–80, 97–9, 70–9, 72, 84, 99, 103, 102. Pocock perhaps exaggerates these advantages (p. 102) because of the strength of his admiration for the boldness and imagination with which Craig and Spelman challenged the distortedly insular approach taken by Coke and the common lawyers. It seems clear, furthermore, that Pocock himself does not question the validity or the usefulness of the term "feudalism."

[4] Ibid., p. 249; see also Robert Boutruche, *Seigneurie et féodalité: Le premier âge des liens d'homme à homme* (Paris, 1959), pp. 15 nn. 16–17, 16 n. 20.

[5] Boutruche, *Seigneurie et féodalité*, pp. 13–14; Marc Bloch, *La Société féodale* (Paris, 1949), vol. 1, pp. 1–3. The English edition, with a foreword by M. M. Postan, was translated by L. A. Manyon and is entitled *Feudal Society* (Chicago, 1961); the corresponding pages are xvi–xviii.

the word "feudalism" was in use. The way was prepared for future scholars to study feudalism – whatever it was conceived to be – scientifically and for others to employ the ism to refer, abusively, to those selected elements of the past that were to be overthrown, abolished, or inexorably superseded.[6]

Since the middle of the nineteenth century the concepts of feudalism and the feudal system have dominated the study of the medieval past. The appeal of these words, which provide a short, easy means of referring to the European social and political situation over an enormous stretch of time, has proved virtually impossible to resist, for they pander to the human desire to grasp – or to think one is grasping – a subject known or suspected to be complex by applying to it a simple label simplistically defined. The great authority of these terms has radically influenced the way in which the history of the Middle Ages has been conceptualized and investigated, encouraging concentration on oversimplified models that are applied as standards and stimulating investigation of similarities and differences, norms and deviations. As a result scholars have disregarded or paid insufficient attention to recalcitrant data that their models do not prepare them to expect.

But let us return to Maitland. Implicit in his assessment of Spelman and the feudal system is a clear objection to applying the label "feudal system" to medieval England, presumably because of a belief that England never underwent a systematization of social and political life – or, as Maitland puts it, never experienced "the development of what can properly be called a feudal system." Less evident, perhaps, is a hesitancy about the propriety of using the phrase "feudal system" at all. That Maitland questioned the wisdom of applying it to conditions of medieval society is hard to dispute, however, for in his lectures he remarks, "The phrase [feudal system] has thus become for us so large and vague that it is quite possible to maintain that of all countries England was the most, or for the matter of that the least, feudalized; that William the Conqueror introduced, or for the matter of that suppressed, the feudal system."[7] Still, having bemoaned the terminological situation, Maitland proceeds to use the term "feudalism," equated by him with "feudal system."[8] He announces that "the feudalism of France differs radically from the feudalism of England, that the feudalism of the thirteenth is very different from that of the eleventh century." He then goes on to give his own definition of feudalism, emphasizing ties of vassalage, fiefs, service in arms owed the lord, and private administration of justice. Using this definition, he discusses the question of the progress toward such an organization that England had been making before the Norman Conquest, and he concludes, "Speaking generally then, that ideal feudalism of which we have spoken, an ideal which was pretty completely realized in France during the

[6] Boutruche, *Seigneurie et féodalité*, pp. 16, 18–23. See also the *Oxford English Dictionary*, s.v. "feudal," "feudalism," and "feudality."
[7] Maitland, *Constitutional History*, pp. 161, 143. See also Sir Frederick Pollock and Frederic William Maitland, *The History of English Law before the Time of Edward I*, 2nd ed., introd. S. F. C. Milsom (Cambridge, 1968), vol. 1, pp. 66–7; and Frederic William Maitland, *Collected Papers*, ed. H. A. L. Fisher (Cambridge, 1911), vol. 1, p. 489.
[8] Maitland does not subject the word "feudalism" to the same critical scrutiny he applies to the phrase "feudal system," and he is far less wary of using the former than the latter. At one point in his lectures he seems to be distinguishing between the two – "we do not hear of a feudal system until long after feudalism has ceased to exist" – but he also uses them as equivalents. In his conclusion he indicates that he considers "the development of . . . a feudal system" the same as the realization of "ideal feudalism." *Constitutional History*, pp. 141–3, 161–3.

tenth, eleventh and twelfth centuries, was never realized in England." Here, he says, "the force of feudalism [was] limited and checked by other ideas."[9]

As these statements show, Maitland's tolerance for unresolved contradictions was high, and other historians have demonstrated a similarly striking capacity for living with inconsistency. Although they attack the term "feudalism," they are still unwilling and perhaps unable – whether from habit, inertia, or simple inattention – to jettison the word. Consider H. G. Richardson and G. O. Sayles. In a book published in 1963 they denounce "feudal" and "feudalism" as "the most regrettable coinages ever put into circulation to debase the language of historians." "We would, if we could," they declare, "avoid using them, for they have been given so many and such imprecise meanings." They confess, however – without apology or explanation – that they cannot "rid [themselves] of the words and must live with them" and therefore proclaim their determination to "endeavor, when [they use] them, to do so without ambiguity." They evidently have some sense of attachment, however grudging, to the terms, and their feelings are reflected in their insistence that "if the concept and the term are to be in the least useful" – thus implying that they can be – "there must be precise definition." Such definition they do not, unfortunately, offer. Nonetheless they doggedly persist in using the words, and they spend a large portion of their book dealing with their "thesis of the relative unimportance of any element of 'feudalism' in post-Conquest England" and of "the essential continuity of English institutions."[10]

Such an approach logically requires isolating those elements that can properly be called feudal from those that cannot. Since Richardson and Sayles never explicitly objectify the enemy, however, their readers are left to deduce from their arguments just what phenomena they consider essential components of feudalism. Homage, "'feudal' incidents [fees and expenses]," honors [baronies and other large fiefs] and honorial courts, knightly service connected with fiefs, and the use of military tenures for military purposes are all linked in one way or another with feudalism, although Richardson and Sayles clearly suggest that, unless found in their Franco-Norman forms, these elements should not be considered truly feudal. Thus the authors attempt to validate their hypothesis by showing either that these or similar institutions existed in England before 1066 – and hence are to be classified as Old English and therefore not Norman feudal – or that they had no real importance after that date.[11] In the end, coming to grips with the problem of definition, they abruptly abandon their previous criteria. So that they can pronounce England safely nonfeudal and therefore non-French, they fall back on what they call "the classical theory of feudalism," described as the idea of lordship diminished by fragmentation or of "sovereignty . . . divided between the king and his feudataries," neither of which was ever found in England. They warn that feudalism should not be defined simply in terms of tenure, since if it is it will be found everywhere.[12]

As their lengthy discussion and conclusion make clear, Richardson and Sayles were never fully convinced, despite their initial volleys, that feudalism was in fact no "more than an arbitrary pattern imposed by modern writers upon men long dead and events long past."

[9] Ibid., pp. 143–64.
[10] H. G. Richardson and G. O. Sayles, *The Governance of Mediaeval England from the Conquest to Magna Carta* (Edinburgh, 1963), pp. 30, 92, 117–18, 30–1, 105, 116.
[11] Ibid., pp. 36–8, 77, 99, 105–12, 115; see also pp. 85–91, 147, and the comments on p. 116: "The Normans were already familiar with much that they found in England, but we are not thereby warranted in terming those familiar things 'feudal' or in asserting that England was already 'feudal.'"
[12] Ibid., pp. 117–18.

Although they end their analysis by remarking of the word "feudal" that "an adjective so ambiguous and so misleading is best avoided," their repeated use of the term belies their alleged distaste.[13]

If numerous arguments in defense of feudalism have been advanced, "utility" and "indispensability" are the chief rallying cries of the term's defenders. Let us turn first to the criterion of utility.

In the introduction to his classic study *Feudalism*, F. L. Ganshof states that he intends his book to facilitate the work of students of medieval society. In analyzing and describing feudal institutions he says he has "endeavoured to bring out as clearly as possible their essential features, since, once these are grasped, it is easy for the student to disentangle the elements that can properly be described as feudal in the institutions of the period or country with which he is primarily concerned."[14] Helping the scholar as well as the student to evaluate, analyze, and categorize the past is also important to Michael Postan, and in his foreword to the English edition of Marc Bloch's *Feudal Society* he argues that the usefulness of "generalized concepts" such as feudalism lies in their ability to "help us to distinguish one historical situation from another and to align similar situations in different countries and even in different periods." For Postan greater complexity apparently means greater utility, and he prefers Bloch's definition of feudalism, which embraces "most of the significant features of medieval society," to "constitutional and legal concepts of feudalism" centering on "military service" and "contractual principles." These latter concepts, he feels, may have some virtue as pedagogical devices, to promote "intellectual discipline," and to serve as "an antidote to the journalistic levities of modern historiography." Still, they cannot validly be considered "an intellectual tool, to be used in the study of society."[15]

If Postan draws a rather unsettling distinction between pedagogy on the one hand and research and sound intellectual endeavor on the other, it is clear that he is not alone in considering appropriate for the student what is decried for the scholar. This "track" approach to feudalism is widespread, even though those who espouse it may differ concerning what should be taught at different levels. Postan envisions progression from a partial to a more complex model, always retaining the term "feudalism" to denote the model. Others, expressing fundamental objections to the misleading impression of simplicity and system they believe inevitably associated with isms, still argue that authors of basic textbooks – as opposed to advanced studies – would be lost without the concept of feudalism. This rather inconsistent attitude apparently springs from two convictions: first, that beginning students are incapable of dealing with complex and diverse development and must for their own good be presented with an artificially regular schema; and second, that the term "feudalism" somehow helps these students by serving as a handy, familiar tag to which to attach consciously oversimplified generalizations. Later, as graduate students, they are presumably to be introduced to qualifications and complications, and finally, as scholars and initiates into the mysteries of the trade, they are to be encouraged to discard the offending ism for purposes of research, if not for purposes of teaching their own beginning students. Charles T. Wood, although not explicitly endorsing the use of the term "feudalism," writes that "the feudal pyramid . . . makes for clear diagrams, and schoolboys have

---

[13]   Ibid., pp. 92, 118.
[14]   F. L. Ganshof, *Feudalism*, foreword F. M. Stenton, trans. Philip Grierson (London, 1952), p. xviii; see also p. 151.
[15]   Postan, foreword to Bloch, *Feudal Society*, pp. xiv, xiii.

to begin somewhere." Still, he admits, "where they do begin is rather far removed from reality."[16]

Postan, and presumably Ganshof, feels that employing the construct has the virtue of enabling scholars to distinguish likenesses among different times and areas. Similarly John Le Patourel advocates formulating a definition of feudalism that could be used "as a measuring-rod,"[17] and such a standard could presumably be relied on not only, as he wants, to clarify "the old argument" over the introduction of feudalism into England but also, as Postan argues, to advance the work of those concerned with comparing developments in different countries.

If feudalism is praised as a teaching device and as a means of understanding societies, it is also said to be "indispensable," and that for a number of reasons. Marc Bloch maintains that scientists cannot function without abstractions and that since historians are scientists, they also require abstractions. The specific abstractions "feudal" and "feudalism" are defended on the grounds that, however awkward and inappropriate in terms of their original connotations these words and others like them may be, the historian is in this respect no worse off than the scientist, who must also make do with inconvenient and unsuitable terminology.[18] Michael Postan goes beyond Bloch to declare that "without generalized terms representing entire groups of phenomena not only history but all intelligent discourse would be impossible," and he maintains that no difference exists between such a word as "feudalism" and other general terms like "war" and "agriculture."[19] Equally positively, if less aggressively, Fredric Cheyette has insisted that the term "feudalism" cannot "simply be discarded – the verbal detours one would have to make to replace it would be strained as well as disingenuous."[20] Otto Hintze argues that the concept is indispensable not only for reasons of practicality and convenience but also because of the deficiencies of the processes of human thought, assumed to be incapable of comprehending the complexities of the real world. Hintze asserts that since "it is impossible to grasp the complicated circumstances of historical life, so laden with unique occurrences, in a few universal and unambiguous concepts – as is done in the natural sciences," historians must use "intuitive abstractions" and create "Ideal Types, and such types indeed underlie our scholarly terminology."[21]

---

[16] Wood's own description of medieval society deals with human beings rather than schemas, but he occasionally uses the terms "feudal" and "feudalism," which are not defined. *The Quest for Eternity: Medieval Manners and Morals* (New York, 1971), pp. 28, 55–6, 177. Wood's index (p. 227) shows that he has not discarded the term "feudalism," which he seems to see as closely linked with vassalage.

[17] John Le Patourel, review of Richardson and Sayles, *Governance of Mediaeval England*, in *English Historical Review* 80 (1965): 117 n. 1; and see also Max Weber, *The Theory of Social and Economic Organization*, ed. Talcott Parsons, trans. A. M. Henderson and Talcott Parsons (New York, 1947), p. 329.

[18] Marc Bloch, *Apologie pour l'histoire ou Métier d'historien* (Paris, 1949), pp. 86–7. The corresponding pages in the English edition – *The Historian's Craft*, ed. Lucien Febvre, trans. Peter Putnam (New York, 1953) – are 169–71.

[19] Postan, foreword to Bloch, *Feudal Society*, p. xiv.

[20] Fredric L. Cheyette, "Some Notations on Mr Hollister's 'Irony,'" *Journal of British Studies* 5 (1965): 4; see also Fredric L. Cheyette, ed., *Lordship and Community in Medieval Europe: Selected Readings* (New York, 1968), pp. 2–3.

[21] Otto Hintze, "Wesen und Verbreitung des Feudalismus" (1929), in Hintze, *Gesammelte Abhandlungen*, ed. Gerhard Oestreich, 1 (2nd ed., Göttingen, 1962), p. 85; for an English translation of the article, entitled "The Nature of Feudalism," see Cheyette, *Lordship and Community*, pp. 22–31. See also the comments of Michael Lane and particularly the enlightening passage quoted from Max Weber, in which Weber describes how ideal types are formulated. *Introduction to Structuralism* (New York, 1970), pp. 25–6.

Even its most eloquent advocates readily acknowledge the difficulties associated with the use of the term "feudalism." Marc Bloch, for one, states that "nearly every historian understands the word as he pleases," and "even if we do define, it is usually every man for himself." He admits that the word is charged with emotional overtones[22] and is in fact "very ill-chosen,"[23] and he acknowledges that, in general, abstractions which are "ill-chosen or too mechanically applied" should be avoided.[24] He goes so far as to declare that the word "capitalism" has lost its usefulness because it has become burdened with ambiguities and because it is "carelessly applied to the most diverse civilizations," so that, as a result, "it almost inevitably results in concealing their original features."[25] Even Postan, whose loyalty to Bloch exceeds Bloch's sense of commitment to his own ideas, grants that comprehensive terms like "feudalism" "over-simplify the reality they purport to epitomize," and he confesses that

> in some contexts the practice of giving general names to whole epochs can even be dangerous, [luring] its practitioners into the worst pitfalls of the nominalist fallacy, and [encouraging] them to endow their terms with real existence, to derive features of an epoch from the etymology of the word used to describe it or to construct edifices of historical argument out of mere semantic conceits.[26]

The variety of existing definitions of the term and the general unwillingness of any historian to accept any other historian's characterization of feudalism constitute a prime source of confusion. The best definition would doubtless be, as Cheyette suggests, one that helped "to make the body of evidence on medieval institutions coherent," but he himself has not found or formulated any definition to accomplish this purpose.[27] In the absence of consensus, the play with meanings has flourished and still continues.

The sweeping perspective adopted by Marc Bloch produced a definition of European feudalism – equated by Bloch with feudal society and, in the translation of his book, with feudal system[28] that in effect summarizes the topics treated in the central section of his *La Société féodale*. It encompasses a wide range of aspects of medieval life:

[22] Bloch, *Apologie*, pp. 89, 87 (*Historian's Craft*, pp. 176, 171).

[23] "Un mot fort mal choisi." Bloch, *Société féodale*, vol. 1, p. 3 (*Feudal Society*, p. xviii).

[24] Bloch, *Apologie*, p. 88 (*Historian's Craft*, p. 173). Bloch comments that the feudalisms which scholars have located in different parts of the world "bear scarcely any resemblance to each other." *Apologie*, p. 89 (*Historian's Craft*, pp. 175–6).

[25] Bloch, *Apologie*, p. 88 (*Historian's Craft*, p. 174). For a fuller, if less extreme, analysis of the similar problems posed by using the terms capitalism and feudalism, see the review of J. Q. C. Mackrell, *The Attack on 'Feudalism' in 18th Century France* (London, 1973), in the *Times Literary Supplement*, February 15, 1974, p. 160.

[26] Postan, foreword to Bloch, *Feudal Society*, p. xiv.

[27] Cheyette, "Some Notations on Mr. Hollister's 'Irony,'" pp. 4, 12; see also pp. 5–6, where he states that the usefulness of the term (he may in fact mean of the definition) "is determined by how it helps to order the evidence."

[28] Bloch, *Société féodale*, vol. 2, pp. 244–9 (*Feudal Society*, pp. 443–5). In the translation (p. 443) "the feudal system" replaces Bloch's "le régime féodal" (vol. 2, p. 245). Similarly, Bloch's "les féodalités d'importation" (vol. 1, pp. 289–92) become in translation "the imported feudal systems" (pp. 187–9). Both Ganshof and David Herlihy have indicated – misleadingly it seems to me – that Bloch perceived a fundamental difference between feudalism and feudal society. Ganshof, *Feudalism*, p. xvi; David Herlihy, ed., *The History of Feudalism* (New York, 1970), p. xix.

A subject peasantry; widespread use of the service tenement (i.e. the fief) instead of a salary, which was out of the question; the supremacy of a class of specialized warriors; ties of obedience and protection which bind man to man and, within the warrior class, assume the distinctive form called vassalage; fragmentation of authority – leading inevitably to disorder; and, in the midst of all this, the survival of other forms of association, family and State, of which the latter, during the second feudal age, was to acquire renewed strength.[29]

Some historians have accepted this inclusive list as a definition of feudalism, but others would prefer to link it only with feudal society, which they feel can and should be distinguished from a more narrowly conceived feudalism, in which the fief is accorded greater prominence than Bloch gives it.[30] Ganshof, for one, believes that in the Middle Ages "the fief, if not the cornerstone, was at least the most important element in the graded system of rights over land which this type of society involved." The definition of feudalism he prefers – "the narrow, technical, legal sense of the word" – concentrates on service and maintenance and emphasizes the fief, while it excludes entirely the private exercise of public justice and jurisdiction. For Ganshof feudalism is envisaged as

a body of institutions creating and regulating the obligations of obedience and service – mainly military service on the part of a free man (the vassal) towards another free man (the lord), and the obligations of protection and maintenance on the part of the lord with regard to his vassal. The obligation of maintenance had usually as one of its effects the grant by the lord to his vassal of a unit of real property known as a fief.

Although Ganshof admits that "powers of jurisdiction [in particular what one normally calls feudal jurisdiction] were . . . very closely bound up with feudal relationships," he states firmly that "there was nothing in the relationships of feudalism . . . which required that a vassal receiving investiture of a fief should necessarily have the profits of jurisdiction within it, nor even that he should exercise such jurisdiction."[31]

Ganshof may have his followers, particularly among historians of the Normans and the English.[32] On the other hand, many scholars insist that the private exercise of public

[29] Bloch, *Société féodale*, pp. 249–50 (*Feudal Society*, p. 446).
[30] Herlihy, *History of Feudalism*, p. xix; Ganshof, *Feudalism*, p. xv. Ganshof's description of feudalism as a form of society on the same page diverges at many points from Bloch's: "a development pushed to extremes of the element of personal dependence in society, with a specialized military class occupying the higher levels in the social scale; an extreme subdivision of the rights of real property; a graded system of rights over land created by this subdivision and corresponding in broad outline to the grades of personal dependence just referred to; and a dispersal of political authority amongst a hierarchy of persons who exercise in their own interest powers normally attributed to the State and which are often, in fact, derived from its break-up." Here there is no mention of peasantry or family; here the state is mentioned only by virtue of its dissolution (although see also pp. 141–51 for a lengthy discussion of feudalism and the state); here there is a stress on landed rights and property missing in Bloch's definition.
[31] Ganshof, *Feudalism*, pp. xvi–xvii, 143, 141.
[32] Similar to but narrower than Ganshof's is the definition of feudalism offered by D. C. Douglas. Since Douglas's works deal primarily with Normandy and the Norman conquests it is understandable that, like Ganshof, he should not consider the disintegration of central control a basic element. For Douglas two ideas are important: "the principle that the amount of service owed should be clearly determined before the grant of the fief" and "the notion of liege-homage." *The Norman Achievement,*

governmental authority – an element rejected by Ganshof – is the single essential component in any definition of feudalism. Several years ago Joseph R. Strayer adopted this position when he advocated a definition focusing on jurisdiction and omitting most of the other factors contained in the definitions just examined. "To obtain a usable concept of feudalism," Strayer argued, "we must eliminate extraneous factors and aspects which are common to many types of society." Having lopped off aristocracy, "the great estate worked by dependent or servile labor," "the relationship between lord and man," and "the system of dependent land tenures," he concluded that it is "only when rights of government (not mere political influence) are attached to lordship and fiefs that we can speak of fully developed feudalism in Western Europe."[33] Subsequently Strayer decided that this definition was defective,[34] and in 1965 he advanced one that included a military as well as a political

---

1050–1100 (Berkeley, 1969), p. 177; see also p. 179. Douglas also emphasizes the idea of contractual military service, isolating this as the core of the "Norman feudal custom," which, he says, William the Conqueror interpreted "in a sense advantageous to himself" when he "[suddenly introduced] military feudalism into England." *William the Conqueror: The Norman Impact upon England* (Berkeley, 1964), pp. 100, 101, 103, 283. See also Cheyette, who counsels historians to "consider feudalism a *technique*, rather than an *institution*, . . . a technique involving above all a relation of personal dependence and service normally sealed by the grant of a dependent tenure or some other form of material support, and confined to that group of professional warriors who in time become the nobility, the *miles* [*sic*], the *domini* – a technique used to achieve certain purposes in certain places at certain times." "Some Notations on Mr. Hollister's 'Irony,'" p. 12.

[33] Joseph R. Strayer, "Feudalism in Western Europe," in Rushton Coulborn, ed., *Feudalism in History* (Princeton, 1956), p. 16, reprinted in Cheyette, *Lordship and Community*, p. 13. A similar definition appears in a lecture presented by Strayer in 1963 and published four years later as "The Two Levels of Feudalism," in Robert S. Hoyt, ed., *Life and Thought in the Early Middle Ages* (Minneapolis, 1967), pp. 52–3, reprinted in Joseph R. Strayer, *Medieval Statecraft and the Perspectives of History: Essays by Joseph R. Strayer*, ed. John F. Benton and Thomas N. Bisson (Princeton, 1971), pp. 63–5. In this essay Strayer maintains that a broader definition, referring to economic and social conditions, "in fact defined nothing," and he asserts that "the narrow, military definition of feudalism" ("a way of raising an army of heavy-armed cavalrymen by uniting the two institutions of vassalage and the fief"), while laudably precise, is "too limited" to be useful, since, if defined in this way, feudalism "would have little historical significance." In Hoyt, *Life and Thought*, pp. 52–3 (in Strayer, *Medieval Statecraft*, pp. 64–5). See also Strayer's comments in *Feudalism* (Princeton, 1965), pp. 13–14. This point of view was again expressed, in modified form, in an essay Strayer published in 1968: "The Tokugawa Period and Japanese Feudalism," in John W. Hall and Marius B. Jansen, eds, *Studies in the Institutional History of Modern Japan* (Princeton, 1968), p. 3, reprinted in Strayer, *Medieval Statecraft*, p. 90. In this essay Strayer states that "in political terms, feudalism is marked by a fragmentation of political authority, private possession of public rights, and a ruling class composed (at least originally) of military leaders and their followers." Note that this definition, explicitly couched "in political terms," does not exclude the possibility of formulating other definitions phrased in different terms.

[34] This modification resulted from a reorientation of approach that occurred in 1962 and 1963, when Strayer established his concept of two levels of feudalism. In reviewing Marie Fauroux's *Recueil des actes des ducs de Normandie, 911–1066* (Caen, 1961), Strayer commented that "many scholars have failed to see that there were really two feudalisms – the feudalism of the armed retainer or knight, and the feudalism of the counts and other great lords who were practically independent rulers of their districts. The two feudalisms began at different times and under different circumstances, and it was a long time before they were fully meshed together." In *Speculum* 37 (1962): 608. Although Strayer did not explicitly define feudalism, his discussion revealed that "Norman feudalism of the classic type" required the holding of "land in return for a definite quota of military service." "Knights and other vassals" were important not only "for military purposes" but also as "part of the governing group," whose aid and counsel the duke needed to rule effectively, and who possessed local administrative authority (pp. 608–9). It is hard to reconcile this analysis with a definition of feudalism that emphasizes

element. Then he presented as "the basic characteristics of feudalism in Western Europe . . . a fragmentation of political authority, public power in private hands, and a military system in which an essential part of the armed forces is secured through private contracts." Thus feudalism was seen not only as "a method of government" but also as "a way of securing the forces necessary to preserve that method of government." It seems clear, however, that Strayer still considered the jurisdictional element fundamental, for in concluding his discussion he wrote that "a drive for political power by the aristocracy led to the rise of feudalism."[35]

Other approaches to the problem of defining feudalism have been taken. In 1953 Georges Duby stated a bit hesitantly that "what one refers to as feudalism" ("*ce qu'on appelle la féodalité*") should be understood to have two aspects, the political – involving the dissolution of sovereignty – and the economic – the constitution of a coherent network of dependencies embracing all lands and through them their holders.[36] Thus he created a bridge of sorts, reconciling the definitions of Strayer and Ganshof. Later, however, Duby turned from government and land to mentalities, and in 1958 he suggested that feudalism might best be considered

> a psychological complex formed in the small world of warriors who little by little
> became nobles. A consciousness of the superiority of a status characterized by
> military specialization, one that presupposes respect for certain moral precepts,

---

the disintegration of central authority and the consequent distribution of political power among numerous members of a ruling group, and in 1963 Strayer acknowledged that in Normandy political fragmentation – an essential element of the political definition of feudalism he described in the same essay as the original and "best" definition – was tardy and incomplete. "Two Levels of Feudalism," in Hoyt, *Life and Thought*, pp. 51–2, see also pp. 63–5 (in Strayer, *Medieval Statecraft*, p. 63, see also pp. 74–5). In addition see Strayer, *Feudalism*, p. 39. Even outside Normandy it was not until the eleventh century – and then not consistently and regularly – that the lower as well as the higher social and military orders distinguished by Strayer can be said to have exercised independent political power. With the inadequacy of the political definition of feudalism exposed, it must have become evident that some additional element or elements would have to be added to produce a satisfactory definition of the term.

[35] Strayer, *Feudalism*, pp. 13, 74. Note, too, that in "The Tokugawa Period," published in 1968, Strayer still laid heavy emphasis on the political aspect of feudalism.

[36] Georges Duby, *La société aux XI*e *et XII*e *siècles dans la région mâconnaise* (Paris, 1953), p. 643, the corresponding page in the reprint (Paris, 1971) is 481. Duby's evasive approach to the word *féodalité* reappears in his book *Guerriers et paysans, VII*e*–XII*e *siècle: Premier essor de l'économie européenne* (Paris, 1973). Here he uses terms reminiscent of those he employed in 1953 as he refers to "ce que les historiens ont coutume d'appeler la féodalité" (p. 179). Calling it "un mouvement de très grande amplitude" ["a movement of wide ramifications"], he does not define it precisely and explicitly, although he says that it was characterized by "la décomposition de l'autorité monarchique" ["the dissolution of monarchical authority"], and coincided with the development of a new sort of warfare and the establishment of a new conception of peace; he discusses "un système économique que l'on peut, en simplifiant, appeler féodal" ["an economic system which one might, by simplifying, call feudal"]; he concludes that "au plan de l'économie, la féodalité n'est pas seulement la hiérarchie des conditions sociales qu'entend représenter le schéma des trois ordres [elsewhere described as "le clergé, les spécialistes de la guerre, et les travailleurs"], c'est aussi – et d'abord sans doute – l'institution seigneuriale" ["On the economic plane, feudalism is not only the hierarchy of social conditions that the scheme of the three orders (those who pray – the clergy; the specialists in war; and those who labor) was meant to represent, but also – and most importantly – the seigneury"] (pp. 179, 184, 185, 187, 191). Thus, on the economic plane, Duby substitutes the development of the lordship for the coherent network of dependencies that he stressed in 1953.

the practice of certain virtues; the associated idea that social relations are organized as a function of companionship in combat; notions of homage, of personal dependence, now in the foreground, replacing all previous forms of political association.[37]

Definitions of feudalism abound, and student and scholar have available to them broad ones that lump together numerous facets of medieval society and narrow ones that center on carefully chosen aspects of that society – tenurial, political, military, and psychical. The possibilities for bewilderment and dispute are dizzying, particularly since a single author's interpretation of the term can undergo marked shifts.

Another difficulty posed by feudalism and its system is the fact that those employing the terms, in whatever sense they use them, are constantly found qualifying and limiting the extent to which they believe them applicable to any particular time and locality in medieval Europe. Marc Bloch writes, "In the area of Western civilization the map of feudalism reveals some large blank spaces – the Scandinavian peninsula, Frisia, Ireland. Perhaps it is more important still to note that feudal Europe was not all feudalized in the same degree or according to the same rhythm and, above all, that it was nowhere feudalized completely." Nostalgically, and with regret only a confirmed Platonist could harbor, he concludes, "No doubt it is the fate of every system of human institutions never to be more than imperfectly realized."[38]

While Robert S. Hoyt could write of the growth and development of feudalism and could state that by the mid-eleventh century "an essentially feudal society had emerged throughout western continental Europe," he felt obliged, first, to deny that there was a "'feudal system' common to all Europe," and second, to assert that "there were endless diversity and variety."[39] In the introduction to *Feudalism* Ganshof notes that he proposes

> to study feudalism mainly as it existed in France, in the kingdom of Burgundy–Arles and in Germany, since in these countries its characteristics were essentially the same, and to concentrate on the regions lying between the Loire and the Rhine, which were the heart of the Carolingian state and the original home of feudalism. Further afield, in the south of France and in Germany beyond the Rhine, the institutions that grew up are often far from typical of feudalism as a whole.[40]

In his foreword to the book, F. M. Stenton praises Ganshof's self-imposed limitations and suggests that they result from a realization "that social arrangements, arising from the instinctive search for a tolerable life, vary indefinitely with varieties of time and circumstance." While it is easy to agree with Stenton that students should be disabused of the idea that "an ideal type of social order" dominated western Europe, it comes as something of a shock to find him readily accepting the doctrine that in the huge area on which Ganshof focuses a single "classical feudalism" was to be found.[41] The expectation of infinite variety in

---

[37] Georges Duby, "La Féodalité? Une mentalité médiévale," *Annales: Économies, Sociétés, Civilisations* 13 (1958): 766. See also the comments of J. M. Wallace-Hadrill in a review of Bloch's *Feudal Society*, in *English Historical Review* 78 (1963): 117.

[38] Bloch, *Société féodale*, vol. 2, pp. 248, 249 (*Feudal Society*, p. 445).

[39] Robert S. Hoyt, *Europe in the Middle Ages*, 2nd ed. (New York, 1966), pp. 190–6, 185.

[40] Ganshof, *Feudalism*, p. xvii.

[41] Stenton, foreword to ibid., pp. vii–viii.

social arrangements seemingly ends for Stenton at the Loire and the Rhine, a good safe distance from the Thames.

The variety of definitions of feudalism and the limitations imposed on their relevance are confusing. Equally disconcerting is the pervasive tendency on the part of those who use the word to personify, reify, and to coin two words, occasionally "bacterialize," and even "lunarize" the abstraction. How often does one read that feudalism, like a virus, spread from one area to another, or that, later on, it slowly waned. In a single study feudalism is assigned a dazzling array of roles. It is found giving birth, being extremely virile, having vitality, being strong, knowing a long tradition, being successfully transplanted, surviving, being replaced, teetering, being routed, declining and falling, and finally dead and in its grave. Another author sees it destroying the Frankish Empire and making a clean sweep of outmoded institutions. For another it makes onslaughts on the power of the kings of France and England; "les forces féodaux" end the confusion of spiritual and temporal authorities. Still another work reassuringly attributes a home to feudalism, which is said to have exercised, rather adventurously, "paralyzing action" over "many forms of royal activity," and, more decorously, to have been "introduced into England in its French form" by the duke of Normandy.[42] In concluding *Seigneurie et féodalité* Boutruche in fact triumphantly proclaims it madness to consider feudalism an abstraction. "In actuality, it is a person. . . . Feudalism is medieval. . . . It is the daughter of the West."[43]

Another problem is the inclination to employ the idea of fully developed, classical, or perfectly formed feudalism as a standard by which to rank and measure areas or societies. Territories are regularly divided into categories: some highly or thoroughly feudalized; others never, gradually, or only partly feudalized.[44] Non-European countries are evaluated in this manner, and the standard has often been applied to Japanese modes of social and political organization.[45] Such assessments can also be made of institutions. The Church in Norman Italy, for instance, has been judged "never feudalized to the same extent as . . . the Church in Norman England."[46]

These examples all involve inanimate phenomena, geographical or institutional, but it is also possible to attribute to an individual or a group the aim of achieving complete feudalization or of introducing an articulated feudal system and then judge the person or

[42] See Bryce D. Lyon, *From Fief to Indenture: The Transition from Feudal to Non-Feudal Contract in Western Europe* (Cambridge, Mass., 1957), pp. 272–3; Georges Duby, *Adolescence de la Chrétienté occidentale, 980–1140* (Geneva, 1967), pp. 61, 83. The corresponding pages in the English edition – translated by Stuart Gilbert and entitled *The Making of the Christian West, 980–1140* (Geneva, 1967) – are 61 and 83. See also Bloch, *Feudal Society*, pp. 59, 142, 443, where the statements found in *Société féodale*, vol. 1, pp. 95, 221 and vol. 2, p. 245, are sometimes given a rather free interpretation. Finally, see Ganshof, *Feudalism*, pp. xvii, 54, 59, 61.

[43] "La féodalité est présentée parfois comme une abstraction. Folie! En vérité, c'est une personne. . . . La féodalité est médiévale. . . . Elle est fille de l'Occident." Boutruche, *Seigneurie et féodalité*, p. 297.

[44] Lyon, *From Fief to Indenture*, pp. 23–4; Joseph R. Strayer, "The Development of Feudal Institutions," in Marshall Clagett, Gaines Post, and Robert Reynolds, eds, *Twelfth-Century Europe and the Foundations of Modern Society* (Madison, 1961), p. 79, reprinted in Strayer, *Medieval Statecraft*, pp. 78–9.

[45] Bloch, *Société féodale*, vol. 2, pp. 250–2 (*Feudal Society*, pp. 446–7); Strayer, "The Tokugawa Period." For hesitations expressed by Ganshof and by Bloch himself concerning the validity of this approach, see Ganshof, *Feudalism*, pp. xv–xvi; Bloch, *Société féodale*, vol. 2, p. 242 (*Feudal Society*, p. 441), and *Apologie*, p. 89 (*Historian's Craft*, pp. 175–6).

[46] Douglas, *Norman Achievement*, p. 176.

group a success or failure in achieving this hypothesized objective. The precise nature of the goal would naturally depend on how the historian making the attribution defined feudalism or feudal system, but such assessments immediately imply that the person or group in question consciously planned and then attempted to implement a system based primarily on the granting of fiefs, but also involving the establishment of a graded hierarchy of status and command and the delegation of sovereign power. D. C. Douglas transposes feudalism from the realm of the abstract into a concretely human framework when he says that in England William the Conqueror "was concerned to establish a completed feudal organization by means of administrative acts" and when he indicates that the conquest of England enabled William to realize the "feudal organization in Normandy." Before 1066, Douglas says, the Normans were "as yet unorganized in any rigid feudal scheme," the feudal structure "had not yet been fully formed," "the structure of Norman society had [not] as yet been made to conform to an ordered feudal plan."[47] A similar transformation of abstract model into consciously held goal occurs as Christopher Brooke asserts that "only in the Norman and the crusading states, colonized in great measure from the homeland of French feudalism, did one find any attempt to live up to a conception of feudalism as coherent as that of northern France."[48]

Appraising in terms of an ideal standard need not involve making value judgments, but such assessments are ordinarily expressed in value-loaded terms. To say that a person or a group is attempting to live up to or realize a standard certainly suggests virtuous dedication on the part of the people in question. To declare that a country which is not feudalized is lagging behind is to indicate that the area is in some sense backward. Even more evidently evaluative are such expressions as decayed, decadent, and bastard feudalism, all of them implying a society's failure or inability to maintain pure principles that were once upheld.[49] One is occasionally struck by a rather sentimental regret that the societies, individuals, and groups which might have been encouraged by high marks to persevere or shamed by low ones into exerting an additional push are unable to benefit from them. Even if formulated in value-free terms, analyses of societies on the basis of their conformity to or deviation from a norm offer little insight into the societies themselves, however much the process of comparison may stimulate and challenge the ingenuity of historians. To produce helpful insights, comparative history must involve the examination of the widest possible range of elements, not those idiosyncratically dubbed essential by the historians devising the standard to be applied.

  Asserting that individual rulers actively and consciously aimed at establishing feudalism and judging them in terms of this aim is, at another level, equally misconceived and

---

[47] Douglas, *William the Conqueror*, pp. 281, 98, 283, 96, 104; see also n. 32 above. See the more convincing analysis presented by Strayer in his review of Fauroux's *Recueil des actes*, pp. 609–10. Like Douglas, however, Strayer concludes that although "Norman feudalism of the classic type was not fully developed until the second half of the eleventh century . . . it was William the Conqueror, more than any other ruler, who gave it definitive form." Note the warnings given by Richardson and Sayles against assuming that William had any "grand designs or well devised plans." *Governance of Mediaeval England*, p. 71. For a clearly integrated account of William's accomplishments – which only once mentions the adjective "feudal" – see D. C. Douglas, "William the Conqueror: Duke and King," in Dorothy Whitelock, D. C. Douglas, C. H. Lemmon, and Frank Barlow, *The Norman Conquest: Its Setting and Impact* (London, 1966), pp. 45–76; see p. 65 for "feudal."

[48] Christopher Brooke, *Europe in the Central Middle Ages, 962–1154* (New York [1963]), p. 100.

[49] See the comments of K. B. McFarlane, "'Bastard Feudalism,'" *Bulletin of the Institute of Historical Research* 20 (1943–5): 161–2.

misleading. That William the Conqueror, the Normans, and the Crusaders wanted to establish control within the areas they conquered as effectively as circumstances permitted is, I think, unquestionable; that they used and molded the institutional forms and arrangements with which they were familiar and which were available to them is equally undeniable. To suggest, however, that they operated on the basis of a definite, preconceived scheme focused primarily on the fief, and to measure their accomplishments by such a standard, is to give a distorted, simplistic picture of their actions and policies, projecting into the minds of people who dealt creatively and flexibly with numerous options and who manipulated a variety of institutional devices to achieve their purposes a degree of calculation, narrowness of vision, and rigidity that the surviving evidence does not suggest characterized them and in which even a contemporary management specialist might have difficulty believing.

What of the other virtues attributed to feudalism as a means of comprehending medieval social and political life? As far as pedagogy is concerned, students should certainly be spared an approach that inevitably gives an unwarranted impression of unity and systematization and unduly emphasizes, owing to the etymology of the word, the significance of the fief. Even if historians agreed to define feudalism as feudal society and included within its scope all facets of social and political development, the practical problem would remain. There are other, more basic, disadvantages. To advocate teaching what is acknowledged to be deceptive and what must later be untaught reflects an unsettling attitude of condescension toward younger students. Furthermore, not only does such a procedure waste the time of teacher and student, but its supporters apparently disregard the difficulty of, as a student of mine puts it, "'erasing' an erroneous concept or fact from the mind of a child who has been taught it, mistakenly or intentionally, at a lower school level." This student, Marie Heinbach, who teaches social studies in a New York junior high school, goes on to point out that "the difficulty becomes almost insurmountable when the amazing retentive powers of a young and impressionable child are considered. In addition, as the amount of time between the learning and unlearning of a concept increases, it becomes nearly impossible totally to correct the misconceptions that a student may have."[50] Experts who knowingly mislead their students appear to be unsure of their own ability to present a simplified account of the conclusions concerning medieval society that historians have now reached. Those of their students who do not progress beyond the introductory stage are denied the knowledge that most medieval historians study the actions and interrelationships of human beings rather than concentrating on the formulation and refinement of definitions of abstractions. Such students are never exposed to the problems of social and family structure and their corresponding etiquettes or to the problems of territorial loyalties and group attachments that historians are now examining. Presented with an abstract model and sternly cautioned against assuming its general relevance and applicability, only the staunchest will be motivated to pursue the individuals and groups lurking behind and beyond the ism.

For scholars the approach has equally little use. Applying an artificially fabricated standard in which certain components are divorced from the context in which they existed is essentially sterile. And those who investigate the workings of medieval society run the risk of having their vision narrowed, their perspective anachronistically skewed, and their receptivity to divergent data consequently blunted, unless they firmly divorce themselves from the preconceptions and sets associated with the oversimplified models and abstractions with which they have been indoctrinated, and which they themselves pass on to their students.

[50] This statement was made in an examination submitted on March 27, 1974.

162   *Elizabeth A. R. Brown*

What of the indispensability of feudalism? Here a distinction must be made. While the creation of intuitive abstractions and simple Ideal Types can indeed be explained by invoking the infinite and confusing variety of human experience, it is quite another matter to suggest that the procedure is obligatory, necessary, or laudable. Alternative modes of classifying and describing exist and can be used. Again, attempting to justify the formulation and use of such models and abstractions by maintaining that scholarly and scientific terminology and common usage assume their existence is patently circular, avoiding as this argument does the obvious fact that scholarly terminology can be revised and common usage clarified. Far more appropriate to express regret and to apologize for measures attributable to the weaknesses and defects of human modes of expression and perception. Historians and social scientists can, like natural scientists, devise multifactor, heuristic models that encompass and account for the available evidence, are reformulated to include newly discovered data, and are not misleadingly labeled so as to suggest either system and conscious organization where none existed or the predominant importance of one element in a situation in which many elements are known to have been significant.[51] Such multifactor models and descriptive, narrative accounts, which emphasize complexity and the unique, can convincingly be said to encourage fuller, less distorted, and hence more acceptable understanding of the past than any "one-sided accentuation of one or more points of view."[52]

The contention that such general terms as "feudalism" are essential for intelligent discourse is also debatable, and those who advance this defense reveal their own discomfiture when they invoke other commonly used abstractions, such as "war" and "agriculture," to serve as buttressing middle elements. Intelligent discourse devoid of general abstract terms is, the argument runs, inconceivable. All abstractions – feudalism, war, agriculture – are similar in nature. Therefore the isms are indispensable if intelligent discourse is to occur. This chain of reasoning is, however, flawed in its second step, for there is an evident difference between, on the one hand, those collective descriptive abstractions arrived at by isolating common features of different phenomena similar enough to permit the use and assure the acceptance of single words to denote them, and, on the other hand, those abstract analytic constructs formulated and defined as a shorthand means of designating the characteristics that the observers consider essential to various time periods, modes of organization, movements, and doctrines. To a degree to which the first type is not, the second sort of general term is inevitably and often intentionally affected by the theories and assumptions of the formulators and users. Disagreements over the exact meaning of "war" or "agriculture" do occur, but they can ordinarily be resolved by introducing greater precision and clarity into the definitions of the terms, whose core signification is not generally contested. In distinction, infinite disagreement about the meanings of the isms is possible and perhaps inevitable, since the terms were not devised to designate the basic elements of fundamentally similar classes of phenomena but rather to refer to selected elements of complex phenomena, the choice of which inevitably involves the idiosyncratic value judgments of the terms' inventors and employers. Thus, however easy it is to say what the words "fief," "capital," and "merchant" mean, it is another thing entirely to seek consensus on the definitions of

---

[51] See, for the natural sciences, N. R. Hanson, *Observation and Explanation: A Guide to Philosophy of Science* (New York, 1971), pp. 77–84; T. S. Kuhn, *The Structure of Scientific Revolutions*, vol. 2, no. 2 of the International Encyclopedia of Unified Science, 2nd ed. (Chicago, 1970), pp. 100–2; George Gamow, *Thirty Years That Shook Physics: The Story of Quantum Theory* (Garden City, 1966), p. 155; and James D. Watson, *The Double Helix* (new York, 1969), pp. 18, 38, 47, 49, 61, 83, 123.

[52] Max Weber, *The Methodology of the Social Sciences* (Glencoe, 1949), p. 90, quoted and discussed in Lane, *Introduction to Structuralism*, p. 25.

"feudalism," "capitalism," and "mercantilism," precisely because of the subjective nature of the definitions of these words. To raise the level of discourse and make it truly intelligent, there should be general agreement to consider the isms no more than the artificialities they are.

Direct expressions of discontent with the term "feudalism" have increased in number and strength over the past two decades. From time to time there has seemed reason to hope that, with a resounding whoop, historians would join together, following the example of the National Assembly, to annihilate the feudal regime and, with the good members of the Legion of Honor, agree "to combat . . . any enterprise tending to reestablish it."[53] At least partly responsible for the mounting volume of protest is the reorientation of perspective that took place in 1953 with the publication of two remarkable books, one French and one English, both dealing with the political and social life of western Europe in the tenth through the twelfth centuries, both concerned with individuals rather than abstractions, and both avoiding the medieval isms.

Of these books the purest – in that it does not, as far as I can tell, contain the word "feudalism" – is Richard W. Southern's study, *The Making of the Middle Ages*. In a section devoted to "The Bonds of Society" Southern presents an illuminating introduction to the political life of the eleventh and twelfth centuries by concentrating on a single, "unusually instructive" example of "what happened where the control exercised by the past was least effective, and where the disturbing elements of trade, large towns and active commercial oligarchies were not conspicuous." Discussing the emergence of the county of Anjou, Southern uses such abstract terms as "the disintegration of authority" and "the shaping of a new political order." He writes, generally, of "an age of serious, expansive wars waged by well-organized and strongly fortified territorial lords." The term "feudal" is sometimes used in a general sense, in contexts in which it clearly implies more than connection or involvement with the fief. When the term is given this broader meaning, however, it seems to be so used out of force of habit rather than from any conscious conviction that it is the most appropriate and meaningful word to be found. "The art of feudal government" and "the early feudal age," neither phrase explicitly defined by Southern, are reminiscent of Bloch's *La Société féodale*, a book Southern recommends, and they strike a jarring note of vagueness and imprecision in a discussion otherwise notable for its concreteness. On the few other occasions when Southern employs the term "feudal" in this general way, alternative expressions that he devises to describe the phenomena in question are strikingly more informative. "Knightly" is one of these alternative terms, and, on a more extended scale, "the straightforward feudal-contract view of society" is far less subtle and suggestive than his evocative description of an "imagination . . . circumscribed by the ties of lordship and vassalage, by the recollection of fiefs and honours and well-known shrines, by the sacred bond of comradeship."[54]

Only a small portion of Southern's book is devoted to social and political ties and the exercise of governmental power, but Georges Duby, in his study of the Mâconnais in the

---

[53] Bloch, *Société féodale*, vol. 1, pp. 2–3 (*Feudal Society*, p. xvii); see also Boutruche, *Seigneurie et féodalité*, pp. 20–1.
[54] Richard W. Southern, *The Making of the Middle Ages* (New Haven, 1953), pp. 90–1, 80–1, 87, 86, 262, 55, 241. When Southern mentions "the straightforward feudal-contract view of society," he associates the term "feudatory" with the "holding [of] land in return for military service" (p. 55); see also p. 56 for a reference to "the formula of feudal government" and p. 242 for "feudal custom" and "feudal etiquette"; for "knightly ideal" see p. 241; see also pp. 55, 243.

eleventh and twelfth centuries, dedicates an entire volume to these subjects. Hence it is all the more noteworthy that in his index, as in Southern's, there is no reference to *féodalité*, although the index does list the indisputably acceptable terms *feudataire, fidèle, fidélité,* and *fief,* which are derived from and accurately reflect the terminology and usage of the eleventh and twelfth centuries.[55] Duby's avoidance of the term *féodalité* is consistent with his avowed purpose in writing his book. In his preface he announces that he is studying a small province in order to approach human beings directly, without isolating them from their milieu.[56] This he does, describing first the state of society in the Mâconnais at the end of the tenth century, then the period of independent castellanies from 980 to 1160, and finally the movement between 1160 and 1240 from castellany to principality. His conclusions are significant, first because of the wealth of data on which they are founded, but even more because the Mâconnais lies within – if at the southern extreme of – the area between the Loire and the Rhine where countless scholars have seen "classical feudalism" emerging, and also because its history does not exemplify the characteristics associated with this development.

Stressing the survival of comital power and superiority until the end of the tenth century, Duby shows that among the higher ranks of society the ties of fidelity linking those agreeing to some sort of mutual support were vague and imprecise, like family ties, and can best be described as confirming a relationship of *amicitia* [friendship]. As the count's power declined and as that of the castellans increased, bonds of dependence among the higher classes became more important, and grants of land were used to solidify the ties, until by 1075 land outweighed loyalty as their determinant. Obligations were still indefinite, however, and military service was not a significant component. Between men of unequal status, dependent relationships were closer, but the strength and meaning of these ties were limited by the small value of the fiefs that lords gave their followers, who generally possessed large allodial holdings, and by the multiplicity of the ties. According to Duby, "feudal institutions" – by which he apparently means not only fiefs but also homage and vassalage – had only superficial importance. They constituted a sort of superstructure that formalized without affecting pre-existing relationships.

> Feudal institutions were adapted to the previous structure of the higher class without significantly modifying it. Between great lords or knights, homage is a simple guarantee, an agreement not to harm; between a small noble and a powerful one, it is a true dedication, an agreement to serve. Vassalage and the fief, customary practices born in private usage, organized the relations that unequal division of wealth and power had already determined; they created no additional ones. In eleventh-century Mâconnais, there was no pyramid of vassals, there was no feudal system.[57]

Duby concludes that for the higher classes "feudalism was a step toward anarchy," but by this he evidently means not that any ill-conceived and abortive attempt had been made to create harmony by introducing homage, vassalage, and the fief, but that the links ordered by

---

[55] Duby, *Société aux XIe et XIIe siècles*, p. 666 (repr., p. 501).
[56] "J'ai volontairement conduit mes recherches dans le cadre étroit d'une petite province. La méthode des monographies régionales permet en effet d'approcher directement les hommes sans les isoler de leur milieu." Ibid., p. ix (repr., p. 7). In his conclusion, Duby again describes his approach: "Pour approcher de plus près les hommes, nous avons concentré notre attention sur une toute petite région" (p. 644 [repr., p. 482]).
[57] Ibid., pp. 94–116, 140–1, 172, 177–85, 194–5, see also 185–93, 291 (repr., pp. 93–108, 124–5, 149, 153–8, 164–5; see also 158–64, 235–36).

these institutions were not strong or meaningful enough to serve as effective restraints. These were instead provided by the teachings and intervention of the Church, by family bonds, and by a variety of oaths. Thus, "although violent and disturbed, the world of lords was not anarchic."[58] In this period the nobility exercised for their own benefit governmental powers over the lower classes, but their actual control over land did not increase.[59]

In the late twelfth and early thirteenth century the economy of the Mâconnais was transformed, and the king of France, long absent from the area, reappeared there. Economic pressures and royal policy produced a proliferation of ties of dependence and a marked decrease in allodial holdings; concomitantly, services may have become more definite and heavier. As far as justice was concerned, "the peace of the prince replaced the peace of God," and judicial procedures developed in the eleventh century were regularized and made more effective.[60]

Duby occasionally uses the word *féodalité*, but the term has no central significance in his book, thanks to his determination to focus on individuals and their actions. In his general conclusion he relates his findings to his own definition of feudalism, which, as has been seen, involves the disintegration of central authority and the development of an inclusive web of dependencies. In the Mâconnais, he reminds his readers, these two characteristics appeared successively rather than simultaneously, since in the eleventh and twelfth centuries, when most lands were freely held, jurisdictional powers were in the hands of private lords, and in the thirteenth century, when most lands were involved with dependent relationships, sovereignty reappeared in the persons of kings and princes.[61] Duby refuses to comment on the districts outside the Mâconnais, and he calls for additional local studies. Nonetheless he notes that "the society of the Mâconnais did not evolve in isolation." Pointing out that the Mâconnais was "a province of feudalism with marked individual characteristics,"[62] he implicitly suggests that other areas lying within the fabled heartland of feudalism were equally distinctive.

Duby does not openly attack the use of the concept of feudalism, nor does he denounce the idea that institutions in the Loire–Rhine region were similar enough to be described as a single phenomenon. Still, his conclusions demonstrate the futility of generalizations that are not based on the study of successive generations of human beings inhabiting a restricted area. They also suggest the inappropriateness of descriptive terms that fail to convey a sense of the variety of experience and development to be found throughout western Europe between the tenth and the late twelfth centuries. When I once asked Monsieur Duby what difference there was between his book on the Mâconnais and Ganshof's study of feudalism, he replied with a modest shrug of the shoulders, "Toute la différence du monde, Madame" ["All the difference in the world, Madame"]. His own book is a testimony to his conviction that understanding the workings of medieval society necessarily involves exploring the intricate

---

[58] Ibid., p. 204 (repr., p. 170). For a full discussion of these restraints see pp. 196–204 (repr., pp. 165–70).
[59] Ibid., pp. 329–30 (repr., pp. 261–2). For the close connection Duby now posits between the development of the ideology of the peace of God and "les premiers phases de la féodalisation" ["the first phases of feudalism"], see n. 36 above and Duby, *Guerriers et paysans*, p. 185.
[60] Duby, *Société aux XIe et XIIe siècles*, pp. 473–569, 571 (repr., pp. 361–427, 429).
[61] Using Bloch's periodization, Duby concludes that only in this sense could there be said to have been "two feudal ages." The second age – a time of fiefs, censives, and feudal principalities – contrasted with the earlier age of independent castellanies, and Duby believes that it began no earlier than 1160 and that it ended in 1240. Ibid., pp. 642–3 (repr., pp. 481–2).
[62] Ibid., p. 644 (repr., p. 482).

complexities of life rather than elaborating definitions and formulas designed to minimize, simplify, and, in the last analysis, obscure these complexities.[63]

Southern and Duby had their predecessors – historians who probed beyond or disregarded the construct feudalism and who concentrated on analyzing and describing the many different ties and modes of dependency binding human beings to one another. Unquestionably, the work of Duby and Southern has acted as an additional, powerful stimulus, prompting more scholars to study the actual functioning of society in different areas. In general, however, and certainly in works directed at a popular rather than a scholarly audience, the situation remains much the same as it has been, and there is virtually universal resistance and opposition to abandoning the term "feudalism" and to confining the word "feudal" to its narrow sense – "relating to fiefs." The reservations regarding the use of the generalized constructs implicit in the books of Southern and Duby have not yet had the widespread effect that might have been hoped.

Exceptions do, of course, exist. In the books he has published since 1953 Southern has consistently employed his brilliant descriptive techniques and has assiduously avoided the term "feudalism."[64] R. H. C. Davis is now following a similar path, having apparently undergone something of a conversion. In the history of medieval Europe that he wrote in 1957 the word "feudalism" occasionally appears. England after William's conquest is called "the best and simplest example of a feudal monarchy." The index refers readers wishing to learn about "fully-developed feudalism" to pages Davis evidently considers relevant to this subject. How refreshing, then, to turn to an article on the Norman Conquest written ten years later and to find there a convincing analysis of William's accomplishments that contains no reference to the ism or its associated forms.[65]

Southern and Davis are unfortunately in a minority. Far more numerous are the scholars who, while attacking the concept [of] feudalism, still use the term and even encourage its propagation by suggesting new and better definitions. The contradictions in the work of

---

[63] See, however, his more restrained comments in "La Féodalité?," pp. 765–6. Duby recommended Ganshof's study of feudalism as a guide and reference work but suggested that the very clarity, simplicity, and Cartesian rigor which are among its chief virtues may give the reader a false impression of order and regularity.

[64] See his book *Western Society and the Church in the Middle Ages* (Harmondsworth, 1970). Under the circumstances it is not difficult to forgive him for translating the word *homo*, which literally means no more than "man," as "vassal" in his edition of the *Vita Anselmi: The Life of St Anselm, Archbishop of Canterbury, by Eadmer* (Edinburgh, 1962), p. 111. Southern recently told me that he thinks "deplorable" not only the term "feudalism" but also the words "humanism" and "scholasticism." He said that he had never knowingly used the word "feudalism" to refer to actual conditions in the Middle Ages. He offered, however, a tentative and qualified defense of the word in *Medieval Humanism and Other Studies* (Oxford, 1970), p. 29. Southern's work suggests that he thinks the words "humanism" and "scholasticism" may have some practical value, however defective he may judge them on a theoretical plane. Medieval humanism is the central subject of his collected essays, and in a lecture, "The Origins of Universities in the Middle Ages," given at Philadelphia on April 8, 1974, Southern emphasized the importance of "scholasticism" and "scholastic" thought, calling the universities "the power house of scholasticism." In his conclusion, however, he warned that "European scholastic development" should be envisioned not as a single whole but as marked by diversity and variety.

[65] R. H. C. Davis, *A History of Medieval Europe from Constantine to Saint Louis* (London, 1957), s.v. "feudalism" in the index, and see also p. 127, where he enclosed the term "feudalism" in quotation marks; and see pp. 295, 414. Davis, "The Norman Conquest," *History* 51 (1966): 279–86, reprinted in C. W. Hollister, ed., *The Impact of the Norman Conquest* (New York, 1969), pp. 123–33.

Richardson and Sayles have already been discussed. Fully as puzzling is the case of Duby himself. Having implicitly questioned the aptness of the term in his study of the Mâconnais, he proceeded in 1958 not only to employ it but also, as has been seen, to advance an alternative definition, unusual and idiosyncratic, which he appears subsequently to have rejected. In a still later work, directed at a less scholarly audience, Duby employs the term *féodal* which, while undefined, clearly refers to something more general than the fief. It is found modifying such nouns as *éparpillement, forces, cours, princes,* and *seigneur;* a section of the book is entitled "Les féodaux," and the construct feudalism is several times personified.[66] A popular work published in 1973 shows that Duby's dedication to and reliance on the term have, in recent years, simply increased. He repeatedly refers to *féodalité* and uses the adjective *féodal* in a vague, indefinite way, and he goes so far as to designate the period from the mid-eleventh to the late twelfth century "les temps féodaux."[67] Saying that feudalism was characterized by the disintegration of monarchical authority and associating it with the institutions of the *seigneurie,* Duby presents feudalism a being implanted and established; he refers to feudalization, a feudal epoch, feudal society, feudal Europe, feudal peace, feudal structures, and a feudal economy and economic system.[68]

Striking inconsistencies appear in Christopher Brooke's five-page discussion of barons and knights in a book he published in 1963. Having begun by declaring that "few historical labels are more ambiguous than 'feudal'" and by proclaiming that he would therefore "use it as little as possible," having then warned that "it is doubtful whether [strict feudalism] ever existed outside the imaginations of historians," he proceeds, without defining the term "feudal," to use it, imprecisely and ambiguously, in writing of "the feudal bond," "feudal conceptions," "the feudal contract," "the feudal oath," and "feudal and quasi-feudal institutions." He also refers to "highly developed" feudalism, "classical feudalism," "French feudalism," and "strict feudalism." Finally he both reifies feudalism and uses the phrase "coherent feudalism" to designate a consciously formulated and adopted set of goals and principles.[69]

---

[66] Duby, *Adolescence de la Chrétienté occidentale,* pp. 60–1, 84. The translation of this book exaggerates these tendencies: see the corresponding pages, *Making of the Christian West,* pp. 61–2, 83–4, and note that the section Duby entitled "Les féodaux" is called "Feudalism" in the translation. In *L'économie rurale et la vie des campagnes dans l'Occident médiéval* (Paris, 1962), Duby may refer to "la seigneurie des temps féodaux" (p. 379), but he generally avoids the term, and *féodalité* is not listed in the index. Note, however, that in the translation of the book published in 1968, "temps féodaux" becomes "the feudal period," and "rente seigneuriale" is transformed into "feudal rent." *Rural Economy and Country Life in the Medieval West,* trans. Cynthia Postan (London, 1968), pp. 171, 232–59.

[67] Duby, *Guerriers et paysans,* pp. 179–204, and see n. 36 above.

[68] See also ibid., p. 194 ("l'implantation de la féodalité"), p. 262 ("l'établissement de la féodalité"), 184 ("l'établissement des structures féodales"), 185 ("la féodalisation"), 278 ("l'époque féodale"), 192 ("la société féodale"), 201 ("l'Europe féodale"), 300 ("la paix féodale"), 184 ("les structures féodales"), 189 ("l'économie féodale"), 187 ("un système économique que l'on peut, en simplifiant, appeler féodal"). It is heartening to note that the review of Duby's *Guerriers et paysans* in the *Times Literary Supplement* does not contain the words "feudal" or "feudalism." August 17, 1973, pp. 941–2.

[69] Brooke, *Europe* in the *Central Middle Ages,* pp. 95–6, 99–100. Brooke writes that "in its origin feudalism provided for the recruitment of vitally needed cavalry troops" (p. 100). See also p. 160 above. Note, too, that having just questioned the validity of the idea of "strict feudalism," Brooke scrupulously encloses "feudal" in quotation marks when he refers to "'feudal' means" of raising troops (p. 100).

The hesitancies, contradictions, and inconsistencies that have been reviewed – and that are wholly typical of statements found in the books on medieval society published in the past 20 years – clearly demonstrate how necessary it is to reassess the value of the words "feudal" and "feudalism." It must be admitted that there is little possibility of ridding the historical vocabulary of them, adopted as they have been by the scholarly community in general and by the economists in particular. The terms exist. They have been and probably will be used for many years. As words students know if they know nothing else about the Middle Ages, they cannot be avoided. But confrontation need not mean capitulation, for it is perfectly possible to instruct students at all levels to use "feudal" only with specific reference to fiefs and to teach them what feudalism is, always has been, and always will be – a construct devised in the seventeenth century and then and subsequently used by lawyers, scholars, teachers, and polemicists to refer to phenomena, generally associated more or less closely with the Middle Ages, but always and inevitably phenomena selected by the person employing the term and reflecting that particular viewer's biases, values, and orientations. Illustrations of the many meanings attached to "feudal" and "feudalism" can be given, and students with a flair for historiography can be encouraged to explore the eccentricities of usage associated with the terms.

Other students will be directed to the study of medieval society and politics, and they and their instructors will be faced with the necessity and challenge of finding an adequate means of describing the elements historians have investigated and should explore and the positive conclusions that have been reached.[70] Throughout, the terminology and word usage of those who lived in the Middle Ages must be emphasized, and attention must be paid to the shifting meanings of key words, as well as to the gulf between actual practice and the formal, stylized records that have survived. Some elements will be pointed to as constants of general importance: the slowness and difficulty of communication, the general insecurity, the sluggish rate of technological change, and the reverence for tradition. The varying effects and significance of terrain, warfare, and violence must be emphasized. Stress must also be given to the resultant regional and diachronic variations in forms of government, modes of military organization, social and family structure, social mobility, the relationship between social class and function, styles of agricultural exploitation and commercial activity, and urban growth. Attention must be called to the different social and political relationships in which human beings were involved, to the ceremonies through which these relationships were fixed and manifested, and to the varying sorts of ties that superficially similar ceremonies could be used to create: bonds of obligation, fidelity, and support between sovereigns and their subjects, created and confirmed by oaths, pledges, and services; ties of loyalty, solidarity, and mutual assistance among people of similar and different social classes, formalized in communes, confraternities, gilds, leagues, and alliances, constituted through mutual undertakings that were sometimes left vague and sometimes clearly defined, solidified through privileges granted to and demanded by these groups; religious ties binding members of local congregations, regional churches, and similar faiths; ties of dependence forged between individuals or inherited from the past, sometimes involving friendship, sometimes service, sometimes protection, reinforced by gestures and oaths, resulting in benefits – material, monetary, territorial, social – to one or both parties; family bonds, revealed and consolidated

---

[70] See Joseph R. Strayer, "The Future of Medieval History," *Medievalia et Humanistica*, n.s. 2 (1971): 182. Only since the appearance in 1968 of Fredric Cheyette's invaluable collection of translated essays, *Lordship and Community*, has it been practically possible to direct beginning students to the recent literature in which this perspective on medieval society is reflected.

in testamentary provisions, marriages, special festivities, and feuds and vendettas. The written and unwritten rules governing these ties and relationships must be considered, as must the ways in which and the different degrees to which these principles were systematized and enforced.

But to be properly understood, these elements must be observed as they developed, interacted, and changed, and thus the importance of presenting searching and detailed descriptions of areas characterized by different forms of governmental and social structure and organization and by different modes of development. Regions where strong monarchies developed and survived must be given as extensive consideration as areas where they disappeared, so that any given region – the Empire, England, Italy, Normandy, the Ile-de-France, the Mâconnais – will be considered neither abnormal nor typical but will be viewed as an instance of the varying ways human beings responded to similar and dissimilar circumstances, whose impact was conditioned by the total pasts of the people they affected. Those who are introduced to the study of medieval social and political life in this way will be far less likely than those presented with definitions and monistically oriented models to be misled about the conditions of existence in the Middle Ages. They will find it difficult to contrive and parrot simplistic and inaccurate generalizations about medieval Europe, and they may be challenged to inquire into subjects and areas as yet uninvestigated and to seek solutions to problems as yet unanswered.

The unhappiness of historians with the terms "feudal" and "feudalism" is, thus, understandable. Far less comprehensible is their willingness to tolerate for so long a situation often deplored. Countless different, and sometimes contradictory, definitions of the terms exist, and any and all of these definitions are hedged around with qualifications. Using the terms seems to lead almost inevitably to treating the ism or its system as a sentient, autonomous agent, to assuming that medieval people – or at least the most perspicacious of them – knew what feudalism was and struggled to achieve it, and to evaluating and ranking societies, areas, and institutions in terms of their approximation to or deviation from an oversimplified Ideal Type.

Despite the examples set by Southern and Duby some twenty years ago and followed in the interim by some scholars, historians have been generally loath to restrict the term "feudal" and discard the term "feudalism," particularly in dealing with general rather than specialized audiences. Feudalism's reign has continued virtually unchallenged, with ambivalence characterizing the attitudes of most historians toward the subject. The situation, however, can and should change. The arguments advanced to defend using the terms as they have been used in the past are weak, based as they are on vaguely articulated assumptions concerning the concept's utility as a verbal and intellectual tool, as a teaching device, or as a mode of evaluation – none of which is convincingly established. Similarly unsatisfactory are justifications founded on hypothesized requirements: the historian's need, as scientist, for abstractions like feudalism; the basic demands of discourse; or necessities created by the fundamental and seemingly insurmountable limitations of the human mind. Preferable alternative perspectives and terms exist, and there seems no reason to delay channeling all available energies to the study of human beings who lived in the past, thus putting an end to the elaboration of arid definitions and the construction of simplistic models. The tyrant feudalism must be declared once and for all deposed and its influence over students of the Middle Ages finally ended. Perhaps in its downfall it will carry with it those other obdurate isms – manorial, scholastic, and human – that have dominated for far too long the investigation of medieval life and thought.

10 Giving Each His Due

Fredric L. Cheyette

What is "Law"? The question has been given many answers.[1] If we are nominalist enough we can list the various ways the word is used, as did Marsiglio of Padua and William of Occam in the fourteenth century. If we are realist enough (in the medieval sense) we can try to construct a definition of the genus. We can define human law with Montesquieu as one variety of the "necessary relations arising from the nature of things." We can define it Positivistically with Austin as the command of the sovereign; or Realistically (in a peculiar modern sense of the word) as "what officials do about disputes," or "a prediction of what courts will do." We can equate law with morals or distinguish the two. We can make justice the defining quality of law or say a law is a law whether just or not.

> Law, says the judge as he looks down his nose,
> Speaking clearly and most severely,
> Law is as I've told you before,
> Law is as you know I suppose,
> Law is but let me explain it once more,
> Law is The Law.[2]

As historians we would probably be inclined to forget the whole matter. Yet I think that would be a mistake. To talk about law as a historical phenomenon without defining it can lead, and has led, only to confusion and occasionally remarkable anachronisms. I therefore want to suggest a couple of definitions that will be useful in exploring the topic at hand: definitions that, I hope, will allow us to use the term in a meaningful way, without getting us embroiled in the philosophical debates to which I have just alluded.

We can use "law," first of all, to denote the ways the members of a society or group in society habitually perform certain acts, whether or not they consciously put those ways into words.

[The old French in this essay has been translated by Anne M. Callahan.]
[1] This paper is drawn from a larger work in progress. Materials were collected under a Social Science Research Council fellowship with additional financial aid provided by the American Philosophical Society and Amherst College.
[2] This and later lines of English poetry are from W. H. Auden's "Law Like Love," *The Collected Poetry of W. H. Auden* (New York, 1945), pp. 74–6 (copyright 1945 by W. H. Auden; reprinted by permission of the publishers, Random House, Inc.).

> Law is the clothes men wear
> Anytime, anywhere,
> Law is Good-morning and Good-night.

If the eldest son in a given society habitually takes over his father's property when the father dies, we can call this a "law" of that society, whether or not the people involved consciously express the habit as a "norm."

This definition, to be sure, makes it impossible to distinguish custom from law, stated rule from observed practice; it also makes it impossible to distinguish law from morals or proper conduct. Were the definition to be used for other purposes these would be serious defects; they are not, however, for analyzing the law of eleventh- and twelfth-century France, when neither distinction was evident in day-to-day practice.

Alternatively, we can call "law" a conscious, verbalized system of norms that people in a society are supposed to observe and that is followed in authoritative settlement of conflicts. What I will be discussing is the shift from the first to the second kind of "law" in thirteenth-century France.

When the men of the thirteenth century make this shift, consciously or unconsciously, they make two choices rich in consequences for European society. Both choices must enter into our definition. First of all, they equate the norms used to make authoritative settlements with the norms that are supposed to govern men's behavior. They identify the law of the courts with the law that "commands what is good and prohibits what is harmful." Though to us this might seem an obvious equation, it is surely not a necessary one. There have been societies in which no courts existed for settling civil disputes: Imperial China, for one. There have also been societies in which courts had functions that did not include enforcing sets of rules, in which dispute settlement served values quite distinct from the network of do and don't, of shall and shall not. Such was the society of eleventh- and twelfth-century France. Secondly, when the men of the thirteenth century define their social norms they use particular sets of concepts: they define their rules in terms of objective criteria of class and situation, in terms of "movables" and "immovables," "inheritance" and "gift," "tenant" and "lord," "nobleman" and "bourgeois," "married woman" and "widow," rather than in terms of the subjective feelings of the persons involved, their pride, honor, or shame.

If we look in the French archives for evidence of conflicts being settled by authoritative courts in accordance with these kinds of objective criteria, what do we find? A large number of such documents exists around 1300. But as we go back into the thirteenth century, we reach a point where the documentary evidence thins out considerably, then suddenly disappears. In the area around Narbonne and Carcassonne, where we have one of the richest thirteenth-century city archives and an important monastic archive, as well as substantial remains from other major collections, this cut-off point is around mid-century. To be precise, the earliest case remaining from the archives of Narbonne is 1252;[3] from Béziers, 1254;[4] from the monastery of La Grasse, 1273;[5] from the archbishop's archives, 1268.[6] This archival phenomenon is not unique to this area. By way of comparison, in the documents from Laon and Saint-Quentin at the Archives nationales, such documents appear only in the reign of Philip III.[7] This is, to be sure, a superficial contrast of wealth and dearth, based

---

[3] Archives communales de Narbonne, AA 105, fo. 36v.
[4] Archives communales de Béziers (unnumbered).
[5] Archives départementales de l'Aude, H 166 (unnumbered).
[6] Arch. dépt Aude, G 21, no. 2.
[7] Archives nationales, L 731–5 (Laon), L 738 (Saint-Quentin).

largely on formal considerations. It nevertheless conforms to the well-known fact that the first continuous records of the Parlement of Paris begin in 1254. Before these dates conflicts are settled by arbitration or compromise when not by violence. This is true after mid-century as well, though, as we shall see, the spirit of the method changes.

Why did this change come about? The most common textbook explanation for the spread of ecclesiastical and royal justice in medieval Europe – I have been guilty of it myself – is based on what might be called the better mousetrap theory of human nature: the world will beat a path to the court that is more just, that is, to the court whose decisions are more "rational" and conform more closely to established objective norms of behavior.[8] Is this tenable? To my knowledge no such general law has ever been demonstrated by psychologists or anthropologists, and it seems dubious on its face. There is no reason to believe that individuals (any more than collectives called "nations") prefer objective neutrality to partiality in their own favor. Indeed, moralists of every age have found ample cause to assert the contrary and denounce its consequences. Neutral, objective order is very much a learned value. An explanation for this thirteenth-century change still remains to be found.

At this point, a few distinctions may help clarify my story.

First of all, in the thirteenth century, as before and after, there are courts and courts, justice and justice. Before mid-century, when members of the "class of rulers" fight over property rights they do not appeal to courts who will judge by impersonal norms to settle their differences. But the members of this class do dominate a subject population. Their domination is expressed, in part, by something called justitia: for *justitia* in the eleventh and twelfth centuries in southern France is, among other things, the name of a customary payment that subject populations in the cities and countryside make to their overlords. It is hard to tell whether some twelfth-century documents employ this term for anything but a customary payment. But the very name of this tallage suggests that some kind of court activity lies, or once lay, behind it. And that activity finally appears clearly when charters distinguish justice-as-dues from justice criminal and civil. One of the earliest to do so in lower Languedoc is the act of 1187 by which Bernard-Ato, viscount of Agde, gave his viscounty to the bishop. His charter lists *justitiae* (plural) among the financial rights, and the *causas criminales et civiles et earumdem executiones* [civil and criminal cases and their enforcement] in a separate clause.[9] Romanized expressions such as this, and the appearance of the Roman phrase *merum et mixtum imperium* around the same time as an equivalent for what is called "high and low justice" elsewhere in France, indicate that the lords had not neglected criminal activities among their subjects and may have taken a hand in settling other kinds of disputes as well. But how far back does this go? And what kind of litigations, procedure, and law were actually involved? These questions the evidence, unfortunately, does not answer. The remainder of this discussion will therefore be devoted to the one group about whom we do have information: the rulers of society.

Secondly, in the Middle Ages, as in our own time, law does not develop evenly on all fronts. Some matters are early made subject to authoritative, objective norms; others remain subject to different values, to different obligations. Property law, for a variety of reasons, is

---

[8] Most flagrantly in my own "La Justice et le pouvoir royal," *Revue historique de droit français et étranger* 4me sér., XL (1962): 373–94. But I had authoritative precedents: Ferdinand Lot and Robert Fawtier, *Histoire des institutions françaises au moyen âge*, II (Paris, 1958), pp. 298–9; George O. Sayles, *The Medieval Foundations of England* (Philadelphia, 1950), p. 342.

[9] *Gallia Christiana*, VI, *instrum.*, cols 331–2.

a late-bloomer. Yet property law deeply influences the structure of late medieval society and government. It is property law that I am concerned with here.

Finally, we may have authoritative norms without authoritative courts and courts without norms. We find both situations in the Middle Ages. When in any area of human activity courts and norms come together, we have created the potential for rapid and radical change. This is exactly what happens in the mid-thirteenth century.

Before the middle of the thirteenth century disputes over property were settled by arbitration and compromise, when not by war. What exactly were these arbitrations? Who performed them? How were they decided?

From the early thirteenth century in the Narbonnais, and by the end of the century everywhere in France, arbiters were given a title from Roman Law; but this should not confuse us. The institution is medieval, not Roman: the fact that their Roman title conflates three different Roman institutions is demonstration enough. They were called *arbiter, arbitrator, seu amicabilis compositor.*[10] People functioning in this composite office were doing the same things their predecessors without the title did in the twelfth and eleventh centuries.

Who were these people, and what did they do? Let us take a brief look at three cases.

In 1071 two groups of people disputed the vicariate of certain lands belonging to the abbey of La Grasse. As arbiter they chose the abbot of La Grasse, referred to as "their lord." He in turn asked the Count of Barcelona (who was in Carcassonne at the time) and the Viscount of Narbonne to join him in deciding the case. They divided the rights and revenues in dispute.[11]

The second case takes us to Béziers, where, sometime before 1078, the abbot of Conques had decided to put an end to the *malis usis* [bad customs] a certain Bermund of Agde was collecting on one of the abbey's "honors" ["estates; fiefs"]. The two parties had at first tried to reach an agreement but without success. They had then asked the bishop of Béziers, the abbot of Saint-Pons, and other "good men" to decide; but Bermund had refused to accept their decision. The abbot thereupon had complained to Raymond of Saint-Gilles and the Viscountess of Béziers, and Raymond had decided to burn down Bermund's house and to give what the recalcitrant nobleman possessed on the abbey's lands to the monastery. This had long since transpired when, in 1078, Bermund's son negotiated a compromise with the abbot, giving up half of what his father had claimed and receiving 50 *solidi* [coins] and the office of the abbot's *viguier* [*vicarius*, or agent] in return. Had the earlier decision of Raymond of Saint-Gilles the force of *res judicata* [a matter determined by the final decision of a court of law], had the decision of the two prelates the force of a rule emanating from an authoritative source, the entire story, but especially the ending, would be quite bizarre; for Bermund's son still had a claim that the abbot of Conques had to meet. In fact, the heir and the abbot took up the dispute where it had originally begun. It was as though the bishop of Béziers, the abbot of Saint-Pons, Raymond of Saint-Gilles, and all those good men had done nothing at all.[12]

[10] A series of arbitral decisions of 1251–3 are the earliest in the archives of Narbonne to use this technical title: AA 99, fo. 12 ("arbitratores seu amicabiles tractatores"); AA 105, fo. 82v; AA 99, fo. 76; AA 105, fo. 36v; AA 109, fo. 22v; but a settlement of 1217, made by individuals entitled *arbitratores*, is called an *amicabilis compositio* (Bibl. nat., ms. Mélanges Colbert 414, no. 71). For a general survey of the use of this title in medieval Europe see Karl S. Bader, "Arbiter arbitrator seu amicabilis compositor," *Zeitschrift der Savigny-Stiftung, Kan. Abt.* XLVI (1960): 239–76.
[11] Bibl. nat., ms. Doat 66, fos 163ff.
[12] *Cartulaire de l'abbaye de Conques en Rouergue*, ed. Gustave Desjardins (Paris, 1879), pp. 25–7.

The final case takes us to La Vaur, a town about halfway between Toulouse and Albi, soon to be famed for its heretics. There in 1139 three brothers were fighting their uncles for possession of part of the town's fortifications and some houses, lands, and a mill. They asked the Viscount of Béziers, one of the Trencavel, to whom they had sworn an oath of security for the fortifications, to settle the dispute. He came to La Vaur with eight men called "judges," whom we can identify as men who were frequently in the Trencavel entourage. The "judges" divided the property between the brothers and their uncles, and the two parties swore to accept the division.[13]

These examples could be multiplied many times over. They indicate, I think, that the arbiters were not definable "institutionally." They were not courts with established jurisdictions. They did not normally decide on the basis of a set of impersonal rules rationally applied. They were individuals or groups capable of pressuring the disputants to accept their judgment, come to an agreement, or recognize that their claims were unjust. They were able to do this either because of their great status or because they were friends, perhaps relatives; in any case, frequent associates.

How did they decide the disputes presented them? On very rare occasions there may have been a charter that they considered decisive; enough to show that this function for the written document had not been totally forgotten. On other rare occasions they might ask the local notables to decide. Most frequently, as in the cases I have just described, they tried to divide the object in litigation, occasionally asking one party to divide the property and giving the other the first choice, thus demonstrating true paternal wisdom. Even when a charter gave the prize to one side the other was almost always paid off. No one left empty-handed. The practice of giving everyone something was indeed so prevalent that it is impossible to reconstruct any objective rules of decision on the basis of arbitral judgments in lower Languedoc, at least before the mid-thirteenth century. It was not the function of these courts to apply objective rules, to "do justice" in that sense. The norm they applied was that both parties should be satisfied. The very categories that the Roman legal tradition had used as the foundation for objective rules, still alive in Septimania in the tenth century, had become cloudy. Their boundaries had disappeared. Sale, gift, and quitclaim became synonymous; for the rules that differentiated one from the other no longer had any consequence in court: in case of dispute, the result did not depend on the technical "nature" of the original transfer. When there were conflicting claims to property, nothing would be settled until everyone was satisfied.

The documents that makers of inventories normally classify as "compromise agreements" were only variants on this main type. Here the arbiters were less in evidence, and are reduced in the documents to the category of "friends and good men" who "counsel" the agreement between the parties. The form of the documents differed but the action they cloaked was the same, at least before the Romanization of the thirteenth century.

What made the system work? We might well ask first what makes our own system work when conflicts are submitted to litigation. Ours works, at least in part, because members of society believe abstract norms should be followed: "there oughta be a law." And the courts ought legitimately to decide in accordance with those norms; even decide what those norms are. We know from recent experience how fragile these beliefs may be. In any event, these were not the assumptions legitimizing the pre-thirteenth-century system. To find out precisely what did legitimize that system I would like to turn briefly to the *chansons de geste* [epic poems: lit., "songs of deeds"], using the general elements of arbitration as our template.

[13] Société archéologique de Montpellier, ms. 11 (*Cartulaire dit "de Foix"*), fo. 19.

In the *chansons de geste*, when a character had been wronged, what sentiment did the poet put on his lips? *Honte*, shame. When Raoul de Cambrai discovered that the Emperor Louis had disinherited him, he exclaimed:

> Des iceste eure, par le cors s. Amant,
> Me blasmeroient li petit et li grant,
> Se je plus vois ma honte conquerant,
> Qe de ma terre voie autre home tenant.[14]

> [From this hour, by the body of Saint Amant,
> Small and great would blame me
> If I could accept further shame
> By seeing another man hold my land.]

In the *Charroi de Nîmes*, when Guillaume discovers that King Louis had left him out of the general distribution of lands, he complained:

> Deus . . . com ge sui mal bailliz
> Quant de demande somes ici conquis.
> Se vos serf mes, dont soie je honiz.[15]

> [God . . . how I am ill treated
> When I am so reduced for a pittance!
> If I serve you now, I am shamed.]

This is but the other side of the shame of which Roland spoke when Olivier asked him to sound the Oliphant, and when he urged his men on to battle. The knight who did not act like one was shamed; so was the knight who was not treated like one. What was this shame? To be a knight and not be considered one:

> Tu es or riche [says Guillaume to Louis] et ge sui po proisie
> Tant com servi vos ai tenu le chief,
> Ni ai conquis vaillissant un denier
> Dont nus en cort mapelast chevalier.[16]

> [You are now rich (says Guillaume to Louis) and I am worth
> little.
> As long as I served you, I held the front line.
> I did not gain a cent from it,
> And no one at court calls me knight.]

A recent commentator has argued that all these heroes are "other directed."[17] I would certainly not go that far: they followed a known internalized code. Nor would I want to get into a metaphysical debate about "shame cultures" and "guilt cultures." But the epic heroes, when they violated their code, or when they were violated, felt opprobium not guilt. They lost their standing in the sight of others.

These were the circumstances in which friends and good men gave wise counsel and arbiters decided the issue. Friends and arbiters were not there to judge according to rules; they were there to get the parties off the hook. They represented *sagesse* [wisdom], the

---

[14] *Raoul de Cambrai*, ed. Paul Meyer and Auguste Longon (Paris, 1882), ll. 702–5.
[15] *Le Charroi de Nîmes*, ed. Joseph L. Perrier (Paris, 1931), ll. 112–14.
[16] Ibid., ll. 252–5.
[17] George Fenwick Jones, *The Ethos of the Song of Roland* (Baltimore, 1963), p. 97.

alternative virtue to overly combative *proece* [prowess], like Olivier in that moment before the great battle began. They must come up with the argument or solution that will remove the threat of violence – as Turpin did when the battle was almost over and Roland and Olivier once again debated whether Roland should sound the horn; as Guillaume's nephew Bertran did when he suggested that Guillaume ask Louis for Spain, Nîmes, and Orange to conquer; as Raoul's vassals did when they tried to patch things up between Raoul and Bernier. They must assuage anger, soothe wounded pride, find the solution that will bring peace. In the *chansons de geste*, people never just changed their minds when in conflict with someone else. Our charters of compromise regularly mention the "good counsel" that brought the result about. For once a position was taken it would be cowardly to retreat unless convinced by the wisdom of others. This was the ritual that must be followed. In real life the status of the arbiters, as great lords, colleagues, friends, and relatives, allowed them to perform this task, assured the parties not only of their wisdom but that public opprobrium would not follow upon their recognition of wrongful claim: for the arbiters were sometimes themselves that very public. The habitual pay-off to the losing side, whether large or symbolic, likewise met the demands of that other virtue much touted by the chivalric poets – *mesure*, moderation.

The arbiters and counsellors had to perform another function, of course, one equally vital: to persuade or to pressure the parties, or one of them, into a peaceful settlement. This may not always have been easy. The charter formula "*cum multa discordia fuit*" ["because there was much discord"] might have often been a euphemism for war as well as for verbal abuse. Occasionally, as in the case involving Conques, the difficulties were glaringly apparent.

What made both functions possible, however, was a social group whose members rubbed each other often enough for their pressure to be effective and the ritual to perform its appointed task. The shame of which the poets sang worked only when people were face to face, when the fighting man really knew that no one called him "knight."

In the thirteenth century the ritual of arbitration and compromise was replaced by the new forms of normative justice; the change, however, was neither smooth nor rapid. Some of our earliest examples in France come from the Paris area, where the *prévot* [a royal official] was already exercising this kind of justice in the second decade of the thirteenth century. In 1218, one Guido of Auxerre, a citizen of Paris, condemned by papal judges delegate to pay a rent of 13*d* to St-Denis, refused to accept the sentence, was excommunicated, and only agreed when a nearly identical decision was made by arbiters.[18] In Normandy, where such justice likewise sprouted precociously, the doctrine that a thing judged was a thing judged was not easily accepted by those whom the Exchequer condemned.[19] But despite this resistance one form did eventually give way to the other.

The change-over, as we might expect, was not sudden. The adoption of Romanized formulae in arbitration agreements early in the century provided one opening. At the beginning, undoubtedly, this new form served mainly to let notaries show off their knowledge of Roman procedure. But the common formula usually said something to the effect that the arbiters were "to inquire about the truth" of the claims, sometimes specifying that this be done "by witnesses and instruments." Most often this possibility was not followed;

---

[18] Archives nationales, LL 1157 (*Cartulaire Blanc* of St-Denis), p. 302, no. 8; p. 303, no. 10. Closer attention to this phenomenon by French legal historians may eventually reveal considerable chronological variance between regions. Professor Henri Gilles of Toulouse informs me that the consuls of Toulouse were already making such authoritative decisions at the end of the twelfth century.

[19] Joseph R. Strayer, *The Administration of Normandy under St. Louis* (Cambridge, Mass., 1932), p. 30.

but sometimes it was, leaving the door ajar for normative judgments to slip in. A second sign of change was the appearance of legal professionals, of men called *jurisperiti* by our southern documents, first in the inner circles of the great lords, then as advisers to the arbiters. It seems likely that their influence was likewise toward objective normative judgment.

Finally, toward mid-century, authoritative courts making normative judgments appeared, and their use expanded rapidly. Arbitration remained, but its meaning changed. More and more the arbiters acted like judges, made inquests, checked charters. Professional lawyers and court officials appeared as arbiters. By the early fourteenth century arbitration had found its place within a hierarchical structure of courts, as decisions from which appeals to higher courts might be made. It was reduced to a technique for avoiding what had become the "ordinary" court.[20]

We must now ask why this happened. The question is not easy to answer. One possibility, at least, may be eliminated. There was no new idea suddenly bursting on mid-century France that might have brought this about. Indeed, the *idea* that a system of norms should govern the settlement of disputes had never completely disappeared from Europe. The clergy, at least, kept it very much alive. Even in the Narbonnais a Gregorian legate, made archbishop, attempted to inject the idea into his relations with lay society at the beginning of the twelfth century.[21] And within the ranks of the clergy, especially where hierarchical relations were concerned, normative decisions by popes, judges delegate, and bishops were common after the mid-twelfth century. Even among the clergy, however, property disputes were often a category apart, to be settled by arbitration.

The introduction of Roman Law was one cause. Its influence in southern France began with the appearance in a document of 1127 of one Adalbertus *"legisperitus"* ["learned in the law"].[22] After that it was revealed in the changing formulae of charters, in the procedure of ecclesiastical courts, in the appearance of notaries: a long and continuing influence, accepted here, resisted there. But it was too vast, too generalized, infusing its spirit into practice over too long a period, to be the sole explanation for the sudden change that occurred in the decades around 1250.

Our search must go in another direction, beginning with the social structures that gave force to arbitration and the attitudes they incorporated. The attitudes were the common property of much of Europe; the structures, however, varied widely in their concrete detail from region to region. It is only on the regional level, therefore, that we can for the moment trace their transformations. My own examples will once again be drawn from the Narbonnais and Carcassès.

In the thirteenth century the old social groupings within the Languedocian seignorial class broke up. At the same time, an alien power spread its shadow across the land. The fellowship of the seignorial court had given force to the old values; but after mid-century, in southern France, the monarchy and its agents began to impose their interests and demands on its members. Lands were confiscated from heretics; more were confiscated after the Trencavel revolt. Permanent seneschals appeared with their bailiffs and *viguiers*, intent on pursuing every scrap of royal right. There agents, as "foreigners," with no ties to the local landed class and with the monarchy to back them up, were not amenable to the pressures and arguments

---

[20] Bernard Guenée, *Tribunaux et gens de justice dans le bailliage de Senlis* (Paris, 1963), pp. 117–20.
[21] Such, at least, is suggested by the talk of the "evil customs of the land" and other precocious uses of *consuetudo* to mean "rule" or "norm." *Histoire générale de Languedoc*, V (Toulouse, 1875), col. 801; Bibl. nat., ms. Baluze 82, fos 55ff.
[22] *Hist. gén. Languedoc*, V, col. 905.

of old-style arbitration. If they were to be fought it could only be on their own ground: in the local royal courts. The old family of Carcassonne disappeared, replaced by the agents of an absentee northern landlord; the viscounts of Narbonne were drawn into the circle of the royal court, as were some of their followers; the archbishop of Narbonne, the abbots of La Grasse and Fontfroide were drawn away toward Paris or Rome. Finally, the monarchy began to demand troops and money. The groups that had gathered around the local greats were broken up; relations among their members were redefined in terms of impersonal norms amenable to judicial decision. Soon after 1300 the major vassals of the Viscount of Narbonne were suing their lord in the king's court to block his claim to their military service.[23] Nothing could more aptly demonstrate how deeply seignorial society had been reshaped.

The process, once started, fed on its own momentum. Village inhabitants, city consuls, lords both minor and great, all discovered that the court machinery provided by the monarchy, once they learned to use it, allowed them to fight those who would impose or continue to impose some kind of dominion over them. With it the consuls of Narbonne could beat the viscount, the viscount the archbishop, the archbishop the consuls; and all of them could use it to beat the king and his agents. The court machinery, in turn, with its special intellectual techniques, led to a further legalization of social relationships. All acts of lordship by one individual over another could then become a legal precedent, fitting into a normative system enforceable by courts, sergeants, fines, and dungeons.

The old ways, the old values, pride in honor and dishonor of shame, could still rouse the hearts of the nobility, but the absolute sway those values had so long maintained when men leveled claims against each other, had weakened. Alternatives long present in the culture of medieval Europe, values promoted in the schools and expressed in the institutions of the Church and the monarchy, took their place. As the groups broke up that had given force to honor and fear to shame, men began to view their "rights" in different terms. Bernier, in the twelfth-century *Raoul de Cambrai*, wronged by his lord, refused to leave him: "tant que tuit dient: 'Bernier, droit en as' " ["Until all might say: 'Bernier, you are in the right' "].[24] By 1300 men thought first of their rights as objectively defined and then strove to have them sanctioned by a court, the king's court if possible.

At the same time, the peasants and urban dwellers, whole classes of men who had had no recourse beyond their lords, were given the means and the reasons to justify a continued petty opposition. People of the seignorial class quickly imitated the monarchy, hired *jurisperiti* to play their judges, established their monopolies of "ordinary" jurisdiction – fighting each other and the monarchy in the process. Within a matter of decades the whole system was worked out.

This was what happened in the low hills and coastal plain between the Massif Central and the Mediterranean during the century when Capetian administration began to impose its unity across the profound diversities of the countryside. But the thirteenth century was also the century of the Albigensian Crusade, when Languedoc became a colony of the North, hounded by the Inquisition, tempted by foreign poles of power, mined by the new-style intellectuals established at Montpellier, Toulouse, and momentarily at Narbonne. The Languedocian experience was thus exemplary. It does not allow us to generalize, however, until we know what variations Poitou and Berry, Burgundy and Picardy, and the other *pays* [regions] of France worked upon the common theme. For their starting points were not identical, nor were the habits and traditions that shaped their acceptance of the new ways. In

[23] Bibl. nat., ms. Doat 49, fos 296, 309.
[24] *Raoul de Cambrai*, l. 1385.

the realm of law and as a school for bureaucrats Languedoc, by the end of the thirteenth century, led the rest of the Capetian kingdom. But imitation and imposition from above explain only a small part of the triumphant legalization of society accomplished by 1300. Only a survey region by region will finally tell the full story.

By the end of the century, nevertheless, men of Languedoïl [the northern part of France, where "yes" was "oui"] as well as men of Languedoc were well on their way to accepting the new ways, to accepting the unity of learned procedures and the necessity of objective norms. It is not surprising that strains should quickly arise, that grumblings against the "encroachments" of royal courts should become loud and clear, that but thirty years after his death Louis IX should symbolize a simpler "golden age." It had been a simpler age. By 1300 its simplicities had disappeared beyond recall. It was now an age of law: of Law "Like love we often weep, / Like love we seldom keep."

11 Strangers and Neighbors

Monique Bourin and Robert Durand

At their root, village solidarities were neighborhood ties. First, we will consider the ties of the rural population as a whole, without taking into account either the dissimilarities which artisanal and professional specialization introduced (compared to the mass majority of farmers), or any differences due to time-period. Considered this way, neighborhood is fundamental because it implies a society of mutual acquaintance, where the behavior of each individual is both transparent and predictable to others, and which is a peculiar fact of village society.

A community of neighbors: the very terms of the charters [legal or quasi-legal documents] evoke this essential proximity. In southwest Europe, from the Basque country to Portugal (with variant forms north of the Adour), members of the same community called themselves "*vicinus*" ("neighbor"). Becoming a member of this community was to be received "*in vicinum.*" The *vézio* was the group of neighbors, the cell of the collective life, whether of a hamlet, a village, or a particular quarter of an agglomeration.

This notion can also be found in northern Europe, particularly in England. It also appears, for example, in the law granted to the village of Prisches in 1158.[1] The success of this law merits a closer study of its notion of neighborhood. At first glance, it seems unimportant, since neighborhood appears only in two articles out of fifty-eight: in the clause which exempts an inhabitant of the village who sells his house to a neighbor from the tax on the transfer of property, and that which authorizes an individual to leave the village once he has assembled all his neighbors, who can affirm that he has paid all his debts. In the context of the charter, and in comparison with the other terms used to designate the inhabitants of the village, the neighbor is someone who lives in any house in the village; thus, the meaning of the word is broader than it is today. Thus defined, the notion has an essential importance in the charter: even if it is possible to enjoy the liberty of Prisches without having a house there, it is important for us to note that the first article begins with the words "whoever has a house in the village of Prisches." Many of the most widespread charters begin with the same words, which suggests that the primitive tie among the inhabitants of the village is in fact this very tangible one, a result of the juxtaposition of the houses they inhabit, rather than of the individuals themselves.

[1.69] L. Verriest, "La fameuse charte-loi de Prisches," *Revue Belge de philologie et d'histoire* 2 (1923): 327–42.

This tangible link associating men and women through the intermediary of their homes appears to have remained, throughout the southern part of Europe, the fundamental glue of village solidarity. Is not the village – with its solid houses pressing close together, often even joined together – the material translation of this idea? As Le Roy Ladurie has shown us, the reports of the inhabitants of Montaillou before the tribunal of the Inquisition manifest clearly the strength of this "*ostal*," which means "at the same time both family and house."[2] The distinction is not clearly made between the building and the people who live there. Solidarities are thus normally woven from house to house.

In northern Europe, especially in Picardy or in the Hainaut, this tangible link seems to have been seconded by a personal link. This is particularly clear in the villages with the most advanced franchises [charters of collective laws and liberties]: their inhabitants are towns-people, and townspeople are linked by a tacit contract which associates their persons, their individualities. This is clear as soon as the village becomes a commune and its members are linked by oath. In other villages, those where solidarity is not sealed by a *conjuratio*, or public oath, a very close collective responsibility is nonetheless evident, which maintains the common peace. Thus the charter of Prisches fixes the territory within which the village law applies: "in the interior of the limits of the peace," which determines, all in all, a code of common life. Though this idea of village peace did not originate in the northern regions (since safe havens were created out of the same concerns in Aquitaine in the twelfth and thirteenth centuries; and it was in the southern regions that the Peace of God was born) the collective responsibility of the Peace is most clearly affirmed by charters from the North.

Village solidarity thus meant both neighborhood and friendship; both existed everywhere, but neighborhood appears to have been a more powerful idea in southern zones, and friendship stronger in the villages of the North.

The Stranger

Solidarities between neighbors, between men and women who know each other, automatically define another group, both complementary and opposed to them: strangers. This is the man "*de fora parte*" seen in Portuguese charters, the "stranger." The solidarity of the village group is very clear in its opposition to this person. In Portuguese villages, villagers were obliged to bear witness for each other against strangers, under penalty of a serious fine. Up to the fourteenth century, in the Dauphiné, a crime committed by a stranger was more severely punished than the same crime committed by a villager, and the fine was lower when a stranger was the victim.[3] However, if the difference was always marked between the stranger and the native, the situation was quite the opposite in certain villages of Gascony near Toulouse at the end of the thirteenth century. There, at certain times, the franchises provided *lesser* fines for the case of a stranger who contravened the common rules and broke the ban on entering onto certain kinds of land: strangers were not expected to know the local rules. At Beaumont in the Argonne, the stranger who damaged vineyards or gardens had to pay only half the fine that a local peasant would pay; the same was true if he broke the peace of the market: his fine was 60 shillings, while a man from Beaumont would owe 100. Whether it was more exigent or more indulgent with its natives, the village group clearly sought to

---

[2] [See Emmanuel Le Roy Ladurie, *Montaillou: The Promised Land of Error*, trans. Barbara Bray (New York, 1978), p. 24.]

[3.70] P. Vaillant, *Receuil de documents relatifs à l'histoire du droit municipal. Les libertés des communautés dauphinoises* (Paris, 1951).

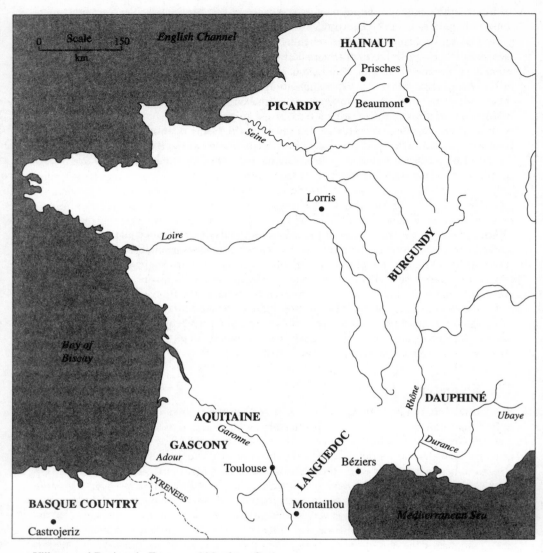

Villages and Regions in France and Northern Spain

Source: Based on Monique Bourin and Robert Durand, *Vivre au village au moyen âge. Les solidarités paysannes du 11e au 13e siècles* (Paris: Messidor/Temps Actuels, 1984), map p. 14.

affirm its difference from the stranger, which confirms that rural solidarities were fundamentally expressed in the village setting.

Just as judicial rules were different for the stranger, so economic exchanges were organized differently. While transactions between villagers were tax-free, those with strangers were always taxed. At Lorris, only men of the parish were free to sell at the market; on the dikes of the Loire, where increased population was encouraged, the privilege was the same. In the Hainaut, strangers continued to pay the taxes on commercial transactions when the villagers were exempted from them, and failure to pay carried a very heavy fine. Judicial solidarity and commercial protectionism thus defined village relations with strangers.

If we can believe the charters of franchise, the definition of the stranger is simple: it is so obvious that it never needs to be defined. Behind this very clear notion, however, lies hidden a much more complex situation.

Passing Through: the Outsider

The stranger could be someone passing through, an outsider. It has become a commonplace to dwell on the fear that the outsider inspired in rural societies, even if this fear was in such sharp contrast with the hospitality enjoined by Christianity. One example is that of a village near Béziers, where during an investigation of the rights of high justice, the witnesses cited only examples of crimes committed by outsiders, whose names they didn't even know.

At the same time, villages often had the right of asylum; not simply church sanctuary, which had to respect any violence at all, but a true asylum for petty criminals under pursuit, though it was not as far-reaching as the more classic kind. Thus, at Beaumont, the criminal and the thief did not escape justice, but the delinquent could remain there in safety while looking for a [different] safe place, and at Prisches, the criminal who sought refuge eventually was brought to inevitable, though milder, justice.

Thus, the outsider was a worrisome being both because he was unknown and often guilty, and because he was an isolated individual, without support, in a difficult situation, and one who needed help to get back on the right track.

From the Village Next Door

The stranger could also be someone from a neighboring village, who was not in the least unknown. Here, village sentiments were ambiguous. Such a person was clearly not subject to the code which regulated village collective life; relations with him (and especially commercial transactions), were according to a different set of mores, which everyone knew and admitted were pragmatic, not moral. Village territory was defended against him, as were common pastures and forest rights. In the valley of the Ubaye, in Haute-Provence, the sheepraisers customarily opposed by force any intruders who tried to dispute their rights on high pastures. In certain regions of the Iberian peninsula where a "frontier society" existed because of the Christian reconquest – a "Far West," we might say, risking anachronism–this violence was perfectly legal. As early as 974, a community like Castrojeriz saw its right recognized to pursue livestock rustlers and punish them by any means up to and including murder. Doubtless they thought it wisest to attack preemptively. In any case, a cycle of violence was begun, one of those never-ending "cattle wars" where reprisals and counter-reprisals fed endlessly off each other.

But in the period we are studying, this affirmation of every man for himself only occasionally turned to violence. There was even a way in which a tissue of relations was woven across borders from village to village – by marriage. Franchise charters often witness to the peasants' desire, and often their success at obtaining the suppression of *formariage*, that is, the ban on marrying outside the seigneury, or more accurately, the authorization of such marriages only at a price. This ban was no doubt especially problematic in villages that grouped together men and women dependent on several different seigneuries. But the suppression of *formariage* assured matrimonial exchanges between villages, even if villages remained largely endogamous.

These external marriages were often the occasion for more or less ritualized discussions. In certain villages in Languedoc, families and their allies would meet at a particular site on the common border and discuss the conditions of the marriage. There were also more official institutions that brought together men from neighboring villages: in Portugal, court cases between members of two different villages were conducted before a tribunal called the "*junta*," which met on the border, and was composed in equal parts of inhabitants of the two villages.

To sum up: in this period, neighbors eyed each other without overt animosity and managed to establish bridges of contact and exchange: a few women might even pass from one clearly understood group to another!

The Immigrant

There was also a third category of stranger, the immigrant, who sought to establish himself in the village, and in time become a villager or townsperson. Different regions and periods treated this individual very differently.

The openness of the village to immigrants is much less simple to define than it would seem, since simply moving to a village did not always entail integration into the village community. The distinction was clearly made in the Gascon villages near Toulouse, where, for a period of a year, the new arrival did not benefit from communal franchises, but neither did he have to participate in financial charges, or village corvées [enforced labor]. It was only after this first year of residence that he became something of a citizen of the village. In Lombard villages in the thirteenth century, this probationary period could last as long as five years. "Naturalization" into the village could thus be either immediate or deferred, and this was an entirely separate issue from how easy or difficult it was simply to move in.

There were villages which very early on fixed a maximum population level which was not to be surpassed. Such was the case in the new villages in Portugal, where the first arrivals imposed this clause on their lord: here, there would not be more than ten settlers, there, the territory would not be cut up in order to found another village. Rare in more well-established areas, this provision was characteristic of the pioneer frontier, where new villages were frequent.

This kind of Malthusianism may well have been related to the migrant's state of mind: his experience of overcrowding in the place he had left, the ambition which prompted his voluntary exile – there are many possible explanations. But even in pioneer regions, this mindset was not a majority one. Rather, the agent who sponsored the move and was followed by the first settlers was no doubt fearful of failure. Thus he determined from the beginning the desirable number of inhabitants so that the new village would acquire sufficient vigor and would keep those who had moved there.

If certain villages preferred to limit immigration by drastic means, the means chosen by the peasants were usually more gentle.

Sometimes, simply an oath was required: an oath of fidelity to the lord in poorly enfranchised communities; an oath to respect village custom and the collective peace, sworn to the mayor and the aldermen in more autonomous villages; oaths to both, in intermediary cases. These oaths sealed the good faith of the new arrival regarding the community and made him a member of the sworn peace.

Elsewhere, it cost money to join a village. The price was merely symbolic in the case of Beaumont in the Argonne, where it was limited to a coin paid to the mayor and another to the magistrates. It was heavier in Burgundy, where the right of admission could frequently be as high as a pound: no penniless vagabond could expect to become a man of the village.

It was also true that being admitted to the village community was usually contingent on the acquisition of a house. The very liberal law of Prisches allows that without a homestead, an "entrance fee" of twelve pennies could be paid in order to enjoy village liberties, but this is a fairly rare case. The new inhabitant had to establish a hearth, which was proof of a desire for stability.

Therefore it was a *prud'homme* whom village communities accepted in their midst: a man of property, who was determined to settle there on a long-term basis, along with his descendants. Some villages emphasized the importance of property, and other villages of long-term intentions.

Except in certain pioneer zones like Portugal, moving to a village did not erase the past, and the new arrival did not suddenly become cleansed of all his sins. At Prisches, the guilty immigrant seeking to evade justice was escorted out of town. But if he submitted to justice, then he benefited from the village's help. Clauses in immigration charters betray an evident fear of introducing hardened criminals into the village, much like those picturesque and menacing signs found in the Far West, but with rather less militant intentions!

Raising the entrance fee and lengthening the probationary period were two possible ways to limit immigration or to hold off its effects. Obviously, charters bent on increasing population, like those of Beaumont or of Prisches, were very liberal. In Picardy, where demographic growth, very lively in the twelfth century, limited interest in immigration, the conditions were less easy, though numerous barriers collapsed after 1240 when natural growth subsided. Lombardy was similar, though the turning point came later. In the twelfth and thirteenth centuries, the community was very jealous of its autonomy, careful to close itself to foreign influences and to reserve for itself the use of its territory. In the fourteenth century, it became more open: at the end of a month of residence, the stranger was already partially assimilated and paid a special tax. With the demographic decline of the second half of the fourteenth century, all restrictions dropped, and the stranger was able to participate fully in communal life, with neither condition nor restriction.

In the south of France, the change went in the other direction, at least before 1350: the laxity of the twelfth century gave way to more rigid attitudes by the end of the thirteenth.

Each community thus had the means to regulate the flow of immigration according to its own interests, but not every community did so. We must not let ourselves be deceived by the charters that have survived. It is true that among the Burgundian charters, only one provides for completely free immigration, and there is only one such charter among those from the Toulouse region of Gascony. But in villages without charters, therefore unenfranchised, immigration was doubtless subject to the lord's whim, and it is hard to imagine why he would object to acquiring new subjects. And out of the countless villages that did have written franchises, how many imposed difficult barriers on immigrant candidates? Very few:

out of the many Burgundian charters, only fifteen. And wasn't the demand for an entrance fee simply a way of imitating the towns? And wasn't the oath of fidelity to the franchise simply reminiscent of the oath to the commune of the town?

Even if it was not really all that difficult to become a villager like everyone else, it took time to gain the confidence of one's fellow-villagers and become integrated into the community, not merely officially, but in fact. How many new men became magistrates in northern villages? None in the case of the consuls of villages near Béziers, and precious few among their counsellors. The man who did not have a particular qualification, a technical competence (a smith, perhaps, in the twelfth century, a notary or a doctor in the thirteenth), had no chance whatsoever of helping to govern his village. The *prud'homme* – not simply the honest man that any villager ought to be – but the genuine *prud'homme*, the man who was adjudged worthy of election by his fellow-citizens, was not a villager by naturalization; he was born in the village, and better yet, from a father native to the village as well. The medieval village was thus at once both open to the newcomer, and slow to legitimize him completely.

Authorization to Emigrate

A relatively simple acceptance of the newcomer and a departure freely granted: the authorization to emigrate was one of the franchises that peasant negotiations had acquired from their lords. The community asked only that the emigrant should settle his debts and leave an honest man. In this period of demographic growth, there was little risk of running short of villagers to pay taxes nor of any consequent rise in the level of those charges on the remaining villagers.

Nevertheless, the departure of a villager posed more problems for the community than the clauses which mention it would at first seem to suppose. Those individuals who left for neighboring villages would naturally keep their goods on site and leave their lands to be cultivated by another villager, usually a relative. But what about those who wished to be rid of their lands: were they free to sell them to a stranger?

In fact, the departure of a villager was little more than a special case of a more general situation: when a piece of land was left vacant by a death without an heir, or by a villager's desire to sell it. Might the village not wish to limit the incorporation of pieces of village land into the patrimony of strangers? Both individual liberty and collective solidarity might indeed oppose it.

Too often we look at the taxes – of *lods* [the lord's approval tax] and sales – collected during the sale of a parcel of land. [We interpret these as] the results of a struggle in which the peasant, who was subject to this tax on the transfer of property, sought to reduce it to a minimum, while his lord, who was the real beneficiary, resisted. The reality was perhaps more complex. At Prisches, the situation was clear: the tax on the transfer of property among villagers did not exist, but no house might be sold to a stranger. Elsewhere, high taxes on transfer did not necessarily indicate a weak community which had been able to acquire only paltry franchises. If they were accompanied by a right of preemption among villagers for vacant lands, or by [the right to] leave such lands fallow for a certain time before granting them to a stranger, as certain charters from Picardy attest, it was because collective solidarities here triumphed over the freedom of the individual, and because the village group chose not to fight for the reduction of the tax in order to avoid losing their potentially cultivable land to strangers. The capacity of the stranger to acquire land in a village, whether free or limited, was thus a good measure of the balance between individualism and collectivity.

Individualism was striking in the South, while the community was stronger in the North and in the region of the Pyrenees.

Equal in Rights

This village community – strong enough to hold onto its territory against the incursions of strangers yet also capable of finding a place for the stranger who wanted it – was anything but a fragile organism on the defensive. This vitality, which pervaded it in the twelfth and thirteenth centuries, showed itself also by absorbing all the various categories of commoners who lived on its territory, and who were not originally an integral part of it.

In certain regions during the twelfth century, one could indeed be a peasant, a free person, living on village territory, and yet not be part of the village community. This was the case of "guests," brought in by the lord in order to cultivate more or less virgin land within the borders of the village. In Picardy until about 1230, such individuals were clearly excluded from the community and did not share in either its juridical statutes – though they often benefited from their own precocious individual franchises – nor financial charges, nor justice. Why this segregation? The fact that they lived outside the village proper was not sufficient reason, since those from the hamlets and even more isolated settlements participated in village franchises. The exclusion of the guests was more likely related to the villagers' original mistrust, their jealousy of the guests' freer juridical status, of their lesser financial charges, and perhaps irritation at the cultivation of previously uncultivated land that the community had intended to reserve for itself.[4]

Though the local courts were denied them in the twelfth century, and though they were originally denied access to peasant clearings, little by little, however, these guests were absorbed by the community in the middle of the thirteenth century. Only those whose meager lands left them out of the general prosperity found their segregation made permanent by social discrimination. After the initial mistrust, it is the enlargement of the village community that tells the story of the relations between guests and villagers.

The integration of serfs into the community was more spectacular because it was more general. [It involved] not only the descendants of the Carolingian *servi* who were, in most regions, little more than residual groups, but also the descendants of all those who had been forced in the course of the eleventh century to enter into dependency on a lord. Due to their real or personal servitude, [whether] enslaved by their birth or by their residence on land considered to be servile [homesteads on great estates were sometimes classified as "free" or "servile"], their belonging to a lord put them clearly outside the community. We have only to reread the simplest charter to see the importance of the oath for the cohesion of the village group. The charter of Beaumont provides almost the caricature of an example, since an accused could purge himself of almost any accusation without witnesses simply by swearing an oath. Even if the village community was able precociously to open certain customary rights to the unfree living on its territory, the first sign of a coming-together of the two groups, the community was still primarily composed of inhabitants subject to seigneurial power globally, not individually.

Much less famous among historians of the nineteenth century than the franchising of urban communes, the role of village communities nevertheless touched a far greater number [of people]. We do not need to spend much time on rural franchises, but simply to underline the process by which rural solidarities erased the juridical differences among the peasants.

[4.71] R. Fossier, *Chartes de coutumes en Picardie* (Paris, 1975).

This is utterly clear for communities with charters similar to that of Lorris, where people were free after residence in the village for a year, the same amount of time as it took to integrate the newcomer into the community.

Even where this phenomenon left no traces, it existed nonetheless. Southern walled villages were founded with a composite population, composed of both the dependants of many lords and of serfs: by the thirteenth century, they were all simply inhabitants of the village. This blurring, and then disappearance, of juridical categories, is easily explained by the conditions of the pioneer frontier, whether in Spain or in Germany, but it also occurred virtually everywhere, generally to the advantage of the unfree, but sometimes to the misfortune of the free. Without falling into the lyricism of the historians of the last century, we can nevertheless underline the originality of this period where social tensions were so weak, and where instead of grasping at their privileges, the free saw more advantages in village solidarity than in antagonism. These solidarities had to be managed for the common good, of course, but this is another story that will be the subject of a later chapter [i.e. in Bourin's and Durand's book].

The Community and the Nobility

As it opened up to the "guests," and welcomed and freed the serfs, the community affirmed its identity as a body of commoners, where all the commoners joined together. Others were excluded, even clerics in the south of France, as we have seen in the chapter on parish solidarities [i.e., in Bourin's and Durand's book]. Knights were also excluded.

From the middle of the twelfth century, it was quite clear in Picardy: there was a formal distinction between inhabitants of the village and knights when it came to participation in collective practices. Probably influenced by urban centers, certain charters went so far as to prohibit knights access to the village, except in times of war in order to go to the castle, and even then on condition that they not dismount from their horses.

In the south of France, it isn't clear whether the exclusion of knights had been so rigorous from the very beginning. By the time we are able to make the point with any precision, towards the end of the thirteenth century, we can see that the knight's situation *vis-à-vis* the community varied, depending on the issue.

As regards agrarian regulations, the knights had long been excluded from the rules of common pasture; their lands were never open to collective pasturing. Or, to be more exact, not the lands which had been in their patrimony for a long time, since the community did its best to retain (more or less successfully) common rights over land that the knights acquired more recently. However, there is nothing to indicate that they were deprived of any rights of use. It is impossible to give a general rule for fiscal matters: not all nobles escaped from all village seigneurial dues, and a certain number contributed just like the villagers.

In summary, the knights sought (and succeeded, for the most part) to benefit from a privileged status that allowed them to escape the charges incumbent on the collectivity, putting forward the argument of their military function regarding each of the taxes owed for the village's defense.

Their participation in the government of the community was also quite variable. At the lord's court in about 1150, knights and other notables were mixed together, all called *prud'hommes*. But by the beginning of the thirteenth century, separation was achieved for villages of middling size; either the knights no longer had any relationship with the village community or they constituted an order apart, electing among themselves their representative to the college of three or four municipal magistrates who governed the village. In smaller villages, knights were frequently the representatives of the village and took over its direction, either because the commoners lacked personalities strong enough to ensure their taking their turn, or because the consciousness of the commoners was less developed there. Only a few of the larger villages, almost small towns, were able to make the knights "common," electors of the consuls just like everyone else (though always listed first in the accounts of the election), and also sometimes elected themselves, like any other village notable.

The general impression, then, is that in the majority of cases, knights were excluded from the community, and that this exclusion was clearly affirmed in the second half of the thirteenth century.

In the few traces that survive of daily life, the social separation of knights and villagers seems to occur later than their institutional separation. Their way of life – even their furniture – hardly distinguished village knight and peasant; many knightly homes were even found in the middle of the village. There may have been a greater difference in apparel. Strategies of naming, which can be so revelatory about the way in which a social group perceives itself in regard to others, did not change until about 1270: at this point, noble titles began to multiply. Up to this point, it had been impossible to tell simply by reading the name of an individual whether he was a knight or a peasant.

In those areas of southern France where collective constraints did not come so early, it is not impossible that the birth of political solidarities within the village accelerated this social gap. It became an opportunity for each group to define itself, one group as noble and *fideles* [loyal men] to their lord, and the other as villagers, members of the community. The prestige of the urban consulate may well have discouraged the village elite from any desire to join the ranks of the nobility, at the very time when it became more difficult to do so.

Who sought this separation? The knights, who found their social identity in distinguishing themselves from the villagers? The villagers, who were mistrustful of individuals tied by hommage not only to the lord but also to many other powers, such as to the bishops, chapters, or other religious establishments from which they held their fiefs? In this society so bound by the strength of the oath, the two different engagements may have been seen as incompatible.

Other villagers also remained excluded from the community and, like the knights, they too had the same allegiance to the lord: his *familia*, that is to say the group of servants and of officials who were responsible for the lord's property interests. Many villages in Picardy placed these individuals resolutely outside the realm of common practices. In the South, it was not the lord's *familia* that was thus anathematized, but those black sheep, the servants of ecclesiastical establishments. Anticlericalism made them enemies of village interests.

Exclusion was the rule for the internal affairs of the village. However, the feeling of belonging to the same village collectivity was stronger than any class solidarity: the knight and the villagers found themselves united in the conflicts which opposed them, together, against any neighboring village. While it may not have affected the lords, whose economic and social position was grander, village particularism animated both knights and commoners, at least in the final years of the thirteenth century.

In the central Middle Ages, and across the greater part of Europe, the history of rural solidarities is thus the history of the gradual growth in consciousness of these solidarities by the population grouped together in the village. And this growth in consciousness came in two parts. First came distinctions against the outside world: the definition of a territory whose use was reserved integrally and exclusively by the community. This is without doubt an essential moment, cutting space into cells whose borders become ever more clearly marked. The second stage involved transcending these differences by the fundamental notion of neighborhood, which allowed the incorporation into the collectivity both of recent immigrants and those of servile status. This essential perception of the common interest of the village was so vital that it led to a paradox: while social segregation between peasants and knights was on the rise, that separation was less strong than the feeling that they belonged to the same village. In summary, village consensus prevailed over centrifugal tensions.

12 Amicitiae [Friendships] as Relationships Between States and People

Gerd Althoff

Making alliances in the general form of a friendship treaty is by no means an invention of the Middle Ages. As early as the Roman period, people recognized the *amicitia* as a possible way to regulate basic relationships with other states, including client-states.[1] In other words, the Roman *amicitia* could also bind and obligate unequal partners. As a rule, however, it was supplemented by exact contractual obligations. In addition, the Romans awarded the honorary title *amicus populi Romani* [friend of the Roman people] primarily to foreign heads of state who had furthered Roman interests. Rome itself boasted the *amici Augusti* [friends of the emperor Augustus], who were divided into different classes. The title embraced those persons permitted an audience with the emperor; it was automatically bound up with certain high offices.[2] In Rome, therefore, we find the tie of *amicitia* already being used, in both foreign and domestic spheres, to regulate relationships fundamentally. This likewise applied to the Byzantine Empire, whose construction of relationships with other states based on the model of kinship is well known. In the Byzantine model of the "family of kings," however, there was also room for the "friend." The Byzantine Emperor Zeno, for example, adopted the Gothic King Theoderic as his "son-in-arms" and labeled him his "friend." He also, however, named him *patricius* [title of someone high in the imperial court] and supreme army commander.[3] Here we see already the combination of ties based on kinship, comradeship, and lordship which appears frequently in the Middle Ages, and which displays a

[1.7] See A. Heuss, "Die völkerrechtlichen Grundlagen der römischen Außenpolitik in republikanischer Zeit," *Klio*, Beiheft 31 (1993), esp. pp. 53–5, as well as in general the *Reallexicon für Antike und Christentum* (1972), s.v. "Freundschaft."

[2.8] See also B. Paradisi, "L' 'amicitia' internazionale nell'alto medio evo," in *Scritti in onore di Contardo Ferrini*, vol. 2, Pubblicazioni dell'Universita cattolica del S. Cuore; nuova ser., vol. 18 (Milan: "Vita e pensiero," 1947), pp. 178–225; W. Fritze, "Die fränkische Schwurfreundschaft der Merowingerzeit. Ihr Wesen und ihre politische Funktion," *ZRG, GAbt* 71 (1954), p. 80.

[3.9] See A. Angenendt, *Kaiserherrschaft und Königstaufe. Kaiser, Könige und Päpste als geistliche Patrone in der abendländischen Missionsgeschichte*, Arbeiten zur Frühmittelalterforschung, vol. 15 (Berlin: de Gruyter, 1984), p. 9. On the problem of adoption in the Byzantine Empire in general see F. Dölger, "Die 'Familie der Könige' im Mittelalter," in *Byzanz und die europäischen Staatenwelt* (Darmstadt: Wissenschaftliche Buchgesellschaft, 1964), pp. 43–5.

mixture of elements aimed at establishing either the equality or the subordination of the partner. It is clear that in such contexts the label "friend" does not simply represent a rhetorical flourish, but rather a serious title expressing a legally fixed position. The scholarship is divided over the question of how far apart the antique and medieval understandings of such *amicitia*-alliances were.[4] Despite the undeniable differences between Roman and Germanic legal conceptions, it does not seem justified to assign to existing differences too fundamental a character. A one-sided explanation of medieval *amicitia* derived from Germanic roots lacks, at least in view of the antique parallels, sufficient basis.

In view of the fact that in the Middle Ages, as in Antiquity, ties in the form of *amicitiae* appear in both the foreign and the domestic political spheres, it seems advisable first of all to present examples from each sphere, in order to ask to what degree the history of such alliances displays change over time. Before beginning, however, several difficulties must be mentioned. Studies, for example of the writers of the Merovingian [*c*.481–751] and the Carolingian [751–*c*.900] periods, have demonstrated that the sources by no means always mean the same thing when they describe relationships and ties with the term *amicitia*. By the same token, one cannot rule out an *amicitia* connection whenever the term fails to appear.[5] Gregory of Tours [d. 594], for example, describes the conclusion of friendships with the phrase *fidem et caritatem promittere* [to promise fidelity and devotion].[6] *Fides* and *caritas* apparently comprised the behaviors and attitudes that friends had to display toward one another. They replace in Gregory's description the term *amicitia*, without, however, describing a different state of affairs. This difficulty, which one by no means finds only in the context under discussion here, makes it advisable to cast as wide a net as possible through the sources for reports of the conclusion of alliances, without too quickly reading different types of alliances and relationships into the use of differing terminology.

Gregory of Tours has reported, in full detail and with the inclusion of the text, the conclusion in the year 587 of a treaty of friendship entered into by the Merovingian kings Guntram and Childebert, as well as Queen Brunhild.[7] *Caritates* (!) *studio*, that is, the striving for mutual *caritas*, brought the kings together; they promised each other "*fidem et caritatem puram et simplicem*" ["pure and simple fidelity and devotion"]. Not just this, however: since

[4.10] See Fritze, "Schwurfreundschaft," pp. 87–9; A. M. Drabek, *Die Verträge der fränkischen und deutschen Herrscher mit dem Papsttum von 754 bis 1020* (Vienna: Böhlau, 1976), pp. 100–2; M. Wielers, "Zwischenstaatliche Beziehungsformen im frühen Mittelalter. *Pax, Foedus, Amicitia, Fraternitas*" (Ph. D. dissertation, University of Münster in W., 1959), pp. 83–5.

[5.11] On this fundamental problem of terminology in the sources see [Fritze, "Schwurfreundschaft," pp. 80–2, 90–2; R. Schneider, *Brüdergemeinde und Schwurfreundschaft: der Auflösungsprozess des Karolingerreiches im Spiegel der Caritas-Terminologie in den Verträgen der karolingischen Teilkönige des 9. Jahrhunderts*, Historische Studien, Heft 388 (Lübeck: Matthiesen, 1964), pp. 86–8, 122–4; O. G. Oexle, "Gilden als soziale Gruppen in der Karolingerzeit," in *Das Handwerk in vor- und frühgeschichtlicher Zeit: Bericht über die Kolloquien der Kommission für die Altertumskunde Mittel-und Nordeuropas in den Jahren 1977 bis 1980*, ed. H. Jankuhn et al., vol. 1 (Göttingen: Vandenhoeck & Ruprecht, 1981), p. 292;] K. Brunner, *Oppositionelle Gruppen im Karolingerreich* (Vienna: Böhlau, 1979), pp. 14–16 on the different expressions for oppositions in the early Middle Ages; P. Michaud-Quantin, *Universitas. Expressions du mouvement communautaire dans le moyen-age latin* (Paris: J. Vrin, 1970) for investigations of community and group terminology, esp. p. 66 and pp. 191–2 for examples of the use of the term *amicitia*.

[6.12] Gregory of Tours, *Historia Francorum*, ed. B. Krusch and W. Levison, *MGH, SSrM* 1, 1 (1951 – henceforward *HF*) IV: 17; IX: 16; IX: 20. See also Fritze, "Schwurfreundschaft," pp. 95–6 and *passim*.

[7.13] *HF*, IX: 20; on this treaty see A. M. Drabek, "Der Merowingervertrag von Andelot aus dem Jahr 587," *Mitteilungen des Instituts für österreichische Geschichtsforschung* 78 (1970): 34–41.

Gregory, who himself as Childebert's legate was entrusted with the consequences of the treaty, copied its text literally into his history, one can also get an overview of the many concrete arrangements that were carried out in the course of this sworn friendship. The parties to the treaty regulated, among many other things, the division of the kingdom, provisions for the death of one of the parties, the treatment of the followers (*leudes*) of both kings, who had each sworn allegiance to the other party, and rights of safe passage through the other's territory. It is evident, in other words, that the partners in this sworn friendship not only promised a general conduct for the future, but also regulated concrete issues.

That this sworn friendship could also demand a certain kind of behavior toward third parties, however, is demonstrated by the discussion between the legates of Kings Childebert and Guntram, which Gregory reports. The discussion concerned, among other things, the relationship of both parties to the treaty to Queen Fredegund. Each side suspected the other of maintaining connections to Fredegund that violated the spirit of the treaty. The legates dealt in addition with a request for help made by Childebert to Guntram for military aid to drive the Lombards out of Italy. The request was turned down, with the justification that a plague then raging in Italy would unnecessarily place Guntram's army in mortal danger. Finally, the legates debated a suggestion by Guntram that a general synod be held. Childebert's legates wanted to know what reasons would support such a suggestion, reasons that Guntram then supplied, without, however, managing to convince the opposing side.

This detailed description of the conclusion of a treaty of friendship, of its contents, and of the reality of its implementation, permits us to make several statements about the nature of Merovingian sworn friendship, statements which should also be valid for other treaties described by the sources in less detail. Sworn friendships in fact possessed the character of a treaty. The treaty on the one hand dealt with concrete arrangements. On the other hand, however, it brought with it obligations that applied fundamentally and generally: a friend was not permitted to cultivate ties with enemies of his friend. We also know this requirement through the formulaic phrase "*amicus amicis inimicus inimicis*" ["a friend to friends, an enemy to enemies"].[8] A friend was approached for military aid, which he evidently could deny only for serious reasons. Friends came together personally or through intermediaries for general consultation. Friends in the final analysis treated each other and their legates with honor, a detail which Greogry points up with the following comment: "after the Mass had ended, the king led us to the table (*convivio nos adscivit*), which was equally laden with dishes and with good cheer."[9] This detail is by no means unimportant, as is demonstrated by the many cases in which insulting behavior transformed an *amicitia* into an *inimicitia* [enmity].[10]

A case from the beginning of the seventh century, reported by Pseudo-Fredegar in some detail, shows admirably the situations that prompted such friendship treaties, and demonstrates that they could very well embrace a wide circle of persons. After the death of King Dagobert (639), the Frankish mayor Pippin (the Elder) and other Austrasian *duces* [military leaders in the Merovingian kingdom of Austrasia] decided in a *unanimis conspiratio* [unanimous agreement] to support King Sigibert. To bring this about,

> Pippin and Chunibert [the archbishop of Cologne] decided once again to preserve firmly and for all time their friendship alliance, just as they had been bound to each

---

[8.14] See L. Wallach, "Amicus amicis, inimicus inimicis," *Zeitschrift für Kirchengeschichte* 52 (1933): 614–15; Drabek, *Verträge*, pp. 91–3.

[9.15] *HF*, IX: 20.

[10.16] See, for example, the case discussed below of the citizens of Tours (n. 13) or the Moravian prince Swatopluk (nn. 33–6).

other earlier by the bonds of friendship. They agreed to maintain friendship with the Austrasian notables for all time by drawing them to their side through adroit and affable behavior, and by governing them mildly.[11]

In other words, an explosive situation – namely the division of the kingdom – prompted the great magnates to secure the basis of their common political action by renewing their *amicitia*, and induced them to extend the bonds of friendship to include their *leudes*, their followers, whom they treated mildly and sensitively because they desperately needed their support.

One can assume that this conduct did not completely set aside the differences in authority between the mayor and the archbishop on the one side and the followers on the other. This example demonstrates rather how flexibly the instrument of the friendship treaty could be used in a precarious situation, precisely by mixing the planes of comradeship and lordship. The consequences that ensued when the "followers" were at one and the same time the "friends" of their lord, however, bear considering. In any case, the lasting influence that such friendship alliances had on political structures in seventh-century Austrasia is demonstrated by the fact that Pippin's son Grimoald, in a difficult situation after the death of his father, concluded a friendship alliance with Chunibert of Cologne, his father's friend.[12] In this context, Grimoald entered into his father's inheritance.

An *amicitia* that arose from a different cause, and which served a different purpose, appears in a report by Gregory of Tours of a long feud between two kindreds in Tours. A compromise between the two parties was eventually reached, in the context of judicial proceedings, after the feud had already produced a number of deaths. This compromise, however, although strengthened by an oath, did not last very long, as Gregory is forced to report two books later: "Sichar had formed with Chramnesind [Sichar's opponent in the feud] an intimate friendship, although Sichar had killed Chramnesind's relatives. They loved each other so deeply that they often took their meals together and slept together in a common bed."[13] Clearly at Tours an attempt was made to secure the peace after the feud had ended by concluding an alliance of friendship. This plan went awry, however, for Sichar angered his friend at a banquet by the awkward reminder that he had become wealthy because he had accepted the wergeld [compensation money] for his relatives. Chramnesind, reminded of his shame, responded by splitting open the head of his opponent with his sword. Despite this ending, the story seems an important piece of evidence for the sort of situation in the early Middle Ages in which people used the friendship alliance. This case in particular clearly demonstrates that it was not a matter of subjective feelings, but rather was a contract designed to secure a certain kind of behavior. Perhaps the very situation most grotesque to modern perceptions, namely that two formerly mortal enemies would share their bed and meals, itself gives an idea of the binding character of such an *amicitia*.

[11.17] *Fredegarii et aliorum Chronica*, ed. B. Krusch, *MGH, SSrM* 2 (1888 – henceforth Fredegar), IV: 85.

[12.18] Ibid., IV: 86.

[13.19] *HF*, VII: 47, IX: 19 (the cited passage); cf. on this famous episode J. P. Bodmer, *Der Krieger der Merowingerzeit und seine Welt: eine Studie über Kriegertum als Form der menschlichen Existenz im Frühmittelalter*, Geist und Werk der Zeiten, vol. 2 (Zurich: Fretz & Wasmuth, 1957), pp. 42–3; R. Wenskus, "Amt und Adel in der frühen Merowingerzeit," in *Mitteilungsheft des Marburger Universitätsbundes 1959* (Marburg, 1959), pp. 40–56; F. Irsigler, *Untersuchungen zur Geschichte des frühfränkischen Adels*, Rheinisches Archiv 70 (Bonn: Rohrscheid, 1969), pp. 178–9; H. Grahn-Hoek, *Die fränkische Oberschicht im 6. Jahrhundert: Studien zu ihrer rechtlichen und politischen Stellung*, Vortäge und Forschungen, Sonderband 21 (Sigmaringen: Thorbecke, 1976), pp. 101–3.

The examples discussed above should suffice to indicate the contexts in which alliances of *amicitia* were used during the Merovingian period. It is important to add, however, that Merovingian kings certainly entered into *amicitiae* with foreign rulers, or offered such alliances to them, as well. Well attested, for example, is a Frankish–Lombard *amicitia* under King Clothar II, from the years 617/18. This *amicitia*, incidentally, was said to have come about through the bribing of the Frankish counselors and of the king. It was a sworn *amicitia perpetua* [perpetual friendship] which replaced the payment of tribute by the Lombards.[14] Tribute payment and *amicitia*, therefore, were mutually exclusive.

The early Carolingians likewise made use of the instrument of *amicitia* in order to regulate their relationships with foreign rulers. Immediately after his elevation to the kingship in 751, King Pippin appears to have striven for a friendship alliance with the Byzantine Emperor Constantine V. The Byzantine likewise sent an embassy to the Carolingian; the embassy handed over a large number of presents, and each side promised mutual friendship and loyalty (*amicitias et fidem*) to the other. Fredegar's Continuator, however, himself added to this report the comment, "I do not know how it happened that this friendship which they had promised to each other afterwards had no effect."[15]

Scholars have also long debated the character of the alliance between the Carolingians and the popes, an alliance first entered into by Pippin with Pope Stephen II in 754. This debate has continued up to the present. After Wolfgang Fritz described the treaty of 754 as a Frankish sworn friendship, and Anna Drabek attributed to it the character of an *amicitia* alliance without a specific Germanic–Frankish orientation, Arnold Angenendt drew attention to the relationship of *compaternitas* [spiritual co-parenthood] that the pope entered into with the Carolingian king when he carried out the sacrament of confirmation for Pippin's sons.[16] By this means, a spiritual kinship, similar to that of godparenthood, was constructed between the pope and the Frankish king, a kinship that derived from Byzantine models based on strict equality between the partners. This, according to Angenendt, formed the basis of their relationship. All of these different attempts at interpretation can appeal to medieval sources and to the terminology used in them. Perhaps the differing interpretations of this epochal alliance, therefore, reflect not least the problem of its medieval interpretation and evaluation, even by the parties to the treaty themselves. For our purposes, the most important point about this case is that securing the Frankish relationship with the papacy necessitated using forms that were also customary in the contexts of private ties, whether spiritual kinship or friendship. It is worth pointing out, incidentally, that the juxtaposition of different kinds of ties was by no means unusual, so that friendship and *compaternitas* by no means need to be seen as alternatives.

For the period of Charlemagne [768–814] and Louis the Pious [814–40] the same picture holds true as for the period of Pippin. Einhard [d. 840] reports that Charlemagne "increased the fame of his Empire through alliances of friendship with many kings and peoples."[17] Identified by name in this context are King Alfonso of Galicia and Asturias; the kings of the Irish; Harun al Raschid; and three Byzantine emperors. Louis the Pious renewed the friendship with the Byzantine emperors immediately after his accession to the throne; the

---

[14.20] Fredegar, IV: 45.

[15.21] Fredegar, *Continuationes*, c. 40.

[16.22] See W. Fritze, *Papst und Frankenkönig. Studien zu den päpstlich-fränkischen Rechtsbeziehungen von 754–824* (Sigmaringen: Thorbecke, 1973), pp. 63–5; Drabek, *Verträge*, pp. 13–15; A. Angenendt, "Das geistliche Bündnis der Päpste mit den Karolingern (754–796)," *Historisches Jahrbuch* 100 (1980): 32–5.

[17.23] Einhard, *Vita Karoli Magni*, ed. O. Holder-Egger, *MGH, SSrG* (1991), c. 16: 19.

friendship was later reinforced several times by ambassadorial missions. Similar missions also renewed the friendship with the popes, as, for example, after the election of a new pope.[18]

The alliance of friendship, in other words, was reserved in the Carolingian period for certain of the ruler's relationships – with foreign kings and emperors as well as with the popes. This conclusion is important, because it changed in the later Carolingian period. There is scarcely any evidence that the early Carolingian kings entered into friendship alliances with their own subjects. Worthy of mention, however, is the title *amicus regis* [friend of the king] from this period, with which several confidants of the ruler were honored. Three years before his death, Charlemagne divided his treasures in the presence of his friends and servants (*coram amicis et ministris*), and charged them to uphold the terms of the division after his death. Two members of the imperial aristocracy from the time of Louis the Pious were also described as *primus de amicis regis* [first among the friends of the king] or *regalium primus amicorum* [first of the royal friends].[19] The *Life* of Sturm, abbot of Fulda, reports of King Pippin that he forgave the abbot a transgression and accepted him into his grace and friendship. The *Vita* describes the relationship between the king and the abbot as *pacati firmiterque in amicitia fundati* [peaceful and firmly grounded in friendship].[20] One might debate the sort of relationship to the king that lay behind these individual formulations – worthy of mention in this context are, for example, possible parallels that appear in other honorary titles[21] – but the fundamental conclusion, that the forging of formal alliances of friendship by kings, in both the Merovingian and the Carolingian periods, took place only within the circle of foreign rulers and the popes, remains untouched. Just as a treaty of friendship between two rulers excluded the payment of tribute, so too a subordinate relationship excluded *amicitia*.

That this changed in the course of the Carolingian period almost certainly reflects the growing influence of the aristocracy on the Carolingian kings. This influence resulted not least from the crises that the Carolingian house itself created, since the stability and the cohesiveness of the family broke apart over questions about the status and inheritance of the sons of Louis the Pious.[22] It is no accident, therefore, that it was these very sons of Louis the Pious who tried to restore and secure their fraternal relationship by binding themselves with mutual oaths, that is, by concluding sworn friendships with each other just as members of the Merovingian house had done. Already famous is one of the first cases of such a sworn friendship, the Oaths of Strasbourg, sworn in 842 by Louis the German and Charles the Bald to each other: "For the love of God, and for the salvation of the Christian people and of us both I wish to behave towards my brother Charles, as one by rights should behave towards

---

[18.24] See Fritze, *Papst und Frankenkönig*, pp. 15–17; on the renewal of the friendship with the Byzantine Emperor see B. Simson, *Jahrbücher des Fränkischen Reiches unter Ludwig dem Frommen*, Jahrbucher der deutschen Geschichte vols. 7–8 (Leipzig: Duncker & Humblot, 1874–6), 1: 30–2.

[19.25] See Schneider, *Brüdergemeinde*, pp. 87–8; see also Brunner, *Oppositionelle Gruppen*, pp. 29–31.

[20.26] Eigil, *Vita Sancti Sturmi. Die Vita Sturmi des Eigil von Fulda. Literatur-kritisch-historische Untersuchung und Edition*, ed. P. Engelbert, Veröffentlichungen der Historischen Kommission für Hessen und Waldeck 29 (Marburg: N. G. Elwert, 1968), c. 18.

[21.27] See in general H. Wolfram, *Intitulatio I. Lateinische Königs- und Fürstentitel bis zum Ende des 8. Jahrhunderts*, MIÖG Ergänzungsband 21 (Vienna: Böhlau, 1967) and *Intitulatio II: Lateinische Herrscher- und Fürstentitel im 9. und 10. Jahrhundert*, ed. H. Wolfram, MIÖG Ergänzungsband 24 (Vienna: Böhlau, 1973); see also Brunner, *Oppositionelle Gruppen*, pp. 27–9.

[22.28] See F. L. Ganshof, "Am Vorabend der ersten Krise der Regierung Ludwigs des Frommen. Die Jahre 828 und 829," *Frühmittelalterliche Studien* 6 (1972): 39–41 Brunner, *Oppositionelle Gruppen*, pp. 109–11.

his brother, under the condition that he does the same for me; and I will enter into no agreement with Lothar that with my volition could redound to his harm."[23] The sources characterize this and subsequent sworn alliances among the Carolingian brothers with the entire spectrum of terminology that we have discussed up to this point: they can be called *pax, foedus, amicitia,* and other things.[24] There is no reason to doubt the fact that these alliances aimed to enhance the ties of kinship by including those of comradeship and friendship as well.

Suprisingly enough, however, the brothers themselves do not appear to have been the driving force behind this fraternal alliance. The historian Nithard, himself a scion of the Carolingian house, fully describes the reasons that lay behind the Carolingians' sworn alliance at Strasbourg. According to Nithard, the elder brother, Louis, declared before the assembled *populus* [here; important men] of both brothers, among other things that "because we believe that you doubt our steadfast loyalty and imperishable brotherly love, we have decided to swear this oath between us before your eyes."[25] The participation of these magnates in the swearing of the oath itself shows that the influence of the followers on the two brothers implied in this statement was no mere rhetorical flourish. Indeed, the magnates swore to withdraw their support from their lord if he broke his oath. This pledge did not directly tie the magnates to the alliance, but it did set them up as its guardians, which amounts to more or less the same thing. This guardian role, of course, only had any real chance of success whenever sufficient solidarity existed among the magnates to permit common action.

The example of the Treaty of Coulaines, which Charles the Bald entered into with the magnates of his kingdom in 843, makes clear just how frequently people made use of alliance forms based on comradeship or friendship during the crisis of the Carolingian Empire.[26] Charles himself described, in a long narrative, the events that led up to the treaty: it was his followers, both ecclesiastic and lay, who had concluded a friendship alliance among themselves (*in pacis concordia et vera amicitia copularent*). They had done so for the good of the kingdom and the king. But Charles joined the *amicitia* (*sociam et comitem fore tota devotione spospondimus*), and ordered the document drawn up, which everyone signed. It contained six sections of provisions for preserving the *honor* [dignity, esteem] of all parties. From our perspective, the individual provisions are completely lacking in the necessary concreteness, as is shown by the frequent addition of the word *debitus* (*a, um*) [ought] to the stipulated ways of behaving. In any given situation, what was due and what befitted the respective *honor* might very well be disputed.[27] But it is very clear that the treaty aimed at preventing those with special connections to the ruler from having a harmful influence on him. The treaty singled out ties (*coniunctiones*) of kinship (*consanguinitas*), comradeship (*familiaritas*), and friendship (*amicitia*), ties which might offend against justice, the dignity of the royal name,

---

[23.29] See Nithard, *Historiarum Libri IIII*, ed. E. Müller, *MGH, SSrG* (1907 – henceforwad Nithard), III, 5: 36.

[24.30] See Schneider, *Brüdergemeinde*, pp. 178–80, with a listing of the terms used in the sources.

[25.31] Nithard, III, 5: 35.

[26.32] See *Capitularia regum Francorum*, ed. A. Boretius, *MGH*, Legum sectio II (1883–97), 2, no. 254: 253; on the interpretation see above all P. Classen, "Die Verträge von Verdun und Coulaines 843 als politische Grundlagen des westfränkischen Reiches," *HZ* 196 (1963): 1–3.

[27.33] This insight into the inherent ambiguity of such provisions was still lacking in the High Middle Ages, as, for example, the use of the term *honor* in the Treaty of Constance of 1153 between Pope Eugene III and Frederick Barbarossa makes clear: *Die Urkunden Friederichs I*, ed. H. Appelt, *MGH*, Diplomata regum et imperatorum Germaniae 10, 1 (1975), nos. 51, 52.

and the king's impartiality. In other words, a friendship embracing *all* of the magnates and the king was intended to protect against the harm done to the peace by kinship and friendship between the king and certain groups or parties. Just as in Nithard's report of the events leading up to the Oaths of Strasbourg, the active role played by the magnates in Coulaines is striking. At Coulaines, the magnates first organized themselves into an *amicitia* alliance before approaching the ruler, while at Strasbourg they brought about an alliance between the kings and then acted as guarantors for it, without entering into an alliance among themselves (Nithard at least does not explicitly mention such an alliance).

This is not the place to decide whether such pithy judgments as "Le roi est descendu de son trône" ["the King descended from his throne"], or "ein bedeutsamer Abstieg für die Monarchie" ["this signified a major setback for the monarchy"][28] match the historical reality of the Treaty of Coulaines. One can also argue that the treaty represented an attempt to exclude capriciousness from the working relationship of the magnates and the king by creating a circle of persons dedicated to cooperation with regard to certain principles – principles which stemmed from the arsenal of comradeship/friendship alliances.

Just as the crisis of the Carolingian Empire in the period of Louis the Pious produced alliances based on comradeship and friendship, so too the ongoing crisis of the Empire brought about and encouraged the conclusion of friendship alliances at the most disparate levels. Members of the Carolingian house itself tried to achieve or secure fraternal or kindred concord through the creation of friendship alliances.[29] Interestingly enough, they did not limit themselves to meetings, to the swearing of oaths, and to political negotiations, but rather in addition proved and "advertised" their friendly intentions through concrete associations. The sources report this in the following way, for example:

> the holy and honorable unity of the brothers surpassed all of their noble character-istics. For they almost always took their meals together, and what each had of value, he gave to the other in brotherly love. They ate and slept in one house; they handled public matters with the same unanimity as their private affairs; and none demanded anything from the other that he did not believe was also useful and of service to him.[30]

In practice, however, the peace associations of the Carolingians also included their follow-ers, with whom, "to exercise the body," they engaged in military games: "and it was worth seeing, because of the lofty feelings and the decorum that reigned there. For not one from among this great multitude and all these different peoples dared to inflict a wound or to insult another, as customarily occurs even in small groups and among acquaintances."[31] Here we see that "friendship" was practiced in a variety of situations. At the same time, the description makes clear what could endanger the peace in the Middle Ages: whenever a large group of armed men gathered in one place, it was only a short step from inflammatory or boastful talk to armed violence.[32]

[28.34] See Classen, "Verdun und Coulaines," p. 26, with the judgment "bedeutsamer Abstieg" ["major setback"], who also quotes the similar citation given in F. Lot and L. Halphen, *Le Règne de Charles le Chauve (840–877)*, Bibliothèque de l'Ecole des hautes Etudes. Sciences historiques et philologiques, 175 fasc. (Paris: H. Champion, 1909), vol. 1, p. 96.

[29.35] See the comparison of the cases in Schneider, *Brüdergemeinde*, pp. 178–80.

[30.36] Nithard, III, 6: 37–8.

[31.37] Ibid., 38.

[32.38] Medieval sources frequently speak of provocation as a cause of conflict, as, for example, with reference to the frequent armed disputes that took place when German armies stayed in Italian cities.

The sources also report friendship alliances in contexts in which the older scholarship constructed nation-state differences. For example, the relationship between Swatopluk of Moravia, the founder of the so-called "Greater Moravian Empire," and the Carolingians and Frankish lords is marked by ties of the comradeship/friendship sort.[33] The tie of *compaternitas* bound Swatopluk to Arnulf, the illegitimate Carolingian and later emperor. Swatopluk had lifted Arnulf's similarly illegitimate son from the baptismal font. The son – we are speaking here of the later King Zwentibold of Lotharingia – even received the name of his godfather.[34] In contrast, the Margrave of Austria, Aribo, concluded a friendship alliance with Swatopluk when he was threatened by Bavarian opponents. In this situation, he did not delay giving his son to Swatopluk as a hostage, to guarantee the continuance of the alliance.[35] This detail can perhaps serve as the best indication of the contractual character of such agreements and their distance from the modern understanding of the word friendship.

In the case of these alliances, we are also in a position to get an overview of their preservation or violation in the context of political confrontation. When Margrave Aribo's opponents expelled him from office, Swatopluk came wholeheartedly to his military aid and drove out the enemies of his friend. Aribo's beaten opponents, however, interestingly enough fled to Arnulf of Carinthia, with whom Swatopluk was bound by the tie of *compaternitas* in the same way that he was with Margrave Aribo. Swatopluk immediately reminded Arnulf of this relationship, and laid down as an ultimatum a demand for appropriate behavior. "You are supporting my enemies," he declared to Arnulf through legates, "and if you do not send them away, you will have no one, not even me, who remains at peace with you." When Arnulf rejected this suggestion, Swatopluk began a feud with his *compater* that was carried on for many years with great bitterness.[36]

At about the same time, there was talk of alliance, godparenthood, and ties of kinship when it came to integrating the Norman Godefrid into the Frankish Empire. Emperor Charles III [Charles the Fat, d. 888] raised the Norman from the baptismal font after he had concluded a treaty with him at Elsloo that contemporaries regarded as disgraceful. It seems that Charles had not only transferred counties and fiefs to Godefrid but had also given him a large amount of gold and silver, which his contemporaries interpreted as tribute payment. It is fascinating to note how different sources represent this state of affairs in entirely different ways. The Regensburg recension of the *Annals of Fulda* writes concerning the events following the baptism: "they cheerfully remained there together for two days; then, after our hostages had been returned from the forts, he was himself sent home again with very great gifts. The gifts were of the following kind: in gold and silver 2,080 pounds or somewhat more, the pound reckoned at 20 solidi."[37] Here we find once again the reference

---

Hincmar of Rheims, therefore, explains in *De ordine palatii* with every justification that the counselor should abstain from causing any provocation through inflammatory speech: Hincmar, *De ordine palatii*, ed. and trans. Th. Gross and R. Schieffer, *MGH*, Fontes iuris Germanici antiqui 3 (1980), c. 31: 86.

[33.39] For the following see G. Althoff, "Zur Bedeutung der Bündnisse Svatopluks von Mähren mit Franken," in *Symposium Methodianum: Beiträge der internationalen Tagung in Regensburg (17. bis 24. April 1985) zum Gedenken an den 1100. Todestag des hl. Method*, ed. K. Trost et al., Selecta Slavica 13 (Neuried: Hieronymus, 1988), pp. 13–21.

[34.40] Regino of Prüm, *Chronicon. Cum continuatione Treverensi*, ed. F. Kurze, *MGH, SSrG* (1890 – henceforward Regino), a. 890, 134.

[35.41] *Annales Fuldenses (Cont. Ratisbonensis)*, ed. F. Kurze, *MGH, SSrG* (1891), a. 884, 111.

[36.42] Ibid., 112; cf. also Angenendt, *Kaiserherrschaft und Königstaufe*, p. 243.

[37.43] See the *Annales Fuldenses (Cont. Mogunt.)*, a. 882, 99 for the defamatory representation of the alleged tribute payment; by contrast, see in the *Cont. Ratisbonensis*, a. 882, 108–9 the interpretation as a gift.

to cheerful fellowship, which so to speak served to demonstrate friendly behavior. And if in fact it was not tribute that Charles III was paying, then they were truly imperial gifts.[38]

One year after his baptism, Godefrid entered into an alliance (*foedus*) with Hugh, the son of Lothar II and an opponent of Charles III. In the course of this alliance, Godefrid married Hugh's sister Gisla. The sources indicate the purpose of this alliance with the sentence, "made bolder by this, that very Hugh sought to bring his father's kingdom under his rule."[39] Regino of Prüm describes in exquisite detail how Hugh, Godefrid, and in reaction Charles III, acted. Even if the selfish motivations attributed to the actors by Regino are overstated, we can establish the following: the alliance and the kinship of Hugh with Godefrid resulted in a request for military aid, which Godefrid was apparently ready to provide against his godfather Charles. On the other side, godparenthood did not prevent Charles III from having Godefrid treacherously murdered after he had heard of the "cunning tricks and conspiracies of their intrigues" (*callida machinamenta et factionum conspirationes*).[40] It must always be remembered, therefore, that ties of kinship, like ties of comradeship or friendship, represented practical alliances that one could also break when it was to one's advantage to do so.

Alliances of friendship during this period, however, were not just entered into by secular lords. We also have contemporary information, from widely differing sources, about alliances involving several bishops, bishops who also, it must be said, held important secular lordships. These were Salomo of Constance, Hatto of Mainz, and Dado of Verdun.[41] The first two in particular wielded the dominant political influence during the reign of Louis the Child [d. 911]. We are first informed in detail about the close friendship alliance between these two men, however, by a source from the eleventh century, namely the "St Gall Monastery Histories" of Ekkehard IV.[42] Ekkehard's account is dominated by anecdotal stories about the two bishops' collaboration, stories that provide only the barest hints about the political dimension of their alliance. The tales are nonetheless valuable, because in a way they reveal individual traits of these bishops – something that is well known to be extremely rare for the earlier Middle Ages. The two men, writes Ekkehard, governed their alliance (*sodalitas*) according to a very curious precept: "each was in the habit of aiming to dupe the other through craftiness in word or deed, whenever he could."[43] Ekkehard also describes how one such deception took place. After Hatto, on the occasion of a journey to Italy, had entrusted all of his treasures to his friend with the injunction to give them all for the salvation

---

[38.44] For the evaluation of these events in the scholarship see H. Keller, "Zum Sturz Karls III," *Deutsches Archiv* 22 (1966): 333–84, esp. 336–8; Angenendt, *Kaiserherrschaft und Königstaufe*, pp. 260–2.

[39.45] *Annales Fuldenses (Cont. Mogunt.)*, a. 883, 100.

[40.46] Regino, a. 885, 123–4; cf. H. Neifeind, "Verträge zwischen Normannen und Franken im neunten und zehnten Jahrhundert" (Ph.D. dissertation, University of Heidelberg, 1971), pp. 89–90.

[41.47] On the political significance of these bishops see U. Zeller, *Bischof Salomo III von Konstanz, Abt von St. Gallen*, Beiträge zur Kulturgeschichte des Mittelalters und der Renaissance, Heft 10 (Leipzig: B. G. Teubner, 1910); J. Fleckenstein, *Die Hofkapelle der deutschen Könige: I. Grundlegung. Die karolingische Hofkapelle*, Schriften der Monumenta Germaniae Historica 16, 1 (Stuttgart: Hiersemann, 1959), esp. pp. 211–13.

[42.48] For an evaluation of Ekkehard see H. F. Haefele, "Tu dixisti. Zitate und Reminiszensen in Ekkehards Casus sancti Galli," in *Florilegium Sangallense. Festschrift für J. Duft zum 65. Geburtstag*, ed. O. P. Clavadetscher et al. (Sigmaringen: Thorbecke, 1980), pp. 181–98.

[43.49] Ekkehard IV, *Casus Sancti Galli*, trans. H. F. Haefele, Ausgewählte Quellen zur deutschen Geschichte des Mittelalters. Freiherr von Stein Gedächtnisausgabe 10 (Darmstadt: Wissenschaftliche Buchgesellschaft, 1980), c. 22, 56–8.

of his soul in case he died, Salomo himself spread the rumor that Hatto had died. There-upon, Salomo had liturgical furnishings made for St Gall from the treasures. Upon his return, the duped Hatto was forced to agree, for good or ill, to this donation of salvific utensils.

Two poems addressed by Salomo of Constance to Dado of Verdun demonstrate that the concern for mutual spiritual salvation indeed constituted a part of such friendship alliances.[44] In the first poem, which consists of a long lament over current conditions in the period of Louis the Child, Salomo asks Dado to accept *nostrum Hattonem* [our Hatto] into their friendship league. Salomo also proposes that they include all other friends in their reciprocal *fides* [good faith]. In the second poem, however, Salomo reports the death of his brother Waldo; he asks his friend to pray for the salvation of Waldo's soul.

These are unusual sources, and what emerges from them is more than the closeness of episcopal *confratres* [colleagues]. It is rather a relationship which is entirely comparable to the friendship alliances discussed previously and which is aimed at gaining aid and support in all areas of life. If we note further that Hatto of Mainz was bound by the tie of *compaternitas* with another important contemporary bishop, Adalbero of Augsburg, and that this Adalbero on a special occasion gave relics to Salomo of Constance, then it becomes clear how similar the web of relationships connecting these spiritual princes was to that which in the same period bound the secular princes.[45] It then also comes as no surprise to see how the influence of these bishops predominated at the turn of the ninth century to the tenth.

Just how widespread the conclusion of friendship alliances was in this period is also shown by the case of the Italian King Berengar, who after his accession to the throne in 898 entered into an *amicitia* with the Empress Ageltruda, the widow of his former opponent Wido. Ageltruda was an extremely capable woman, which she had proven not least in 896 by ordering the gates of Rome closed before the advancing army of Arnulf of Carinthia and by placing the city in readiness to be defended. It was also she, according to circulating rumors, who brought about Arnulf's death by means of a poisoned drink. Berengar allied himself, therefore, with a very influential woman, to whom he promised "from this hour on to be a friend, as rightly a friend should be to his friend."[46] Moreover, he conceded her everything that her husband and son had granted her. Though only Berengar's *promissio* [charter that makes a promise] has survived, there can be no doubt that this was a mutual alliance, one aimed at eliminating the imperial widow's opposition.

Charles the Simple [the west-Frankish King] and Henry I [the east-Frankish King] likewise used the same formula at the conclusion of their friendship alliance on the Rhine at Bonn in 921: "*ero huic amico meo regi orientali Heinrici amicus, sicut amicus per rectum debet esse suo amico*" ["I will be a friend to my friend the eastern King Henry, just as a friend by rights

---

[44].50 *Salomonis et Waldrammi carmina*, ed. P. v. Winterfeld, *MGH*, Poetae latini IV, 1 (1899), 296–314; see G. Althoff, "Unerforschte Quellen aus quellenarmer Zeit (III). Necrologabschriften aus Sachsen im Reichenauer Verbrüderungsbuch," *Zeitschrift für die Geschichte des Oberrheins* 131 (1983): 91–108, esp. 105–7.

[45].51 See on further aspects of such webs of connection G. Althoff, "Der Corveyer Konvent im Kontakt mit weltlichen und geistlichen Herrschaftsträgern," in *Der Liber Vitae der Abtei Korvey. Studien zur Corveyer Gedenküberlieferung und zur Erschließung des Liber Vitae*, ed. K. Schmid and J. Wollasch (1989), pp. 29–38, and "Der Adel Alemanniens im früheren Mittelalter," in *Archäologie und Geschichte des ersten Jahrtausends in Südwestdeutschland*, ed. H. U. Nuber et al. (Sigmaringen: Thorbecke, 1990).

[46].52 See *Capitularia regum Francorum* pt 2, no. 231; on Empress Ageltruda see T. Leporace, "L'imperatrice Ageltrude," *Samnium* 9 (1936): 5–46, 142–66.

ought to be to his friend"].[47] This treaty also stands in the tradition of Carolingian royal friendship alliances, insofar as magnates of both rulers participated in it and guaranteed its permanence with an oath (*"collaudando acceptaverunt et manibus suis sacramentum firmaverunt nunquam a se destruendam"* ["they received it with great praise and confirmed the oath with their own hands: the pact would never be destroyed by them"]). The *narratio* [narrative part of the charter] tells how this treaty came about. Legates from both sides negotiated an arrangement that stipulated that the two kings meet at Bonn on November 4. On this first day, the kings were only to show themselves on the opposite banks of the river and look at each other, whereupon the legates could regard their sworn obligations as fulfilled. Only on the third day did the kings step out of their ships into a third, which was anchored in the middle of the Rhine. There they held a *colloquium*, in the course of which they confirmed with an oath the *unanimis pactum* [unanimous agreement] and the *societatis amicitia* [friendship of their union]. One cannot go wrong in assuming that the initial eye-contact represented a ritual action by means of which each one demonstrated, at first approach, his peaceful intentions. The action thus stood in a line with the previously mentioned common meals, living together in the same house, or sleeping together in the same bed, all of which served to create and to reinforce a friendly atmosphere. The fact that both treaty texts and the short descriptions by medieval historians mentioned such rituals makes clear how important contemporaries considered them.

This particular friendship alliance clearly did not fulfill its purpose. A short time later, Henry I concluded a similar *amicitia*-alliance with the west-Frankish anti-king against Charles the Simple. We can hardly describe this as anything other than a breach of the Bonn friendship treaty. It did Charles the Simple little good while in captivity to send his friend Henry the relics on which Henry had sworn friendship to him.[48] In this period of crisis, ties of friendship were as little inviolable as those of vassalage or of kinship.

Charles the Simple was taken captive by his vassal Count Herbert of Vermandois, who not only played an important, though thoroughly obscure, role in this period, but whom the sources also describe as striving to secure his own political influence via a web of kinship and friendship connections. Herbert can in fact serve as an excellent example of the degree to which people used both kinds of connection. Herbert was himself, as a descendant of Bernard of Italy, a scion of the Carolingian house. One of his sisters married the later King Robert, a second the east-Frankish Conradine Udo. The daughters of Herbert and Adela married Arnulf of Flanders and the Norman Duke William.[49] Over and above these kinship ties, however, the sources describe Herbert as entering into *amicitiae*, not only with the same

[47.53] See *Constitutiones et acta publica imperatorum et regum*, ed. L. Weiland, *MGH*, Legum sectio IV, vol. 1 (1893 – henceforward *Constitutiones*), no. 1; see K. Schmid, "Zur amicitia zwischen Heinrich I und dem westfränkischen König Robert," in *Festschrift für Berent Schwineköper zu seinem siebzigsten Geburtstag*, ed. H. Maurer and H. Patze (Sigmaringen: Thorbecke, 1982), pp. 119–20.

[48.54] See Widukind of Corvey, *Sachsengeschichte*, ed. P. Hirsch, *MGH, SSrG* (1935 – henceforward Widukind), I: 33, with the legate's speech: *"Hoc* [i.e. the relics] *habeto pignus foederis perpetui et amoris vicarii"* ["These you should have as a pledge of our perpetual alliance and mutual love"]. The connection with the Bonn treaty and the political situation is not explicitly referred to, but is nonetheless obvious; cf. H. Beumann, *Die Ottonen* (Stuttgart: W. Kohlhammer, 1987), p. 38.

[49.55] See K. F. Werner, *Die Nachkommen Karls des Grossen bis um das Jahr 1000 (1.–8. Generation)*, Karl der Grosse. Lebenswerk und Nachleben 4, ed. W. Braunfels and P. E. Schramm (Düsseldorf: Schwann, 1967), p. 458, with the genealogical table on the cover; in general, K. F. Werner, *Untersuchungen zur Frühzeit des französischen Fürstentums (9.–10. Jahrhundert)*, Die Welt als Geschichte 20 (Stuttgart: Kohlhammer, 1960), pp. 87–119.

Norman Duke William Longsword, with Hugh the Great, and with Gilbert of Lotharingia, but also with Henry I and Otto the Great. Since Herbert's son Odo, according to the testimony of Flodoard and Dudo, lived at the court of the Norman Duke Rollo, it is entirely likely that an *amicitia* also bound Herbert and Rollo.[50] All of these connections served to construct a position of lordship, which was equally true of the attempt to have Herbert's son Hugh made archbishop of Reims.

By contrast, Charles the Simple did not bind himself to the great lords of his kingdom with *amicitiae*, if one can believe the surviving sources. He likewise did not use his daughters to build up kinship connections with his magnates.[51] Just the opposite: he provoked the magnates by raising up advisors of unimportant heritage.[52] Charles's attempt to build up his rule in the style of the early Carolingians, that is, by relying on the loyalty of vassals and remaining at a distance from the magnates, failed as a result. When we consider that the loyalty of vassals had no priority in the spectrum of available ties during this period, then this failure is hardly surprising. It should be contrasted with the otherwise multivalent interweaving of the ruling classes, of which the natural and artificial ties formed by Herbert of Vermandois serve as but one example. But we must not forget that even in his case ties of kinship and *amicitiae* could be broken when doing so would produce a more favorable constellation in the struggle for power.

Henry I [d. 936] developed a plan for consolidating his rule that differed entirely from that of Charles the Simple. In his scheme, alliances of friendship played a central role. The sources describe Henry, while still a duke, blending lordly and comradely ties and bonds in virtuoso fashion. For his wedding to Hatheburg, Henry gathered all of his neighbors (*vicinos*) together and bound himself to them by such *familiaritas* that they loved him as a friend and honored him as a lord. Thietmar of Merseburg, who roughly a century later still knew about it, called the "settlement" that Henry reached in the year 915 with his opponent King Conrad I an *amicitia*.[53] One consequence of this alliance was that Henry gained the kingdom, since Conrad designated him as his successor. It also brought with it, however, a noticeable promotion of members of the Conradine kindred by the Ottonians [as Henry I's

---

50.56 See L. Buisson, "Formen normannischer Staatsbildung," in *Studien zum mittelalterlichen Lehenswesen. Vorträge gehalten in Lindau am 10.–13. Oktober 1956*, Konstanzer Arbeitskreis für Mittelalterliche Geschichte, Vorträge und Forschungen, Bd. 5 (Lindau: Thorbecke, 1960), pp. 142–4; G. Althoff [*Amicitiae und Pacta. Bündnis, Einung, Politik und Gebetsgedenken in beginnenden 10. Jahrhundert*, Schriften der *MGH*, 37 (Hanover, 1992)].

51.57 See Werner, *Nachkommen*, p. 461, with the genealogical table on the cover.

52.58 The resistance of the princes was above all provoked by the Lotharingian Hagano, who wielded an especial influence on Charles the Simple; see Flodoard of Reims, *Annales*, ed. Ph. Lauer, Collection de textes pour servir à l'étude et à l'enseignement de l'histoire 39 (Paris: A. Picard & fils, 1905 – henceforward Flodoard), a. 920; A. Eckel, *Charles le Simple* (Paris: E. Bouillon, 1899), pp. 106–8.

53.59 On the marriage celebration see Thietmar of Merseburg's formulation with respect to Henry I: "*Nupciis ex more peractis, sponsus cum contectali ad Merseburch venit; omnesque convocans vicinos, quia vir fuit illustris, tanta familiarite sibi adiunxit, ut quasi amicum diligerent et ut dominum honorarent*" ["The wedding having been carried out according to custom, the husband came with his bride to Merseburg; since he was a man of rank, he called together all those in the vicinity, and bound them to him by such familiarity, that they loved him as a friend and honored him as a lord"]. *Die Chronik des Bischofs Thietmar von Merseburg und ihre Korveier Überarbeitung*, ed. R. Holtzmann, *MGH, SSrG*, Nova ser. 9 (1955 – henceforward Thietmar), I: 5. The label *amicitia* for the relationship between Henry and Conrad appears in Thietmar I: 7. Cf. in general H. Büttner and I. Dietrich, "Weserland und Hessen im Kräftespiel der karolingischen und frühen ottonischen Politik," *Westfalen* 30 (1952): 133–49, esp. 146; the authors speak here of a "compromise."

progeny would later be called].[54] It is likewise by no means an accident that an alliance with Eberhard, the brother of the dead King Conrad, was forged at the beginning of Henry I's elevation to the kingship. This alliance contained elements of lordship and friendship together.[55]

The list of *amicitiae* attested for Henry I during his reign as king is long. He entered into these alliances first of all with other kings, such as Charles the Simple, as discussed previously, but also King Robert of France, Rudolf of Burgundy, and Hugh of Italy.[56] In addition, Henry concluded them with the magnates of other kingdoms, such as the previously mentioned Herbert of Vermandois or Gilbert of Lotharingia. In the case of Gilbert, the juxtaposition of different sorts of bonds is especially clear. After Gilbert had been handed over into Henry's custody, Henry treated him *liberaliter* [generously, nobly], and bound himself to Gilbert as a kinsman as well as a friend by giving him his daughter Gerberga in marriage. In addition, however, ties of lordship were created when Henry bestowed on Gilbert the *regnum Lotharii* [realm of Lothar – i.e. Lotharingia].[57] Henry entered into similar relationships with the dukes of his own kingdom, as is demonstrated, among other ways, by the example of Eberhard of Franconia.[58]

Amicitia appears, however, to have played an even more central role within the framework of Henry I's efforts to consolidate his royal authority. It was reported of the king that in the year 931 he had himself invited into the homes of all the bishops and counts of Franconia and engaged in *convivia* [feasts] with them, and that everyone reciprocally honored each other by exchanging gifts.[59] This is exactly the way one concluded friendship alliances, and there is no reason to doubt that this report deals with exactly that.

[54.60]   Examples for this include the elevation of Hermann to Duke of Swabia, the installation of Conrad the Red as Duke in Lotharingia and his marriage to the royal daughter Liudgard, as well as the later ducal offices held by members of the Conradine kindred in Swabia; cf. G. Tellenbach, "Vom karolingischem Reichsadel zum deutschen Reichsfürstenstand," in *Adel und Bauern im deutschen Staat des Mittelalters*, ed. Th. Mayer (Leipzig: Koehler & Amelang, 1943), pp. 35–7; H. Maurer, *Der Herzog von Schwaben. Grundlagen, Wirkungen und Wesen seiner Herrschaft in ottonischer, salischer und staufischer Zeit* (Sigmaringen: Thorbecke, 1978), pp. 30–1.

[55.61]   This is shown very clearly by the formulation in Widukind, I: 26: "*Evurhardus adiit Heinricum seque cum omnibus thesauris illi tradidit, pacem fecit, amicitiam promeruit; quam fideliter familiariterque usque in finem obtinuit*" ["Eberhard went to Henry, and handed himself over to him with all of his treasure, made peace, and promised friendship; this he maintained faithfully and intimately to the end"].

[56.62]   See Schmid, "Zur amicitia zwischen Heinrich I und dem westfränkischen König Robert," 136–8.

[57.63]   See Widukind, I: 30: "*liberaliter eum coepit habere, ac postremo desponsata sibi filia nomine Gerberga affinitate pariter cum amicitia iunxit eum sibi, sublegato omni ei Lotharii regno*" ["he began to treat him more graciously, and finally he betrothed him to his daughter named Gerberga, thus binding himself to him by kinship as well as friendship, and he gave to him the entire realm of Lothar"].

[58.64]   Cf. n. 55 above. Widukind uses the following formulation with respect to Arnulf of Bavaria (I: 27): "*egressus est ad regem, tradito semet ipso cum omni regno suo. Qui honorifice ab eo susceptus amicus regis appellatus est*" ["he went out to the king and surrendered himself with his entire realm. He was honorably taken up by the king, and called a royal friend"]. With reference to Burkhard of Swabia (Ibid.): "*tradidit semet ipsum ei cum universis urbibus et populo suo*" ["he surrendered himself with all of his castles and people"]. On the free rein that Henry I gave to the dukes see most recently Beumann, *Die Ottonen*, pp. 34–5.

[59.65]   See the *Continuatio Reginonis*, a. 931: "*Eodem anno rex ab Eberhardo aliisque Franciae comitibus seu episcopis in Franciam vocatus singillatim ab unoquoque eorum in domibus suis vel ecclesiarum sedibus regem decentibus est conviviis et muneribus honoratus*" ["In the same year, the king was called into Franconia by

Henry I did not just conclude alliances and bring about unions by himself, however. He sent out confidants for this purpose, with instructions to lead quarreling parties in a given region back to peace and unity.[60] It is only natural, therefore, that all of the chroniclers of his reign emphasize precisely these efforts in their comprehensive judgments of this king's rule. Never did a greater concord and love bind humanity than during his reign; he was a man who refused his friends nothing.[61] Pacify, assemble, and unify are the verbs used to describe his performance as a ruler, a performance that was successful both at home and abroad: at home, feuds ceased abruptly, and by dint of common efforts successes were achieved in the defensive war against the Hungarians.[62]

These stepped-up efforts by the king to settle differences through peace unions and friendship alliances did not leave their mark only in the historiographical sources. Memorial sources show just as clearly – though in a completely different manner – that during this period new groups were dedicated to memorial prayer. One can speak directly of a wave of entries that flooded the confraternity books in a relatively short time.[63] Various characteristics of these new entries clearly indicate their connection with the efforts to bring about peace, efforts we have seen reflected in the historiographical sources. In many case, it is possible to identify representatives of the political leadership in the entries. These representatives appear in different entries, each time in different surroundings [i.e., groups of names]. The number of persons contained in each entry is so large that kinship ties cannot entirely explain them. Moreover, in a series of cases, Henry I and his family can be shown to appear among those entered; in each of these cases, they appear in different company. In other words, the royal family was directly involved in the [social] movement visible in the entries. This is not the place to discuss these complex findings in detail. It must be emphasized, however, that rich opportunities for observing the structures of connection and

---

Eberhard and other counts and bishops of Franconia; he was specially received by each of them into their homes or ecclesiastical sees and honored with appropriate banquets and gifts"].

[60.66] Cf. Flodoard, a. 926: "*Ebrardus quidam Transrhenensis in regnum Lotharii mittitur ab Heinrico, justitiam faciendi causa, et Lotharienses inter se pace consociat*" ["a certain Eberhard from across the Rhine was sent into the realm of Lothar by Henry, for the purpose of rendering justice, and he united the Lotharingians together in peace"].

[61.67] See, for example, Ruotger, *Vita Brunonis archiepiscopi Coloniensis*, ed. I. Ott, *MGH, SSrG*, Nova ser. 10 (1951), c. 3: "*tantus amor colligavit domesticos, ut nihil umquam in quolibet potentissimo regno coniunctius videretur*" ["so great a love bound the members of the court, that it surpassed any ever seen in the mightiest kingdom whatsoever"]. Widukind, I: 39 agrees: "*Ipse enim rex talis erat, qui nihil negaret amicis*" ["He was namely the sort of king who could deny his friends nothing"]. For a complete treatment of the judgments of Henry I rendered by Ottonian historiographers see Althoff [*Amicitiae und Pacta*].

[62.68] The famous chapter in Widukind (I: 35) concerning the *agrarii milites* [farmer-soldiers] shows that forms of organization based on comradeship were used in the defence against the Hungarians; see most recently J. Fleckenstein, "Zum Problem der *agrarii milites* bei Widukind von Korvey," in *Beiträge zur niedersächsischen Landesgeschichte. Festschrift für H. Patze*, ed. D. Brosius and M. Last (Hildesheim: Lax, 1984), pp. 26–41.

[63.69] See the documentation [in Althoff, *Amicitiae und Pacta*]. Examples appear in Schmid, "Zur amicitia zwischen Heinrich I und dem westfränkischen König Robert" and "Unerforschte Quellen aus quellenarmer Zeit (II): Wer waren die 'fratres' von Halberstadt aus der Zeit König Heinrichs I?," in *Festschrift für Berent Schwineköper*, as well as in G. Althoff, "Unerforschte Quellen aus quellenarmer Zeit (IV): Zur Verflechtung der Führungsschichten in den Gedenkquellen des frühen 10. Jahrhunderts," in *Medieval Lives and the Historian. Studies in Medieval Prosopography*, ed. N. Bulst and J. P. Genet (Kalamazoo: Medieval Institute Publications, 1986), pp. 37–71.

alliance in this period are opened up by the fact that the names of persons who bound themselves together by comradeship or friendship were entrusted to memorial prayer.

We see, therefore, that the old institution of the friendship alliance was used with increasing frequency during the crisis of the Carolingian Empire to build up a network of personal connections that would guarantee help in all areas of life. It is useless to speculate whether the tie of kinship or the tie of friendship had the greater weight. It is impossible to provide a general answer to this question; the effectiveness of a connection was much more a matter of individual circumstance. The lack of any hierarchy governing these connections is amply demonstrated by the observation that kinship ties were not infrequently strengthened by alliances of friendship, as conversely, friendship ties were by subsequent marriage alliances. The most noticeable innovation that the development sketched here brought with it, however, is that dependence on a lord ceased to exclude ties of friendship or kinship; indeed, in not a few cases, friendship alliances were created in an attempt to stabilize relationships involving lordship.

Already the Danish King Horich could offer Louis the Pious *obedientia* [obedience] and *amicitia* together. Eberhard of Franconia handed himself over (*tradidit*) to Henry I and at the same time bound himself to the king by friendship, which he maintained as *fidelis* and *familiaris* to the last.[64] These phenomena characterized a rulership in which the prestige of the ruler no longer sufficed to mobilize a following large enough to hinder internal dissent and at the same time ward off external dangers. It can be no accident, therefore, that the royal reign which proved most successful was that which most consistently relied on alliances. And that was the rule of Henry I. Yet we should not forget that the conclusion of friendship alliances and the unification and reconciliation of divided groups did not solve every problem. Real divergences of interest certainly could not be resolved by this means alone. A form of rulership that emphasized elements of comradeship or friendship was indeed suited to initiate a phase of consolidation. Whether it could in the long run iron out differences better than the superiority and subordination implicit in the term "lordship" may at least be doubted.

Contemporaries themselves appear to have seen this problem. It was already Otto the Great [son of Henry I; d. 973] – even in the earliest phase of his rule – who refused to engage in reciprocal alliances (*pacta mutua*) like his father's *amicitiae* with the magnates of his realm. This refusal was limited solely to the magnates of his kingdom, for Otto indeed continued to conclude friendship alliances with foreign kings as well as with foreign magnates, such as the Norman William Longsword and Herbert of Vermandois.[65] These refusals brought a severe crisis to Otto's reign, for those affected perceived them, as well as other royal actions aimed at pushing through a strengthened royal prerogative, as an *offensio*, as an insult; they reacted by starting several feuds, each of which reached significant proportions.[66] Similarly, just as

64.70 On Eberhard see n. 55 above; on Horich see the *Annales Bertiniani*, ed. G. Waitz, *MGH, SSrG* (1883), a. 836: "*Sed et Horich rex Danorum per legatos suos in eodem placito amicitiae atque oboedientiae conditiones mandans*" ["But Horich king of the Danes, who through his legates at that assembly offered the terms of friendship and obedience"].

65.71 See for the discussion of Otto's refusal to engage in *pacta mutua* H. Naumann, "Rätsel des letzten Aufstandes gegen Otto I. (953–4)," *Archiv für Kulturgeschichte* 46 (1964): 133–84; G. Althoff, "Zur Frage nach der Organisation sächsischer coniurationes in der Ottonenzeit," *Frühmittelalterliche Studien* 16 (1982): 130–2; on the *amicitiae* with foreign magnates see Buisson, "Formen normannischer Staatsbildung," pp. 144–5.

66.72 See on this G. Althoff and H. Keller, *Heinrich I. und Otto der Große. Neubeginn auf karolingischem Erbe* (Göttingen: Muster-Schmidt, 1985), pp. 135–7. With respect to the study of medieval conflicts,

Otto the Great tried to establish royal rule in the East once more on its old basis by refusing ties of friendship, so too in the West one can observe phenomena aimed at establishing the preeminence of lord-dependent relations over all other bonds. When the Norman Duke William commended himself to the west-Frankish King Louis IV in 940, he promised him *fidem contra omnes* [fidelity against all], thus securing by means of an oath the priority of his dependence on his lord.[67] Nonetheless, this dependence was softened, so to speak, by spiritual kinship: William lifted the son of Louis IV, Lothar, from the baptismal font.[68] A long period of time would pass before the ties of dependence on the king were granted priority over all other bonds by reserving allegiance with respect to him alone.[69]

In the course of the tenth century, therefore, there were two ways in which kings attempted to control the prevalence of ties based on comradeship or friendship, and the consequent blurring of man–lord dependence. On the one hand, kings bound themselves in friendship only to a circle of persons who were not themselves the kings' dependants. On the other, they strove to win absolute priority for the tie to the king over all other bonds. It goes without saying that such efforts could hardly bring about quick, and certainly not sudden, change in the customs that had up to that time governed relationships. Nevertheless, the east-Frankish/German kings, beginning with Otto the Great, appear indeed to have distanced themselves from their magnates to such a degree that they managed to avoid ties such as *amicitia*. Although the term *amicus regis* does still appear in a few exceptional cases, it seems to have taken on once more the character of an honorary title. It was used, for example, by Thietmar of Merseburg to describe the relationship between Henry II and his competitor for the throne, Duke Hermann of Swabia, after Hermann had recognized Henry as king: "*miles et amicus eius fidus efficitur*" ["he became his faithful knight and friend"].[70] It seems more than questionable whether Thietmar intended this formulation, which placed the feudal tie first and added the word *fidus*, to indicate a connection of equal partners. The term was possibly also used by Otto III, who in the course of his political program in the East was said to have bestowed the title *amicus populi Romani*, which clearly looks back to Roman custom, on Boleslav Chrobry.[71] This too, however, indicated a different kind of connection than that which obtained in the ninth and early tenth centuries.

---

it must be stressed that terms in the sources such as *offensio/offensus*, but also *tristis/tristitia* [sad/sadness] or *aegre ferens* [vexed] and the like, must be given careful attention, because contemporaries used them to indicate circumstances that had a fixed place in the rituals of dispute processing; cf. G. Althoff, *Verwandte, Freunde und Getreue. Zum politischen Stellenwert der Gruppenbindungen im Mittelalter* (Darmstadt: Wissenschaftliche Buchgesellschaft, 1990), c. 5.3, and "Königsherrschaft und Konfliktbewältigung im 10. und 11. Jahrhundert," *Frühmittelalterliche Studien* 23 (1989): 272 and n. 22.

[67.73] See Buisson, "Formen normannischer Staatsbildung," p. 144, with further references in n. 243.

[68.74] Ibid., p. 145; see also Angenendt, *Kaiserherrschaft und Königstaufe*, p. 122.

[69.75] See Heinrich Mitteis, *Lehnrecht und Staatsgewalt. Untersuchungen zur mittelalterlichen Verfassungsgeschichte* (Weimar: Bohlaus, 1958), pp. 562–4; W. Kienast, *Untertaneneid und Treuevorbehalt in Frankreich und England. Studien zur vergleichenden Verfassungsgeschichte des Mittelalters* (Weimar: H. Böhlaus Nachfolger, 1952), pp. 43–5, 205–7; F. L. Ganshof, "Les relations féodo-vassaliques aux temps post-carolingiens," in *I problemi comuni dell'Europa post-carolingia. Spoleto* 2 (Spoleto: Presso la sede del Centro, 1955), pp. 67–114, esp. 70–2.

[70.76] Thietmar, V: 22.

[71.77] On the problems posed by this title, which appears only in the so-called Gallus Anonymous (*MGH, SS*, 9, 428) see C. Erdmann, "Die Würde des Patricius unter Otto III," in C. Erdmann, *Forschungen zur politischen Ideenwelt des Frühmittelalters*, ed. Friedrich Baethgen (Berlin: Akademie-Verlag, 1951), pp. 99–102, and H. Appelt, "Die angebliche Verleihung der Patriciuswürde an Boleslaw Chrobry," in

Of course this "holding back" that the kings practiced did not bring about a complete abandonment of *amicitia* as a bond between equal partners with a claim on support in all areas of life. Below the level of the kings, it appears to have continued among the politically important classes as a means of broadening the available possibilities for action. "*Amici facti sunt, nam antea inimici erant ad invicem*" ["they were made friends, where before they had been mutual enemies"], we learn, for example, of Duke Conrad the Red and Archbishop Frederick of Mainz, when these attached themselves to a political grouping around Liudolf, the son of Otto the Great.[72] The existing enmity was apparently formally ended and replaced by a friendship alliance. In the eleventh century, Archbishop Adalbert of Bremen concluded a friendship alliance with a Danish king. As was likewise customary among the Danes, this alliance was reinforced by an extended feast, which allegedly lasted eight days.[73]

Amicitia as a relationship between two people and a basis for common political action may also be seen in the case of Margrave Ekkehard of Meissen. Ekkehard managed to force the Polish Duke Boleslav, by means of "promises and threats," to become his *amicus familiaris*.[74] This connection between the Ekkehardines and the Piast dynasty, although strengthened further by a marriage alliance, nonetheless did not endure, because by this point the consciousness of the feudal tie's priority had apparently risen considerably. This conclusion stems from Thietmar's report of the negotiations between Boleslav and the Margrave Ekkehard's brother, Gunzelin, in the year 1002. Boleslav was at this point engaged in a feud with the king and therefore wanted to renew his old friendship (*pristina amicitia*) with Gunzelin. Gunzelin, however, recalled his feudal obligations, and answered Boleslav that, "vassals of my lord are with me who make such a thing impossible. If it were to become known, my life and all of my possessions would be in danger."[75]

This argument is very much like the one employed a short time later by the vassals of Duke Ernest to justify withdrawing their fealty when the duke decided to rise up against King Conrad II.[76] Ernest himself, however – and this made him famous to his contemporaries – did not yet consider his tie to the king, his stepfather, higher than all his other attachments. Urged by Conrad to fight his own vassal Werner because the latter had allegedly injured the king, Ernest refused, and perished together with his vassal.[77]

Although it was deemed thoroughly honorable in the eleventh century to promote the affairs of your relatives and friends with all your might as if they were your own (as Wipo, for example, says of Conrad II before the latter became king), the importance of the *amicitia* alliance in the context of political competition seems to have declined instead. This judgment does not exclude the possibility that in certain situations it could represent an adequate bonding mechanism. This is demonstrated by the example of the Saxon magnates, who in

---

Geschichtliche Landeskunde und Universalgeschichte, Festgabe für H. Aubin (Hamburg, 1951), pp. 65–81.

[72.78] Regino, *Continuatio*, a. 952. Cf. the similar formulation in Liudprand of Cremona, "Antapodosis," in *Opera omnia*, ed. E. Dümmler, *MGH, SSrG* (1877), IV, 25 concerning the friendship alliance between Kings Henry I and Rudolf of Burgundy: "*facti sunt amici in illa die, qui prius inimici erant*" ["they, who had previously been enemies, became friends on that day"].

[73.79] Adam of Bremen, *Hamburgische Kirchengeschichte*, ed. B. Schmeidler, *MGH, SSrG* (1917), III: 18.

[74.80] Thietmar, V: 7.

[75.81] Ibid., V: 36.

[76.82] See Wipo, "Gesta Chuonradi II. imperatoris," in *Opera*, ed. H. Bresslau, *MGH, SSrG* (1915), c. 20; on the problem see Kienast, *Untertaneneid*, pp. 111–13.

[77.83] Wipo, "Gesta Chuonradi," c. 25; on the problems posed by this conflict see Althoff, "Königsherrschaft," pp. 278–80.

the course of their conflict with Henry IV [d. 1106], concluded an alliance with magnates from Swabia.[78] The Saxons, it must be said, paid no attention to this alliance when they made peace with Henry IV some time later. The Swabians in turn regarded this as a breach of treaty, and thus were transformed from faithful friends to the bitterest enemies (*ex amicis fidelibus hostes atrocissimi*).

Interestingly enough, there were bishops active during the same difficult period who took steps to secure the best possible mutual support by concluding friendship alliances among themselves. Archbishop Siegfried of Mainz wrote along these lines to Bishops Werner of Magdeburg and Burchard of Halberstadt, asking them to mediate an alliance between himself and Archbishop Anno of Cologne. Siegfried and Anno were not enemies, the archbishop declared, but up to that point no reliable friendship had linked them that sufficed for them to share each other's secrets.[79]

The *Life* of Bishop Benno of Osnabrück provides an excellent witness to the fact that it was perfectly customary in the eleventh century for bishops to reach out for friends in precarious situations. Benno first revealed to his friends his plan to request back from the king the tithes for the diocese of Osnabrück; these friends then proceeded to open the necessary doors for him.[80] The *Life* also describes the arguments with which Benno armed his friends, so to speak, as well as certain royal advisors, in order to push through his plan. The friends and royal advisors expressed their opinion that Benno had already earned "a royal reward" because he had abandoned his "very considerable property" out of loyalty to the king. It would also strengthen the fealty of others, they went on to say, if this loyalty were rewarded with an appropriate counter-gesture from the king. Moreover, the tithes in question were held by enemies of the kingdom, who deserved nothing but punishment. Finally, the king had every reason to reconcile himself with God (whom he had up till that point offended by his many sins) by a just decision in this matter.

The mental world here was completely dominated by the principle of service and counter-service. This principle, as it pertained to the relationship between kings and imperial princes, began from the twelfth century on to be captured in writing.

Legal historians have observed that from the twelfth century on rulers concluded alliances with their subjects, without, however, taking into account the cases from previous centuries sketched above. These scholars regarded as alliances the written treaties, which laid down in

---

[78.84] For Wipo's judgment of Conrad II see "Gesta Chuonradi," p. 104 – the "Cantilena in Chuonradum II factum": *"propinquorum causas et amicorum haud secus quam suas desideravit cunctis viribus iuvare pro possibilitate"* ["he desired to promote, to the best of his ability, the affairs of his relatives and friends with all men no less than his own"]. On the alliances of the Saxons with the Swabians see Bruno's *Buch vom Sachsenkrieg*, ed. H.-E. Lohmann, *MGH*, Deutsches Mittelalter 2 (1937), c. 31 (incl. the breach of treaty mentioned in the following sentence), 35, 87, 88, with the interesting detail of a "trust-building measure": *"Tunc omnes facti ex hostibus amici fideles, castra posuerunt tam prope, ut vicissim populus uterque sermones utriusque non difficile posset audire"* ["Then all were turned from enemies into faithful friends; they placed their camps so close to each other, that each host could hear what was said on both sides without difficulty"]. Cf. Althoff, *Verwandte*, c. 5.
[79.85] Bruno, *Buch vom Sachsenkrieg*, c. 18.
[80.86] Norbert von Iburg, *Vita Bennonis II. episcopi Osnabrugensis*, ed. H. Bresslau, *MGH, SSrG* (1890), c. 16: *"propriis primitus amicis, deinde regis familiaribus tantae controversiae querimoniam insinuando detexit"* ["he revealed and made known the complaint that had caused such controversy, first to his own friends, then to the intimates of the king"]. Cf. Althoff, *Verwandte*, c. 5 n. 28. On *insinuatio* as a technical term belonging to the discipline of rhetoric see P. von Moos, *Geschichte als Topik. Das rhetorische Exemplum von der Antike zur Neuzeit und die historiae im "Policraticus" Johanns von Salisbury*, Ordo, vol. 2 (Hildesheim: G. Olms, 1988), *passim* (index, p. 646).

advance the obligations due from each side.[81] These treaties are certainly analogous to the early medieval alliance, but they also display substantial differences. In the period of time discussed up to this point, an alliance created an obligation for the future for full support in all areas of life, not, as in the twelfth century, exclusively with respect to concrete provisions. This difference appears enormous; the notion of the "juridification" that the twelfth century is supposed to have brought with it hardly describes it adequately.[82]

Frederick Barbarossa, the first king for whom such written alliances have survived, concluded a treaty with Duke Berthold IV of Zähringen, which laid down exact obligations for both sides and even fixed their duration in time.[83] This treaty inaugurated a long series of similar ones; there was no more talk of friendship or the like. What would early medieval rulers and magnates have done in similar situations? We do not have a comparable written treaty from the early Middle Ages. This does not exclude the possibility that such treaties could have been orally concluded. The surviving sources, however, speak for another interpretation. In the early Middle Ages, people generally tried to regulate relationships between persons and groups through marriage, godparenthood, or friendships. They appear to have employed, not utilitarian alliances with concrete and exactly circumscribed limitations, but rather a fundamental and at the same time only generally formulated statement of intent: one agreed to behave in the future as a relative or a friend *per rectum* ought to behave.

The history of alliances based on comradeship or friendship, therefore, reflects to a certain degree a learning process undergone by medieval people. The path goes from alliances that vaguely bound the treaty partners in all cases and for all time, to the concrete, written establishment of rights, obligations, and duration, that bound the partners only with respect to that which was laid down in writing. This history also reflects, however, phases in which ties of comradeship or friendship were promoted more intensively, as well as attempts to create a hierarchy of connections, and thereby gain priority for the ruler.

[81.87] See H. Mitteis, "Politische Verträge im Mittelalter," *ZRG, GAbt* 67 (1950), pp. 76–140; G. Rauch, *Die Bündnisse deutscher Herrscher mit Reichsangehörigen vom Regierungsantritt Friederich Barbarossas bis zum Tod Rudolfs von Habsburg* (Aalen, Scientia Verlag, 1966).

[82.88] See in general J. Fried, *Die Enstehung des Juristenstandes im 12. Jahrhundert: zur sozialen Stellung und politische Bedeutung gelehrter Juristen in Bologna und Modena* (Cologne: Böhlau, 1974); *Recht und Schrift im Mittelalter*, ed. P. Classen, Vorträge und Forschungen 23 (Sigmaringen: Thorbecke, 1977); extensive references are provided by H. Jakobs, *Kirchenreform und Hochmittelalter, 1046–1215*, Oldenbourg Grundriss der Geschichte, Bd 7 (Munich: Oldenbourg, 1984), esp. pp. 159–61.

[83.89] *Constitutiones* 1, nr 141: 199. See most recently G. Althoff, "Die Zähringer Herrschaft im Urteil Ottos von Freising," in *Die Zähringer. Eine Tradition und ihre Erforschung*, ed. K. Schmid (Sigmaringen: Thorbecke, 1986), pp. 49–51; H. Heinemann, "Untersuchungen zur Geschichte der Zähringer in Burgund," pt 1, *Archiv für Diplomatik* 29 (1983): 42–192 (pt 2 of this Marburg dissertation appears in ibid., 30 [1984]: 97–257).

Part III Gender

Part III Gender

The very modern topic of "gender" has extremely old roots in histories of women and the family.[1] Such studies began in Italy with the writings of Vico in the early eighteenth century; and they became important in Germany later in the same century, under the inspiration of Johann Gottfried Herder, who considered the *Volk* (an untranslatable term; the best approximation is possibly "the common people") the proper subject of scholarly study. French historians lacked comparable theoretical foundations, but that did not prevent those of the nineteenth-century Romantic movement, such as Jules Michelet, from celebrating women of virtue and action alongside their male counterparts. In England, later in the nineteenth century, lively interest in the topic of women's history arrived largely with the women's suffrage movement.

Yet events and attitudes in the first half of the twentieth century conspired to put an end to these traditions and forays. Fascist Italy glorified conquering men; Nazi Germany uprooted and depopulated its university history departments. In France between the wars (and then dominating the historical scene thereafter), the *Annales* school, in every other respect pathbreaking in its insistence on underlying structures and the "long haul" over time, nevertheless largely ignored women. Marc Bloch's book, *Feudal Society*, a prime example of this new historiography and dazzling in its scope, nevertheless mentioned only two women by name, while he included 233 men with titles and names. In England, the threat of Continental totalitarianism sparked a particular interest in the origins of English democracy, a process in which women were thought to have played no part. In the United States, medievalists largely followed the methods, subjects, and interests of European historians.

Thus there was everywhere a hiatus in the sorts of studies that would, in the 1970s and thereafter, come to the forefront of historical research. In the new research on women and families that characterized this more recent period it is fair to say that – standing on the shoulders of Vico and Michelet, of course – American scholars took the lead in the 1970s, though the debate has been joined (and was from the start) by many European historians.

The reasons for the resurgence of the 1970s are not difficult to uncover. The women's movements of the 1960s, in some ways an outgrowth of the civil rights movement in the United States and the movements towards post-war decolonization in western Europe, were of key importance. As blacks and others mobilized their political energies and formulated

---

[1] The essential book for the historiography of the field is Susan Mosher Stuard, ed., *Women in Medieval History and Historiography* (Philadelphia: University of Pennsylvania Press, 1987), from which a good deal of the historiographical discussion below is borrowed.

strategies for "empowerment," women became self-conscious and organized as well. In addition, interest in "mass" society, in demographic issues, and in the use of new methodologies and technologies (such as computers) to chart changes in population over time, led to redefining the subject matter of history. No longer would it be narratives of public action; it would be analyses of everyday conditions and private family structures of ordinary people, both men and women. Finally, the studies of anthropologists on kin groups, marital customs, life-cycle rituals, and sexual behavior in non-Western cultures inspired medievalists to consider these topics in their own field.

Women's Experience

The earliest work of the newly revived research was spurred above all by the desire to know about the experience of past women. At first these studies sought simply to bring to light the existence of outstanding women. This built upon a long tradition. Queens and saints, in particular, had been studied long before the twentieth century, were the subject of scrutiny even during the hiatus in the first half of that century, and continue today to be extremely attractive subjects. The two women who had earned a place in Bloch's study were Joan of Arc, a perennial heroine both for the Catholic Church and for French nationalists; and Edith, queen of England, who, because of her royal status, played an undeniably political and active role. Both of these women had been "actors" on the public stage; they were not out of place in any history, however masculine its orientation.

But in the 1970s and 1980s new studies appeared that also discovered or made much of largely forgotten women, especially those whose achievements were undeniable. Scholars uncovered women musicians, writers, and visionaries.[2] Margaret Wade Labarge ended her book, *Women in Medieval Life: A Small Sound of the Trumpet*, with a fanfare: a chapter entitled "Women's Contributions to Medieval Culture," devoted to nuns' intellectual and artistic accomplishments.[3]

For some historians, however, the subject of achieving women was all too fully parallel to the agenda of traditional male histories. These scholars challenged the search for greatness; they were interested in what obstacles even ordinary women had overcome and what opportunities they had seized. Even in the traditional domain of medieval queens, the spotlight was cast differently. A good example of this new work was an article by Janet Nelson on two relatively obscure early medieval queens (chapter 13). Nelson was quick to point out at the very beginning of her study that these women had been "very active and intelligent."[4] But she was concerned to show more than that; indeed, Nelson demonstrated,

---

[2] Some examples: Ann Bagnall Yardley, "'Ful weel she soong the service dyvyne': The Cloistered Musician in the Middle Ages," in Jane Bowers and Judith Tick, eds, *Women Making Music: The Western Art Tradition, 1150–1950* (Urbana: University of Illinois Press, 1987), pp. 15–38; Maria V. Coldwell, "*Jougleresses* and *Trobairitz*: Secular Musicians in Medieval France," in Bowers and Tick, eds, *Women Making Music*, pp. 39–61; Peter Dronke, *Women Writers of the Middle Ages: A Critical Study of Texts from Perpetua (†203) to Marguerite Porete (†1310)* (Cambridge: Cambridge University Press, 1984); Elizabeth Alvilda Petroff, ed., *Medieval Women's Visionary Literature* (New York: Oxford University Press, 1986).

[3] London: Hamish Hamilton, 1986.

[4] Chapter 13: Janet Nelson, "Queens as Jezebels: the Careers of Brunhild and Balthild in Merovingian History, "*Medieval Women: Essays Dedicated and Presented to Professor Rosalind M. T. Hill*, ed. D. Baker, *Studies in Church History: Subsidia*, vol. 1 (Oxford: Blackwell, 1978), pp. 31–77, reprinted in Janet Nelson, *Politics and Ritual in Early Medieval Europe* (London: Hambledon Press, 1986), pp. 1–48.

with the queens serving largely as exemplars, the advantages, hazards, attitudes, and images that Merovingian women had to negotiate as they made their way in the world.

This approach also contained an implicit challenge to those who sought, in their discussions of women's past, to find a female "golden age." That search was fueled by the conviction that some historical periods had been more favorable for women to exercise social, economic, and/or political autonomy than others. Thus Marian K. Dale applauded the late medieval London silkwomen, for they worked as real wage-earners and traders, and they had a gild-like organization.[5] Rodney Hilton emphasized the way that late medieval peasant women held land, drove the plow animals, and pled at court.[6] More recently, P. J. P. Goldberg argues that in England the period after the Black Death offered new and better choices for women both in work and marriage;[7] while Caroline M. Barron emphasizes the fact that women in fourteenth- and fifteenth-century London could manage their own businesses, supervise apprentices, and make money.[8]

On the other side of the "golden age" debate are, for example, Maryanne Kowaleski and Judith M. Bennett, who emphasize the low status of most female workers, their subordinate place in any gild they might belong to, and – with regard to Dale's thesis – the extremely temporary status of the London silkwomen's gild-like structure.[9] Bennett also counters the picture of rosy medieval country life in her book on the manor of Brigstock.[10]

The debate on golden ages is especially sharp with regard to the Anglo-Saxon period. Some historians consider that period to have been a golden age for women, brutally shattered by the Norman Conquest of 1066.[11] Vigorously disputing this view is Pauline Stafford (chapter 14).[12] One implication of her argument (which may also be drawn from Nelson's article) is that historians would be better off not trying to find golden ages or their opposite, as different women profited (or lost out) in any given period.

Yet the search for a golden age has also been the cutting edge of a critical method in some hands. Some feminist historians have used it to prod and counter at every point the old narrative of progress. Did traditional histories celebrate the Renaissance as a great step forward? The celebration would have to stop while historians figured out whether it had

[5] Marian K. Dale, "The London Silkwomen of the Fifteenth Century," *Economic History Review* 1st ser., 4 (1933): 324–35, reprinted in Judith M. Bennett et al., *Sisters and Workers in the Middle Ages* (Chicago: University of Chicago Press, 1976), pp. 26–38.

[6] Rodney H. Hilton, *The English Peasantry in the Later Middle Ages* (Oxford: Clarendon Press, 1975), pp. 95–110. If theirs was hardly a golden life, yet "there is reason to believe that peasant women enjoyed a measure of relative independence, a better situation in their own class than was enjoyed by women of the aristocracy, or the bourgeoisie, a better situation perhaps than that of the women of early modern capitalist England" (p. 105).

[7] For marriage, P. J. P. Goldberg, "'For Better, For Worse': Marriage and Economic Opportunity for Women in Town and Country," in P. J. P. Goldberg, ed. *Woman is a Worthy Wight: Women in English Society c. 1200–1500* (Wolfeboro Falls, NH: Alan Sutton, 1992), pp. 108–25; for work, P. J. P. Goldberg, *Women, Work, and Life Cycle in a Medieval Economy: Women in York and Yorkshire, c. 1300–1520* (Oxford: Clarendon Press, 1992).

[8] Caroline M. Barron, "The 'Golden Age' of Women in Medieval London," *Reading Medieval Studies* 15 (1989): 35–58.

[9] Maryanne Kowaleski and Judith M. Bennett, "Crafts, Gilds, and Women in the Middle Ages: Fifty Years after Marian K. Dale," in Bennett et al., *Sisters and Workers in the Middle Ages*, pp. 11–38.

[10] Judith M. Bennett, *Women in the Medieval English Countryside: Gender and Household in Brigstock Before the Plague* (New York: Oxford University Press, 1987).

[11] See the historiographical survey at the beginning of chapter 14.

[12] Chapter 14: Pauline Stafford, "Women and the Norman Conquest," *Transactions of the Royal Historical Society* 6th ser., 4 (1994): 225–37, 249.

been a Renaissance for women as well.[13] Were there medievalists convinced that the Carolingians ushered in a more peaceful, orderly, and innovative era? Suzanne Fonay Wemple argued that its very "advances" thwarted women's opportunities in church and family life.[14]

Forces Shaping Women's Lives

Some historians choose to view women's history more as the product of past social forces and structures than as the story of women's achievements or experiences. Goldberg, who saw decided advantages for women in post-plague England, argued that that "age of choice" was in fact a result of demographic and economic factors quite out of anyone's control. Women's new options were explained by depopulation during the Black Death and consequent labor shortages in the towns.

One important and much discussed example of the ways in which outside forces shaped the lives of women is the shift from "brideprice" to "dowry." Brideprice was a gift that the groom offered to his bride or his bride's kin. It was often accompanied, and sometimes even supplanted, by *morgengabe*, a gift that the husband gave his wife after the consummation of their marriage. In the Mediterranean world, beginning around the twelfth century, the dowry – a gift given by the bride's family to its daughter – came to replace these marital gifts. The classic study of this shift was written by Diane Owen Hughes, who suggested that the new dowry system was a response to a "crisis of status" brought about by economic and social changes.[15] The *morgengabe* had often been in the form of land bequests, enough to support a woman after her husband's death. However, the dowry, which was often the only portion of the paternal inheritance a woman could expect to get, was generally given in cash. The wife's family (that is, her father and brothers) not only held on to their real property, but also – even while her husband controlled and managed her dowry – supervised the way that dowry was invested. The dowry gave a woman's family perpetual rights over her and her offspring; it reflected and buttressed the new patrilineal kin groups of the High Middle Ages. Indeed, the amount of dowry a father offered for his daughter came to signify his family's status; it was key to his ability to make alliances and climb the social ladder. One result of this tie between dowry and familial honor was a great inflation in the dowry's size, as families competed with one another for high status even as they lamented the outlay that they were forced to make to do so.

The new dotal system had pervasive and sometimes unanticipated consequences. Christiane Klapisch-Zuber, a French historian who works in Italian archives on issues of women and the family, considers how the dowry plunged widows into a painful dilemma. They were pressed by their natal family to take their dowry into a new marriage, but if they did so, they risked the opprobrium of their sons (chapter 15).[16]

[13] Joan Kelly, "Did Women Have a Renaissance?," in Renate Bridenthal and Claudia Koonz, *Becoming Visible: Women in European History* (Boston: Houghton Mifflin, 1977), pp. 137–64 (and reprinted in the second ed. of *Becoming Visible* on pp. 174–201).
[14] *Women in Frankish Society: Marriage and the Cloister, 500 to 900* (Philadelphia: University of Pennsylvania Press, 1981).
[15] Diane Owen Hughes, "From Brideprice to Dowry in Mediterranean Europe," *Journal of Family History* 3 (1978): 262–96, here 288. Some elements of Hughes's account have recently been disputed by Régine Le Jan-Hennebicque, "Aux origines du douaire médiéval," in Michel Parisse, ed., *Veuves et veuvage dans le haut moyen âge* (Paris: Picard, 1993), pp. 107–22.
[16] Chapter 15: Christiane Klapisch-Zuber, "The 'Cruel Mother': Maternity, Widowhood, and Dowry in Florence in the Fourteenth and Fifteenth Centuries," in her *Women, Family, and Ritual in Renaissance Italy*, trans. Lydia Cochrane (Chicago: University of Chicago Press, 1985), pp. 117–31.

Recently the idea that cultural forces shape women's lives and images has shaded into the "social constructionist" view of men and women. The theory of social construction posits that there is no innate (or, at least very little innate) male or female nature; that the roles men and women take, the sexualities they express, the emotions they feel – in short, the very cores of their gender – are the products of the pressures and norms of the societies in which they live.[17]

The Female Shaping of History

The ultimate goal of many feminist historians is not only to make women and their history visible, nor yet just to show the forces that shaped it, but also to illuminate thereby the history of men. That is, they argue, the full history of human beings is incomplete unless it includes the way that women have been constructive of their society *across* gender.

One of the first and most important ways in which this goal was met was by talking about the feminine elements of male culture. In *Jesus as Mother* Caroline Walker Bynum explored images – such as a nurturing and maternal God – that had been largely associated with female piety; she placed them instead at the center of male Cistercian monastic spirituality.[18] In this way she showed that the full nature of twelfth-century piety could not be understood without thinking about gender. In her book *Holy Feast and Holy Fast*, which was largely an exploration of the meaning of food and the Eucharist to religious women in the Late Middle Ages, Bynum went further. In the portion of her book reproduced here as chapter 16, she argued that "female imagery" was experienced and used differently by men than by women.[19] She thus illuminated how medieval people of different sexes participated in a common culture in divergent ways.

Another way to meet the goal of dual-gender history was advanced in Clare A. Lees's collection of essays, *Medieval Masculinities*. The authors of the articles in this book agreed that the critical methods of women's history had to be applied to the history of men as well; that the history of men was as much at the mercy of social and cultural forces as that of women; and that traditional "male" histories in fact degendered men by making them emblematic of humanity as a whole. In Lees's book, in an article on the dowry, Susan Mosher Stuard showed the way in which this institution, so important in the lives of women (as we have seen), had impact on the lives, roles, and opportunities of men as well (chapter 17).[20]

The subject of gender is of keen interest not only to historians but also to literary scholars. Its importance to medievalists in general was recently recognized by the Medieval Academy of America, which published an entire special issue of its journal, *Speculum*, on the topic in 1993.[21] There the contours of the current debate are clearly etched. There is no question any

---

[17] For example, essays in David M. Halperin, John J. Winkler, and Froma Zeitlin, eds, *Before Sexuality: The Construction of Erotic Experience in the Ancient Greek World* (Princeton: Princeton University Press, 1990). See also Thomas Laqueur, *Making Sex: Body and Gender from the Greeks to Freud* (Cambridge, Mass.: Harvard University Press, 1990).
[18] Caroline Walker Bynum, *Jesus as Mother: Studies in the Spirituality of the High Middle Ages* (Berkeley: University of California Press, 1982), pp. 110–59.
[19] Chapter 16: Caroline Walker Bynum, *Holy Feast and Holy Fast: The Religious Significance of Food to Medieval Women* (Berkeley: University of California Press, 1987), pp. 282–94.
[20] Chapter 17: Susan Mosher Stuard, "Burdens of Matrimony: Husbanding and Gender in Medieval Italy," in Clare A. Lees, ed., *Medieval Masculinities: Regarding Men in the Middle Ages*, Medieval Cultures 7 (Minneapolis: University of Minnesota Press, 1994), pp. 61–72.
[21] Nancy F. Partner, ed., *Studying Medieval Women: Sex, Gender, Feminism*, special issue, *Speculum* 68 (1993): 305–471, reprinted in book form (Cambridge: Medieval Academy of America, 1993).

longer of *whether* gender issues should be part of history. Who would write a history of medieval society today that included only two women? The debate is rather *how* to include women. As helpmates in the processes traced in the traditional (and originally male) narrative? Or as subjects of a counternarrative? As socially constructed beings whose distinguishing characteristics depend on cultural assumptions? Or as human beings with innate and individual psychological needs and responses? Like most debates in medieval history, this one is not simply "academic." Indeed, the last essay in the *Speculum* collection calls on scholars to come out of the library and get involved in their communities.[22]

[22] Allen J. Frantzen, "When Women Aren't Enough," in Partner, *Studying Medieval Women*, pp. 445–71.

13 Queens as Jezebels: the Careers of Brunhild and Balthild in Merovingian History

Janet L. Nelson

Since they got a toe-hold in universities, the achievement of women in the field of medieval history has been high. Some female historiography may have been justly criticized for a certain breathlessness of style, a narrowness of concern, a subjectivity, even romanticism, of approach: faults produced, no doubt, by the pressures of most women's early socialization.[1] But the work of Rosalind Hill has shown an exemplary freedom from the faults and contributed substantially to the achievement. The combination of good sense and judgment with breadth of vision might perhaps have been expected from that rare person (of either sex) who can combine scholarly excellence with prowess in mountaineering. And so, despite its title, the paper that follows, in which I deal with the careers of two very active and intelligent women who commanded both the respect and the affection of many contemporaries (however unfairly posterity has treated them) will not, I hope, be thought a wholly inapt tribute.[2]

That women played a "large role" in Merovingian society is a commonplace of the historiography of the period. Queens Brunhild and Balthild[3] have been cited as cases in point. But if it is important to stress at the outset the obvious point that queens are not typical of women in this or any other period, it is also worth pursuing a little further the banal observation about the "large role" of women to inquire *which* women appear as significant actors in the later sixth and seventh centuries, and why they do so. Some women sometimes found themselves in positions of wealth and potential power: they were those who belonged to a land-based aristocracy whose members generally married within their own ranks.[4] These women – as wives, bringers of dowries and receivers of bride-wealth, as

I am very grateful to Ian Wood, John Gillingham, and Pauline Stafford for friendly criticism, and to Paul Fouracre for keen discussion of Merovingian matters.
[1] On some problems (if not the faults) of historical work by and about women, see the comments of [Susan Mosher] Stuard in her introduction to *Women* [*in Medieval Society*] (Philadelphia, 1976), pp. 1–12. For some lively criticisms of the male-dominated historiography of women, see the remarks of Ria Lemaire in *CCM* 20 (1977): 261–3.
[2] [This article was originally published in a volume honoring Rosalind Hill.]
[3] For the sake of simplicity I have used anglicized spelling of these and other familiar names.
[4] This statement seems to me essentially true both for the Gallo-Roman and barbarian aristocracies in the period covered in this paper. On the former, see [K. F.] Stroheker, [*Der senatorische*] *Adel* [*im*

widows and mothers (or stepmothers) custodians of family estates, as daughters heiresses to some or all of their parents' wealth – shared the status of their male kin, and had to be protected and provided for. If women loom so large in the history of Columbanan monasticism in seventh-century Gaul, this was not, I think, because "women, especially, were seduced by the rigours of Columban's teaching,"[5] but because, rather, these were new monastic structures eminently adapted to, and thus adopted by the managers of, land-based familial structures in which women already and necessarily occupied key positions. The number of sixth-century women's houses had remained low partly because monasticism on an urban, or suburban, episcopally-directed model could not readily be accommodated to the requirements (for solidarity and biological continuity) of aristocratic families: witness the complaint of the mother of Rusticula, her only child, who had entered the convent of St John at Arles: "I look at the possessions of our house, the innumerable multitude of our *familia* [household] and whom I shall leave it all to, I don't know. . . . Who will look after me in my old age, now that the one daughter I had is lost?"[6] In the seventh century, Sadalberga, whose hagiographer writes glowingly of contemporary foundations *per heremi vastitatem* [throughout deserted wasteland], established her first convent *in hereditate paterna* [on her paternal inheritance], having first conveniently converted husband and children to the monastic life;[7] while Moda, widow of the magnate Autharius, moved in with her own kin to take over control of her stepson Ado's recent foundation at Jouarre.[8] The importance of such family

---

spätantiken Gallien] (Tübingen, 1948); on the latter, [R.] Sprandel, [Der] *merovingische Adel* [*und die Gebiete ostlich des Rheins*], *Forschungen zur oberrheinischen Landesgeschichte* 5 (Freiburg-im-Breisgau, 1957), and "Struktur und Geschichte des merovingischen Adels," *HZ* 193 (1961): 33–71; K. F. Werner, "Bedeutende Adelsfamilien im Reich Karls des Grossen," in *Karl der Grosse, Lebenswerk und Nachleben*, ed W. Braunfels, 5 vols (Düsseldorf, 1965–8) 1, pp. 83–142, with full bibliography. The jural status of women differed as between Roman and various barbarian laws, but the long-term trend was toward heavy influence on the latter by the former and by canon law. Changes from the second half of the sixth century onward made for an improvement in the status of women under the Salic law, especially in the matter of inheritance of ancestral land in which females could now share under certain circumstances, and in the women's control of her own *dos* or bride-price. On all this see [F. L.] Ganshof, "[Le] statut [de la femme dans la monarchie franque]," *Recueils Jean Bodin* 12 (1962): 5–58, esp. 15–17, 25–35. The specific political and social developments which, as Ganshof observes, (p. 57) lie behind these legal changes have yet to be thoroughly examined. But see meanwhile F. Beyerle, "Das legislative Werk Chilperics I," *ZRG GAbt* 78 (1961), esp. pp. 30–8. For particular aspects of women's legal position see K. F. Drew, "The Germanic Family of the *Leges Burgundionum*," *Medievalia et Humanistica* 15 (1963): 5–14 and [J.-A.] McNamara and [S. F.] Wemple, "[Marriage and] Divorce [in the Frankish kingdom]," in Stuard, *Women*, pp. 95–124. For a broader comparative view see two recent works of J. Goody: *Production and Reproduction* (Cambridge, 1976), and his introductory chapter to *Family and Inheritance: Rural Society in Western Europe, 1200–1800*, ed. J. Goody, J. Thirsk, and E. P. Thompson (Cambridge, 1976), both offering characteristically stimulating insights and analysis for historians as well as social scientists. See also his *Succession [to High Office]* (Cambridge, 1966), esp. pp. 1–56.

[5] [P.] Riché, *Education [and Culture in the Barbarian West, Sixth through Eighth Centuries]*, trans. J. J. Contreni (Chapel Hill, 1976), p. 329. For details of women's participation in monasticism, see [F.] Prinz, [*Frühes*] *Mönchtum* [*im Frankenreich*] (Munich and Vienna, 1965); the good short survey in the first chapter of [G. A. de Rohan Chabot, marquise de] Maillé, [*Les Cryptes de*] *Jouarre* (Paris, 1971). There remains, however, a basic problem of explanation.

[6] *MGH SSrM* 4, cap. 5, p. 342. See P. Riché, "Note d'hagiographie mérovingienne: la *Vita S. Rusticulae*," *AB* 72 (1954): 369–77, showing this to be a seventh-century text.

[7] *MGH SSrM* 5, caps 8 and 12, pp. 54, 56. For the site, a *villa* in the *pagus* of Langres, see Krusch's comments, ibid. pp. 43, 56 n. 2. Could paternal *saltus* be classed as *eremus*?

[8] J. Guerout, "Les Origines et le premier siècle de l'Abbaye," in *L'Abbaye royale Notre-Dame de Jouarre*, ed. Y. Chaussy (Paris, 1961), pp. 1–67.

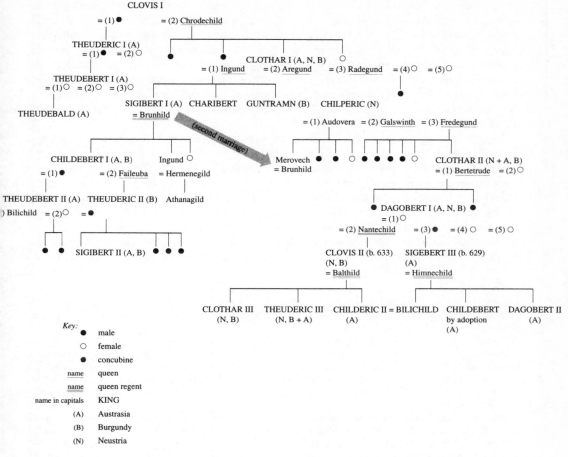

Table showing the Merovingians, their queens and concubines, dealt with in this paper

connections is equally, and poignantly, shown in the case of Wulftrude, daughter of Grimoald and abbess of the Pippinid foundation at Nivelles, whose removal from office was attempted by Merovingian *reges* [kings] and *reginae* [queens] "out of hatred for her late father," their family's enemy.[9]

No *Frauenfrage* [a reference to the problem of a surfeit of unmarried females in the Late Middle Ages] of the deprived or alienated arises, then, in reference to the seventh-century nuns and abbesses of Gaul. It is rather a matter of families' deployment of their personnel. The one function that critically distinguished masculine from feminine roles, that of warfare, was conspicuously absent from the monastic life: monks, like women, were *inermes* [without arms]. Conversely, within the monastery, a woman could transcend the "weakness" of her

---

[9] *Vita Geretrudis*, cap. 6, *MGH SSrM* 2, p. 460. For *Sippenkloster* ("kin-group monasteries") as aristocratic cult-centres, see Prinz, *Mönchtum*, pp. 489–503.

sex and become, not perhaps "virilized,"[10] but desexualized. Thus the same literary and spiritual culture was offered in monasteries to both girls and boys; and in this same asexual milieu, a woman as abbess of a double monastery[11] could exercise the political authority which in the secular world, at all levels including the monarchic,[11a] was formally monopolized by men. The point to stress is the absence of any principle of matriarchy.[12] Aristocratic women propose and dispose *ex officio* in a context where their sex is irrelevant. If through the contingencies of mortality or inheritance they temporarily wield power in secular society, they do so primarily in virtue of, and by means of, biologically-ascribed status which marital status will normally match and reinforce.[13]

To all of this, the position of a Merovingian queen, at any rate from the later sixth century, stands in something of a contrast. For it *could* be (not necessarily, but usually – and the mere possibility is what matters here) achieved and constituted exclusively through her husband. This happened when it became royal practice, first in Burgundy, then in Austrasia and Neustria, to choose as consort a low-born woman or even a slave.[14] From this same period we have evidence that the birth or status (whether queen or concubine) of a king's bed-fellow could not affect the status or succession-rights of her sons,[15] and it may be that the principle enunciated by Gregory of Tours reflected a new situation. Certainly, from the time of Guntramn and Chilperic, the typical Merovingians king expressed the uniqueness of his

---

[10] So, Riché, *Education*, p. 457, with, however, valuable comments on the place of women in monastic culture.

[11] See Guerout, "Origines," esp. pp. 34 *seq.*; also J. Godfrey, "The Double Monastery in early English history," *AJ* 79 (1974): 19–32.

[11a] Ganshof, "Statut," p. 54, stresses the inability of women, despite their *Rechtsfähigkeit* [legal capacity] in private law, to receive or transmit royal power in their own right: kingship was an *hereditas aviatica* [ancestral inheritance]. (For one small caveat, see below, pp. 224–5.) Ganshof's point must modify the notion that the Merovingians treated their realm simply as personal property, in view of the changes made in inheritance law by Chilperic I (561–84), on which see Ganshof, pp. 34–5.

[12] This is certainly not to deny the importance of ties with and through maternal kin. See K. Leyser, "The German aristocracy from the ninth to the early twelfth century," *PP* 41 (1968): 25–53, and "Maternal kin in early medieval Germany: a reply," *PP* 49 (1970): 126–34, though Leyser deals with periods later than the Merovingian.

[13] This seems true of the seventh-century marriages on which details are given in hagiographic sources. I have found only one clear case of an asymmetrical marriage in Gregory of Tours's *L[ibri] H[istoriarum]* (the so-called *History of the Franks*) and here the mother's status is higher than the father's: see *LH* x, 8, ed. B. Krusch and W. Levison, *MGH SSrM* 1 (2nd ed., Berlin, 1937–51), p. 489 (the parents of Tetradia – *nobilis ex matre, patre inferiore* [noble through her mother, but of humbler father]). For an alleged attempted exception to this conjugal matching by a Frankish aristocrat see below, p. 231.

[14] For details see [E.] Ewig, "Studien [zur merowingischen Dynastie]," *Frühmittelalterliche Studien* 8 (1974): 15–59 at 39 *seq. LH* iv, 25 and 26, pp. 156–7, provides confirmation that low-born queens were not usual in the mid-sixth century.

[15] *LH* v, 20, p. 228. See [Ian] Wood, "Kings, [Kingdoms and Consent]," in *Early Medieval Kingship*, ed. P. H. Sawyer and I. N. Wood (Leeds, 1977) pp. 6–29 at p. 14. On the distinction between queen (*regina*) and concubine (*concubina*) in Gregory and Fredegar, see Ewig, "Studien," pp. 38–9, 42–4. There is only one certain case of a concubine's son succeeding to the kingship in the later sixth century and through the whole later Merovingian period: Theudebert II. See below, p. 229. But Sigibert III is another probable case. Pauline Stafford rightly points out to me that the queen–concubine distinction is too simple, betraying an ecclesiastical perspective: matters were often more complicated. But in the light of the very scarce Merovingian evidence it seems impossible to say how much more so in the cases that have concerned me here.

monarchic status, his freedom from the norms that constrained his aristocratic subjects, by marrying a woman who, far from bringing him potent affines or rich dowry, owed everything to her relationship with him. Even if the royal bride was, as occasionally in the sixth century, a foreign princess,[16] her situation in practice might be little different from the ex-serving maid's. Her dependence on her husband's generosity and favour, when her own kin were far away and her people reckoned, perhaps, the enemies of the Franks, might be similarly complete. A Visigothic princess (Spain being one source of foreign brides for Merovingians) might keep in touch with her fatherland, but dynastic discontinuity there might in the fairly short run cut her personal link with the reigning house.[17] The fate of the Spanish princess Galswinth at Chilperic's hands[18] was no different from that of the ex-slave Bilichild at Theudebert II's.[19] And Galswinth did not find her avenger in any Spanish king.

The wife of a Merovingian, then, enjoyed a position both dependent and precarious, resting as it did on her personal, sexual association with a husband whose interests or fancy could all too easily attach him to her supplanter. A Merovingian ex-wife often cuts a pathetic figure, especially if she was sonless, or if her sons quarrelled with, or predeceased, their father.[20] Radegund, opting for ascetic virtuosity,[21] is an exception that also proves the rule. A Merovingian wife might have the title of queen, but there is no evidence that she underwent any special inauguration ritual (apart, presumably, from the marriage-ritual itself) that would have paralleled her husband's to his kingship.

Yet the very limitations on the extent to which the queen was enmeshed in political and familial structures could also give her, under certain conditions, a paradoxical freedom. We can look at this under two aspects: the economic and the sexual–genetic. Whereas a female aristocrat usually inherited some wealth in land or retained a stake in family estates, a queen of low or servile birth acquired wealth exclusively from or through her husband; and because a fair proportion of such acquired wealth tended to be in movables,[22] there was probably rather less contrast in practice between the resources of a Bilichild and a Galswinth than the difference in original status might seem to suggest. The association of queens with treasure is a recurrent theme of Merovingian history, and the uses of treasure were manifold. First as gold-bringer or gold-receiver, then as guardian of the royal hoard in a primitive "capital" during the king's absences at war, a queen could personally control sufficient treasure to support political activities on her own account. Fredegund was generous enough in

---

[16] Ewig, "Studien," p. 39.

[17] See below, p. 226.

[18] *LH* iv, 28, pp. 160–1.

[19] [*The Fourth Book of the Chronicle of*] *Fred.* [*egar*], ed. J. M. Wallace-Hadrill (London, 1960), cap. 37, p. 30.

[20] *LH* iii, 27 (Deuteria – though she did have a son, Theudebald); iv, 25 (Marcatrude – childless); iv, 26 (Ingoberg – sonless); v, 39 (Audovera – see below, n. 29). Nantechild, ex-wife of Dagobert, retained her queenly status and reemerged to prominence at her husband's death because she had an infant son (Clovis II) for whom she became regent, whereas the two queens who superseded her in Dagobert's favours both seem to have been childless: *Fred.*, caps 60, 79, pp. 50, 67.

[21] *LH* iii, 7, p. 105. It is probably significant that Radegund was childless. On her spirituality see E. Delaruelle, "Sainte Radegonde, son type de sainteté et la chrétienté de son temps," *Études Merovingiennes*, Actes des Journées de Poitiers, 1952 (Paris, 1953), pp. 65–74.

[22] This seems to have been true of the bride-price (*dos* – to be distinguished from dowry) in barbarian laws: see Ganshof, "Statut," p. 28 with nn. 66–8. It is not clear from *LH* ix, 20, p. 437 what proportion of the five *civitates* [cities] given to Galswinth by Chilperic constituted the *dos* and what was morning-gift. But it is clear that kings gave land as well as moveables to their wives: see *LH* vi, 45, p. 318 (Fredegund). For Balthild's estates, see below, n. 204.

deploying hers to taunt the Franks for their niggardliness;[23] plotters against Clothar II solicited his queen's alliance, asking her to send them secretly "all the treasure she could."[24] Given the indispensability of treasure to political success in the Merovingian world, in the seventh and the eighth centuries no less than in the sixth,[25] the queen's access to such resources could put her in a strong position, despite her relative weakness in terms of the direct control of land. Politically as personally, a queen's "rootlessness" might mean the advantage of greater freedom of manoeuvre.

The queen's initial offer to her husband of sexual services could obviously serve as a power-base as long as she retained his affections. Fredegund's is probably the best-documented case of a king's passion giving his consort long-term political ascendance.[26] Aside from such personal predilections, however, the strength of the conjugal bond – a point on which Germanic and ecclesiastical attitudes converged, though from different premises[27] – meant that a monarch's status rubbed off on his bed-fellow so that, while no queen could reign in her own right, a queen as widow could become a repository of royal powers for the time being apparently quiescent, a vehicle on which claims to the royal succession could be carried to a second husband. Admittedly, in every such case known to me, the queen was not low-born but herself of noble or royal family.[28] Still, her capacity to transmit a claim to rule

[23] *LH* vi, 45, p. 318. Compare *LH* iv, 26, p. 159 (Theudechild), and vii, 4, p. 328 (Fredegund again).

[24] *Fred.* cap. 44, pp. 36–7. The bishop of Sion asks Bertetrude "ut thinsauris quantum potebat secretissime ad Sidonis suam civitatem transferrit, eo quod esset locum tutissimum" ["to transfer as much of the treasury as she could secretly to his city of Sion, which would be the safest place"]. Perhaps episcopal treasuries had something of the function of banks. On the Burgundian background to this episode see E. Ewig, "[Die fränkische] Teilreiche [im 7. Jahrhundert 613–714)]," *Trierer Zeitschrift* 22 (Trier, 1953): 85–144 at 106.

[25] *Fred.* cap. 45, p. 38; cap. 67, p. 56; cap. 75, p. 63; cap. 84, p. 71. The Continuator of Fredegar, ibid., cap. 9, p. 88 shows the importance of treasure for Plectrude, widow of Pippin II, in 714–15. Hincmar, *De Ordine Palatii*, cap. 22, *MGH cap.* 2, p. 525, shows the continuing intimate connection of the queen with treasure in the ninth century. See below, n. 234. For the continuance of taxation and tolls throughout this period, see F. Lot, *L'Impôt foncier et la capitation personnelle sous le Bas-Empire et à l'époque franque* (Paris, 1928), and F. L. Ganshof, "A propos du tonlieu sous les mérovingiens," *Studi in honore di Amintore Fanfani* (Milan 1962), I: 291–315.

[26] *LH* iv, 28, p. 161; v, 18, p. 240 (Fredegund has 200 pounds of silver to offer as a bribe); v, 34, p. 220; etc. For a caution about Gregory's bias, see below, p. 226. Fredegund is vividly evoked in the novel of M. Brion, *Frédégonde et Brunehaut* (Paris, 1935).

[27] Ganshof, "Statut," pp. 15 seq, cites evidence not only from the laws but from legal acts (wills; land-grants) showing the rights of wives and widows in conjugal property. Roman law here influenced barbarian laws. Of course divorce was allowed in barbarian as in Roman codes. But McNamara and Wemple, "Divorce," pp. 98 *seq.*, seem to overstress both the disadvantaged position of wives as compared with that of husbands, and the importance of the divergence between barbarian and ecclesiastical law on this point. Divorce and inheritance need to be treated together, as do law and practice, in both areas. I am not convinced by those who argue that the cases of Clothar I (*LH* iv, 3) or Dagobert (*Fred.* cap. 60, p. 50) show the practice of royal polygamy, though these two kings offer the most conspicuous examples of serial monogamy.

[28] For the Lombards, see *Fred.* caps 51, 70, pp. 42, 59; and the comments of [K. A.] Eckhardt, *Studia [Merovingica]*, *Bibliotheca Rerum Historicarum* 11 (Aalen, 1975), p. 141. For the Anglo-Saxons, the evidence is conveniently assembled by W. A. Chaney, *The Cult of Kingship in Anglo-Saxon England* (Manchester, 1970), pp. 25–8, though the inferences there drawn concerning matrilineal royal succession are quite unwarranted. For the Merovingians, see *LH* iii, 6; iv, 9; and perhaps *Fred.* cap. 44, p. 37; also below, pp. 226–7. The men concerned in all these cases where information is available already had a claim to the kingship, which suggests that marriage with the late king's widow strengthened, but did not constitute, such a claim. See also [R.] Schneider, *Königswahl* [*und Königserhebung im Frühmittelalter*] (Stuttgart, 1972), pp. 246–8, where, however, the notion of *Einheirat* ("endogamy") seems of doubtful relevance.

seems to have arisen from her association with a reigning king; and in the interregnum created by his death, given an indeterminate succession system (whether dynastic or elective), the queen would function as an inhibitor of conflict if her second husband could make his claim stick.

In Gaul, however, unlike Lombard Italy or Visgothic Spain, filial succession remained normal. Thus the only way a queen could secure her position, both in her husband's lifetime and especially after his death, was to produce a son who survived.[29] Because of the frequent succession of minors, regents might govern for relatively long periods (even though the age of majority was fifteen)[30] and a queen-mother clearly had a strong claim to the regency. Hers was not the only claim: the role of *nutritor*, literally "male nurse," which in fact contained that of a regent, thereby illustrating once again the political significance of personal closeness to the king even when he was a child,[31] was appropriated by mayors of the palace on several occasions in the sixth and seventh centuries.[32] But a dowager queen could normally hope to act as regent for her own son. If a dowager queen were childless or had only daughters, then her husband's death would obviously mean her exclusion from power. But even if she had a young son, she might have difficulty in maintaining that physical proximity to him on which a regent's power depended. An infant prince might be reared on a country estate;[33] he would probably be in the care of a nurse. The moment of his father's death might find his mother far away. In any event, what determined a boy-prince's success in claiming the royal succession also directed his mother's future: namely, the attitude of the aristocracy, or, immediately, of a few well-placed aristocrats. A widowed queen was thrown back on the personal ties she had formed during her husband's lifetime, and on her own political skill: for on these depended how much treasure and influence (the two were not unconnected) she might be able to salvage. Throughout Merovingian history, the fates of widowed queens in interregna highlighted the persisting power of bishops and *leudes* [aristocrats around the king].[34]

So far I have laid stress on the precariousness and contingency of queens' positions rather than any inherent advantages accruing from their associations with monarchy, and on the relatively small extent to which the queen's powers were integrated into ongoing political or social structures: beyond personalities, episcopacy, aristocracy, kingship can be said to have existed as institutions, but it is much harder to identify anything that could be called "queenship." I want now to consider in more detail two queenly careers, not simply to illustrate but to amplify, and perhaps qualify, the above generalizations, and by exploring more fully the mechanisms of queenly activity to get at what seem to me some of the main forces and fundamental continuities in Merovingian politics. I begin with some basic biographical information on each.

---

[29] For the position of a widowed queen with only daughters, see *LH* iv, 20 (Ultrogotha). For the risks of sonlessness during the husband's lifetime see *LH* iv, 26 (Ingoberg) and possibly iii, 7 (Radegund). See also below, p. 231, and for another probable seventh-century example (Gomatrude), see *Fred.* cap. 58, p. 49. There were the additional risks of very high infant mortality (Fredegund lost four sons in infancy) and of sons growing up to quarrel with their father and being killed on his orders (Audovera lost two of her three sons this way, and the third also predeceased his father).

[30] Ewig, "Studien," pp. 22–4.

[31] For the potential importance of the nurse's position, see *LH* ix, 38, pp. 458–9, where a royal nurse and her male assistant conspire with powerful aristocrats.

[32] Venantius Fortunatus, *Carmina* vii, 16, *MGH AA* 4, pp. 170–1 (Condan, preceptor of Theudebald and *de facto* mayor of the Austrasian palace); *LH* v, 46, p. 256 (Gogo – see below, p. 227); *Fred.* caps 86, 88, pp. 72, 75 (Otto; Grimoald). On Otto see [H.] Ebling, *Prosopographie [der Amtsträger des Merovingerreiches (613–741)]* (Munich, 1974), pp. 66–7.

[33] *LH* vi, 41, p. 314.

[34] *LH* v, 1, p, 194; vii, 7, p. 330. See Wood, "Kings," pp. 6–7, 10–11; also below, pp. 227, 232.

First: Brunhild.[35] A Visigothic princess who maintained links with Spain till her last years, Brunhild's kinship link with the ruling dynasty there was severed when Liuva II was murdered in 603. Sisebut (612–21) whose *Vita* [*Life*] of Desiderius of Vienne[36] is the earliest surviving source for Brunhild's regency and is also violently hostile, was therefore no relative of hers. Nor was Witteric (murderer of Liuva II), whose daughter Ermenberga was sought as a bride for Brunhild's grandson Theuderic in 607.[37] These facts, I shall argue, are relevant to the unfolding of Brunhild's Spanish connection.

Born *c.*545–50, Brunhild was sought in marriage by Sigibert (apparently continuing an Austrasian tradition of foreign dynastic marriages)[38] in 566. Her Arianism was no obstacle, and she swiftly abandoned it. Gregory of Tours, our chief source for Brunhild's life up to 591, has no unfavourable comment to make on her: he introduces her on her arrival at Sigibert's court as good-looking and shrewd with a large dowry of treasures.[39] But Gregory's view of Brunhild must be set in a literary as well as an historical context: Chilperic figures in Gregory's drama as "the Nero and Herod of our time,"[40] Fredegund is his female counterpart in villainy, and Brunhild, for whose sister Galswinth's death the evil pair are responsible,[41] is therefore an avenger on the side of the angels. Twenty years after Galswinth's murder, the mutual hatred between Brunhild and Fredegund was as strong as ever.[42] Clearly the pursuit of this vendetta is one main theme in Brunhild's whole life.[43]

But another, equally significant, is Brunhild's identification with the family into which she had married. Of the various aspects of her collaboration with her husband and, later, her son praised in the courtly verse of Venantius Fortunatus, none is more revealing than her patronage of the cult of St Martin, the Merovingians' *Reichsheiliger* [royal saint].[44] It was said after Sigibert's death that she had "held the realm under her husband."[45] She had joined him on his last campaign against Chilperic, bringing treasure to him at Paris. She was there, with treasure and children, when the news of his assassination arrived.[46] But though deprived of this treasure and of the custody of her children and exiled to Rouen, she retained an

[35] The best scholarly study remains [G.] Kurth, "[La reine] Brunehaut," in *Etudes Franques*, 2 vols (Paris and Brussels, 1919), 1, pp. 265–356, with full references to the nineteenth-century literature (Kurth's paper first appeared in 1891). See also E. Ewig, "[Die fränkischen] Teilungen [und Teilreiche (511–613)]," *AAWL*, Geistes- und Sozialwissenschaftlichen Klasse 9 (Wiesbaden, 1952), pp. 689 *seq.* For the chronology of Brunhild's life, I have relied on Ewig, "Studien."
[36] *MGH SSrM* 3, pp. 620–7. See below, p. 239.
[37] *Fred.* cap. 30, p. 20.
[38] Ewig, "Studien," p. 40.
[39] *LH* iv, 27, p. 160: "puella elegans opere, venusta aspectu, honesta moribus atque decora, prudens consilio et blanda colloquio . . . cum magnis thesauris" ["a girl refined in behavior, lovely in appearance, honorable and seemly in her way of life, prudent in counsel, and charming in speech . . . with a great treasury"]. For Gregory's own personal relations with Brunhild, see below, n. 59, and p. 236. He is hardly, therefore, a dispassionate witness.
[40] *LH* vi, 46, p. 319.
[41] *LH* iv, 28, p. 161.
[42] *LH* ix, 20, p. 439: "odium, quod inter illas olim statutum est, adhuc pullulat, non arescit" ["hatred which grew up between them long ago sprouts new shoots and does not wither"].
[43] This is rightly stressed by [J. M.] Wallace-Hadrill, [*The*] *Long-haired Kings* (London, 1962), pp. 134–5, 205.
[44] Venantius Fortunatus, *Carmina* x, 7, pp. 239–41. See Prinz, *Mönchtum*, pp. 32–3.
[45] *LH* vi, 4, p. 268.
[46] *LH* v, 1, p. 194.

impressive quantity of personal treasure[47] as well as the special association with kingship adhering even to the widow of a Merovingian king. Very soon, Merovech, son of Chilperic and stepson of Fredegund, came to Rouen and married her.[48] *Aima-t-elle réellement Merovée?* [Did she really love Merovech?][49] Kurth's delightful question must remain unanswered. But it is not fanciful to guess that Merovech's motive was the staking of a claim to Sigibert's kingdom.[50] As it turned out, Sigibert's young son Childebert proved more acceptable to a majority of the Austrasian magnates. Brunhild herself commanded enough personal loyalty from some of those magnates for them to request and get her liberation from Chilperic.[51] And Merovech's rejection by "the Austrasians" when he attempted to rejoin Brunhild (577) may not, as Kurth surmised, have meant her humiliation but the carrying out of her wishes. For as long as her son was king, she could hope to retrieve her position. Kurth portrays the period 576–84, that is, until Childebert attained his majority, as "eight years of humiliation" for Brunhild at the hands of the Austrasian aristocracy.[52] But there is no evidence that Childebert's *nutricius* [tutor] Gogo was hostile to her: he may, indeed, have been her appointee both in this capacity and in the royal chancery.[53] Brunhild could conduct her own relations with Spain, using the bishop of Châlons as an envoy.[54] Even the driving into exile of her "faithful supporter" Duke Lupus of Champagne was the work of a faction, not an "anti-royal" aristocracy as a whole. Brunhild had been strong enough to prevent faction-fighting from erupting into open warfare in a threatened attack on Lupus when, in Gregory's fine phrase, "girding herself manfully, she burst into the midst of the opposing ranks," and her *industria* [perseverance] prevailed. Against these facts, Ursio's taunt that Childebert's realm "is being kept safe by our protection, not yours" should not be understood as implying Brunhild's eclipse.[55]

When Childebert reached his majority in 585[56] however, Brunhild's position became a commanding one. Dispensing with a "tutor," she now took over her son's guidance herself,[57]

---

[47] *LH* v, 18, p. 221: Brunhild had left five bundles with the bishop of Rouen for safe-keeping, of which two were alleged to be stuffed with "species et diversis ornamentis . . . quae praeciebantur amplius quam tria milia solidorum; sed et saccolum cum nummismati auri pondere, tenentem duo milia" ["precious things and all sorts of jewels . . . valued at more than 3,000 coins and also a sack which, by weight, must have held 2,000 gold coins"].

[48] *LH* v, 2, p. 195.

[49] Kurth, "Brunehaut," p. 280.

[50] Ewig, "Studien," p. 33.

[51] *LHF* cap. 33, p. 299. See Kurth, "Brunehaut," pp. 281–2.

[52] Kurth, "Brunehaut," p. 28.

[53] For the letter written for Childebert to the Lombard king Grasulf by Gogo, see *MGH Epp.* 3, no. 48, p. 152. Riché, *Education*, p. 222, suggests that Brunhild "brought Gogo into the royal chancellery." For Gogo as *nutricius*, see *LH* v, 46, p. 256. According to the *Chronicle of Fredegar*, iii, cap. 59, *MGH SSrM* 2, p. 109, Gogo was one of the envoys sent to Spain to fetch Brunhild.

[54] *LH* v, 40, p. 247. The date is 580.

[55] *LH* vi, 4, p. 268: "'Recede a nobis, o mulier. Sufficiat tibi sub viro tenuisse regnum; nunc autem filius tuus regnat, regnumque eius non tua, sed nostra tuitione salvatur. . . .' Haec et alia cum diutissime inter se protulissent, obtenuit reginae industria, ne pugnarent" ["'Begone woman! Be content that you held the kingdom under your husband. Now your son reigns, and his kingdom is preserved by our protection, not yours.'. . . They said these and other things to each other for a very long time until, by her perseverance, the Queen made sure that they would not fight"].

[56] Ewig, "Studien," p. 22.

[57] *LH* viii, 22, p. 389: "regina mater curam vellit propriam habere de filio" ["the queen mother wanted to rear her son herself"]. As Ewig points out this did not, of course, involve a formal legal position, but rather a personal relationship.

and Pope Gregory the Great would soon afterwards treat "both the government of the realm and the education of your son" as evidence of Brunhild's qualities.[58] A family compact between the Austrasian and Burgundian branches of the dynasty was achieved at Andelot (586) where her continuing hostility to Fredegund is transparent.[59] Fredegar makes her responsible for Chilperic's assassination and names the man she hired for the job.[60] Against this, the argument from Gregory's silence, given his bias, may not be as telling as Kurth supposed – which is only to say that Brunhild carried out her family duties according to her Germanic lights. Family duty marched with political interest within Austrasia: those Austrasian magnates who had opposed Brunhild not surprisingly found support in Neustria.[61] But now able to back her aristocratic supporters with the full weight of royal resources, the queen mother crushed her opponents within Austrasia, demonstrating then and later her capacity to exercise the eminently royal virtues of rewarding loyalty, avenging wrongs done to those under her protection, and revenging herself on personal enemies.[62] Her famous "foreign relations" with Spain and with Constantinople were in fact extensions of family relations, on the one hand forging further links with the royal dynasty in Spain and, after her daughter Ingund's marriage to Hermenegild and his unsuccessful revolt against his father Leuvigild,[63] trying to recover her little grandson Athanagild from the Byzantine imperial protectors to whom he had fled;[64] on the other hand identifying with a new Frankish assertiveness expressed as clearly in Baudonivia's *Vita* of Radegund[65] as in the diplomatic exchanges of earlier Austrasian kings,[66] and now epitomized in Brunhild's appeal to the empress Anastasia (wife of Maurice) to join with her in bringing the benefits of peace "between the two peoples"!;[66a] Beneath the Roman verbiage of *pax* and *caritas* is a thoroughly gentile consciousness of Frankish-Roman parity.

[58] Gregory the Great, Ep. vi, 5, in *MGH Epp.* 1, p. 383: "Excellentiae vestrae praedicandam ac Deo placitam bonitatem et gubernacula regni testantur et educatio filii manifestat." The date is 595.
[59] *LH* ix, 20, pp. 434–9, for the text. For the date, see [W. A.] Eckhardt, "[Die] *Decretio Childeberti* [und ihre Uberlieferung]," *ZRG GAbt* 84 (1967): 1–71 at 66 *seq.* In the subsequent diplomatic exchanges between Guntramn and Childebert and Brunhild, Gregory of Tours himself served as the latter's envoy. This closeness to the Austrasian court is noteworthy.
[60] *Fred.* iii, 93 in *MGH SSrM* 2, p. 118: "ab homine nomen Falcone" ["a man named Falco"].
[61] *LH* ix, 9, p. 421.
[62] *LH* ix, 9–12, pp. 421–7. Brunhild's relations with Lupus, Ursio, and Berthefried, illustrating the varieties of just deserts, should be compared with the earlier episode recounted in *LH* vi, 4, pp. 267–8. Brunhild's concern for someone under her protection is shown in the story of Sichar, *LH* ix, 19, pp. 433–4.
[63] See J. N. Hillgarth, "Coins and chronicles: propaganda in sixth-century Spain and the Byzantine background," *Historia* 15 (Wiesbaden, 1966): 483–508; and E. A. Thompson, *The Goths in Spain* (Oxford, 1969), pp. 64–73.
[64] The evidence is contained in the *Epistolae Austrasicae*, nos 25–48, *MGH Epp.* 3, pp. 138–53.
[65] *MGH SSrM* 2, pp. 358–95, II cap. 16 at p. 388: in acquiring a piece of the true Cross, Radegund tells King Sigibert she will act "pro totius patriae salute et eius regni stabilitate" ["for the welfare of the entire fatherland and the stability of his kingdom"]. "Sicut beata Helena . . . quod fecit illa in orientali patria, hoc fecit beata Radegundis in Gallia" ["What St Helena did in the Eastern fatherland, St Radegund did in Gaul"], comments Baudonivia. Radegund commends her foundation, ibid., p. 389, "praecellentissimis dominis regibus et serenissimae dominae Bronichildi" ["to the most excellent lord kings and to the most serene lady, Queen Brunhild"].
[66] *MGH Epp.* 3, nos 18, 19, 20, pp. 131–3, esp. no. 20, p. 133, where Theudebert I lists "quae gentes nostrae sint, Deo adiutore, dicione subiectae" ["the peoples who, with God's help, are ours, subject to our jurisdiction"], and asks Justinian "ut . . . in communi utilitate iungamur" ["that we join in common purpose"].
[66a] *MGH Epp.* 3, no. 29, p. 140: "dum inter utramque gentem pacis causa conectitur, coniuncta gratia principum subiectarum generer beneficia regionum" ["since the grounds of peace between the two

Childebert, who had inherited Burgundy on Guntramn's death in 593, himself died aged only twenty-six in 596, leaving Austrasia to the ten-year-old Theudebert, Burgundy to nine-year-old Theuderic.[67] Brunhild, as de facto regent for both young kings, now entered the last and most active phase of her career. She and her son had had their Austrasian supporters. Now she needed, and found, support from members of a more southerly aristocracy, of mixed "Roman" and barbarian origins, long used to collaboration with kings. Asclepiodotus, former head of Guntramn's chancery, had carried his expertise to Childebert, whose great *Decretum* of 596 he probably drafted, and he remained influential during Brunhild's regency.[68] I shall examine presently other bases of the old queen's continuing power, but here briefly consider her position in the royal family. She had vetoed Childebert's marriage to the Agilolfing Theodelinda (the pair had been betrothed before 589), presumably to counter the hostile influence of that princess's Austrasian and Lombard connections.[69] But she seems to have approved Childebert's eventual marriage with his ex-mistress Faileuba, who may possibly have been a woman of low birth.[70] If this was so, and Childebert was following Guntramn in raising a low-born concubine to queenship, we might speculate that Brunhild assented the more readily because Faileuba, lacking powerful aristocratic connections of her own, posed less of a threat to Brunhild's ascendance than a noblewoman might have done. Over the marriage of her elder grandson Theudebert II, a concubine's son,[71] Brunhild had no control. His coming-of-age in 600 saw, hardly coincidentally, her expulsion from Austrasia,[72] presumably because magnates hostile to her found the young king ready to assert himself. Soon after, he married Bilichild, a former slave of Brunhild herself with no kind feelings for her former mistress.[73] Once queen, Bilichild's position could not be affected by Brunhild's taunts about her base origin – so long as the Austrasian magnates approved of her. Had withdrawal of that approval, and perhaps also her lack of a son, anything to do with her murder in 611?[74] The case of Bilichild could show that a queen who was an ex-slave was just a bit more vulnerable to changing currents of aristocratic support than was a princess like Brunhild: certainly her fate was unusually harsh. Theuderic II (Faileuba's son)[75] provides a marked contrast to his half-brother. Having given a welcome to his grandmother when she sought his court in 600,[76] Theuderic remained close to her for

---

peoples are connected, let them engender, by the mutual good-will of their princes, the well-being of subject regions"], and no. 44, p. 150, another appeal to the empress to return Brunhild's little grandson Athanagild "et inter utramque gentem per hoc, propitiante Christo, caritas multiplicetur et pacis terminus extendatur" ["and through this, by Christ's favor, let love be multiplied and peace prolonged between the two peoples"]. These letters date from 584 and 585.

[67] *Fred.* cap. 16, p. 11, Paulus Diaconus, *Historia Langobardorum* iv cap. 11, *MGH SSrL* p. 120: "Brunichildis tunc regina cum nepotibus adhoc puerulis . . . regebat Gallias" ["At that time Queen Brunhild was ruling over Gaul with her grandsons, who were still children"].

[68] Eckhardt, "*Decretio Childeberti*," pp. 70–1.

[69] *Fred.* cap. 34, p. 22. I accept the interpretation of Ewig, "Studien," p. 40, n. 145.

[70] Ewig, "Studien," p. 42.

[71] L[iber] H[istoriae] F[rancorum], cap. 37, *MGH SSrM* 2, p. 306.

[72] *Fred.* cap. 19, p. 12. The attempt of Kurth, "Brunehaut," p. 310, to gloss over this is unconvincing.

[73] *Fred.* cap. 35, pp. 22–3. On the probable date of this marriage (601–2), see Ewig, "Studien," p. 26.

[74] *Fred.* cap. 37, p. 30: "Belechildis a Teudeberto interfecitur" ["Bilichild was killed by Theudebert"].

[75] *LHF* cap. 37, p. 306. Both Theudebert and Theuderic were sons of Childebert according to *LH* viii, 37 and ix, 4. But there seems no reason to doubt that Brunhild goaded Theuderic to attack Theudebert by alleging that the latter was a gardener's son and thus no kin at all to Theuderic: *Fred.* cap. 27, p. 18. If Theuderic believed this, his subsequent treatment of Theudebert and his sons is even less surprising: *Fred.* cap. 38, p. 32, and *LHF* cap. 38, pp. 307–9.

[76] *Fred.* cap. 19, p. 13.

the rest of his life. That he never married was due to Brunhild's influence (I see no reason to reject the evidence of the *Vita Columbani* on this point):[77] the raising of a concubine to queenly status would have created a new power in the *aula regis* [king's court] and so weakened Brunhild's position in general and her freedom to choose Theuderic's heir(s) in particular. This freedom played a crucial part in the network of personal loyalties which upheld the old queen, for loyalty required long-term prospects dependent, in turn, on predictions of who would control the royal succession. I shall return to this point below. Only one other action of Brunhild needs mentioning here: her renunciation in 613 of the allegedly "traditional" practice of dividing a Merovingian's realm between his sons. Theuderic in 612 had defeated Theudebert and gained control of Austrasia. His sudden death just as he was marching against Clothar II of Neustria (Fredegund's son) created an interregnum of the usual dangerous kind. How did Brunhild respond? "Her endeavour was to make Sigibert [Theuderic's eldest son, then aged eleven] his father's successor,"[78] in other words, to maintain, at least for the time being, the union of Austrasia and Burgundy. By this date there was no question, I think, of dividing Theuderic's inheritance among his *four* sons. But why was the twofold division of 596 (already foreshadowed in 589) not followed in 613? Should not Brunhild have bought off the Austrasian "separatists" and so forestalled their alliance with Clothar? The answer, in my view, lies not in the old queen's alleged "centralizing" ambitions nor in her adherence to *Romanentum* against *Germanentum*,[79] but in a short-term bid to rally her old and new supporters among the Burgundian and Austrasian aristocracy in a final thrust against Clothar II. There is nothing to suggest that, had she won, she would have resisted the inevitable pressures – since young princes were available – to redivide the *regnum* [kingdom] by allocating kings to the Neustrians and Austrasians. Her supporters among them would surely have expected such a pay-off. Brunhild's mistake in 613 was, as Ian Wood has recently pointed out,[80] to overestimate the support she commanded among the aristocracy, especially and fatally the very Burgundian office-holders she had believed loyal. The politics were as ever those not of *raison d'état*[81] but of family interests, of self-preservation, of maneuvering among shifting aristocratic loyalties. Brunhild's game was the old one, only now she made her first bad miscalculation and lost all.

Before looking more closely at some key aspects of Brunhild's success, I turn now to

---

[77] V[ita] C[olumbani] I, cap. 18, *MGH SSrM* 4, p. 86. This chapter and much of the next two are borrowed almost verbatim by *Fred.* cap. 36, pp. 23–9.

[78] *Fred.* cap. 40, p. 32: "Brunechildis . . . Sigybertum in regnum patris instituere nitens."

[79] So, Ewig, "Teilungen," pp. 705–8, 715. For a similar view, see H. Löwe, "Austrien im Zeitalter Brunichilds. Kampf zwischen Königtum und Adel," in H. Grundmann, *Handbuch der deutschen Geschichte* (9th ed., rev. B. Gebhardt, Stuttgart, 1970), pp. 124–7. This view seems standard in German historiography. The alleged evidence (the *chaussées Brunehaut* [Brunhild's roads]) for Brunhild as a "Roman" road-builder or maintainer was demolished by Kurth, *Histoire poétique des Mérovingiens* (Paris, 1893), pp. 424 *seq.*

[80] Wood, "Kings," p. 13.

[81] So, Kurth, "Brunehaut," pp. 306, 350–1: "elle prétendit soumettre à l'autorité d'une femme des gens qui ne reconnaissaient pas même celle d'un homme" ["she aspired to subject to a woman a people who did not even recognize the authority of a man"]. Kurth's contrast between the would-be despot Brunhild, an inevitable failure, and the *monarchie temperée* [moderate monarchy] of the Carolingians seems to have had a strong influence on francophone historiography: see H. Pirenne, *Mohammed and Charlemagne*, trans. B. Miall (London, 1939), pp. 265 *seq.* and F. Lot, in F. Lot, C. Pfister, and F. L. Ganshof, *Les Destinées de l'Empire en Occident de 395 a 888* (2nd ed., Paris, 1940–1), pp. 265–6, 297–8, 314–15.

Balthild,[82] and a sketch of her career which, much shorter than Brunhild's, is also less variously documented, the main source being the *Vita Balthildis* written soon after her death (in 680 or soon after).[83] Born in England probably in the early 630s, Balthild was brought as a slave-girl to Gaul and bought (in 641 or after) by Erchinoald, mayor of the palace of Neustria.[84] Her hagiographer's stress on her low birth (she was one of those "poor" whom God "raises from the dust and causes to sit with the princes of his people," and a "precious pearl sold at a low price")[85] must be taken seriously, in view of the usual contemporary hagiographical delight in noble ancestry.[86] She was good-looking (had doubtless caught Erchinoald's eye) and she was also canny – *prudens et cauta*.[87] Erchinoald himself is said to have wished to marry her after his wife's death, but this seems implausible, given all the other evidence of aristocratic marriage patterns.[88] The hagiographer introduced this detail, I suggest, in order to deploy the chastity motif obligatory in the *Vitae* of female saints[89] and otherwise unusable in the special case of Balthild. Divine providence caused the girl to spurn the king's minister so as to be saved for the king himself – Clovis II, son of Dagobert. Clovis probably married Balthild as soon as he came of age in 648.[90] "Astute" as ever, Balthild had no illusions about her position. Pregnant in 649, she confided her anxieties to Eligius, most influential of Dagobert's courtiers and a holy man still evidently at the heart of royal affairs: what would happen to the realm (did she mean, to herself?) if she carried only a girl-child? Eligius reassured her that she would give birth to a son, and put his money where his mouth was: "he had a piece of metalwork made which was suitable for a boy-baby and ordered it to be kept for his use until he was born."[91] Balthild duly had her son – the future Clothar III,

---

[82] The only usable biography remains [M. J.] Couturier, *Sainte Balthilde*, [*reine des Francs*] (Paris, 1909), which, despite its devout and rather rambling style, should not be dismissed as by [L.] Dupraz, [*Le*] *Royaume* [*des Francs et l'ascension politique des maires du palais au déclin du VIIe siècle (656–680)*] (Fribourg en Suisse, 1948), p. 223, n. 3. For useful preliminary remarks on Balthild, see [W.] Levison, *England* [*and the Continent in the Eighth Century*] (Oxford, 1946), pp. 9–10 with a full bibliography of the source materials at p. 9, n. 4.

[83] *MGH SSrM* 2, pp. 475–508, version "A," with the ninth-century reworking, "B," in parallel columns. For the dates of both versions, see Krusch's introduction, ibid., pp. 478–9. The "A" *Vita* was evidently written by a nun at Chelles, and commissioned by some monks – perhaps those of Corbie?

[84] *MGH SSrM* 2, cap. 2, p. 483.

[85] Ibid. These are standard topoi in references to low-born holy people: the references are to I Kings 2: 8 and Ps. 112: 7, as is observed by [F.] Graus, [*Volk, Herrscher und*] *Heiliger* [*im Reich der Merowinger. Studien zur Hagiographie der Merowingerzeit*] (Prague, 1965), pp. 411–12. For another example, Gerbert writing of himself, see *Lettres de Gerbert, 983–887*, ed. J. Havet (Paris, 1889), no. 217, p. 229.

[86] See Prinz, "Heiligenkult [und Adelsherrschaft im Spiegel merowingischer Hagiographie]," *HZ* 204 (1967): 529–44. Low birth was perceived as hard to reconcile with holiness. Version "B" of the *Vita* makes Balthild into a noble lady: *claro sanguine* [noble blood]; and she was later depicted as belonging to an Anglo-Saxon royal family! See Couturier, *Sainte Balthilde*, p. 2, n. 2.

[87] *MGH SSrM* 2, cap. 2, p. 483; cap. 3, p. 485: "prudens et astuta virgo" ["a sensible and astute virgin"].

[88] Ibid., cap. 3, p. 484. Ian Wood suggests to me, however, that Erchinoald, a kinsman of Dagobert on his mother's side, may have been deliberately imitating royal practice.

[89] Graus, *Heiliger*, pp. 410 *seq*. The authoress of this *Vita* clearly had before her Venantius's *Vita Radegundis*.

[90] *LHF* cap. 43, p. 315. On the date, see Ewig, "Studien," p. 26.

[91] *Vita Eligii*, ii, 32, *MGH SSrM* 4, p. 717. Riché, *Education*, p. 231 with n. 354, seems slightly to misinterpret this passage: I cannot see that Eligius's present for the baby can possibly have been "a teething-ring" which would have been equally suitable for a boy or a girl.

followed by Theuderic (III) and Childeric (II).[92] Already during her husband's lifetime, her great influence was evident: she seems to have organized the care of the king's entourage of young aristocrats at the court – that cradle of royal servants; and she controlled, with the help of her almoner Genesius, quantities of treasure for disbursement to the poor and other pious causes.[93] The hagiographer paints the picture of a *palatium* in which all revolves around the queen. Other sources stress the role of Erchinoald in maintaining peace throughout Clovis II's reign.[94] Balthild and her former master probably coexisted by each concentrating on different areas of activity, and the Neustrian aristocracy, whether dazzled still by Dagobert's glories or gratified by the restitution of his unjust exactions after his death during the conciliatory regency of Nantechild (died 641/2),[95] were satisfied. But the best argument for silence for Bathchild's strong position during Clovis II's lifetime might be that despite his womanizing, he did not endanger her position (as Dagobert had done Nantechild's) by raising another woman to the status of queen.[96] Both the moral and the political backing of Balthild's ecclesiastical connections must have helped her here.

Balthild's situation changed with the deaths of Clovis and, soon after, Erchinoald (657, 758/9).[96a] She now became regent for her son Clothar III, who significantly, succeeded to an undivided realm, excluding at least for the moment his two little brothers. The *Vita Balthildis* and the *Liber Historiae Francorum*[97] both stress the decisive roles of the Neustrian aristocracy. No doubt the many personal bonds forged during Balthild's years as "nurse to the young men" in the *palatium* [palace] now stood her in good stead. The Neustrians' choice of Ebroin, a former *miles palatinus* [palace warrior], to succeed Erchinoald as mayor must have had Balthild's consent.[98] It has been alleged that Balthild and Ebroin between them pursued a

---

[92] For the birth-order of the three boys, I follow that implied by the near-contemporary *Passio Leudegarii* I, cap. 5, *MGH SSrM* 5, p. 287, in preference to that given by *LHF* cap. 44, p. 317. See [L.] Levillain, "[encore sur la] Succession [d'Austrasie au VIIe siècle]," *BEC* 106 (1945–6): 296–306 at p. 305, n. 1. The *filiola* ["little daughter"] who lived with Balthild at Chelles and died just before she did must, as the "B" Vita and Krusch agree, have been a god-daughter. (After all, Clovis II had died in 657!) Although Clovis II is said to have had other women (*LHF* cap. 44, p. 316) he is not known to have had any children except by Balthild.

[93] *MGH SSrM* 2, [cap. 4] pp. 485–7. "Auri vel argenti largissima munera" ["very generous gifts of gold and silver"] are disbursed. On the role of Genesius, see Ewig, "[Das Privileg des Bischofs Berthefrid von Amiens für Corbie von 664 und die] Klosterpolitik [der Königin Balthild]," *Francia* 1 (1973): 63–114 at pp. 107–8 with n. 86: "eine Art Grand Aumônier" ["a sort of Grand Almoner"].

[94] *Fred.* cap. 84, p. 71. Compare the aggressive and tightfisted Erchinoald depicted in the *Vita Eligii*, i, caps 20, 27, *MGH SSrM* 4, pp. 711, 714.

[95] Ibid., cap. 80, p. 68.

[96] Ibid., cap. 84, p. 71.

[96a] Clovis II died between 11 September and 16 November 657: see Levison, "Das Nekrologium von dom Racine," *NA* 35 (1910): 45. For the date of Erchinoald's death, see Dupraz, *Royaume*, p. 245 with n. 1.

[97] *Vita* cap. 5, *MGH SSrM* 2, p. 487; *LHF* cap. 44, p. 317.

[98] *LHF* cap. 45, p. 317; *Fred.* (Continuator) cap. 2, p. 80, *Vita Balthildis*, cap. 5, p. 487. See [J.] Fischer, [*Der Hausmeier*] *Ebroin* (Bonn, 1954), pp. 82 *seq.*, whose case for Ebroin's low birth seems, however, unproven and his explanation of Ebroin's rise therefore unconvincing. (His picture of the regent and "her" mayor as two *Willensmenschen* [people of strong wills] risen from nothing through their own energies yet fated to clash because of the very strength of their wills, has a splendidly Wagnerian quality, at once romantic, epic, and sexist: "Früher oder später musste es zwischen ihnen zur entscheidenden Auseinandersetzung kommen, und der weniger Starke musste dem Stärkeren weichen" ["sooner or later, a decisive clash was bound to take place; the lesser strength had to submit to the stronger"].)

systematic policy of reunifying the Merovingian *regnum*, first by imposing the Neustrian prince Childeric II on the Austrasians, then by abolishing the Burgundian mayoralty of the palace thus uniting Neustria and Burgundy.[99] On an alternative hypothesis, the unification-policy was "only neustro-burgundian, not pan-frankish."[100] Neither view offers an entirely convincing interpretation of the *Vita*'s account of Balthild's actions. The complications surrounding the export of Childeric II boil down to Merovingian family politics with two dowager queens playing typical roles. It is possible that the coup of Grimoald and his son Childebert III was even part of the same family politics, in a broad sense, if indeed they too had Merovingian blood in them.[101] The most plausible reconstruction of the events of 662, in my view, is that Childebert's childless death left Grimoald in a dangerously exposed position rather like that of a dowager queen. He had exiled Dagobert, son of Sigibert III, in 656[102] and to recall him would have been, at best, difficult and time-consuming for Grimoald. With Austrasian enemies to cope with, Grimoald had little time to afford. But he did have custody of Dagobert's sister Bilichild and perhaps also of her mother, Sigibert's widow Himnechild. To play this "trump-card," Grimoald needed to find a Merovingian husband for Bilichild. There was no alternative but to seek him in Neustria. Thus the initiative in 662 was an Austrasian one,[103] and the outcome was a Merovingian family compact: the seven-year-old

---

[99] Dupraz, *Royaume*, pp. 239 *seq.*, 351 *seq.*

[100] Fischer, *Ebroin*, p. 87. See also Ewig, "Teilreiche," pp. 121 se*q.*

[101] On the evidence for Grimoald's coup. Levillain, "Succession," remains fundamental, and for a cogent restatement of his views in the light of subsequent research, see Ewig, "Noch einmal zum 'Staatsstreich' Grimoalds," *Speculum Historiale, Festschrift J. Spörl* (Munich, 1965), pp. 454–7. But in what follows I have accepted some revisions suggested by H. Thomas, "Die Namenliste des Diptychon Barberini und der Sturz des Hausmeiers Grimoald," *DA* 25 (1969): 17–63, and further modified by Eckhardt, St*u*dia, pp. 152 *seq.*, who also argues that Grimoald was descended in the maternal line from the Austrasian king Theudebald. But even if Levillain and Ewig are right, and Grimoald was killed in 657 rather than 662 (see following note) my view of Balthild's actions in the latter year would be unaffected.

[102] *LHF* cap. 43, p. 316: "Decedente vero tempore, defuncto Sighiberto rege, Grimoaldus filium eius parvolum nomine Dagobertum totundit Didonemque Pectavensem urbis episcopum in Scocia peregrinadnum eum direxit, filium suum in regno constituens. Franci itaque hoc valde indignantes Grimoaldo insidias preparant, eumque exementes ad condempnandum rege Francorum Chlodoveo deferunt. In Parisius civitate in carcere mancipatus, vinculorum cruciatu constrictus, ut erat morte dignus, quod in domino suo exercuit, ipsius mors valido cruciatu finivit". ["After some time, King Sigibert died, and Grimoald tonsured Sigibert's young son, who was named Dagobert, and sent him to Dido, bishop of Poitiers, to make a pilgrimage to Ireland; and he put his own son on the throne of the kingdom. The Franks, however, were very indignant at this and planned to ambush Grimoald. They took him away and brought him to Clovis, King of the Franks, to be condemned. Grimoald was taken to prison at Paris and bound with painful chains like a man worthy of death, because he acted against his own lord. Horrible torture ended his life"]. Levillain argues that the *LHF* account must be accepted entirely: thus, Grimoald's death must precede Clovis (II)'s, in autumn 657. Those who argue that Grimoald's death must be dated to 662, on the grounds that his son Childebert III could not otherwise have been sustained as king in Austrasia until that date, must emend the *LHF*'s "Chlod*oveo*" to "Chlod*ochario*" or "Chl*othario*," that is, Clothar III. This emendation is not merely "arbitrary" as Levillain alleges: for evidence of just this confusion of names in seventh- and eighth-century *diplomata*, see Dupraz, *Royaume*, pp. 382–4.

[103] *Vita Balthildis* cap. 5, p. 487: "Austrasii pacifico ordine, ordinante domna Balthilde, per consilium quidem seniorum receperunt Childericum, filium eius, in regem Austri" ["By arrangement of Lady Balthild and certainly with the advice of their magnates, the Austrasians peacefully received her son Childeric to rule Austrasia"]. Only by mistranslating "ordinante" could Dupraz, *Royaume*, p. 355, infer that Balthild "gave orders" and "imposed" her own solution. See further, Schneider, *Königswahl*, pp. 163–4.

Childeric II was sent (perhaps it was Balthild's decision to choose her third in preference to her second son) to be betrothed to his first cousin Bilichild – a unique case of Merovingian in-marriage – while her mother assumed the regency,[104] all with the backing of a powerful section of the Austrasian aristocracy.[105] At this point, Grimoald became expendable and thus the sole victim of these arrangements. In him Merovingian blood, if any, was much diluted. Perhaps the narrower family of Dagobert I's descendants closed ranks against more distant kin, the *indignatio* of the Neustrians against Grimoald was genuine, and his execution in Paris a kind of vengeance for the exile of Dagobert's grandson.[106] In all this, it is impossible to see Balthild as imposing her son – still less Neustrian control – on the Austrasians. She acts within limits defined by the Austrasians themselves, and her response restores harmony within both family and *regnum*. The *Vita's* depiction of her as a peace-bringer is not mere hagiographical convention.

As for her "neustro-burgundian policy", it is possible to interpret Clothar III's succession in both Neustria and Burgundy as evidence of aristocratic interests in *both* regions, rather than only of royal design. The gradual cessation of the practice of dividing the realm in the course of the seventh century was not the result of kings' (or queens') decisions alone.[107] The *Burgundofarones* [Burgundian notables] had something to gain from access to the *palatium* of a king who was theirs and the Neustrians' alike.[108] Nor can I see much evidence for a formal extinction of the Burgundian mayoralty by Balthild. It is arguable, anyway, that their laws and customs mattered more to the Burgundians than a mayoralty.[109] Scholarly discussion of the whole issue has turned on the interpretation of a phrase in the *Vita Balthildis*: "The Burgundians and the Franks were made as one."[110] What seems to have been unnoticed hitherto is that not merely this sentence but the whole final section of chapter 5 of the *Vita* echoes a remarkable passage in the Book of Ezekiel. The context (Ezekiel chapter 36) is a divine promise to the prophet that the *gentes* [peoples] shall be put to shame and Israel renewed and exalted. In the following chapter, God sets Ezekiel down in the valley of the bones and brings them to life. He then tells the prophet to take two sticks, one to signify Israel and the other Judah:

> And join them one to another into one stick; and they shall become one in thine hand. . . .
> And when the children of thy people shall speak unto thee saying, Wilt thou not shew us what thou meanest by these?
> Say unto them, Thus saith the Lord God. . . . Behold, I will take the children of Israel from among the heathen. . . .
> And I will make them one nation . . . and one king shall be king to them all: and

---

[104] Himnechild continued to subscribe Childeric II's *diplomata* until he came of age: see Ewig, "Studien," p. 23. For the assassination of Childeric and Bilichild in 675, see *LHF* cap. 45, p. 318.

[105] For the role of Wulfoald, see Ewig, "Teilreiche," p. 123.

[106] Above, n. 102.

[107] This is a basic assumption in Dupraz's book. See also Ewig, "Teilreiche," pp. 110 *seq.*

[108] *Fred.* cap. 44, p. 37; cap. 55, p. 46. For later Burgundian resistance to Ebroin because he denied them direct access to the *palatium*, see *Passio Leudegarii* I, cap. 4, *MGH SSrM* 5, p. 287.

[109] *Fred.* cap. 54, p. 46: the Burgundians decide to do without a mayor of the palace after the death of Warnacher (626), preferring *cum rege transagere* [to deal directly with the king]. *Passio Leudegarii* I, cap. 7. p. 289, shows the Burgundians' concern to preserve their *lex vel consuetudo* [law and custom]. The Burgundian mayoralty seems not to have been revived after the death of Flaochad, a Frankish appointee of Nantechild, in 642. See also Ewig, "Teilreiche," pp. 106–7, 120.

[110] *Vita*, cap. 5, pp. 487–8: "Burgundiones vero et Franci facti sunt uniti."

they shall be no more two nations, neither shall they be divided into two nations any more at all. . . .

Moreover I will make a covenant of peace with them; it shall be an everlasting covenant with them: and I will place them, and multiply them, and will set my sanctuary in the midst of them for evermore.[111]

The hagiographer's purpose throughout his fifth chapter is to show Balthild as the instrument of divinely-ordained concord between the once-warring kingdoms. The queen is presented, not as the author of specific new constitutional arrangements, but – in almost apocalyptic terms – as the inaugurator of a new era of peace. There is a significant contrast, as well as a similarity, here with the note caught by Ewig in the early eighth-century *Continuator* of Fredegar's identification of the Franks with Israel and of their war-leader Charles Martel with Joshua:[112] clearly the insistence on the Frank's providential role is a common theme, but a female ruler cannot be the lieutenant of a God of Battles. Here, in a warlike age, the obstacles to an ideology of "queenship" are as evident as the hagiographer's ingenuity.

One final point to make here concerns Balthild's loss of power, which, as with Brunhild in Austrasia, coincided with her son's coming of age. Like Brunhild, Balthild found regency imposed its own time-limit and tenure was non-renewable. Balthild's retirement to her foundation of Chelles in late 664 or 665 was no voluntary move. Though her hagiographer glosses over it,[113] the threat of force is strongly suggested by the *Vita Eligii*.[114] Whether or not Ebroin was directly involved,[115] those responsible were clearly a powerful section of the Neustrian aristocracy. The very violence of these *principes'* reaction implies the reality of Balthild's power: as her *Vita* puts it, they had acted against her will and feared her vengeance.[116] But their success also showed how precarious was a queen-mother's

---

[111] Ezekiel 37: 17–18, 20–2, 26 (Authorised Version). The Vulgate reading of verse 17 is: "Et adjunge illaunam ad alterum tibi in lignum unum; et erunt in unionem in manu tua."

[112] Ewig, "Zum christlichen Königsgedanken im Frühmittelalter," *Das Königtum*, ed. T. Mayer, *Vorträge und Forschungen* 3 (Konstanz, 1956): 7–73 at 51 *seq.*

[113] *Vita Balthildis* cap. 10, p. 495: "Erat enim eius sancta devotio, ut in monasterio [Chelles] . . . conversare deberet. Nam et Franci pro eius amore hoc maxime dilatabant nec fieri permittebant. . . . Et exinde . . . permiserunt eam subito pergere ad ipsum monasterium. Et fortasse dubium non est, quod ipsi principes tunc illud non bono animo permississent" ["For it was her holy vow to retire to the monastery of Chelles. But the Franks, for love of her, delayed this for the longest time, nor would they have permitted it. . . . And from this (see n. 116) . . . they suddenly permitted her to go to the monastery. And there is little doubt that these princes permitted this without good will"].

[114] *Vita Eligii* ii, 32, p. 717: "iure regio exempta" ["she was removed by order of the king"]. The last of Clothar III's *diplomata* subscribed by Balthild is dated September 6, 664: *MGH DD* 1, no. 40, p. 38.

[115] Judgments on this point have been very subjective. See Fischer, *Ebroin*, pp. 98–104.

[116] *Vita* cap. 10, p. 495: "nec fieri permittebant, nisi commotio illa fuisset per miserum Sigobrandum episcopum, cuius superbia inter Francos meruit mortis ruinam. Et exinde orta intentione, dum ipsum *contra eius voluntatem* interfecerunt, metuentes *ne hoc ipsa domna contra eos graviter ferret ac vindicare ipsam causam vellet*, permiserunt eam subito," etc. (above, n. 113.) ["nor would they have permitted it except that there was an insurrection caused by the contemptible bishop Sigobrand, whose pride towards the Franks earned him deadly ruin. And strife arose from this, since they killed him *against her will*. Fearing *that this lady would hold it very much against them and want to vindicate his cause*, they suddenly permitted her," etc.]. A few lines further on, p. 496, the *Vita* gives a further revealing glimpse of Balthild's position: "Habuit enim tunc non modicam querelam contra eos, quos ipsa dulciter enutriverat, pro qua re falso ipsi eam habuissent suspectam, vel etiam pro bonis mala ei repensarent.

position if those "whom she had tenderly nurtured" should turn against her. Her elimination could be more decorously handled, but, like Grimoald, she had become expendable. The dowager's phony vocation, the mayor's judicial murder, could be arranged without the political upheavals of an interregnum.

So far, I have portrayed two queens acting in a thoroughly secular context of kingly courts and counsels, treasure, armed force, and aristocratic politics. But other, equally important, non-secular types of power in the Merovingian world must now be considered if we are fully to appreciate these queens' activities, or their posthumous reputations. The saints – the holy dead – were believed to incorporate supernatural power which could seem random, inexplicable in its operations.[117] Those who could claim to mediate such power, to render it intelligible, to enable "human strategy [to be set] at work on the holy"[118] were the bishops, the holy men and the monks in the towns and countryside of Gaul. Both the power and the exponents thereof predated the Merovingians: Clovis and his successors had to come to terms with them. We must now examine how, first, Brunhild and then Balthild did so.

If the Frankish kings from the fifth century onwards wielded a territorial authority from city bases, the collaboration of bishops was indispensable. Appointments of, and relations with bishops remained key aspects of royal action through the sixth and most of the seventh centuries:[119] and rulers had scope for action precisely because, though episcopacy was part of the "Establishment," bishops, especially prospective ones, needed outside support to secure their local positions. Had "senatorial blood, episcopal office and sanctity" *really* "presented a formidable united front,"[120] Merovingian kings – and queens too – could never have been as formidable as they sometimes were. Brunhild is a case in point. As a consort, she, like other sixth-century queens, had probably used her influence in episcopal elections, notably, according to Venantius, that of Gregory of Tours himself.[121] Better documented is her intervention at Rodez in 584, where her influence was invoked by one of the participants, Count Innocentius, in a power-struggle in the nearby city of Javols. When the count

---

Sed et hoc conferens cum sacerdotibus citius, eis clementer cuncta indulsit" ["For she harbored not a small complaint against those whom she herself had sweetly nurtured, because they had suspected her falsely and even repaid her good with evil. But conferring quickly with priests, she clemently pardoned them for everything"]. For the Sigobrand episode, see below p. 249.

[117] For a fine account, full of fresh insights, see now [P.] Brown, "Relics [and Social Status in the Age of Gregory of Tours]," The Stenton Lecture for 1976 (University of Reading, 1977), with references to previous work. Also indispensable is Graus, *Heiliger*. Brown's paper must be supplemented for the seventh century by Prinz, "Heiligenkult," and *Mönchtum*; and Ewig, "Milo [et eiusmodi similes]," *Bonifatius-Gedenkgabe* (Fulda, 1954), pp. 412–40, at 430 *seq*.

[118] Brown, "Relics," p. 14.

[119] D. Claude, "[Die] Bestellung der Bischöfe [im merowingischen Reiche]," *ZRG KAbt* 49 (1963): 1–77. For some general aspects of episcopal collaboration, see Wood, "Kings." It is tempting to correlate the absence of queenly regencies in England in the seventh century (the year-long reign of Seaxburh, widow of Cenwalh of Wessex, apparently in her own right, in 672–3 is quite exceptional) or later, with the relative weakness of episcopal power there as well as with the ubiquity of warfare: there was no substitute therefore for an adult warrior king. An obvious further correlation would be with the persistance of dynastic discontinuity in the English kingdoms into the ninth century. See below, n. 235.

[120] So, P. Brown, *Religion and Society in the Age of Saint Augustine* (London, 1972), p. 131, quoted and renounced, with admirable open-mindedness, by Brown himself: "Relics," p. 17. See also his reservations, "Relics," pp. 19–20, about Prinz, "[Die bischöfliche] Stadtherrschaft [im Frankenreich]," *HZ* 217 (1974): 1–35, which, however, remains an important article.

[121] Venantius Fortunatus, *Carmina* v, 3, ll. 11–15, p. 106 "Huic Sigibercthus ovans favet et Brunichildis honori" ["Sigibert, rejoicing, promotes him to this honor, and Brunhild too"].

transferred his interests to the see of Rodez, Brunhild's support secured him the bishopric in an election which scandalized even Gregory by the fierceness of the competition.[122] Brunhild's own interest here might have been connected, I suggest, with her continuing efforts to secure the restitution of her sister Galswinth's morning-gift which included the city of Cahors.[123] The dioceses of Rodez and Cahors were contiguous, and Bishop Innocentius's harrassment of the neighbouring see[124] may have exerted some of the pressure which achieved the transfer of Cahors into Brunhild's possession in 586. Her continuing interest in this region, in which Frankish and Visigothic powers competed, and the key position of Rodez are still evident twenty years later.[125] The other vital area for the queen's control of episcopal appointments after 600 was Burgundy proper. She must surely have been behind the elections of Aridius to Lyons and of Domnolus to Vienne in 603. She appointed Desiderius to Auxerre in 605.[126] Gregory the Great complained in 595 that no one obtained a bishopric in the *regnum Francorum* [Kingdom of the Franks] without paying for it.[127] Assuming twelve to fifteen vacancies per annum, Claude has made the interesting calculation that the royal profits from simony over the *regnum* as a whole could have reached ten thousand solidi in the later sixth century.[128] Despite later accusations, I do not think that Brunhild's practice here was unusual, nor that she was responsible for a peculiarly bad attack of this "contagion" in the late sixth century.[129] Of course the money was useful to her, as to the other strong rulers who profited from this source. But it was not the chief consideration. Whether or not they proved their devotion in hard cash, Brunhild needed episcopal allies and servants. They if anyone could control the cities, their very simony being proof of one vital attribute of power;[130] they could influence their aristocratic lay kinsfolk; and they could

---

[122]   *LH* vi, 38, p. 309. For the previous context at Rodez see *LH* v, 46.

[123]   *LH* ix, 20, see above, n. 22.

[124]   *LH* vi, 38, p. 309.

[125]   The evidence lies in three letters, two of them apparently addressed to the bishop of Rodez, by Bulgar, count of Septimania during the reign of the Visigothic king Gunthimar (610–12): *MGH Epp.* 3, *Epp Wisigothicae* nos 11, 12 and 13, pp. 677–81. The letters to the bishop of Rodez are violently hostile to Brunhild and Theuderic, accusing them of making an alliance with the pagan Avars, and making it clear that Gunthimar was sending money to Theudebert. The Auvergne region was, of course, an Austrasian enclave. Bulgar's third letter, evidently addressed to a Burgundian bishop (here Brunhild and Theuderic are *gloriosissimi reges* [most glorious rulers]), reveals that Brunhild was negotiating with Gunthimar for two towns in Septimania which had been granted to her personally by her cousin king Reccared but taken back by the Visigoths, presumably after Reccared's death in 601 or his son's in 603. Brunhild was meanwhile holding two Visigothic envoys captive as a bargaining counter. For anti-Brunhild propaganda in this festering Visigothic–Frankish conflict, see below, p. 239. The treatment of Bulgar's letters by Kurth, "Brunehaut," pp. 313–14, is rather confused.

[126]   *Fred.* cap. 24, p. 15; cap. 19, p. 13 with Wallace-Hadrill's n. 1. The case of Desiderius of Auxerre, and the inaccuracy of Fredegar's "legendary" account, are discussed by Kurth, "Brunehaut," pp. 308–10.

[127]   Ep. v, 58, *MGH Epp.* 1, p. 369. Compare *Ep.* ix, 213, *MGH Epp.* 2, p. 198.

[128]   Claude, "Bestellung der Bischöfe," p. 59, n. 290.

[129]   *Vita Eligii* II, 1, p. 694: "Maxime de temporibus Brunehildis infelicissimae reginae . . . violabat hoc contagium catholicam fidem" ["This contagion infected the catholic faith most greatly from the time of the wretched Queen Brunhild"]. A similarly harsh view of Brunhild ("le mauvais génie de la maison de Sigebert" ["the evil genie of the house of Sigibert"]!) is taken by E. Vacandard, "Les elections episcopales," in *Etudes de Critique et d'Histoire* (Paris, 1905), pp. 159 *seq.*

[130]   For a nice example from the 660s, of wealth as a qualification for episcopal office, see the contemporary *Passio Praejecti*, cap. 12, *SSrM* 5, p. 232: when Praejectus solicits the bishopric of Clermont, the *plebs* ask him "si se sciebat tantam pecuniam auri argentique metalli habere, unde hoc opus

serve as counsellors and envoys, deploying their useful network of personal connections. The bishops, for their part, could achieve no concerted action, could undertake no moral reform, without royal sponsorship. This pope Gregory understood very well when he directed his appeals to Brunhild.[131] The collaboration of queen, bishop and pope is apparent in Brunhild's foundations at Autun: a nuns' house dedicated to the Virgin, a *Xenodochium* [hospice] associated with a male convent whose abbot was to be royally appointed, and a church dedicated to St Martin served by secular clergy and destined to provide the queen's tomb.[132] Brunhild's interest in Autun is significant. Continuing the eastward reorientation of the "Burgundian" kingdom implicit in Guntramn's choice of Chalon for his *sedes regia* [royal seat],[133] Brunhild, while cultivating links with the Rhône cities, especially Lyons, also entrenched royal influence firmly in a major centre of sixth-century cult and culture, a point of articulation between the two broad zones of Martinian and Rhône-based monasticism, a citadel, finally, of Gallo-Roman aristocratic power which was close to the frontier with "barbarian" Gaul.[134]

Brunhild's association with Syagrius of Autun is only the most striking instance of what must be seen as a characteristic and inevitable mode of royal government in the Merovingian *regnum*. Bishops were there in the *civitates* [cities], and kings, from Clovis onwards, who wanted to govern in and from cities therefore had to work with bishops. This rather than any common commitment to *Romanentum* and Roman governmental principles, or any adherence to a "*parti romain*" ["Roman faction"],[135] or any absolutist ambitions on the part of a cultured Visigoth grown into a "Burgundian 'lady-centralist,'"[136] accounts for Brunhild's relations with the bishops of the realms she ruled and, beyond them, with the pope. In Burgundy, naturally, the bishops were *Romani*, but it was not their Romanity which determined Brunhild's favour, any more than ethnic affinity governed her choice of lay officials: her alleged partiality to "Romans" is belied by the number of Frankish and Burgundian appointments mentioned by Fredegar.[137]

The exception to the record of harmony between Brunhild and her bishops is the case of

queat subire" ["if he knew that he had enough money in gold and silver to be able to attain that position"].

[131] *Epp.* viii, 4; ix, 213; xi, 46, *MGH Epp.* 2, pp. 5–8; 198–200; 318–19.

[132] *Epp.* xiii, 11–13, *MGH Epp.* 2, pp. 376–81, where also the editor, L. M. Hartmann, convincingly defends the authenticity of these privileges, and suggests that Gregory based his wording on that of Brunhild in her original request. For Brunhild's tomb, see Kurth, "Brunehaut," pp. 347, 352–6.

[133] Ewig, "Résidence [et capitale pendant le haut Moyen Age]," *RH* 230 (1963): 25–72, at p. 48.

[134] See Gregory the Great, *Epp.* ix, 214, 218 and 222 *MGH Epp.* 2, pp. 200, 205–10, 213–14 (contacts with Syagrius of Autun) and *Epp.* ix, 208 and 230, pp. 195–227 (contacts with Spain via Autun). Riché, *Education*, pp. 179 *seq.*, 268–70, with maps on pp. 170 and 269; Prinz, *Mönchtum*, pp. 60–1, 136, 140 with maps 5, 6 and 9; and Stroheker, *Adel*, pp. 121–2, 163–4 (for the Syagrii and Desiderii).

[135] So, Delaruelle, "L'Eglise romaine et ses relations avec l'Eglise franque jusqu'en 800," *Spoleto* 7, i (1960): 143–84, at 160.

[136] So, Prinz, *Mönchtum*, p. 542.

[137] *Fred.* caps 24, 28, 29, pp. 16, 19, mentions Protadius, Claudius, and Ricomer as "Romans by birth"; but he also mentions the promotions of the Franks Quolen (cap. 18, p. 12), and Bertoald (cap. 24, p. 15), while the constable Eborin and the chamberlain Berthar (caps 30, 38, pp. 20, 31–2) were also presumably Franks. Duke Rocco, probably a Burgundian, served as Brunhild and Theuderic's envoy to Spain in 607 and only turned against her in 613 (caps 30, 42, pp. 20, 34). Among bishops, the Austrasian Frank Leudegasius of Mainz was an ally of Theuderic in 612 (cap. 38, p. 31) while Lupus of Sens, deposed after 614 for his previous loyalty to Brunhild, came from a Frankish family in Orléans: *Vita Lupi, MGH SSrM* 4, caps 1, 11, pp. 179, 182.

Desiderius of Vienne, first exiled, later stoned to death, according to Fredegar, on "the wicked advice of Aridius of Lyons and of . . . Brunhild."[138] If all we had was Fredegar's threadbare account of this apparently arbitrary action, it might be tempting to explain Desiderius's fate in terms of factionalism in the Burgundian episcopate and the traditional rivalry between Lyons and Vienne. But the remarkable *Vita Desiderii* written by the Visigothic king Sisebut (612–21), and a second *Vita* written in the eighth century by a cleric of Vienne throw more light on the affair.[139] Sisebut is violently hostile to Brunhild, not I think because he held her responsible for the dismissal of Theuderic II's Visigothic bride (who after all was no relation of Sisebut's)[140] nor through any genuine concern for the sanctity of Desiderius, but because he is writing propaganda for Septimanian consumption. His *Vita* is, as Fontaine has brilliantly shown, "a hagiographic pamphlet" designed to show how a Toledan king could respect a Gallo-Roman aristocrat and to incite opposition to Frankish rule.[141] And here, significantly, as in the letters of Count Bulgar of Septimania (written about 610)[142] Brunhild the "nurse of discords" is completely identified with the Merovingians. Sisebut stresses the role of Brunhild's protégé, the mayor of the palace Protadius in bringing about Desiderius's exile and suggests that the terror of Brunhild and Theuderic at Protadius's death made them avenge themselves on Desiderius. The eighth-century *Vita* hints at popular opposition to Desiderius in Vienne. But both *Vitae* agree that the basic reason for Desiderius's loss of royal favour and eventual death was his sharp criticism of royal *mores* – specifically of Theuderic's concubines.[143] How credible is it that Brunhild would have let such an issue embroil her in an uncharacteristic conflict with a leading bishop? Why did she not ensure that her grandson took a wife and became respectable in the eyes of an ecclesiastical moralist? Such a marriage, argued Kurth, could not have endangered Brunhild any more than concubines already did: "will anyone seriously maintain," he asked, "that a sensual king submits more willingly to the influence of his wife than that of his mistress?"[144]

To understand Brunhild's motives, we must look at one more episode: her relations with St Columbanus. She must have met him long since, when he first arrived in the *regnum Francorum* c.591 and found patronage from her son Childebert.[145] From the outset Columbanus's *peregrinatio* [pilgrimage] had a strong inner-worldly objective, namely the restoration (or application) of *religio* to *fides*,[146] which could only be achieved with political support. It was a matter of building up a network of personal relations and loyalties, of education: and this took time. The history of Luxeuil is obscure until quite late in Theuderic's reign but it is clear that some Austrasian and Burgundian aristocrats had been patronizing the monastery in the 590s,[147] and there is no sign of any royal hostility. The first

---

[138] *Fred.* cap. 32, p. 21.

[139] Both *Vitae* are edited by Krusch in *MGH SSrM* 3, pp. 630–45.

[140] [*Fred.*] cap. 30, p. 20: Ermenburga was the daughter of Witteric, murderer of his predecessor and himself murdered by Gunthimar in 610.

[141] J. Fontaine, *Isidore de Séville et la culture classique dans l'Espagne wisigothique* (Paris, 1959), p. 841 nn. 1, 2.

[142] *MGH Epp.* 3, pp. 677–81, at 677: "iurgiorum auctrix."

[143] *MGH SSrM* 3, pp. 635, 640–1.

[144] Kurth, "Brunehaut," p. 322.

[145] Jonas, *VC* cap. 6, *MGH SSrM* 4, p. 72 with Krusch's n. 3. See [G. S. M.] Walker, [*Sancti Columbani Opera*], *Scriptores Latini Hiberniae*, 2 (Dublin, 1957), introd., pp. x–xi, xxi *seq.*

[146] *VC* cap. 5, p. 71. Compare Columbanus's ep. 2, Walker, pp. 12–23.

[147] *VC* I, caps 10, 14 and 15, pp. 76, 79 and 81. For another possible case (Agilus) see Prinz, *Mönchtum*, pp. 126, 217, 356–7.

mention in the *Vita Columbani* of Theuderic's attitude to the saint stresses his veneration: "he had often come to [Columbanus] at Luxeuil and with all humility begged the help of his prayers."[148] Brunhild too recognized his support as worth having. Columbanus seems to have been in the habit of coming to visit Brunhild and the royal family. In 609 she sought the holy man's blessing for her great-grandsons, the eldest of them born in 602.[149] We should note the lateness of the evidence for conflict between the queen and the saint. If for years he had been complaining about Theuderic's failure to marry, it was only in 609 that the political conse-quences of his objections became explicit when he denied the claim of Theuderic's sons to succeed to the kingship. Now and only now Brunhild appears as "a second Jezebel,"[150] her sin the primal one of pride: but it is pride of a specific kind, which fears to lose long-held status, power and wealth, and it has a specific manifestation of hostility to the *vir Dei* whose moral-izing threatens that position. Theuderic had nothing to lose by compliance and indeed, Brunhild "could see that he was yielding to the man of God." But for her, what might be at stake was control of the *aula regis*, the court, and thus the real power and influence which made a queen's position worth having. Columbanus's hagiographer Jonas, for all his bias, had hit the nail squarely on the head: being the king's bed-fellow, even being the mother of his sons, was not at all the same thing as being queen. Brunhild knew this. She must have known it when in Childebert's reign she had had a queen as daughter-in-law. But in such situations, personalities counted for much, and Faileuba did not strike contemporaries as considerable. And in any case that was all long ago when perhaps Brunhild herself had had little choice. In the early 600s she was old, had long grown used to power and did not want to retire: there was no contemporary sentiment against gerontocracy. Her aim now was to secure the future for her line; thus to get Theuderic's sons accepted as his prospective heirs. And there was a final element in her motivation, perhaps still an essential one: Fredegund's son lived and ruled in Neustria. Could Theuderic be counted on, without Brunhild at his side, to pursue the vendetta to its necessary end? Desiderius had already been eliminated, probably by means of an intended exile that went wrong.[151] Columbanus too must now be exiled – for Brunhild rightly judged that the abrasive old Irishman would never be pressurized into silence when he saw principle at stake. The initiative was hers. The allegedly "fundamental" hostility of the bishops, or, alternatively, of "the monasticism of the Rhône region," have in my view been exaggerated. Despite Columbanus's rudeness, despite the awkward dispute over the dating of Easter,[152] the bishops of Brunhild's realm had left the Irish to their eccentricities; as for "monasticism," the delay in the appearance of Luxeuil's influence in southern Gaul (neatly demonstrated in Prinz's maps) had more to do with pre-existing deep-rooted traditions and patterns of aristocratic patronage and monastic practice than with positive or principled "opposition."[153] Jonas should still be believed, I think, when he says that it was Brunhild

---

[148]   *VC*, I, cap. 18, p. 86; *Fred.* cap. 36, p. 23.

[149]   *VC*, I, cap. 19, p. 87. *Fred.* cap. 21, p. 14 gives the date of Sigebert's birth.

[150]   *VC*, I, cap. 18, p. 86: "mentem Brunechildis . . . secundae ut erat Zezebelis, antiquus anguis adiit eamque contra virum Dei stimulatam superbiae aculeo excitat quia cerneret viro Dei Theudericum oboedire" ["the ancient serpent entered the mind of Brunhild as if she were a second Jezebel, and turned her, aroused by the sin of pride, against the man of God because she saw that Theuderic obeyed the man of God"]. It is worth noting that Sisebut, despite his violent antipathy to Brunhild, does not label her a "Jezebel." But his *Vita* is stylistically very different from Jonas's work.

[151]   Kurth, "Brunehaut," p. 329, argues this on the basis of the second *Vita Desiderii*, *MGH SSrM* 3, cap. 9 p. 641.

[152]   Columbanus, epp. 1–3, Walker, pp. 12–25, with Walker's comments, pp. xxv–vi.

[153]   Prinz, *Mönchtum*, p. 148 and n. 137, stresses this "opposition." Reservations similar to mine, though based on other evidence, are voiced by Ian Wood, "A Prelude to Columbanus[: the Monastic Achievement in the Burgundian Territories," in *Columbanus and Merovingian Monasticism*, ed. H. B.

herself who "worked upon the bishops" and on the lay magnates and *auligae* [courtiers] as well as the king, to coordinate an anti-Columbanan front. It was natural for Jonas to see a parallel with the biblical archetype of the wicked queen who sought to destroy God's mouthpiece, the holy man. Knowing as he did the details of Brunhild's life and death, Jonas must have relished other reminiscences of Jezebel: like her, Brunhild was a foreigner and a king's daughter; like her, Brunhild attacked a personal enemy (Naboth = Desiderius) by bringing false charges against him and then had him stoned to death; like her, Brunhild met a dreadful fate – *et equorum ungulae conculcaverunt eam* [the hooves of horses trampled her underfoot].[154] Jonas's audience, likewise connoisseurs of the Books of Kings, could readily supply these motifs, once given the identification of Brunhild with Jezebel; and readers of the *Vita Columbani* who wrote about Brunhild subsequently gained access to useful new "material." In the *Liber Historiae Francorum*, the aged Brunhild titivates herself in a pathetic attempt to seduce her conqueror Clothar II, just like Jezebel who, hearing of king Jehu's arrival, *depinxit oculos suos stibio et ornavit caput suum* [painted her eyes with antimony and adorned her head];[155] while in the eighth-century *Vita* of Desiderius, Brunhild becomes Jezebel in this second context, *alone* responsible for the bishop's death in which the motif of stoning is emphasized.[156] So influential, indeed, was Jonas's work, so definitive his portrayal of Brunhild that in Frankish hagiography she came to rank with Ebroin as a stereotype of villainy.[157] If in one tenth-century *Vita* she appears in a less awful light when, struck by the saint's power she becomes his patron, this simply proves that a hagiographer could best show the greatness of *his* holy man by pitting him successfully against the wickedest of Wicked Queens.[158]

Brunhild, then, had not been born bad, but nor had she exactly had badness thrust upon her: in the hagiographer's terms, she deserved her reputation and had indeed challenged the authority of a saint and opposed heavenly with earthly power. That this action was untypical of her, that it was forced on her in a particular time and situation by the need to survive politically, could not concern the monks who reviled her memory. That she was very unlucky to have crossed the path of the one great charismatic of her age and that her posthumous fate was in a sense accidental: none of this could concern the generations of monks in whose collective memory this Jezebel lived on. But it must concern modern historians and cause us to rethink some of the sweeping generalizations and value-judgments out of which our predecessors, two or three generations ago, fashioned their own improbable images of Brunhild as benevolent despot or great soul.

Balthild's image is, of course, timeless: she was and is a saint.[159] But she was also, for some contemporaries, a Jezebel. The paradox, and the apparent contrast with Brunhild, invite our attention. Balthild's *Vita* makes it clear that she had grasped the uses of piety, both as a means to secure personal status and as a political instrument. There is a touch of Uriah Heep about her oft-praised "humility" but this may be the hagiographer's fault, not hers. What is new and

Clarke and M. Brennan (Bar International Series 113, Oxford, 1981), pp. 3–32]. I am very grateful to him for letting me see this paper in advance of publication.

[154] 3 Kings 16: 31; 19: 1–2; 5–16, 23; 4 Kings 9: 30–7. For Jonas's use of typology in the *Vita Columbani*, see J. Leclercq, "L'univers religieux de St Columban," in *Aspets du Monachisme hier et Aujourd'hui* (Paris, 1974), pp. 193–212 at 201 *seq.*

[155] *LHF* cap. 40, p. 310, influenced by 4 Kings 9: 30–3.

[156] *MGH SSrM* 3, cap. 9, p. 641.

[157] Graus, *Heiliger*, pp. 373–4.

[158] *Vita Menelei, MGH SSrM* 5, cap. 3–11, pp. 150–4.

[159] *Lexicon für Theologie und Kirche* 2, col. 50 (Ewig) *sv* "Balthildis." Her feast-day is 30 January. If we may trust Ewig, "Klosterpolitik," p. 62, she is still capable of making a nocturnal visit to reprove a detractor!

remarkable here is the depiction of a specifically royal sanctity.[160] This is apparent first in her activities as Clovis II's consort. In the intimate atmosphere of the court, Balthild structures her personal relationships "correctly" in terms both of the hagiographer's values and of her own interests: "to the great men she showed herself like a mother, to the bishops like a daughter, to the young men and boys like the best sort of nurse." In a rather wider context too, she has the right priorities, loving "bishops as fathers, monks as brothers and the poor as their pious nurse"; she does not infringe the magnates' sense of status but accepts their counsels when appropriate, she encourages the young men to monastic studies, and uses her influence with the king "humbly but persistently" on behalf of churches and the poor.[161] Clovis assigns her the chief of his palace clerks, his *fidelis famulus* [faithful servant] Genesius, to administer her charitable works: as the *Vita's* term *assiduus* implies, he was a force to be reckoned with in the Neustrian palace at this time. Further promotion was assured: he would become bishop of Lyons, "on Christ's orders" (and doubtless Balthild's) in 660.[162]

Already during Clovis's lifetime, Balthild had had close ties with Eligius, bishop of Noyon from 641, and probably also Audoenus (Dado), bishop of Rouen from 641.[163] These men were at the centre of a friendship-network which spanned the entire *regnum Francorum* and had a remarkable capacity to persist and to reproduce itself over generations – from the 620s through to the 660s and probably later.[164] In so far as it transcended the boundaries of the *Teilreiche* [divided kingdom], it could be troublesome for a king: Sigibert III forbade Desiderius of Cahors to attend a council at Bourges because that was in his brother's realm, and Desiderius could invite only his Austrasian friends to celebrate the foundation of the monastery of St Amantius at Cahors.[165] But Clothar II and Dagobert had made the network work for them, using its members first as lay officials and close advisers, later as bishops in major *civitates*. A hefty attack on simony made by the bishops themselves was directed against local aristocratic, rather than royal malpractice.[166] Control of episcopal appointments, simoniac or otherwise, remained essential for rulers. It seems likely, for instance, that Chrodobert became bishop of Paris late in Clovis's reign because of his already close connections with Audoenus and with Balthild.[167]

---

[160] This is most evident in her remission of the capitation-tax and her prohibition of the slave-trade in Christian captives: "datasque praeceptiones per singulas regiones, ut nullus in regno Francorum captivum hominem christianum penitus transmitteret" ["and she issued decrees throughout each region commanding that no one at all was to send a captive Christian into the Kingdom of the Franks"], *Vita* caps 6 and 9, pp. 488, 494.

[161] *Vita* cap. 4, pp. 485–6.

[162] Ibid., pp. 486–7.

[163] *Vita Eligii*, ii, 32, p. 727. See also Vacandard, [*Vie de*] *Saint Ouen*, [*evêque de Rouen*] (Paris, 1902), pp. 249–55.

[164] The main evidence lies in the letter-collection of Desiderius of Cahors (d. 650) *MGH Epp.* 3, pp. 191–214. Audoenus survived until 684. For the friendship-circle, see Levison's introduction to the *Vita Audoini*, *MGH SSrM* 5, pp. 536–7; Sprandel, *Adel*, pp. 16–17, 33; Riché, *Education*, pp. 236 *seq.* Wallace-Hadrill, *Long-Haired Kings*, pp. 222–3.

[165] Desiderii, *Ep.* ii, 17, p. 212; *Ep.* i, 11, p. 199.

[166] Council of Chalon-sur-Saône (647–53) cap. 16, *Concilia Galliae 511–695*, ed. C. de Clercq, *CCSL* 148A (Turnhout, 1963), p. 306.

[167] He seems to have belonged to Audoenus's circle, if the "bishop Chrodobert" to whom Audoenus sent a copy of his *Vita Eligii* can be identified with the then bishop of Paris: see Krusch's comments in *MGH SSrM* 4, pp. 650–1 and Vacandard, *Saint Ouen*, pp. 236–7. But Vacandard's apparent identification of the bishop with a Rodebert, mayor of the palace in 655, is mistaken for the latter was still addressed as mayor in 663: see Ebling, *Prosopographie*, pp. 112–13. The mayor and the bishop could well be relatives however.

When Clovis died late in 657, Balthild as queen mother naturally had a good claim to the regency, but her established friendships, especially with Genesius, allowed her to make the claim effective. There is no evidence of any demand at this point for a division of the Neustro-Burgundian realm, which, while suggesting the absence of any strong Burgundian secessionist movement, could also indicate the smoothness of the transmission of royal power. Audoenus and Chrodobert are named in the *Vita Balthildis* as the key supporters of the regency,[168] and Ebroin's appointment as mayor some months afterwards must have been made on their, as well as the queen's, "advice." In 657–8, then, the *regnum Francorum* remained at peace – no mean tribute to the degree of governmental stability and continuity which episcopal underwriting helped ensure.

But the maintenance of royal power was not just a simple matter of keeping inherited episcopal allies. The trouble was, there were bishops and bishops: the "good" ones, as the *Vita* engagingly terms them (they certainly included Eligius and Audoenus) urged the queen on to prohibit simony specifically in episcopal appointments,[169] where the "bad" ones, by implication, preferred to work the familiar systems. Whatever financial profits this meant foregoing Balthild continued to exercise her power to appoint. Politics based on personalities, families and factions were the reverse of static: to remain in any sort of control, a ruler had to be able to place his/her supporters in key positions. Earlier Merovingians had been able to exercise considerable freedom in appointing patricians, dukes, and counts. The development of hereditary offices, restricting the scope of royal action,[170] heightened the need to secure the right bishops. Against this background, the scanty evidence for Balthild's episcopal appointments becomes significant. Three cases are known. In the first is recorded only the bare fact that through her influence Erembert, who came originally from the Chartres region, became bishop of Toulouse.[171] Aquitaine was clearly not yet outwith the scope of royal intervention. The second and third cases relate to Burgundy which contained, in my view, not a separatist movement, but aristocratic factions operating in cities as well as countryside. As in Brunhild's time, Autun and Lyons were two key cities in the region. In Autun, faction-fighting kept the see vacant for two years (probably 660–2)[172] until Balthild took the initiative. She had already provided herself with the man for the job when she summoned to the court a learned, experienced, and above all *strenuus* [effective] man from Poitiers – Leudegarius. It is tempting to suggest that Balthild needed a replacement for Genesius in the royal chapel and, probably on Audoenus's advice, sought an "outstanding teacher of clerics." His subsequent move from chapel to bishopric replicated that of Genesius. In the short run he proved the wisdom of Balthild's choice by restoring Autun to peace and good government.[173]

Balthild's interventions in Toulouse and Autun evoked little contemporary comment. But the third case involved more complications: Genesius's appointment to Lyons followed a

---

[168] *Vita* cap. 5, p. 487: "suscepit ilico . . . Chlotharius quondam Francorum regnum, tunc etenim precellentibus principibus Chrodobertho episcopo Parisiaco et domino Audoeno seu et Ebroino maiore domus" ["right away the late king Clothar took up the Kingdom of the Franks, then truly with the excellent princes Chrodobert, bishop of Paris, and lord Audoenus and Ebroin, mayor of the palace"].

[169] *Vita* cap. 6, p. 488: "exortantibus bonis sacerdotibus" ["at the urging of good priests"].

[170] A. R. Lewis, "The Dukes in the *Regnum Francorum*, A. D. 550–751," *Speculum* 51 (1976): 381–410 at 398–9; Sprandel, "Struktur and Geschichte," pp. 43–7, 60–1.

[171] *Vita Eremberti, MGH SSrM* 5, p. 654. This *Vita* was composed *c.*800, but its accuracy on this point is accepted by Ewig, "Teilreiche," p. 127.

[172] *Passio Leudegarii* I, cap. 2. p. 284.

[173] Ibid., I, caps 2, 3, pp. 284–6. See also Riché, *Education*, pp. 363–4.

violent episode in which his predecessor was killed. According to *Acta* which seem to have a genuinely seventh-century base,[174] Bishop Aunemundus and his brother, the prefect of Lyons, were sons of a previous prefect and the family had built up a virtual monopoly of local power through using their influence at the courts of Dagobert and Clovis II. There Aunemundus had had a typically successful career as a lay office-holder before being appointed to Lyons, surely with royal support, about 650 (he baptized the infant Clothar III who was born in that year). But the *Acta* stress envy in what sounds like a local context as the cause of Aunemundus's downfall.[175] The bishop and his brother were accused of treason (*infidelitas*) and summoned to appear before the boy-king Clothar and the regent Balthild at an assembly at Mareuil, a royal *villa* near Orléans. The brother appeared, was found guilty and executed. When Aunemundus himself failed to appear, pleading illness, the regent sent *duces* [dukes] with instructions to bring him to the royal court and to kill him only if he resisted. On their way there, near Chalon, Aunemundus was murdered one night by two armed men whose action was deeply regretted by the *duces* themselves.[176] Now the local tradition about these events had got fairly confused by the time the surviving (late-medieval) texts were written.[177] But the crucial points so far as Balthild is concerned are, first, that these *Acta* ascribe to her neither the initiative in Aunemundus's accusation nor the responsibility for his death, and second that the identity or gentile origin of Aunemundus's accusers is ˙not stated. To erect on this basis a theory of a "Burgundian autonomist party" who had "conspired against the Neustrian *palatium*" in sharp reaction against Balthild's "programme of compulsory 'union'"[178] is to pile figment on fantasy. We simply know too little about the alleged treason of Aunemundus and his brother and have no indication that any others but these two were involved. It is more likely, I think, that the episode belongs in a context of family or factional rivalries in and around Lyons, and that the accusers of Aunemundus and his brother were other local aristocrats, not Neustrian centralists. The whole affair is reminiscent of a situation recorded in the *Passio Praejecti*, where a dispute over land in the Auvergne between the bishop of Clermont and a local magnate is brought to the king's court and settled, but the royal decision is soon followed by violence on the spot when the bishop is murdered by other local enemies.[179] The interplay, rather than conflict, between royal and

---

[174] *Acta sancti Aunemundi, AASS* Sept. vii (Brussels, 1760), pp. 744–6. See A. Coville, *Recherches [sur l'histoire de Lyon du Vme au IXme siècle]* (Paris, 1928), pp. 366 *seq.*

[175] *Acta* p. 744: "nullusque de aliqua re ad suum profectum quidquam valebat impetrare, nisi sua suggestione (that is, Aunemundus's) Clotario tertio principi deportaret. . . . Ideo dum sublimitatis suae gloriam ac brachium vindicaret extentum, nec non et a fratribus celsior videretur in coetu, cunctis incidit in odium. Qui tractare eum seditiose coeperunt sub clandestina accusatione dicentes, quasi regnum ejusdem Clotarii . . . evertere moliretur occulte" ["And no one could ask for anything on their account at all unless Aunemundus conveyed it by his own petition to the prince, Clothar III. But since he claimed the glory of his high position with arm extended, he was seen by the brethren as too high in society, and he came to be hated by all. They began to treat him treacherously, making clandestine accusations, as if he were striving to overturn the kingdom of Clothar secretly"]. Dupraz, *Royaume*, p. 343 n. 1, and Fischer, *Ebroin*, p. 92, both state, citing the *Acta*, that the bishop's accusers were *maiores natu ducesque* [nobles by birth and dukes]. But what the *Acta* in fact say is that these magnates appeared at the assembly at Mareuil, as one would expect. The *Acta* imply, rather, the identity of accusers and *fratres* – presumably the "brethren" of the church of Lyons. A few lines later, the *Acta* tell how Aunemundus asked forgiveness from the *fratres* [brethren] at Lyons for any injuries he had done them, including unfair seizure of their goods. For further evidence of Aunemundus' local power, see below, n. 181.

[176] *Acta* p. 745. The *duces* had promised the abbot of Luxeuil that Aunemundus would be safe.

[177] Coville, *Recherches*, pp. 372 *seq.*

[178] So, Dupraz, *Royaume*, pp. 342–4, 352–4; Fischer, *Ebroin*, pp. 90–8.

[179] *MGH SSrM* 5, caps 23, 24, pp. 239–40.

aristocratic interests, the circulation of power from court to provinces and back, seem to me as characteristic of Merovingian politics in the 660s and 670s as in the days of Gregory of Tours. In our Lyons case, anyway, the death of Aunemundus left the way open for Balthild to appoint Genesius, who not only survived but established a strong base for intervention in the politics of the *regnum* over the next twenty years.[180]

Unmentioned in any contemporary Frankish source, apparently without repercussions in the history of the *regnum Francorum*, the Aunemundus affair might seem irrelevant to Balthild's reputation. But because the young Wilfrid happened to have established close relations with Aunemundus and to have stayed for three years in Lyons, whence he subsequently acquired some information about the bishop's death, the story was translated in a new "Wilfridian" version to an Anglo-Saxon literary milieu.[181] Thus, strangely, Balthild who had begun life in England returned there in posthumous tradition, not as a saint – but as a "malevolent queen . . . must like the most impious queen Jezebel."[182] Eddius may have borrowed the motif from the *Vita Columbani*, but he could equally well have used it independently, for his *Vita Wilfridi* is rich in biblical typology. Jezebel was the obvious type for a queen who persecuted a holy man, and Eddius actually used the same motif again later in his work in reference to the "wicked" queen Iurminburg, second wife of Ecgfrith of Northumbria and Wilfrid's violent enemy until her later *conversio*.[183] Eddius wrote over half a century after Aunemundus's death, and based his account of it upon Wilfrid's reminiscences. He asserts that the "evil-wishing queen Balthild" persecuted the church of God; that she had nine bishops put to death ("not counting priests and deacons"!) and one of these was "bishop Dalfinus" (= Aunemundus)[184] whom certain dukes had most malignly ordered to come before them; and that Wilfrid not only was present at the bishop's "martyrdom" but offered himself to the same fate, only to be spared by the dukes when they learnt that he was "from overseas, of the English race from Britain." So, concludes Eddius, Wilfrid, though denied a martyr's palm, was already a confessor – "just like John the apostle and evangelist who sat unharmed in a cauldron of boiling oil."[185] Eddius's aim here is not factual reporting,[186] but the establishment of Wilfrid's saintly credentials at an early point in his *Vita*.

---

[180] Genesius died in 679. For his career, see Coville, *Recherches*, pp. 416–21.

[181] Eddius, *Vita Wilfridi*, ed. Levison, *MGH SSrM* 6, cap. 6, p. 199; ed [B.] Colgrave, p. 14. Bede *H*[*istoria*] *E*[*cclesiastica gentis Anglorum*], ed. [C.] Plummer (Oxford 1896) v, 19, p. 325. Plummer, vol. 2, pp. 316–20, established the chronology of Wilfrid's life. During Wilfrid's first visit to Lyons on his way to Rome in 653, the bishop of that city offered him his niece in marriage together with "a good part to Gaul" (*bona pars Galliarum*); *Vita* cap. 4, ed. Levison, p. 197.

[182] *Vita Wilfridi* cap. 6, p. 199 (Levison). One of the two manuscripts of Eddius gives the reading "Brunhild" instead of "Balthild," as do some manuscripts of Bede, *HE*: see Levison's comment here p. 199 n. 3, and Colgrave's, p. 154. Colgrave's suggestion that this may be a reminiscence of the Brunhild of the Volsung saga is surely incorrect.

[183] *Vita Wilfridi*, cap. 24, p. 218 (Levison), p. 48 (Colgrave). I am grateful to Joan Nicholson for reminding me of Eddius's other Jezebel.

[184] The name "Dalfinus" is not, as often alleged, evidence of Eddius's inaccuracy. Coville, *Recherches*, pp. 381–5, shows that Aunemundus's brother is not named at all in any early Lyons source, that Aunemundus, typically in this period, had two names, and that his second name (Dalfinus) was simply "borrowed" for his brother by late medieval reworkers of the story.

[185] *Vita Wilfridi* cap. 6, pp. 199–200 with n. 2 (Levison); p. 14 (Colgrave, who gives a possible source of the St John anecdote in the note on p. 155.)

[186] For pertinent views on Eddius's method, see R. L. Poole, "St Wilfrid and the see of Ripon," *EHR* 34 (1919): 1–22, and H. Mayr-Harting, *The Coming of Christianity to Anglo-Saxon England* (London, 1972), pp. 139 *seq.*

Now if we date Aunemundus's death to 660 with Levison and Ewig,[187] there is clearly a chronological problem involved in accepting Eddius's story, for Wilfrid left Lyons, at the latest, in 658.[188] Further, the details of place, time, and circumstances recorded in the *Acta* (where of course Wilfrid is not mentioned at all) actually contradict those of Eddius's account. Levison observed these discrepancies but left the matter unresolved; while Coville claimed the discrepancies were insignificant and on Eddius's "authority" dated Aunemundus's death to 658.[189] I suggest another conclusion, namely, that Wilfrid was not in fact present at Aunemundus's death, and that Eddius's account therefore derives from information which Wilfrid acquired on one of his subsequent visits to Gaul (or perhaps from some other *peregrinus* [pilgrim]) on which either Eddius or Wilfrid himself superimposed the tale of Wilfrid's youthful heroism – satisfying to upholders of Germanic and monastic values alike.[190] The motivation behind this tale need not concern us further, though Wilfrid's later connection with Dagobert II and Eddius's very hostile attitude to Ebroin[190a] are no doubt relevant. Here the point is simply that the *Vita Wilfridi*, and Bede who depends on it, while they explain Balthild's otherwise surprising "bad name in her native country,"[191] need not seriously affect our assessment of Balthild's regency and, more particularly, of her interventions in local politics and her relations with bishops. Ewig has seen "the conflict between Aunemundus and Balthild" as signifying a new development in the Neustro-Burgundian realm: the diocese was changing from an "area associated with an office" to "the area of a lordship" and Balthild, so Ewig implies, was thus engaged in a new struggle against episcopal "territorial politics."[192] I have argued, however, that the fate of Aunemundus was the result rather of a local conflict than of one between centre and province; that Eddius should not be invoked to suggest, as Ewig does, that Aunemundus's case is typical of many others during Balthild's regency; and that the relationship between ruler and *civitas*-politics evident in this case is not a new but a rather traditional one. Evidence of a "structural change" in the seventh century must be sought elsewhere.

One last aspect of Balthild's dealings with the holy, its custodians and interpreters, remains to be considered: her *Klosterpolitik* [monastic policy].[193] Since the evidence for it begins in 655 and continues throughout the regency, we can fairly assume that she was at least partly responsible for it already as Clovis II's queen. The extant text of the privilege of

---

[187]   Levison, *Vita Wilfridi*, pp. 163–4; Ewig, "Teilreiche," p. 95.

[188]   *Vita*, ed. Colgrave, pp. 14–15; Plummer at p. 317 of Bede, *HE*, vol. 2.

[189]   Coville, *Recherches*, p. 389; also Fischer, *Ebroin*, pp. 95–6. But there is a further difficulty in accepting that Wilfrid, if he had really experienced Balthild's malevolence at first hand, could have been consecrated bishop in 664 at the Neustrian royal villa of Compiègne, by courtesy of Clothar III and presumably also Balthild: Bede, *HE* iii, 28, p. 194, with Plummer's notes, vol. 2, pp. 198, 317.

[190]   R. Woolf, "The ideal of men dying with their lord in the *Germania* and in The Battle of Maldon," *Anglo-Saxon England* 5 (1976): 63–81; Graus, *Heiliger*, pp. 63–4, 101.

[190a]   *Vita*, caps 25, 27, 33, pp. 219–20, 228 (Levison); 50, 52, 68 (Colgrave). Poole, "St Wilfrid," pp. 4 seq., notes some inaccuracies in Eddius's information on Frankish affairs.

[191]   Levison, *England*, p. 10. Balthild might have been expected to have had a glowing reputation in England, given the close links of Chelles and Jouarre with various English houses: see A. Lohaus, *Die Merowinger und England, Münchner Beiträge zur Mediavistik und Renaissance-Forschung* (Munich, 1974), pp. 53 seq., and P. Sims-Williams, "Continental influence at Bath monastery in the seventh century," *Anglo-Saxon England* 4 (1975): 1–10.

[192]   Ewig, "Milo," pp. 430–3. (His terms are *Amtsgebiet, Herrschaftsgebiet*, and *Territorialpolitik*.)

[193]   On what follows, Ewig. "Klosterpolitik," is fundamental, as also is his "Beobachtungen zu den Klosterprivilegien des 7. und frühen 8. Jhdts," *Adel und Kirche. Festschrift G. Tellenbach* (Freiburg, 1968), pp. 52–65.

Bishop Landericus for St Denis has been tampered with by later forgers, but its genuine parts can be supplemented by Clovis II's confirmation of it which has survived in the original dated 22 June 655.[194] Clearly the bishop gave up certain rights he had formerly exercised in respect of the monastery: he could no longer exact payment for certain liturgical functions, nor interfere in the disposition of the monastic revenues, nor dip into the monastic treasure. What prompted such substantial concessions of wealth and power? Landericus is explicit enough: he grants his privilege "because the request of the king is for us like a command which it is extremely difficult to resist."[195] During Balthild's regency this episcopal privilege was complemented by a grant of royal immunity, whereby the king took the monastery under his protection and put himself under the saint's protection, in return for releasing the monastery from fiscal obligations and other public services, making it "immune" to the entrance of public officials in the performance of fiscal or judicial functions.[196] What was taking place was a redistribution of resources between three parties, bishop, monastery, and king. The bishop's loss was the monastery's gain: so much the privilege made clear. But when at the same time the monastery became an immunist, the king, while reallocating the burdens of royal administration, could also hope to gain in terms of close, permanent, mutually-beneficial relations with the monastery and more effective control through, for example, royal intervention in abbatial appointments.[197] Finally, and also of vital importance from the king's standpoint, the establishment of the *laus perennis* [liturgy of ceaseless prayer] at St Denis, which Dagobert seems unsuccessfully to have attempted,[198] was achieved in 655 by the introduction there of the *sanctus regularis ordo* [holy order of the Rule], that is, the mixed Benedictine–Columbanan Rule of Luxeuil.[199] The monks' prayers were the instrument by which their royal protector on earth sought the benefits of heavenly protectors: Ewig is surely right to stress the importance "for the court, [of] the cultic-liturgical business of monasticism."[200]

The new arrangements at St Denis not only foreshadowed but provided the model for a whole series of similar ones precisely during Balthild's regency. On the one hand, there were two new foundations: Corbie, founded by Balthild and Clothar III between 657 and 661 and granted a privilege by the bishop of Amiens in 664 at Balthild's "pious request,"[201] and Chelles, effectively refounded on a royal *villa* where Chrodechild (Clovis's queen) had long ago established a little convent of nuns and a church dedicated to St George.[202] For Corbie,

---

[194] Landericus's privilege: [J. M.] Pardessus, [*Diplomata, Chartae . . . et instrumenta aetatis Merovingicae*], 2 vols (Paris, 1843–9) 2, no. 320, pp. 95–7. Clovis II's confirmation: *MGH DD* 1, no. 19, pp. 19–21; facsimile in P. Lauer and C. Samarin, *Les Diplômes originaux des Merovingiens* (Paris, 1908), no. 6.

[195] Pardessus, p. 96: "quia supradicti domni Clodovei regis petitio quasi nobis iussio est, cui difficillimum est resisti."

[196] For the significance of privilege and immunity, see Levillain, "Etudes [sur l'abbaye de Saint-Denis a l'époque mérovingienne]," *BEC* 87 (1926): 21–73. Clothar III's concession of immunity during Balthild's regency is not extant.

[197] Explicitly stated in the privilege of the bishop of Amiens for Corbie, ed. Krusch in *NA* 31 (1906): 367–72 at p. 369: "quem unanimiter congregatio ipsius monasterii . . . dignum elegerint, data auctoritate a praefato principe vel eius successoribus" ["a worthy (abbot) whom the congregation of the monastery will have elected, by the authority granted by said prince and his successors"].

[198] *Fred.* cap. 79, p. 68.

[199] See Prinz, *Mönchtum*, pp. 105–6, 167–9, and Wood, "A prelude to Columbanus", pp. 3–32.

[200] Ewig, "Klosterpolitik," pp. 112–13.

[201] *NA* 31 (1906): 367. *Vita Balthildis* cap. 7, pp. 490–1.

[202] *Vita Balthildis* cap. 7, pp. 489–90, cap. 18, pp. 505–6, *Vita Bertilae*, *MGH SSrM* 6, cap. 4, p. 104.

Balthild had monks and abbot imported from Luxeuil, for Chelles, nuns and abbess from Jouarre. On the other hand there was the reorganization of the communal life of old basilicas by the introduction therein of the *sanctus regularis ordo*. The *Vita Balthildis*, remarkably detailed and explicit on this topic, lists the main basilicas and makes it clear that Balthild's actions were coherent and well-planned – in Ewig's word, a "policy":

> throughout the senior basilicas of the saints, lord Dionisius [St Denis near Paris], lord Germanus [St Germain at Auxerre], and lord Medardus [St Medard at Soissons], and also St Peter [St Pierre-le-Vif at Sens] and lord Anianus [St Aignan at Orléans] and also St Martin [at Tours], and everywhere else that her attention affected, she commanded the bishops and abbots, persuading them for the sake of zeal for God, and directed letters to them to this end, that the brethren settled in these places should live under the holy regular discipline. And in order that they [that is, the brethren] might willingly acquiesce, she ordered that a privilege should be granted them, and at the same time she granted them immunities, so that it might please them the better to pray for the mercy of Christ the highest king of all on behalf of the king and for peace.[203]

If we accept Ewig's plausible suggestion that "everywhere else" probably included St Marcel at Chalon-sur-Saône, St Symphorien at Autun, St Bénigne at Dijon, St Hilary at Poitiers, St Lupus at Troyes and St Sulpicius at Bourges,[204] then with the *Vita's* six we have a list of nearly all the major cult-sites of seventh-century Gaul. Brunhild had cultivated St Martin's patronage and Dagobert St Denis's. But Balthild was mobilizing a whole regiment of saints, enlisting the forces of the holy in every *civitas*. Perhaps still more confidence-inspiring was the placing of such forces right within the *palatium* itself: Clovis II (at Balthild's instigation?) had appropriated the arm of St Denis for the palace-oratory, outraging the monks thus deprived;[205] and it may well have been Balthild herself who acquired St Martin's *cappa* for the royal relic-collection[206] (it is first documented there in 679)[207] though in this case no opposition is recorded. Thus in the burial-places of the royal dead[208] and in the home-base of the living king, direct contacts were made between the Merovingian family and the sources of supernatural power – contacts which superimposed new centripetal forces on a previously localized field.

Playing for such high stakes, Balthild knew the risks she ran. Not every bishop was enthused by the new monasticism; and even if a bishop happily granted privileges to his own

---

Chelles's function of prayer for king, queen, and *proceres* [great men of the kingdom] is stressed by the dying Balthild herself: *Vita*, cap. 12, p. 498, urging the abbess to maintain this "consuetudo, ut ipsa domus Dei bonam famam, quam coeperat, non amitteret, sed amplius semper in affectu caritatis cum omnibus amicis . . . permaneret in dilectione" ["custom, so that this house of God would not let slip the good reputation that it had begun to have, but would always remain more fully in the affection of all its friends"].

[203] *Vita* cap. 9, pp. 493–4.

[204] "Klosterpolitik," p. 111, with n. 43. Balthild's generosity to a group of Norman monasteries in the diocese of Rouen, to Luxeuil and "the other monasteries of Burgundy," to Jouarre and Faremoutiers, and to the monasteries of Paris itself is stressed in *Vita* cap. 8, pp. 493–4, listing forests, *villae*, and *pecuniam innumerabilem* [immeasurable amounts of money].

[205] *LHF* cap. 44, p. 316.

[206] So, Ewig, "Klosterpolitik," p. 112.

[207] *MGH DD* no. 49, p. 45.

[208] Their significance is indicated by Ewig, "Résidence," pp. 48–52.

new foundation in the countryside, it would be naive to assume that he granted the same privileges equally gladly to the ancient basilica on his own doorstep in or by the city.[209] I am struck by the documents' emphasis on the bishop's economic loss, especially the renunciation by Bishop Landericus of what was evidently an existing practice of carrying off from the monastery and into the city gold and silver bullion and cash which had been placed in the monastery.[210] The bishop of Amiens expressly renounced the same practice in the Corbie privilege,[211] but in his case the profit or loss was hypothetical. The bishops of Paris, Auxerre, Soissons, and the rest must have faced a real loss of resources. The *Vita Balthildis* gives no hint of any compensation. For the brethren who served the basilicas, on the other hand, the new obligations Balthild laid on them were offset by new "freedoms" which included financial incentives.[212] Balthild's policy then, might have been expected to arouse opposition, if anywhere, from bishops, which would make royal control of episcopal appointments all the more essential. Perhaps it is in this context that Balthild's "fall" should be understood. Sigobrand, presumably her appointee to the see of Paris, alienated some powerful aristocrats by his *superbia* [pride]:[213] was he trying to recoup some of the losses his see had suffered because of his predecessor Landericus's enforced concessions to St Denis? Did the "commotion" which caused Sigobrand's death signify the limits set by aristocratic interests to Balthild's policy in a situation of fierce competition for scarce resources (especially around Paris)? Balthild's wealth was clearly vast, both in treasure and in land; but had she enough to sustain lavish generosity to monasteries all over Neustria and Burgundy and at the same time to maintain bishops in their powerful yet dependent positions as linchpins of royal government? In the event, the precariousness of her position as mere regent was exposed, and those whom she had "sweetly nurtured" in the palace – including, probably, Ebroin decided to dispense with her. Personal bonds held only so long as they were reinforced by real or prospective benefits. Balthild's regime had not been anti-aristocratic, nor, if she had gained prestige, had she done so at the aristocracy's expense; but their benefits were not apparent. With deadly accurate irony, the "prince," according to Balthild's hagiographer, now "suddenly permitted her"[214] to retire to Chelles which she had so richly endowed. There she died, perhaps in 680, after fifteen years of exemplary humility in the convent;[215] there she

---

[209] Ewig, "Klosterpolitik," p. 109, rightly stresses that bishops might perceive Balthild's demands as "an unheard-of imposition."

[210] *MGH DD* 1, no. 19, p. 20.

[211] *NA* 31 (1906): 369. The broader economic context which these references hint at cannot be discussed here. But for some archaeological and artistic evidence that might suggest continuing Neustrian prosperity, see Maillé, *Jouarre*, pp. 112–14, p. 206 *seq.* and for other evidence, F. Vercauteren, "La vie urbaine entre Meuse et Loire du VIe au IXe siècle," *Spoleto* 6, ii (1959), pp. 453–84 at pp. 478–9.

[212] *Vita Balthildis* cap. 9, pp. 493–4 (quoted above) suggests that the inducements to the *fratres* [brethren] were well-planned: "ut hoc libenter adquiescerent, privilegium eis firmare iussit [!], vel etiam emunitates concessit, ut melius eis delectaret pro rege . . . exorare" [translated above, on p. 248].

[213] Above p. 235, and n. 116.

[214] Above ibid., and p. 235 n. 113. The role of the *sacerdotes* [bishops] at this point is interesting: they intervene, not to save Balthild but to reestablish peace between her and the *seniores* [magnates] and thus to nip in the bud her *non modica querela* (feud?) against them. The implication is that she might have pursued the quarrel even in "retirement."

[215] For the date, see Krusch's introduction to the *Vita*, p. 476. In describing Balthild's convent years, her hagiographer lavishly deploys the motifs of female asceticism: the influence of Venantius's *Vita Radegundis* is clear, and we are assured no less than thrice that Balthild was an *exemplum humilitatis* [model of humility] (caps 11, 12, 16, pp. 496, 498, 502).

soon found her hagiographer and there her memory was kept green and her cult defended against the skeptical.[216]

Balthild had attempted, as Ewig observes, "a structural change in the Merovingian church."[217] But this could not fail to have consequences also for non-ecclesiastical politics. To be sure of this, we need only recall the implications of the Carolingians' *Reichskirche* [imperial Church] for their whole political position, especially in the ninth century when royal exploitation of the Church's resources replaced, to a significant extent, an eroded secular power-base.[218] Ewig thinks that Balthild's fall made her attempted "structural change" quite abortive.[219] I am not so sure. True, we lack the evidence which might show whether or not a Childeric II or even a Theuderic III landed himself and his court more often than his predecessors had done on the hospitality of monastic communities, or used monastic lands to reward trusty warriors, or dipped into monastic treasuries when need arose. We do know, however, that toward the end of the seventh century, there were "organizational connections" between Corbie and the royal chancery[220] and that there were similarly close and continuous links between the ruling dynasty and both St Denis[221] and Chelles.[222] After Balthild, there were still powerful Merovingians – the more powerful, I suggest, because of what she had done. The real threat to such rulers was not bad blood but assassination. Against that the only remedy in the Early Middle Ages, so the Carolingians' experience implies, was the dynastic prestige that came of contact with supernatural power. Precisely that contact was what Balthild had effected so forcefully. But it took time and a more thorough Christianization of Frankish society for sentiments of legitimacy to grow, and so the Carolingians reaped what Balthild had sown. It was apt enough, therefore, than in the time of Louis the Pious, the abbess of Chelles, who was also the emperor's mother-in-law, staged in the imperial presence a splendid *translatio* [formal transfer] of Balthild's remains into a fine new church dedicated to the arch-protectress, the Virgin.[223] Ewig's claim that "not constitutional or political but religious aspects primarily determined [Balthild's] actions"[224] seems to me in one sense a truism, in another misleading. For those "religious" aspects were at one and the same time political: to appropriate relics, to commandeer prayers, to pressurize bishops, to make dependents and allies of urban as well as rural monastic communities – all this was to gain power at once this-worldly and other-worldly. Balthild's tenure of that power was brief, partly, at least, because of the inherent weakness of her position as a mere regent, a married-in woman. But in terms of what she attempted, she must be judged a rarely gifted and creative early medieval politician.

In sketching the careers of Brunhild and Balthild, I have tried to grasp both the fortuitous and the significant in their reputations as "Jezebels." I have therefore had to consider some aspects of royal power and of its interrelations with what in the sixth and seventh centuries

[216] Their existence must be inferred from the reference in the *Vita* cap. 1, p. 482 to *detractores*. In caps 18–19, pp. 505–7, the hagiographer tries to establish Balthild's saintly credentials by setting her in a line of holy queens: Chrodechild, Ultrogotha, and Radegund.
[217] "Klosterpolitik," p. 113.
[218] See C.-R. Brühl, *Fodrum, Gistum, Servitium Regis* (Cologne, 1968), pp. 50 *seq.*
[219] "Klosterpolitik," p. 113.
[220] See Prinz, *Mönchtum*, p. 174 and works cited there, n. 114.
[221] Ewig, "Résidence," p. 52; Levillain, "Etudes," *BEC* 87 (1926): 21–73; 91 (1930): 1–65.
[222] B. Bischoff, "Die Kölner Nonnenhandschriften und das Skriptorium von Chelles," *MStn*, 2 vols (1966), 1, pp. 16 *seq.* at 26–7.
[223] *Translatio Balthildis*, MGH SS 15, pp. 284–5.
[224] "Klosterpolitik," p. 113.

was believed to be the power of the holy. Though we in the twentieth century tend to place these two types of power in separate compartments, it is precisely their interrelations which make for some fundamental continuities in the Merovingian period. If it is hard to make "a clear distinction between religion and politics"[225] in establishing the motivations of Brunhild, Balthild, and their contemporaries, perhaps, without discarding useful categories, rather than seeking lines of division, we should look for points of intersection and ask how far we can understand the religious *as* political, and vice versa, in the Merovingian world. It is in the changing location of such points of intersection that we can find evolution, and a kind of dialectic. In the sixth century, there are important cult-sites mainly in *civitates*, in which royal and episcopal power mutually reinforce each other, in the early seventh century, land-based aristocratic power creates new religious centres in the countryside; and in the mid-seventh century royal power is redefined and extended (in intent, at least) in relation to rural as well as urban centres. Thus from the activities of Brunhild and Balthild, which serve so conveniently to identify two of these three phases, we can make some useful inferences about the modes of Merovingian royal power and its adaptation, by means of new religious forms, to economic and social changes.

Can we also make any useful inferences about women, or about royal women, in the sixth and seventh centuries? There is no simple answer. In comparing her position with that of a female aristocrat, we observed the queen's special character. And while her position had its disadvantages these are hard to attribute specifically to her femininity. The weakness of ineligibility for kingship she shared with all non-Merovingian men; that of the non-institutionalization of her power, with even very powerful male contemporaries, including mayors of the palace. A queen who possessed the right personal qualities could command the loyalty of warriors, and if, as a woman, she could not wield armed force herself, she could direct armies in a strategic sense. Wallace-Hadrill once asked how women could have prosecuted a feud except by using hired assassins;[226] but I have suggested that her grandson's campaign against Clothar II may have been instigated by Brunhild precisely to prosecute her feud against the son of Fredegund. Balthild, on the other hand, used her power most effectively without recourse to armed force. All this prompts the question of whether the exercise in person of command on battlefields was always so indispensable a function of successful early medieval rulership as is usually assumed. Perhaps even a seventh-century Merovingian queen, like a Byzantine emperor (or, in the eighth-century, an empress)[227] or most modern rulers, could either like Brunhild have her battles fought for her, or like Balthild use political as an alternative to military action.

Our discussion of these two queens' careers has indicated less the alleged drawbacks of a woman's position than a kind of strength inherent precisely in its domestic location. A king might win or confirm his power on the battlefield, but he exercised it in the hall, and this we have seen to be the prime area of the queen's activity. Here in the royal *familia* the distribution of food, clothing, charity, the nurturing of the *iuvenes* [young men], the maintenance of friendly relations between the *principes*, the respectful reception of bishops and foreign visitors: all fell to the queen's responsibility. Thus the organization of the household,

---

[225] Ibid., where Ewig himself recognizes the problem.
[226] *Long-Haired Kings*, p. 135. Men, including kings, used assassins sometimes: Gregory and Fredegar give several examples.
[227] See Sir Steven Runciman's paper in the present volume. [Steven Runciman, "The Empress Irene the Athenian," in *Medieval Women*, ed. Derek Baker (Oxford, 1978), pp. 101–18.]

the woman's sphere, became a political function in the case of the *aula regis*. The centrality of *Hausherrschaft* [household lordship] to early medieval kingship has long been recognized.[228] But its implications for the queen's position, perhaps less clearly appreciated hitherto, have emerged in strikingly similar ways in both Brunhild's and Balthild's careers: Brunhild braves even Columbanus's wrath to preserve all the *dignitates* and *honor* that only control of the *aula regis* has given her, while Balthild makes the *palatium* her power-house as long as she controls the network of friendships and clientage that radiates from it. In so far as later Merovingians remained powerful, it was their activity in the palace that made them so. Wallace-Hadrill lists the judgments, the confirmations, the arbitrations, the confiscations and the exemptions which had been, and in the late Merovingian period remained, the peacetime functions of kingship.[229] In all these queens could be active too: Brunhild ransomed captives.[230] Balthild remitted taxes,[231] and behind the dry *diplomata* [royal charters] how often can a queen's influence be suspected? Praejectus owed to Himnechild the favourable outcome of his land-dispute.[232] Indeed episcopal *Stadtherrschaft* [city lordship], and the whole complex of relations between bishops and rulers, need to be linked to the *Hausherrschaft* of kings and queens. When Chilperic sought the support of one bishop against another "traitorous" one, the whole exercise was conducted through face-to-face contact in the palace; and though the king's first move was a threat to sabotage the bishop's local power-base in his own *civitas*, his second was a conciliatory offer of an alfresco snack of specially-cooked chicken and pea soup.[233] If banquets still play an important role in modern diplomacy, how much the more useful instruments were food-prestations and commensality to an early medieval king. The distinction between public and private action becomes redundant in the context of the royal hall. All this explains why in the case of a queen, domestic power could mean political power.[234] Their realization and effective exploitation of this possibility go far to explain the achievements of Brunhild and Balthild.

But in the end, it is not just as female but as royal figures that the pair have commanded our attention. That both were able to function as regents at all is significant. In no other early medieval kingdom did queen regents recurrently rule as they did in the late sixth- and seventh-century *regnum Francorum*.[235] It could be argued that such regencies are symptom-

---

[228] W. Schlesinger, *Beiträge zur deutschen Verfassungsgeschichte des Mittelalters* (Göttingen, 1963), 1, pp. 9 *seq.*, partly translated in F. L. Cheyette, *Lordship and Community in Medieval Europe* (New York, 1968), pp. 64 *seq.*

[229] *Long-Haired Kings*, pp. 237–8.

[230] Paulus Diaconus, *Historia Langobardorum* iv, 1, *MGH SSrL*, p. 116.

[231] *Vita* cap. 6, p. 488: the capitation-tax had apparently been causing parents to prefer infanticide to rearing offspring, so Balthild by removing, the *impia consuetudo* [impious custom] also removed the inducement to an impious crime. Her financial loss would of course be compensated by a *copiosa merces* of a heavenly kind.

[232] *Passio Praejecti* cap. 24. *MGH SSrM* 5, pp. 239–40.

[233] *LH* v, 18, pp. 219–20.

[234] This equation, and its relevance to the queen's position, was made explicitly by Hincmar in reference to ninth-century *palatium* organization, in his *De Ordine Palatii* cap 22, *MGH Capit.* 2, p. 525: "De honestate vero palatii seu specialiter ornamento regali necnon et *de donis annuis militum* . . . ad reginam praecipue et sub ipsa ad camerarium pertinebat" ["Regarding the riches of the palace and especially the royal ornaments, not to mention the annual gifts of the warriors, these pertain above all to the queen and, under her, the chamberlain"]. Thus the king could be freed "ab omni sollicitudine *domestica vel palatina*" ["from all domestic and courtly cares"] to turn his mind to the *status regni* [state of the Kingdom]! Here again, Carolingian arrangements show continuity with Merovingian.

[235] The contrast with seventh-century England was noted by Wallace-Hadrill, *Early Germanic Kingship in England and on the Continent* (Oxford, 1971), p. 92.

atic of aristocratic power. For whereas elective monarchy tends to produce a sequence of mature kings who may consolidate royal power at the expense of their magnates (and even of many magnates' lives'),[236] hereditary monarchy, with son(s) succeeding father, though it may exclude princes who had hitherto been eligible, in practice ensures that there will be minorities during which those princes and other magnates can collaborate with the queen-mother in ruling the kingdom. On this view the regimes of Brunhild and Balthild would represent the product of aristocratic interests. But the very fact that those interests are centred still on the royal *palatium* suggests that our queens' regencies are also symptomatic of dynastic strength. The long-term Merovingian monopoly of Frankish kingship should be explained primarily in terms of concentrations of monarchic power from Clovis to Sigibert and Chilperic, and during the reigns of Clothar II and Dagobert, and only secondarily in terms of aristocratic reactions to that power. If magnates exploited minorities, they did not create the conditions for them: filial succession became normal as a consequence of the activity and the will of kings.

The careers of Brunhild and Balthild, therefore, highlight the Merovingians' monopoly of kingship, as well as some of the modes and potential resources of royal government in the Frankish realm which made that monopoly possible and conditioned its operation in practice. The extent of these queens' political success thus helps confirm what the work of Ewig and others have shown of the fundamental structures of Merovingian politics in *palatium* and *civitas*. At the same time, Brunhild and Balthild focus our attention on the ebb and flow of power through those structures, on the dynamic relationships and the personalities that shaped the course of Merovingian history. Both queens, acting in areas of life dominated by men, were depicted as having masculine traits: Brunhild defied a posse of armed enemies *viriliter*[237] – "like a man" – while to Balthild was attributed that most manly of virtues – *strenuitas* [energy].[238] Each ruled like a Merovingian, with a Merovingian's authority. Each earned the ill-name of "Jezebel" in certain quarters not because female rulership was seen as a monstrous incongruity but because these particular rulers in the exercise of their power offended particular influential men. If we want to redress the gross unfairness of their posthumous reputations, we shall do them less than justice to consider them *only* as women. Like their contemporary female saints[239] – or like any climber of the Matterhorn – they are distinguished as *homines*: as human beings.

---

[236] For the spectacular bloodbath following the accession of the Visigothic king Chindaswinth in 641, see *Fred.* cap. 82, pp. 69–70. On the differing consequences of indeterminate and hereditary father-son succession, see Goody, *Succession*, pp. 29 *seq.*; compare also the remarks of Pauline Stafford, ["Sons and Mothers: Family Politics in the Middle Ages," in Baker, *Medieval Women*,] pp. 79–100. I am grateful to John Gillingham for discussion of this point.

[237] *LH* vi, 4, p. 268.

[238] *LHF* cap. 43, p. 315: "pulchram omnique ingenio *strenuam*" ["beautiful and *energetic* in every skill"]. Compare *Vita Bertilae* cap. 4, *MGH SSrM* 6, p. 104: "[Baltechildis] ... *viriliter* gubernabat palatium" ["Balthild ruled the palace like a man"].

[239] See the evidence assembled by Kurth, *Etudes Franques*, 1, pp. 161–7, for women *homines* in Merovingian texts.

14 Women and the Norman Conquest

Pauline Stafford

Anglo-Saxon England has [been seen as] a Golden Age variously of women's domestication, women's legal emancipation, women's education, and women's sexual liberation. The length of a tradition which has changed so fundamentally [as it has been dealt with by various historians] over time is no guarantee of its veracity. A cursory view of a range of evidence from either side of the 1066 divide casts immediate doubt on the idea of a brutal Norman ending of the Golden Age. The raw statistics of Domesday, for example, suggest a different picture of England on the eve of the Norman arrival. No more than 5 percent of the total hidage of land recorded was in the hands of women in 1066. Of that 5 percent, 80–85 percent was in the hands of only eight women, almost all of them members of the families of the great earls, particularly of earl Godwine, or of the royal family.[1] By the tenth and eleventh centuries women other than the queen are virtually absent from the witness lists of the royal charters,[2] and thus apparently from the political significance such witness lists record.

By contrast, Norman and Anglo-Norman women strike an early English historian by the range and prominence of their activity. In Musset's edition of the acts of William the Conqueror and Matilda for the abbeys of Caen, for example, 30 documents are printed. Twenty-three of them mention women either as signatories, grantors, consenting to grants, or as involved in some way in the making of the grant.[3] No collection of pre-1066 English documents shows the same proportions.[4] Twelfth-century Anglo-Norman charters regu-

---

[1.20] Figures calculated by M. A. Meyer, "Women's Estates in later Anglo-Saxon England: the politics of possession," *Haskins Society Journal*, Studies in Medieval History, ed. R. B. Patterson, III (1991), pp. 111–29, at 113–17.

[2.21] Queens as witnesses: A. Campbell, ed., *Encomium Emmae Reginae*, Camden Soc., 3rd ser., LXXII (1949), appendix 2; F. Barlow, *Edward the Confessor* (London, 1970), pp. 77, 93, 163 and S. Keynes, *The Diplomas of King Æthelred "the Unready", 978–1016* (Cambridge, 1980), p. 187. Note in addition the witness list of S 582 [S = P. H. Sawyer, *Anglo-Saxon Charters, an annotated list and bibliography* (London, 1968)] where Ælfgyth *magistra* of Wilton witnessed a charter of AD 955 in favour of the nuns of Wilton.

[3.22] L. Musset, ed., *Les Actes de Guillaume le Conquérant et de la Reine Mathilde pour les Abbayes Caennaises*, Memoires de la Société des Antiquaires de Normandie, XXXVII (Caen, 1967), nos 2–16, 18–22, 25, 27. No. 17 is a list of parishioners of Bourg l'Abbé, including six women out of some 67/68 people. The above list includes many *signa* [signatures or marks in lieu of them] and activities of Queen Matilda, but also covers many transactions involving other women. I am grateful to Dr David Bates for pointing out the utility of the Caen charters for the study of women.

[4.23] The *Libellus Æthelwold* is the only English collection which approaches this for evidence of female activity. Like the Norman charters, it covers private grants and disputes rather than royal. Forthcoming edition by S. Keynes; see for the present *Liber Eliensis*, ed. E. O. Blake, Camden Soc., 3rd Ser., XCII (1962).

larly record the consent of wives, of mothers, and sometimes even of daughters to land grants. It was only after 1066 that an English king attempted to arrange the succession for his daughter. Henry I should not be remembered in women's history as the English king who produced more known bastards than any other, but as the man who tried to pass the throne to his daughter Matilda.[5] He may well have been the first English king to put down in written form the right of a daughter to inherit land.[6]

This evidence sits ill with a periodization which would see 1066 and the coming of the Normans as heralding a decline in women's status. As does the career of such a Norman woman as Mabel, daughter of Talvas, heiress of Bellême in the eleventh century. The mothering of nine children did not prevent her from actively defending her inheritance, traveling, we are told, with a retinue of 100 armed men when necessary. She seized at least one castle and disposed of rivals, accidentally poisoning her own brother-in-law in the process. She was finally murdered, resting after her bath, by a man whom she had deprived of land. Her death, Orderic tells us, occasioned rejoicing at her ruin. Her epitaph described her as "A shield of her inheritance, a tower guarding the frontier; to some neighbours dear, to others terrible. She died by the sword, by night, by stealth, for we are mortals all. . . . Pray for her." It was not her low-status activities which called for such intercession.[7] All this evidence needs careful interpretation and discussion. None of it speaks transparently about the status of women as a group or as individuals. Yet it begs for reconsideration of the tradition of seeing pre-1066 England as a sort of Golden Age of women and of deterioration with the arrival of the Normans.

That tradition unites two important Golden Ages, that of high-status Germanic women and of the Norman Yoke on Anglo-Saxon liberties. High-status Germanic women dated back to first-century Rome. The idea of Anglo-Saxon liberties goes back to the seventeenth century. The two traditions made ideal partners in the context of nineteenth-century Teutonism. The status of women had already emerged in the late eighteenth and early nineteenth centuries as a litmus test of civilization and a marker for change and

---

[5.24] The most recent discussion of Matilda's claim and Henry's plans is Marjorie Chibnall, *The Empress Matilda*[: *Queen Consort, Queen Mother and Lady of the English*] (Oxford, 1991), pp. 50–3. Gilbert Foliot, abbot of Gloucester, felt able in 1142–3 to make a case for a daughter's inheritance based on divine, natural, and human law which is unparalleled pre-1066. Chibnall, *Empress Matilda*, pp. 84–7 discusses this letter and its arguments. It is printed in *The Letters and Charters of Gilbert Foliot*, ed. A. Morey and C. N. L. Brooke (Cambridge, 1967), pp. 60–6. [. . .]

[6.25] This is how the implications of the *Statutum Decretum* may be interpreted. This lost royal decision, referred to as a *Statutum Decretum* in *Regesta Regum Anglo-Normannorum*, iii, ed. H. A. Cronne and R. H. C. Davis (Oxford, 1967), p. 39, no. 106, was concerned with the division of land among daughters. Cf. S. F. C. Milsom, "Inheritance by women in the twelfth and thirteenth centuries," in *On the Laws and Customs of England, Essays in Honor of S. E. Thorne*, ed. M. S. Arnold, T. A. Green, S. A. Scully, and S. D. White (Chapel Hill, 1981), pp. 77–8. Milsom remarked that "it took some step beyond Henry I's coronation charter in establishing female inheritance itself." J. C. Holt, "The heiress and the alien," *TRHS*, ser. 5, XXXV (1985): 11–14 argues convincingly for a date for this decision between 1130 and 1135. M. Chibnall, *Anglo-Norman England* (Oxford, 1986), p. 174 sees it as the preservation of traditional custom rather than deliberate change. What it did provide was the first recorded written acceptance of daughters' inheritance. It is worth speculating whether such a change was politically important to Henry I in securing the throne for his daughter.

[7.26] V. Chandler, "Intimations of authority: notes on three Anglo-Norman countesses," *Indiana Social Studies Quarterly* (1978): 5–17; Orderic Vitalis, *The Ecclesiastical History*, ed. M. Chibnall, esp. vol. 3, bk 5 (Oxford, 1972), pp. 134–8 for her death and epitaph.

periodization.[8] It pleased Kemble that his admired Teutonic ancestors, the Anglo-Saxons, treated their women better than the French Normans.[9] The Saxons never purchased their wives in the "truly gross and vulgar sense of such purchases among those whom writers of Romances represent as the chivalrous Normans." In claiming a loss of status for women at this alleged critical turning point of English history, [Florence] Buckstaff [writing in the 1890s,] made overt what Kemble left implicit. Women's status was linked to the idea of 1066 as a turning point of great significance, to a view of Anglo-Saxon England as the land of lost content, and to a debate long framed in legal and constitutional terms. Were it not for that critical tradition, late eleventh- and twelfth-century women might have been seen differently and the period before 1066 would not have been treated as a unity in women's, nor in any other area of English history.[10]

Writing, whether about Germanic, Anglo-Saxon, or Anglo-Saxon and Norman women, has always been in the context of debate – the history of women has been written when "women" and their status were issues.[11] Although the tradition has developed with the advancing state of the evidence,[12] the most fundamental differences lie not in the evidence but in the criteria used for the definition of status. All have been in agreement that Anglo-Saxon women were of high status; they differ in what they understand by "high status." All the writers quoted were responding in some way to a "woman-question," in which the subject of the question has already been generalized as "woman."[13] Change after 1066 has been the explicit formulation of the question; questions about status and women have often been left insidiously implicit or unasked. Some historians were aware of the problems of these terms. Doris Stenton carefully restricted her comments about deterioration to upper-

---

[8.27] Thus, for example, Fourier, "As a general proposition: social advances and changes of period are brought about by virtue of the progress of women towards liberty and social retrogression occurs as a result of a diminution in the liberty of women. . . . The extension of privileges to women is the fundamental cause of all social progress." *Théorie des Quatre Mouvements et des Destinées Générales* (Paris, 1846), in *The Utopian Vision of Charles Fourier*, ed. J. Beecher and R. Bienvenu (London, 1972), pp. 195–6.

[9.28] [J. M. Kemble, *The Saxons in England: A History of the English Commonwealth till the Period of the Norman Conquest* (London, 1849)], vol. II, p. 97. For Kemble's commitment to German scholarship and his correspondence with Jakob Grimm see R. A. Wiley, "Anglo-Saxon Kemble: the life and works of John Mitchell Kemble, 1805–1857, philologist, historian, archaeologist," *Anglo-Saxon Studies in Archaeology and History*, BAR British Ser., LXXII (Oxford, 1979): 165–273.

[10.29] I shall be concerned particularly with the questions of "status" and "women." It should also be pointed out that "Anglo-Saxon" is an equally debatable term in this tradition. Abbess Hilda from the seventh century is too readily cited alongside the landholding women of the tenth and eleventh centuries in a common category "Anglo-Saxon women," which does little justice to the differing circumstances necessary to an understanding of either.

[11.30] B. A. Hanawalt, "Golden Ages for the history of medieval English women," in *Women in Medieval History and Historiography*, ed. S. M. Stuard (Philadelphia, 1987), pp. 1–24. For a similar history of writing about Greek women see M. Katz, "Ideology and 'the Status of Women' in Ancient Greece," *History and Theory* XXXI (1992): 70–97.

[12.31] If Doris Stenton's views [Stenton wrote in the 1950s] differ from those of Kemble, it is in large part because of the growth of knowledge of legal and social history in the intervening years. The evidence on which so many of these statements, particularly since Kemble, have been based requires careful consideration, not blanket rejection.

[13.32] For the question of whether there can or should be a history of women see D. Riley, *Am I That Name, Feminism and the Category of "Women" in History* (London, 1988), H. Bloch, *Medieval Misogyny and the Invention of Western Romantic Love* (Chicago, 1991), Introduction.

class women, and Eileen Power asked whether there was such a thing as "the position of medieval women."[14] Their caution is essential.

If Anglo-Saxon England was an age of high status for women, which women are we discussing? Noble women only? Noble daughters, wives, or widows? An individual noble woman in a particular family context? Was there any common legal status of daughters, wives, or widows which would encourage such generalization? And if there was, should we not allow for the enormous variation which a particular legal framework allows as it intersects with political, economic, and individual family situations?

If Anglo-Saxon England was a period of high status for women, how do we judge that status? Of its nature the tradition has no agreed set of criteria, nor have modern historians. Should we judge by landholding rights, or by power through the family?[15] Since different statuses need not coincide, these approaches are not necessarily mutually exclusive.[16] Perhaps no agreed set of criteria is possible as long as the "status of women" is a live political issue. But can we proceed by bundling all existing ones together when the criteria themselves are debatable, when few are transparent guides to status? When Marjorie Chibnall states that Norman and Anglo-Norman women were "effective and powerful by virtue of their position in the family," she does not have in mind that sacred and separate family sphere which underlies Kemble's ideology. For her and others, it is precisely the lack of that clear distinction of public and private spheres which allows, if not requires, women like Mabel of Bellême to be both the mother of nine children and the active shield of her inheritance.[17] We must ask not merely was 1066 a turning point, but were women a group and how is status to be measured.

Since Buckstaff much debate has centered on landholding and legal questions, the long-standing terms of the 1066 debate. Although some have continued to speak of "women," the central issue has been the status of *noble*women as landholders. The social, economic, legal, and political similarities of this group have justified some generalization of them. But it can be questioned whether the legal and political framework of this group and its landholding

---

[14.33] [D. M. Stenton, *The English Woman in History* (London, 1956), p. 348] and Eileen Power's opening remarks in "The position of women," in *The Legacy of the Middle Ages*, ed. G. C. Crump and E. F. Jacob (Oxford, 1926), p. 401, reprinted in her *Medieval Women*, ed. M. M. Postan (Cambridge, 1975).

[15.34] Stenton, e.g., judges by landholding and legal rights. Marjorie Chibnall, "Women in Orderic [Vitalis," *Haskins Society Journal*, II (1990)]: 120 and n., has recently criticized this approach for a failure to take account of status within or through the family.

[16.35] For the problems of measuring female status H. Moore, *Feminism and Anthropology* (Cambridge, 1988), ch. 2; S. C. Rogers, "Woman's place: a critical review of anthropological theory," *Comparative Studies in Society and History*, XX (1978): 122–62; discussion in C. Meyers, *Discovering Eve, Ancient Israelite Women in Context* (Oxford, 1988), pp. 33–7 and P. Reeves Sanday, *Female Power and Male Dominance, on the Origins of Sexual Inequality* (Cambridge, 1981), pp. 114, 120–1, 163, etc.

[17.36] Chibnall, ["Women in Orderic Vitalis," p. 120]. For Kemble, the family was the private world in which women belonged. The more recent views of, e.g., J. McNamara and S. Wemple, "The power of women through the family in medieval Europe," in *Clio's Consciousness Raised*, ed. M. Hartmann and L. W. Banner (New York, 1974) and much reprinted, or P. Stafford, "Sons and mothers, family politics in the early middle ages," in *Medieval Women*, ed. D. Baker (Oxford, 1978), pp. 79–100 take issue openly or implicitly with the idea of a clear public/private distinction in the Early Middle Ages. For specific discussion of this issue see J. Nelson, "Review Article, The problematic in the private," *Social History*, XV (1990): 355–64.

changed dramatically in and after 1066, whether they can be generalized as a group, and whether their landholding can be translated simply into their status.

Over the past 20 years and more Professor Holt's work has brilliantly demonstrated the dialogue of royal power, noble inheritance, family organization, and politics in the Anglo-Norman period.[18] From 1066, or more correctly from 1087, he sees a situation where challenge to noble inheritance was possible, where there was significant royal interference in that inheritance opened up by distant and debatable claims, but chiefly by the political incentive for the king to intervene, and at the same time where the means to resist that intervention existed. All this left noble inheritance in a state of flux and flexibility not ended until 1154 and after. Henry I's coronation charter and Magna Carta were major statements in this dialogue, the mid-century civil war its violent expression. The results of this for noble women were diverse. Both families and king sought to control their inheritance and marriage. But, between the two, some individual women were able to act more independently. Both Holt and Doris Stenton have hailed Magna Carta clauses 7 and 8, and the earlier proffers a widow made to the king to choose her fate, as steps forward in the legal emancipation of English women.[19] This dialogue was older than 1066; royal intervention begins as early as the late ninth century; already succession dispute and foreign invasion allowed noble resistance, already attempts were being made to find agreements on this issue between the king and other groups.[20] What were the ramifications of this for women?

There is evidence to suggest that the king was already interfering in noble marriage by 1016 and before. Cnut's laws forbade the marrying-off of widows and demanded that women consent to marriages; this implies that some widows and daughters at least were married off without their consent.[21] Cnut's statement comes in a section dealing with the abuses of the king's power and, by extension, that of other lords.[22] Individual cases reinforce the view that Cnut was dealing here with an established practice of royal intervention in noble marriage.

In the mid-tenth century Ælfgar ealdorman of Essex left two daughters as his heirs. I deliberately do not state that he had no sons; we do not know. The wills of Ælfgar himself and of the two women concerned have survived.[23] The elder daughter, Æthelflæd, married first the king, Edmund, and then a south Midlands ealdorman; the younger, Ælfflæd, married Ælfgar's replacement as ealdorman of Essex, Byrhtnoth, an incomer sent to Essex

---

[18.37] J. C. Holt, "Feudal society and the family, I to IV," *TRHS*, ser. 5, 32–5 (1982–5); his "Politics and property in early medieval England," *PP* LVII (1972): 3–52, and *Magna Carta* (Cambridge, 1965).

[19.38] Holt, *Magna Carta*, p. 46 saw the proffers by which widows gained some freedom of choice in marriage as "one of the first great stages in the emancipation of women," though as J. S. Loengard remarked, much depends on the size of the proffer, "'Of the gift of her husband': English dower and its consequences in the year 1200," in *Women of the Medieval World*, ed. J. Kirshner and S. Wemple (Oxford, 1985), p. 235n. Doris Stenton, *The English Woman in History*, p. 51 hailed Magna Carta clause 8 as a "tentative beginning of the emancipation of English women from the legal subservience which had followed the Norman Conquest."

[20.39] P. Stafford, "The Laws of Cnut and the history of Anglo-Saxon royal promises," *Anglo-Saxon England*, ed. P. Clemoes et al., X (1981), pp. 173–90 and *Unification and Conquest, a Political and Social History of England in the Tenth and Eleventh Centuries* (1989), especially chs 2, 8, 9, 10.

[21.40] II Cnut 73 and 74, printed in F. Liebermann, *Die Gesetze der Angelsachsen* (Halle, 1903–16), vol. I, and with translation in A. J. Robertson, ed., *The Laws of the Kings of England from Edmund to Henry I* (Cambridge, 1925).

[22.41] I have argued a case for seeing Cnut's laws as, if not a coronation charter, at least the expression of a political agreement between king and nobles in "The Laws of Cnut."

[23.42] D. Whitelock. *Anglo-Saxon Wills* (Cambridge, 1930), nos 2, 14, 15.

by the king. Ælfgar's will made his daughters great heiresses, but also tied their inheritances to grandchildren, and in the event of failure of heirs, provided for reversion to the Church. The case strongly suggests the manipulation of female inheritance in political ways. Did Byrhtnoth have the good fortune to fall in love with one of the richest women in Essex, or was pressure involved in the marriage of the daughter of one ealdorman to his successor?[24] Was that pressure the king's? Did royal pressure extend to pressure on the father to endow his two daughters so liberally? Can we even rule out a choice of women as heirs with a view to such important marriages? The difficulty of reconstructing the full circumstances of tenth-century documents make all these hypotheses. But it would be unwise to assume that the Normans brought to England the practice of the king or others manipulating the inheritance and marriages of noble women.[25] One of the grand narratives of medieval social history, that of the interaction of lord, family, and inheritance, was already in place.

Some noble families were already reacting by attempting to tie up future inheritance, to see women as conduits of land rather than as heirs. Ælfgar tied the succession of his land via his daughters to his grandchildren, and in their absence, to the Church. Ælfgar was passing his inheritance in the direct female line at the expense of collateral male heirs and attempting to ensure the next stage of that direct succession.[26] He was doing so under possible pressure of external interference, perhaps in fear of future interference to the detriment of his direct heirs. He was simultaneously using the protection of that external power, the king, to secure such a narrowing of the inheritance. Post-1066 historians might call this a shift toward patrilineal primogeniture and the narrowing of the inheriting family to the direct heirs in each generation.

[24.43] The witness lists indicate a gap between Ælfgar and Byrhtnoth, but the idea of a politically arranged marriage is not thereby invalidated. The king may have had plans for Ælfgar's daughters, including his own marriage to one of them, whilst their father was ealdorman, and his plans may have included the future succession of the ealdormanry. Ælfgar's disappearance from the witness lists does not necessarily argue for his death, and if there was an ealdorman whose office separates that of Ælfgar and Byrhtnoth, the appointment of a new man and his marriage to a woman whose landholding has been confirmed for his benefit may mark renewed royal intervention in Essex. We may be misled in seeing a tenth- or eleventh-century will as a simple arrangement of post-obit bequests rather than the confirmation of a series of gifts and arrangements, some already made *inter vivos*, dowry possibly among them.

[25.44] Two cases in the *Chronicon Abbatiae Ramesiensis*, ed. W. D. Macray, Rolls Series (1886), p. 49, where Archbishop Oda received lands for petitioning Eadred that Edwyn might marry the daughter of Ulf, and p. 135, where a follower of Cnut receives royal permission to marry an English widow. For another probable case see A. Williams, "The king's nephew: the family and career of Ralph, earl of Hereford." *Studies in Medieval History Presented to R. Allen Brown*, ed. C. Harper Bill, C. Holdsworth, and J. Nelson (Woodbridge, 1989), pp. 327–43. Williams sees Ralph's English fortunes founded on an advantageous arranged marriage. Her identification of his wife Gytha links her with a family which certainly had male members and thus potential male heirs in 1066. A choice of the woman as heir followed by her marriage to a royal relative seems possible here. J. Nelson, "Commentary on the papers of J. Verdon, S. F. Wemple and M. Parisse," in *Frauen in Spätantike und Frühmittelalter, Lebensbedingungen – Lebensnormen – Lebensformen*, ed. W. Affeldt (Sigmaringen, 1990), p. 332 suggests Alfred may already have been interfering in the fate of noble women, directing them, for example, to nunneries.

[26.45] Cf one of the earliest wills, that of ealdorman Alfred in the late ninth century, ed. F. Harmer, *Select English Historical Documents of the Ninth and Tenth Centuries* (Cambridge, 1914), no. 10 for a similar attempt to pass land to a female heir in the direct line, but allowing for the repurchase of the land by paternal relatives in the event of her failure to produce an heir. This case is muddied by the existence of a son whom some have argued as illegitimate.

Ælfgar negotiated all this in his will, with the agreement of the king. Already the dialogue of noble inheritance and royal power was producing individual agreements, and by 1016 collective ones. The prehistory of Magna Carta should include not only the coronation charter of Henry I after 1066, but before that date the laws of Cnut, the specific agreements recorded in the shire and borough customs in Domesday which derive in part or in whole from the pre-Conquest situation,[27] and arguably the wills of the tenth century. This series of agreements between individual nobles and the king, between noble, shire, and town communities and English kings, chart the painful evolution of inheritance toward closer definition in the face of royal interference.

When those agreements were collective, "women," or at least groups of women, were generalized: widows and unmarried women in the laws of Cnut; widows in the coronation charter of Henry I;[28] daughters in families without direct male heirs in the mid-twelfth-century *statutum decretum*.

But turning from collective agreements to individual royal interventions, before or after 1066, a more complex picture emerges in which individual women benefit and lose. Royal interference worked both for and against noble women. The king intervened to ensure the successful outcome of the widow Æthelgifu's dispute over dower in the tenth century, at a price.[29] And for an even higher price Henry I allowed Countess Lucy to administer her own lands in the late 1120s.[30] The king guaranteed many of the women's wills from the tenth and eleventh centuries, after suitable payment.[31] But the king's involvement in inheritance and land dispute worked differently for different women. Whilst some benefited from protection of their wills or intervention in land dispute on their behalf, others lost. In the 990s, Æthelred II refused to accept the heriot or death payment proffered by one noble widow for the control of some or all of her husband's lands.[32] Her husband was accused of treason. The truth of the accusation cannot be known, though the delay in prosecution of the case until the widow came forward is suspicious. The woman was forced to seek an advocate, the archbishop of Canterbury, and paid for his support in loss of land. This noble widow was vulnerable to the king's intervention and had to relinquish land to gain a powerful protector.

None of these examples supports a simple statement about high or low status for women, before or after 1066. The series of collective agreements shows some definition of groups of

---

[27.46] Stafford, "The Laws of Cnut"; S. Reynolds, "Towns in Domesday," *Domesday Studies*, ed. J. C. Holt (Woodbridge, 1987) pp. 295–309; and P. Stafford, *Unification and Conquest*[: *a Political and Social History of England in the Tenth and Eleventh Centuries* (London,] 1989), chapter on "Ruling the Kingdom," and pp. 213, 159–61.

[28.47] Coronation Charter of Henry I, caps 3 and 4, *Stubbs Select Charters*, 9th ed. (Oxford, 1913), p. 118.

[29.48] *Will of Æthelgifu*, ed. D. Whitelock, Roxburgh Club (Oxford, 1968).

[30.49] *Magnum Rotulum Scaccarii vel magnum rotulum pipae de anno tricesimo primo regni Henrici Primi*, ed. J. Hunter (London, 1833), p. 110.

[31.50] The similarity between such payments and proffers for dower after 1066 would bear exploration. Few women testators proffered the heriot [a type of inheritance dues], which was the normal payment made by men, but most proffered some combination of land and cash to the king, and occasionally to the queen. The relevance of the queen to noble women's landholding in the tenth century and the significance of heriot in gender definition are issues to which I hope to return elsewhere.

[32.51] Whitelock, *Wills*, no. 16.2. It is not clear whether Ætheric's widow was seeking all his land, or merely her dower. The outcome involved her gift of her morning-gift to Christ Church Canterbury, and it may be that it was chiefly this and her dower with which she was concerned.

women, as heiresses, or as widows, which legitimizes a qualified discussion of at least "noble women" in a general way. That series begins before 1066 and the stimulus to definition was a debate over inheritance and women as carriers of it forced in large part by royal intervention, which spanned the tenth to twelfth centuries. The individual cases, however, illustrate the difficulty of generalizing the impact even of a specific factor, here royal intervention in inheritance, for a specific social group, noble widows. The collective agreements may allow us to speak of the "rights" of widows or heiresses, though with the heavy qualifications such a statement must have before the existence of a legal profession. Either side of 1066 we are dealing with the implications for noble women of a flexible legal situation[33] and of royal interference within it. If a turning point is to be sought, and all such are debatable, it might be found in the restriction of flexibility in inheritance of the late twelfth century; in the working of the possessory assizes and the attempts at legal standardization.[34]

Tracing the relationships of individual noble women with kings also reveals the importance of family circumstances in understanding their lives. The paucity of evidence for the period before 1066 makes family reconstruction and history almost impossible. Where reconstruction can be achieved, its critical importance in interpreting what is happening becomes clear. My discussion of the family of Ælfgar of Essex was speculative; ironically 1066 itself, a foreign conquest, allows the fullest examination of individual family circumstances. The Norman Conquest had a dramatic effect on the production and survival of documents. The early English noblewomen whom we can see most clearly are those who lived on either side of and in the thick of these great events.

Domesday Book shows how far women's enrichment paralleled that of their families in general; the widows of earls Harold and Godwine stand out from the rest. Domesday and the fuller chronicle sources reveal how far women shared the fate of their families. Gytha, Godwine's widow and Harold's mother, was rapidly dispossessed – perhaps as Harold's mother, perhaps for her support of her grandsons in rebellion. Earl Leofric's widow and daughter-in-law, by contrast, seem to have retained some of their lands for longer, mirroring the political fortunes of their sons and grandsons.[35] Women, even of the same social group, are divided by the differing fortunes of the families of which they form part.

Women are also individuals, more than the expression of roles within families. No eleventh-century evidence permits a full assessment of individual action, but the sources after 1066 provide tantalizing glimpses. Gytha, Godwine's widow and Harold's mother, carved a political role for herself. She sought her dead son's body, supported her grandsons, was involved in rebellion and then went into exile in Flanders, the traditional retreat of eleventh-century English malcontents; from there she appears to have contacted other of William's enemies in Scandinavia.[36] Her actions were those of a mother, of a widow, of an eleventh-century English noble; of Harold's mother, and Godwine's widow and a Scandinavian noble woman; of an individual woman at a particular critical point in eleventh-century history. Her career demonstrates those family roles which shaped and allowed women's

[33.52] [See Stafford, "Women and the Norman Conquest"] n. 75 for more discussion of the legal framework.
[34.53] S. F. C. Milsom, "Inheritance by women in the twelfth and thirteenth centuries," *On the Laws and Customs of England*, ed. M. S. Arnold et al. (Chapel Hill, 1981), pp. 60–89 and *The Legal Framework of English Feudalism* (Cambridge, 1976).
[35.54] P. Stafford, "Women in Domesday," *Medieval Women in Southern England*, Reading Medieval Studies, XV (Reading, 1989), pp. 75–94.
[36.55] The fullest account of Gytha remains the various references in vols I to IV of E. A. Freeman, *The History of the Norman Conquest of England, its Causes and Results* (Oxford, 1870–9).

actions, roles which remain constant over a long historical period which spans 1066.[37] It demonstrates those roles within a specific family and political context. But it strongly suggests that an active individual woman seized, utilized, and developed the opportunities of her roles and her context. Gytha is no proof of the specially high status of Old English noble women. To generalize her even as "Anglo-Saxon noble woman," let alone as "Anglo-Saxon woman," is to do some violence to historical understanding.

Either side of 1066 noble women had claim to land as heiresses, and often held it as widows. It is not easy to move from such a statement to an assessment of their status. The situation of the heiress exemplifies this. Shifts towards patrilineal primogeniture and the narrowing of the inheriting family to direct heirs produces heiresses. There is a constant proportion of failures in the direct male line; as the claims of collateral males were restricted, so the likelihood of female heirs increases.[38] The Empress Matilda's claim on the English throne is the most obvious example. It resulted from a desire to cut out collateral heirs, in this case Henry I's nephews, coupled with the accidental death of her only legitimate brother in the disaster of the White Ship.

Does the heiress's land make her a high-status woman? The more land a woman holds the more likely she is to be controlled and manipulated by male relatives or lords.[39] This point is readily conceded for the pathetic heiresses of the High Middle Ages, passed from hand to hand and bed to bed as the pawns of male politics. What reason is there to suppose that heiresses before 1066 were any different? Indeed Ælfgar's daughters suggest the similarities. Before and after 1066 women had claims on land which could make them vulnerable and manipulable. Their claims could also be challenged or overridden. If the Empress Matilda was the greatest English heiress of the twelfth century, she did not secure her inheritance. Her cousin Stephen was crowned king. Direct primogeniture was far from triumphing over collateral claims when the direct heir was a woman, on either side of 1066. About AD 1000 the great midland noble, Wulfric Spott, passed over his daughter and left the bulk of his land to his brother, nephews, and Burton abbey; so much for the special position of Anglo-Saxon women. It is easy to see the heiress as victim, not a high-status woman.

But that is too simple. Æthelflæd and Ælfflæd may have been manipulated heiresses in their youth, but they made wills which show at least a limited freedom of action over their inheritance as widows. Matilda's failure to secure coronation does scant justice to the impact of her claim to the throne on her life. That claim legitimized and allowed extensive political, even military, activity. It affected her relationship with her sons, if not with her husband Geoffrey.[40] It is impossible to generalize to all heiresses from Matilda or from Æthelflæd; it

[37.56] P. Stafford, "Sons and Mothers," and *Queens, Concubines and Dowagers, the King's Wife in the Early Middle Ages* (London, 1983). There are important similarities in the opportunities which the roles of wife, widow, and mother allow women throughout the medieval period as the growing literature on noble and royal women demonstrates, e.g. J. Ward, *English Noblewomen in the Later Middle Ages* (London, 1992); M. K. Jones and M. G. Underwood, *The King's Mother, Lady Margaret Beaufort, Countess of Richmond and Derby* (Cambridge, 1992).

[38.57] J. Martindale, "Succession and politics in the Romance-speaking world, c. 1000–1140," in *England and her Neighbours, 1066–1453,* essays in honour of Pierre Chaplais, ed. M. Jones and M. Vale (London, 1989), pp. 19–41.

[39.58] J. Nelson, "Commentary on the papers of J. Verdon, S. F. Wemple and M. Parisse," in Affeldt, ed., *Frauen in Spätantike und Frühmittelalter,* p. 331, arguing that the property claims of women already made them manipulable in ninth-century Frankia.

[40.59] The claim and its negotiation may have contributed both to the breach and reconciliation with Geoffrey: see Chibnall, *The Empress Matilda,* pp. 55–62. Some Angevin chroniclers stress that she

is against such generalization that I have argued. But a balance sheet on the status of heiress would have to include opportunities as well as manipulations.[41]

These women realized some of the opportunities of the heiress as a wife and mother or widow. Land, its provenance, and claims on it affect the dynamics of power within families. So, too, does emphasis on legitimacy, which is a corollary of emphasis on direct lineal descent. The woman who is the vehicle of that descent, the wife, the legitimate bearer of heirs, takes on a new prominence. An ecclesiastical reform movement which was stressing legitimate Christian marriage reinforced that status. In the private charters of post-1066 England the consent of wives to gifts is commonplace, their involvement in joint gifts regular. Consent and involvement cover their claims to dower, dowry, or their own inheritance. The wife's prominence also defines that narrow inheriting family in which the wife and mother is a key figure. The inheritance structures which produced some heiresses and excluded other daughters brought wives to the fore.[42] Can a particular inheritance practice or even women's landholding be taken as a simple guide to the status of women when the implications of landholding and inheritance practice can be ambiguous and varied, not only for different women, but at different stages of the same woman's life?

[. . .]

[T]here are many [arguments] for abandoning the idea of 1066 as a turning point of great significance in the history of English women, and for jettisoning the Anglo-Saxon Golden Age. Both ideas are more a product of the political concerns of past historians than of the experience of the eleventh century. They threaten to obscure the continuities of the English Early Middle Ages. They generalize women and ignore problems of status measurement. Even in their most sophisticated forms they have long diverted attention from the experience of 1066 by the women who lived through it, and from the gendered discussion of it by near contemporaries. A wider framework would allow for the continuities, though it must include latitude for varied interpretation in individual women's lives. Within that framework, and without preconceptions of deterioration or Golden Ages, changes between the tenth and the twelfth centuries may well be discovered. The evidence on either side of 1066 will need careful scrutiny to explore the power as well as the limitations on women, both in the twelfth as in the tenth century. The powers of tenth- as of twelfth-century women will look more complex when seen in full context, but that complexity will reveal more about what gives power to women, about how and when they are able to exercise it. Women's history is now too sophisticated for "Golden Ages" or for simple stories of advance or retreat. It is time to restore the lives of tenth-, eleventh-, and twelfth-century women to them.

---

brought the promise of power to Geoffrey. Their joint action on the Continent is discussed in ibid., pp. 62–72. Henry II and her other sons were brought up in her household, often in her own land of Normandy. Relations between mother and sons are discussed in ibid., esp. pp. 143–63.

[41.60] Including the advantages of a higher degree of male commitment to marriage to an heiress and a greater intensity in the husband and wife relationship, J. Gillingham, "Love, marriage and politics in the twelfth century," *Forum for Modern Language Studies*, XXV (1989): 292–303.

[42.61] They had different implications for another group of women, concubines.

The "Cruel Mother": Maternity, Widowhood, and Dowry in Florence in the Fourteenth and Fifteenth Centuries

15

Christiane Klapisch–Zuber

In Florence, men *were* and *made* the "houses." The word *casa* designates, in the fourteenth and fifteenth centuries, the material house, the lodging of a domestic unit, and it is in this sense that many documents of a fiscal, legal, or private nature use the term. But it also stands for an entire agnatic kinship group. The *casa* in this case designates all ancestors and living members of a lineage, all those in whose veins the same blood ran, who bore the same name, and who claimed a common ancestor – an eponymic hero whose identity the group had inherited.[1]

"Houses" were made by men. Kinship was determined by men, and the male branching of genealogies drawn up by contemporaries shows how little importance was given, after one or two generations, to kinship through women. Estates also passed from one generation to another through men. Among the goods that men transmitted jealously, excluding women from ownership as far as they could, was the material house, which they "made" also, in the sense that they built it, enlarged it, and filled it with children who bore their name. The Florence of the early Renaissance, the Florence of the great merchants and the first humanists, was not a tenderly feminine city. Family structures and the framework of economic, legal, and political life remained under the control of level-headed males, bastions of solidarity, and family values were inspired by a severely masculine ideal.[2]

In these *case* [*case* is the plural of *casa*], in the sense of both physical and the symbolic house, women were passing guests. To contemporary eyes, their movements in relation to the *case* determined their social personality more truly than the lineage group from which they came. It was by means of their physical "entrances" and "exits" into and out of the "house" that

Originally published as "Maternité, veuvage et dot à Florence," *Annales ESC* 38, no. 5 (1983): 1097–109. A first version of this essay was presented at the colloquy at Sénanque organized by Georges Duby in July 1981 on the topic "Maisons et sociétés domestiques au Moyen Age"; it was later revised for the workshop "La femme seule," held 1980–82 at the Centre de Recherches Historiques.
1 D. Herlihy and C. Klapisch-Zuber, *Les Toscans et leurs familles* [: *Une étude du catasto florentin de 1427* (Paris, 1978)], pp. 532ff. [Published in English as *The Tuscans and Their Families: A Study of the Florentine Catasto of 1427* (New Haven, 1985).]
2 See R. C. Trexler, *Public Life in Renaissance Florence* (New York: Academic Press, 1980).

their families of origin or of alliance evaluated the contribution of women to the greatness of the *casa*.[3] The marriage that brought a woman out of the paternal house and lineage, the widowhood that often led to her return, these incessant comings and goings of wives between *case* introduced a truly indeterminate quality in the ways they were designated: since reference to a male was necessary, a woman was spoken of in relation to her father or her husband, even when they were dead.[4] It is clear that the mere reference to the name of the lineage into which she was born or into which she married situated a woman much more clearly than the place where she was living at the moment. Women, then, were not permanent elements in the lineage. Memory of them was short. An important woman, a benefactress for her kin, for example, would eventually be known under her own name and brought to people's attention; but the family chronicler or the amateur genealogist would feel obliged to explain *why*, since the process fit so poorly within their definition of kinship. Thus Paolo Sassetti, noting in his journal the death of a female relative in 1371, writes, "Let special mention be made here, for we considered her to be like a beloved mother, and in all of her works she has been and was among the beloved women who have gone forth from our house."[5] As one who had both "come into" and "gone out of" the house, this exceptional "mother" must have stood out for her fidelity to the family into which she was born. Equally worthy of "special mention" but marked with the seal of the lineage's disapproval were the women who usurped an inheritance and persuaded a husband on his deathbed to disinherit his own kin.[6] More often, the family chroniclers keep the memory of an alliance with a certain lineage, but forget, a few generations after the marriage, the given name of the woman on whom the alliance was built.

The determination of a woman's identity thus depended on her movements in relation to the "houses" of men. The corollary was that upper-class Florentines found females who remained in their house of birth just as intolerable as females who lived independently. "Honorable" marriages were what regulated the entries and exits of the wives, and the normal state, the state that guaranteed the honor of the women and the "houses," could be no other than the married state. Any woman alone was suspect. An unmarried woman was considered incapable of living alone or in the absence of masculine protection without falling into sin.[7] Even if she were a recluse and lived a holy life,[8] even if she retired to a room on the

[3] Thus several tables drawn up by genealogists of the fifteenth and sixteenth centuries categorize women under *uscite* [exits] and *entrate* [entrances] according to lineage.

[4] [Christiane Klapisch-Zuber, "The Name 'Remade': The Transmission of Given Names in Florence in the Fourteenth and Fifteenth Centuries," in her, *Women, Family, and Ritual in Renaissance Italy*, trans. Lydia Cochrane (Chicago, 1985), ch. 13.]

[5] Archivio di Stato, Florence (henceforth abbreviated ASF), *Strozziane*, 2nd ser., 4, Ricordanze di Paolo Sassetti (1365–1400), fol. 34 (11 February 1371). Dates are given in modern style.

[6] Ibid., fol. 68v (24 September 1383); ASF, *Strozz.*, 2nd ser., 13, Ricordanze di Doffo di Nepo Spini, fol. 83 (7 July 1434).

[7] In the *catasto* of 1427 there are only 70 unmarried women among the 1536 female heads of household in Florence.

[8] On the suspicion that greeted *pinzochere* (women who took the habit of third order nuns to live in communities or, worse, alone), see below, n. 22, and R. Davidsohn, *Storia di Firenze* (Italian trans., Florence, 1965), vol. 6, pp. 66ff. On church attitudes concerning *pinzochere*, see R. C. Trexler, *Synodal Law in Florence and Fiesole 1306–1518*, Studi e Testi no. 268 (Vatican City, 1971), pp. 121–2, 142. On the various forms of religious life for women, in community or in seclusion, see the works of A. Benvenuti-Papi, esp. "Penitenza e penitenti in Toscana: Stato della questione e prospettive della ricerca," *Ricerche di storia sociale e religiosa* nos 17–18 (1980): 107–20; R. Pazzelli and L. Temperini, eds, *Prime manifestazioni di vita comunitaria maschile e femminile nel movimento francescano della penitenza* (Rome, 1982), pp. 389–450.

upper floor of the paternal house,[9] she placed the family honor in jeopardy by the mere fact of her celibacy. The convent was the only way out, although terrible doubts about the security of the cloister continued to torment her parents.[10] Among the "best people," therefore, families did not include females over twenty years of age who were not married.[11]

The widow's solitude was hardly less suspect. Although the Church advised the widow with a penchant for chastity not to remarry and to practice the related virtues of *mater et virgo* [mother and virgin], secular society did not set much store by her chances of remaining chaste.[12] The problem of where the widow was to live became crucial in such a case, for she was a threat to the honor not only of one family but of two. Given that a wife must live where her father or her husband lived (since they were the guarantors of her good conduct and her social identity), where should a wife be when she lost her husband?

On the Dwelling Place and the Virtue of Dowered Widows

Theoretically, a widow had some choice in the matter. She could live in her husband's family, by her children's side; she could live independently without remarrying, but near her children; or, finally, she could remarry and leave the first family that had received her. But in practice a widow, if young, was barred from the second option and found herself subjected to contradictory pressures that prevented her from quietly choosing between the other two possibilities. Young widows were in fact the target of a whole set of forces struggling fiercely for control of their bodies and their fortunes.

The statistics of the *catasto* show that widows in 1427 were much more numerous in the general population than widowers (13.6 percent and 2.4 percent, respectively). In Florence these percentages doubled (25 percent and 4 percent).[13] Widowers tended to be older men (14 percent of the age classes of 70 years old and older were widowers), for men remarried promptly up to a late age. Definitive widowhood came much earlier for women: at 40 – that

---

[9] On women who were nuns *in casa*, see Herlihy and Klapisch-Zuber, *Les Toscans*, pp. 153–5, 580. In Florence, thirty such women made a declaration to the *catasto* in their own name, but many more were part of a family. (In Arezzo, four out of eleven *suore in casa* or *pinzochere* declared their wealth independently.) See below, n. 40, on Umiliana dei Cerchi.

[10] R. C. Trexler, "Le célibat à la fin du Moyen-Age. Les religieuses de Florence," *Annales ESC 27*, no. 6 (1972): 1329–50.

[11] Among Florentine women who belonged to the age group of 20–24 years of age, 92 percent were married; the proportion is even higher among the wealthier classes.

[12] See J. Kirshner, *Pursuing Honor while Avoiding Sin: The Monte delle Doti of Florence*, Quaderni di *Studi Senesi* 41 (Milan, 1978), p. 7, n. 22; A. Burguière, "Réticences théoriques et intégration pratique du remariage dans la France d'Ancien Régime, XVIIᵉ–XVIIIᵉ s.," in J. Dupâquier et al., eds, *Marriage and Remarriage in Populations in the Past* (London, 1981), p. 43. On popular treatment of remarriage, see J. Le Goff and J.-C. Schmitt, eds, *Le charivari* (Paris and The Hague, 1981). See also "De la vie des veuves," in E. C. Bayonne, ed. and trans., *Oeuvres spirituelles de J. Savonarole* (Paris, 1879–80), pp. 5–51.

[13] Herlihy and Klapisch-Zuber, *Les Toscans*, appendix V, tables 1 and 2. [The *catasto* of 1427 was a public record, made during the period 1427–30, of the tax declarations of all subjects of Florence, which at the time meant nearly all people living in Tuscany. Covering about 265,000 persons and including information on age, wealth, family relations, property holdings, household goods, and many other topics, it has been exploited since the 1960s by historians (Klapisch-Zuber and Herlihy in particular) seeking to understand in detail the society and economy of the region during the fifteenth century.]

is, at an age at which they might still give children to their new husband – 18 percent of Florentine women appear in the census as widows, and at 50, nearly 45 percent do so. Furthermore, according to the statistics on couples drawn from family diaries, two-thirds of the women who became widows before 20 found a new husband, one-third of those widowed between 20 and 29, but only 11 percent of those widowed between 30 and 39 – when their numbers grow. We might conclude that after 40 they no longer had much chance of remarrying, while from 75 to 100 percent of all men up to 60 years of age took another wife.[14] Even if they hoped for remarriage, then, widows' liberty of choice was singularly limited by their age.

The social group to which they belonged added other constraints. According to the statistics on households, it was easier, in 1427, for a widow to live independently in the city than in the country. In Florence itself, nearly 14 percent of the heads of household were at that time widows, as opposed to 4 percent who were widowers. The difference between the two was smaller in rural areas: 7.6 percent widows and 4.4 percent widowers. What is more, among wealthy Florentines the probability of a widow's living alone collapses: 2 percent of the 472 wealthiest households (which represent less than 5 percent of all Florentine households) were headed by a woman (an even lower percentage than in the country), and rich widows who lived really autonomously were the exception at the upper levels of urban society.[15]

Since it is strikingly obvious that a widow's ability to live alone or simply to head the household of her minor children was correlated to her wealth, we need to raise questions concerning the processes that tied her fate to that of the family estate. By processes I mean legal mechanisms as well as individual and collective behavior that affected the widow or motivated her decisions.

It was of course the dowry that tangled the threads of a woman's fate. In principle, the dowered goods that a wife brought her husband were attached to her for life: they had the double function of providing for the expenses of the household and, when the household dissolved at the husband's death, of providing for the surviving wife.[16] Since she could not inherit her father's estate, which went to her brothers,[17] a woman looked to her dowry to assure her subsistence: she could "keep her estate and her honor" before transmitting to her children, male and female, the dowry she had received at marriage. This lovely scheme was unfortunately often belied by the facts. Every widowhood threatened the economic equilibrium the domestic group had achieved during the father's lifetime. If the widow was 40 years old or older, the difficulty of finding her a new husband discouraged her own parents from

---

[14] For comparative data on the problem of remarriage and its implications for fertility, see Dupâquier et al., eds, *Marriage and Remarriage*.

[15] Many widows who made independent declarations of their worth to the *catasto* of 1427 in reality lived in their children's household but took this opportunity to have their rights to their personal estate recognized (see Herlihy and Klapisch-Zuber, *Les Toscans*, p. 61).

[16] M. Bellomo, *Ricerche sui rapporti patrimoniali tra coniugi* (Milan, 1961), pp. 61ff.

[17] And, in the absence of brothers, to the agnates of the intestate father, up to three-quarters of the total estate. A daughter could inherit only in the absence of agnates to a stipulated degree of consanguinity. (For examples of how this right was put into effect and how it affected lineage ties, see R. Bizzochi, "La dissoluzione di un clan familiare: I Buondelmonti di Firenze nei secoli XV e XVI," *Archivio storico italiano* 140, no. 511 [1982]: 3–45.) See *Statuta populi et communis Florentiae (1415)* (Fribourg, 1778–81), vol. 1, pp. 223ff. A father could, of course, leave more to his daughters in his will; for example, ser Alberto Masi left one-third of his estate to his two brothers and the other two-thirds to his two daughters (ASF, *Manoscritti*, 89, fol. 15).

intervening. It was up to her husband's heirs to persuade her to remain with them and not to "leave with her dowry" to live independently. What is more, her husband would do his utmost, on his deathbed, to encourage her to give up any such idea. He would agree to assure her a lifetime income and supplementary advantages, over and above the income from her own estate, if she would remain under his roof, and he would make his heirs swear to show her all consideration and to consult her in the management of the holdings in which her dowry would continue to be sunk.[18] All of this was not unique to Florence, or to Italy.[19] Clearly, well-off Florentines did succeed in dissuading their wives from flying with their own wings, since there were very few rich and elderly widows who lived independently. If a widow, however, did not get along with her husband's heirs and preferred her freedom, she had no claims other than to her dowry. The suits initiated by widows to regain their dowry show that the heirs did not always see matters her way. In the fifteenth century, however, widows had the law and judicial institutions on their side: if they were not discouraged from the start, they ended up by taking back what they had brought to their marriage.

Finally, if the heirs – who were not always her own children – did not want to keep her under their roof or give her back her dowry, the Florentine widow could fall back on the *tornata*, a right of refuge in her family of birth. It was the obligation of her close kin or their heirs to receive her and assure her board and lodging.[20] In the fifteenth century, some Florentines, anxious to assure shelter to the widows of their blood after the extinction of their male descendants, provided in their will that one of their houses be devoted to "taking in, in the future, all of our women 'gone out' [of the house] and widowed, and assuring them the *tornata*." Thus, veritable old people's homes for family members were created, in which women rejected by their family by marriage could end their days honorably, knowing they could count on the solidarity of those of their blood even unto the next generation.[21]

These arrangements attest to an anxiety among men – who were deeply committed to maintaining the honor of their "house" – at the thought that a woman of their kin might not be included in a familial group. Even when old, a widow represented a threat to the reputation of good families. Since she had tasted the pleasures of the flesh, she was consid-

---

[18] See the example cited in Herlihy and Klapisch-Zuber, *Les Toscans*, p. 557 n. 21 (year 1312). For another example: Barna Ciurianni stipulates that his widow share in all of the revenue of the family and that she "be in all things honored as it is appropriate, and [that she be] trustee, with Valorino [her son], without having to give accounts" (ASF, *Manoscr. 77*, fol. 19, 1380). Giovanni Niccolini, who died in 1381, left his wife a share in the administration of his estate, with his children, as long as she lived with them, and, after ten years, if she wanted independent widowhood without taking back her dowry, he left her the profits from a farm, or half of the latter if she preferred to take back her dowry – the choice that the widow seems to have preferred after 1382 (C. Bec, ed., *Il libro degli affari proprii di casa de Lapo Niccolini de' Sirigatti*, Paris, 1969, pp. 62ff.). See also the case of Matteo Strozzi in 1429 (ASF, *Strozz.*, 5th ser., 12, fol. 25).

[19] See M. T. Lorcin, "Retraite des veuves et filles au couvent: Quelques aspects de la condition féminine à la fin du Moyen-Age," *Annales de Démographie historique* (1975): 187–204; Lorcin, *Vivre et mourir en Lyonnais à la fin du Moyen Age* (Paris, 1981), pp. 65–73.

[20] On the right to support and on the *tornata* see *Statuta*, vol. 1, pp. 135, 223–5.

[21] Conflict with the male heirs could result from the *tornata*: see ASF, *Strozz.*, 5th ser., 1750, Ricordanze di Bartolomeo di Tommaso Sassetti, fols 181, 154v. For examples of these houses for retirement within the family, see ASF *Strozz.*, 5th ser., 12, Ricordanze di Matteo di Simone Strozzi, fol. 25 (1429), and *Strozz.*, 5th ser., 15, fol. 96 (the will of Matteo's widow in 1455) and fol. 97 (1464); ASF, *Conventi soppressi*, 83, 131, fol. 100 (1548). See also Biblioteca Centrale Nazionale, Florence (henceforth abbreviated BNF), Magliab. VIII, 1282, fol. 122v (1367).

ered prone, like the hideous merry widow portrayed in Boccaccio's *Corbaccio*, to fall into debauchery.[22] If the heirs let their material interests pass before defense of their honor, the widow's kin, their allied family, felt sufficient responsibility toward her to take her back under their charge – not always without recriminations. Piero di Bernardo Masi, a copper-smith, gave solemn instructions to his progeny, in 1512, to take all precautions to avoid what had happened to his own father and to get guarantees for the dowries they gave their daughters. For fifteen years – until she died – his father had had to maintain at his own expense a sister whose husband had left her penniless.[23]

In this game, a married woman embodied stakes that were fully revealed only if she was widowed young. Early widowhood revived the claims of the widow's family of birth on the goods brought as a dowry. As these were irrevocably attached, by law, to the physical person of the woman for the duration of her life, widowhood forced her own kin to use her as a pawn by making her "come out" of her husband's family. When she remarried, her family could join a new circle of affines. By the remarriage of a widow of their blood, Florentines affirmed that they had never totally relinquished control over the dowries that they had given their daughters or their sisters.[24] At the same time, they claimed a perpetual right to the women's bodies and their fertility. Marriage alliance did not obliterate blood kinship; it did not signify a definitive break between the wife and her family of origin. When the widow returned to her family of birth and once again became part of its matrimonial strategies, the family took back cards it had already played, with every intention of making the most of a second deal of social prestige bought by the conclusion of a new alliance.

As soon as the husband had been buried and the funeral ceremonies had ended, the wife's kin came to claim her if she was young. They brought her back to their own house: such is "the custom of Florence," Paolo Sassetti says in 1395,[25] and a contemporary asserts that it was less than honorable for the widow to leave before the ceremony, but that it was understood as proper and accepted by all that she do so immediately afterward.[26] The right of families of birth to take back their widows was stronger than the desires the deceased had expressed in his will. The Sassetti "extracted" (the verb *trarre* is used) a sister in 1389, a niece of this same Paolo, and they remarried her promptly, even though she had "three little boys of very young age," for whom her husband had named her guardian and of whose inheritance she had been named coadministrator. But, Paolo Sassetti says, "as we had to remarry M[adonn]a Isabetta, she could not, and we did not want her to, take on this guardianship, and she renounced it 7 December 1389." The maternal uncles then took over responsibility for their sister's sons.[27]

---

[22] A debauchery that was all the more repugnant because it was hidden behind the state of *pinzochera* and because the widow opened her door to mendicant friars, "great consolers of widows" (Giovanni Boccaccio, *Corbaccio*, ed. P. G. Ricci, Classici Ricciardi, 44 [Turin, 1977], pp. 71–2).

[23] ASF, *Manoscr.*, 88, fol. 160v.

[24] On the remarriage of widows and the recycling of their dowry or their dower, see G. Duby, *Le chevalier, la femme et le prêtre* (Paris, 1981), pp. 88, 96, 283.

[25] ASF, *Strozz.*, 2nd ser., 4, fols 74ff.

[26] BNF, *Panciatichi*, 120, fol. 156 (1377). Here the widow leaves "although she had four children and she was pregnant and she failed to pay him honor in the church." In the same manner the Bolognese mason, Gasparre Nadi, notes that the neighborhood gossiped a good deal when a widow went to a second husband too quickly (*Diario bolognese*, ed. C. Ricci and A. Bacchi della Lega, Bologna, 1886, p. 47).

[27] ASF, *Strozz.*, 2nd ser., 4, fols 74, 103.

The Widow's Defection and the Abandonment of Children

A departure like Madonna Isabetta's constituted a double threat: to the children of the couple broken up by the death of the father, and to the children of a previous marriage. If their mother or their stepmother left them abruptly for a second marriage, their economic situation underwent a much more brutal shock than when an aged widow demanded her dowry in order to retire where it suited her. The heirs could put many an obstacle in the way of an older widow, for she would find less support from her own kin than if they had decided to remarry her. Remarriage was an honorable objective – so honorable, in fact, that long delays in the restitution of the dowry were frowned upon. For this reason testators who left minor children and a young widow made every effort to stave off the danger by including many dissuasive stipulations. Giovanni Morelli, in devoting many pages of his *Ricordi* (around 1400) to the fate of the widow after her husband's death, testifies to his own dread of leaving his heirs and their guardians the frightening obligation of a sudden restitution of a dowry.[28] That possibility also explains the recurring advice in Florentine writings that the sums demanded for dowries be kept within reasonable limits. Otherwise their restitution would jeopardize the children's future.[29] Since an inflationary movement inexorably carried urban dowries upward in the fourteenth and fifteenth centuries, these repeated appeals have an almost desperate tone. Nothing could be done about it, however; contemporaries saw the size of a dowry as an indicator of their social status, and they were little inclined to receive a dowry that was less than "honorable."[30] Testators set up barriers to keep a dowry from ebbing from their house toward the house that had given and was taking back the widow, but they could do little to counter the perverse effects of the dotal system in a society in which patrilineal transmission of estates tended to dominate.[31]

"Give a thought, reader," writes one hard-pressed guardian, "of the expenses that have fallen to me in order to satisfy the widows so that they will not abandon their children, especially Neri's widow, who was 25 years old."[32] The remarriage of a widow cast the shadow of a second threat: the abandonment of the children. In fact, the children belonged to the lineage of their father.[33] Thus, boys all their life and girls until their marriage resided with their agnatic kin. Statistics on households, like the daily events chronicled in family journals, show that children rarely stayed for long periods with their maternal kin. If the latter did take

---

[28] Giovanni di Pagolo Morelli, *Ricordi*, ed. V. Branca, 2nd ed. (Florence, 1969), pp. 213–23.

[29] Ibid., p. 211. L. B. Alberti, *I Libri della famiglia*, ed. R. Romano and A. Tenenti (Turin, 1969), 135–6. A study by Julius Kirshner ["*Maritus Lucretur Dotem Uxori Sue Premortue* in Late Medieval Florence," *ZRG* 108 (1991): 111–55], clarifies changes in attitudes regarding the remarriage of widows, which eventually, in 1415, introduced a notable change in the statutes.

[30] See Kirshner, *Pursuing Honor*.

[31] See ["The Griselda Complex: Dowry and Marriage Gifts in the Quattrocento," in Klapisch-Zuber, *Women, Family*, ch. 10].

[32] Bonaccorso Pitti, *Cronica*, ed. A. Bacchi della Lega (Bologna, 1905), p. 200.

[33] There is one case that is a tragicomic example of belonging to the father's lineage: a pregnant woman is widowed, her family "retracts" her after the husband's burial but sends her back to the husband's lineage until the child is born. When this happens, the family takes her back to remarry her (ASF, *Acquisti e Doni*, 8, Ricordanze di Jacopo di Niccolò Melocchi, fol. 56 [1517]). See also the squabbles of the Minerbetti family: one of them quarrels with his brothers to marry a woman whom he leaves pregnant when he dies. The mother sees her newborn baby whisked off by her brothers-in-law; then her own family has the baby snatched from his nurse. It takes a court decision to get him restored to his paternal uncles, who, when all is said and done, return him to his mother (Biblioteca Laurenziana, Florence, *Acquisti*, 229, fol. 69 (1508).

them in, they were paid for the children's keep, or they took on management of the children's estates, since children had no rights to goods that belonged to a lineage not their own. Children who followed their remarried mother were even rarer.[34] The documentation shows that arrangements permitting a widow to establish the children of her first marriage (also with payment of their keep) under the roof of the second husband were usually provisional.[35] Although the stepmother was a very familiar figure in Florentine households, the stepfather was practically unknown.

When a widow left a house in order to remarry, she left with her dowry but without her children. In 1427, many of the tax declarations deplore the abandonment of orphans whose mother had "left the family, taking away her dowry," leaving her husband's heirs in the charge of guardians and of paternal kin.[36] The Florentine family journals, too, overflow in the fourteenth and fifteenth centuries with such situations, brutally initiated by the departure of a widow. The paternal kin had to take charge of orphans "of whom it can be said that they are orphaned on both the father's and the mother's side," one Florentine orphan reiterates, "since it can well be said of those who still have a mother that they have none, given the way she has treated them and abandoned them."[37] Giovanni di Niccolaio Niccolini left four orphaned children in 1417, and his uncle Lapo notes bitterly that the widow "left the house [with her dowry of 900 *fiorini*] and left her children on the straw, with nothing."[38] When Bartolo di Strozza Rucellai's mother remarried, he threw himself, with his brothers, on the mercy of the tax officials, declaring, "See what a state we are in, without a father and, one could also say, without a mother, having no one else on earth, abandoned by everyone."[39]

Young widows would certainly have to have had singular tenacity and a good deal of courage to resist the contradictory pressures of their two families. Umiliana dei Cerchi, at the beginning of the thirteenth century, who hoped to live out her life in holy seclusion,[40] and Tancia, the daughter of the notary ser Giovanni Bandini, who wanted to enter a convent in 1450,[41] came into conflict with the desires and the maneuvers of relatives eager to bed them

---

[34] One exception, notable because it is so well known, is that of Giovanni Morelli and his young brothers and sisters, who lived with their maternal grandparents for seven or eight years after their mother's remarriage (see below, n. 49).

[35] Antonio Rustichi remarried his widowed sister in 1418, and he reached an agreement with his new brother-in-law that the children of the first marriage who accompanied their mother would renounce all claim to the dowry, probably in compensation for the expenses of their upbringing, assumed by the stepfather (ASF, *Strozz.*, 2nd ser., 11, fols 12v, 13v).

[36] As examples: in the Pisan countryside the three heirs of Giovanni di Biagio, ranging from 1 to 7 years of age, were abandoned by their mother (Archivio di Stato, Pisa, *Ufficio dei Fiumi e Fossi*, henceforth abbreviated UFF, 1542, fol. 400); so were the two daughters, aged 9 and 12 years old, of Giovanni di Corsetto (UFF, 1559, fol. 580), and the two children of Battista di Giovanni Guideglia, 3 and 10 years old (UFF 1538, fol. 479).

[37] ASF, *Strozz.*, 2nd ser., 15, Ricordanze di Cambio di Tano and di Manno di Cambio Petrucci, fol. 64v (1430).

[38] Bec, ed., *Il libro degli affari proprii*, p. 135.

[39] Cited in F. W. Kent, *Household and Lineage in Renaissance Florence* (Princeton, 1977), p. 36. We might also cite the case of Bernardo di Stoldo Rinieri, who lost his father in 1431 and whose mother remarried eight months later, leaving him with his two young sisters when he was 3 years old (ASF, *Conventi soppressi*, 95, 212, fol. 150).

[40] "Vita S. Humiliane de Cerchis," by Vito da Cortona, *Acta sanctorum*, May, IV, col. 388. For Umiliana's life, see also A. Benvenuti-Papi, "Umiliana dei Cerchi: Nascita di un culto nella Firenze del Dugento," *Studi francescani 77* (1980): 87–117.

[41] ASF, *Conv. soppr.*, 102, 82, fol. 15.

down with new husbands. Umiliana had her way (she was subsequently beatified), but Tancia failed (she was to remain an anonymous housewife). Some women – extraordinarily few – seem to have succeeded in their desire for independence, though there is no way of knowing how widespread this desire might have been.[42] Often, widows really did want to remarry.[43] Nevertheless, what contemporary reports emphasize above all is the irresolution of widows, and they leave an impression of widows' abject submission to the demands of their kin. Widows had few legal weapons, their whole upbringing had inculcated docility in them, and only in exceptional circumstances could they avoid remarriage if their relatives had decided in favor of it.[44] The widow of Barna di Valorino Ciurianni, to the immense displeasure of her stepsons, "leaves the house with her dowry" the minute her husband was in the ground, probably with remarriage in mind, since she was young. In spite of her promises to Barna and the advantages assured her in his will, she left her twelve-year-old son in the charge of his half brothers.[45]

Manno di Cambio Petrucci's narration, in 1430, of the days following the death of his father, who was carried off by the plague, offers a striking example of the anguish to which a widow could be subjected when her brothers wanted her to remarry. We see her here at the age of thirty-four torn between her aunt – probably sent by her family – and her children and stepchildren, who beg her to remain with them. "Madonna Simona," Manno, the eldest of her stepchildren implores her,

> your own children are here. We will treat them as our brothers and you, Madonna Simona, as our mother. Alas! our mother, I beg of you and throw myself at your mercy, for you know our situation. Left without father or mother, if you do not come to our aid we will go headlong into ruin.

The widow, however, bowed to her family's wishes: "I will do what my family decides," she says, and Manno adds, "for Madonna Pipa, her aunt, had done her job well overnight." It is a poignant tale, and one in which the children's dismay at the threat of being abandoned is expressed in protestations of respect and fidelity. The children avoid frankly broaching the question of what was most at stake in the conflict, however: the dowry that they might have to give back. Manno admits as much once the break was irreversible: "If Madonna Simona had agreed to remain with us, we would not have had to sell our things at half their price, wasting our substance so that we could give her back some of her dowry."[46]

---

[42] D. Herlihy has focused on widows' desire for independence and on the role that the new autonomy brought by their widowhood allowed them to assume in urban society. See his "Mapping Households in Medieval Italy," *Catholic Historical Review*, 58 (1972): 14; "Vieillir à Florence au Quattrocento," *Annales ESC* 24, no. 6 (1969): 1342ff. For a discussion of these positions, see Kirshner, *Pursuing Honor*, 8 and n. 23.

[43] This is the case with the anonymous widow cited by Vespasiano da Bisticci in his *Vite di uomini illustri del sec. XV*, ed. L. Frati (Bologna, 1892), vol. 3, p. 261, who, "desiring to remarry and take back her dowry, which was great," left her four young children with their paternal grandmother. See also below, n. 47.

[44] Some mothers must have ended up by regaining the children from whom they had been separated, like the widow Minerbetti cited in n. 32, but for one case of this sort, how many scenarios must there have been in which the mother seems to fall in line without the slightest complaint – or at least, with no complaint that succeeds in piercing the thick cloak of male narration of their behavior.

[45] ASF, *Manoscr. 77*, fol. 19. She had married Barna in 1365, when he was 43 years old, and had been widowed less than three years before.

[46] ASF, *Strozz.*, 2nd ser., 15, fols 61v–65.

"Good Mothers" and "Cruel Mothers"

When one famous orphan, Giovanni Morelli, became an adult, he accused his mother (who remarried when he was three years old) of having been "cruel" to him and to his brothers, though he does say the epithet was prompted by the Evil One in a moment of doubt and despair.[47] But what did a man of the fifteenth century mean by this accusation? Did it perhaps signify an affective abandonment, a case in which a mother would leave young children who needed her "love" and her "maternal" care? This is the way we spontaneously understand the situation today.[48] The texts of the time suggest this meaning, but they emphasize, perhaps even more strongly, the financial debacle, the ruin that the remarried widow left behind her. The "cruel mother" was the woman who left her young children, but it was above all the mother who "left with her dowry." There is no better evidence of this than this same Giovanni Morelli, who lived a good part of his childhood and adolescence in his stepfather's house, brought up by the very mother whom he nevertheless accuses of having "abandoned" him.[49] The abandonment was economic as much as affective, and what abandoned children complained of explicitly was the financial implications of their mother's remarriage. The mother who deserted the roof under which her children lived placed the interests of her own lineage and her own family above her children's interests, and that is why she was stigmatized. The clearest reproaches on the part of children or children's guardians rarely dwell on anything other than this consequence of remarriage.

The positive image, that of the "good mother," shows *a contrario*, the range of functions that the "cruel mother" who left to remarry failed to fulfill. There is truly no "good mother" who is not "both mother and father." This is the widow who refuses to remarry, no matter how young she might be, "in spite of the objurgations of her entire family," "so as not to abandon her children," "in order not to lead them to ruin," and who is both "a father and a mother for her children."[50] Just like the father, she assured, by her stability, a transmission that was first and foremost a transmission of material goods, without which there was no family. "Remaining," "staying," "living with" her children, bequeathing them the wealth that was theirs – such was the primary paternal obligation in a system of residence and transmission of patrimony organized by patrilineal filiation. The virtues of an exceptional mother are from this point of view all manly virtues.

---

[47] Morelli, *Ricordi*, p. 495. See especially L. Pandimiglio, "Giovanni di Pagolo Morelli e le strutture familiari," *Archivio storico italiano* 136, nos 1–2 (1978): 6. R. C. Trexler, in *Public Life in Renaissance Florence*, ch. 5, gives a long analysis of the case of Morelli and (particularly p. 165 n. 27) sees one of the reasons for the abandoning of children by their mother in her desire "to establish her *persona*." The fact that the wife's kin in most cases take the initiative in encouraging her departure seems to me to contradict this hypothesis.

[48] See the debate about maternal love prompted by E. Badinter's book, *L'amour en plus* (Paris, 1980) and the colloquy of the Société de Démographie historique in November 1981 devoted to the theme "Mothers and Wet Nurses."

[49] As noted by Pandimiglio, "Giovanni Morelli e le strutture familiari," p. 6. For relations with the maternal grandmother, see also the *ricordanze* of Morello Morelli, Giovanni's brother, in ASF, *Carte Gherardi*, Morelli, p. 163.

[50] Giovanni Rucellai, cited in Kent, *Household and Lineage*, p. 40, n. 64, and in G. Marcotti, *Un mercante fiorentino e la sua famiglia nel sec. XV* (Florence, 1881), pp. 49, 59–60. "Memorie di Ser Cristofano di Galgano Guidini da Siena," ed. C. Milanesi, *Archivio storico italiano* 4 (1843): 25–30., BNF, *Panciatichi*, 134, Memorie Valori, fol. 4 (1438).

274   *Christiane Klapisch-Zuber*

The widow qualified as a "good mother" was also one who devoted herself to the upbringing of her children with firmness and discipline.[51] Perhaps she could not compete with the father on the terrain of pedagogy. She could not offer a boy all the models of behavior that a father offered his sons, and her inexperience in public and political life constituted a vexing handicap. Her culture was often limited, and worse yet, she was unable to transmit to her sons the values and the spiritual heritage of the lineage, to talk to them of "what happened to their ancestors and of their actions, of those from whom they had received gifts and services and those by whom they had been badly used, of who was their friend in need and, conversely, the vendettas they had engaged in and of recompenses given to those to whom they were obliged."[52] A uniquely maternal upbringing had lacunae and was necessarily incomplete. Nevertheless, if undertaken with constancy and rigor, it could be comparable to the education administered by a father. When widowhood precluded other choices, the "good mother" was an acceptable substitute for the father. The "love" she bore her orphaned children took its full value from its masculine connotations.

Conversely, the bad mother, the "cruel mother," violated the values and the interests of her children's lineage when she showed too much docility toward her family of birth. In this she demonstrated the traditional vices of woman in exaggerated form. "Inconstant," "light," "flighty," she swings from one family to the other, she "forgets" her children and the husband she has just buried to seek pleasure in the bed of a second husband; she shifts shamelessly between the rigid structures of the contending masculine lineages. There is no doubt that the growing misogyny and mistrust of women at the dawn of the Renaissance were reinforced by structural contradictions that made it difficult to combine dotal system with patrilinearity. Among jurists, moralists, and those who reflected on the family, stereotypes presented woman as avid and capricious, eager to appropriate male inheritances for herself or other women, without pity for her children, whom she abandoned the moment she was widowed; a creature inconstant in her family loyalties, of immoderate attachments and inordinate sexuality, insatiable, and a menace to the peace and honor of families.[53] In short, a creature intent on destroying the "houses" that men had constructed.

The tensions caused by the problem of the autonomy or the remarriage of widows did not simply blacken the image of woman in the collective consciousness. They also generated positive but contradictory images of women to serve the opposing interests of the lineage that gave and the lineage that received the wife. The image of the mother loyal to her children countered that of the sister or the daughter faithful to her blood relatives; the wife

[51] Donato Velluti found in his mother the equivalent of a father, since his father was "nearly continually absent" on business (*Cronica domestica*, ed. I. Del Lungo and G. Volpi [Florence, 1914], pp. 119–20).
[52] Such are some of the merits of a paternal upbringing, as enumerated by G. Morelli, *Ricordi*, esp. p. 269. Conversely, the wife who harangues her husband continually about the great actions of her own lineage is a stock figure in contemporary literature (as in Boccaccio, *Corbaccio*, 46, 61) – a figure perhaps linked to the social hypergamy of men common at the time.
[53] The statutes of the city of Pisa in the middle of the twelfth century accuse mothers of manifesting an "impietatem novercalem" (stepmotherly impiety) toward their children rather than their "maternum affectum" (maternal affection) when they take back their dowry and their *antefactum*, and the female sex is frequently qualified by jurists as "genus mulierum avarissimum atque tenacissimum promptius . . . ad accipiendum quam ad dandum" ("most avaricious female sex, much more tenacious . . . in receiving than in giving") (texts cited by D. Herlihy in "The Medieval Marriage Market," *Medieval and Renaissance Studies* 6 (1976): 27, nn. 58–9). Let me note once more Boccaccio's *Corbaccio* as the most complete broadside on the vices and misdeeds of women, the root of which is sensuality and greed.

attentive to the interests of her household contrasted with the woman who remembered her own lineage; the good mother who nearly equaled a father was the counterpart of the good daughter, nearly as good as a son. Even more than the somber image of the concupiscent widow or the "cruel mother," this ambivalence, this double and deep-rooted source of qualities appreciated in women provoked masculine resentment of them for their "inconstancy." No woman was perfect: a man attached to only one woman would be perpetually disappointed with her. Only the male sex, backed up by the law and by the structure of society and the family, could boast of perfection that was seen primarily as fixity and permanence.

Few contemporaries grasped the reasons for these tensions and tried to look beyond their lineage-inspired and antifeminist prejudices. One, however, puts a fine defense of remarried widows into the mouth of a young Florentine. In the *Paradiso degli Alberti*, written around 1425 by Giovanni Gherardi of Prato,[54] a courtly discussion arises among a group of people of polite society.[55] The problem posed is whether paternal love or maternal love is the better. One young man argues heatedly that mothers are not worth much since, contrary to fathers, they abandon their children. In any event, as they are inferior beings, their love could not possibly be as "perfect" as that of men. One young woman "of great wit and of most noble manners" is then charged by the women to respond to him. She cleverly turns his arguments against him by placing herself in his logic: since women are less "perfect" than men, they must obey men and follow them; and

> since [women] cannot take their children, nor keep them with them, and they cannot remain alone without harm, especially if they are young, nor remain without masculine protection, it is almost perforce that mothers see themselves constrained to choose the best compromise. But it is not to be doubted that they think constantly of their children and remain strongly attached to them in spite of this separation.[56]

In this demonstration the young woman throws back to her male interlocutor the very contradictions in which he – along with the whole society of his time – let himself be trapped. For how could the "honor" and the "status" of a lineage be increased by taking back a woman and her dowry in order to give them elsewhere, without offending the honor and the standing of the family to which she had given children? How could such a family reassert its rights over the person and the wealth of a woman without depriving another family of those rights? How could the separation of mother and child be avoided when the mother's identity was always borrowed and the child could belong only to his paternal kin? How could a woman be reproached for her docility before men when society denied her economic and legal autonomy?

---

[54] Giovanni Gherardi da Prato, *Il Paradiso degli Alberti*, ed. A. Lanza (Rome, 1975), pp. 179–84.

[55] The debate on the preeminence of paternal love is a commonplace that runs from the preachers to Alberti, who classes it among scholastic stylistic exercises (see Alberti, *I libri della famiglia*, p. 349).

[56] For the masculine argument, see Herlihy and Klapisch-Zuber, *Les Toscans*, p. 558 n. 22. What the young woman has to say – which occupies three times the space of the young man's argument – astonishes the master of ceremonies: "Per nostra donna, per nostra donna vergine Maria, che io non mi credea che le donne fiorentine fossono filosofe morali e naturali né che avvessono la rettorica e la loica così pronta come mi pare ch'abbino!" ("By our Lady, by our Lady the Virgin Mary, I had no idea that Florentine women were moral and natural philosophers, nor that they had such ready rhetoric and logic as it seems to me they have!"). He then gives the victory to the ladies (*Il Paradiso degli Alberti*, pp. 183–4).

But the young woman's words go farther. When she evokes the mother's attachment to her children – an attachment that the males of her time either failed to express, rejected, or sublimated into "paternal love," according to whether they stood on one side or the other of the dowry fence – our clever Florentine exposes the mechanisms by which a society that manipulated woman and the wealth attached to her attempted to prove its own innocence by reinforcing the image of the insensitive and destructive female.

16 Men's Use of Female Symbols

Caroline Walker Bynum

When we look at male writing in the later Middle Ages we find that symbolic dichotomies and reversals were at its very heart. Men tended to use the male/female dichotomy to underline male/female differences (father versus mother, teacher and disciplinarian versus nurturer, tough versus soft, etc.) and to castigate or romanticize female weakness. As I have demonstrated elsewhere, men tended to associate a clearly delineated set of social and biological characteristics with each gender, even when they were using gender as a symbol, and they tended to see these sets of characteristics as opposites. For example, Guerric of Igny (d. *c*.1157) wrote: "The Bridegroom [Christ] ... has breasts, lest he should be lacking any one of all duties and titles of loving kindness. He is a father in virtue of natural creation ... and also in virtue of the authority with which he instructs. He is a mother, too, in the mildness of his affection, and a nurse."[1] An anonymous Franciscan, describing Francis and Elizabeth of Hungary as parents of the friars minor, wrote: "He was the father ... and she was their mother. And he guarded them like a father, she fed them like a mother."[2] In their symbolic universe, men tended to use the male/female dichotomy not only as symbol of authority/nurture, spirit/flesh, law/mercy, strong/weak, but in a broader sense as a way of expressing the contrast between God and soul, divinity and humanity, clergy and laity.[3] To medieval men, God was (as he has been to most of the pious throughout the long

1.[11] Guerric of Igny, Second Sermon for SS Peter and Paul, ch. 2, in *Sermons*, vol. 2, ed. J. Morson and H. Costello, SC 202 [Série des textes monastiques d'Occident], 43 ([Paris,] 1973), p. 384, trans. the monks of Mount St Bernard Abbey, in Guerric of Igny, *Liturgical Sermons*, vol. 1, Cistercian Fathers Series 32 (Spencer, Mass.: Cistercian Publications, 1971), p. 155. See also [Caroline Walker] Bynum, [*Jesus as Mother: Studies in the Spirituality of the High Middle Ages* (Berkeley: University of California Press, 1982), henceforth Bynum,] *JM*, p. 122.

2.[12] [. . .]. It is worth noting that the only passage in which Hadewijch [a thirteenth–century Flemish mystic] employs a clear distinction between *father* as an image of authority and discipline and *mother* as an image of nurture and affection is one that borrows the dichotomy in question from a male author, William of St Thierry. [. . .].

3.[13] I have demonstrated this in twelfth-century Cistercian writing in Bynum, *JM*, ch. 4. I have suggested that the pattern extends into the thirteenth and fourteenth centuries in "'. . . And Woman His Humanity'[:Female Imagery in the Religious Writing of the Later Middle Ages," in Caroline Walker Bynum, Stevan Harrell, and Paula Richman, eds *Gender and Religion: On the Complexity of Symbols* (Boston, 1986), pp. 257–88, reprinted in Caroline Walker Bynum, *Fragmentation and Redemption: Essays on Gender and the Human Body in Medieval Religion* (New York: Zone Books, 1992), pp. 151–79.] [. . .].

Christian tradition) metaphorically male – father or judge, bridegroom or friend – and the soul (partly because of the linguistic gender of *anima*) was frequently symbolized or described as female. Moreover, the gender dichotomies we find in men's writings were reinforced by other gender dichotomies that were implicit in the ways people lived. Men were food receivers, women food preparers and generators. Men were priests and women laity. Men were authoritative by office or ordination; women's religious power derived from inspiration, from ecstatic visitation.

Whatever other patterns lie behind these dichotomies, one is clear. If male is to female as spirit is to flesh, food receiver to food generator, clergy to laity, office to inspiration, law to mercy, and divine to human, then that which is symbolized by *male* is in some sense a product of culture, cut off from nature or biology. Thus, although it may at first appear incoherent or even contradictory that *the female* should symbolize *both* inspiration versus office *and* flesh versus spirit, there is a consistent dichotomy behind these pairs. The fundamental contrast seems to be between (a) constructs of laws, patterns, forms, erected at some distance from, if not in opposition to, nature, and (b) a more instinctual, internal, biological "human nature." In this sense, flesh is natural and spirit cultural just as prophetic inspiration is interior, subjective, natural, whereas clerical authority is an external, cultural structure independent of personal moral, experiential qualifications.

Structuralist anthropologists have recently taught us to see such a dichotomy as a basic contrast in human symbol systems. I have been influenced by their formulations, above all by Sherry Ortner's,[4] but I do not mean here what they mean. I agree with Ortner's critics that her theory is universalist in undesirable ways, ignoring the possibility that subgroups in a society, especially women, may hold differing and even disagreeing perspectives on the symbolic dichotomies used by dominant cultural groups.[5] Thus I am not here saying that the culture/nature dichotomy was an objectively true dichotomy between male and female. Nor am I saying that medieval women espoused such a dichotomy. I am merely pointing out that this is the pattern symbols fell into in male writing and religious practice between 1200 and 1500.

Such a symbolic pattern was, to men, profoundly disturbing. For the same male writers who came to see the church as the clergy, to see their gender as the symbol for God's divinity, to argue that male, clerical mediation was the necessary bridge between heaven and earth, knew they partook of fallen humanity. They knew Christ had preached: "Blessed are

---

4.14   [Sherry] Ortner, "[Is] Female to Male [as Nature Is to Culture?,]" [in Michelle Rosaldo and Louise Lamphere, eds, *Women, Culture and Society* (Stanford: Stanford University Press, 1974), pp. 67–87]. For a somewhat similar argument, see Edwin Ardener, "Belief and the Problem of Women," and "The Problem Revisited," in Shirley Ardener, ed., *Perceiving Women* (New York: Wiley, 1975), pp. 1–28. See also Michelle Rosaldo, introduction and "Women, Culture and Society: A Theoretical Overview," in Rosaldo and Lamphere, *Women, Culture and Society*, pp. 1–42; and Eric Wolf, "Society and Symbols in Latin Europe and in the Islamic Near East," *Anthropological Quarterly* 42 (1968): 287–301.

5.15   See Eleanor Leacock and June Nash, "Ideologies of Sex: Archetypes and Stereotypes," *Issues in Cross-Cultural Research*, Annals of the New York Academy of Sciences 285 (New York: New York Academy of Sciences, 1977), pp. 618–45; Carol P. MacCormack and M. Strathern, eds, *Nature, Culture and Gender* (Cambridge: Cambridge University Press, 1980); and Judith Shapiro, "Anthropology and the Study of Gender," *Soundings* 64.4 (1981): 446–65. Ortner has attempted to deal with some of this criticism in Sherry Ortner and Harriet Whitehead, introduction to Ortner and Whitehead, eds, *Sexual Meanings: The Cultural Construction of Gender and Sexuality* (Cambridge: Cambridge University Press, 1981), pp. 1–27; see esp. preface, p. x. See also [Caroline] Bynum, "[The] Complexity of Symbols," in [*Gender and Religion*, pp. 1–20.].

the meek." Their piety reflected their ambivalence. Increasingly they stressed not God's authority but Jesus' accessibility, not Judgment Day or Resurrection but a man laying down his life for his friends. They had recourse to visionary women for comfort and counsel – and for the direct inspiration they were afraid they no longer received.[6] And they spoke (as a definitely subordinate but nonetheless highly charged theme) of Jesus as mother and of themselves as women.

Sometimes, in calling themselves women, male writers used *woman* as a term of opprobrium. Helinand of Froidmont castigated his brothers: "Behold God compares men to women . . . and not merely to women, but to *menstruating* women!"[7] But more frequently they used *woman* as a symbol of dependence on God – both as a way of describing themselves as cared for by God and as a way of underlining their own renunciation of worldly power and prestige. In his "Letter to all the Faithful" Francis of Assisi said, describing virtuous friars:

> It is they who are the brides, the brothers and the mothers of our Lord Jesus Christ. A person is his bride when his faithful soul is united with Jesus Christ by the Holy Spirit; we are his brothers when *we do the will of* his *Father who is in heaven* [Matthew 12:50], and we are mothers to him when we carry him in our hearts and bodies by love with a pure and sincere conscience, and give him birth by doing good deeds which enlighten others by example.[8]

Speaking of friars who go in groups of three or four to hermitages, he wrote:

> Two of these should act as mothers, with the other two, or the other one, as their children. The others are to lead the life of Martha; the other two, the life of Mary Magdalen. . . . The friars who are mothers must be careful to stay away from outsiders. . . . The friars who are sons are not to speak to anyone except their mother or their custos [superior].[9]

[6.16] See [. . . André] Vauchez, *La Sainteté* [*en Occident aux derniers siècles du moyen âge d'après les procès de canonisation et les documents hagiographiques* (Rome, 1981), pp. 439–41; published in English as *Sainthood in the Later Middle Ages* (Cambridge: Cambridge University Press, 1997)]. Thomas of Cantimpré's Life of Lutgard is a particularly good example of male recourse to visionary women. Thomas repeatedly describes Lutgard as "mother" and "nurse" to himself, to secular men, and to friars (*AASS* June, vol. 4, pp. 202–3, 205, 207). He reports that Lutgard, a frequent recipient of visions, enables a priest to have a vision by praying that he be granted one (p. 202). He also reports that a certain man brought to Lutgard by the abbot of Afflighem was struck with horror at his sin when he looked into her face "as if into the face of God's majesty" (p. 201).

[7.17] See Helinand of Froidmont, Sermon 27, *PL* 212, col. 622b. See also Sermon 20, cols 646–52, and Helinand of Froidmont, *Epistola ad Galterum*, col. 753b. For other male writers who use *woman* to mean physically or morally weak, see Bynum, *JM*, pp. 148–49, and [Georges] Duby, *The Knight, the Lady and the Priest*, trans. B. Bray (New York: Pantheon Books, 1983)], esp. pp. 22, 45–6.

[8.18] Francis of Assisi, "Letter to All the Faithful," [in Francis, *Opuscula sancti patris Francisci Assisiensis*, ed. Fathers of St Bonaventure's College (2nd ed., Quaracchi, 1949) (hereafter *Opuscula*), trans. Benen Fahy in Marion A. Habig, ed., *St Francis of Assisi: Writings and Early Biographies: English Omnibus of Sources* (3rd ed., Chicago: University of Chicago Press, 1973) (hereafter *Omnibus*], p. 96, with my changes. The concern for giving birth to others by example is typically Franciscan; see Bynum, *JM*, pp. 105–6.

[9.19] Francis of Assisi, "Religious Life in Hermitages," *Opuscula*, pp. 83–4; trans. Fahy, *Omnibus*, pp. 71–2. Francis repeatedly refers to the love of friars for each other as maternal. See, for example, Rule of 1221, ch. 9: "Begging alms," in *Opuscula*, p. 38: "Et quilibet diligat et nutriat fratrem suum, sicut mater diligit et nutrit filium suum" ["He who loves and feeds his brother (friar) is like a mother loving and feeding her son"].

Suso saw himself as a maiden picking roses, a baby nuzzling its mother's breast. Ruysbroeck wrote: "Man's nature is the bride [of Christ]."[10]

When a male writer described another man as a woman (for example, Bonaventure speaking of Francis of Assisi) or when a man (for example, Richard Rolle or Suso) described himself that way, he was using symbolic reversal. Man became woman metaphorically or symbolically to express his renunciation or loss of "male" power, authority, and status. He became woman, as Eckhart said, in order to express his fecundity, his ability to conceive God within.[11] Such reversal seemed necessary in a religion at whose heart lay contradiction and Incarnation: God-become-man. When Tauler sought a symbol of the soul's utter self-abasement before God, its utter denuding and emptying, he not only chose the poor Canaanite woman of Matthew 15:21–8, who referred to herself as lower than a dog, he also cited a contemporary woman who received a vision in which she was abandoned by all intermediaries between creation and Creator and who therefore cried aloud to God that she would accept condemnation to hell itself if it was his will.[12] In such a sermon, "woman" is a symbol and an example not only of the utterly contemptible and of the redeemed but also of the great reversal at the heart of the gospel: the fact that it is the contemptible who *are* redeemed.

The food and flesh imagery I examine in [earlier chapters] is, as I have explained above, a particular case of such symbolic inversion. Much about the priest's role and about the theology of *imitatio Christi* [imitation of Christ] in the later Middle Ages involves a reversal of cultural assumptions about gender. On the one hand, of course, given the symbolic patterns, the priest was "male" and the communicant "female"; the priest was God and the recipient human. As is well known, Bonaventure argued that women could not be priests because the priesthood, the authority of God, had to be symbolized by a male.[13] But, in another sense, as I have demonstrated, God's dying body was female – a birthing and lactating mother – and the priest was female too. He was Mary, for in his hands, as in her womb, Christ was incarnate; he was food preparer and distributor to recipients who ate. In the central moment of the mass the male celebrant waited, ready to care for and distribute a heavenly food, a vulnerable body, provided by a father-mother God for the benefit of human children.

Iconographic evidence, too, suggests that the mass implied gender reversal. Pictures of Christ distributing food and washing the feet of guests at the Last Supper outnumber visual representations of Christ as king or priest in the later Middle Ages. In such paintings Christ is depicted in one of society's most admired *female* roles: the role of food preparer and servant. A fifteenth-century retable from Ulm [. . .] shows just such a reversal. On the outer

[10.20] [Jan van Ruysbroeck, *The Spiritual Espousals*, trans. Eric Colledge (New York: Paulist Press, n.d.), p. 43.].

[11.21] See Vauchez, *La Sainteté*, p. 446 n. 511; and Eckhart, Sermon 2, in *Meister Eckhart: The Essential Sermons, Commentaries, Treatises, and Defense*, trans. Edmund Colledge and Bernard McGinn (New York: Paulist Press, 1981), pp. 177–9.

[12.22] Tauler, Sermon 9 for Second Sunday in Lent, in [John] Tauler, *Die Predigten [Taulers: Aus der Engelberger und der Freiburger Handschrift sowie aus Schmidts Abschriften der ehemaligen Strassburger Handschriften*, ed. Ferdinand Vetter (Berlin, 1910)], pp. 40–6. [. . .] Men also took female saints as models of penitence; see Acta alia, ch. 2, of John of Alverna, *AASS* August, vol. 2 (Paris, 1867), pp. 471–2, where John is seen as another Magdalen.

[13.23] [Francine] Cardman, ["The Medieval Question of] Women and Orders," [*The Thomist* 42 (1978)]; J. Rézette, "Le Sacerdoce et la femme chez saint Bonaventure," *Antonianum* 51 (1976): 520–7.

wings (when closed), we find Christ as servant and food distributor, testing Judas with the wafer (as many mystical women tested false priests). When opened, the retable displays the Eucharist represented both as a body in the chalice and as flour ground through a mill. Mary and the four evangelists pour the grain into the funnel (i.e., celebrate). Apostles turn the crank. It is the prelates of the church, garbed in all their splendor, who wait quietly below as recipients.

Thus male writers, artists, worshipers, and priests in the later Middle Ages made use of sharp symbolic dichotomies, and many of their most profound and moving images were symbolic reversals. Moreover, men's own life stories tended to be stories of crisis and conversion. They enacted the reversals they used as symbols, stripping themselves naked (as did Francis of Assisi before his father), putting on the clothing of a child, a beggar, or a woman (as Richard Rolle did in becoming a hermit), suddenly and dramatically renouncing wealth, influence, and wife to take up poverty and chastity (as did John Colombini).[14] As I pointed out in chapter 1 [of *Holy Feast and Holy Fast*], many more medieval men than women underwent abrupt changes of lifestyle during adolescence. Having greater access to power and family wealth, men were able to abandon them more abruptly and flamboyantly, and medieval boys seem to have been older on average than girls when stricken by the impulse to abandon the world.

Many explanations can be suggested for the fact that men tend to use images, and live lives, of contrast, opposition, and reversal. Structuralist anthropologists have sometimes argued that dichotomous images of hard/soft, male/female, law/mercy, reason/unreason tend to appear in cultures with strongly patrilineal inheritance patterns, because the female (although necessary for procreation) tends in fact to be a disruptive force in such societies, a force outside law and structure.[15] Such explanation, though plausible, appears to reflect none of the subtlety of late medieval imagery, and it does not explain reversal, although it may explain dichotomy. Another way of relating imagery to social structure seems more convincing. This is simply to note that most gradations of status in the later Middle Ages were gradations of male status. The growing consciousness of the multiplicity of statuses and roles that characterizes twelfth- and thirteenth-century writing is predominantly a growing awareness of a variety of male roles. As Georges Duby has pointed out, women were outside the "three orders" of medieval society: those who pray, those who fight, and those who till the soil.[16] Even in the Church, although nuns were "clergy" in one sense (that is, they were "regular"; they took vows), in another sense all women were laity – that is, outside orders. Women, as I said in chapter 1 [of *Holy Feast and Holy Fast*], often shied away themselves from highly structured institutional forms, avoiding rules and vows; and male characterization of women was usually according to their marital or sexual status – widow, virgin, married woman – rather than their institutional affiliation. Thus women were not "on" a ladder of roles and statuses in the same sense that men were.[17] It is hardly surprising

---

[14.25] See [Donald] Weinstein and [Rudolf M.] Bell, [*Saints and Society: The Two Worlds of Western Christendom, 1000–1700* (Chicago: University of Chicago Press, 1982)], pp. 114–19; see also Giovanni Battista Proja, "Colombini, Giovanni, da Siena," *BS*, vol. 4, cols 122–3.

[15.26] See, for example, Victor and Edith Turner, *Image and Pilgrimage* [in *Christian Culture: Anthropological Perspectives* (Oxford: Oxford University Press, 1978)], pp. 161, 199.

[16.27] Georges Duby, *The Three Orders: Feudal Society Imagined*, trans. A. Goldhammer (Chicago: University of Chicago Press, 1980), pp. 89, 95, 131–3, 145, 209.

[17.28] For example, when Francis of Assisi in ch. 23 of his Rule of 1221 lists "everyone" who should persevere in faith and penance, he writes as follows: "We beseech . . . all those who serve our Lord and God within the holy, catholic, and apostolic Church, together with the whole hierarchy, priests,

therefore that complex imagery of role reversal, of inversion of power and status – of fool become king, boy become pope, man become woman or woman become man – appealed more to men, for whom the precise gradations of society were self-definitions that might bear down with a psychological weight that demanded periodic release.

There may also be psychological and theological reasons for men's preference for dichotomy and reversal. As several theorists have recently pointed out, the maturation of a boy (in western culture, medieval and modern) requires a fundamental break in self-image: a boy must learn that he cannot be the mother who is his first projection of self, his first love, his first model.[18] A boy's growing up is therefore a learning to be other than female – a learning both to reverse his own desires and self-definition and to see the female as "other." Small wonder therefore that reversals and conversions become central in male ways of thinking about and symbolizing spiritual growth.

Moreover, the nature of the symbolic dichotomies men generated contained within itself pressure for reversal. Not only did Christian theology state that the humble, the lowly, "the last," were eventually to come first, thus dictating that men must find reversed symbols to speak of progress toward God (for example, the soul as woman, child, fool).[19] The male symbols themselves, in referring to that which is cut off from nature, that which is cultural construct, forced recognition of their opposites, for men knew themselves to be not merely "divine," "clerical," "spirit," and "authority." Because the symbols associated "the male" with culture, with "more than" and "other than" human nature, these symbols implied that in order to *be* human nature the male must take opposites to himself in symbol. The particular group of cultural activities, responsibilities, and symbols associated with *the male* by men itself implied contrast and reversal. The set of activities, responsibilities, and

---

deacons, subdeacons, acolytes, exorcists, lectors, porters, and all clerics and religious, male or female; we beg all children, big or small, the poor and needy, kings and princes, labourers and farmers, servants and masters; we beg all virgins and all other women, married or unmarried; we beg all lay folk, men and women, infants and adolescents, young and old, the healthy and the sick, the little and the great, all people, tribes, families, and languages, all nations and all men everywhere, present and to come" (*Opuscula*, pp. 59–60; trans. Fahy, *Omnibus*, p. 51). Although it is sometimes unclear how generic the categories are, it *is* clear that all religious women are lumped into the category "religious," that the statuses that reflect occupations are male (kings, princes, laborers, farmers, masters, possibly even servants), that women are categorized by sexual or marital status whereas men are not, and that only "lay folk" includes male and female equally.

18.29 Nancy Chodorow, *The Reproduction of Mothering: Psychoanalysis and the Sociology of Gender* (Berkeley and Los Angeles: University of California Press, 1978). See also Carol Gilligan, *In a Different Voice: Psychological Theory and Women's Development* (Cambridge, Mass.: Harvard University Press, 1982), chs 1, 2, 6. Chodorow's theories have been creatively applied to women saints in India in A. K. Ramanujan, "On Women Saints," in J. Hawley and D. M. Wulff, eds, *The Divine Consort: Rādhā and the Goddesses of India* (Berkeley: Berkeley Religious Studies Series, 1982), pp. 316–24. For a different version of this argument, found in the research of John and Beatrice Whiting, see [Peggy Reeves] Sanday, *Female Power and Male Dominance*[: *On the Origins of Sexual Inequality* (Cambridge: Cambridge University Press, 1981)], pp. 182–5. There has been much criticism of the essentialist overtones of Gilligan's work, however. See Judy Auerbach et al., "Commentary on Gilligan's *In a Different Voice*," *Feminist Studies* 11.1 (1985): 149–61; Debra Nails et al., eds, *Women and Morality*, special issue of *Social Research* 50.3 (1983); Joan W. Scott, ["Gender: A Useful Category of Historical Analysis,"] *American Historical Review* [91 (1986): 1053–75].

19.30 For New Testament passages that require reversal, see, among others, 1 Corinthians 1:20 ("Hath not God made foolish the wisdom of this world?") and Mark 10:31 ("But many that are first shall be last").

symbols associated with *the female* did not, in the same way, imply its obverse. That which *the female* symbolized – nurture, body, laity, humanity, inner inspiration – did not require anything else – for example, power, spirit, office, divinity – in order to conjure up person. Nor did it imply that reversal was necessary in order for person, for that-which-is, to be given religious meaning. Woman already *was* that which is, in Christianity, given religious meaning. For woman was, in fact as well as symbolically, human.

Thus the very set of dichotomous symbols that clustered around male/female in the western tradition suggested that men – powerful, clerical, authoritative, rational, "divine" men – needed to become weak and human, yet spiritual, "women" in order to proceed toward God. And male writers in the later Middle Ages used much such reversed imagery for self. Moreover, they often assumed that reversed imagery and dichotomous symbols were appropriate ways of reflecting on female experience. Male writers urged women to "become male" or "virile" in their rise to God.[20] Male hagiographers and chroniclers were fascinated by stories of women's cross-dressing in order to enter religious houses – probably to the point of fabricating such incidents.[21] Male writers devoted much attention to female weakness, both by underlining women's sexual temptations and by expatiating upon the inappropriateness of asceticism to women's soft, tender, and inconstant bodies. Suso wrote to a spiritual daughter: "You are weaker than Eve in paradise." The compiler of the Life of Ida of Louvain praised her by saying she was "not a woman or lazy, but like a man in constancy."[22]

There is much evidence that religious men in the thirteenth, fourteenth, and fifteenth centuries were fascinated by women – both by the female visionaries who became, through their very lowliness, the mouthpieces of God on high and by the ordinary mothers, house-wives, laundresses, and maidservants who were signs of the depths to which Jesus stooped in redeeming humankind. As I suggested in chapter 3 [of *Holy Feast and Holy Fast*] above, male mystics such as Bernard, Francis, Rolle, Suso, Tauler, Eckhart, and Gerson advised women, admired women, and abhorred women. They adopted the image of woman – woman who was more humble and more fleshly than they – to speak of their own approach to God. In describing themselves as nursing mothers or suckling babes, these men were describing the self they became in conversion as the opposite of adult and male. In speaking of their conversions as the espousing of nakedness, poverty, suffering, and weakness, they were, even more generally, renouncing and reversing the prerogatives of wealth, strength, and public power that their world connected to adult male status. If male writers were fond of seeing themselves as brides, mothers, and children, such reversed images were only one set of metaphors in a symbolic world in which the man had to see his basic religious commitment

---

[20.31] [. . .] For secular histories by male authors that depict virtuous women as "virile," see Duby, *The Knight, the Lady and the Priest*, pp. 234–5. Even male biographers do not always see the spiritual progress of women as increasing "virility"; the hagiographer of Umiltà of Faenza says (ch. 1, par. 5, *AASS* May, vol. 5, p. 208), that after her conversion she was transformed into "another woman."

[21.32] [John] Anson, "The Female Transvestite [in Early Monasticism: The Origins and Development of a Motif," *Viator* 5 (1974): 1–32]. See also Vern Bullough, "Transvestites in the Middle Ages," *American Journal of Sociology* 79 (1974): 1381–94.

[22.33] See [Henry Suso, *Briefbüchlein der Ewigen Weisheit*, Letter 4 in Henry Suso, *Heinrich Seuse: Deutsche Schriften im Auftrag der Württembergischen Kommission für Landesgeschichte*, ed. Karl Bihlmeyer (Stuttgart, 1907), p. 369; Life of Ida of Louvain, *AASS* April, vol. 2 (Paris, 1865), p. 159.] Needless to say, women writers did not generalize about the nature of "man" (used non-generically), although they did both revere and castigate the clergy as a group [. . .].

as flight from power and glory – for Jesus himself had fled power, no matter how much kings and prelates might wield it in his name.

Women's Symbols as Continuity

Female writers, expressing their religious desires and fears in the same symbolic tradition as men and worshiping in the same rituals, also in some ways used and reflected the clusters of dichotomies I have just described. Some of women's images of food and flesh were not only expressions of such dichotomies but profound reversals as well. In both Eucharist and mystical union, women inverted what the culture assumed them to be. Just as Christ's death on the cross was a symbolic reversal – for he became, not *male* (king or priest or recipient of nurture), but *female* (a lactating and birthing mother, nurturer of others) – so the female communicant experienced gender reversal. She became not nurturer and feeder of others but receiver. In the mass, the roles of clergy and laity reversed ordinary social roles. The celebrant became food preparer, the generator of food, the pregnant mother of the incarnate God; the woman recipient feasted, with eyes and palate, on a food she did *not* prepare or exude. Woman's jubilant, vision-inducing, intoxicated eating of God was the opposite of the ordinary female acts of food preparation and of bearing and nursing children.[23]

Yet, on a deeper level, women's eating of God was not a reversal at all. For in the mass and in mystical ecstasy women became a fuller version of the food and flesh they were assumed by their culture to be. In union with the dying Christ, woman became a fully fleshly and feeding self – at one with the generative suffering of God. Woman's eating, fasting, and feeding others were synonymous acts, because in all three the woman, by suffering, fused with a cosmic suffering that really redeemed the world. And these three synonymous acts and symbols were not finally symbolic reversals but, rather, a transfiguring and becoming of what the female symbolized: the fleshly, the nurturing, the suffering, the human.

Women's food images and food practices thus reflect a larger pattern. For women's way of using symbols and of being religious was different from men's. It appears as a kind of subtext within a larger text, dominated by dichotomous symbols and symbolic inversions, and it is always aware of male/female oppositions and of images of reversal. But women's sense of religious self seems more continuous with their sense of social and biological self; women's images are most profoundly deepenings, not inversions, of what "woman" is; women's symbols express contradiction and opposition less than synthesis and paradox.[24]

This quality of women's religious writings has been consistently noted by the greatest scholars who have studied them, although it has not been placed in a theoretical framework. Baron von Hügel, commenting on Catherine of Genoa's use of simultaneity of opposites or paradoxes, says, "For it was the element of simultaneity, of organic interpenetration of the

[23.34] Iconographic evidence supports this point, but ambiguously. [. . .] [Depictions of women's visions show woman as recipient.] Even here, however, the emphasis on woman's receiving undoubtedly arises more from her status as lay (as opposed to clerical) than from any reversal of her social role as cook.

[24.35] [. . .] Although French feminist writing has been determinedly atheistical and some French feminists will no doubt reject the subject of this book as uninteresting, what I suggest about the continuity of woman's sense of self into her symbolic language in medieval texts could be explained very much as Luce Irigaray has explained present feminist discourse in "The Sex Which Is Not One," trans. Claudia Reeder, in Elaine Marks and Isabelle de Courtivron, eds, *New French Feminisms: An Anthology* (Amherst: University of Massachusetts Press, 1980), pp. 99–106.

God-like *Totum Simul*, which chiefly impressed her in these deepest moments."[25] Brant
Pelphrey, in his exposition of the theology of Julian of Norwich, suggests that Julian saw sin
as a necessary (if painful) part of being human and that her theory of union with God did not
involve "stages" the soul "passed beyond" but, rather, a continuity of self, a becoming fully
human with Jesus.[26] Peter Dronke, writing on Margaret Porete and the female heretics of
Montaillou, comments both on the originality of women's approach to evil and on the lack
of "apriorism" in women's writings, pointing out their avoidance of rules of either/or and
their substitution of singular, existentially appropriate solutions.[27]

All this is not to say that male mystics never use paradox (one thinks of Nicholas of Cusa)
or that male theologians never push such paradoxical synthesis to the point of reconciling
heaven and hell (one thinks of Origen) or that male penitents never substitute continuity of
self in Jesus for passage up the hierarchy of the cosmos to God (one thinks of Francis).[28] But
the explosion of paradox in a Hadewijch, a Margaret Porete, or a Catherine of Genoa, the
agonized rejection of the existence of hell in a Mechtild of Magdeburg or a Julian of
Norwich, the delicious groveling in the humiliations of being human that characterizes
virtually every religious woman of the later Middle Ages – these form a consistent pattern
that is found only infrequently in religious men. And behind the pattern lies a confidence
that all is one – all is, as Julian said, a hazelnut held in the palm of God's hand – because it
is finally the humanity that we most despicably are that is redeemed.[29] It is our "Me" that
becomes God.[30]

To argue this is to argue that religious women saw themselves as human *because* they were
women, as redeemable *because* they were women. It may appear a very odd argument in light
of certain recent feminist claims. Jo Ann McNamara, Rosemary Reuther, Marie Delcourt,
and Marina Warner have, for example, argued that because male was in western culture
superior to female, woman had to take on symbolic maleness (or, at the very least, abandonment of femaleness) in order to signify spiritual advance.[31] They cite not only a few scattered

[25.36] [Friedrich] von Hügel, [*The*] *Mystical Element* [*of Religion as Studied in Saint Catherine of Genoa
and Her Friends*, 2 vols (London, 1908)] vol. I, p. 238; see also [D.C.] Nugent, ["The"] Annihilation of
[St.] Catherine of Genoa," [*Mystics Quarterly* 10.4 (1984):] 185. [. . .]

[26.37] Brant Pelphrey, *Love Was His Meaning* [: *The Theology and Mysticism of Julian of Norwich*
(Salzburg: University of Salzburg, 1982)]. This reading of Julian makes her *Showings* a more conceptually and theologically subtle statement of the kind of "continuity of self" I find in other women's
writing from the period. [. . .]

[27.38] See [Peter] Dronke, [*Women Writers of the Middle Ages: A Critical Study of Texts from Perpetua
(+203) to Marguerite Porete (+1310)* (Cambridge: Cambridge University Press, 1984), henceforth
WW], p. x. For further comments on the significance of Dronke's observations, see my review of his
book in *Modern Language Quarterly* [46 (1985): 386–9].

[28.39] But Francis, of course, achieves such an emphasis on his self as human through a series of
extravagant reversals, seeing himself as poor, naked, female, leprous, etc.

[29.40] Julian [of Norwich], [*A*] *Book of Showings* [*to the Anchoress Julian of Norwich*, ed. Edmund
Colledge and James Walsh, 2 parts (Toronto: Pontifical Institute of Medieval Studies, 1978)]. The
Long Text, ch. 5, revelation 1; pt 2, p. 299.

[30.41] The French feminist Julia Kristeva, in a brilliant discussion of women's discourse, suggests that
women's language "traverses" – it expresses process – whereas man's bifurcates and opposes. She also
writes of woman's movement beyond "I" in language – her sense of self as a "subject-in-the-making"
– in ways that echo Catherine of Genoa's rejection of the "I" (for very different reasons). See interview
with Kristeva by Xavière Gauthier, "Oscillation du 'pouvoir' au 'refus,'" trans. Marilyn August, in
Marks and de Courtivron, *New French Feminisms*, pp. 165–7.

[31.42] Jo Ann McNamara, "Sexual Equality [and the Cult of Virginity in Early Christian Thought,"
Feminist Studies 3.3/4 (1976): 145–58]; [Rosemary] Reuther, ["Misogynism and Virginal Feminism in

references in the patristic period to women seeing their courage as "male" but also the many (predominantly patristic) stories of transvestite saints – of women masquerading as men, and sometimes even growing beards, in order to escape marriage (or rape) or to enter monasteries. They also cite Joan of Arc. Such work tends to suggest that gender reversal was a powerful symbol to women. Moreover, recent research demonstrates that cross-dressing by males was extremely rare in the Middle Ages (and sometimes persecuted as sexual perversion).[32] Although historians who focus on Joan of Arc have not tended to find parallels to her cross-dressing in the later Middle Ages (thus weakening their case), it is in fact true that late medieval women did adopt male dress, especially in order to run away from their families or to go on pilgrimages.[33] Why, then, do I suggest that reversals, especially gender reversals, were *not* crucial in women's religiosity?

My argument is basically that cross-dressing was for women primarily a practical device, whereas to men it was primarily a religious symbol. Women sometimes put on male clothes in order to escape their families, to avoid the dangers of rape and pillage, or to take on male roles such as soldier, pilgrim, or hermit. But, once freed from the world by convent walls or hermitage, by tertiary status, by the practice of continence, by mystical inspiration, or even by miraculous inedia, women spoke of their lives in female images. They saw themselves, metaphorically speaking, not as warriors for Christ but as brides, as pregnant virgins, as housewives, as mothers of God. Perhaps exactly *because* cross-dressing was a radical yet practical social step for women, it was not finally their most powerful symbol of self. For men, on the contrary, who did not cross-dress as a practical step and could have gained

the Fathers of the Church," in Rosemary Reuther, ed., *Religion and Sexism: Images of Women in the Jewish and Christian Traditions* (New York: Simon & Schuster, 1974), pp. 150–83]; Marie Delcourt, "Le Complexe de Diane dans l'hagiographie chrétienne," *Revue de l'histoire des religions* 153 (1958): 1–33; and [Marina] Warner, *Joan of Arc[: The Image of Female Heroism* (New York: Knopf, 1981)]. For a sensitive criticism of the approach of these articles, see Evelyne Patlagean, "L'Histoire de la femme déguisée en moine et l'évolution de la sainteté féminine à Byzance," *Studi medievali*, 3rd ser., 17, fasc. 2 (1976): 597–623. Both Delcourt and Patlagean contain references to the important early work by Usener and Delehaye on transvestite saints.

[32.43] Bullough, "Transvestites." John Boswell, [*Christianity, Social Tolerance and Homosexuality: Gay People in Western Europe from the Beginnings of the Christian Era to the Fourteenth Century* (Chicago: Chicago University Press, 1980)], has little to say about cross-dressing. The fifth-century translator of Soranus, Caelius Aurelianus, sees male cross-dressing as a sign of homosexuality; see Helen R. Lemay, "William of Saliceto on Human Sexuality," *Viator* 12 (1981): 179.

[33.44] Caesarius of Heisterbach tells a few such stories from the late twelfth century, but they are imitated from patristic tales. See Caesarius [of Heisterbach, *Dialogus miraculorum*, ed. Joseph Strange, 2 vols (Cologne, 1851)], Distinctio 1, chs 40–3, vol. 1, pp. 47–54. For three other examples, see [Michael] Goodich, "Contours of Female Piety [in Later Medieval Hagiography," *Church History* 50 (1981):] 25, and Matthew Paris, *Historia major [juxta exemplar Londinense 1571 verbatim recusa*, ed. William Wats (London, 1640)], for the year 1225, pp. 325–7 (adapted from the chronicle of Roger of Wendover). Other examples are Christina of Markyate, who escaped her family in male garb, and Margery Kempe, who wore male clothes on pilgrimage. The girl described by Matthew Paris, who took refuge with the friars, used the opportunity provided by male clothing to preach: "et Evangelium pacis per civitates et castella, et praecipue sexui muliebri praedicare studuerat" ["she was zealous to preach the Gospel of peace throughout the cities and castles, above all to the woman"] (p. 326). For a fifteenth-century story of a woman who disguised herself as a man in order to attend university, see Martin of Leibitz (or of Zips) (d. 1461?), "Senatorium sive dialogus historicus Martini abbatis Scotorum Viennae Austriae," in Hieronymus Pez, ed., *Scriptores rerum Austriacarum veteres ac genuini* . . . , 2 vols (Leipzig, 1725), vol. 2, col. 629ff., cited in Michael H. Shank, "A Female University Student in [late] Medieval [K]racow," *Signs* [12 (1987): 373–80].

nothing socially by it except opprobrium, gender reversal was a highly charged, even frightening symbol.[34]

In any case, whatever the reason for the fascination felt by medieval men with female cross-dressing – a fascination apparently shared by modern historians of both genders – the evidence concerning imagery is clear. Women's basic images of religious self were *not* inverted images, not male images. Where women used gender as image they usually spoke of themselves as female to a male God or as androgynous. Mechtild of Magdeburg, Hildegard of Bingen, Catherine of Siena, and Margery Kempe referred to themselves as poor women, unlettered and weak. Hildegard actually dressed her nuns as brides when they went to receive communion. Margery gloried in relating to God as wife and mother. Catherine reported that she had wanted, as a child, to imitate one of the early transvestite saints, but as an adult she heard directly from Christ in a vision that such reversal was not necessary: God preferred her to teach and inspire others as a lowly woman.[35]

As I explained in chapter 9 [of *Holy Feast and Holy Fast*], women's use of female images did not express any incapacity for godliness or for approach to God. Indeed, Peter Dronke has pointed out that the topos of the "poor little woman" was sometimes an ironic claim to divine inspiration, to being the vessel or mouthpiece chosen by God.[36] And some women writers passed beyond even such irony. Julian of Norwich, for example, deleted her reference to female incapacity when she expanded her *Showings* into their longer, more theologically audacious and sophisticated version.[37] Moreover, women's images for self were frequently androgynous, for they frequently included qualities the larger culture stereotyped as male (such as discipline or judgment) in their understanding of "motherly" or "womanly." Gertrude of Helfta, Hadewijch, Catherine of Siena, and Julian of Norwich all mix gender images and personality characteristics (such as tenderness, severity, love, discipline) so thoroughly in describing both the soul and God that one can only intermittently see in their writings the common association of soul with female and God with male. Finally, where women's own symbols did associate with self activities or characteristics that the broader culture saw as female (for example, lactation and food preparation, weakness and fleshliness), women tended to broaden these symbols to refer to all people rather than to underline the opposition of male/female. As we saw above, women's sense of themselves as symbolizing the "humanity of Christ" carried the concept *human* beyond any male/female dichotomy.

Hildegard of Bingen, for example, did write that male and female are different in social, biological, and religious roles (although even here she stressed complementarity more than

---

[34.45] In the popular festivals of late medieval Europe, men sometimes masqueraded as women (see [Natalie Z.] Davis, *Society and Culture* [*in Early Modern France* (Stanford: Stanford University Press, 1975)], pp. 124–31), and such practices were frequently disapproved of by moralists and theologians. (For an example of disapproval, see Salimbene's chronicle in [G.G.] Coulton, [*From St.*] *Francis to Dante* [: *Translations from the Chronicle of the Franciscan Salimbene* . . . , 2nd ed. (1907; repr. Philadelphia: University of Pennsylvania Press, 1972)], p. 220.) Moreover, the idea of female cross-dressing was a threatening symbol to men; and there is reason to suspect that the tales of transvestite women that circulated in monastic circles were sometimes expressions of male anxiety and prurience without basis in historical fact (see Anson, "Female Transvestite").

[35.47] See [Raymond of Capua, *Life of Catherine of Siena*, pt 2, ch. 1 pars. 121–2, *AASS* April, vol. 3, p. 892]. We should not forget that although Catherine spoke of men as courageous and women as weak, she applied the adjectives *manly* and *womanly* to people of both genders [. . .].

[36.48] Dronke, *WW*, passim, esp. pp. 66, 82.

[37.49] Julian, *Book of Showings*, ed. Colledge and Walsh, The Short Text, ch. 6; pt 1, p. 222; the reference is deleted in The Long Text.

did the male theologians of her day). But her most profound use of woman as symbol drew no contrast to men at all. "Woman" was what modern writers sometimes call "mankind." In Hildegard's vision of salvation, the "image of woman" – that is, humanity – stands below the cross and receives Christ's blood [. . .]. Two centuries later, Catherine of Siena did criticize women as weak. But she said, of herself and other women, that they were all children, drawing the milk of suffering from the breast of Christ's humanity. And by suffering she meant Christ's suffering and their own. Thus the soul was a suckling child who became one with a mother whose feeding was suffering, and that suffering saved the world. The child *was* the mother; the eating *was* feeding others; the suffering *was* fertility. Such images go beyond dichotomies, yet they arise from and express ordinary female experiences. Women's images, although informed and made possible by the symbolic oppositions of the dominant theological tradition, are themselves neither dichotomies nor inversions.

Just as men's lives show much actual conversion and reversal, paralleling the strongly dichotomous nature of their symbols, so women's actual life stories show less reversal, paralleling their use of symbols of continuity. As I noted in chapter 1, [of *Holy Feast and Holy Fast*], Weinstein and Bell have demonstrated that the pattern of women's lives shows fewer ruptures; instead, there is gradually dawning vocation, voiced earlier and consolidated far more slowly.[38] This difference does not appear to be entirely a matter of women's greater powerlessness, of the extreme difficulty they sometimes faced in rejecting suitors, husbands, children, or parental dictates if a vocation to chastity or deprivation came to them in adolescence or adulthood. Survey of a large number of medieval saints' lives suggests that girls (unlike boys) often knew before the age of eight that they wished to avoid marriage. To such women, virginity and humble service of family members or of sister nuns was as much a continuation of childhood as it was an escape from the adult status "married woman."

The same sort of explanation I suggested for male use of symbols may explain female usages as well. Girls' more continuous self-development, involving no fundamental need to develop a concept of "other," may help explain women's avoidance of dichotomous imagery and their tendency to elaborate as symbols aspects of life closer to ordinary experience (eating, suffering, lactating). Recent feminist psychological theory has suggested that the profoundly asymmetrical patterns of child-rearing in western culture may influence female children toward a less acute sense of binary oppositions and of "otherness."[39] Moreover, women's place in some sense outside the *ordines* (statuses) of late medieval Europe may suggest why images of status reversal seemed to them less pertinent and interesting. Structuralist anthropologists have recently shown the ways dichotomous symbols – especially the fundamental dichotomy culture/nature – tend to express *and support* the power of those identified with "culture."[40]

Whatever explanation one proposes, it is clear that women's way of using and living symbols was different from men's. The difference lay not merely in what symbols were

---

[38.51] [In *Saints and Society*, analyzed by Bynum, *Holy Feast*, on pp. 24–5. Peter] Dinzelbacher, *Vision und Visionsliteratur* [*im Mittelalter* (Stuttgart: Hiersemann, 1981)], pp. 24–5. Dinzelbacher, *Vision und Visionsliteratur*, p. 229, sums up differences between early medieval visions, characteristic of men, and later visions, characteristic of women, in a way that underlines this point. Women's visions were expected and sought for; men's occurred suddenly. Women's visions confirmed them in an already chosen way of life; men's marked the onset of a new life.

[39.52] See above, n. 18.29. See also Judith Van Herik, "The Feminist Critique of Classical Psychoanalysis," in David Tracy and Steven Kepnes, eds, *The Challenge of Psychology to Faith* [*Concilium: Revue internationale de théologie* 156] (Edinburgh: Clark, 1982), pp. 83–6.

[40.53] See above, nn. 4.14, 5.15.

chosen but also in how symbols related to self. Where men stressed male/female contrasts and used imagery of reversal to express their dependence on God, women expressed their dependence on God in imagery at least partly drawn from their own gender and avoided symbolic reversals. Although men wrote about the nature of woman, women tended to write, not about gender (male versus female), but about the soul or about humanity. There is thus a sense in which women's use of metaphors and images took a shape of its own, oblique to a male tradition of spiritual writing in which the male/female dichotomy was a symbol for many other oppositions. And yet it is clear that women's sense of self was formed within and influenced by the symbolic dichotomies of the dominant theological tradition. It was from age-old notions that God, mind, and power are male whereas soul, flesh, and weakness are female that women drew inspiration for a spirituality in which their own suffering humanity had cosmic significance.

[. . .]

17 Burdens of Matrimony: Husbanding and Gender in Medieval Italy

Susan Mosher Stuard

If there is received opinion on husbanding as a determinant of gender for men in medieval times, I suppose it was supplied by David Herlihy in 1983 when he argued from art and literature that the last figure set into the constellation of holy child and devoted mother to form the ideal family was the self-denying husband, modeled upon Joseph. Herlihy saw Joseph's entry into iconography as a relatively late medieval phenomenon; Joseph began to figure prominently in urban Italian art in the fifteenth century.[1] Yet Joseph's bent and weary figure, relegated to the periphery of the scene, seems to have held few attractions for men in the vigor of their youth. It is in fact difficult to imagine any success at all for Joseph as a male ideal except in a struggle where age triumphs over youth. Perhaps then, a search for husbanding as a determinant of gender must be undertaken by investigating generational relations among men rather than by studying changing patterns of husband–wife relations.

To turn attention to the early stages of this generational conflict – perhaps I should call it taming men to behave like Joseph – is to take the quest to the twelfth century. In the middle years of that century, at the University of Bologna and in civil and church courts, teaching on a husband's financial obligations to his wife suddenly narrowed to the crucial task of husbanding a wife's natal family inheritance, that is, in Roman law, the wife's Falcidian quarter, or full share of inheritance from her natal family, paid to her upon her marriage in the form of a dowry. It has been generally assumed that this reversal in the direction in which marital gifts moved favored husbands with unencumbered access to their wives' wealth, rather than requiring husbands to pay to marry as had been the case both in Germanic and late Roman customary practice. But, I would argue, men who married did not solely gain at the expense of their wives;[2] instead, elders found legal ways to tie up money flowing to youth, their stated aim being to assure the young couple always had the means on hand to support the "burdens of matrimony." Clearly, marriage changed a man's relationship to his father, uncles, and elder brothers, admitting him to the decision-making body of those who con-

---

[1] David Herlihy, "The Making of the Medieval Family: Symmetry, Structure, and Sentiment," *Journal of Family History* 8 (1983): 116–30; see esp. 127–8.
[2] For the analogue of this argument featuring gender and married women, see Susan Mosher Stuard, "From Women to Woman: New Thinking about Gender, c. 1140," *Thought*, 64 (1989): 208–19.

trolled the patrimony, a personal rearrangement of the practical effects of patriarchy. At the same time, however, a wife's dowry established a contractual relation between a new husband and his father-in-law, possibly too the bride's brothers, uncles, and cousins, an acquired kin group the Florentines honored with the name *parentado*. The complexity of responsibilities in a man's life increased substantially with marriage; so did the numbers of persons who looked over a husband's shoulder to see that he behaved responsibly.

Relations between wife and husband were not, of course, left unaltered by such momentous changes. Because gender encompasses the system of social relations between women and men, the tightening of the definition of woman before the law, which was a component of the new legal controls, also restricted, or tightened, gender assumptions about men. Gratian asserted that "it is the natural order among mankind that a woman serves her husband as children do parents; the justice in this is that the lesser serve the greater," and also, "woman should be subject to her husband's rule and has no authority, either to teach, to bear witness, to give surety, or to judge." He defined woman's condition categorically for canon law, basing his case upon a married woman's condition.[3] A woman's resulting "incapacity" before the law mandated certain "capacities" from her husband, first among them being his obligation to preserve her dowry. A husband was answerable before church courts and, in time, before civil courts, if he failed to act for his wife. What a man had to do was as constrained by gender assumptions as were his wife's choices, albeit in opposite ways.

Before the twelfth century, husbands had, by and large, profited from the traditional gift giving prompted by marriage, if we consider men's roles within the orbit of their own natal families. To illustrate this I would like to turn to some important new research by Barbara Kreutz on Lombard charters in tenth-century South Italy. Kreutz cites a charter drawn up in 940 in which a husband declared that if he should predecease his father, his wife was to have her *morgengabe*, a quarter share of any inheritance from the father, over which she was to have complete control.[4] This was generous – a Lombard wife generally expected the *morgengabe*, a *quarta* (one-fourth her husband's estate, which she owned unencumbered).[5] But what I find interesting in this 940 Cava charter is the control of wealth a husband gained from his natal family when he wed. Clearly this husband had already secured sufficient family funds to allow him to marry with the required resources, so his kin had themselves assumed the "burden of matrimony" by sharing out to him part of the family estate well before the death of his father (men generally married in their twenties in this era). This man came from a landowning family, and the charter's provisions are consonant with general practice among propertied families before eleventh-century European society began to enforce the right of primogeniture.

[3] Gratian, *Decretum, Causa* 33, *Questio* 5, *Corpus juris canonici*, ed. E. Freidburg (Graz: Bernard Tauchnitz, 1911), vol. 1, cols 1254–5. This is my translation from the Latin; the original is as follows: "Est ordo naturalis in hominibus, ut feminae serviant viris, et filii parentibus, quia in illis hec iusticia est, ut maiori serviant minor"; and "Mulierem constat subiectam dominio viri esse, et nullam auctoritatem habere; nec docere potest, nec testis esse, neque fidem dare, nec iudicare."
[4] Barbara Kreutz, "Lombard Women, Lombard Law, Lombard Reality in the Ninth and Tenth Centuries," paper presented at the Medieval Academy of America, Madison, Wisconsin, April 1988; to be published in expanded form as "The Twilight of *Morgengabe*" in a festschrift for David Herlihy, forthcoming. See nn. 36, 49. The author cites *Codex Diplomaticus Cavensis*, 8 vols (Milan: Hoepli, 1873–93), 1 : 166 (940).
[5] See Diane Owen Hughes, "From Brideprice to Dowry in Mediterranean Europe," *Journal of Family History* 3 (1978): 263–96.

Following Harry Brod's dictum that "traditional scholarship's treatment of generic man as human norm systematically excludes from consideration what is unique to men *qua* men,"[6] I wish to examine how this devolution of wealth to young men at marriage might have affected their masculine identity. First, it effectively marked off youth from adulthood. With the late marrying pattern now applied over most of Germanic Europe,[7] not just the northwest, this was likely an event of the third decade of life for young men. Men were launched into adulthood at this rite through gaining wealth and responsibility simultaneously. Households may have been virilocal, but they were seldom patrilineal. A young couple set up their own modest quarters, perhaps the first of a number of moves if they prospered. Responsibilities came in large, but not overwhelming, measure with marriage; others descended over the course of married life with the birth of children, further inheritances, and age. Marriage did not even deter men from wandering off in search of their fortunes. One explanation for European expansion in this sparsely settled age was that women administered resources at home so effectively that their husbands were freed to seek out new opportunities abroad.[8] This was not be a lasting feature of European life, however. Footloose adventures tended to cease with marriage by the twelfth century, Georges Duby relates.[9] The wandering years in which young men sought their fortunes terminated with marriage, allowing an advantageous marriage to a propertied widow or an heiress to signify the making of a fortune and an end for youth's caprice, at least among the propertied classes.

When husbanding merely marked a passage in life – that is, until the twelfth century – it lacked the force to define a man in relation to his wife. As a result, the traits that composed identity remained multivalent for men. This was the age of epic, when oral tradition had the power to define. A nickname or epithet often individuated a man according to his physical attributes (Harald Bluetooth), his idiosyncrasies (Notker the Stammerer), or his behaviors (Robert the Crafty), and none too kindly. Honorifics (the Great, the Bold, the Debonair) belonged to a later feudal age, although they were reflected back upon the remembered heroes of this earlier time. Until the end of the first feudal age, the eleventh century in Marc Bloch's chronology, even an ordinary man earned a sobriquet to distinguish him from his fellows, as early charters reveal in plenty.[10] A patronym or a matronym might serve to distinguish a man, but he was not known as a spouse. Foibles, skills, or attributes were encoded in nicknames that stuck like glue even in the formal space of a notary's registers, but marriage lacked such an eponymous role while it merely signified a passage in life.

---

[6] Harry Brod, ed., *The Making of Masculinities* (Boston: Allen & Unwin, 1987), p. 2.
[7] David Herlihy, *Medieval Households* (Cambridge, Mass: Harvard University Press, 1985), pp. 109–11.
[8] David Herlihy, "Land, Family and Women in Continental Europe, 700–1100," *Traditio* 18 (1962): 89–120.
[9] Georges Duby, "The Youth Culture of Twelfth Century France," in *Social Historians of Contemporary France*, ed. Marc Ferro, trans. The staff of Annales, Paris (New York: Harper, 1972), pp. 87–99.
[10] Marc Bloch, *Feudal Society*, trans. L. A. Manyon (New York: Harper, 1972); for nicknames in charters, see Robert S. Lopez and Irving I. Raymond, *Medieval Trade in the Mediterranean World* (New York: Columbia University Press, 1955): "Malfiliastro" (Genoa) (p. 181); also "Porchetto Streiaporco" – the surname was a long-standing name for a prominent family of the Genoese merchant aristocracy (p. 172); in Venice the patrician Giovanni Loredan was called merely *vacca* (cow) in the body of a contract – no other name was supplied (p. 283).

Marriage Law and New Values

The new set of values associated with marriage law in the twelfth century placed gender distinction at the heart of the matter of a man's definition, fixing him firmly in relation to his wife. Gratian stated, "Woman is subject to her husband," which he explained is the natural order *in hominibus* (among mankind). *Vir* and *homo* took on distinct meanings with the gendered association of husbanding attached to the former – *vir*. Gratian's arguments about a woman's incapacity followed this phrase.[11] Thus the incapacity argument, which held such power for defining women as passive and dependent in subsequent centuries, also established a new identity for a husband by creating a polar interdependence between husband and wife. Because a man was a husband, he bore responsibility for both. [Whether he wants to or not], he must supply the capacity, directing "head," or public *persona*, for both himself and his wife. Context is all in Gratian, and the context of this discussion is the issue of a man leaving his marriage to enter holy orders without his wife's consent. Gratian's answer is, clearly, no, he may not leave. A husband found no escape from the demands a capacity justification placed upon him. As Gratian's argument was applied in ecclesiastical courts and, perhaps more to the point, by civil lawyers in civil courts after the passage of new statute laws in towns that appropriated this capacity argument, husbands, in contrast to their peers who were priests, monks, or unmarried bachelors, were firmly pinned to their responsibilities based upon the gendered understanding that they spoke for their wives according to natural law.[12]

There was no necessary application of this capacity argument to property settlements in marriage, let alone to dowry, but civil lawyers saw a relevance in Gratian's arguments that they linked to property rights arguments. Furthermore, Gratian was studied in schools of law, and his phrase "without dowry there is no marriage" grew famous in time.[13] Later lawyers simply linked what Gratian said about marriage, that it required a Roman dowry, to what he had said elsewhere about married women, that they had no legal capacity. Once these two ideas were joined, control over a woman's dowry and natal inheritance neatly fell to the husband for the span of his lifetime. Women came more and more under legal guardianship with a reimposition of what Roman law had termed the *tutela*, that is, a male right to represent a woman before the law at all times and under all circumstances.[14]

Scholars are of two minds on the implications of the husband's new obligations before the law. Manlio Bellomo sees little here other than a new statutory permission for the *capo di famiglia* [head of the family] to condense a woman's dowry into the patrimony to the benefit of his lineage. Bellomo cites the thirteenth-century laws of cities that eased the way for this strengthening of a husband's financial control.[15] Julius Kirshner is not so certain, and he cites the late medieval Italian jurists who insisted that husbands did not own their wives' dowries

---

[11] Gratian, *Decretum, Causa* 33, *Questio* 5, c. 12, *Corpus juris canonici*, vol. 1, cols 1254–5. "Mulieres viris suis debent subesse."

[12] See, for example, the *Constitutem Legis: Constitutum Usus*, Pisa. Ms. 415, Beinecke Rare Book Library, Yale University. Comparable changes occurred in the law in Siena; see Eleanor Riemer, "Women in the Medieval City: Sources and Uses of Wealth by Sienese Women in the Thirteenth Century" (Ph.D. dissertation, New York University, 1975), pp. 71–3. For change to Roman dowry in Genoa, see Hughes, "From Brideprice to Dowry," pp. 290ff.

[13] Gratian, *Decretum, Causa* 33, *Questio* 5, c. 6, *Corpus juris canonici*, vol. 1, col. 1106. "Sine dote non facit coniugium."

[14] Gigliola Villata di Renzo, *La tutela: Indagini sulla scuola dei glossatori* (Milan: Giuffre, 1975).

[15] Manlio Bellomo, *Ricerche sui rapporti patrimoniali tra coniugi* (Milan: Giuffre, 1961), pp. 8–25.

but managed them instead, and that a dowry must be intact if a wife predeceases her husband. Other directives in consonance with this principle meant dotal goods always stood in a husband's custody and that he was answerable to a woman's father as donor and a woman's children as heirs.[16] Heaven help the husband found "verging toward insolvency" for, as Kirshner points out, his wife may, nay must, sue him for her dowry. If this principle was enforced in courts, then there was a convergence of husband's financial obligations in marriage and man's authority, or his legal capacity for his wife as Gratian defined it, that has important implications for gender.

Examples from the Archives

It is useful to take this problem to cases. Perhaps Venice, whose late twelfth- and thirteenth-century legal practices are known through surviving records, may shed some light on how husband's roles came to be understood. The *Procuratoria* of San Marco became a repository for married women's dowries in Venice by the twelfth century. As guardians, the procurators took their responsibilities seriously. They allowed some husbands "authority" over their wives' dowries – that is, husbands could remove amounts of dotal goods – but under stringent restrictions. Reinhold Mueller states:

> Since dowries were often brought to the marriage in the form of real estate [real estate was good as gold in Venice, whereas gold itself was the preferred gift of dowry elsewhere], special provisions restricted the alienation of such property. The doge Pietro Ziani in 1226 saw to the approval of regulations for the sale of real estate [in dowry] *ad usum novum* [for another use]. After the extent and worth of the dowry had been demonstrated under oath, the husband or seller of the real estate was required to deposit in the *Procuratoria* a sum equal to the appraised value of the dowry. While this provision guaranteed the dowry, it immobilized the capital.[17]

This wrinkle in Venetian law supports Kirshner's contention that the law held husbands liable for the awarded sum or its equivalent.[18] But thinking changed over time in Venice and, in this market-oriented society, practice moved in the direction of increasing liquidity for the sums tied up in dotal gifts. Over the following decades, the requirement to leave sums with the procurators of equal value to the dowry was relaxed. Men might then invest dowry funds, but only in low-risk ventures. They still had to account to the procurators for their investments' success.

Dowries were the cause of constant litigation. In Ragusa (Dubrovnik) in 1319, the Small Council distrained Anna de Bodacio's dowry along with the private wealth of her husband, Peter Paborra, in order to satisfy foreign creditors. Heedless of the Italian revival of Roman law that forbade this expedient move, the councilors trusted close kin and other members of the affluent aristocratic circle to buoy up these victims of the uncertainties of long-distance trade.[19] Meanwhile, in Venice, Mueller states that in 1338,

[16] Julius Kirshner, "Wives' Claims against Insolvent Husbands," in *Women of the Medieval World*, ed. Julius Kirshner and Suzanne F. Wemple (Oxford: Basil Blackwell, 1985), pp. 256–303. *Vergere ad inopiam* was the legal phrase.

[17] Reinhold C. Mueller, "The Procurators of San Marco," *Studi Veneziani* 13 (1971): 176.

[18] The phrases is *dos estimata*.

[19] *Libri Reformationes, Monumenta spectantia historiam slavorum meridiolium*, ed. Fr. Racki (Zagreb: Sumptibus Academiae Scientiarum et Artium, 1879–97), vols 10, 13, 27, 28, 29, known consecutively as *Monumenta Ragusina*, 1–4, vol. 5, p. 93.

having sold real estate bound in dowry, Andrea Boldu was to deposit the dowry in the Procuratia; instead lent the 1,000 lire to a German count, who deposited jewels in the Procuratia as surety for the dowry. Each year for 17 years he had received 5 per cent plus a "gift" of 12 lire, so that the return totalled 6.2 per cent. When Boldu purchased more real estate, he put a part in his wife's name, and withdrew the jewels.[20]

With such close surveillance of a husband's custodial role, there was little flexibility in Boldu's investment strategy. In Florence, where prosecution before the law made misman-agement of dowry a scandal, Giovanni Morelli could ruin his brother-in-law's name merely by complaining angrily that his sister was too obedient to her husband. As Thomas Kuehn relates, "[The sister's] husband would suddenly appear at home with a notary and witnesses in tow, explaining that she must consent to some deal." Morelli had reason for anger because the obligation to support his sister eventually fell on his shoulders, but not before his hapless brother-in-law was ruined beyond repair.[21] In Italian city-states there was scant opportunity to escape from the capacity argument that the revival of Roman law had pinned on husbands.

The key to what was expected of husbands may lie in how a husband's custodial role reflected current understandings of that newly popular medium of exchange of the twelfth and early thirteenth centuries: silver coin. Here, in preserving dotal wealth, valued and also frequently awarded in good coin, husbands faced an increasingly difficult task as custodians. This occurred against all received wisdom, because coin – that is, the new medium of currency – was not constant in value but fluctuated, decreasing in purchasing power, often through devaluation, much more commonly than it increased in value. Devaluation was a fact of medieval urban life, as there was never sufficient silver to support the currency needs of the age.[22]

Dowry was awarded in coin whenever possible (although Venice continued to favor real estate). In fact, it became a matter of family honor in most Italian cities to award dowry in the best coin obtainable. Pierre Bonnassie has gone so far as to say that dowry was the first of all intrafamilial exchanges commuted to coin because a woman's kin were loath to divide assets more essential to the patrimony for the purpose of endowing a bride and groom.[23] Further-more, there is ample proof that then, as now, people thought the newly wed couple should receive the very best gifts. Applied to dowry given in currency, that meant the best coin available: the best groats of silver or, when minted, florins or ducats of gold. By the late Middle Ages in Florence, for example, dowry was paid in special bagged florins guaranteed to be full-weight coin.[24] It is worth suggesting, perhaps, that the movement to gold coinage owes some debt to affluent families's quest for specie that accurately conveyed their prestige and worth in marital exchanges. Good coins were saved up over a lifetime for a dowry, and

[20] Mueller, The Procurators of San Marco," 178–9 n. 141.
[21] Thomas Kuehn, "'*Cum Consensu Mundualdi*': Legal Guardianship of Women in Quattrocento Florence," *Viator* 13 (1982): 322. Kuehn cites Giovanni Morelli, *Ricordi*, ed. Vittore Branca (Florence: F. Le Monnier, 1956), pp. 187–8.
[22] Peter Spufford, *Money and Its Uses in the Middle Ages* (Cambridge: Cambridge University Press, 1988), pp. 240–88.
[23] Pierre Bonnassie, "A Family of the Barcelona Countryside and Its Economic Activities around the Year 1000," in *Early Medieval Society*, ed. Sylvia Thrupp (New York: Appleton-Century-Crofts, 1967), pp. 103–23; see esp. pp. 120–1.
[24] Mark Phillips, *The Memoir of Marco Parenti* (Princeton: Princeton University Press, 1987), pp. 23, 150–68. Phillips gives one detailed example of how two families in Florence felt about the quality of wedding gifts.

it is possible that merchants and bankers might recognize a husband verging on insolvency who spent his wife's dowry by the sudden presence of very good coin in circulation. If so, dowry wealth was as marked as the larger influx of coin brought by a visiting ruler from silver-rich Goslar or later, Hungary, whose presence in a big city was broadcast by a marked change for the better in specie in circulation.[25]

In this new cash economy husbands became an accountable personal line of defense against the vicissitudes of a money economy when they were vested with the obligation to preserve the worth of dowry valued in a currency that, understood or not, refused to maintain its own value. The reintroduced Roman law that stood as the foundation for husbands' custodial roles had not been designed to deal with this dilemma. The economy of late Rome had been sufficiently stable, if not static, that dotal wealth had a reasonable chance of maintaining its value over the life of a marriage. The twelfth and thirteenth centuries placed husbands up against expectations at odds with the volatility of money in an emerging commercial economy. Yet, medieval Italian jurists apparently still clung to the outmoded notion of fixed monetary values without modification through at least the fourteenth and fifteenth centuries.[26] Under these circumstances, a husband faced some very difficult choices. As husband, he must invest the dowry in his custody because that was the only way to keep up with the devaluation of money. On the other hand, he must not risk dowry because he was accountable for it, but what was a commercial investment if not risk? Dowry must not sit idle, for it would lose value, but it must not be lost in speculation; by force of circumstances a husband was enjoined to "make" money. Through failure to acknowledge, and very possibly to understand, the proclivities of their own medium of exchange, the enforcers of the law had placed married men in the position of being "in authority" and husbanding a wife's wealth against all realistic expectation of consistent success.

In application to daily life, the law came to mean that a husband kept dowry funds separate from other capital. Often a husband was restrained from investing dowry abroad in long-distance trade, with its inherent risk, but that meant he was also forbidden from investing dowry in the most lucrative ventures open to men in marketing towns and cities. By the late Middle Ages, it was accepted practice that dowry was to be invested near home, that is to say, within the town, in every sense inhabiting a special category of "domestic capital." Efforts to corner this capital source may be seen in Florence, where a *Monte della Dote* [public dowry fund] was established so fathers might invest in city funds over decades to raise dowry. Husbands were encouraged to leave dowries invested in the fund instead of withdrawing them after marriage. "Pursuing honor while avoiding sin" was touted as a fine reason for investing in the city's debt as the fund's agents became new interested parties in scrutinizing men's performance at preserving their wives', and daughters', wealth.[27]

Over three centuries, the formative influences of the law upon the understanding of a husband's role had gone some distance toward creating a new *persona* for men. The privileged position in which husbands stood before the law, because they possessed legal capacity for themselves and their wives, had been revealed to entail a clear burden. Other features of a man's identity paled before the court-enforced obligation to perform a custodial role in the family.

[25] See Spufford, *Money and Its Uses*, pp. 240ff.
[26] Kirshner, "Wives' Claims," pp. 266–75.
[27] See Julius Kirshner, " 'Pursuing Honor while Avoiding Sin': The Monte della Dote of Florence," *Quaderni de Studi senesi*, 87 (Siena, 1977): 177–258.

Implications for Gender Identity

Under the principles of law laid out by Gratian in his *Decretum*, man received his identity in polar opposition to a woman, just as woman received her definition in opposition to man. Note that the singular was used, not the plural. Gratian spoke generically, using categorical imperatives, thus authority of a husband was not equivocal but absolute and the use made in case law, in church law, in civil courts, and in restitution of dowries in cities made an unequivocal, albeit frequently unrealistic, demand on husbands.

Next, this categorization simplified the diverse components of identity for married men to the single issue of a husband's legal capacity and responsibility. Gender often connotes a simplification of understandings, whether applied to women or to men. What was lost in terms of complex understandings, the multivalent nature of personality, was never as complete, I believe, as with the new gendered understanding of woman, nor was gender ever as negatively construed. However, for men as well as for women this change represented a powerful simplifying force in understanding what it was to be a man. Husbanding might come to outweigh all other considerations when a man was judged by his society.

Also, this new gendered understanding was applied to men's lives, or enforced, within an increasingly urban society. Through the actions of civic bureaucracies, the *Procuratoria* of Venice, the *Monte della Dote* of Florence, or their equivalents, and the law courts, both civil and ecclesiastical, married men found new legal definitions affecting their lives. From Italy the concept of Roman dowry spread over most of western Europe in subsequent centuries. It was often accompanied by the justifications originally offered by Gratian and later applied to civil law.

And, in truth, most men in European society were married men. The age of marriage for men rose steadily through the medieval centuries, which may be related in part to the burden marriage had come to represent in the eyes of young bachelors.[28] Because most men did marry eventually, there was a high probability that these gendered arguments were applicable to them at some point. Propertied citizens, the *meliores* or *sapientes*, as they were called – the better sort, wise or grave – were men who could not, in matter of fact, escape marriage often as not because marriage signified that they had become the responsible, mature adults the community demanded to shoulder the burdens of governing and overseeing the welfare of others.[29] The dialectic of privilege and burden had become an institutionalized feature of men's lives. It comes as no surprise then that when Francesco Barbaro condemned marriage he attacked it as an institution bringing unsupportable personal burdens to men. His quarrel lay with his elders rather than with women.[30]

Changes in gender assumptions about men figured in the secularization of European society. Increased consequence of the married estate accompanied the spread of the ideals of humanism in the early Renaissance centuries. The gradual transition from an ideal based

[28] David Herlihy and Christiane Klapisch-Zuber, *Tuscans and Their Families* (New Haven: Yale University Press, 1985), pp. 202–31.
[29] As Stanley Chojnacki notes in ch. 5 of [*Medieval Masculinities*], some prominent men began to resist marriage by the late Middle Ages.
[30] See Francesco Barbaro, "De re uxoria," ed. A. Gnesotto, *Atti e Memorie della R. Accademia di Scienze, lettere ed arti di Padova*, n.s. 32 (1915), pp. 23–7, 62–100; trans. Benjamin Kohl as "On Wifely Duties," in *The Earthly Republic*, ed. Ronald Witt and Benjamin Kohl (Philadelphia: University of Pennsylvania Press, 1978), pp. 189–228.

upon celibacy to an ideal based upon a life solidly lived "in the world" carried with it, in most instances, the assumption that a man marry. In matter of fact, the man who married and carried off his gendered husbanding role well was often the man most in possession of dignity as Renaissance ideals defined dignity. As Stanley Chojnacki notes in his essay in [*Medieval Masculinities*], "The dynamic driving [Venetian] patrician culture from generation to generation can thus be seen as the fusion of patriarchal, patrilineal, and patrimonial objectives into a triptych of gender principles that guided, by blending, the domestic and official worlds of the governing class."[31] This was the bargain struck between privilege and burden. It ascribed a narrow hierarchical pyramid of ascent, where few aspirants achieved a level near the ideal.

For these reasons we need to take a second look at the power over and access to money men gained through the award of their wives' dowries and the complex laws that grew up about this marital assign. Through them, gender came to restrict men's lives. The perception of what it was to be a man, and in time men's identities, began to change, just as surely here as did the identities of women in the Middle Ages. Joseph had taken up his background pose, an icon of responsibility.

[31] Stanley Chojnacki, "Subaltern Patriarchs: Patrician Bachelors in Renaissance Venice," in Clare A. Lees, ed., with the assistance of Thelma Fenster and Jo Ann McNamara, *Medieval Masculinities: Regarding Men in the Middle Ages*, Medieval Cultures, vol. 7 (Minneapolis: University of Minnesota Press, 1994).

Part IV Religion and Society

Part IV   Religion and Society

Gibbon's succinct summation of his own work was that Rome's fall came about through a dual triumph of barbarism and superstition. Having dealt with the question of Rome and "barbarism" in Part I, here we turn to what Gibbon meant by "superstition," which was religion, in particular the Christian religion. This he saw as a force subversive of the military, civic, and moral underpinnings of Roman culture. His views were typical of Enlightenment intellectuals, who, hostile to religious institutions and the clergy, clashed with their contemporaries in the religious orders, which had been reinvigorated by the Counter-Reformation in Catholic countries. Among these monks could be found many of the pioneers of the study of the Middle Ages, and for them religion was of prime importance.

Gibbon, like Voltaire and other *philosophes*, gave great attention to religion, but mainly as a negative force in human affairs, as an impediment to human progress. Their anti-clerical heirs in the nineteenth century, among them republicans, liberals, and socialists, tended instead to downplay religion in the histories they wrote, presenting an ever-more secular Middle Ages and leaving religious and ecclesiastical history largely in the hands of clerical writers. This bifurcation remained in place beyond the middle of the twentieth century. In a widely read textbook, *The Middle Ages, 395–1500*, issued in 1959 by the eminent American expert on French political institutions, Joseph R. Strayer, religion was not really present at all except in the guise of the Church, by which Strayer seemed to mean mainly the Roman papacy.[1] At about the same time, clerical historians, with their nearly exclusive hold on church history, were developing an interest in the different ways that various religious orders defined their respective ways of life. An authoritative example of their work from 1961 is a history of spirituality in the Middle Ages, written in French by three monks, Jean Leclercq, François Vandenbroucke, and Louis Bouyer.[2] The history of theology similarly remained a virtually exclusive clerical occupation, carried out in Catholic universities and seminaries in such places as Rome, Louvain, and Toronto. Much the same could be said for the history of liturgy, a forbiddingly arcane field practically inaccessible to outsiders.

In the Soviet-bloc countries, meanwhile, some medieval historians adopted a third approach, one that had more in common with Gibbon's views than with those of either their secularist or religious colleagues in the West. They gave considerable attention to religion, which, however, they interpreted as a means exploited by the propertied, controlling classes of society for repressing and manipulating the lower classes. A school of such historians

---

[1] Joseph R. Strayer, *The Middle Ages, 395–1500*, 4th ed. (New York: Appleton Century Crofts, 1959).
[2] Jean Leclercq, François Vandenbroucke, and Louis Bouyer, *La spiritualité du Moyen Age* (Paris: Aubier, 1961).

flourished under Ernst Werner at Leipzig in East Germany from the 1950s to the 1980s. Sharp rebuttals to the conference papers and publications of Werner and his associates came regularly from German, Italian, and French Catholic scholars. A probable, albeit unintended, effect of this eastern European Marxist school was to impede or at least discourage the development in the West of a way to analyze religious phenomena from a social standpoint.[3]

Beginnings

The integration of religion into the mainstream of medieval history nonetheless came about, and from a number of independent initiatives. One of these was the German historian Herbert Grundmann's book on religious movements in the Middle Ages, published first in 1935 but not widely known or discussed until the late 1950s. While raised as a Protestant but professing no religion as an adult, Grundmann received training that prepared him to see religion as one essential component intertwined with others in the totality of human culture. Where Catholic clerical historians saw mainly differences among various religious groups, and especially between those regarded by the hierarchy as heretical and those accepted as orthodox, Grundmann saw the similarities. The descriptive subtitle of his book reads: "Studies on the Historical Connections among Heresy, the Mendicant Orders, and the Feminine Religious Movement of the Twelfth and Thirteenth Centuries."[4]

Grundmann found a sympathetic audience among liberal, reform-minded lay Catholic historians in Italy, notably Rafaello Morghen, Arsenio Frugoni, Raoul Manselli, and Cinzio Violante. Their works did not shy away from showing how the religious history of the age was inseparable from rural–urban tensions, economic change, social stratification, the attempts of German kings to exercise lordship over most of Italy, and the desperate struggles of urban governments, especially in the North, to gain or maintain their independence.[5] Manselli gave voice to their views of the significance of social factors but took care to avoid making these the cause of religious expression or change. Writing about Grundmann in his preface to the Italian translation of *Religious Movements* (1974), Manselli noted,

[3] Ernst Werner, *Häresie und Gesellschaft im 11. Jahrhundert* (Berlin: Akademie-Verlag, 1975); *Stadtluft macht frei: Frühscholastik und bürgerliche Emanzipation in der ersten Hälfte des 12. Jahrhunderts* (Berlin: Akademie-Verlag, 1976); and *Stadt und Geistesleben im Hochmittelalter, 11. bis 13. Jahrhundert* (Weimar: Böhlaus, 1980). Although none of his works was translated into English, for a representation of the views of this school in English one could consult the translation of a general book on heresy by one of his colleagues, Martin Erbstösser, *Heretics in the Middle Ages*, trans. Janet Fraser (Leipzig: Edition Leipzig, 1984).
[4] Herbert Grundmann, *Religious Movements in the Middle Ages: The Historical Links between Heresy, the Mendicant Orders, and the Women's Religious Movement in the Twelfth and Thirteenth Century, with the Historical Foundations of German Mysticism*, trans. Steven Rowan (Notre Dame: Notre Dame University Press, 1995). Whereas Grundmann showed center-left democratic leanings as a young man, he claimed to support the Nazi regime in 1933, but was denied an academic post until his appointment to Königsberg in 1939. For this and other information on Grundmann's career, see the introduction to the Rowan translation by Robert E. Lerner, pp. ix–xxv.
[5] Examples of their work: Rafaello Morghen, *Medioevo cristiano* (Bari: Laterza, 1951); Arsenio Frugoni, *Arnaldo da Brescia nelle fonti del secolo XII* (Rome: Istituto Storico Italiano per il Medio Evo, 1954); Raoul Manselli, *L'eresia del male* (Naples: Morano, 1963); Cinzio Violante, *La Pataria milanese e la Riforma ecclesiastica* (Rome: Istituto Storico Italiano per il Medio Evo, 1955).

He, however – make no mistake about it – did not ever underestimate the social importance of these religious movements . . . but he accepted no prefabricated track, whether social or economic or cultural, that somehow determined the events of history. His work thus appears to be an exaltation of the creative liberty of man in the area of religion.[6]

In addition to these German and Italian scholars, yet another influential innovator was a French historian of theology, Marie-Dominique Chenu, a member of the Dominican Order and an expert on both Thomas Aquinas and the development of the discipline of theology in the twelfth and thirteenth centuries. A man frequently embroiled in controversy, Chenu readily conceded that most religious manifestations, excepting only the essential elements of doctrine, were socially determined. He worked out a historical view in which the urban and commercial developments of the twelfth century bypassed the Church, leaving it without either a theology or a clergy adequate to the new social situation. The Church was then rescued, in his view, and brought up to date by the foundation and successful growth of the Dominican and Franciscan orders. This historical view ran parallel to his view of the Church in his own time, the decades to either side of World War II, which he believed to be an institution detached from social realities and in need of revitalization. The common element in his views of the past and the present was the permanence and fundamental rightness of the Christian Gospel, which he believed manifested itself differently, sometimes prominently and sometimes subtly, in differing social, economic, political, and cultural – in brief, historical – circumstances. Chenu's firmly held beliefs (upon which he acted consistently) are apparent in "The Evangelical Awakening," which was one of a collection of his essays published in 1957 (chapter 18).[7]

The international community of medieval scholars soon started to build on the foundations laid by these German, Italian, and French innovators. A group of German experts on Cluniac monasticism published essays on the social origins of the monks in *New Research on Cluny and the Cluniacs*, edited by Gerd Tellenbach, in 1959. An early work of synthesis with a social orientation was the work of an English specialist on St Anselm, R. W. Southern, who published *Western Society and the Church* in 1970. The book was to be a volume in a series on the traditional theme of the history of the Church. Southern states candidly that it became a quite different kind of book: "In the course of time, however, the relations between ecclesiastical development and social change took so strong a hold on the work that the plan had to be altered."[8] There followed in 1974 an article by the editors of this volume, which we called "Social Meaning in the Monastic and Mendicant Spiritualities." We sought

---

[6] *Movimenti religiosi nel Medioevo*, trans. Maria Ausserhofer and Lea Nicolet Santini (Bologna: Il Mulino, 1974), p. xiv.

[7] Chapter 18: Marie-Dominique Chenu, "The Evangelical Awakening," in his *Nature, Man, and Society in the Twelfth Century: Essays on New Theological Perspectives in the Latin West*, trans. Jerome Taylor and Lester K. Little (Chicago: University of Chicago Press, 1968), pp. 239–69. As for the reception of Chenu in Italy, see the remarks of Giovanni Miccoli, whose *Chiesa Gregoriana: Ricerche sulla Riforma del secolo XI* (Florence: Nuova Italia, 1996) contains eleven references to Chenu and six to Grundmann, in his appreciation of one of his professors, "Gli *Incontri nel Medio Evo* di Arsenio Frugoni," *Studi Medievali* 24 (1983): 469–86, at 470: "It was Frugoni who brought me to Pisa and made me read, early in 1955, the study for a theology of the laity by Père Congar, and to steer me towards some of the medieval studies by Père Chenu."

[8] R. W. Southern, *Western Society and the Church in the Middle Ages* (Harmondsworth: Penguin, 1970), p. 11.

to be as explicit as we could in stating our assumptions and methods, beginning with this definition:

> Spiritualities – the ideals, beliefs, and practices of persons who devote themselves fully to religion – are integral components of the societies in which they appear. The task of the social historian is to determine the precise nature of this integration in particular instances. . . . But establishing that a spirituality fits, in a general way, into its social context still leaves unanswered the question of how a specific form of spiritual life is causally related to particular social phenomena.

The answer to that question is then sought by isolating the unique features of particular spiritualities and correlating them with the unique features of the societies that respectively incorporated them.[9]

None of the works cited thus far had much or anything at all to say about the laity. Even Southern's survey, which was organized by various constituencies in the Church, such as the papacy, the bishops, the priests, and the religious orders, left out the largest group of all, that of the lay faithful. This gap was soon attended to by André Vauchez, a French historian, who in the preface to his *The Spirituality of the Medieval West, 8th–12th Centuries* (1975) promises:

> Rather than spiritual doctrines and schools, which have already been the object of intensive study [here a note refers to the book of Leclercq, Vandenbroucke, and Bouyer], our focus will be the possible impact of the Christian message on the minds and behaviour of the greater number. In other words, we will attempt to bring the history of spirituality down from the summits where it has too often been pleased to dwell, and to place it within the social and cultural history of the medieval West.[10]

Vauchez has gone on to write several articles on lay people, of which some were gathered in two collections.[11] Of course the laity is not an undifferentiated mass, but one of its largest parts, the poor, held center-stage from 1962 to 1977 in a seminar conducted at the Sorbonne by Michel Mollat. Among the many works spawned by this seminar is Mollat's own work of synthesis, which appeared in 1978, on poverty and the poor in the Middle Ages.[12] Better-off town-dwellers often found a spiritual outlet in the confraternity, a subject pioneered by the Dominican scholar G. G. Meersseman, whose lifetime scholarly effort was assembled in a three-volume work on confraternities and lay piety in 1977.[13] Definitive as such a work can seem, this one has had the effect of opening a field rather than closing it. A Society for

---

[9] Barbara H. Rosenwein and Lester K. Little, "Social Meaning in the Monastic and Mendicant Spiritualities," *PP* 63 (1974): 4–32.

[10] André Vauchez, *La Spiritualité du Moyen Age occidental, VIIIe–XIIe siècles* (Paris: Presses universitaires de France, 1975); English trans. by Colette Friedlander (Kalamazoo: Cistercian Publications, 1993), pp. 9–10.

[11] *Religion et société dans l'Occident médiéval* (Turin: Bottega d'Erasmo, 1980), and *Les laics au Moyen Age: Pratiques et expériences religieuses* (Paris: Cerf, 1987); *The Laity in the Middle Ages*, trans. Margery J. Schneider (Notre Dame: Notre Dame University Press, 1993).

[12] Michel Mollat, *The Poor in the Middle Ages: An Essay in Social History*, trans. Arthur Goldhammer (New Haven: Yale University Press, 1986).

[13] G. G. Meersseman, *Ordo Fraternitatis: confraternite e pietà dei laici nel medioevo*, 3 vols (Rome: Herder, 1977).

Confraternity Studies was formed in Toronto and started publication of a newsletter, *Confraternitas*, in 1990.[14]

This inclusion of everyone within the scope of religious history has been accompanied by parallel attempts to include everything, that is, everything in the way of religious ideas and practices. The resulting studies are too numerous even to list here, but attention will be given to four areas: saints (including their relics and cults), the monastic practice of praying for the dead, heresy, and liturgy and doctrine.

Saints

Of all the aspects of medieval religious life, one of the best documented has to do with those model Christians, the saints. There are the biographical accounts (*vitae sanctorum*, saints' lives) especially, but also in some cases their own writings or histories of religious organizations they founded or inspired, testimonies to saintly miracles, descriptions in sermons or in narratives of cult centers and particular devotions, iconographic representations, and from the late twelfth century on, canonization hearings. Peter Brown's 1971 essay on "The Rise and Function of the Holy Man in Late Antiquity" marked an important moment because of the central role he gave to function – not theological, spiritual, didactic, or ecclesiastical, but social function. By asking why holy men came to play such an important role in society, and what light their activities cast on a society that was prepared to concede them such importance, Brown reestablished the ties connecting these saints with their respective social settings.[15]

Peter Brown and André Vauchez published immensely influential books on saints and sainthood in 1981: Brown's on the rise and function of the cult of the saints in Latin Christianity and Vauchez's on sainthood in the West, especially as represented in canonization proceedings from their origins in 1185 until their considerable modification after 1431.[16] There has been an explosion of specialized studies in this field, such as those by Patrick Geary on relic theft, Jean-Claude Schmitt on the cult of a greyhound named Guinefort, a martyr to baby-sitting who specialized in curing (or quickly dispensing with) sickly children, Benedicta Ward on miracles, Stephen White on gifts to saints, Thomas Head on saints' cults in the diocese of Orléans, and Julia Smith on the peculiar nature of female sanctity in Carolingian times.[17]

---

[14] Note also a review of work in the field by André Vauchez, "Les confréries au Moyen Age: Esquisse d'un bilan historiographique," *RH* 275 (1986): 467–77.

[15] Peter Brown, "The Rise and Function of the Holy Man in Late Antiquity," *JRS* 61 (1971): 80–101, reprinted in his *Society and the Holy in Late Antiquity* (Berkeley: University of California Press, 1982), pp. 103–52; see Brown's modifications of his own arguments in "The Saint as Exemplar in Late Antiquity," *Representations* 2 (1983): 1–25. See also *Agiografia altomedioevale*, ed. Sofia Boesch Gajano (Bologna: Il Mulino, 1976). This is a collection of scholars' essays on early medieval hagiography; the editor's introduction traced the historiography of this field and gave indications of how it was then rapidly changing. Cf. Patrick J. Geary, "Saints, Scholars, and Society: The Elusive Goal," in his *Living with the Dead in the Middle Ages* (Ithaca, NY: Cornell University Press, 1994), pp. 9–29.

[16] Peter Brown, *The Cult of the Saints: Its Rise and Function in Latin Christianity* (Chicago: University of Chicago Press, 1981), and André Vauchez, *La Sainteté en Occident aux derniers siècles du Moyen Age* (Rome: Ecole française, 1981).

[17] Patrick J. Geary, *Furta sacra: Thefts of Relics in the Central Middle Ages* (Princeton: Princeton University Press, 1978); Jean-Claude Schmitt, *Le saint lévrier: Guinefort, guérisseur d'enfants depuis le XIIIe siècle* (Paris: Flammarion, 1979), *The Holy Greyhound: Guinefort, Healer of Children since the Thirteenth Century*, trans. Martin Thomas (Cambridge: Cambridge University Press, 1983); Benedicta

When a group of scholars gathered in Rome in 1991 to take stock of how hagiography had developed, the resulting volume of essays bore the revealing title: *The Functions of Saints in the Western World (3rd to 13th Centuries)*. Sofia Boesch Gajano's contribution on the use and abuse of miracles covers such topics as saints, holy places, clerical and lay attitudes, the relationship of the miraculous to the sacred, and the clerical ambition to maintain control of both. These reflections led her to reject the "historiographical negation of the miracle," involving as that does its "elite theological ghettoization," and to conclude that "the miracle can truly be a privileged observatory for the history of a society – and surely not only of early medieval society" (chapter 19).[18]

Cult of the Dead

Another major area is the monastic cult of the dead. The principal sources are books maintained by monasteries that contained hundreds, and in some cases thousands, of names of deceased persons for whom prayers were to be said on a regular basis. Through painstaking analysis of these sources and of the liturgies performed in monasteries, monastic religion has come to be understood in part as a highly organized cult of the dead. These studies were first concentrated in Freiburg-im-Breisgau and then more recently in Münster, fostered by two of Tellenbach's disciples, Karl Schmid and Joachim Wollasch, and several of their students and collaborators. Some of their results have appeared in nearly every issue of the German annual publication on early medieval studies, *Frühmittelalterliche Studien*, starting in 1967 with a major article by Schmid and Wollasch on the community of the living and the dead in medieval sources. These two set forth the problems of definition and purpose of memorial books and necrologies, which contain the names of the deceased for whom prayers were to be said; in addition, they gave several specific examples of such books with the numbers of names they contain (e.g. 10,000 at Marcigny-sur-Loire, 40,000 at Reichenau) and of the peculiarities and significance of the various ways they are arranged.[19]

An example of how these highly specialized studies have been built upon and integrated into the mainstream of religious history is given by Dominique Iogna-Prat in an essay on the dead in the celestial accounting of the Cluniac monks around the year 1000. He shows how the dead constituted the central element of – even the motivation for – the socioeconomic mechanisms that coordinated funerals, burials, donations, liturgical commemorations, assistance to the poor, and construction of sanctuaries. For the Cluniacs, he concludes, "the cult of the dead is the keystone of their theocracy" (chapter 20).[20]

Ward, *Miracles and the Medieval Mind: Theory, Record, and Event, 1000–1215* (Philadelphia: University of Pennsylvania Press, 1982); Stephen White, *Custom, Kinship, and Gifts to Saints: the Laudatio Parentum in Western France, 1050–1150* (Chapel Hill: University of North Carolina Press, 1988); Thomas Head, *Hagiography and the Cult of Saints: The Diocese of Orléans, 800–1200* (Cambridge: Cambridge University Press, 1990); Julia M. H. Smith, "The Problem of Female Sanctity in Carolingian Europe, c.780–920," *PP* 146 (1995): 3–37.

[18] Chapter 19: Sofia Boesch Gajano, "Uso e abuso del miracolo nella cultura altomedioevale," in *Les Fonctions des saints dans le monde occidental (IIIe–XIIIe siècle)*, Collection de l'Ecole française de Rome, 149 (Rome: Ecole française, 1991), pp. 109–22.

[19] Karl Schmid and Joachim Wollasch, "Die Gemeinschaft der Lebenden und Verstorbenen in Zeugnissen des Mittelalters," *Frühmittelalterliche Studien* 1 (1967): 365–405.

[20] Chapter 20: Dominique Iogna-Prat, "Les morts dans la comptabilité céleste des Clunisiens de l'an mil," in *Religion et culture autour de l'an Mil: Royaume capétien et Lotharingie*, ed. Jean-Charles Picard and Dominique Iogna-Prat (Paris: Picard, 1990), pp. 55–69. Other works that seek to clarify the

Heresy

The study of heresy in recent decades goes back to a conference held near Paris in 1962. Among those attending were Chenu, Grundmann, Morghen, Manselli, and Violante. The ensuing volume, *Heresies and Societies in Pre-industrial Europe*, was edited by Jacques Le Goff. It deals with such questions relating to heresy as tradition and resurgence, origins and transmission, definitions and sanctions, urban and rural, learned and popular, and mystical and rationalist. In its time, the book was less a compendium of results achieved than a program of research and reflection to be carried out.[21]

Of the many scholars who subsequently became engaged in the study of heresy, few have advanced the inquiry so interestingly and consistently as R. I. Moore of Newcastle. His early work, in the 1970s, established the close ties between heresy and church reform; dissent, in his view, grew simultaneously with, and of course in opposition to, new attempts at asserting authority. In the next decade, he shifted the focus to the cultural processes that produced conceptions of and bureaucratic practices for the defining, separating out, and punishing of marginal people believed to be threats to Christian society. In Moore's view, license for official violence and procedures for persecution, unmistakable attributes of the modern state, were put in place and legitimized in the twelfth and thirteenth centuries as they had not been since the Roman Empire.[22]

In the meantime the Toronto historian Brian Stock published a book on the implications of literacy in the eleventh and twelfth centuries. Among Stock's contributions were his notion of "textual communities," groups whose identity was formed by adherence to a particular body of texts, and his application of this notion to some groups of heretics.[23] Moore's recent contribution to a book of essays on heresy and literacy builds on this work by Stock, as well as upon those by such anthropologists as Jack Goody, Ernest Gellner, and Mary Douglas, to formulate a thesis about the separate textual communities of bishops and of heretics, and of the role of the parish as the locus of mediation between the two. His striking conclusion argues that parish priests and heretics had much in common, as did parishes and heretical sects (chapter 21).[24]

Liturgy and Doctrine

Finally, the history of liturgy and doctrine has also undergone change. This should cause no surprise, given the changes in all the other areas discussed above. And yet liturgy and

---

social role of the dead are Otto Gerhard Oexle, "Die Gegenwart der Toten," in *Death in the Middle Ages*, ed. Herman Braet and Werner Verbeke, Mediaevalia Lovaniensia, ser. I, studia IX (Louvain: Leuven University Press, 1983), pp. 19–77, and Patrick Geary, "Exchange and Interaction between the Living and the Dead in Early Medieval Society," in his *Living with the Dead*, pp. 77–92.

[21] *Hérésies et sociétés dans l'Europe pré-industrielle, 11e–18e siècles*, ed. Jacques Le Goff (Paris: Mouton, 1968).

[22] R. I. Moore, *The Origins of European Dissent* (London: Allen Lane, 1977); *The Formation of a Persecuting Society: Power and Deviance in Western Europe, 950–1250* (Oxford: Blackwell, 1987). The teleology implied in these titles and in much other scholarship on heresy has been criticized by David Nuremberg, *Communities of Violence* (Princeton: Princeton University Press, 1996).

[23] Brian Stock, *The Implications of Literacy: Written Language and Models of Interpretation in the Eleventh and Twelfth Centuries* (Princeton: Princeton University Press, 1983).

[24] Chapter 21: R. I. Moore, "Literacy and the Making of Heresy, c.1000–c.1150," in *Heresy and Literacy, 1000–1530*, ed. Peter Biller and Anne Hudson (Cambridge: Cambridge University Press, 1994), pp. 19–37.

doctrine by their very nature are peculiar. Because their legitimacy and efficacy depend on their appearing to be ancient in origin and unchanging through time, when change did occur those responsible sought to minimize the shock by citing venerable authority for whatever they were introducing. Thus the positivist method of reliance upon exactly what the sources say is hardly sufficient in this area. One example is the earliest written plainchant, i.e. from the ninth and tenth centuries, which was then credited to a pope of several centuries earlier, Gregory I (590–604), and is accordingly called "Gregorian."[25]

Even so, historians have forged ahead in these delicate matters, some equipped with insights that anthropology offers into ritual, to study the fundamental liturgical celebrations of medieval Christianity. John Bossy wrote on the Mass, Miri Rubin on the Eucharist, and Peter Cramer on baptism.[26] The sacralization of marriage has also received much attention, for example from Georges Duby, as have rituals concerning death, for example by Frederick Paxton.[27] Rituals that did not survive beyond the Middle Ages, such as the humiliation of saints' relics, have been mined by historians.[28] And as for doctrine, one could hardly find a topic that touched more lives than the whole nexus of sin, guilt, repentance, confession, penance, forgiveness, and salvation that is associated with purgatory. Jacques Le Goff made clear his view that purgatory began at a particular time (he places it in the late twelfth century), by naming his book *The Birth of Purgatory*.[29]

The new trends catalogued here have not gone unopposed. A particularly sharp reaction appeared in 1986 in a lengthy and comprehensive historiographical essay by John Van Engen, who characterized recent trends generally as marking a "dramatic shift downward." More specifically he wrote: "the examination of 'popular religion' now threatens to eclipse work on popes, theologians, and bishops"; or, "doctrinal disputes and papal policies have given way to relics, the cult of saints, pilgrimage, miracles, purgatory, and the like." The names cited as most representative of the new historians are Jacques Le Goff and Jean-Claude Schmitt, the ones chiefly responsible for the notion of two distinct religious cultures, one clerical and bookish, the other popular, oral, and customary, the first accessible through traditional intellectual and spiritual categories, the second mainly through cultural anthropology and comparative religions. So much effort "to dredge up from the bottom, as it were,

---

[25] To cite an unfortunate vestige of this medieval notion in recent decades: when the American historian of canon law Brian Tierney published his study of the origins of the doctrine of papal infallibility, which he located with precision in the thirteenth-century debates about apostolic poverty, the then head of the Vatican Library, in defending the view that this doctrine goes back to Peter, wrote a condescending review that warned Tierney and other historians to keep their "purely rational criteria of research" away from theology. Brian Tierney, *Origins of Papal Infallibility, 1150–1350: A Study on the Concepts of Infallibility, Sovereignty, and Tradition in the Middle Ages* (Leiden: Brill, 1972); and the review by Alfons Stickler in the *Catholic Historical Review* 60 (1974): 427–41.

[26] John Bossy, "The Mass as a Social Institution," *PP* 100 (1983): 29–61; Miri Rubin, *Corpus Christi: The Eucharist in Late Medieval Culture* (Cambridge: Cambridge University Press, 1991); and Peter Cramer, *Baptism and Change in the Early Middle Ages, c.200–c.1150* (Cambridge: Cambridge University Press, 1993).

[27] Georges Duby, *Love and Marriage in the Middle Ages*, trans. Jane Dunnett (Chicago: University of Chicago Press, 1994), a translation of essays published between 1967 and 1986; and Frederick S. Paxton, *Christianizing Death: The Creation of a Ritual Process in Early Medieval Europe* (Ithaca, NY: Cornell University Press, 1990).

[28] Patrick J. Geary, "Humiliation of Saints," in his *Living with the Dead*, pp. 95–115 (the essay was first published in 1979).

[29] Jacques Le Goff, *La naissance du Purgatoire* (Paris: Gallimard, 1981); published in English as *The Birth of Purgatory*, trans. Arthur Goldhammer (Chicago: University of Chicago Press, 1987).

the residues of peasant religious 'folklore,'" has in Van Engen's view diverted attention from the faith that was essential to medieval religion.[30]

A reply by Jean-Claude Schmitt spoke directly to this point, warning against an anachronistic use of the term "religion," which according to Schmitt is here used in the sense that it acquired in the nineteenth century. He cites as an example this sentence of John Van Engen: "In medieval Christendom, religious culture rested ultimately on 'faith' or 'belief,' meaning professed assent to certain propositions as well as inner conviction."[31] Schmitt then comments:

> That this was the ambition of certain clerics, or in any case of certain theologians, is probable. But the "religion" of the Middle Ages was above all participation in rituals and even more generally participation in an entire social organization and in the sum of symbolic practices and of relationships of meaning among men, between men and nature, and between men and the divine. (Chapter 22)[32]

This debate is not over. The old-style political, institutional, and doctrinal histories of the Church still have life in them, but they can no longer be confused, any more than the history of theology or the history of monasticism can, with the history of the religious beliefs and practices of the great majority of the people who lived in Europe in the Middle Ages.

[30] John Van Engen, "The Christian Middle Ages as an Historiographical Problem," *American Historical Review* 91 (1986): 519–52, passages cited on 530 and 535. Cf. Michel Lauwers, "'Religion populaire', culture folklorique, mentalités. Notes pour une anthropologie culturelle du Moyen Age," *Revue d'histoire ecclésiastique* 82 (1987): 221–58, esp. 255–7; and André Vauchez, "Les orientations récentes de la recherche française sur l'histoire de la vie religieuse au moyen âge," *Ricerche di storia sociale e religiosa* 40 (1991): 25–44.

[31] Van Engen, "Christian Middle Ages," p. 545.

[32] Chapter 22: Jean-Claude Schmitt, *Religione, folklore e società nell'Occidente medievale*, trans. Lucia Carle (Bari: Laterza, 1988), pp. 1–20.

18 The Evangelical Awakening

Marie-Dominique Chenu

> If anyone should ask you to what religious order you belong, tell him the order of
> the gospel, which is the basis of all rules. And let this always be your answer to any
> inquirers. As for me, I would not allow myself to be called a monk, or a canon, or
> a hermit; these titles are so exalted and holy that it would be presumptuous to
> apply any of them to myself.[1]

This was the firm resolution of Stephen of Muret, leader of the self-styled *pauperes Christi*
[Poor of Christ], a group that became the order of Grandmont. Stephen died in 1124, but
countless episodes and nearly a century had passed before his resolution assumed institutional form. At that time, though Innocent III was bound by the canons of the Fourth
Lateran Council [1215] to admit no new orders, Francis of Assisi came before him to plead:
"I do not come here with a new rule; my only rule is the gospel." Thus did the Gospel
confirm its inalienable vitality and relevance, in galvanizing both human understanding and
even ecclesiastical foundations. It is the common inspiration of all Christians of all times and
all milieux, but its abrupt recrudescence periodically provokes a spiritual and institutional
crisis against which it is clearly preferable to measure the pace and standards of the life of the
Church.

   This particular opening of a new evangelical period was marked by an acute sensitivity to
the appearance and to the forms of the primitive Church. With its poverty and humility, the
religious life of the primitive Church became an ideal, indeed a sort of mystique that engaged
the productive energies of men.[2] Often it served a violent reform movement, and occasionally a lunatic fringe. In the midst of the twelfth century, when there flourished a politically
involved and propertied Church, ever ready to engage in diplomatic or even military
ventures, Otto of Freising asked which was preferable for the Church: the humility and

---

[1] Stephen of Muret, *Sermo de unitate diversarum regularum*, cited in E. Martène, *De antiquis ecclesiae
ritibus* (Antwerp, 1738), IV: 877.

[2] From many available facts and accounts it suffices to cite a particularly qualified text of James of
Vitry, witness and historian of the period (his *Historia occidentalis* contains a celebrated description of
the apostolic movements), who declared in a model sermon designed for regular canons: "tempore
scilicet primitivae Ecclesiae et Apostolorum. In eis [ordinibus] enim ad statum priorem Ecclesia
reformatur, quando omnia temporalia tanquam stercora reputabant" ("the time of the primitive church
and of the apostles. In these orders, the church is restored to its original condition, when all worldly
things were regarded as dung"). Text cited in [P.] Mandonnet [and M.-H. Vicaire, *Saint Dominique.
L'idée, l'homme et l'oeuvre*, 2 vols (Paris, 1938)], I: 236; II: 197–8; [translated by M.B.] Larkin [as *St
Dominic and His Work* (St Louis, 1944)], pp. 286–7.

poverty of the primitive period or the grandeur of the present. The earlier condition, he replied with melancholy, was better, but the second was more agreeable.[3] That Otto, member and chief apologist of the imperial family, should have taken that position is no surprise; but a generation was about to appear which would not consent to an "agreeable" Church, that instead aspired to restore it to its primitive state. This aspiration not only provoked a drive to moral reform, but also nourished a deep inquiry into the Christian faith that brought significant advances in theology.

The Social Context of Apostolic Poverty

For a century already, from the original impetus given it by Gregory VII, this evangelical revival had tended increasingly to take institutional form, carrying its demands beyond moral reform to reform of the political and economic structure of society. Liturgical reform was brought about as well, both by a return to early Christian practices and by a loosening of the hitherto rigid clerical caste system. The canonical movement in the twelfth century launched this program into a social and ecclesiastical sphere, thereby assuring its success and expanding its intellectual and institutional dimensions well beyond those conceived by the Gregorian reformers. The *vita apostolica* (apostolic life), a juridical as well as a spiritual concept, became the principal theme of the new movement. Thus fortified, the movement deprived the monastic order of its traditional primacy, precisely on the ground of its own derivation from the early Church, and also because it was so much better received by a new society which cried out for baptism. By proselytizing in the cities, the new reformers transubstantiated the Gregorian ideal; and the remarkably long list of their foundations covering a half-century demonstrates the extent and variety of the renewal they achieved.

The movement itself was in turn expanded and greatly strengthened by the proliferation of groups of laymen who, though part of the new society, had sufficiently broken with the world to proclaim the absolute and literal value of the Gospel – and to proclaim it even at the risk of causing institutions fundamental to the Church to be questioned. The story of these groups is well known. To the great benefit of the word of God, they led to the formation of numerous orders of "poor men" on the eve of the Lateran Council, and shortly thereafter to the foundation of the mendicant orders, which not only brought evangelism and the Church into happy equilibrium but, in the field of *doctrina sacra* (sacred teaching), blended study of the Bible with theological construction.

If I call attention to this conjunction of evangelism and the Church, of bible study and theological construction, it is because there was latent within it great potential for doctrinal development. This potential stemmed from the vital sources of the faith itself, and not so much from the appropriation by this faith of rational methods that could equip it to cope with the developing renaissance of secular culture and thought. Aristotle was not the prime mover in the evolution of sacred doctrine any more than, in the case of St Francis, it was

---

[3] *Chronica*, iv, prol. ([Otto of Friesing, *Chronica sive historia de duabus civitatibus*, ed. W.] Lammers [and A.] Schmidt (Berlin, 1960)], p. 294; [translated by C.C.] Mierow [as Otto of Friesing, *The Two Cities, A Chronicle of World History to the Year 1146 A.D.* (New York, 1928)], p. 274): "Ego enim, ut de meo sensu loquar, utrum Deo magis placeat haec ecclesiae suae, quae nunc cernitur, exaltatio quam prior humiliatio, prorsus ignorare me profiteor. Videtur quidem status ille fuisse melior, iste felicior" ("Speaking frankly, I do not really know whether the current prosperous condition of the church is more pleasing to God than its earlier humility. That earlier condition was perhaps better but the present one is more agreeable").

sociopolitical aspiration that determined the lay, apostolic movement, even where he took over that aspiration and evangelized it.

It would be well to review the principal traits of this conjunction, traits that gave institutional shape to this heralding of the word of God. The point of impact was obviously poverty, considered now not merely as moral asceticism among members of a fraternity that held their goods in common, but as the proper institutional condition of the kingdom of God in this world. Such an outlook was not unambiguous, as the facts show; but at least it went well beyond the political provisions of the Concordat of Worms (1122). In distinguishing between temporal and spiritual investiture, the Concordat preserved by law the essential ecclesiastical institutions, to the benefit of their liberty, and accommodated the Gregorian demands to the feudal regime, which was, after all, accepted by the Church itself. The "poor men," however, sought the liberty of the Church, not any longer in terms of delicate feudal arrangements, but in the disengagement of the Church from a situation wherein supposedly apostolic institutions had assumed the forms and in turn the mentality of temporal society. That great feudal prince, Innocent III himself, lent these "poor men" his support and, after administering appropriate correction, gave them status in a Church where episcopal princes had once fought against the reforms of Gregory VII. Innocent reconciled the Humiliati, communities consisting mainly of artisans, but having a few priests; he authorized the Poor Catholics of Durand of Huesca; and at Milan he protected Bernard Prim against the local clergy, placing him "under the protection of St Peter."

Moreover this conjunction of poverty and Christian liberty found its theatre and effectiveness among that clientele of the Church that was susceptible to the apostolic message, among the poor who became the privileged object of its ministry. All of the new apostles, from Robert of Arbrisselles (d. 1117) to Francis of Assisi, addressed their wonderful message to the little people of the shops and the cellars – "in the winecellars, in weavers' shops, and in other such subterranean hovels" (*"in cellariis et textrinis et hujusmodi subterraneis domibus"*) – to the unfortunate ones with neither fire nor shelter, to the serfs bound to the soil. "Robert preached the gospel to the poor, he called the poor, he gathered the poor together."[4]

It was not, however, only economic poverty that was in question here but, more than that, the social poverty of those who for one reason or another were living on the fringes of society – feudal society based on territorial stability – and who were consequently outlaws. Such, to begin with, were the merchants who had abandoned all feudal ties. They were ready customers for itinerant preachers who, in similar fashion, had broken with the system of ecclesiastical benefices, including the possession of churches. It was precisely this break that led to the practice of mendicant poverty by such preachers. Going out to beg for food became for them merely a way to get a footing among those groups who were sympathetic with their new style of life. The lay apostolic movement developed in this new urban class, tied to the economy of the market and of trade, not without resentment against feudal society. Cadet sons without land, progeny who in the overpopulation of the twelfth century could find neither status nor property and who thus organized their lives on the margins of society, wage earners living on commerce, dusty-footed (piepowder) merchants – all these constituted a homogeneous milieu for the "poor men" of Christ. Waldo was the son of a merchant from Lyons, and Francis the son of a cloth-maker from Assisi, one among those cloth-makers who, as a group, were noted above others for a critical spirit that included a sharp anticlericalism directed against feudal prelates and rich monasteries.

---

[4] "Iste [Robertus] revere pauperibus evangelizavit, pauperes vocavit, pauperes collegit" (*PL*, CLXII, 1055).

A few nobles and rich men entered into the movement, however, as against the great majority of feudal lords, lay and clerical, who sought to rid their Christendom of these dangerous reformers. Some entered into it by a sudden and total conversion; others supported it in local struggles against their adversaries, not without political advantage to themselves; in both cases they attacked what they had long held dear. Intellectual circles became especially involved, in particular the clientele of the rapidly growing urban schools of which the University of Paris would become, early in the thirteenth century, the prototypical fulfillment. As always, students were at the center of a most active ferment in which intellectual culture and fresh spirituality collaborated and even produced new institutions. In 1201 the Order of the Valley of Students was founded by William Langlois and three other teachers from Paris, with thirty-seven students, all committed to the total rejection of property and of temporal lordship.

Thus poverty, beyond its ascetic purport, emerged as a disruptive force in this social agglomeration known as feudal Christendom, so that in fact the Church had to use interdicts to protect the feudal regime from which it benefited. It is not as if the "poor men" of Christ attacked social problems directly. It was their evangelical purity that set their objective; and the temporal effects of their striving toward that objective, however powerful these were in the civilization then emerging, were not at all the determining factor in their inspiration. All this, as it turned out, did not keep their poverty from being formidable and double-edged – so effective a dissolvent was their rejection of earthly goods. Seen in this light, papal policy, in the course of several apparently incoherent steps, demonstrated an admirable faculty for selecting the pure and well-balanced parts of an evangelical reformism whose socially disruptive elements menaced the Church as much as they did civil society.

The most telling and most characteristic trait of this poverty was sensitivity to the distress of sinners, the poor among the poor before the Lord, for such sensitivity, too, was an integral part of the evangelical life. Vitalis of Mortain, a hermit-preacher of the early twelfth century, specialized in bringing women of ill repute back to a virtuous life. Henry of Lausanne, to whose career St Bernard called attention, exhorted his listeners to marry prostitutes in order to save them. Fulks of Neuilly also, in the late twelfth century, dedicated much of his preaching effort to the saving of prostitutes.

The preaching of the word of God was central to this evangelical revival and determined the spiritual and social shape it took; and the *vita apostolica*, in the new sense of the term, governed the whole of this preaching, its inspiration as well as its formal structures. This portion of the program succeeded, for after the papacy had been insisting emphatically on the importance and necessity of preaching for a half-century, the Christian people were finally going to hear the gospel. Peter the Chanter had denounced the "most dreadful silence" ("*pessima taciturnitas*") of the clergy, and both Peter and Innocent III had invoked a phrase from Isaiah (56:10) to repudiate "these muted dogs who don't have it in them to bark" ("*canes muti non valentes latrare*").[5] But in fact, neither the episcopacy nor the monastic orders, not even Cîteaux, had the desire or the means to take on this mission. The story is well known, indeed its import has been overinflated, of how Dominic relieved the Cistercian mission to Narbonne and established in its place, instead of the machinery of the prelates with their political procedures, a program based on Luke 9:1–6 and 10:1–16: "acting and

---

[5] Peter the Chanter, *Verbum abbreviatum*, lxii (*PL*, CCV, 189); Innocent III, *Reg.* iii.24 (*PL*, CCXIV, 904). Cf. [Marie-Dominique Chenu, *Nature, Man, and Society in the Twelfth Century: Essays on New Theological Perspectives in the Latin West*, trans. Jerome Taylor and Lester K. Little (Chicago, 1968)], pp. 202–38.

preaching as had the master, going on foot, without gold and without silver, imitating in everything the way of the apostles." As for the prelates and monks, they were not only, or always, ignorant or even lacking in zeal; rather, they were somehow unable to speak the same language as these Christian people. With their feudal orientation, these prelates and monks felt completely turned about in urban society as if they were in a strange land, whereas the new apostles bore their testimony among men with whom they had established close human relationships and of whom they had intimate knowledge.

No less important for this social context were the institutional forms into which the apostolic movement more or less rapidly crystallized. Their variety and their maneuverability in encounter render classification difficult; but, looking over the movement as a whole and despite crossbreeding in it, one can discern two basic patterns of foundation on the level of action in the Church. One was a special adaptation of the Christianized feudal institution of knighthood; the Knights Templar and Knights of the Holy Sepulchre served, both within Christendom and on its frontiers, as a militia of Christ, with the approval and active support of St Bernard. The other was the fraternity, the penitential order, based on institutional poverty, lacking a hierarchy of authority, owning no material possessions, disaffected from the trappings of ecclesiastical life – even from the traditional liturgy – in brief, little inclined to conform to any classical patterns.

The final trait, of yet more dubious value, in this social disestablishment of the Church was one that sometimes seriously compromised the very truth of the unbreakable tie between the Holy Spirit and the visible Church. The evangelical revival represented for some the work of the Holy Spirit operating through earthly agencies in a Church henceforth purged of all worldly defect and headed towards the end of time. As formerly in the Old Testament, so now again the poor were the born prophets of the Messianic kingdom; and in the New Testament, it was the Book of the Apocalypse that nourished hopes and odd desires, not all of them healthy. This it did not so much by its predictions, which fostered temptations to millenarism, as by the promise of an eternal judgment upon the contingencies of time. In the divine plan, the best means were not to be confused with ends, nor were external forms to be observed for their own sake. From Peter Damian and the Gregorian reform to Francis of Assisi and the mendicant orders, a continuous prophetic tradition held many people firm in their resolve not to compromise, for example, in their resistance to formalism. The first generations of Franciscans and Dominicans exploited to their advantage the views of Joachim of Flora. But the very mention of the name of this Calabrian monk recalls the spurious value of the prophetic bent of the "poor men" of Christ. It also recalls the discernment of the Roman Church, which, while respectful of personal sanctity, was determined to protect the authentic institutional guardians of the biblical and sacramental heritage against extravagant spiritualist movements.[6]

The Evangelical Theology

It is desirable to abstract the doctrinal implications of these apostolic impulses and activities; for the new apostles, whether in groups or as individuals, elaborated their faith in a self-

[6] For a bibliography of numerous works on "apostolic" heresies, see L. Sommariva, "Studi recenti sulle eresie medievali (1939–52)," *Rivista storica italiana* LXIV (1952): 237–68. [Cf. J. B. Russell, "Interpretations of the Origins of Medieval Heresy," *Medieval Studies* XXV (1963): 26–53; J. B. Russell, *Dissent and Reform in the Early Middle Ages* (Berkeley and Los Angeles, 1965); and Raffaello Morghen, "Problèmes sur l'origine de l'hérésie au moyen âge," *RH* CCXXXVI (1966): 1–16.]

conscious, organic system of theology. Indeed it was the faith itself that was in question in the evangelical message and the tensions it stirred up. Though seemingly little inclined to intellectualism, these "poor men" of Christ were to revitalize the resources of theology, even in the schools. They were the ones who would become tomorrow's masters in the new universities, leaving monastic traditionalism to its fate, while creating within the Church a new theological method as well as a new exemplar of sanctity.

If the *vita apostolica*, in the literal sense of the term, was the decisive force and model of these new groups, it was because the word of God took priority in their thought as in their zeal. Alan of Lille, in his brief tract on the art of preaching, undoubtedly based on his missionary experience among the Cathars (after 1185), placed preaching at the top of his ladder of perfection, as the seventh degree, over the investigation of doubts (fifth degree), and the exposition of sacred scripture (sixth degree), a marked change for those familiar with the usual categories of the classical ladder.[7]

This awakening to preaching towards the close of the twelfth century, an awakening that led to the founding of an Order of Preachers, is all the more striking when compared with the deadly silence that prevailed in the Church during the previous decades despite pathetic appeals from Rome. The awakening to preaching was not simply the result of zeal – the Cistercians had surely had enough of that – but the concomitant effect of Christian witness as such, for the letter of the gospel insured a radical dynamism of spirit. For St Francis, the gospel was, in absolute terms, the rule of his religious fraternity; and one had to read it and practice it *sine glossa*; that is, without any of those explanations that dilute the meaning in order to accommodate it to passing conditions.[8] Personal witness was the only suitable medium for this communication; it existed only by and in an exchange where the sociological situation rendered human dialogue possible. The evolution of preaching during this century, leaving aside those geniuses who would excel in any period, expressed this law singularly well. It would be misleading to pay attention only to little episodes, after the fashion of chroniclers and hagiographers, without appreciating the broad significance of preaching for both institutional life and theology. Moreover, in official documents as well as in solemn pronouncements by the leaders of the movement, the very phrases of the Gospel regained their original sharpness and their compelling force. The apostolic letters of Innocent III contain, beneath their legal language, some flashes that are as striking and forceful as the appeals of St Bernard or the prophecies of Joachim of Flora.

---

[7] *Summa de arte praedicatoria*, praef. (*PL*, CCX, 111). [The ladders, for example, of St Benedict, St Bernard, and Hugh of St-Victor, though not identical, have in common their goal of personal perfection, whereas the ladder of Alan has a social orientation. For Benedict, see *Regula monachorum*, vii, ed. J. McCann (London, 1952), pp. 36–49; for Bernard see G. B. Burch, trans., *The Steps of Humility* (Cambridge, Mass., 1940); for Hugh, see the *Didascalicon*, v.9, 10 ([Hugh of St Victor, *Didascalicon de studio legendi*, ed. C. H.] Buttimer [(Washington, 1939)], pp. 109–12; [translated by J.] Taylor [as *The Didascalicon of Hugh of St Victor* (New York, 1961)], pp. 132–4).]

[8] Cf. the *Testamentum* of St Francis (D. Vorreux, ed., *Les opuscules de Saint François d'Assise* [Paris, 1955], pp. 152–4): "ut non mittant glossas in regula neque in istis verbis dicendo 'Ita volunt intelligi'; sed, sicut dedit mihi Dominus simpliciter et pure dicere et scribere regulam et ista verba, ita simpliciter et sine glossa intelligatis et cum sancta operatione observetis usque in finem" ("let them not add glosses to the rule or to my words here, saying: 'This is what they mean'; rather, just as God gave it to me to speak simply and purely, and to write the rule and these words, so should you understand them simply and without glosses, and so should you keep them to the very end in holy conduct"). (For the pejorative meaning of *glossa*, already signifying "glossing over," see [B.] Smalley, [*The Study of the Bible in the Middle Ages* (Oxford, 1952)], p. 271.)

The needs arising from preaching the word in true apostolic fashion led not only to a broad diffusion of biblical texts but to translations of at least parts of the Bible into the vernacular languages. The history of these versions has been studied at great length.[9] The fact of such translations, exemplified by the translation made by Waldo and presented to the pope in 1179, is recalled here only for the spiritual, apostolic, and doctrinal principle it implied, and implied far more forcefully than would a legal pronouncement on bible reading. Innocent III made official note of this fact and these implications as well as of the conditions governing the use of scriptural translations in the Church, as against all the procedures followed in conventicles. He took such a stance in his famous letter to the faithful at Metz in 1199, and this in turn became general church policy by its insertion in the Decretals.[10] The University of Paris was soon to undertake a translation of the entire Bible after completing a revision of the Latin text in 1226.

To keep these principles in balanced perspective, one should note that since the diffusion of the gospel was a pastoral task, it was tied to the conditions of pastoral enterprise, i.e. it tended, in the twelfth century, to be spread as much by the spoken word, by visual representations, and by liturgical drama and spectacle, as by the written and read text, or perhaps more. Thus, between 1168 and 1175, the bishop of Paris, Maurice of Sully, published a series of homilies that he had given each Sunday, first summarizing and then commenting upon the gospel; these soon gained wide distribution in French and other languages.[11]

The pontiffs' insistence on the urgency of sacred teaching is not to be seen strictly as an insistence upon the founding of schools, but, as was everywhere evident, and typically in the affair of the Humiliati,[12] as an insistence upon the preaching of the gospel, a task that various preparatory agencies came to subserve. In this way theology came into the service of preaching the word of Christ to the Christian people; and this reinforced the *vita apostolica*, which met its responsibilities more and more as the Christian people became increasingly aware of their needs by their access to the scriptures.

---

[9] See, for example, H. Rost, *Die Bibel im Mittelalter. Beiträge zur Geschichte und Bibliographie der Bibel* (Augsburg, 1939).

[10] Innocent III, *Reg.* ii.141 (*PL*, CCXIV, 695); *Decretal.* lib. 5, tit. 7, c. 12 (Friedberg, II, 784–7). "The very terms of this juridical text," comments M.-L. Congar, *Jalons pour une théologie du laïcat* (Paris, 1953), p. 437, "and all that we know, furthermore, of the open attitude of Innocent III (cf. [H.] Grundmann, [*Religiöse Bewegungen im Mittelalter*, 2nd ed. (Hildesheim, 1961),] pp. 70–2; 87; 100 n. 55; 114 n. 89; 129) show that L. Hardick is correct in ascribing to Innocent a sort of inner joy and receptiveness." Cf. L. Hardick, "Franziscus, die Wende der mittelalterlichen Frömmigkeit," *Wissenschaft und Weisheit* XIII (1950): 135. It would be easy to document with contemporary testimonies the judgment of Innocent III on the danger represented by these conventicles, in which an ignorant man would set himself up as a learned authority. See, for example, the *Débat d'Yzarn et de Sicart*, ed. P. Meyer (Nogent-le-Rotrou, 1880), cited by P. Alphandéry, *Les idées morales chez les hétérodoxes latins au début du XIIIᵉ siècle* (Paris, 1903), p. 91. The Waldensians, who prescribed learning scripture by heart, urged their faithful to preach, claiming to follow the message of James 4:17. Cf. G. de Lagarde, *La naissance de l'esprit laïque au déclin du moyen âge*, I (Paris, 1956), pp. 82–90.

[11] C. A. Robson, *Maurice de Sully and the Medieval Vernacular Homily, with the Text of Maurice's French Homilies* (Oxford, 1952).

[12] Excommunicated by Lucius III in 1184, the Humiliati, who represented in northern Italy a phenomenon similar to that of the Waldensians in southern France, were reconciled in 1201 by Innocent III who gave them – even laymen – the power to preach; i.e. to give witness to faith (*verbum exhortationis*) but not to teach doctrine (*articuli fidei*). The Humiliati then organized schools to offer training in this giving of witness.

Another indication of the same concerns and needs, but in another sector, is seen in the widespread popularity of the *Historia scholastica [Scholastic History]* of Peter Comestor (d. *c*.1179), both in its Latin form, which circulated in various redactions, and in several translations as well. This history sanctioned and extended the current usage, in the schools and in preaching, of the historical-literal method of St-Victor; it was to become, along with the *Sentences* (but without provoking controversy as Peter Lombard's work had done), one of the basic books of the century. The *magister historiarum* [master of histories] should not be separated from the *magister sententiarum* [master of the sentences]. Its importance can be seen, for example, in Anthony of Padua (d. 1231), who in his sermons, despite occasional contaminations of allegory, frequently cited the *Historia* of Comestor and in fact relied upon it extensively. The biblical reform of the Victorines thus lent a scientific support to the evangelical movement. It furnished the elements for a transition from the monastic interpretation of the Bible (in the *collatio*, collection and comparison of texts) to the scriptural theology of the mendicants (in the *lectio*, systematic explication by their masters).

For the *magister in sacra pagina* (master who taught scripture) was not, as an expositor of scripture, in every respect a direct descendant of the *abbas* (abbot), of whom St Gregory remained the venerated prototype. To be sure, as between abbot and master, a continuity of aim and of scriptural faith remained, but not without a certain evolution in method that paralleled the transition from monastic to scholastic theology. When Philip of Harvengt (d. *c*.1182), abbot of the Premonstratensian monastery of Bonne Espérance near Cambrai, addressed students in Paris, he did not seem to perceive this evolution, for he gave them an exhortation that would have been suitable for monks: "Schola claustrum alterum dici debet" ("The school ought to be considered another cloister").[13] But the Parisian master Robert of Courçon, who prepared his *Summa* between 1204 and 1207, declared that "whoever reads out the sacred scripture in public chooses for himself a path of greater perfection than does any monk from Clairvaux."[14] In the generation between these two men, the influence of the evangelical awakening of the *vita apostolica* intervened, following upon the work of the regular canons and the doctrinal enterprises of the three great masters Peter Comestor, Peter the Chanter, and Stephen Langton. In the same interval, the ministry of the word of God regained, in various forms and before various audiences popular and scholarly, the dynamism of its dialogue with the world. Its regained dynamism took the form of proclaiming the gospel, controversy with heretics,[15] and the absorption of reason into theology. The persistence of old literary genres and intellectual traditions, themselves good and useful, partially concealed this new dynamism; yet it was not to be without effect on the treatment of the word of God, which was at work like a leaven in the minds of the faithful.

---

[13] *Epp.* xviii (*PL*, CCIII, 158–9). Cf. *Epp.* iii (*PL*, CCIII, 31): "volo te non tam litteraliter quam spiritualiter erudiri, sic scripturas capere, ut internam illarum dulcedinem diligas experiri" ("I want you to become not so much textually educated as spiritually formed, to study scripture in such a way that you will love tasting its inner sweetness";) also *Epp.* xx (*PL*, CCIII, 165): "habes quod ad refocillandum animam expedire perhibetur, divinae series lectionis" ("you have the means for rekindling your soul – repeated reading of scripture").

[14] MS Paris BN lat. 14524, fol. 74, cited by C. Dickson, "Le cardinal Robert de Courçon, sa vie," *Archives d'histoire doctrinale et littéraire du moyen-âge* IX (1934): 73: "Qui legit publice sacram scripturam iter maioris perfectionis arripuit quam aliquis clarevallensis."

[15] It would be worthwhile to analyze the ways and means, the spirit, the techniques, and the contexts of the encounters between St Dominic and the heretics in southern France. The accounts by chroniclers have greater theological significance than the *Contra haereticos* of Alan of Lille, who was in the same region at about the same time.

We have elsewhere remarked on the close bond existing between the evangelical movement and the flowering of the *quaestiones* [questions] in the biblical *lectio* [reading] and culminating in scholastic theology, principal instance of the tie between grace and nature among these theologian-apostles. It is no accident that these mendicants turned out to be both the harbingers of the new Christianity and the masters of the new universities.[16] The transformation that was accomplished at the same time in scriptural understanding (biblical theology, we would call it today) was more subtle, but not less significant. The pivotal point of this transformation was the essential relationship between the fundamental literal sense and the construed spiritual sense as it had been worked out by the Victorines against the allegorical idealism that so delighted the monastic mind.[17] Further and more precisely, the new relationship involved definition of the proper nature, use, and limits of the spiritual sense. All plainly considered the spiritual sense to be coterminous with a valid understanding of scripture, both in its history and in its doctrine. But whereas in the monastic *collatio* allegory was more or less a way for secret and aristocratic initiation into the mystical meaning in the style of the Alexandrians, now the primacy of the letter was respected and upheld through the techniques developed bit by bit by the new generations of *scholares*.

The master – a common name among the new evangelists for a teacher in the schools or for the leader of an apostolic group[18] – had to accomplish three operations in order to bring the word of God into full exercise: *legere, disputare, praedicare* (to explicate, to dispute in the sense of resolving *quaestiones*, and to preach). Thus did Peter the Chanter (d. 1197), whose *Verbum abbreviatum* [*The Abbreviated Word of God*] was the *summa* of pastoral and institutional theology for the late twelfth century, formulate a master's threefold function in a division that would long remain a classic.[19] One must not think of this, however, as an inviolable division. In fact, in the works of the masters of that time, it is difficult to

---

[16] See Chenu, pp. 202–38.

[17] While the reputation of Gregory the Great as the leading monastic exegete remained high, as with Guibert of Nogent, *De vita sua* i.17 (*PL*, CLVI, 874; *The Autobiography of Guibert, Abbot of Nogent-sous-Coucy*, trans. C. C. S. Bland [London, 1926], p. 70) and Hugh of St-Victor, *Didascalicon*, v.7 (Buttimer, p. 105; Taylor, p. 128), Richard of St-Victor did not hesitate to point out the weaknesses in Gregory's method: *In visionem Ezechielis*, prol. (*PL*, CXCVI, 527) and *Expositio difficultatum*, prol. (*PL*, CXCVI, 211). See Chenu, pp. 310–30.

[18] *Magister* was the common twelfth-century term for the leader of a group of itinerant preachers. It was used, for example, in reference to Robert of Arbrisselles, Norbert of Xanten, and Bernard of Thiron. Cernai called Diego d'Osma and his companion Dominic "praedicationis principes et magistri" ("leaders and masters of preaching"). Of St Francis himself, James of Vitry, a contemporary, wrote in his *Historia occidentalis*, xxxii (Douai, 1597), p. 352: "Vidimus primum hujus ordinis fundatorem magistrum, cui tanquam summo priori suo omnes alii obediunt" ("We saw the order's founder and first master whom all the others obey as the highest and first among them"). This term "master" had over others such as "lord" or "abbot" the advantage of being free from implications of power or temporal responsibilities. In the *Vita* of Robert of Arbrisselles (*PL*, CLXII, 1052), Baudry of Dol wrote: "Praelatum suum magistrum tantummodo vocabant, nam neque dominus, neque abbas vocitari solebat" ("They called their prelate master only; they did not call him either lord or abbot"). Cf. Mandonnet, I: 53, 130; Larkin, pp. 38, 141.

[19] *Verbum abbreviatum*, i (*PL*, CCV, 25): "In tribus igitur consistit exercitium sacrae scripturae: circa lectionem, disputationem et praedicationem. . . . Lectio autem est quasi fundamentum et substratorium sequentium, quia per eam ceterae utilitates comparantur. Disputatio quasi paries est in hoc exercitio et aedificio, quia nihil plene intelligitur, fideliterve praedicatur nisi prius dente disputationis frangatur. Praedicatio vero, cui subserviunt priora, quasi tectum est tegens fideles ab aestu et a turbine vitiorum" ("The study of sacred scripture consists in three operations: in explication, disputation, and preaching. . . . Explication is a sort of foundation or base for what follows, because upon it other uses

distinguish explication from the two other exercises; the line separating explication from preaching was seldom drawn clearly.[20]

What we need to sense in this instructional formula, as much as the specification of functions, which showed up noticeably in the new statute of teaching and in the diversity of its methods, is the necessity that a full coordination of these functions be achieved in order to promote a total and active understanding of God's word. True mastery *in sacra pagina* called for preaching. The theology of the word of God could be accomplished only in the transmission of its message. Exegesis, dogmatics, and preaching could not be separated for one who would master the gospels, because they could be fully comprehended only by participation in the immediate action of the word. Did not Alan of Lille consider the preaching of the word of God the highest act of the Christian advanced in perfection? We have come far from the monastic program, not only by the steady introduction of *quaestiones*, but by the treatment of a divine word that now appeared as a word directed to men.

A new equilibrium was thus about to be established, one that the Victorine reform had not been able to accomplish. That it had not been able to accomplish this in practice is shown by the typical case of Stephen Langton's work. Its reputation was assured only by his development of *quaestiones* and his proliferation of *moralitates* – but not by his sense of religious history. His biblical scholarship was not sound; and men were led astray by its errors, even in their preaching. Neither had the Victorines achieved this equilibrium in principle, and their ultimate failure was written into their position on allegory. One could not base a scientific understanding of scripture, St Thomas was later to say, on the symbolism of the spiritual senses.

It was the mendicants who were finally to establish this equilibrium. Its establishment was signaled and accomplished in two facts: first, St Francis proclaimed in thought and action the literal appreciation of the mystery of Christ; and second, the earliest generation of Dominicans at the Convent of St-Jacques in Paris surprised "moralists" and "questionists" alike by organizing the direct study of scripture in its textual simplicity.[21] "The old allegories and moralities were fading before an intense realization of the literal meaning."[22] By a kind

---

of the text rest. Disputation is a sort of wall in this exercise, this building, because nothing is fully understood or faithfully preached unless first analyzed by disputation. Preaching, however, which the previous ones support, is a sort of roof protecting the faithful from the raging storms of vice"). Cf. Smalley, p. 208.

[20] Smalley, p. 209, analyzes the literary genre of the *Summa super Psalterium* of Prepositinus of Cremona, a work that was undoubtedly "preached," and of the *Distinctiones super Psalterium* by Peter the Chanter and Peter of Poitiers. In the face of this apostolically oriented combination of the master's three functions, one ought to reexamine the history of preaching in this period. One can presume that such an effort would bring into relief, alongside popular preaching, a literary genre almost entirely perverted by dialectic to the detriment of sacred rhetoric. Cf. T. M. Charlier, *Artes praedicandi, contribution à l'histoire de la rhétorique au moyen âge* (Paris and Ottawa, 1936).

[21] Hugh of Saint-Cher, the leader in this vast undertaking, told of the double opposition encountered by the friars (*Postillae in Bibliam* [Paris, 1530–45], VI, fol. 86): "Hi sunt reprehensores fratrum studentium qui nimis sunt intenti circa studium scripturarum. Dicunt morales: non est bonum in theologia tot questiones implicare. Dicunt questioniste: non est bonum tot moralitates fingere. Et quilibet reprehendit quod nescit" ("These are the critics of the friar-scholars who are wholly intent upon the study of scripture. The moralists say, 'It is not good to concoct so many questions in theology.' The questionists say, 'It is not good to contrive so many moral interpretations.' And each side criticizes what it does not understand"). Cf. Smalley, p. 269.

[22] Smalley, p. 284. See esp. ch. 5, "Masters of the Sacred Page: The Comestor, the Chanter, Stephen Langton" and ch. 6, "The Friars" for a full discussion of the development which is being discussed briefly here.

of scriptural monophysitism, decadent symbolism would still too often swamp the *lectio* of the schools with allegory and public preaching with tropology; but this double, dead weight could not stifle the power of the Gospel to move, a power rediscovered both in the apostolic life of the Church and in its theological reflection.[23] The theological and apostolic programs, each defined by the other, overlapped in their subservience to the primacy of the word of God. By this meeting, both the vital center of pastoral theology and even the superficial aspects of the pastoral ministry were modified. Despite his basically impeccable reputation, Gregory the Great, author of the hitherto supremely influential *Regula pastoralis* [*Book of Pastoral Care*] and inspirer of the monastic *collatio*, found his authority eclipsed by such an approach as that taken in Peter the Chanter's *Verbum abbreviatum*, and even more by the spiritual style of the new apostles.

   Faith meant assent to the word of God; and according to that word, faith was the prime and characteristic act of the Christian. It was certainly not by chance that, in keeping with their custom of reviving evangelical terms, these men of faith called themselves properly and, so to speak, technically, *credentes* (believers), imitating the expression *multitudo credentium* [whole body of believers] of the first Christian community (Acts 4:32).[24] By itself alone the term "believer" properly expressed the ideal of the apostolic life in contrast to the ideal that inspired the reform of the canons: the crucial point in the activity, the itinerant poverty, of the new apostles was the force of a believing witness that ignored any distinction between clergy and laity, whereas the other reforms had involved clerics searching for virtue and effectiveness within settled and observant communities. And the difference between their two approaches to poverty – between subjecting clerical avarice to moral control and rejecting out of hand an entire economic system[25] – emphasized the differences underlying their inspiration and their proselytism.[26]

   It is at this critical juncture that one can see the connection between the evangelical reformers with their literalism and the exegetes who were faithful to the historical letter, as against the old-style Gregorian allegorizers who considered this "history" superficial. St Gregory had written in his *Hom. XXII in evang.* (*PL*, LXXVI, 1174–5): "Lectio sancti evangelii, quam modo, fratres, audistis valde in superficie historica est aperta, sed ejus nobis sunt mysteria sub brevitate requirenda. *Maria Magdalena, cum adhuc tenebrae essent, venit ad monumentum* (John 20:1): juxta historiam notatur hora; juxta intellectum vero mysticum requirentis signatur intelligentia" ("The reading of the holy gospel which you have just heard, my brothers, is sufficiently clear on the historical level, but its mystical meaning has to be searched for by us for a while. 'Mary Magdalen, while it was still dark, went to the tomb': according to a historical reading, this tells us the hour; but by a mystical understanding, this tells us the state of mind of one seeking the Lord").

[23] Maurice of Sully, bishop of Paris (d. 1196), took up the *Allegoriae* of Richard of St-Victor in his French homilies. See above, n. 11. But soon Francis of Assisi was to speak a clear, evangelical language.

[24] Cf. Mandonnet, II: 187 n. 58; Larkin, p. 276 n. 54: "One attributes perhaps too readily the giving of the name *credentes* to the Cathar faithful to the fact that their apostles preached a new faith, distinct from the catholic faith; and one rejects on the same account the usage of the chroniclers who nearly all apply the term *credentes* to the Waldensians, who were *not* heretics." The crucial text of Acts 4:32 reads: "Now the company of those who believed were of one heart and soul, and no one said that any of the things which he possessed was his own, but they had everything in common." ·

[25] St Bernard's morally severe criticism of avarice did not go to the heart of the new monetary and commercial economy, which it simply condemned as perverse; this criticism could have been just and effective only in the feudal agrarian society to which the monk belonged. The new poverty expressed the break between evangelical principles and the old regime and thus put itself in a good position from which to denounce the disorders wrought by the new regime.

[26] Cf. Mandonnet, II, 190; Larkin, p. 279: "Whereas among reformed priests, entry into the Augustinian Order, with the life of poverty which that entailed, was considered the proper means of achieving the life of apostolic perfection, it signified nothing of the kind for the masses of people involved in the

On this theological plane the old moral reformism was discredited, at least relatively, and its methods were easily criticized. In an astonishingly strong chapter, "Contra traditionum onerositatem et multitudinem" ("Against the Burdensome Host of Traditions"), Peter the Chanter, citing a phrase from Acts 15:10 about the "unbearable burden which neither we nor our fathers have been able to carry," proclaimed the primacy of the gospel and of its spiritual liberty as against the proliferation of precepts, however useful they might have been. To this he added a long list of stultifying burdens, especially those found in monastic life. He recalled that St Anthony, when his disciples asked him for a rule and observances, was content to hand them the gospels.

There are other traditions that are allowable, even inoffensive in any least way to God's commandments. And yet when they are numerous they weigh heavily upon those who uphold them and upon those who transgress them; unless such traditions are kept brief and few and have been instituted for the most obvious and useful reasons, they become an obstacle to obeying divine precepts. They restrict the liberty of the gospel. . . .

Note that the Apostle had no traditions except a few venerable and mystical ones. Also when certain religious came to the hermit Anthony seeking a rule and a model for the religious life, he gave them a copy of the gospels. At the Lateran Council [the Third Lateran, 1179], John of Salisbury said to the assembled fathers who were discussing some decrees: "God forbid that any new ones be set up or a lot of old ones resurrected and renewed!"

We are oppressively burdened with a multitude of contrived practices, although authority speaks, because even some useful things have to be tossed aside or we get borne down by them. We ought rather to teach and work to get the gospel observed, since so few now observe it. . . .

[Next, after citing the words of Christ against the legalism of the Jews and texts from St Paul against Judaizing Christians, he continues:] Do not abandon the vital spirit of the letter in favor of anybody's tradition or refinement or obscure explanation.[27]

---

various apostolic movements. For these people, the practice of the common life and of poverty dated from much further back than the foundation of the Augustinian regular life. The establishment of a juridical organism added nothing to their imitation of the primitive church. The regular life represented for them not so much religious progress as social stabilization and, for the church, a recuperation, insofar as this stabilization saved wandering masses from anarchy or even heresy. The tremendous success of the apostolic movement, its immense Christian vigor maintained in spite of its stormy history, gave this recuperation its great value."

[27] *Verbum abbreviatum*, lxxix (*PL*, CCV, 233–9; punctuation altered): "Sunt et aliae (traditiones) licitae, nullumque offendiculum mandatis divinis parientes, et tamen prae multitudine sua gravant constituentes, et inobedientes illis transgressores[;] nisi in parcitate et paucitate, et nonnisi pro manifestissima causa et utili instituendae essent[,] obicem videntur praebere divinis praeceptis. Hae evacuant evangelicam libertatem. . . .

Vide Apostolum nonnisi paucas traditiones honestas et mysticas instituisse. . . . Antonius etiam eremita quibusdam religiosis quaerentibus ab eo regulam et formam religiose vivendi. tradidit eis codicem Evangelii. In Lateranensi etiam concilio, sedentibus patribus ad condenda nova decreta, ait Joannes Carnotensis: Absit, inquit, nova condi, vel plurima veterum reintigi et innovari!

Multitudine etiam inventorum praegravamur, cum dicat auctoritas, quia etiam de utilibus aliqua post ponenda sunt, ne multitudine utilium gravemur. Imo ideo potius praecipiendum et laborandum esset, ut Evangelium observaretur, cui nunc pauci obediunt. . . .

Non reliquas spiritum litterae vivificantem, propter traditionem, determinationem, vel remotam alicujus expositionem."

As it happened, the new apostolic movements shunned the classical forms of the religious life. The Humiliati refrained from drawing up complex regulations. Francis of Assisi would not agree "to be diverted into the monastic or eremetic life."[28] It was Innocent III who guided these movements firmly but gently to a more organized mode of life. In any case, the rule of St Francis was far different from that of St Benedict. The *Expositio quattuor magistrorum super regulam fratrum minorum* (*Explanation of the Rule of the Friars Minor by Four Masters*)[29] displayed a mentality utterly foreign to monastic paternalism. Without any prejudice against the classic term *regula* [rule], the elaboration of what the Preachers chose to call their *Consuetudines* or *Institutiones* [customs] did not present itself as a commentary upon an already established rule.

In the interpretation of texts and, even more, in the application of these texts to daily life, the new apostles experienced a balancing-off of letter and spirit of the kind which, once the Church became engaged upon its apostolate, solved for it the problem of relating mystery and institution without violating the unity of the spirit. The seemingly simplistic literalism of their reading of the gospels (think, for example, of their custom of traveling two-by-two, of their eating whatever was given them, of their obsession with the number 12, of their rigorous application of evangelical poverty, pardon, and fraternity) paradoxically guaranteed their most absolute apprehension of the spiritual sense, if it is true that that sense is contained within the letter. Thus always has understanding of scripture proceeded to coordinate letter and spirit in passages susceptible of both literal and spiritual interpretation but often restricted to the latter by allegorization of details. The literature of the new apostles of the twelfth and thirteenth centuries gave a new example of this law. As concerns institutions, the labored development of the Franciscan order, in particular the affair of the Spirituals (how significant the very name of these men who objectified the letter in the service of a shaky Spiritualism!), ought to illustrate not only the risks involved in this coordination of letter and spirit, but also its pervasive vitality, which derives from the very heart of the law of grace.

A whole theology of law, of its role and its subservience to grace, grew out of this interaction of thought and behavior. For example, whereas for St Benedict any transgression of the rule constituted a fault, the laws of the Dominicans and later on of other groups did not as such oblige in conscience – "*non obligant ad culpam sed ad poenam*" ("they do not entail

---

[28] Thomas of Celano, *Vita prima S. Francisci*, xiii (*Analecta Franciscana* [Florence, 1926–41], X: 26): "ut ad vitam monasticam seu heremeticam diverteret." One recalls here the famous scene in which St Francis, under pressure from Cardinal Ugolino to go back to the legislation of St Benedict or of St Augustine, led Ugolino silently before his brothers and then, from the depths of his soul, cried out: "Fratres mei, fratres mei, Deus vocavit me per viam simplicitatis et humilitatis, et hanc viam ostendit mihi in veritate pro me et pro illis qui volunt mihi credere et me imitari. Et ideo nolo quod nominetis mihi aliquam regulam, neque sancti Benedicti, neque sancti Augustini, neque sancti Bernardi, nec aliquam viam et forman vivendi, praeter illam quae mihi a Domino est ostensa misericorditer et donata" ("My brothers, my brothers, God has called me by the way of simplicity and of humility, and He has pointed out this way as being the true way, both for me and for those who wish to believe me and imitate me. So don't talk to me about some rule or other, neither that of St Benedict, nor of St Augustine, nor of St Bernard, nor about any life or way of living other than that which the Lord has mercifully shown and given to me"). *Speculum perfectionis*, lxviii, ed. P. Sabatier, vol. 1 (Manchester, 1928), p. 196. Cf. Thomas of Celano, *Legenda secunda*, cxli (*Analecta Franciscana*, X: 237–8).

[29] Ed. L. Oliger (Rome, 1950). In the midst of a very significant crisis, four masters of theology were officially summoned for consultation.

a fault but only a correction").[30] At the time that the rules of the order were taking shape, in 1220, Dominic declared that if anyone thought otherwise he would himself go ceaselessly about the Preachers' convents erasing the regulations with his own knife.[31] The Gregorian reformers could not have imagined such a violation of the binding force of law, just as they could not have aroused such an evangelical enthusiasm for obedience as the new friars showed. When St Bernard was asked by the Carthusians of St Peter in 1140 whether all monastic regulations obliged in conscience, he had replied that some obliged gravely, others lightly, but never once suggested that there could be any whose violation involved no sin.[32]

It was no accident that the apostolic movements, unlike the Gregorian reform and the canonical movement, thrived as well if not better among laymen than among the clergy. The evangelical shock reverberated throughout the Christian body of the Church wherever it encountered the world, especially at those points where laymen bore witness in secular society. Waldo of Lyons and Francis of Assisi were laymen. The Humiliati formed mixed lay and clerical communities. The Poor Catholics set up religious houses (1212) to accommodate members of both the clergy and the laity, women as well as men. The clericalization of Franciscan brotherhoods (1210), which incorporated their members into the ecclesiastical hierarchy, did not go unchallenged, nor was it accomplished without qualms of conscience for Brother Francis. The penitential orders spread sporadically in the thirteenth century as third, or lay, orders.

The principle and the laws of this apostolic shock in fact transcended the clerical–lay distinction. The pontiffs, through express legislation, sought to build them into the structure of a Church in which apostolic initiatives would not be limited to the sacramental and priestly apparatus, to which, from a conventional point of view, they belonged. Here we have the Church's long struggle to give juridical and sacramental authenticity to the apostolic drive, which in dissident groups tended to corrupt rapidly. This was especially the history of the first Franciscan brotherhood, as foreshadowed by the case of the Lombard "poor men." And the key to these developments lay in the legislation and executive directives gradually worked out for the preaching of the word, which, arising from the evangelical force of the faith, could be exercised only within the apostolic magisterium. The "poor men" of Lombardy, the Humiliati, like the Waldensians, refused all control, to the point where they found themselves excommunicated by decree of Lucius III in 1184. But by 1201 a good many of them had been reconciled, and Innocent III gave them permission to preach. He made explicit the distinction between the preaching of doctrine ("*articuli fidei et sacramenta*"), which was reserved, and giving witness to faith and morals ("*verbum exhortationis*").[33] In 1207 some Waldensians, led by Durand of Huesca and persuaded by

[30] *Constitutiones Ordinis Praedicatorum*, prol., in H. Denifle, "Die Constitutionen des Predigerordens in der Redaction Raimunds von Peñafort," *Archiv für Literatur- und Kirchengeschichte* V (1889): 534. Humbert of Romans said that St Dominic enunciated this principle at the chapter of 1220; see Humbert of Romans, *De vita regulari*, ed. J. J. Berthier (Rome, 1889), II: 45.

[31] Ibid., p. 46; "si hoc crederetur, ipse (Dominicus) vellet ire semper per claustra, et omnes regulas cum cultellino suo delere."

[32] *De praecepto et dispensatione*, i (*PL*, CLXXXII, 861–2).

[33] G. Tiraboschi, ed., *Vetera Humiliatorum Monumenta* (Milan, 1776), II: 133–4: "singulis diebus dominicis ad audiendum Dei verbum in loco idoneo convenire, ubi aliquis vel aliqui fratrum probate fidei et expertae religionis, qui potentes sint in opere ac sermone, licentia diocesani episcopi verbum exhortationis proponent iis qui convenerint ad audiendum verbum Dei, monentes et inducentes eos ad mores honestos et opera pietatis, ita quod de articulis fidei et sacramentis ecclesiae non loquantur.

Dominic that they could keep to their former way of existence within the Church, were reconciled and granted permission to engage in this same limited form of preaching (*"licentia exhortandi"*); the same happened in 1210 with a group of priests and laymen led by Bernard Prim.[34] And in fact these various people did exercise the *verbum exhortationis* each Sunday.[35] In the same year the companions of St Francis received the same privilege, to be administered at the discretion of Francis himself, free of all episcopal control. "The pope gave Francis and his brothers permission to preach penance everywhere, provided that whoever was going to preach got approval from the blessed Francis. And to any of the brethren, layman or cleric, who had the spirit of God, he gave permission to preach."[36] Thus under these formulations a consistent policy was developed; it was not merely a casuistical solution but a substantive discrimination in the laws and titles governing the apostolic transmission of the faith within the institutional magisterium.

Apart from these lay groups with their authorized witness within the apostolic movement,[37] certain confraternities and brotherhoods became a vehicle for the religious and social expression of the new Christianity. Themselves ancient institutions, they now became caught up in the general forward movement of the temporal and spiritual economy. They had always been established on a ground where sacred and secular met. From this recrudescence of the religious confraternity, craft and trade and professional guilds now drew a religious inspiration that related meaningfully to their temporal involvements and their most material preoccupations. Here, wholly outside the framework of canon law, the Church encountered concrete realities and, to its satisfaction, societies based on occupation and devoted to mutual aid and entertainment. Confraternities, guilds, charitable enterprises, festivals – all sponsored and organized independent meetings and ceremonies that, as ecclesiastical authorities complained, upset the traditional order of things in the churches and cluttered every church with one altar after another.[38]

It is in this context that one must appreciate the new and consistent expression given to Christian prayer, penitence, fraternal charity, and morality, whether by active participants in

---

Prohibemus autem ne quis episcopus contra praescriptam formam impediat hujusmodi fratres verbum exhortationis proponere, cum secundum Apostolum, non sit Spiritus extinguendus" ("every Sunday they assembled in a suitable place to hear the word of God, and there, one or more of the brethren of approved faith and experience in religion and powerful in deed and word, with permission of the bishop of the diocese, exhorted those who had gathered to hear the word of God, admonishing them and leading them toward upright conduct and pious works – but not speaking of the articles of the faith or of the sacraments of the church. We forbid any bishop to violate the prescribed rule and interfere with the exhortations given by such brethren, for, as the Apostle says: 'The Spirit is not to be extinguished').

[34] Innocent III, *Reg.* xiii.94 (*PL*, CCXVI, 293).

[35] Grundmann, p. 112.

[36] *Legenda trium sociorum* (*AAAS*, Oct., II: 737–8): "Dedit eidem licentiam praedicandi ubique paenitentiam ac fratribus suis, ita tamen quod, qui praedicaturi erant, licentiam a beato Francisco obtinerent. . . . Quicumque ex ipsis spiritum Dei habebat, sive clericus, sive laicus, dabat ei licentiam praedicandi." Cf. H. Felder, *Geschichte der wissenschaftlichen Studien im Franziskanerorden bis um die Mitte des 13. Jahrhunderts* (Freiburg-im-Br., 1904), pp. 33–57.

[37] One would here have to take into account the works written in defense of the faith by laymen, right in the thick of the apostolic movement with all its variations and ambiguities – works such as the *Disputatio inter catholicum et paterinum* by a certain George, the *Liber supra stella* by Salvo Burci, etc.

[38] G. LeBras, "Les confréries chrétiennes," in *Etudes de sociologie religieuse* (Paris, 1956), II: 423–62. See also E. Coornaert, "Les ghildes médiévales, V^e–XIVe siècles," *RH* CXCIX (1948): 22–55, 208–43. For complaints at the Council of Rouen, 1189, see [J. D.] Mansi, [ed., *Sacrorum conciliorum nova et amplissima collectio*, 31 vols (Florence and Venice, 1759–98)], XXII, 585–6.

the confessional societies organized by occupation or by the little people whom Chrétien of Troyes celebrates in his lament of the weavers.[39] It is in this context especially, rather than in light of occasional scepticism concerning doctrine, that one ought to see the sometimes rather violent outbreaks of anticlericalism that continued on the rise into the thirteenth century. At times this anticlericalism was reformist in tendency and could thus be used openly by the Church. At other times, in its critique of the social sluggishness of the Church, it directly and firmly opposed the Church itself. This major theme of a return to the primitive Christian community, to its poverty and humility, nourished more than the reforms of the regular canons and the several manifestations of apostolic movements. Its ambiguity was exploited by Arnold of Brescia and by the Patarini. In the midst of one of his disputes with the papacy, Frederick II (emperor from 1212 to 1250) proposed that all clerics of whatever rank or order, but especially the higher clerics, be reduced to the status they held and the functions they performed in the primitive Church. The same proposition was expressed by the French barons in 1246, with the approval of King Louis IX (reigned 1226–70).

These polemics, which fed diplomatic quarrels and military engagements with a mixture of partisan ideology and sincere faith, tended to relocate the border between the sacred and the secular, not without endangering orthodoxy. The development of new political entities (the new national kingdoms against the Holy Empire, for example) and a naturalistic philosophy of man, including man-in-society, bolstered one another more or less consciously; together they took on the character of secondary causes autonomously at work in the kingdom of God on earth. No one formulated this into an explicit principle, either as a philosophy of society or as a theology of the Church. Yet the popes, especially Alexander III and Innocent III, in the very midst of their struggles against the princes, developed in their official writings, as close analysis of these will reveal, a delicate but decisive recognition of the elements comprising Christendom. The term *Christianitas* was henceforth charged with a concrete meaning that embodied these elements – cosmic, ethnic, cultural, political.[40]

The evangelical fraternities were sensitive to such secular elements, to the point of being susceptible to their influence. Instinctively, on the other hand, and in virtue of the spiritual mission to society of these fraternities, the Roman pontiff, in addressing directives to them, avoided the term *Christianitas*; for that Christendom was no proper part of their apostolic business.[41] Once again, a new border between sacred and secular: the fraternities invalidated after a fashion the traditional and more or less sacred tripartite division of society into clerics, knights, and peasants.[42] That division offered no sociological or religious identity to their clientele, who included merchants and urban artisans. They were not averse to a certain desacralizing of authority, however divine it was thought to be in ultimate principle. In their electoral system there was never any thought of consecrating their priors in the way that

---

[39] See Chenu, pp. 228–9.
[40] Cf. J. Rupp, *L'idée de Chrétienté dans la pensée pontificale, des origines à Innocent III* (Paris, 1939). Also, G. B. Ladner, "The Concepts of *Ecclesia* and *Christianitas*, and Their Relation to the Idea of Papal *plenitudo potestatis*, from Gregory VII to Boniface VIII," *Miscellanea Historiae Pontificiae* XVIII (Rome, 1954): 49–77.
[41] In making a systematic survey of the use of *Christianitas* and its related forms, J. Rupp found no mention of such terms in pontifical texts addressed to the fraternities and new orders. Neither St Francis nor St Dominic belonged to this "Christendom."
[42] Adalbero of Laon, *Carmen ad Robertum regem francorum* ccxcvii–ccxcviii (*PL*, CXLI, 771–86): "Triplex Dei ergo domus est, quae creditur una;/Nunc orant alii, pugnant, aliique laborant" ("Thus the Lord's house, which is thought to be one, is really threefold;/while some pray, others fight, and still others work").

abbots were consecrated. On another plane and reflecting the same tendency, while the anointing of kings continued to be an awe-inspiring religious rite which brought great political prestige to the monarchy, the popes made every effort to strip monarchy of its sacramental character. Innocent III, at the end of a long evolution to which canonists and liturgist-theologians had contributed, went against popular beliefs[43] and against the weight of Old Testament texts to make official a distinction between two kinds of anointing. Kings were to receive princely power (*potestas principis*) by being anointed on the arm with the oil of catechumens; prelates were to receive pontifical authority (*auctoritas pontificis*) by being anointed on the head with the holy chrism.[44]

The dubbing of a knight, a "sacrament" of feudal society, acquired the formalism of liturgical pomp as the social function of the knight became increasingly a matter of privilege; it became the initiation rite of a caste ("O, God, you have constituted in nature three degrees among men," declared the eleventh-century pontifical of Besançon) and no longer the sanctifying of a social value. This anointing of outdated privilege was the sin of a Christendom whose ceremony, bereft of religious value, survived as a symbol devoid of human relevance. At the same time, merchants – despised, held suspect in moral and religious thought – remained profane by birth in the new society.

The oath (*sacramentum*) of vassalage – the institutional keystone of feudal society, of social morality (*fides*, the virtue of fidelity), and of a sacral society – was bit by bit stripped of its threefold relevance. Its decline was regarded by traditionalist theologians as scandalous both because emancipation from it necessitated infidelity to the oath and because society was now being built upon non-sacralized agreements. The new formations – guilds, communes, fraternities – substituted a horizontal and fraternal agreement for vertical and paternalistic fidelity, and this agreement was affirmed not in a religious rite but in the solidarity of the "brothers" and in democratic deliberation. And the new evangelists stupefied the feudal ecclesiastics with their bold claim that the new regime no less than the old was in accord with the faith, with the good news of the gospel, and with the love of charity.

This process of desacralization extended to the political order itself. The scaling-down of the imperial anointment was a liturgical indication of the scaling-down of the idea of a *sacrum imperium* [holy empire]. At a time when the papacy under Innocent III reached the height of its power, realizing to some extent Gregory VII's program for papal aggrandizement; at a time when the papacy was able to manipulate feudal forms to its own advantage *vis-à-vis* the princes; at a time when the papacy seemed to be turning into a giant theocratic monolith engrossing both the sacred and the secular spheres – the most consistently reliable expressions of its power implied the conception of an empire completely stripped of its "sanctity,"

---

[43] Cf. M. Bloch, *Les rois thaumaturges* (Paris, 1924). The Gregorians had failed in their attacks on the popular belief in the supernatural powers of kingship. Otto of Freising, *Gesta Frederici*, ii.3 ([Otto of Friesing, *Gesta Frederici I imperatoris*, ed. B. de] Simson [(Hanover, 1912), pp. 103–4; [translated by C. C.] Mierow [and R.] Emory [as Otto of Friesing, *The Deeds of Frederick Barbarossa* (New York, 1953)], pp. 116–17) still spoke, on the occasion of the coronation of Frederick I in 1152, of the *sacramentum unctionis* (sacrament of anointing) and of the emperor as *Christus Domini* (the anointed of the Lord).

[44] Innocent III, *Reg.* vii.3 (*PL*, CCXV, 284); *Decretal.* lib. 1, tit. 15, c. 1 ([E.] Friedberg, [*Corpus juris canonici*, 2 vols (Leipzig, 1888–92)], II, 131–4). Even if one insists upon the synonymous connection between *potestas* (power) and *auctoritas* (authority), which this text would seem to split apart, the distinction did already appear in the letter of Pope Gelasius I (494) to the Emperor Anastasius: *Epp.* viii (*PL*, LIX, 42): "Duo quippe sunt, imperator Auguste, quibus principaliter mundus hic regitur: auctoritas sacrata pontificum, et regalis potestas" ("There are two means, august emperor, by which this world is mainly ruled: the sacred authority of the priesthood, and the royal power").

functional and political, while at the same time of course the imperial jurists claimed a sacred role for their sovereign. The polemical texts of this most tangled debate are highly revealing. The efforts to desacralize the Empire and those to force the papacy out of politics had in common a recognition of the autonomy of the temporal, and this recognition ran throughout the debate as a leitmotif.[45] The exclusive dedication to the apostolate on the part of the mendicant orders took into account this new type of relationship even before it had been defined, a relationship in which the Gregorian principles concerning *libertas ecclesiae* found a workable sociological base as well as a proper theology.[46]

All this would have consequences. One important political yet implicitly religious consequence was that the new monarchies would be emancipated not only from the pretensions of the Empire, but from the pseudoreligious myth of a political oneness of the world deriving necessarily from the catholic oneness of Christians. The *Ludus de Antichristo* [*Game of Antichrist*], wherein the king of France finally submits to the emperor in the Church triumphant, had been convincing back in the 1160s. But when Frederick II tried to revive the theme, the mystical pretensions of the Hohenstaufen seemed anachronistic in a Church now animated by the mendicants and no longer by monastic feudalism. The universalism of the Church was opportunely shaken free from its political matrix at the very moment when it seemed to have realized that universalism in a new empire of its own conceived as the *respublica christianitatis* [Republic of Christendom]. The relations between Innocent III and the emancipated monarchies could now take into account passing circumstances or personal political options; the relations so determined would soon find expression in theological writings, to the great advantage of the liberty of the kingdom of God. The remains of the Holy Empire would continue to drag along with a few jurists, and even some poets, to say nothing of genuine partisans. But the theologians would here and there retain only an occasional verbal or fossilized trace of it.

Of the several indications of this shift in frontiers, to the advantage of the apostolic faith, not the least significant was the rejection of the myth of Constantine. It was replaced, especially in Germany, by the myth of Charlemagne, the loyal protector of Christianity in the guise of the ideal knight. Constantine had been first the author and next the symbol of the confusion – ideological, mystical, and political – of two traditions: the papacy as heir of the Roman Empire, and the Empire as consecrated by a religious mission. The liturgy had incorporated this symbol by having the pope receive, in token of investiture on the day of his election, the purple mantle given by Constantine to Sylvester; and the official imperial theology had embroidered it with allegory.[47] All the reformers, St Bernard included ("In these things you have succeeded not Peter but Constantine," he said in reproaching

---

[45] Among other sources one could cite are R. Folz, *L'idée d'empire en occident du Ve au XIVe siècle* (Paris, 1953); A. Dempf, *Sacrum Imperium* (Munich, 1929); and P. E. Schramm, "Sacerdotium und Regnum im Austausch ihrer Vorrechte," *Studi Gregoriani* II (Rome, 1947): 403–57.

[46] [For *libertas ecclesiae*, see Gerd Tellenbach, *Church, State, and Christian Society at the Time of the Investiture Contest*, trans. R. F. Bennett (Oxford, 1959), ch. 5. The notion was conceived wholly within the feudal age and so did not extend to a disengagement of the Church from the holding of property. Only after certain important sectors of the Church had left the land and become disenchanted with the money economy, which served in place of land, did the notion *libertas ecclesiae* include freedom from all entanglements in property. (Added with author's concurrence.)]

[47] Cf. Honorius of Autun, *Gemma animae*, iv. 58, 60 (*PL*, CLXXII, 710–11), where the parallelism Solomon–Constantine is presented in the most fantastic symbolism amidst the texts on the seventh Sunday after Pentecost. Or, in Adam of Dryburgh, *De tripartito tabernaculo*, ii.13 (*PL*, CXCVIII, 713), for an exaltation of the conversion of Constantine and its extraordinary results.

Eugenius III[48]), denounced this confusion. The new apostles treated it with contempt. Joachim of Flora wove his anathema of the first corrupter of the spiritual Church into his prophetic scheme of history. Thus the apostolic movement came to inject its evangelical views into the dialogue of the two swords.[49]

The final trait of this theology, let us say of this politics of grace and nature, was that the evangelical revival brought a sharpened sensitivity to eschatology. This was an expected reaction, since the success of monastic Christianity had led many souls into the subtle temptation of surrendering themselves complacently to heavenly contemplation, as if to get a foretaste of glory. The Church, they said, had sanctified the world. Evoking the three stages of church history, called Zion, Jacob, and Jerusalem, Adam of Dryburgh had said: "What now remains except that the church, endowed with the tranquility of peace, should turn from the name 'Jacob,' which expressed its toilsome struggle, to that name which heralds peace, namely 'Jerusalem.'"[50] According to the Cistercian Otto of Freising, Constantine had inaugurated an era of sacred peace, extending to secular princes;[51] it was now reaching fulfillment in a radiant Church.

As it settled down in the world, this monastic eschatological ideal withdrew into its secure fantasies, inattentive to the drama of life, to the desperate call of the Church in a state of rapid expansion and in peril. It was the apostolic movement which renewed the Messianic hope, seeking to detect the advance signs of the time, signs at least of the urgency imposed by that consummation. Here again we see an instance of that troubled ferment wherein the worst is mixed with the most pure in the critical rebuke given to institutions conspicuously too well established. "*Peregrinamur a Domino*" ("We are straying from the Lord"). Here come the laborers of the eleventh hour, who are going to relieve the faltering first teams. Here are the true people of Israel, decidedly liberated from terrestrial servitude. Here is the new Jerusalem, triumphing over the antichrists foretold by the apocalypses. And here, near at hand, is the coming of the spirit. In manifestoes, in programs, in pontifical approbations, in sermons, in polemical tracts, in chronicles, these scriptural themes of the Messianic era were exploited to convey with unction the message of hope about to be realized. The allegorization of history, however customary, was not simply a literary device; it was a means of explaining the working-out in time of the kingdom of God by successive stages.[52] The way was perhaps open to interpretations by a delirious Messianism;[53] at least it was an entirely different eschatology, which called for reflection upon the course of history and which drew understanding and drive for the present from the future.[54]

---

[48] *De consideratione*, iv.3 (*PL*, CLXXXII, 776): "In his successisti non Petro sed Constantino"; Eugenius III was trying to maneuver between the senate and the emperor. The force of Bernard's outburst stemmed from moral, not institutional, concern.

[49] On the contexts of this development – on the one hand economic, social, political, and on the other hand doctrinal – see Georges de Lagarde, *La naissance de l'esprit laïque au déclin du moyen âge*, vol. 1: *Bilan du XIIIe siècle*, 3rd ed. (Paris, 1956).

[50] Adam of Dryburgh, *De triplici sanctae Ecclesiae statu*, sermo 8 in adventu Domini (*PL*, CXCVIII, 144): "Quid jam superest, nisi ut dum ei [ecclesiae] pacis tranquillitas indulta est, a nomine quod est Jacob, in quo laboriosa ejus expressa est lucta, ad nomen illud pacis insigne prae se ferens conscendat, quod est Jerusalem."

[51] Otto of Freising, *Chronica*, v. prol., vii prol. (Lammers [and] Schmidt, pp. 374, 496; Mierow, pp. 323, 404).

[52] See Chenu, pp. 162–201.

[53] For examples see P. Alphandéry, "Notes sur le messianisme médiéval latin (XIe–XIIe siècles)," *Rapport de l'Ecole pratique des hautes études* (Paris, 1912), pp. 1–29.

[54] This eschatological accent of the mendicants is lacking in John of Garland, *De triumphis ecclesiae* (first half of the thirteenth century; ed. T. Wright [London, 1856]).

Like St Peter speaking to the community at Jerusalem (Acts 2:14–21), the leaders of the apostolic movements took up the text of Joel on the day of the Lord: "I will pour out my spirit upon all of mankind, and your sons and daughters will be prophets. Your young men shall see visions, and your old men shall dream dreams." This prophetic attribution, common enough in tradition and liturgical anointing, had a special vigor for these generations. Teaching, the ministry of the word under ecclesiastical mandate, took among them the form of testimony, which gave it a prophetic accent. Honorius III's use of the word "prophets" to describe the Dominicans was not merely pious verbiage. This was not a matter of making predictions about the future, even if a taste for the exotic turned it into that in some Franciscan and Dominican chronicles. Instead it was an understanding of faith that gave to the teacher an aptitude for presenting in all its urgency the present working-out of God's plan, especially since that urgency was experienced while awaiting the Lord's return. From such a perspective, the interpretation of events left itself open, as always, to all sorts of infantile or shameful fantasies; but even with fantastic elaborations it remained the manifestation of an inner charisma within the ordinary magisterium of the Church (as in the case of a Francis or a Dominic). One should analyze all the chronicles or legends here, for they are all in their own way, both in content and as a literary genre, good witnesses to theological and apostolic activity in the midst of contemporary social stagnation.

Thus, one can define this evangelical awakening as an active presence of the gospel, not only because men took up the text and read it directly in its literal fullness, but also because, at the same time, the word of God was announced as real and present by action of the Holy Spirit in a vibrant Church and a revitalized theology.

19 The Use and Abuse of Miracles in Early Medieval Culture

Sofia Boesch Gajano

My point of departure is a text: a letter written by Archbishop Agobard, Ildigisus a priest, and Florus a deacon to Bishop Bartholomew of Narbonne, probably in 828–9.[1] The archbishop of Lyons is a figure of such political and cultural importance that he needs no introduction. I wish only to mention, as a preface to what I will shortly talk about, the archbishop's tendency to assume an authoritarian and repressive stance toward individuals he considered abusive of orthodox religious theories and practices (some of whom were favored by the political power, as can be seen in his letters relating to Jews) or toward those deviating from or resisting orthodox practices (pagan and folkloric remnants).[2] This letter has received less attention than other works by the archbishop, such as *De imaginibus sanctorum* [*On Saints' Images*] and *De grandine et tonitruis* [*On Hail and Thunder*], which can be considered true treatises in epistolary form.

Agobard had been asked his opinion on the interpretation (*quonam modo accipi debeat* [how ought one to interpret]) of certain *percussiones* [misfortunes] that afflicted some people in the manner of epileptics or what the populace referred to as *demoniaci* [demoniacs] and others in the form of burn marks [*stigmata exustionis*], as if they had been scalded by sulfur on certain parts of their bodies. This happened, according to what he had learned, in certain churches, and in particular in a church where the body of a saint by the name of Firmin was venerated: the church of St Firmin of Uzès. Men and women of all ages flocked to the places where these phenomena occurred, bringing gifts of gold, silver, animals, and other objects according to their means. These men and women were neither exhorted nor admonished to do so, but rather brought the gifts out of an irrational fear. The letter, after describing the place, the event, the reaction, and the reparation, turns to interpreting the nature of the phenomenon, its religious and moral meaning, and the comportment, some mistaken and some correct, of those reacting to it.

[1] Agobardi Lugdunensis, *Opera omnia*, ed. L. van Acker (Turnhout, 1981) (*Corpus christianorum, Continuatio medievalis*, 52), n. 15, pp. 237–43. See the introduction and the bibliography (particularly pp. LXVI–LXVII) for the author and his works as well as for secondary literature on him.
[2] For his relationship to Jews, see "Indicazioni bibliographiche," collected by S. Boesch Gajano in *Aspetti e problemi della presenza ebraica nell'Italia centro-settentrionale* (Rome, 1983), pp. 366ff. For some comments on this topic, see S. Boesch Gajano, "Identità ebraica e stereotipi cristiani: riflessioni sull'Alto Medioevo," in *Atti del VI Congresso internazionale dell'Associazione italiana per la storia del giudaismo* (Rome, 1988), pp. 45ff, which also contains additional bibliography.

The letter first passes judgment on the nature of the phenomenon. The archbishop does not provide any conceptual definitions, sustained by theological argument, but rather provides a sort of explanation extrapolated from scriptural tradition. No one would be so ignorant not to know that God punishes people, both visibly and invisibly, in order to teach them and convert them (*ad eruditionem et conversionem*). When doing so, God uses all the instruments he has at his disposal: men, demons, and animals, including small and vile ones such as snakes, frogs, flies, spiders, and locusts, as well as inanimate objects, such as hail, lightning, rain, and drought. The archbishop of Lyons, confident in his religious authority and even more so in his cultural prestige, sanctions the supernatural event as "positive," as having a divine origin, buttressing his argument with numerous examples found in the biblical tradition.

The letter then moves on to a moral interpretation. If the phenomenon's origin is divine, the instrument used is the devil who, in his desire to harm, directs his actions against the ones over whom he knows to have power, those who are of little faith and are weak in reason (*exigue fidei et vacui pondere rationis*). As a result he strikes and marks with burns *pueros, et puellas, et hebetes* [boys and girls, and the dim-witted]. The faithful who possess reason, upon seeing and hearing such things, are led to fear God and, pushed by terror, they run to the very churches where such events have happened and give as much as they can.

In the letter the archbishop criticizes the interpretation of the event as well as the reaction of fear, claiming both to be signs of ignorance. As a result he strongly condemns this type of reparation since the offerings are made thoughtlessly (*perdito consilio meliore* [better advice having been squandered]) and do not render honor to God. They do not aid the poor but merely satisfy the cupidity and avarice of a few individuals. So what was the right reparation? According to the bishop it was giving one's possessions to the poor, going to the clergy to be anointed with oil according to evangelical and apostolic precepts, and accompanying these acts with fasts and prayers. Moreover, if it had been a matter of *signa sanitatum* [healthy signs], healings conceded by God through his saints, then it would be just and fruitful to visit the churches and bring offerings *more ecclesiastico et secundum dispositionem patrum* [in the ecclesiastical manner and according to the teachings of the Fathers]. In conclusion, the letter states how reprehensible it is not to distribute to the poor that which belongs to the poor, and how fruitless an offering is that is not accompanied by due reverence for the Church.[3]

After this long summary, I now wish to make a few remarks about the actors, the theatrical space, the subject, and the recitation. Beginning with the actors, there is first of all a division between the clergy and the laity. Clerics are the repositories of tradition, culture, and orthodoxy. They are the only ones authorized to define the religious nature of the phenomenon. However, clerics are in all likelihood the "avaricious ones" who are profiting from the offerings made by the naïve and terrorized believers. This is testimony to the different cultural levels within the clergy and in this specific case reveals different forms of perception and practice, which in any case are already implicit in the request of an opinion from the clergy of Lyons. The laity is not socially defined: if the gifts of gold and silver suggest wealth, terminological analogy points to a cultural image in the text that is generally used in ecclesiastical literature to characterize the rural population. In any case, the laity's culture is depicted as subordinate.

Concerning the "stage" of action, the insistence on specifying that it is in churches, the sacred place par excellence, leads one to believe that precisely this place has been, since the beginning, the strongest cause of concern for the hierarchy. The "plot" seems to enjoy the

---

[3] See pp. 237, 238, 242, 243 in the edition cited in n. 1.

same credibility among the actors, the audience, and the writers insofar as the nature of the event is concerned, while the way in which it is recited differs profoundly. Both the fear and the offerings are judged negatively in the letter as an expression of a culture that is anthropologically different and, what is more serious, autonomous. The offering as reparation appears to be the most blameworthy element due to its lack of conformity to church regulations.

The event is considered supernatural and is described in a text that is neither hagiographical, ecclesiastical, nor normative, which makes it a good observation point for the numerous problems posed by miracles in early medieval ecclesiastical culture. It provides a good pretext for launching some considerations that I attempt to center, for organizational reasons, around three themes: first, the "ambiguity" of miracles with respect to how they are defined, perceived, used, and managed; second, the "autonomy" of miracles with respect to hagiographical discourse, and I use this in a double sense: the miracles' autonomy from hagiographical writings and from the primary object of hagiographical discourse, holiness, of which miracles manifest themselves as "antecedents" instead of "consequences"; third, the "instruments" of miracles, meaning the places, the objects, and the individuals, in which or through which, or whom, it is judged that an event considered outside of the natural course of events has taken place, since its impact on or modification of nature can only be attributed to supernatural power, making it what we can call an impact point between the natural and supernatural.

The theme of "ambiguity" can be approached through a large variety of problems ranging from theory to practice, from conceptual definitions to unconscious use, from ways of perceiving miracles, linked to the knowledge and interpretation of man and nature, to modes of managing them, connected to religious norms and rituals of control over and intervention in natural and social contexts. The development of Christian thought on miracles allows us to follow the evolution and difficulties of establishing a new conception of the marvelous, which permeated the ancient world not only in a religious but also in a political and cultural dimension.[4] Ambiguity is found in the patristic controversies, which discussed biblical antecedents and influenced the theological, pastoral, and hagiographical traditions of the Early Middle Ages,[5] as well as in the numerous "external" analyses found in a literature of the "other," which reflects a view on manifestations of Christian holiness that is both deformed and at the same time realistic.[6] Ambiguity is seen in the evolution, both quantitative and qualitative, of the holiness–miracle relationship, which becomes easier to detect once procedures of control are set down and then more precisely defined over time.[7] Finally it appears in the relationship between official and popular religion, the multiple segments of which at times stand in opposition, at times overlap, and at times intertwine across chronological and spatial nodes that are sometimes evident and sometimes hidden.[8]

---

[4] L. Cracco Ruggini, "Il miracolo nella cultura del Tardo Impero: concetto e funzione," in *Hagiographie, cultures et sociétés (IVe–XIIe siècles)* (Paris, 1981), pp. 161–204.

[5] M. van Uytfanghe, "La controverse biblique et patristique autour du miracle, et ses répercussions sur l'hagiographie du haut Moyen Age latin," in ibid., pp. 205–33.

[6] G. Dagron, "Le saint, le savant, l'astrologue: étude de thèmes hagiographiques à travers quelques recueils de 'Questions et réponses' des Ve–VIIe siècles," in ibid., pp. 143–56.

[7] On this vast issue see first of all, A. Vauchez, *La sainteté en Occident aux derniers siècles du Moyen Age d'après les procès de canonisation et les documents hagiographiques,* 2nd ed. (Rome, 1988) [published in English as *Sainthood in the Middle Ages* (New York: Cambridge University Press, 1997)].

[8] The bibliography on this subject has become so large that it is impossible to mention everything. I will limit myself to the following: in addition to essay collections cited in bibliographies, see *Agiografia*

The miracle has been taken away from the realm of credulity of an era (the medieval) and of a class (the popular) – the final blow in this direction must certainly be attributed to Peter Brown – and instead has entered a dimension that is constantly problematical.[9] This can be seen not so much in the effort to provide conceptual definitions as in the concern to recognize miracles religiously and ecclesiastically on the basis of their conformity to set criteria and to a functionality compatible with institutional order. The miracles of fifth- and sixth-century holy Italian fathers were chosen and set down by Gregory the Great in a context that was narrative, exegetical, and theological at the same time.[10] These miracles were wisely measured out, both quantitatively and qualitatively, in hagiographical literature from Gregory of Tours to Jonas of Bobbio,[11] then afterward in the hagiography of the Ottonian era[12] and in the production linked to the eleventh-century reform [13] and connected

---

altomedievale, ed. S. Boesch Gajano (Bologna, 1976); *Saints and their Cults*, ed. S. Wilson (Cambridge, 1983); S. Boesch Gajano, "Il culto dei santi: filologia, antropologia e storia," *Studi storici* 1 (1982): 119–26; P. Golinelli, "Agiografia e storia in studi recenti," *Società e storia* 19 (1983): 103–20; *Histoire des miracles* (Angers, 1983), two volumes devoted specifically to miracles and interesting for their diachronism and their thematic diversification, even if marked by a confessional imposition; *Les miracles miroirs des corps*, ed. H. Gélis and O. Redon (Paris, 1983) also arranged diachronically and innovative in its approach; *Culto dei santi, istituzioni e classi sociali in età preindustriale*, ed. S. Boesch Gajano and L. Sebastiani (Rome and L'Aquila, 1984); the monograph by P.-A. Sigal, *L'homme et le miracle dans la France médiévale (XI'–XII' siècle)* (Paris, 1985); and above all the synthesis found in B. Ward, *Miracles and the Medieval Mind. Theory, Record and Event, 1000–1215*, 2nd ed. (Trowbridge, 1987), which contains a large bibliography. Pierre Boglioni, who for some time has been developing individual and collective ideas concerning popular culture in the Middle Ages (including conventions organized by the Institut d'études médiévales of Montreal) is preparing a general study. On miracles see an interesting chapter found in J. Bossy, *Christianity in the West, 1400–1700* (Oxford, 1985).

[9] P. Brown, *The Cult of Saints* (Chicago, 1981). The historian's most recent book is *The Body and Society. Men, Women and Sexual Renunciation in Early Christianity* (New York, 1988), which contains an up-to-date bibliography.

[10] On this interpretation see my "Gregorian" articles: "La proposta agiografica dei Dialogi di Gregorio Magno," *Studi Medievali*, 3rd ser., 21 (1980): 623–64; "«Narratio» e «expositio» nei Dialogi di Gregorio Magno," *Bullettino dell'Istituto storico italiano per il Medio Evo e Archivio Muratoriano* 88 (1979): 1–33; "Dislivelli culturali e mediazioni ecclesiastiche nei Dialogi di Gregorio Magno," in *Religioni delle classi popolari*, ed. C. Ginzburg, in *Quaderni storici* 41 (1979): 398–415. There are many older or contemporary studies that I cite and discuss in these works, including the edition by A. de Vogué for the SC, which contains a rich Introduction. I would also like to mention the Acts of the Colloque international du Centre national de la recherche scientifique held in Chantilly in September 1982, *Grégoire le Grand* (Paris, 1986), and two recent monographs (both of which offer comprehensive interpretations of Gregory's hagiographical work in light of his culture), which unfortunately I am not able to discuss here: J. Petersen, *The Dialogues of Gregory the Great in their Late Antique Cultural Background* and W. D. McCready, *Signs of Sanctity. Miracles in the Thought of Gregory the Great*, both published in Toronto by the Pontifical Institute of Mediaeval Studies, *Studies and Texts*, vols 69 (1984) and 91 (1989), and both containing large bibliographies.

[11] See S. Boesch Gajano, "Il santo nella visione storiografica di Gregorio di Tours," in *Gregorio di Tours* (Todi, 1977), pp. 29–91 and "La tipologia dei miracoli nell'agiografia altomedioevale. Qualche riflessione," in *Aspetti dell'agiografia nell'Alto Medioevo. Schede medievali* 5 (1983): 303–12. For Jonas see A. de Vogué, Introduction to *Jonas de Bobbio. Vie de Saint Colomban et des ses disciples* (Abbaye de Bellefontaine, 1988), pp. 19–90, with a bibliography on pp. 13–15.

[12] For the hagiography of the Ottonian era, along with a bibliography, see P. Corbet, *Les saints ottoniens. Sainteté dynastique, sainteté royale et sainteté féminine autour l'an Mil* (Sigmaringen, 1986).

[13] The most recent reference point for the eleventh century is P. Golinelli, *"Indiscreta sanctitas". Studi sui rapporti tra culti, poteri e società nel pieno Medioevo*. Istituto storico italiano per il Medio Evo, *Studi Storici* 197–8 (Rome, 1988)

to the birth and development of the mendicant orders.[14] An evident expression of the need for recognition (beside other meanings, such as one to counteract possible forms of disbelief) is the authentication of the miracle, attested to frequently in the urban world of Italy in the High Middle Ages.[15] The miracle as a moment in which God intervenes directly in the world without mediation between human and divine is inevitably an anomalous element and could even be dangerous to a church historically directed toward interpretation and mediation of the holy.

> The ambiguous reality of the extraordinary event can only become certainty of faith thanks to the objectivity of a judicial "rite" to which the church . . . attributes the capacity to confer the status of a miracle upon any extraordinary event, transforming in this way the unlikely suspension of natural laws into a precise, divine action, turning it irrevocably into a precise moment and place of human history.[16]

The cultural contrast does not emerge so much from the belief in the miraculous event as in the forms of the perception, use, and management of it. The feelings of fear, respect, and hope, which find expression in the principles of the gift, which Sigal rightly considers to be the basis of the relationship between saint and believer, are also present in the reactions to the *percussiones* about which Agobard speaks to us.[17] Yet the very spontaneity of these feelings recalls a different cultural code in which the archbishop intervenes not in order to contest the reality of the supernatural event, which in fact has been assimilated into the Christian universe, but to distinguish it from the normal and correct relationship between saint and believer and to set down a different and more controlled form of reparation.

The research of Aline Rousselle has identified numerous interacting traditions, depicting Christianization as an active process not only on the part of the converters but also of the converted, who are capable of judging what portion of their traditions can be accepted and integrated and what portion constitutes a separate culture.[18] The rural world is not merely the realm of folkloric traditions and a natural, pagan religiosity, a world that offers a sort of passive resistance to learned religion, but is also a place for elaborating cultural choices. This illuminates what Andrea Giardina has spoken of as a "slippage" between the figure of Bacauda the bandit-hero and that of the Christian martyr described in the *Vita Martini* [*Life of St Martin*], slippage which continued into the eleventh century.[19] The hagiographical documents relative to the Subiacan cult of the anchorite Chelidonia (from the end of the

---

[14] See A. Vauchez, *La sainteté*. Also worth remembering are Vauchez's articles in *Les laïcs au Moyen Âge. Pratiques et expériences religieuses* (Paris, 1988).

[15] Numerous cases are recorded by A. Vauchez in *La saintété* (see the index entry "notaire"). Worth noting among recent editions is N. Occhioni, ed., *Il processo per la canonizzazione di S. Nicola da Tolentino* (Rome, 1984), which contains a preface by A. Vauchez and an introduction by Domenico Gentili.

[16] L. Odorisio, "La 'narrazione miracolosa'. I miracoli di santa Rita da Cascia," *Dimensioni e problemi della ricerca storica. Rivista del Dipartamento di studi storici dell'Università di Roma "La Sapienza"* 18 (1988): 51–67.

[17] P. Sigal, *L'homme*, in particular pp. 79ff.

[18] A. Rousselle, "Deux exemples d'évangélisation à la fin du IVe siècle: Paulin de Nole et Sulpice Sévère," in *Béziers et le Bitérrois* (Montpellier, 1971), pp. 91–8 and "Paulin de Nole et Sulpice Sévère hagiographes e la culture populaire," in *Les saints et les stars*, ed. J.-Cl. Schmitt (Paris, 1983), pp. 27–40.

[19] A. Giardina, "Banditi e santi: un aspetto del folklore gallico tra tarda Antichità e Medioevo," *Anthenaeum* 61 (1983): 374–89.

eleventh century to the middle of the twelfth century) allow us to see what can be defined as a true contrast between the interests of monastic institutions and those of the population of a place, be it in the rural areas or in the *castrum* [walled town] of Subiaco. This contrast does not relate to the saint herself, her miracles or the virtues of her relics, but rather to the where, how, and when to venerate her. This dispute was not to be resolved until the Counter-Reformation when the body, which already once had been transferred from the cave on the mountain but then afterward brought back, where it remained the object of a non-institutionalized devotion, was definitively transferred to the Church of St Scolastica and transformed into an official cult.[20]

Another problematic aspect of the miracle is what I have called "autonomy," and by this I mean autonomy as related to both holiness and hagiographical discourse. A quantitative and qualitative analysis of the miracles found in saints' lives is perhaps the best way of revealing the characteristics of a text, including its author/setting, its purpose, its audience (readers and/or listeners), and its beneficiaries (both direct and indirect). The classification of miracles has been the object of close study making use of grids: reflexive and transitive miracles, practical or material miracles, and exonerating and spiritual miracles, among others. Such grids have made it possible to capture, for example, the hierarchy of miracles in its interconnection with the spiritual progress of the saint, or to show the function of miracles in the construction of holiness.[21]

What characterizes most of these studies, however, is the univocal interpretation established for the relationship between holiness and miracles. Certainly in hagiographical texts there is a constant concern to establish, or perhaps better, to reestablish, the correct theological relationship, that of the miracle as an external *signum* [sign] of a spiritual holiness that the saint constructs through practicing virtues. This insistence itself seems to reveal that the miracle is perceived as more autonomous. In fact the same hagiographical narratives at times allow us to discern a relationship [between miracle and holiness] that is not defined in linear fashion, but always intertwined and at times even reversed. Miracles keep their characteristic as *signum* but often in the sense of a "revelation" of holiness rather than a "manifestation" of a holiness that has already been revealed. If in early medieval hagiography holiness often works itself out in a miracle, meaning that the saint has no other biographical or religious consistency except that of miracle worker, the miracle can present itself both narratively and conceptually as a *primum*, as an antecedent to holiness rather than its consequence, a first building-block in the "making" of a saint, insofar as it reveals the *virtus* [excellence, power] of a body.

A glance outside of hagiographical literature allows us to confirm these intertwinings and inversions, directing us to follow the lead of Gilbert Dragon who suggested using "alternative" sources.[22] It also strengthens our insistence on the theme of "autonomy." In his *Historia gentis Anglorum* [*Ecclesiastical History of the English People*], Bede constructs the holiness of Oswald, king of Northumbria. He constructs it on the field in the sense that the battlefield

---

[20] S. Boesch Gajano, "Monastero, città, campagna. Il culto di s. Chelidonia a Subiaco (sec. XI–XVI)," in *Culto dei santi*, pp. 229–60 and by the same author the forthcoming book *Chelidonia. Storia di un culto*.

[21] Again I remind readers of the article by J.-L. Derouet, "Les possibilités d'interprétation sémiologique des textes hagiographiques," *Revue d'histoire de l'Eglise de France* 62 (1976): 153–62, to which I owe much for some of my elaborations on typological suggestions. Also see the articles already cited: Boesch Gajano, "Narratio" and "La tipologia." Also see the wonderful contribution of B. Flusin, "Miracle et hiérarchie," in Ruggini, *Hagiographie*, pp. 299–317.

[22] G. Dagron, "Le saint, le savant, l'astrologue."

is the theater that consecrates Oswald as a saint, at the same time that it is consecrated by his blood. A horse, having collapsed on the ground, unexpectedly drags itself toward a precise spot where, suddenly, he stands up and is healed. The rider in this way understands that *aliquid mirae sanctitatis* [something of wondrous sanctity] has taken place there. Bede's story is testimony to the perception of miracles as independent from holiness. Sacredness can emanate from objects and only a religious explanation can bring it back to the presence of a saint, in this case the king who died in that place, whose blood bathed the earth and whose holiness the writer constructs piece by piece through a series of episodes in the chronicle.[23] A similar example is found in the story narrating the rediscovery of the holy lance in Guibert of Nogent's *Gesta Dei per Francos* [*The Deeds of God through the Franks*], which offers much material for reflection on miraculous events and the perception of them.[24]

Turning to another historical work, the *Liber pontificalis* [*The Book of Pontiffs*] of the Roman Church (even though defining the literary genre of this work is problematic), we can discern an evolution in the work's narrative structure as well as in its political–ecclesiastical purpose, noticeable in the way it provides and stratifies biographical information. It is immediately apparent that the hagiographization of the medallion [portrait, biographical entry] takes place not by means of enumerating, augmenting, and spiritualizing virtues but by the sudden appearance of a thaumaturgical *virtus*, which is directly linked not to the person but to the institutional function of a pontiff, Gregory II [715–31], who is endowed with holiness by comparison with his two enemies, one internal (the iconoclasts) and one external (the Muslims).[25] Only gradually does personal holiness become an important element in papal biographies, finding a happy moment of equilibrium in the unfolding of the miraculous in the biography of Pope Zachary [741–52].[26]

Paying attention to the "autonomy" of miracles in the dual sense mentioned above, narrative autonomy and hagiographical autonomy, allows for a decisive deepening in the relationship between the natural and the supernatural in medieval society. Such a relationship is consciously established and structured within a theological context or more simply accepted, utilized, and reproposed in written form. This relationship corresponds to means felt to be traceable to less explicit although not unknown sociocultural parameters. In this schema miracles, far from appearing as a simple manifestation of the sacred made possible by the "credulousness" of an entire society, become the best means of revealing different levels or relationships among different "levels," to use a term favored by Peter Brown.

Miracles likewise reveal conflicts. One need only think of the frequency with which ecclesiastical writers, in sources that are typologically quite varied, worry about miracles and seek to exert control over them or even to repress them. This happens when one "discovers" cultic forms that have been absorbed into Christian ones, the object of which was chosen outside of ecclesiastical jurisdiction; these are therefore autonomous objects and forms of devotion. This is the case of the cult of the martyr-bandit, mentioned above, which was discovered, condemned, and destroyed by Martin. It is also the case of the cult raised on the

[23] Bede, *Historia gentis Anglorum*, III: 9, ed. B. Colgrave and R. A. B. Mynors (Oxford, 1969), pp. 144ff. For a brief reference to Oswald in a different context from this see S. J. Ridyard, *The Royal Saints of Anglo-Saxon England. A Study of West Saxon and East Anglian Cults* (Cambridge, 1988), pp. 92–3, 242–3, with a useful bibliography on pp. 311–26.
[24] Guibert, *Gesta Dei per Francos* (PL 156, coll. 768, 784, 785). On the history of the rediscovery of the holy lance see S. Runciman, "The Holy Lance found at Antioch," *Analecta Bollandiana* 68 (1950): 197–209. For an analysis of Guibert's attitude see B. Ward, *Miracles*.
[25] *Liber pontificalis*, ed. L. Duchesne, vol. 1 (Paris, 1955), pp. 396–410, in particular pp. 401 and 412 for some historical and chronological information.
[26] Ibid., pp. 426–35.

tomb of a child, the son of a *miles* [knight] who died two days before Easter, a sanctifying time ("*coepit mortuo illo pro sacra illa in qua obierat de gratuita sanctitas imputari*" ["sanctity began to be attributed to the deceased on account of the sacred day on which he died"]), perhaps also sanctifying the boy's age?). The cult was started by peasants who were "*rerum novarum cupidi*" ["greedy for novelties"]: "*oblationes et cerei*" ["offerings and candles"] were brought from the surrounding countryside and "*tumba superstruitur, locus ille domo aedificata praecingitur*" ["the tomb was built up and that site was enveloped in a shrine"]. Only the *rustici* [peasants] showed this devotion, with no member of the upper classes becoming involved. However, the abbot, seeing the profits, closed an eye to and tolerated the *infecta miracula* [fake miracles].[27] In this story Guibert of Nogent offers us a multidimensional reality made up of many levels, many interests, which are not necessarily in contrast, and many interconnections. Above all he offers us, through his lamentations and condemnations, a certainty: that his preoccupation arises not from the differences but from the similarities. It is the cultic and ritual similitude itself that renders more difficult both control and actual intervention directed toward reestablishing a proper relationship among holiness of life, the external signs of holiness, and cult; while, in this case, it must be added, it renders easier opportunistic indulgence.

All of this becomes even more evident when we go on to a consideration of the "instruments" of miracles: the places and objects capable of transmitting sacredness. Once again I take an example from Bede, found in his *Ecclesiastical History*, a reading of which offers an inexhaustible amount of food for thought, even more so if read alongside his hagiography. In the same way that the place bathed in the blood of Oswald is soaked in thaumaturgical *virtus*, so the slivers of wood that were driven into his head are bearers of a sacredness both material (capable of serving the body) and spiritual (capable of serving the soul). Thus they are "instruments" in the true sense of the word, since they are objects suitable for mediating a supernatural power and transferring it into a human reality. "I beg you," says an elderly, dying monk to one who was spreading the news of Oswald's holiness, "if you have any of his relics with you, bring them to me, so that the Lord may perhaps have mercy on me through his merits." The response is as follows: "If you truly believe with all your heart, God, in His grace, can prolong life by means of the merits of such a great man and render you worthy of entering into eternal life." Thus the old, sick monk receives the holy water "consecrated" by a sliver of the holy wood.[28] A sliver of wood as host?

Certainly this example brings to mind the relationship between miracles and "the" miracle of the Eucharist, act, moment, and object in which the sacred, continually and daily, materializes and remains permanently available.

> The process of distinction among events called *mira* in this period (the period under consideration by Benedicta Ward in this quotation is the eleventh to early thirteenth centuries) is seen particularly clearly in relation to the supernatural events called sacraments. In one sense the sacraments always have been "miracles" *par excellence*, insofar as they were the supreme instances of the regular but mysterious intervention of God in the created order: *quotidiana miracula* [daily miracles]. . . . The real emphasis on a sacrament as miraculous, however, was to be found in connection with the Eucharist. Unlike the other sacraments, the Eucharist involved the use of bread and wine, natural objects that could be observed and discussed in terms other than those of psychology.[29]

[27] Guibert, *De pignoribus sanctorum* (*PL* 156), 621.
[28] Bede, *Historia*, III: 2–13, pp. 128ff.
[29] Ward, *Miracles*, p. 13. Also see Ward for bibliography on this topic.

Thus the theological and historical dimension of the issue must be linked to the knowledge and interpretation of nature and to the entire perception of the sacred in a specific sociocultural context.[30]

The consecrated host can thus become an "instrument," perhaps even an instrument endowed with a particular kind of sacredness and, as a result, more effective. As a consequence, there are Eucharistic miracles, in the telling of which the internal holiness is sometimes superimposed – it is the proof of transubstantiation, almost a "reflexive" miracle, according to a typology that I mentioned above – upon the active, transitive *virtus*, used in a variety of ways, and not always correctly.[31]

Peter Damian [*c*.1007–72] tells the story of a woman who, betrayed by her husband, decides to receive the body of the Lord "*quasi communicatura*" ["as if she were taking communion"], keeping it intact in her mouth: "*quod caute reservans, viro suo postmodum non sine quibusdam maleficiis propinaret*" ["holding on to it carefully, after a short while she gave it to her husband to eat, not without a certain malevolence"]. A miracle prevents this sacrilege: half of the host is transformed into human flesh while the other half does not change its "*panis speciem*" ["appearance as bread"].[32] Is this a sort of spell, or merely the use for everyday ends of an object whose sacredness the woman believes in, as most likely her husband does, too? Is this an example of witchcraft or only an improper use?

A peasant in a story told by Peter the Venerable [1092–1156] is accused of having "abused" the sacrament of the Eucharist by means of magic. According to the story, the peasant kept the wafer in his mouth and brought it intact to a beehive, where he blew it into the hive because he had been told that the body of the Lord could protect his bees ("*nulla deinceps moreretur, nulla recederet, nulla deperiret*" ["that none die off in turn, none go away, none perish"]) and increase his production of honey ("*de augmento fructus multo amplius quam ante gauderet*" ["that he benefit from the increase of the fruit much more than before"]). The bees, demonstrating a natural devotion, preserved the wafer intact. The man, however, "*in vindictam sceleris sui*" ["out of revenge for his own wickedness"], killed the bees, which he had wanted to protect with evil magic. As proof of the sin, the host, appearing in the form of a newborn baby, vanished as soon as it was touched by those unworthy hands.[33]

The miracles told by Peter the Venerable confirm the *virtus* of objects sanctified by the clergy, the Eucharist and holy water, certainly as a way to affirm priestly power, which was a necessary intermediary between man and God and the only one capable of managing the sacred and of constructing the correct vehicles for distributing and spreading it.[34] A similar intention can be found in Peter Damian, even if the dossier is slimmer. In the punitive use of the first example and in the protective use of the second, elements of misbelief are not to be found. Proof of the "real presence" appears as an "added" element – a reaffirmation of the

---

[30] For the relationships among miracles, physical knowledge, and medical science see Ward, *Miracles*, as well as Occhioni, ed., *Il processo per la canonizzazione di S. Nicola da Tolentino* (look in index under "scienza medica"). Also interesting are the pages dedicated to the issue by E. Brambilla, "La medicina del Settecento: dal monopolio dogmatico alla professione scientifica," in *Storia d'Italia, Annali 7: Malattia e medicina*, ed. F. Della Peruta (Turin, 1984), pp. 81ff.

[31] Numerous examples can be found in Ward, *Miracles*.

[32] Peter Damian, *Op. XIII* (*PL* 145), pp. 571–3.

[33] Peter the Venerable, *De miraculis libro duo*, ed. D. Bouthiellier, *Corpus christianorum, Continuatio medievalis* 83 (Turnhout, 1988), I/1: 7–8.

[34] J.-P. Valery Patin and J. Le Goff, "A propos de la typologie de miracles dans le 'Liber de miraculis' de Pierre le Vénérable," in *Pierre Abélard-Pierre le Vénérable. Les courants littéraires et artistiques en Occident au milieu du XIIᵉ siècle* (Paris, 1975), pp. 181–7.

orthodoxy of faith, which does not appear to have been put into discussion – and the narratives concentrate on the object of condemnation itself, its "evil" use. In this episode, one can instead clearly see a different use of the holiness and power that are recognized in that "instrument," which does not exclude but could even combine with the ecclesiastical instrument, which in turn can present several differentiations and be at times an object of disciplinary intervention. An "instrumental" use of the Eucharist seems implicit in the prohibition against taking it outside of churches.[35]

The control over the use of the sacred seems in these examples connected to one prevalent preoccupation, which we can define as a "mingling."[36] In the face of this mingling, the distinction between positive holiness, correctly used, and negative holiness, used for evil ends, must be made clear. The miracle–magic relationship thus returns to the foreground, just as the problem of the concept itself does along with the terminology relating to miracles. I wish here only to express the need to formulate and articulate this. Miracles have many forms and degrees of intensity, or perhaps it would be better to say that people in every era possess or create numerous ideas aimed at obtaining that which reality does not offer them, including material necessities, instruments to fight disease, and protection against physical pain, anxiety, and the fear of death.[37] It is obvious in this sense that the miracle can truly be a privileged observatory for a history of a society – and surely not only of early medieval society. The historical "negation" of the miracle, in which it is thrown into an imaginary realm void of all cultural consistency, or its elitist theological ghettoization (at times purposefully manipulated), in which it is placed into the sphere of badly tolerated "popular" credulousness, contrary of course to its "explanation" and utilization as a sign of God's intervention (thus its "ahistoricization"), both serve to impoverish history, perhaps in the hope of rendering it less complex and worrisome. And it is to this topic that I hope to turn in the near future.

---

[35] See, for example, the prohibition formulated at the Fourth Lateran Council (XX), Mansi, 21: 1077. Seventeenth-century examples of the clergy's "improper" use of the Eucharist against fires and storms are found in P. Guidotti, *Dall'Appennino all'Oltralpe sulle tracces della religiosità popolare* (Bologna, 1988), pp. 33–4.

[36] I have also used this term in other contexts: see my "Identità."

[37] Interesting ideas come out of the coincidences, the superimpositions, and the ambiguities found in the analysis of some specific cases: see for example the wonderful article by A. Rousselle, "Du sanctuaire au thaumaturge: la guérison en Gaule au IVe siècle," *Annales ESC* 31 (1976): 1085–1107 and the recent research by G. Ferzoco, "Historical and Hagiographical Aspects of the Religious World of Peter of Morrone," in *S. Pietro del Morrone Celestino V nel Medioevo monastico* (L'Aquila, 1989), pp. 227–37. On the "degrees" of miracles, many interesting ideas came to me upon reading the article by F. Koch, "Il 'buon mercato': utile e religione in una confraternita romana di fine Ottocento," *Movimento operaio e socialista* 11 (1988): 21–34.

20 The Dead in the Celestial Bookkeeping of the Cluniac Monks Around the Year 1000

Dominique Iogna-Prat

At the beginning of the 1050s, Jotsald, monk of Cluny, reported the following story in a passage of his *Life of St Odilo*:

> One day . . . a monk from the Rouergue was coming back from Jerusalem. In the very middle of the sea that lies between Sicily and Thessalonica, he met with a violent wind, which pushed his ship towards a rocky little island where a hermit lived, a servant of God. As soon as our man saw the wind lessen, he spoke of this and that with the hermit. The man of God asked him of what nationality he was, and he answered that he was from Aquitaine. Then, the man of God wanted to know if he knew a monastery called Cluny, and the abbot of that place, Odilo. He answered, "I have known him, and indeed, known him well, but why do you ask?" And the other answered, "I will tell you, and I entreat you to remember what you are going to hear. Not far from us are places that spit out most violently a burning fire, by the manifest will of God. For certain periods of time, the souls of sinners purge themselves with various tortures. It is the task of a multitude of demons constantly to renew their torments: reviving their pains from day to day, making

This study was originally presented as a paper at the twelfth Rencontre d'histoire religieuse organized by the Société des idées et d'histoire religieuse, at the Centre culturel de l'Ouest, at the Abbey of Fontevraud, October 14–15, 1988. I would like to thank Father Crouzel, and Professors J. de Viguerie and E. Magnou-Nortier for their judicious remarks, as well as F. Neiske and E. Palazzo, who kindly read and commented on a first draft of this text. I am also more than grateful to Anne L. for her stimulating reflections on reading it.

[This essay originally had two prefatory epigraphs. The first makes reference to the year in which the conference it was read at was held: "For Dante, who died nine hundred and eighty-eight years after the year 1000. Does he know in which circle Odilo of Cluny, accountant of the afterlife, is hovering?" The second is: "Madan Danoze, welcome to the prison of thoughts and dreams. Your home from now on will be this central building where a thousand good little angels, locked up for eternity for a vast variety of reasons, wander in peace. This place of detention has been arranged to accommodate the bottled-up souls of living Christians condemned to a sentence depriving them of spiritual freedom. Their daily work consists of bottling up the imagination of those individuals changed into the living dead."] See R. Depestre, *Hadriana dans tous mes rêves* (Paris, 1988), p. 161.

their agony more and more intolerable. I have often heard the lamentations of these men who complain bitterly: for God's mercy allows the souls of these prisoners to be delivered from their pains by the prayers of monks, and by the alms offered to the poor in holy places. In their pleas, they address themselves especially to the community of Cluny and to its abbot. So, I entreat you by God, if you are fortunate enough to return to your home, let the community know everything you have heard from my lips, and exhort the monks to multiply their prayers, their vigils, and their alms, for the repose of these souls cast into misery, so that joy in Heaven may increase, and that the Devil may be vanquished and frustrated.[1]

These were the circumstances that, according to Jotsald, led Odilo of Cluny to introduce the commemoration of all the dead, All Souls, on November 2, the day after All Saints, in the 1030s.[2] This famous episode has been reported, and commented on, many times since. Peter Damian, James of Voragine, Vincent of Beauvais – to mention only a few of the most important – all helped to make the efficacity of Cluniac prayers for the dead legendary.[3] Later, the Roman martyrology accepted and reinforced this tradition, which made Odilo the saint of all the faithful departed.[4] Recently, Jacques Le Goff, commenting on Jotsald's text, has underlined the importance of this Cluniac landmark in the prehistory of the idea of Purgatory.[5]

From the fundamental book of W. Jorden[6] to the more recent studies of O. G. Oexle, K. Schmid, J. Wollasch, and their disciples of the Münster School, many scholars – especially German scholars – have scrutinized and analysed the wealth of Cluniac documentation dealing with funerary matters.[7] On the basis of these works, and in tribute

---

[1] Jotsald, *Vita Sancti Odilonis*, *PL* 142, cols 926 C–927B, cited in J. Le Goff, *La naissance du purgatoire* (Paris, 1981), pp. 171–2 [published in English as *The Birth of Purgatory*, trans. Arthur Goldhammer (Chicago, 1984), p. 201].

[2] The date 1030 is the most commonly accepted; discussion can be found in *Liber tramitis aevi Odilonis*, ed. P. Dinter, Corpus Consuetudinum Monasticarum 10 (Siegburg, 1980), 126, pp. 186–7.

[3] Peter Damian reworked the biography of Odilo written by Jotsald. This new *Life of St Odilo* has since become the text of reference (*PL* 144, cols 925–44; the passage concerned here is found in cols 935 C–936 C). This is the text that inspired James of Voragine, for example, in *La légende dorée*, trans. J.-B. M. Roze (Paris, 1967), 2, p. 322 [published in English as *The Golden Legend*, trans. William Granger Ryan (Princeton, 1993), vol. 2, p. 280]; the same is true for Vincent of Beauvais, *Speculum historiale*, bk 25 (Douais ed., 24), 105, cols 102–5. I would like to thank M. Paulmier-Foucart for having provided me with this reference.

[4] "*Apud Silviniacum sancti Odilonis abbatis Cluniacensis, qui primus commemorationem omnium fidelium defunctorum prima die post festum Omnium Sanctorum in suis monasteriis fieri praecepit; quem ritum postea universalis ecclesia recipies comprobavit*" ["Near Souvigny of St Odilo the abbot of Cluny, who first began to celebrate the commemoration of all the faithful departed on the day after All Saints in his monasteries; this rite was later approved by the universal Church"], *Martyrologium Romanum . . . , Propylaeum ad Acta Sanctorum decembris* (Brussels, 1940), p. 1.

[5] See above, n. 1.

[6] W. Jorden, *Das cluniazensische Totengedächtniswesen vornehmlich unter den drei ersten Äbten Berno, Odo und Aymard (910–954). Zugleich ein Beitrag zu den cluniacensischen Traditions-Urkunden*, Münstersche Beiträge zur Theologie 15 (Münster in W., 1930).

[7] We can follow the thread of this impressive German production thanks to the synthetic volume *Memoria. Die geschichtliche Zeugniswert des liturgischen Gedenkens im Mittelalter*, ed. K. Schmid and J. Wollasch, Münstersche Mittelalterschriften 48 (Munich, 1984). Besides the essential articles that are assembled in this volume, I have especially used the following works: N. Huyghebaert, *Les documents nécrologiques*, Typologie des Sources du Moyen Age occidental 4 (Turnhout, 1972) (updated by J.-L. Lemaître, 1985); J. Ntedika, *L'évocation de l'au-delà dans la prière pour les morts. Étude de patristique et*

to the German School, I would like to paint a general picture of how Cluny managed (and I will explain my use of this accounting term) the memory of the dead around the year 1000.

Odilo was the fifth abbot of Cluny, and presided over the abbey between 994 and 1049.[8] The monastery had been founded in 910 by William the Pious, duke of Aquitaine, under conditions that rapidly ensured its success. He had placed the establishment under the protection of Peter and Paul, which guaranteed its independence through a direct attachment to Rome. Under the abbacy of Odilo, Cluny underwent two major transformations:

1. In the context of the crumbling of public power (royal, ducal, and comital), which affected the western kingdom of Francia in the years 980–1020, the monastery became an independent lordship.[9]
2. In 998, Cluny received a privilege of exemption from Pope Gregory V freeing the sanctuary from diocesan control and coercion.[10]

This acquisition of liberties (temporal and spiritual) represents a kind of second birth for Cluny. For more than half a century, Odilo sovereignly organized the monastery, both its interior life and its relations with the "world." He developed the activities of its scriptorium, which had already been very active since the 960s.[11] There, copies of all kinds were produced: at Cluny, the monk was both scribe and notary. Hence the great coherence of contemporary Cluniac sources, which invites the historian to consider the whole, passing from texts copied in the scriptorium (especially the numerous scriptural commentaries of the Fathers, or of Carolingian masters), to the original productions of Odilo and his disciples

---

de liturgie latines (IVe–VIIIe siècles) (Louvain and Paris, 1971); O. G. Oexle, "Memoria und Memorialüberlieferung im früheren Mittelalter," *Frühmittelalterliche Studien* 10 (1976): 70–95; D. Poeck, "Laienbegräbnisse in Cluny," *Frühmittelalterliche Studien* 15 (1981): 68–179; D. Sicard, *La liturgie de la mort dans l'église latine des origines à la réforme carolingienne*, Liturgiewissenschaftliche Quellen und Forschungen 63 (Münster in W., 1978), as well as the numerous and important works of J. Wollasch, which include: "Gemeinschaftsbewusstsein und soziale Leistung im Mittelalter," *Frühmittelalterliche Studien* 9 (1975): 268–86; "Kaiser und Könige als Brüder der Mönche. Zum Herrscherbild in liturgischen Handschriften des 9. bis 11 Jahrhunderts," *Deutsches Archiv für Erforschung des Mittelalters* 40. 1 (1984): 1–20; "Les Obituaires, témoins de la vie clunisienne," *CCM* 22 (1979): 139–71; "Wer waren die Mönche von Cluny vom 10. bis zum 12. Jahrhundert?", *Mélanges J. Stiennon* (Liège, 1982), pp. 663–78. I have also profited greatly from reading M. Lauwers. "La mémoire des ancêtres, le souci des morts. Les relations entre les vivants et les morts au diocèse de Liège (XIe–XIIIe siècles)" (DEA thesis under the direction of J. Le Goff, École des hautes études en Sciences sociales, Paris, 1987).

[8] On St Odilo, see J. Hourlier, *Saint Odilon, abbé de Cluny*, Bibliothèque de revue d'histoire ecclésiastique 40 (Louvain, 1964).

[9] See G. Duby, *La société aux XIe et XIIe siècles dans la région mâconnaise*, 2nd ed. (Paris, 1971), pp. 145ff.

[10] See J.-F. Lemarignier, "L'exemption monastique et les origines de la réforme grégorienne," in *A Cluny. Congrès scientifique, fêtes et cérémonies liturgiques en l'honneur des saints abbés Odon et Odilon (9–11 juillet 1949)* (Dijon, 1950), pp. 288–334; and "Structures monastiques et structures politiques dans la France du Xe et des début du XIe siècle," in *Il monachesimo nell'alto Medioèvo e la formazione della civiltà occidentale*, Spoleto 4 (Spoleto, 1957), pp. 357–400.

[11] On this question, see the important studies of M.-C. Garand, "Copistes de Cluny au temps de saint Maïeul (948–994)," *Bibliothèque de l'École des Chartes* 136 (1978): 5–36; and "Une collection personnelle de saint Odilon de Cluny et ses compléments," *Scriptorium* 33 (1979): 163–80.

(primarily hagiographic, homiletic, and historiographical texts),[12] to the customary and the cartulary.

It is these last two sources that will particularly concern us here. In the 1030s, Odilo gave the monastery a set of customs to which his name is quite rightly attached: the *Liber tramitis aevi Odilonis* [*Book of the Way of Life in the Age of Odilo*]. This customary represents the first systematic organization of the life of the monastery, which thus fits into the important movement of monastic codification that the Latin West saw between 950 and 1040. It is therefore a document of considerable importance, curiously underused by historians, no doubt because until recently, there was no critical edition of the text.[13] I will use it abundantly, because it minutely describes the activities of the monastery, expecially its rich liturgical life in the second monumental abbey, Cluny II, built slowly after 948, that is to say, essentially under the abbacies of Mayeul (954–94) and Odilo. In particular, it was Odilo who had constructed the famous "Galilee," that is, the "ante-church" built on a part of the atrium that preceded the major basilica.[14]

The first attempt to organize the entire Cluniac demesne, documented in the cartulary, also dates from the abbacy of Odilo.[15] This is an extremely rich source, well known to historians since the works of A. Deléage[16] and G. Duby,[17] which have allowed us to follow the management of this sanctuary/lordship, and its relations with the "world" – both its friends and benefactors, and its despoilers.

The customary and cartulary together provide irreplaceable testimony on the manner in which the memory of the dead was managed at Cluny around the year 1000. The cartulary registers the movement of donations, with, among others, donations *ad sepulturam* [for burial]. In a very searching study, D. Poeck has followed the movement of donations made to Cluny from its foundation to the end of the abbacy of St Hugh in 1109. Let us simply mention a few significant statistics. Under the abbacy of Mayeul, for 637 donations, 72 were donations *ad sepulturam*; under Odilo, the movement grew: 1,018 acts in all, including 704 donations of which 124 were *ad sepulturam*. The corresponding figures under Hugh's administration are 898 acts, 654 donations of which only 73 are *ad sepulturam*. The phenomenon of donations *ad sepulturam*, which had been known at Cluny from the beginning, therefore attained its peak under the abbacy of Odilo.[18]

A study of Cluny's customs confirms this observation. Anyone who goes through the *Liber Tramitis aevi Odilonis* guided by the table of contents, or better yet, the index, is bound to be struck by the importance of the entry for *defunctus* [deceased], and by the number of cross-references (*matutinae, missa, officium, psalmus, uesperae, uigiliae* [matins, mass, office, psalm, vespers, vigils]). The conclusion is inescapable: Odilo and his brothers gave an important place in the conventual liturgy to the celebration for the dead. It ought to be

---

[12] I have provided a rather cavalier overview of the narrative production of Cluny in the abbacy of Odilo in my study titled *Agni immaculati. Recherches sur les sources hagiographiques relatives à saint Maïeul de Cluny (954–994)* (Paris, 1988), to which I refer the reader.

[13] See above, n. 2.

[14] On Cluny II, see K. J. Conant, *Cluny, les églises et la maison du chef d'ordre* (Mâcon, 1968), pp. 53–67; more recently, C. Sapin, *La Bourgogne préromane* (Paris, 1986), pp. 67–70.

[15] *Receuil des Chartes de l'abbaye de Cluny*, ed. A. Bernard-A. Bruel, 1–4, Collection de documents inédits sur l'histoire de France (Paris, 1871–87); A. Bernard and A. Bruel date the earliest cartulary of the monastery to the abbacy of Odilo; see ibid., 1, preface, pp. 14–15.

[16] A. Deléage, *La vie rurale en Bourgogne jusqu'au début du XIe siècle*, 3 vols (Mâcon, 1942).

[17] See above, n. 9.

[18] Poeck, "Laienbegräbnisse" (above, n. 7), p. 101 (Mayeul), 122, 176 (Odilo), 152 (Hugh).

possible for us to confirm this observation by a study of one last source, the necrology. Unfortunately, this document has been lost, but we can partially reconstitute it by means of the necrologies of other establishments dependent on Cluny. The closest to the lost version is that of Marcigny-sur-Loire, a monastery of nuns founded by Hugh. The reconstitution of the Cluny necrology has been attempted by J. Wollasch and his team from Münster in the form of a *Synopsis*,[19] which I will refer to as necessary.

Was it really so obvious that the monks should thus take charge of the dead? Not if we look at the Rule of St Benedict, which, as J. Wollasch points out, does not once speak of the memory of the dead, or the commemoration of the defunct.[20] In fact, the reforming monks of the tenth and eleventh centuries inherited a relatively recent funerary tradition. Let us look at the beginning of this tradition so that we may judge the importance of the Cluniacs' taking it over.

Gregory the Great provides the first significant reference point. The enormous influence of this pope-monk on the monastic communities of the Early Middle Ages was simultaneously doctrinal, hagiographical, and liturgical.[21] His *Dialogues* took up and illustrated the old Augustinian thesis about the utility of suffrages for the dead. But Gregory added to this a doctrine of expiation, and of purification by fire. Distinguishing three categories of sins, he maintained that the least serious sins are remissible, and, like wood, hay, and straw, they are combustible. These little doctrinal developments are illustrated by miraculous stories and apparitions. Thus Gregory tells the tragic but edifying story of a brother, Justus, poorly named, who broke his vow of poverty by hiding two pieces of gold.[22] At the hour of his death, he begged for the help of the brothers, but no one dared to come near him; his blood-brother, Copiosus, finally told him why he was "the abomination of all." On Gregory's order, [the body of] Justus was thrown, without any further attention, into a ditch filled with manure. After 30 days, Gregory invited the brothers to help the deceased by means of a liturgical service equivalent in length (30 days) to the "penitence" imposed on the deceased.[23] At the end of this 30-day period, Justus appeared to Copiosus to attest to the efficacy of the liturgical service. There can be no doubt that this tale, known to all the monks, contributed effectively and durably to entrenching the notion that assistance was necessary in order to accompany the dead into a blessed afterlife.

But it was especially in the Carolingian period that this assistance became more organized. Remember first of all that All Saints, a feast especially beloved of Alcuin, appeared in England in the eighth century, and spread throughout the Carolingian Empire during the next century.[24] And it was also in this period that the idea emerged to associate all the deceased with the celebration of all the saints. This was the idea expressed by Amalarius in his *Liber de ordine antiphonarii* [*Book on the Order of Antiphons*]: "After the offices of the saints, I have inserted an office for the dead. Many are those who, having left this world, are

---

[19] W. D. Heim, J. Mehne, F. Neiske, and D. Poeck, *Synopse der cluniacensischen Necrologien*, ed. J. Wollasch, Münstersche Mittelalter-Schriften 39, 2 vols (München, 1982).

[20] J. Wollasch, "Les moines et la mémoire des morts," in *Religion et culture autour de l'an Mil: Royaume capétien et Lotharingie*, ed. J.-C. Picard and D. Iogna-Prat (Paris, 1990), pp. 47–54, p. 47.

[21] See the essential work of Ntedika, *L'évocation de l'au-delà* (above, n. 7), especially pp. 58ff, 105ff.

[22] *Dialogues* 4.57, 8–15, ed. A. de Vogüé, SC 265 (Paris, 1980), pp. 188–92.

[23] It is J. Ntedika, *L'évocation de l'au-delà* (above, n. 7), p. 109, who judiciously noted the penitential "tricenaire" inflicted on the deceased brother.

[24] See H. Delehaye, *Martyrologium Romanum* . . . (Brussels, 1940), pp. 488–9; *L'Eglise en prière*, ed. A.-G. Martimort, 2nd ed. (Paris, 1983), 1: 67; 4: 133 as well as L. Pietri, "Les origines de la fête de la Toussaint," *Les Quatres Fleuves* 25–6 (1988): 57–61.

not immediately gathered unto the saints."[25] A similar idea obeyed a liturgical logic clearly expressed in the *communicantes* [a prayer of the mass that lists several saints] which put the dead in "communion" with the saints.[26] St Odilo's introduction of the commemoration of all the deceased, All Souls, November 2, is thus directly in line with this tradition. Around the year 1000, the idea was clearly in the air; thus the *Mirabilia Urbis* [*Marvels of the City*], a guidebook to Rome at the time of the Ottonian Renaissance, associated all the dead with all the saints who surround Mary, honored at the Pantheon in the place and in place of Cybele, mother of the gods.[27]

In the history of the Early Middle Ages, the Carolingian period also represents the great moment when Christian society solidified its doctrine. It was in this period that the *ordines ecclesiae* [orders of the Church] were defined and organized in the traditional form of a moral hierarchy: virgins, the continent, and the married, or, following the organic image of three functional orders: clerics, warriors, and farmers.[28] The distributive logic of these classifying schemes insists that each order has its own norms of behavior, and a specific task to accomplish in the service of the whole of the *Ecclesia* [Church]. The clerics are the *oratores* [those who pray], that is, the liturgical professionals at a time when laymen were increasingly cut off from perception of the mysteries.[29] And the eighth and ninth centuries represent an extremely important stage in the movement towards the clericalization of monasticism.[30] It is thus that monks logically became, through their assiduous prayer and their celebration of the Eucharist, the representatives of salvation. In another study, I tried to show the receptivity of Cluniacs around the year 1000 to Carolingian ecclesiological reflection.[31] They lived in the eschatology that meditating on Haymo of Auxerre's *Commentary on the Song of Songs*

---

[25] Amalarius, *Liber de ordine antiphonarii*, c. 65, in *Opera liturgica omnia*, ed. J.-M. Hanssens, 3, Studi e Testi 140 (Vatican City, 1950), p. 98.

[26] See J. A. Jungmann, *Missarum sollemnia. Explication génétique de la messe romaine*, Théologie 19 (Paris, 1964), 3, p. 83.

[27] "*et in isto die (sc. in kalendis novembris) omnes sancti cum matre sua Maria semper virgine et celestibus spiritibus habeant festivitatem et defuncti habeant per ecclesias totius mundi sacrificium pro redemptione animarum suarum*" ["on this day (i.e. on the kalends of November), all the saints with their mother the always-virgin Mary and the celestial spirits have their feast, and the deceased have their sacrifice for the redemption of their souls through all the churches of the whole world"], *Mirabilia Urbis*, ed. C. D'Onofrio (Rome, 1988), p. 67. On the date when the text was written, see D'Onofrio's argument in ibid., pp. 14–30.

[28] See D. Iogna-Prat, "Le 'baptême' du schéma des trois ordres fonctionnels: l'apport de l'École d'Auxerre dans la second moitié du IXe siècle," *Annales ESC* 41 (1986): 101–26; E. Ortigues, "L'élaboration de la théorie des trois ordres chez Haymon d'Auxerre," *Francia* 14 (1986): 27–43.

[29] On this point, see J. A. Jungmann, *Missarum sollemnia* (above, n. 26), 1, pp. 114ff.

[30] On this important problem, see O. Nussbaum, *Kloster, Priestermönch und Privatmesse. Ihr Verhältnis im Westen von den Anfängen bis zum hohen Mittelalter*, Theophania Beiträge zur Religions-und Kirchengeschichtes des Altertums 14 (Bonn, 1961); A. Häussling, *Mönchskonvent und Eucharistiefeier*, Liturgiewissenschaftliche Quellen und Forschungen 58 (Münster in W., 1973). These two authors, while they agree on the phenomenon, do not explain it in the same manner. O. G. Oexle, *Forschungen zu monastischen und geistlichen Gemeinschaften im Westfränkischen Bereich* (Munich, 1978), magisterially described the phenomenon using the examples of St-Germain-des-Prés and St-Denis; see especially pp. 101–6, 110–11. On the relationship between eschatology and the multiplication of private masses (and therefore, of monk-priests), see C. Vogel, "Deux conséquences de l'eschatologie grégorienne: la multiplication des messes privées et les moines-prêtres," in *Grégoire le Grand* (Paris, 1986), pp. 267–76.

[31] See above, n. 12.

(a work dear to Odilo[32]) invites. In their eyes, the *Ecclesia* was beautiful and peaceful, the one and only city of the living, temporarily divided into two parts. The terrestrial half endeavours to march toward the heavenly Jerusalem in order and harmony, each individual in his place, correctly accomplishing the work which is his. Laymen ritually sacrifice their terrestrial riches in alms, thus buying their place in the afterlife; clerics, and especially monk-priests, assure liturgical service with assiduity and in purity. These spiritual individuals lead the pilgrim Christians; through their prayers and their celebrations, they are the bridge that assures the easy path for the assembly of the faithful into the choir of angels.

It was also in the Carolingian period that new forms of solidarity were created: the confraternities. To be brief, let us understand by these a kind of corporation, which could take the form of a political union, *amicitia* [friendship], which guaranteed to its members both fraternity here below and memory in the beyond.[33] Books, called *libri confraternitatum* [confraternal books], *libri memoriales* [memorial books], or *libri vitae* [books of life], registered the names of members both living and dead so that they might be remembered during the celebration of the Eucharistic sacrifice.[34] The monastic *familia* [family] of the year 1000, that is to say, the brothers and their friends and family, inherited from the Carolingian confraternity and its necrologies a kind of book of life.

Which dead were honored at Cluny? The *Liber tramitis aevi Odilonis* codifies funerary usages that went well beyond the convent itself. Odilo's constitution instituting the commemoration of all the dead was inserted in the customs of the monastery in two places. First of all in chapter 14, at its place in the calendar, after Pentecost;[35] then, in chapter 15, where the degrees of solemnity of all the major feasts celebrated at Cluny are recapitulated. Their enumeration finishes with All Saints, with which the commemoration of the dead is so closely and organically linked.[36] The two versions are only marginally different. But the repetition gives a marked flavor of insistence. It is a "decree," unanimously taken, which seeks to honor the memory of all the faithful departed with precise liturgical and charitable services. This "constitution" has a very legislative character, which is underlined by the terms of the directive, "we want, we ask, and we enjoin" ("*uolumus et petimus et praecipimus*"), and is to be applied within the Cluniac congregation ("*apud nos*") [among us], that is to say, at Cluny itself, and in its dependent establishments. But it allows for the possibility that this Cluniac "invention" could be used by all the faithful. The text contains a reference in the preamble to the "Universal Church." And in fact, the rest of Christianity did not wait long to follow Cluny's lead. As early as the 1020s, papal decrees given in favor of Cluny

---

[32] Odilo had this text (written in the 840s by the first great master of the Carolingian School of Auxerre) inserted in his personal collection related to the Virgin and virginity (Paris, Bibliothèque Nationale, ms lat. 17275); see Garand, "Une collection" (above, n. 11). A copy of this precious commentary was given by Odilo to the emperor Otto III [Bamberg manuscript, Patr. 88 (B IV 20)]; see A. Ripberger, *Der Pseudo-Heronymus-Brief IX "Cogitis me,"* Spicilegium Friburgense 9 (Freiburg, Switzerland, 1962).

[33] I take this description from F. Neiske, *Communities and Confraternities in the Ninth and Tenth Centuries*, a paper presented at the conference in Kalamazoo (May 1988), in a session presided over by B. H. Rosenwein: *Continuities and Discontinuities between the Ninth and the Tenth Centuries*. The notion of *amicitia* is discussed by K. Schmid, "Unerforschte Quellen aus quellenarmer Zeit: Zur 'amicitia' zwischen Heinrich I. und dem westfränkischen König Robert im Jahre 923," *Francia* 12 (1984): 119–47; see also G. Althoff-H. Keller, *Heinrich I. und Otto der Grosse* (Göttingen, 1985), 1: 65. I would like to thank F. Neiske for having brought these references to my attention.

[34] See Huyghebaert, *Les documents nécrologiques* (above, n. 7), pp. 13–14.

[35] *Liber tramitis* (above, n. 2), 126, pp. 186–7.

[36] Ibid., 138, p. 199.

insist upon that monastery's special place within the Church. One simple example is in a passage of a letter sent by Benedict VIII to the bishops of Burgundy, Aquitaine, and Provence in April 1021 or 1023, which invites them to defend the Cluniac demesne from any aggression:

> In this place [i.e. Cluny], the uninterrupted prayers and celebrations of the mass, as well as the alms given, are for the maintenance of the holy Church of God, for the salvation and the repose of all the faithful, both living and dead; this is why any damage done to Cluny does wrong both to us, and to the whole community.[37]

It makes for an especially juicy tale to remember that the supposed author of these lines, Pope Benedict VIII, needed the support of Cluniac suffrages himself in order to escape from "chaos" and "to fly up towards the heavenly beatitudes," if we can trust the *Vita sancti Odilonis*.[38] Thus, it is perfectly within the logic of these pontifical measures that Odilo's constitution ought to have received approval in Rome. In reality, such approbation never came by decree. J. Mabillon thought this was due to John XIX, among other hypotheses.[39] But there is no really decisive evidence, to my knowledge, of pontifical approval before these lines from the *Vita sancti Bertulfi* [*Life of St Bertulf*], written by an anonymous monk of St-Peter of Ghent between 1073 and 1088: "You know that a fitting memorial of the faithful departed is flourishing today in the Church. As we read in the Life of the Blessed Odilo, this memorial developed in the Church after divine revelation; shortly thereafter, thanks to the authority of the venerable pope Leo, it spread to nearly all the churches."[40]

If we can believe this text, Leo IX (1049–54) was the papal relay for this Cluniac "invention." In Normandy, it was the *Liber de officiis ecclesiasticis* [Book of Ecclesiastical Offices] of John of Avranches (d. 1079)[41] and then the *Decrees* of Lanfranc, successively monk of le Bec, abbot of St-Stephen of Caen, and archbishop of Canterbury between 1070 and 1089, which ensured the diffusion of the feast of All Souls in England.[42] With these various testimonies, we can say that within a relatively short period of time after its institution within the *Ecclesia cluniacensis* [Cluniac Church], Odilo's initiative was adopted by a good part of the Latin Church, even if the commemoration of November 2 was not generally adopted until the end of the twelfth century.[43]

Help for the dead *extra monasterium* [outside of the monastery], which is so manifest in Odilo's constitution, is also very well documented. Cluniac necrologies make a division

---

[37] H. Zimmermann, ed., *Papsturkunden, 896–1046*, 2 vols (Vienna, 1984), 2, 530, p. 1009.

[38] Jotsald, *Vita sancti Odilonis, PL* 142, col. 928 D-929 A.

[39] J. Mabillon, *Sancti Odilonis Clunicacensis abbatis V elogium, PL* 142, cols 880–1.

[40] *Vita sancti Bertulfi* (*Bibliotheca hagiographica latina* (henceforth *BHL*) 1316), *Acta Sanctorum Ordinis Sancti Benedicti*, 3, 1st edn, 1672, p. 58; *MGH, SS*, 15, p. 637; on the author, see N. Huyghebaert, "La '*Vita secunda sancti Winnoci*' restituée à l'hagiographie gantoise," *Revue bénédictine* 81 (1971): 227ff., 258. On the closeness of Leo IX and Cluny, see Iogna-Prat, *Agni immaculati* (above, n. 12), pp. 379–80; Wibert, the pope's biographer, noted that the "venerable abbot Odilo" had appeared to Leo IX in a dream (*Vita sancti Leonis, PL* 143, col. 486C).

[41] Ed. R. Delamare (Paris, 1923), p. 47 (*PL* 147, col. 60 C); cited by F. Plaine, "La fête de morts du 2 novembre. Dates et circonstances de son institution à Cluny et de son extension à l'Église universelle," *Revue du clergé français* 7 (1896): 445.

[42] *Decreta Lanfranci*, ed. D. Knowles, Corpus Consuetudinum Monasticarum 3 (Siegburg, 1967), 71, p. 54, ll. 17–27.

[43] According to Plaine, "La fête des morts" (above, n. 41), p. 446, this was done by the time of Durand of Mende.

between the "monks of our congregation" and "our familiars." We may wonder, with Franz Neiske, whether Cluny's primitive necrology made such a distinction.[44] Reading the examples given by the *Liber tramitis*, in the passage concerning the inscription to the martyrology, it would seem so. It concerns "monks or friends," these latter identifiable by their titles.[45] In any case, the presence of individuals external to the monastery, either listed separately or mixed in with the "*turme*" ["company"][46] of the monks, is well established.

The *Liber tramitis* devotes an entire chapter (chapter 34) to "those who die outside the monastery."[47] One by one, it deals with the monks to be helped (*ad succurrendum*), then with the brothers of another monastery (doubtless one linked to Cluny by an association of prayer), and finally with the relatives of Cluniac monks. In the following chapter (chapter 35), the customs sketch different circles of solidarity. Notably, they mention particular memorials: the abbot of the monastery, the king and the queen, the deceased diocesan [bishop], as well as the founder of the monastery, William the Pious. Another lay figure is the object of particularly attentive care: Emperor Henry II, who is mentioned twice: just after the second insertion of Odilo's constitution, and in the passage of chapter 35 that we are looking at. This sovereign is distinguished in particularly strong terms: "the august Emperor Henry, very dear friend of our society and our fraternity."[48] He is also associated with other major solemnities of the monastery. This "very dear friend" had given the jewels, apple, scepter, crown, and cross that were ritually exhibited at the Nativity, the Purification of the Virgin, Palm Sunday, Ascension, and Assumption.[49] After these particular memorials come the bishops, laypeople – both great and *mediocres* [ordinary] – and then, more generally, the relatives of monks or familiars. It is important to note carefully the degrees of the Cluniac memorial hierarchy. Besides the brothers of the monastery, it honors with memorial those individuals particularly dear because of their function (the abbot, the king and the queen, the diocesan) or because of the ties they have made with the monastery (William the Pious, the founder; Emperor Henry II; the monastery's benefactors whether clerical or lay; the relatives of the monks). These individual memorials, mentioned in the necrology and celebrated once a year, melt into the general commemoration of all the "relatives or familiars" in three places: on the second feast after the first Sunday of Lent, on July 6 (the octave of Apostles Peter and Paul), and on November 2.[50] Finally, on this very November 2, the monastic fraternity expanded to the entirety of the faithful departed. Like a mirror, certain pieces of the Cluny cartulary sketch out the very same circles of solidarity. Thus, in an act from June 995, Aylaldus and his wife Tetza make a donation "for the repose of [their] souls, and those of all [their] relatives, as well as of all faithful Christians."[51]

[44] See above, n. 33.
[45] *Liber tramitis* (above, n. 2), 208, p. 286.
[46] This term, which comes from military vocabulary ("troop," in its accepted understanding), is often found in the Cluny cartulary to designate the community of brothers; see, for example, *Receuil des chartes de Cluny* (above, n. 15) 806, from April 7, 951.
[47] *Liber tramitis* (above, n. 2), 196–202, pp. 278–81. The first cases (196, 197) concern the brothers of Cluny who die outside the monastery or in one of its dependences.
[48] Ibid., 207, p. 285, ll. 22–3.
[49] Ibid., 13.4, p. 23 (Nativity); 31.3, p. 42 (Purification of the Virgin); 54.2, p. 68 (Palm Sunday); 72, p. 108 (Ascension); 100.4, p. 151 (Assumption). The *Vita Henrici II* (twelfth century) states that the emperor had given Cluny a crown that was to be used for the *Cathedra sancti Petri, MGH, SS*, 4, p. 809.
[50] *Liber tramitis* (above, n. 2), 207, p. 285, ll. 15–16; 42.1, pp. 55, l. 22–56, l. 2 (second feast after the first Sunday in Lent); 86, p. 134, ll. 16–18 (July 6); 127, p. 189, ll. 16–24 (November 2).
[51] *Receuil des chartes de Cluny* (above, n. 15), 2302. Following Hourlier, *Saint Odilon* (above, n. 8), we should note the precocity of their mentioning "all the faithful [departed]."

The Cluniac memorial horizon, both familial and ecclesial, which frequently mixes together particular memorials with more general commemorations, is perfectly within Augustinian logic. When Paulinus asked him about the care that one ought to give to the dead, Augustine remarked (in the *De cura gerenda pro mortuis* [*On Taking Care of the Dead*]) that the Church took care of all deceased Christians. "She gathers them up, without even knowing their names, in her general commemoration. And when parents, children, relatives, and friends forget their duty, like a pious mother, she assumes it, and, alone, provides for all."[52]

What this means in medieval translation is that death is the affair of the *familia*, but that the Church, metaphorically mother, widens the circle of fraternity.

This opening was especially important for those laypeople who used the Cluniac sanctuary as a cemetery. The fact is sufficiently unusual for us to pause here a moment. To be sure, there are examples in the Early Middle Ages of lay burials in monasteries. The originality of Cluny is that the *Liber tramitis* mentions the existence of two cemeteries: one for the brothers, the other for laypeople ("*populare cimiterium*"). K. J. Conant situates the latter in the north, next to the great basilica.[53] Whom exactly might we find in this "people's cemetery"? We can eliminate right away those cases of *professio in extremis*, that is to say, those who have died in the habit and are therefore buried with the monks. This other cemetery was indeed reserved for simple laypeople, both men and women, like Oda, who in an act from August 958, asked to be received into the monastic society as "one of yours."[54] Even the excommunicated could find a place there. In a passage from his 1024 privilege, John XIX asked:

> Let the just man find a place, and may the unjust who wishes to do penance not be pushed away. Offer to the innocent the charity of a mutual fraternity, but do not refuse the hope of salvation, and the indulgence of piety to those who have offended. If someone who has been subjected to the anathema comes to this place either to be buried, or to receive the grace of salvation or for any other good thing, do not refuse him pardon and the awaited mercy. Welcome him instead with benevolence, and grant him the comfort of saving care. It is indeed just, that in the house of goodness [*in domo pietatis*], one should at least offer the love of a holy fraternity, and to the sinner in search of forgiveness, do not refuse the medicine of indulgence, and of salvation.[55]

D. Poeck justly notes that this disposition is linked to Cluny's exemption.[56] The monastery is a space for reconciliation – an idea strongly implied by the expression "*domus pietatis*," so difficult to translate because of the many meanings of the word *pietas*: honor due to God, true faith, benevolence or goodness, even pontifical title.[57] This privilege confirms and prolongs the exemption granted in 998 by Gregory V. From now on, it is all the Cluniacs "wherever they may be" ("*ubicumque positi*") who are freed from the power of control and of

---

[52] Augustine, *De cura gerenda pro mortuis*, 4.6, trans. G. Combès, Bibliothèque Augustinienne 2 (Problèmes moraux) (Paris, 1948), p. 477.

[53] *Liber tramitis* (above, n. 2), 142, p. 206, ll. 2–3; 200, p. 280, l. 11; 206, p. 284, l. 28. See Conant, *Cluny* (above, n. 14), pl. 4. C. Sapin's recent work has shown, however, that Conant's plans should be used with circumspection.

[54] *Recueil des chartes de Cluny* (above, n. 15), 1051, cited by Poeck, "Laienbegräbnisse" (above, n. 7).

[55] Zimmermann, *Papsturkunden 896–1046*, 2, 558, pp. 1053–4.

[56] Poeck, "Laienbegräbnisse" (above, n. 7), p. 179.

[57] See A. Blaise, *Dictionnaire latin–français des auteurs chrétiens* (Turnhout: Brepols, 1954).

coercion of bishops: not simply Cluny itself, but also its dependencies. Any brother "wherever he may be" is responsible only to his abbot. The *Ecclesia cluniacensis* was thus born; and the privilege that established it also opened it simultaneously to the world. This space, protected from any potential episcopal interdict, was a fraternity as open to the repentant sinner as it was to the most faithful. The monastery, which spiritually was responsible to none save pontifical authority, was juridically bound to reconcile to the article of death he who had been excluded from the communion of the faithful by anathema, and to offer him a place in eternity. In these times troubled by struggles for power over land and men, where spiritual men, in the absence of public control, sought to regulate violence by interdict and the force of the anathema, such a disposition was by no means only a formality, and could only add to the attraction of the Cluniac sanctuary. And so large numbers of laypeople (several hundred, if we can believe the numbers arrived at later)[58] sought the company of the brothers either for their own remains, or for those of a relative. D. Poeck has observed that all lordly levels are represented in the acts of donation.[59] The *Liber tramitis* only mentions the great, honored more or less like the monks themselves, and the *mediocres*, who receive less attention.[60]

What did these benefactors want? First, the safety of a community. The Cluniac monk died surrounded by the greatest possible spiritual aid. The *Liber tramitis* stipulates that "everyone, including the deans and the other brothers living within one or two leagues should, in charity, hasten to help with the vigils and the burial."[61] "In charity": Haymo of Auxerre meditates, in a key passage of his *Commentary on the Song of Songs*, on the "Church, as beautiful as a well-ordered troop" ["*acies*"],[62] well ordered by virtue of charity, as strong "as glue"[63] and "terrible for malicious spirits."[64] It is this logic that mobilized the convent at the hour when one of their own was in his final agony. Collectively and ritually, they thwarted the forces of evil, and assured the passage of the deceased to the assembly of saints and of angels. Such was the goal of the voyage; this is what the prayers recited in such circumstances repeat, such as the prayer *Deus uitae dator* [O God, giver of life], a supplication addressed to God asking Him to spare the deceased "the cruelties of Hell" and to "place him among the troops [*agmina*] of his saints."[65]

All possible solidarities were invoked. They called upon the Virgin, whom the Cluniacs call "mother of mercy," and visited her altar with the body of the deceased brother.[66] At this moment, when community ties were being tightened, they invoked Mary (following the Augustinian tradition), as "the greatest part of the Church."[67] Within the logic of "All Saints," the saints were solicited just as they were celebrated, collectively.[68] They were

---

[58] See above, n. 18.

[59] Poeck, "Laienbegräbnisse" (above, n. 7), pp. 106, 127.

[60] *Liber tramitis* (above, n. 2), 206, p. 285, ll. 9–12.

[61] Ibid., 195.5, p. 276, ll. 12–14, cited by Poeck, "Laienbegräbnisse" (above, n. 7), p. 74.

[62] Haymo of Auxerre, *Expositio in Cantica Canticorum*, PL 117, col. 336 D–337 A-B (=*Cant.* 6:3).

[63] Ibid., col. 355 D.

[64] Above, n. 62.

[65] *Liber tramitis* (above, n. 2), 195.2, p. 273, l. 27. (=*Sacramentaire grégorien*, ed. J. Deshusses, 1407).

[66] Ibid., p. 274, l. 1. On the expression "mother of mercy," see Iogna-Prat, *Agni immaculati* (above, n. 12), p. 329.

[67] "*Maria portio maxima est Ecclesiae*"; Augustine's phrase is cited by M.-L Thérel, *A l'origine du décor du portail occidental de Notre-Dame de Senlis: le triomphe de la Vierge-Eglise. Sources historiques, littéraires et iconographiques* (Paris, 1984), p. 121 n. 262.

[68] On the collective cult of the saints, attested to in Rome by the middle of the eighth century, see P. Jounel, "Le culte des saints," in *L'Eglise en Prière* (above, n. 24), 4, p. 131 and *Le culte des saints dans les basiliques du Latran et du Vatican au douzième siècle* (Rome, 1977), pp. 9–12.

entreated to come to the aid of the deceased along with the angels; thus, in the antiphon *Subuenite*: "Bring your help, saints of God, Come, angels of the Lord, welcoming his soul, and presenting it as an offering in the sight of the Most High."[69] It is therefore easy to understand why laymen sought to approach the monks so as to incorporate themselves into the troop of the angels. In an act from 983, a certain Vuido asked the brothers to receive him into their society so that once he had died, "they would place his body in the heart of the earth, and give to his soul a place among the angels" ("*animam coetibus angelis adsignent angelicis*").[70]

The voyage could be tortuous. How could wandering souls be helped? The *Liber tramitis* in fact anticipates a difficult situation. The deceased appears in dreams to his familiars, that is to say, to those of the brothers who have known him, and to his relatives. Actually, the customs of Cluny do little more than to codify certain teachings of the Fathers. Doubtless, Odilo and his brothers remembered the passage in Gregory the Great's *Dialogues* in which the deceased Justus appears in a dream to his blood-brother Copiosus.[71] They would also have known the *De excessu fratris* [*On the Death of a Brother*], the sermon preached by Ambrose of Milan at the funeral of his brother Satyrus.[72] In reading this authority, they would have learned, had they needed to, just how dreams could put the living in contact with the world of the dead;[73] they would have noted the importance of fraternal recommendations in the text, and the necessary distinction between private and public, which cemented the Christian community at the moment of weeping for the dead.[74] At the heart of the Cluniac convent, the narrow circle of close relations expanded with prayers and masses; the *Liber tramitis* maintains that this service, "without any doubt, will incline the Lord."[75] In such circumstances, efficacity is primarily familial.

We should also note the flexibility of the various references to relatives. The monastic *familia* assisting the deceased has two horizons: the immediate is that of blood relatives and familiars; more largely, it includes the spiritual family of the convent, a prelude to the fraternity of the afterlife itself. The customs distinguish between these registers of public and private. They regulate the usages of the collectivity, by providing personal slots for meditation, prayer, and especially, the private mass, that key liturgical innovation of the Early Middle Ages that was coming into play under monastic influence in precisely the

---

[69] *Liber tramitis* (above, n. 2), 195.2, p. 273, l. 29; 203, p. 282, l. 8; 205, p. 284, l. 6; 206, p. 284, l. 23 (= *Corpus Antiphonalium Officii*, ed. R.-J. Hesbert, 4, 7716).

[70] *Recueil des chartes de Cluny* (above, n. 15), 1199, April 966; cited by Poeck, "Laienbegräbnisse" (above, n. 7), p. 109.

[71] Above, n. 22.

[72] The *De excessu fratris* can be found on fo. 146ff. of Paris, Bibliothèque de l'Arsenal, ms. 1244, very probably copied at Cluny around the year 1000. I would like to thank M.-C. Garand for this information.

[73] A possibility denied by Tertullian; on the importance of Ambrose and the *De excessu fratris* on this subject, see the very detailed study of J. Amat, "Songes et visions. L'au-delà dans la littérature latine tardive," *Etudes augustiniennes* (Paris, 1985), p. 213. On the question of the *commendatio*, see P. Brown, *The Cult of Saints: its Rise and Function in Latin Christianity* (Chicago, 1981), pp. 65–6. See also P. Geary, "Echanges et relations entre les vivants et les morts dans la société du Haut Moyen Age," *Droit et cultures* 12 (1986): 3–17; F. Neiske, "Vision und Totengedanken," *Frühmittelalterliche Studien* 20 (1986): 137–85, especially pp. 164ff., which puts the Cluniac "visions" in perspective.

[74] A distinction clearly expressed in the following formula: "*Itaque licet privatum funus, tamen fletus est publicus,*" Ambrose, *De excessu fratris*, I, 5, ed. O. Faller, *Corpus scriptorum ecclesiasticorum latinorum*, 73, p. 212, ll. 15–16.

[75] *Liber tramitis* (above, n. 2), 195.8, p. 277, l. 27.

period that interests us.[76] Liturgy – especially funerary liturgy – added to the solemnity of communal celebrations or the intimacy of personal devotions. Each brother could thus honor his own dead, and could also celebrate all of the faithful departed. It was at the same time distinct, and all one. The monastic community was an elective family in which blood families could reside, and could put down the roots of their lineages. The necrology and the cartulary preserve the different parts of familial memory distinctly: the names of certain ancestors, the pieces of the patrimony that have passed into the possession of the Cluniac sanctuary, but with their origin clearly noted. We should note this phenomenon especially closely, since the tenth and eleventh centuries represented a particularly turbulent time for the aristocracy. In the definition of power and honor, ancestry played a primordial role, to the detriment of alliance. As G. Duby pointed out forcefully, monastic writings, powerful "conservators of memory," stimulated a new, vertical, disposition of familial relations, like a "tree of Jesse."[77]

Let us now look more precisely at the nature of this monastic aid so sought after by laypeople.

The God of the year 1000 was a formidable judge.[78] At Cluny, at the moment that the grave was being prepared, the brothers recited Psalm 93, *Deus ultionum*, among others.[79] This invocation of the "God of vengeance" distinguishes, in a very medieval fashion, between a cursed part and a good part. The wicked "have brought low thy people, and they have afflicted thy inheritance. They have slain the widow and the stranger: and they have murdered the fatherless." On the other side, "blessed is the man whom thou shalt instruct, O Lord: and shalt teach him out of thy law. That thou mayst give him rest from the evil days: till a pit be dug for the wicked." In these years when assemblies of the Peace were attempting to institute places and times without violence, excluding violators of this Peace from the community of the faithful, this psalm must have seemed stingingly contemporary. At the hour of death, it was best to repose in a safe haven, in the company of the professionals of penitence. In this space of peace, the deceased layman could hope to be purified of all his sins; here, supplicant pleas for divine mercy were both more numerous and better than anywhere else.[80]

But from these monk-priests, they were mostly seeking a viaticum. In a justly famous passage from his *Histories*, Ralph Glaber tells of the benefits given by the Eucharistic mystery to the souls of the faithful departed.[81] An anchorite from a "distant country" (Africa) thus reveals that Cluny "has no equal in the Roman world, especially for delivering souls that have fallen under the power of the devil. The vivifying sacrifice is consumed there so often, that no day passes but that this incessant commerce allows souls to be ripped away from the power of the evil demons."

---

[76] See *L'Eglise en prière* (above, n. 24), 2: 154–5.

[77] G. Duby, "Le lignage Xe–XIIIe siècle," in P. Nora, ed., *Les lieux de mémoire*, 2. *La nation* (Paris, 1986), esp. pp. 31–7.

[78] See Sicard, *La liturgie* (above, n. 7), pp. 402–3.

[79] *Liber tramitis* (above, n. 2), 195.2, p. 273, l. 23.

[80] We should note in particular the importance of the psalms of the "*misericordia*," among others, in the Cluniac liturgy: Ps. 56 (*Miserere mei deus miserere mei, Liber tramitis* (above, n. 2), 203, p. 282, l. 2; 205, p. 283, l. 27); 66 (*Deus misereatur nostri*, ibid., 203, p. 282, l. 3; 205, p. 283, l. 28); 69 (*Deus in adiutorium meum intende*, ibid., 203, p. 282, l. 3); 129 (*De profundis*, ibid., 127, p. 189, l. 13; 139, p. 200, l. 4).

[81] Ralph Glaber, *Historiarum libri quinque*, ed. M. Prou, Collection de textes pour servir à l'étude et à l'enseignement de l'Histoire (Paris, 1886), 5, 1, 13, pp. 124–5.

And Glaber comments:

> We have ourselves been witness in this monastery to a custom made possible by the large number of monks, which has masses being celebrated without interruption from the first hour of the day to the hour of the meal; and there is there so much dignity, so much piety, and so much veneration, that we almost thought they were angels rather than men.

This frequently cited extract deserves to be placed in its context. The story of the anchorite appears in chapter 13 of book 5 of the *Histories*.[82] At the beginning of this book, Glaber tells of the misdeeds of evil spirits, and he shows interest first in prodigies and then in the strength of the saints. As he so often does, as he passes from a popular story to speculative refinements, he broaches a theological question: "in the period of the new covenant, why do we no longer have signs?" Because we have Christ, our living bread. Thus, the developments that follow are devoted to the Eucharistic mystery: the virtues of the chrism; how important it is to handle the chalice carefully; and the extreme attention with which the Eucharistic rite should be accomplished. Any carelessness brings divine resentment in its wake; therefore, attention and consideration ensure an abundance of good. This little theological lesson thus is illustrated practically and hagiographically by considering Eucharistic miracles, among which may be found their very great help for the dead.

The *Liber tramitis* confirms Glaber's testimony. Odilo's constitution recommends that on November 2, "all priests should celebrate private masses for the repose of all souls."[83] In service to the dead, the priests of the community form a waterwheel of masses, like a Eucharistic chain – except on Sundays, which are consecrated "without mixing" [i.e. exclusively] to the unique celebration of the Lord.[84] When a monk dies, the customs anticipate that six brothers, without interruption up to the thirtieth day, "should offer consecrated hosts daily to God for this soul. As soon as one of them should have said five masses, he should let this be known in chapter, so that another can succeed him."[85] In this way six times five masses are said during 30 days: a trifling 900 masses!

At Cluny, the liturgy of the dead was accompanied by a charitable service designated generically throughout the *Liber tramitis* by the expression *iustitia dare*, "to give justice." By this, the customs mean the ritual support of the poor. For example, Odilo's constitution allows for feeding 12 paupers on November 2.[86] At the death of a brother, one pauper was supported for 30 days.[87] The same tricenaire was given for the three annual celebrations for the relatives of the monks or of the familiars.[88] On the occasion of the anniversary of the "deposition" of Emperor Henry II, July 30, 12 paupers were supported for seven days.[89]

Monastic aid also ensured memory after death. Brother, relative, or member of the monastic family, the deceased was inscribed in the necrology. He thus figured in the Book of

---

[82] On the composition of the *Histories*, see E. Ortigues and D. Iogna-Prat, "Raoul Glaber et l'historiographie clunisienne," *Studi Medievali*, 3rd ser. (1985): 566–7.
[83] *Liber tramitis* (above, n. 2), 126, p. 187, ll. 15–16.
[84] Ibid., 204, p. 283, ll. 18–23.
[85] Ibid., 195.6, pp. 276, l. 31–277, l. 2.
[86] Ibid., 126, p. 187, ll. 18–19.
[87] Ibid., 195.6, p. 277, ll. 4–5.
[88] Ibid., 207, p. 285, ll. 19–20.
[89] Ibid., p. 285, ll. 23–4.

Life mentioned in Luke 10:20: "Rejoice, in this, that your names are written in heaven."[90] His entirely individual memory was honored every year on the same date.

This memorial service calls for two remarks. Above, we tried to place the Cluniacs of the year 1000 in the continuity of Carolingian tradition. Having done this, we must not forget the extremely important change that occurred between the ninth and the eleventh centuries: the birth of individual memory. We have passed, effectively, from the global recommendation of the living and the dead registered in the Carolingian *Libri uitae*, to the personal commemoration of individual deceased persons written down in necrologies, remembered on specific dates.

We should also note that the deceased, so honored, belonged evermore to the "good part"; the part that was celebrated, rather than to the "wicked part," which was cursed. Two aspects of Cluniac documentation stand out. On one side, the "faithful," individually named in the necrology, or collectively in the customs; on the other, the "wicked", cursed, frequently by name (along with their lands), in one or another papal bull that was now part of the cartulary,[91] or even in bulk in the formulas found in the charter, and the "clamors" of the *Liber tramitis*; the wicked are named in order to abolish their remembrance, to deprive them of memory, and to deliver them to the devil.[92] In this age of uncertainty, faced with a God of judgment, in these years of tension linked to the one-thousandth anniversary of the birth and the passion of Christ, it was hardly a matter for indifference to be honored or cursed in the monastic books.

Apart from the communal, liturgical, charitable, and memorial aid that Cluny offered, its attraction in funerary matters was in no small part due to one of the two patrons of the monastery: St Peter.

The second of the three annual commemorations of the relatives of monks or of familiars of the monastery took place on July 6, that is, as the *Liber tramitis* itself points out, the octave of the holy apostles Peter and Paul.[93]

---

[90] See Wollasch, "Kaiser" (above, n. 7), pp. 7–8.

[91] Particularly significant is the letter addressed by Benedict VIII to the bishops of Burgundy, Aquitaine, and Provence mentioned above (n. 37): "*Sunt autem crudeliores sepe nominati loci habitatorum persecutores: Hildin[us] omnis bonitatis inimicus*" ["These very cruel individuals are often named as the persecutors of the inhabitants of this place: Hildinus is the enemy of all good"]. A list of names follows, along with invitations to reform, and then long formulas of malediction: "*Sintque a liminibus sanctae Dei aecclesie procul repulsi et a consortio fidelium alienati et excommunicati. Sint maledicti stantes et ambulantes, vigilantes et dormientes, ingredientes et egredientes. Sint maledicti manducantes et bibentes. Sit maledictus cybus et porus. Sit maledictus fructus ventris eorum fructusque terre eorum*" ["And let them be repulsed far from the threshold of the holy Church of God and alienated and excommunicated from the company of the faithful. May they be cursed in their standing still and in their walking, in their staying awake and in their sleeping, in their coming in and in their going out. May they be cursed in their eating and in their drinking. May their very food and drink be cursed. May the fruit of their wombs, and the fruit of their lands be cursed"]. Zimmermann, *Papsturkunden* (above, n. 37), pp. 1009–10.

[92] *Liber tramitis* (above, n. 2), 174, pp. 244–7: "*Pro aduersa preces faciendam*"; on monastic maledictions, see the fine studies of P. Geary, "L'humiliation des saints" and L. K. Little, "La morphologie des malédictions monastiques," *Annales ESC* 34 (1979): 27–42 and 43–60, respectively. [Geary's article can also be found in English in his *Living with the Dead in the Middle Ages* (Ithaca, NY, 1994), pp. 95–115.]

[93] Ibid., 207, p. 285, ll. 15–16; see Guy de Valous, *La monachisme clunisien des origines au XVe siècle*, 2 vols (Paris, 1970), 1: 404.

Donations *ad sepulturam* were often made directly to saints. Donors were looking for protectors, especially in Peter. Remember that Peter had long been seen to be intimate with the dead. One of his feasts, the Throne of St Peter, documented by the first third of the fourth century, commemorates the beginnings of his episcopacy, and is celebrated on February 22. Thus, this anniversary day was celebrated on the same day, and soon came to be associated with the *Cara cognatio*, the familial feast of the dead in pagan Rome.[94] As P. Jounel has recently pointed out, the "throne" of St Peter was therefore funerary before it was episcopal.[95] The liturgy long preserved the memory of these origins. At Cluny until 1030, the reading for the office of February 22 was taken from Sermon 109 of Pseudo-Augustine.[96] The first part of the text justifies the feast: it celebrates Peter, foundation of the Church. The second part, however, has an entirely different tone. The author exerts himself to denounce the pagan superstitions still attached to the Throne of St Peter. Apparently, libations were offered to deceased relatives – a practice still being denounced by John Beleth [a twelfth-century liturgist].[97] Pseudo-Augustine thus explains that the souls of the faithful do not need to be refreshed; they do not loiter around their tombs; they are in the company of Christ. There is no reason for us to believe that such funerary meals were practiced in Burgundy around the year 1000. We simply note, nevertheless, that the liturgy transparently allowed the memory of a privileged link uniting St Peter and the dead to endure.

In an act from 1027 that invited King Robert II to support Cluny, Jean XIX formulated the strength of St Peter's patronage in a manner that is practically canonical: "Is it not a very slim folly to growl (*mutire*: like a dog) against him, who, as protector and patron, holds the keys to the kingdom of heaven?"[98] This patron is a celestial solicitor. Thus, toward 1010, Vuldricus, in the presence of his wife and children, made a donation "to God and to St Peter,

---

[94] This feast is attested to by the Chronography of 354, which transmits the earliest known calendar of the Roman Church; see *MGH, AA*, 9, p. 71. Amidst an abundant bibliography, see F. Cabrol, "Chaire de saint Pierre (Fête de)," in *Dictionnaire d'archéologie chrétienne et de liturgie*, 3, pt 1, col. 77; P.-A. Février, "Natale Petri de Cathedra," *Comptes rendus de l'Académie des inscriptions et belles lettres* (1977), pp. 514–31, which expresses some reserve concerning the reality of the link between the *Cathedra sancti Petri* and the cult of martyrs or of the dead; Ch. Pietri, *Roma christiana. Recherches sur l'Église de Rome, son organisation, sa politique, son idéologie de Miltiade à Sixte III (311–440)* (Rome, 1976), p. 382, and on the term *cathedra*, pp. 301–14, 351–7, 1454–9. With this feast, Cluny – directly attached to Rome – rooted itself in the ancient and powerful tradition of the *prima sedes Ecclesiae*. See also P. Jounel, "Le sanctoral du sacramentaire de la collection Phillipps," in *Mélanges offerts au Père P.-M. Gy* (Paris, 1990).

[95] A paper given at the twelfth Rencontre d'histoire religieuse (see p. 340).

[96] See the first lectionary of the office of Cluny, Paris, Bibliothèque National, ms. lat. 13371, f. 89v.: "*In cathedra sancti Petri. Institutio sollemnitatis hodierne*"; = Dekkers n. 368, *PL* 39, cols 2100–1; the *Liber tramitis* [cit. (above, n. 2), p. 49, l. 6] notes that after 1030, the *Tractatus* 4 of Leo the Great was used instead (ed. A. Chavasse, Corpus Christianorum Series Latina 138, pp. 16–21). The attribution to Augustine was rejected by G. Morin, *Sermons apocryphes du Bréviaire*, in *Etudes, texts, découvertes* (Maredsous and Paris, 1913), p. 493 n. 25; this sermon is of uncertain date (*c.*460?); we note that it is also included in the *Sermo Clementis papae in Petri apostolorum principis sessione qua cathedre sublimatur anthiocena* transcribed in f. 137r–139v. (= ff. 137v–138r) of Paris, Bibliothèque Nationale, ms. lat. 18304 (eleventh century), which comes from the Cluniac priory of St-Arnoul in Crépy-en-Valois.

[97] See F. Cabrol, *Chaire de Saint Pierre* (above, n. 94).

[98] Zimmermann, *Papsturkunden 896–1046*, 2, p. 1087. John XIX wrongly attributes this formula to Leo the Great (on this point see H. Fuhrmann, *Einfluss und Verbreitung der pseudoisidorischen Fälschungen. Von ihrem Auftauchen bis in die neuere Zeit*, Schriften der Monumenta Germaniae Historica 24 (Stuttgart, 1972), 2: 352 n. 174).

for the care of his soul, in order to obtain burial" ["*in locum sepulture*"] and in the hope that "St Peter would be a good advocate [*advocatus*] on the day of Judgment."[99]

This point is important: being buried at Cluny is to repose on the very foundations of the Church. From the 980s on, Cluny was a monastery with relics, which it had not been at the beginning. From Rome, the brothers had brought the relics of popes Marcellus and Gregory;[100] the very arrival of their relics at Cluny was celebrated.[101] A portrait-reliquary of St Peter contained remains of the holy apostle, among others.[102] The relics of the apostles Peter and Paul had in fact been transferred from St-Paul's-Outside-the-Walls (a monastery earlier reformed by Odo). In 981 they were solemnly placed under the high altar at the consecration of Cluny II by Hugh, archbishop of Bourges. A late text, the *Epistola Hugonis* [letter of Hugh], addressed to Abbot Pons of Melgueil (1109–1122), conserves the memory of this through the narrative of Pope Calixtus II, which is in direct speech.[103] The pontiff, who is addressing Pons, tells the long story of the venerable apostolic relics from the beginning: the removal of the bones from the catacombs by order of Pope Cornelius, their transfer to the Ostian Way and the Vatican Hill, to St-Paul's-Outside-the-Walls, and then to Cluny.[104] Thus a slow transfer of legitimacy from Rome to the Mâconnais, where the apostles would hitherto be honored.[105] This is why Cluny represented a kind of ersatz pilgrimage to Rome.[106] One went to Cluny to venerate and implore St Peter, "foundation of the Church," as Odilo proclaimed him in his *Sermon for the Vigil of Sts Peter and Paul*.[107] Thus, Cluny was

---

[99] *Receuil des chartes de Cluny* (above, n. 15), 2676, around 1010; cited by Poeck, "Laienbegräbnisse" (above, n. 7), p. 178.

[100] *Liber tramitis* (above, n. 2), 189, pp. 261–2: "*De reliquiis sanctorum.*"

[101] Ibid., 92, p. 141 (Gregory); 108, p. 161 (Marcellus).

[102] Ibid., 189, p. 260.

[103] *Epistola Hugonis monachi cluniacensis* (= *BHL* 4011), ed. H. E. J. Cowdrey, "Two Studies in Cluniac History 1049–1126," *Studi Gregoriani* 11 (1978): 111–17 (the passages that interest us here are on pp. 116–17).

[104] "*Nosti, pater, quia papa Cornelius martyr gloriosus Petri et Pauli ossa de catachumbis leuata, Pauli via Hostiensi, Petri in Vaticano sagaciter posuit. Eorum vero cineres studiose congruo recondens uasculo in monasterio sancti Pauli tradidit uenerandos. Hoc autem monasterium sequentibus annis commissum est sancto Oddoni tuo predecessori, ubi per eum aliquandiu Cluniacensis uigor ordinis radiauit. Tandem seditiosis urbe turbata motibus quos illa ciuitas infausto usus creberrime patitur, malis urgentibus monachi discedentes uas illud apostolicorum cinerum sacra secum pignora detulerunt, sicque Cluniacum propere peruenerunt*" ["Know, father, that when Pope Cornelius the glorious martyr raised up the bones of Peter and Paul from the catacombs, he placed them wisely, Paul on the Ostian Way, and Peter on the Vatican Hill. Then, truthfully, put into a small vessel with all the appropriate zeal, their remains were brought to the monastery of St Paul in order to be venerated. Then after many years, this monastery was given to St Odilo your predecessor, whence for a long while the vigor of the Cluniac order was able to radiate. However, when the city was disturbed by seditious movements, by which the city was brought most frequently to unfortunate use, monks fleeing the urgent evil brought away the vase with the holy relics of the remains of the apostles, so that they might come without delay to Cluny"]. *Epistola Hugonis* (above, n. 103).

[105] ["There (where you are), Father, the apostolic remains, an inestimable treasure, can be frequently visited with reverence. Since you are obliged to pray before them often, I beg of you, although nervous about doing so and yet encouraged by your compassion, that before these holy apostolic remains you deem it worthwhile to remember me from time to time, you who do not cease to have pity on your own (people)"] "*Ibi cineres Apostolici, thesaurus, pater, inaestimabilis, frequenti reuerentia visitantur. Quos quia saepius orando requiris, te precor, licet trepidus, sed tua misericordia roboratus, ut ante sacrosanctos cineres illos Apostolicos mei aliquando memorari digneris, qui tuorum miseri non desinis*" ibid.

[106] I have given several examples in *Agni immaculati* (above, n. 12), p. 356 n. 178.

[107] *PL* 142, col. 1022 B.

not just any place to be buried. Here, one was in the most intimate part of the communion of the faithful, which was symbolically recalled when during the death agony of a brother, the entire convent recited the symbol of Nicea, *Credo in unum Deum* [I believe in one God], the foundation of the Christian community.[108]

The Cluny cartulary records transactions. Some of them, the donations *ad sepulturam*, sought in exchange the acquisition of a part of the afterlife. The acts assembled in this accounting document offer an excellent illustration of what a sociology of the gift might be in the so-called feudal era. Let us be clear: at Cluny around the year 1000, a "donation" was no longer – as had been the case in Roman law – a free gift. In his study of the Cluny cartulary, G. Chevrier showed that "the donation, previously equal to liberality, becomes a matter of prototype of the juridical act."[109] The distinction sale/donation tends to blur; goods are no longer sold (or less and less): they are acquired. It is important to note that this change happens precisely during this period of the tenth and eleventh centuries, that is to say, in the period when the "donation" for relief of the soul (*pro remedio animae*) becomes increasingly frequent. The acquisition of a piece of the afterlife is not a liberality; nevertheless, the specific qualities of the act (neither sale nor gift) could not be easily expressed in the practical vocabulary of exchange. How can we translate the idea of self-interested charity? Disguised by the old term "gratuity," and by the deliberately vague expression "unnamed contracts" (to use the words of G. Chevrier),[110] a very specific juridical category lies hidden: the "donation" remunerated in the afterlife, or, the exchange of material gifts against spiritual counter-gifts.

And this exchange sealed alliances. At the Christian origins of the *tumulatio ad sanctos* [burial close by the saints] studied by Y. Duval (third and fourth centuries),[111] all the nuances of late antique vocabulary are used in the very limited space of funerary inscriptions to describe these relationships: one associates oneself (*sociari*) with a saint, ties oneself strongly to him (*coniugere*: as in a marriage), becomes his companion (*comes*) or his ally (*foedari*). In the Cluniac charters, the terms for this alliance are no less interesting. By covenant (*conuentum; conuenientia*), the donor is seeking the peace of his soul, for later; but here below, he is also getting good neighbors, and the fidelity and friendship of the monks; he is looking to enter into association (*consortium*) with their society, and to participate in their community.[112] Without entering into this lexical proliferation, let us simply retain that in a time of redistribution of power, and thus of the definition of alliances, material gifts and spiritual

---

[108] *Liber tramitis* (above, n. 2), 195.1, p. 273, l. 6.

[109] G. Chevrier, "L'évolution de la notion de donation dans les chartes de Cluny du IXe à la fin du XIIe siècle," in *A Cluny*, p. 203. On the idea of the gift *pro anima*, see also P. Jobert, *La notion de donation. Convergences: 630–750*, Publications de l'Université de Dijon 49 (Paris, 1977), especially pp. 213ff., 219ff.

[110] G. Chevrier, "L'évolution de la notion de donation" (above, n. 109), p. 208.

[111] Y. Duval, "Auprès des saints corps et âmes. L'inhumation *ad sanctos* dans la chrétienté d'Orient et d'Occident du IIIe au VIIe siècle," in *Etudes Augustiennes* (Paris, 1988), pp. 145ff.

[112] For a convenient approach to this question, see the table of Poeck, "Laienbegräbnisse" (above, n. 7), pp. 131–43, no. 7 [*Recueil des chartes de Cluny* (above, n. 15), 2116] and 86 (ibid., 2838): *societas*; no. 50 (ibid., 926), 66 (ibid., 2738), 71 (ibid., 2760), 96 (2083), 103 (ibid., 2879): *pars et societas*; no. 97 (ibid., 2090): *particeps et consors + societas et caritas*; no. 107 (ibid., 2905): "*ut supradicti seniores nos et successores nostros, ut fideles amicos et vicinos, diligant; et illi ex nostra parte quamdiu vixerimus fidelitatem et amicitiam habeant, et cum mortui fuerimus, animas nostras Deo commendent et corpora nostra sepulturae tradant*" ["so that the above-mentioned seniors might love us and our successors as faithful friends and neighbors; and that they might have our faithfulness and friendship as long as we live, and that when we should come to die, they might commend our souls to God, and carry our bodies to burial"].

counter-gifts founded a "community"[113] – a Christian community that is, after all, nothing more than the monastic side of the lordship. This is the "gift society" woven around the Cluniac convent, in the hope of eternal life.

In funerary matters, the monks were professional and effective intermediaries. Professionals, because in the distribution of tasks defined at least by the Carolingian era by the schema of the three functional orders, they were in position in order to pray; around the year 1000, these monk-priests become more and more exclusively the order of *oratores*.

And effective *oratores*, at that. The dead manifested this truth, and the Cluniacs wrote it down so that it might be known. Earlier, we alluded to the help brought by Odilo to the deceased Pope Benedict VIII. Jotsald, who reports the episode, gives us the terms in which the pontiff thanked the Cluniacs. In a dream, a brother saw the following:

> A person in a magnificent habit, in a long and white procession, entered into the cloister of the monastery, and headed toward the chapter, where Master Odilo was in the company of the holy senate, and he kneeled down humbly before this father. The brother asked who this resplendent person was. It was answered that it was Benedict, the Roman pontiff, bishop of the first seat, giving thanks for his liberation; it was thanks to the intervention of Odilo and his brothers that he had been able to escape from the monstrous chaos, and to fly toward the celestial beatitude.[114]

We can measure the persuasive force of such "fables" by reading the cartulary. Certainly, all the acts were written down by Cluniac notaries. But the benefactors, even lay and illiterate, were conscious of the document, and adhered to the formulas it contained. The pope himself needed the help of Cluniac suffrages. How then could they do without them? On the map of the afterlife, Odilo and his brothers marked the place of a purgatorial halt – in the South, on the left, alongside the barbarous Midi[115] – which ought to be populated; but once it had been populated, it was also important to help the unfortunate to leave in order to attain more favorable climes.

The monks charged for their services. By prayers, masses, and assistance to the poor, these spiritual men produced eternity. This was a saleable product. One had to buy one's part of the afterlife, given material expression here as a "prebend" (from the Latin *praebere*: to give) – revenue which provided for the needs of a pauper, a symbolic substitution for the dead. On May 30, 953, Raymonde, mother of Mayeul, future abbot of Cluny, made a donation of goods situated in the region of Mâcon "for the love of God, in hope of eternal retribution, for the soul of her father Mayeul, of her mother Landrade, of all her brothers living or dead, as well as for all Christians." In a passage of the act, she specifies the funerary goal of her donation: "so that in the place of justice I may have a fraternal prebend just like any one of the brothers of that place."[116] This offering permitted her to do "justice" to the poor whose maintenance in her memory is assured by the "prebend."

Let us note in passing that the gift, here considered as a funerary foundation, was an

[113] As O. G. Oexle has justly noted, "Memoria" (above, n. 7), pp. 87ff.: "Gebet als Gabe."
[114] Above, n. 38.
[115] Jotsald, *Vita sancti Odilonis* (above, n. 1ff.); in my opinion, this localization in the South ought to be considered together with the "*constitutio crucis*" at the end of book 1 of the *Historiae* of Ralph Glaber (above, n. 81), 1, 5, 24, p. 23: "*sic quoque omnipotentem . . . levam gentibus Barbarorum tumultuosus sortitur meridies.*"
[116] "*ut . . . in loco iustitie, et fratrum prebendam habeam sicuti unus ex fratribus eiusdem loci.*" *Receuil des chartes de Cluny* (above, n. 15), 843.

almost functional obligation in the society of the year 1000. In the extract already cited from his *Commentary on the Song of Songs* about the "orders of the Church," Haymo of Auxerre notes that if the Church is beautiful, it is because each order contributes in its own way: the holy doctors, by preaching; the continent (that is, the monks), by divine service; the married (that is, laypeople), by alms and their terrestrial activities.[117] The lay benefactor helps to make the monastery more beautiful, and thus participates in the brilliance of the Church. The cumulative effect of these penitential gestures was enormous. Without lay liberality, without this great zero-sum game seeking to prepare for death, and divestiture in favor of the monks and the poor, no more monastic foundations, nor ecclesiastical finery. The Church was beautiful thanks to fear of the afterlife. On the macroscopic scale, this was a considerable phenomenon: Christian society was built by these exchanges prompted by the dead.

These transactions of a funerary nature generated the most minute accounting.[118] The Cluniacs watched over the interests of their lordship. D. Poeck has thus noted that, under the abbacy of Mayeul, 18 out of 72 donations *ad sepulturam* resulted in land "districts" of the Cluniac sanctuary.[119] At times, the documents hint at the monastic appetite; for example, in an act from March 18, 1014, a certain Oddo specified that at the hour of his death, the monks should not ask for anything more, "without any other gift."[120]

On their side, the donors made their own demands, especially regarding burial. Some gave lands in order to be buried on them. Others asked that the brothers come to get their bodies in order to bury them at the monastery. Sometimes, the limits of deplacement are set. In a charter from February 979, Robert, "thinking of the future, and recognizing the enormity of his sins," gave, in order to obtain burial, some chattels (serfs), and some land; also concerned for the salvation of his wife Walburga, he indicated that the monks were bound to come get her body "either at Châteauneuf, or at a place sufficiently close that it is possible to bring her to Cluny."[121] In fact, the *Liber tramitis* anticipates and organizes the ceremony for the transfer of the body of a deceased person: the psalms that the brothers should sing as they go, the marching order (the young before, the priors after), the rite for lifting the body, and the return to the monastery.[122] This convoy is a kind of transmigration. And once the body has arrived at Cluny, it crosses the ante-Church, the Galilee, that transitional space *par excellence*, whose very name symbolically evokes the Paschal period and Christ's migration.[123]

[117] Above, n. 62.
[118] I am, of course, here indebted to J. Chiffoleau, who has masterfully elaborated the notion of the "accountancy of the afterlife" in his book *La comptabilité de l'au-delà: les hommes, la mort et la religion dans la region d'Avignon à la fin du Moyen Age, vers 1320–1480* (Rome, 1980).
[119] Poeck, "Laienbegräbnisse" (above, n. 7), pp. 106, 176.
[120] "*sine aliquo alio dono.*" *Receuil des chartes de Cluny* (above, n. 15), 2688 (18-3-1014); cited by Poeck, "Laienbegräbnisse" (above, n. 7), p. 127.
[121] *Receuil des chartes de Cluny* (above, n. 15), 1471; cited by Poeck, "Laienbegräbnisse" (above, n. 7), p. 107.
[122] *Liber tramitis* (above, n. 2), p. 282.
[123] See Matthew 28:16. The first explicit Cluniac testimony on this subject is very late; it is a passage from the *Miracula sancti Hugonis* (*BHL* 4013), where the basilica constructed by St Hugh is described in these terms: "*Haec (sc. habitatio gloriae Dei) eius decoris et gloriae eius, quam, si liceat credi coelestibus incolis in huiusmodi usus humana placere domicilia, quoddam deambulatorium dicas angelorum. In hac uelut eductos de carcere monachos refouet libera quaedam planicies, ita se monasticis accommodans institutis, ut angustia chori necesse non sit permisceri ordines, non stationes confundi, vel foras quemlibet euagari. Verum omni die quasi pascha celebrant, quia transire meruerunt in quandam Galileam, et libertatis nouae gaudio laetari, non murmurantes depressura, sed gratulantes ex latidunis copia, qua possunt uacare contemplationi*

This accounting of the afterlife was minutely regulated on the terrestrial scale. As G. Duby has magisterially taught us, the entire society of the Mâconnais of the eleventh and twelfth centuries swarms through the Cluny cartulary: clerics and monks, castellans and *milites* [knights], freemen and serfs.[124] To fix the degree of solemnity of one's funeral was to affirm one's social rank to those present and to posterity. We have seen that among the familiars, the Cluniac customs distinguish between the great and "*mediocres*."[125] This is why certain charters specify the "honor" claimed by the donor. Thus Wido, in 1020: "when my death is announced to you, bury me with honor."[126] As the act was being written, the Cluniac notary, so very keen on social classification, was informed of the precise kind of "death-style" expected.

Such assistance to the deceased was not without certain perverse effects in the middle term, which we will mention in order to conclude. In doing this, we can also see more clearly in what ways the Cluniac eleventh century was exceptional.

Like his predecessors, Peter the Venerable, abbot of the monastery from 1122 to 1156, became a propagandist for Cluniac efficacity in the matter of death. In a passage of his *De Miraculis* [*On Miracles*], he reported the apparition of Bernard Legros.[127] This castellan, a contemporary of Odilo, belonged to one of the most powerful lineages of the Mâconnais, a lineage that had been very intimately linked to the abbey of Cluny since the middle of the tenth century.[128] In addition, two of Bernard's sons had become monks there; one of them, Josseran, had even become prior of the monastery. The story related by Peter the Venerable is only the more exemplary for these facts. Here is his tale:

> After having greatly sinned, Bernard decided to go on pilgrimage to Rome, where he poured out prayers and alms. He died as he was on the road home, at Sutri. Several years later, Bernard appeared to the master of a Cluniac demesne, in the forest of Uxelles, near a castle that he had built many years before in order to pillage the area nearby. Bernard was on a mule, covered in fox skins. To his interlocutor, who was astonished at the apparition of a dead man, he confessed that he was expiating his past sins, especially the construction of this castle. His

---

diuinae absque tristitia" ["This (house of the glory of God) is made for His honor and His glory, which, if we were allowed to believe that human habitations are pleasing to heavenly inhabitants, we might call a deambulatory of the angels. In this church, a broad, open expanse revives the monks, as if they had been released from prison; this space is so well adapted to the monks' offices that it is not necessary to mix together the ranks because of the narrowness of the choir, or to mix up the stations, or make anyone stand outside. In truth, every day it is as if they were celebrating Easter, for they rightly pass through the Galilee and rejoice in the pleasure of a new freedom, no longer murmuring because of crowdedness but thanking God for the ample space in which they can devote themselves to divine contemplation without sadness"], *Bibliotheca Cluniacensis*, col. 958 B–C; text indicated by K. J. Conant, *Cluny* (above, n. 14) p. 60. On the problem of the Galilee, see C. Heitz, *Recherches sur les rapports entre architecture et liturgie à l'époque carolingienne* (Paris, 1963), pp. 206–9, which relates this term (and its architectural incarnation) to the Paschal drama (Jeu de la résurrection).

[124] See above, n. 9.

[125] See above, n. 60.

[126] *Receuil des chartes de Cluny* (above, n. 15), 2729; cited by Poeck, "Laienbegräbnisse" (above, n. 7), p. 128.

[127] Peter the Venerable, *De Miraculis*, 1, 11, ed. D. Bouthilier, Corpus Christianorum Continuatio Medievalis 83 (Turnhout, 1988), pp. 40–2 (= *PL* 189, col. 874, C–876 A). I would like to thank M. Zerner-Chardavoine for having pointed out this text to me.

[128] See Duby, *La société* (above, n. 9), pp. 336ff.

repentance *in extremis* had saved him from eternal damnation, but he still needed Cluniac suffrages. The cloak made of skins, which he had once given to a poor man, brought him an indescribable refreshment for the hour. Informed of this apparition, Abbot Hugh accepted the deceased's mandate, and full of the spirit of charity, gave many alms, and celebrated many masses to come to the aid of the soul who was carrying the weight of the eternal judgment of God.

The case of Bernard Legros could be multiplied by the thousands. The dead, and their symbolic doubles, the poor, were so well taken care of that the charge became unbearable for the monastery.[129] When the author of this tale, Peter the Venerable, became abbot in 1122, the convent had between 300 and 400 monks. However, as J. Wollasch has remarked, "more than 10,000 dead brothers shared the table of these 300 or 400 monks by the presence of the 10,000 paupers who received 10,000 prebends in memory of the deceased brothers."[130] These are enormous figures, tantamount to a city of the twelfth century.

We can therefore understand that Peter the Venerable found himself constrained, in these conditions, to reduce drastically the number of inscriptions to the necrology (a maximum of 50 per day). For the same reasons, the new orders – notably the Cistercians – refused to commemorate the dead individually. Other forms of solidarity took their places – especially the urban confraternities.

In concluding this study, is the historian (and not simply those drawn by funerary exoticism) recompensed for his pains? Why should we be interested in these affairs of the afterlife, at this period, in this particular place of Christendom? Because the Cluniacs of the year 1000 and their dead represent an exceptional observational field for so-called feudal society in the years of its birth.

Odilo and his brother were certainly the inheritors of an ancient tradition. Their doctrinal references were taken as much from the writings of the Fathers as from the works of Carolingian masters. They found in them especially useful frames for social classification, such as the schema of the three functional orders, with its origins in the depths of Indo-European history, and Christianized in the ninth century.

By using such authorities, the Cluniacs of the year 1000 certainly knew, as did all those who were lettered, that the ideal society was distributed in three parts that were unequal, but with complementary functions. The only things missing so that the system could function properly were the dead. It was the dead, in fact, who ordered the gifts. By exchanges or concessions of land, by prayers, through the building of sanctuaries, the redistribution of seigniorial benefices, and the maintenance of the poor, the dead were in some ways the very motor of this society that aspired to the afterlife. Without the socio-economic dynamic that the dead engendered, these ideals would have had no hold on reality. Therefore, we can understand why it was so essential for Odilo and his brothers to manage eternity. The cult of the dead was the touchstone of their theocracy; it was the driving force of their system of domination. Studying it allows us to understand how a sanctuary around the year 1000 could have all the functions of a lordship.

---

[129] On Cluny's economic difficulties at the arrival of Peter the Venerable, see the classic work of G. Duby, "Le budget de l'abbaye de Cluny entre 1080 et 1155. Economie domaniale et économie monétaire," in *Hommes et structures du Moyen Age* (Paris and The Hague, 1973), pp. 71ff.; "Un inventaire des profits de la seigneurie clunisienne à la mort de Pierre le Vénérable," in ibid., pp. 87ff.
[130] Wollasch, *Les moines* (above, n. 20), from which I have drawn a large part of this conclusion.

In the immediate term, and especially in the long term, the effects derived from the monastic management of the memory of the dead were hardly small. In the cemetery of the sanctuary, or in the books of the monks, begin the descendants who receive from Peter himself, "the keymaster of heaven," foundation and legitimacy.

Thus, in this period of the privatization of public power, the dead offer a marvellous inverted image of the society of the living. Among other things, they reveal the power that, here below, was conferred by the control of memory.

21 Literacy and the Making of Heresy, c.1000–c.1150

R. I. Moore

> The writing down of some of the main elements in the cultural tradition in Greece brought about an awareness of two things: of the past as different from the present; and of the inherent inconsistencies in the picture of life as it was inherited by the individual [with] the cultural tradition in its recorded form.[1]

What Goody and Watt describe as the consequences of the appearance of literacy in classical Greece are also fundamental to the religious reform movement of eleventh-century western Europe, whose manifold expressions included the first assertions of popular heresy since Antiquity. Hardly a source or a secondary account of that period fails to remind us that "reform" meant first and foremost a drive to recover the ancient purity and vigor of the early Church, as revealed by the lives and writings of its Fathers, and through them the spirit of the Gospels and apostles. If ever a movement was inspired by books (irrespective of its origins in radically changing social relations), it was this one. Anxious that monastic communities were failing to live in strict observance of the Rule of St Benedict, the spiritually ambitious left to live in the forests and on the mountainsides, emulating the heroes of the *vitae patrum* [lives of the Fathers]. Leo IX and his successors on the throne of St Peter appealed continually to the writings and pronouncements of their founding fathers to give form and legitimacy to their revolutionary claim to authority over the western Church and its ministers and members, and their antagonists replied in kind. Bernard of Chartres's famous image of the scholars as dwarfs on the shoulders of giants[2] asserted that the present was different from the past – and implied that the future would be different again, since by virtue of their elevated position the dwarfs could see a little further. The much humbler people who were arraigned as heretics before the Christmas synod of Bishop Gerard of Cambrai at Arras in 1024–5 replied serenely: "Lex et disciplina nostra, quam a magistro accepimus, nec evangelicis decretis nec apostolicis sanctionibus contrarie videbitur, si quis eam diligenter velit intueri" ("The teaching and rule that we have learned from our master will be seen to contravene neither the precepts of the gospels nor those of the apostles by

An earlier version of this paper was delivered at the annual meeting of the Medieval Academy of America at Columbus, Ohio, in March 1992. I wish to express my gratitude to the Medieval Academy, the organizer of the session, Richard Landes, and many participants in the meeting.
[1] Jack Goody and Ian Watt, "The consequences of literacy," in *Literacy in Traditional Societies*, ed. Jack Goody (Cambridge, 1968), pp. 27–68, p. 56.
[2] In John of Salisbury, *Metalogicon*, ed. C. C. J. Webb (Oxford, 1929), p. 136; cf. Brian Stock, *The Implications of Literacy. Models of Interpretation in the 11th and 12th Centuries* (Princeton, 1983), pp. 517–21.

anybody who is prepared to examine them carefully").[3] They spoke for their age in measuring their belief and conduct against the text, confident that virtue and orthodoxy consisted in stripping away the encrustations and deformations of tradition which literacy alone (though in their case indirectly) enabled them to recognize as departures from the historically authenticated canon upon which they took their stand.

The literacy of the eleventh century was the restricted literacy of all traditional societies, and had its usual corollaries – the mystification of the book, the social and political aggrandizement of those who had access to it, the consequent extension and reinforcement of social hierarchy, the identification of orthodoxy with privilege and illiteracy with unfreedom, and the elaboration of a concept of heresy to police the frontier between them.[4] Guy Lobrichon has recently discovered a new text, in an early eleventh-century manuscript from St Germain at Auxerre, of the letter in which a monk named Heribert describes *quamplurimi heretici* (numerous heretics) who had appeared in the Périgord.[5] They would not eat meat, drink wine, or accept money, despised the mass and hated the cross. They also possessed distinctly sinister capacities. Heribert had been present when "ferreis compedibus victi fuerunt missi in tonnam uinariam, fundum patentem habens, sursum clausum, deorsum custodibus adhibitis. In crastinum non solum sint inuenti sed nec semita eorum est inventa usquequo se representaverunt" ("they were loaded with chains and put in a great wine-barrel. It had an open bottom, its top was shut, and guards had been set over it. In the morning they were gone, and furthermore they left no tracks until their next appearance"). Heribert's letter has long been well known, but had been associated with a much later date. Lobrichon's revision, however, is not merely chronological. He argues powerfully that "Heribert" was not describing real heretics at all; the letter was part of a debate within the Cluniac order, and satirizes certain internal critics of the dramatic developments of the liturgy, and of the organization of the abbey's estates and relations with other Cluniac houses, which were taking place under the "imperial" abbacy of Odilo.[6]

This conclusion does not remove the Heribert letter from the list of sources for the birth of popular heresy. It only transfers it from the history of those who deliberately and publicly repudiated Catholic teaching and authority to that of the apprehensions and expectations about heresy and heretics which were entertained by Catholics themselves. Those expectations were largely formed and nourished by the warnings of the scriptures and the Fathers, but were expressed in response to contemporary anxieties and experiences, which sometimes but by no means always included encounters with real dissenters. The relationship between these two histories, logically and in fact quite distinct from one another, of heresy and the apprehension of heresy, is casual, fluctuating and often nonexistent. The value of Heribert's letter is not that it tells us what any real heretics were like, but that it shows what they were expected to be like, just at the moment when dissent was in fact taking shape among the people of northern Europe for the first time.

[3] *Acta synodi atrebatensis, PL* 142, col. 1272.
[4] Goody, ed., *Literacy*, pp. 11–20; cf. Patrick Wormald, "The uses of literacy in Anglo-Saxon England and its neighbours," *Transactions of the Royal Historical Society* 5/27 (1977): 95–114.
[5] Guy Lobrichon, "The chiaroscuro of heresy in early eleventh-century Aquitaine. A letter from Auxerre," in *The Peace of God: Social Violence and Religious Response in France around the year 1000*, ed. Thomas Head and Richard Landes (Ithaca, 1992), pp. 80–103.
[6] See also D. Iogna-Prat, *Agni immaculati: recherches sur les sources hagiographiques relatives à saint Maieul de Cluny (954–994)* (Paris, 1988); Barbara Rosenwein, *To be the Neighbor of St Peter* (Ithaca and London, 1989).

According to Heribert, "nemo namque tam rusticus se cum eis iungit, qui non infra octo dies sit sapiens, litteris verbis et exemplis, ut nec superari a quoquam ulterius ullomodo possit" ("no one, no matter how rustic, adheres to their sect who does not become, within eight days, wise in letters, writing and action, so that no one can overcome him in any way"). In this he anticipated the complaint of Bishop Roger of Châlons-sur-Marne, c.1043, about some people discovered in his diocese. "Si quos vero idiotas et infacundos huius erroris sectatoribus adiungi contingeret, statim eruditissimis etiam catholicis facundiores fieri asseverabat" ("He asserted that if simple, uneducated people happened to become followers of this heresy they immediately become more eloquent than the most learned Catholics).[7] The same nervousness is represented by the shadowy figures to whom the spread of heresy was sometimes attributed – the Italian Gundolfo, who (according to Gerard of Cambrai) was quoted as their leader by the men examined at Arras in 1024–5, or the woman, also Italian, whom Radulfus Glaber credited with the seduction of the clerks burned at Orléans in 1022.[8] Radulfus is also our source for the sad story of Leutard of Vertus, who some years earlier discarded his wife, attacked his parish church and embarked on a career of heretical preaching until he was exposed as a charlatan by the bishop and threw himself into a well in despair at the loss of his following. Radulfus lays heavy emphasis both on Leutard's madness (*vesania, insaniens*) and on his fraudulent claim to familiarity with scripture.[9] Although he does not overtly make a causal connection between the two, his story may remind us of the man whom Esther Goody encountered in Bole (northern Nigeria), whose madness was thought to be the result of his reading certain parts of the Koran without taking the appropriate precautions.[10]

The combination of anxiety that heresy would result from unauthorized access to the Scriptures with nervousness of the magical properties associated with books and their use is nowadays seen to be connected with restricted literacy, and particularly with the desire to sustain the restriction.[11] Even though (as seems probable) the actual diffusion of literacy in most or all of its forms was increasing during the eleventh and twelfth centuries, the principle of restriction was articulated far more clearly and asserted far more aggressively than formerly. In the ninth century the famous requirement of the *admonitio generalis* [General Admonition, an edict issued by Charlemagne in 789] that education should be available to the children of the unfree (though subsequently restricted to prospective monks), echoed in Theodulf of Orléans's insistence that priests should hold schools *per villas et vicos* (in every farm and district), confirms that there was no sharply delineated conceptual boundary between the literate and the illiterate, or any sense that literacy was inappropriate or undesirable in the poor or unfree.[12] By the twelfth century, when western Europe was changing from a warrior into a clerical society, the enormous power represented by the ability to read and write made literacy – Latin literacy, that is – not only an invaluable personal asset but an increasingly visible social marker. It was coming to be regarded, with celibacy, as a defining attribute of the clerical class which provided not only spiritual but administrative and governmental services and leadership, at a time when the power and

---

[7] Anselm of Liège, *Gesta episcoporum Leodicensis*, ed. R. Koepke, *MGH, SS* vii, 226.

[8] *PL* 142, col. 1271; *Rodolphus Glaber Opera*, ed. John France, Neithard Bulst, and Paul Reynolds (Oxford, 1989), p. 138.

[9] *Rodolphus*, pp. 88–91.

[10] Goody ed., *Literacy*, p. 13.

[11] Ibid., pp. 11–20, 199–241.

[12] Rosamond McKitterick, *The Carolingians and the Written Word* (Cambridge, 1989), p. 220; P. Riché, *Daily Life in the World of Charlemagne* (Liverpool, 1978), p. 199.

status associated with those functions was growing rapidly.[13] Since at the same time the perfection and promulgation of the seigneurial ban scored a universal division sharp and deep across western society, subsuming the manifold gradations of freedom and obligation among the *pauperes* [poor people] of the Carolingian world into a single servile class, it was bound to follow that literacy would be associated not only with clerisy but also with freedom.

Nervousness of heresy tended to exaggerate its power and sophistication. The rustics who questioned the necessity of church marriage, or the capacity of their priest to absolve in others the sins of which he had so manifestly failed to purge himself, were quickly discovered on interrogation to have been infected by the emissaries of a hidden but universal sect which preached a sophisticated doctrine of theological dualism. Clement of Bucy, near Soissons, revealed under interrogation by Guibert of Nogent in 1115 that he thought that *beati eritis* ["You shall be blessed." John 13:17 (not Matthew 5)] in the Sermon on the Mount meant "blessed are the heretics," but the sect to which he belonged "certe cum per latinem conspersi sint orbem" ("are undoubtedly dispersed throughout the Latin world"). Guibert knew how to account for that: "si relegas haereses ab Augustino digestas, nulli magis quam manichaeorum reperies convenire" ("if you look up the heresies summarised by Augustine you will find that this resembles none more than that of the Manichees").[14]

Guibert was rather ahead of his time. In general the myth of the medieval Manichee was a creation of the period after the middle of the twelfth century.[15] Until then those who encountered dissent usually accounted for it by postulating sources external to their own communities, but did not generalize whatever contamination they identified into an elaborate or universal stereotype. If, in the manner of Mary Douglas, we see this sensitivity to contamination as an indication of insecurity about social boundaries,[16] it would follow that, while such insecurities were certainly rife in the earlier period, the new social order which they sought to protect was not yet clearly envisaged as a coherent and overarching whole, as it came to be by the end of the twelfth century.[17] As society began to settle into a regular and clearly articulated hierarchy premised on absolute and unbridgeable distinctions between servile and free, clerical and lay, male and female, heir and younger son, the divisions between those organizing categories, crevices vulnerable to penetration by contaminating agents of one sort or another, themselves assumed a regular and articulate form, like the lines of mortar in a well-built wall. The Bogomil church, with its hierarchically organized missionaries, its elaborate mythology and theology, its deacons (of both sexes), bishops and pope, as they came to be imagined in the thirteenth-century West, was in that sense a conceptual counterpart of the society of the three orders. The parts (the Black Pope excepted) were real enough, but their sum was far less than the constructed whole.[18]

---

[13] Michael J. Clanchy, *From Memory to Written Record* (London, 1979), pp. 175–201; Alexander Murray, *Reason and Society in the Middle Ages* (Oxford, 1978), pp. 112–30, 213–44.

[14] Guibert de Nogent, *Autobiographie*, iii. 17, ed. E.-R. Labande (Paris, 1981), pp. 428–30.

[15] R. I. Moore, *The Origins of European Dissent* (Oxford, 1986), pp. 243–6.

[16] Mary Douglas, *Purity and Danger* (London, 1966), applied to Guibert by R. I. Moore, "Guibert of Nogent and his world," in H. Mayr-Harting and R. I. Moore, eds, *Essays in Medieval History Presented to R. H. C. Davis* (London, 1985), pp. 107–17.

[17] Georges Duby, *The Three Orders* (Chicago, 1980), pp. 271–353.

[18] Cf. the famous comment of Antoine Dondaine, "Le *De heresi catharorum in Lombardia*," *Archivum fratrum praedicatorum* 19 (1949): 280–312, pp. 292–3: "l'on parle du catharisme comme d'*une* réligion. . . . C'est là une erreur historique grave. Il y a eu *des sectes* dualistes, aussi bien en Orient qu'en Lombardie" ("people speak of Catharism as *a* religion. . . . That is a serious historical error. There were *dualist sects*, as much in the East as in Lombardy").

How the concept of literacy, no less than the fact, became in this period the great instrument of the power and influence of the *clerici* who appropriated it as a possession and prerogative of their class has been clearly established by the work of Clanchy, Murray, Stock, and others. The equation of illiteracy with the notions of paganism, rusticity and heresy itself served to discredit popular acclaim, as opposed to clerical authority, in other contexts besides the imputation of heresy, including, for example, the veneration of relics and trial by ordeal.[19] Thus heretics were effectively characterized in terms of the two great axes of the social revolution of the eleventh century, as those who lacked both freedom and learning, the defining attributes of legitimate secular and spiritual power, and who challenged the moral basis upon which that power was founded. Conversely, the same process helped, much more broadly, to establish a sense of solidarity and community among the clerks themselves, and to associate them firmly with the ranks of privilege, in contradistinction from the despised and terrifying world of the ignorant and brutish peasantry.

Popular heresy in the eleventh and twelfth centuries was in this sense a social construction. That it was also a great deal more is most obviously attested by its capacity to rally people to ways of life and courses of action which were different from those they would otherwise have followed, and often exposed them to real danger and hardship. As Eberwin of Steinfeld reported to St Bernard, of the first Cathars detected in the West and burned at Bonn in 1143, "Quod magis mirabile est, ipsi tormentum ignis non solum cum patientia, sed etiam cum laetitia introierunt et sustinuerunt" ("The amazing thing was that they entered and endured the torment of the flames not merely courageously but joyfully").[20] In the preceding decades Catholic observers had often been shocked by what crowds might do under the inspiration of heretical preachers, when Tanchelm of Antwerp had mocked the figure of the Virgin, for example, and his follower Manasses expelled the priest from St Peter at Ghent and took over the church, when Henry of Lausanne had precipitated an insurrection against the clergy of Le Mans, after which he apparently controlled the city for several weeks, or when Peter of Bruys presided over the burning of crosses and the destruction of holy images.[21]

Both the sneers of the clerks and the obduracy of the heretics illustrate Brian Stock's invaluable insight that literacy in this period not only marked communities, but made them. The clerical elite which was now in the process of formation (or, as it preferred to say, re-formation) and the groups which gathered around preachers and leaders like Leutard, Henry, or the early Cathars, are equally examples of Stock's "textual communities," for whom allegiance and association founded on kin or lordship, locality or vocation, were expressed in or superseded by those based on common loyalty to a particular body of texts as mediated by a particular leader.[22] They differed, however, in another and fundamental respect. The Europe created in the eleventh and twelfth centuries conforms very closely (even though it did not constitute a single polity) to Ernest Gellner's model of what he calls the complex agro-literate society, in which a very large number of producing communities, relatively undifferentiated in their internal structure and generally communicating with one another only at the level of local exchange, are dominated by an elite which is sharply differentiated internally (the three orders again) but owes its unity to a cosmopolitan high

[19] Stock, *Implications*, pp. 244–52; Robert Bartlett, *Trial by Fire and Water* (Oxford, 1986), p. 86.
[20] *PL* 182, col. 677.
[21] R. I. Moore, "New sects and secret meetings: association and authority in the eleventh and twelfth centuries," *Studies in Church History* 25 (1986): 47–68.
[22] Stock, *Implications*, pp. 88–92.

culture which it shares and monopolizes, and through which it exercises its hegemony.[23] It will be convenient to refer to these respectively as the "small" (or "little") and the "great" communities. Some of the connotations of Redfield's terminology are unacceptable,[24] but the terms themselves describe better than any alternative Gellner's essential contrast between the everyday social homogeneity and cultural particularity of the one, and the necessary commitment to cultural universality and social differentiation of the other.

The people examined at Arras in 1024–5, possibly weavers but more probably peasants (though seemingly prosperous enough to foreswear the use of domestic servants[25]), belonged among the producers, whose values they articulated clearly when they told bishop Gerard of Cambrai that the tenor of their teaching was "mundum relinquere, carnem a concupiscentiis frenare, de laboribus manuum suarum victum parare, nulli laesionem quaerere, charitatem cunctis quos zelus huius nostri propositi teneat, exhibere" ("to abandon the world, to restrain the appetites of the flesh, to prepare our food by the labour of our own hands, to do no injury to any one, to extend charity to every one of our own faith").[26]

The "textual community" of the clerks who confronted them, by contrast, was nothing less than the high culture itself, and Gerard was one of its most articulate spokesmen in his time, as he demonstrated in an elaborate and wide-ranging response which paid very little attention to what had actually been said by the defendants. His concern was rather to defend the external forms and rituals of the traditional Church against the intellectually innovative and socially destabilizing tendencies within the ranks of the elite which were represented by neoplatonist theologians, Cluniac monks, and the Peace movement.[27]

Gerard's fears that Cluny and the Peace of God constituted a threat to social hierarchy turned out to be the opposite of the truth. In that respect he made the same mistake as the free tenants and small landholders who flocked to the relics at the great peace rallies in Aquitaine and the Auvergne of the 990s. They answered the summons to defend the *pauperes* – that is, the monks – against the depredations of the universally reviled *milites* (warriors), only to find that the purpose of the canons which they swore on these occasions to uphold was not to overturn the seigneurial regime which was being constructed through the privatization and extension of the powers of the ban to support castle-building, forced labour services, and a vast range of new pecuniary exactions, but to ensure that control over it remained in the hands of the churches themselves and those laymen whom they recognized as legitimate.[28]

I have suggested elsewhere[29] that the bitter accusations of a popular heresy in the 1020s which Richard Landes has so skilfully set in context in his examination of the writings of

---

[23] Ernest Gellner, *Nations and Nationalism* (Oxford, 1983), pp. 8–13.

[24] Cf. Goody, ed., *Literacy*, pp. 6–9.

[25] Neither I nor, so far as I know, anyone else had previously noticed this implication of these people's insistence on preparing their food with their own hands: despite the concurrence of Walter L. Wakefield and Austin P. Evans, *Heresies of the High Middle Ages* (New York, 1969), p. 84. I cannot defend my previous translation of *parare* as "earn" (R. I. Moore, *The Birth of Popular Heresy* (London, 1975), p. 17). Nonetheless, the reference to the *supplicia* (torture) to which they were subjected before the hearing clearly implies that they were unfree.

[26] *PL* 142, col. 1272.

[27] Moore, *Origins*, pp. 12–16; Duby, *Three Orders*, pp. 28–43.

[28] R. I. Moore, "The peace of God and the social revolution," in Head and Landes, eds, *Peace of God*, pp. 308–26.

[29] R. I. Moore, "Heresy, repression and social change in the age of Gregorian reform," in *Christendom and its Discontents: Exclusion, Persecution, and Rebellion, 1000–1500*, ed. Scott L. Waugh and Peter Diehl (Cambridge, 1995), pp. 19–46.

Adémar of Chabannes arose from mutual disillusionment between Church and people upon the realization of that contradiction. Landes has shown how in the space of a few years Adémar, who had been an enthusiastic advocate, even architect, of the alliance between Church and people, became an embittered fanatic.[30] Disillusionment was completed by the humiliation which he endured in public debate at the hands of a wandering monk named Benedict of Chiusa, in 1029. Adémar had devoted his energies and writings for thirty years to establishing the apostolicity of St Martial of Limoges and building up popular support for his cult. To the vociferous delight of the assembled populace Benedict denounced it all as mere cover for the greed of the monks, and Adémar's life's work collapsed around his ears. In a subsequent rewriting of his history he uncoupled from a description of a tragedy that took place in 1018 (when the newly enlarged shrine of St Martial collapsed and some fifty people were trampled to death) the famous paragraph which announced the appearance of popular heresy in Aquitaine: "Paulo post exorti sunt per Aquitaniam Manichaei, seducentes plebem" ("Soon after Manichees appeared in Aquitaine, leading the people astray").[31] Instead of appearing as in some degree a response to this tragedy, popular hostility to clerical authority and avarice thus became the fortuitous consequence of contamination from without.

In that context we may see not only that the "Manichees" were Adémar's rationalization of the disenchantment between Church and people which succeeded the initial rapture of the peace movement, but also that here in Aquitaine, as in Champagne where Leutard had inveighed against tithes, and as at the synod of Arras, the expression of sentiments which churchmen construed as heresy stood for the assertion of the values and interests of the little community against the great. There was a contradiction in the ethos of "reform" which long remained unresolved. It had to appeal, both for spiritual respectability and intellectual coherence, to a universal ideal derived from the neoplatonist spirituality of the late Carolingian schools and given programmatic form and European-wide circulation by the Gregorian papacy and its agents, and for practical support in local conflicts to popular indignation arising from grievances which, though doubtless very widely shared, were nonetheless to each community peculiarly its own – demands for tithes and payments for services, the unfitness of priests, and so on. It was one of the fruits of the victory which had been largely secured by the first decades of the twelfth century that this contradiction could increasingly be resolved by designating as heresies those whose professed loyalties remained with the small community. The point is illustrated by the life and teaching of Henry of Lausanne,[32] not only the best documented, but the most articulate and successful dissenting preacher of the age.

Henry enters the record in 1116 when, having been admitted to preach in Le Mans during Lent, the vigour of his assault on the misdeeds of the cathedral clergy precipitated a popular rising. When Bishop Hildebert returned from the Easter synod at Rome he was able to expel Henry only with great difficulty.[33] This looks very much like a spiritual equivalent of the process of disillusionment over the wealth of the Church which had taken place in Aquitaine

---

[30] Richard Landes, "The dynamics of heresy and reform in Limoges: a study of popular participation in the peace of God," in Head and Landes, eds, *Peace of God*, pp. 184–218.

[31] Adémar of Chabannes, *Historiarum libri iii*, ed. G. Waitz, *MGH, SS* iv, 138.

[32] There is even less justification for calling him "of Lausanne" than "the monk" – the authority is Bernard in each case – but if it is untrue, the implications are much less misleading.

[33] *Gesta domini Hildeberti episcopi* in *Actus pontificum Cenomannis in urbe degentium*, ed. G. Busson and A. Ledru, *Archives historiques du Maine*, vol. 11 (Le Mans, 1901), pp. 407–15; Moore, *Origins*, pp. 83–90.

100 years earlier. That Henry approached Hildebert, before his departure, for permission to preach in the city – not the action of a heretic – and that it was granted, suggests that neither initially saw the other as an antagonist. For 20 years and more itinerant preachers had toured this rather backward region denouncing a conspicuously unreformed clergy. Hildebert had long supported one of the fieriest, Robert of Arbrissel, founder of Fontevrault, who had died in the previous year. To each man, in other words, the other initially appeared to be on the same side. Both were "reformers," for whom the clergy of Le Mans (one of whom was nicknamed William "Qui-non-bibit-aquam" – "who-doesn't-drink-water") represented the self-evident source of present evil as plainly as the *milites* of late tenth-century Aquitaine had done in their time. It was the intensity of the reaction to Henry's sermons which brought them to the parting of the ways, forcing each of them to stare down the barrel, as it were, at the prospect of popular insurrection and the overthrow of clerical authority.

The ancient choice which confronted them, between the light of conscience and the voice of authority, also had profound social implications. Hildebert of Lavardin, classicist, poet, and ecclesiastical statesman, represented to perfection a new and cosmopolitan clerical elite which was defined by ordination, but distinguished and united by its common Latin culture. The story of his journey to Rome and return in the nick of time to save his flock from the wolf which had been devouring its souls in his absence underlines not only the ultimate source of Hildebert's authority but his citizenship of the wider world by which the reforms he was introducing in Le Mans were inspired. Henry was as fitting a spokesman for the little community as Hildebert was for the great. He possessed a formidably articulate and consistent theology, characterized by stark individualism and uncompromising rejection of large and abstract structures of authority in favor of those firmly rooted in the community itself. He denounced clerical vice and avarice, and repudiated most sources of clerical income and power. He denied the authority of the Fathers to interpret the scriptures and insisted on his own right to do so. He maintained that marriage was entirely a matter for those concerned and not a sacrament of the Church. He advocated the baptism of adults, not of infants, and confession in public before the community, not in private to priests. In short, the faith he preached plainly affirmed the values of a world in which small groups of men and women stood together as equals, dependent on each other, suspicious of outsiders, and hostile to every external claim upon their obedience, allegiance, or wealth.[34]

Henry's impact on the people of Le Mans was not transient. "Eos enim Henricus sic sibi illexerat," concludes the hostile chronicler, "quod vix adhuc memoria illius et dilectio a cordibus eorum deleri valeat vel depelli" ("They had become so devoted to Henry that even now his memory can scarcely be expunged, or their love for him destroyed or driven from their hearts").[35] For another 30 years he ranged across southwestern France, reducing it, according to Bernard of Clairvaux, to a land where "Basilicae sine plebibus, plebes sine sacerdotibus, sacerdotes sine debita reverentia sunt . . . moriuntur homines in peccatis suis . . . parvuli Christianorum baptismi negatur gratia" ("Churches are without people, people without priests, priests without the deference due to them . . . men dying in their sins and children denied the grace of baptism"). "O infelicissimum populum!," Bernard continues, expressing with his own eloquence exactly the point I have been making so laboriously, "Ad vocem unius haeretici siluerunt in eo omnes propheticae et apostolicae voces, quae de

---

[34]   Raoul Manselli, "Il monaco Enrico e la sua eresia," *Bulletino dell'Istituto storico italiano per il medio evo* 65 (1953): 1–63, 41, 63 (Engl. trans. Moore, *Birth*, pp. 46–60); for fuller discussion, Moore, *Origins*, pp. 96–101.

[35]   *Gesta domini Hildeberti*, ed. Busson and Ledru, pp. 414–15.

convocanda in una Christi fide e eunctis nationibus Ecclesia, uno veritatis spiritu cecinerunt" ("Unhappy people! At the voice of one heretic you close your ears to all the prophets and apostles who with one spirit of truth have brought together the Church out of all nations to one faith in Christ").[36]

Henry is described by Bernard, in that same letter, as *litteratus*.[37] It is plainly no accident that we find this alternative cosmology most clearly articulated by the only dissenting leader of our period of whom it can be asserted with some confidence that he possessed a significant level of literacy. His capacity for abstract thought, and the acumen with which he handled himself in the debate with the monk William from which our knowledge of his teaching derives, would be hard to account for otherwise. Peter the Venerable read a book of which Henry was said to be the author, presumably the same one to which William refers during the debate: "De ecclesiis vero, quas in primo capituli posuisti dicis quod non sunt lignee vel lapidee faciende" ("In your first chapter you say that churches should not be made either of wood or of stone"), etc.[38]

Predictably, most (but not all) of the other dissenting and enthusiastic movements of the period are described as being founded or spoken for by disillusioned clerks or priests, who presumably possessed at least a measure of pragmatic literacy. Nevertheless, it would be quite wrong to describe the formation of these movements, the formulation of their ideas, and their capacity to attract support, entirely in terms of the impact of literacy (or even the semi-literacy of the ordinary priest or choir monk) on a nonliterate population. That would be to overlook the enormous influence of literate usages, especially in law and government, on the habits of thought and social action of those affected by them, even when they are not literate themselves – of what is called, logically if in some degree misleadingly, passive literacy. The point is very simply made if, returning to Stock's conception of the textual community, we ask upon what conditions it is likely that a text will gain such authority as Stock describes, obviously correctly, among those who cannot read it. The circumstances which assist a new religious leader to gain influence in any small community – social dislocation, exceptional need for impartial mediation, loss of trust by former leaders, and so forth – are quite familiar and have been exhaustively applied to the religious movements of the eleventh century.[39] But nothing in the theory of the holy man requires him to display, in addition to sanctity of character, the ability convincingly to claim textual authority for his prescriptions.

It is unnecessary to labor the extent to which, in Nelson's words, "a crucial feature of the cultural context of Carolingian literacy was the church's commitment to the practice of the written word."[40] It is perhaps not so readily appreciated, as she shows with great learning and subtlety, quite how widely and for what a variety of purposes writing and written instruments were used in Carolingian government, not only in the royal household but everywhere that imperial authority aspired to reach. Consequently, the Carolingian world experienced

---

[36] Epistolae, ccxli, *PL* 182, col. 434.

[37] *PL* 182, col. 435.

[38] *Petri Venerabilis contra Petrobusianos hereticos*, ed. J. V Fearns, *Corpus Christianorum, Continuatio Medievalis* 10, p. 5; Manselli, "Enrico," p. 61.

[39] Peter Brown, "The rise and function of the holy man in late antiquity," *JRS* 61 (1971): 80–101; Janet L. Nelson, "Society, theodicy and the origins of heresy," *Studies in Church History* 9 (1972): 65–77; T. Asad, "Medieval heresy; an anthropological view," *Social History* 11 (1986): 354–62; Moore, *Origins*, pp. 270–7.

[40] Janet L. Nelson, "Literacy in Carolingian government," in McKitterick, *Carolingians*, pp. 258–96, at p. 265. See also Mitchell and McKitterick in that volume, pp. 186–225, 297–318.

some aspects of the transition "from memory to written record" which Clanchy explored so brilliantly in Anglo-Norman and Angevin England. The subjects of Charles the Bald were accustomed not only to seeing written inscriptions and hearing bibles and service books read (or at least recited) in their churches, but in their workaday lives to swearing fidelity to written affirmations, seeing law preserved in and pronounced from written texts, having their dues and obligations recorded (and thereby limited) in written surveys, and title to land and the perquisites associated with it in written diplomas. All of these documents would be produced, read out and if necessary translated on the appropriate public occasions. In short, the conditions existed for a high degree of passive literacy. People were accustomed to hearing, understanding, and acknowledging the authority of the written word – and also, therefore, had a clear view of the conditions in which it ought be heard and understood, and on which it might be accepted as authoritative.

Once again the synod of Arras illustrates these points almost to perfection. When bishop Gerard had completed his long rebuttal of errors they had not professed, they were required to subscribe a confession of faith. "Haec quae Latina oratione dicebantur, non satis intelligere poterant" ("they did not fully understand it because it was in Latin"), it was translated into the vernacular, they swore that they accepted its tenets, and "ad confirmandum suae fidei testamentum, unusquisque eorum in modum crucis hujusmodi [cross in the text] quemdam characterem conscripsit" ("to confirm this attestation of their faith each of them inscribed a mark in the shape of the cross, like this").[41] The procedure is exactly that by which they would have witnessed a charter, or seen one witnessed.[42]

In associating the extent of passive literacy with the emergence of popular heresy at the time when Carolingian authority was in the last stages of its disintegration we may particularly note two further points in Nelson's discussion. First, she specifically includes among those in whom a high degree of passive literacy might be expected "the mass of free or freedmen landholders"[43] – just the people whose late tenth- and early eleventh-century descendants were finding their freedom subverted and their lands commandeered in the process of seigneurialization against which the earliest dissent was directed. Second, in discussing regional variations in the ways in which written texts and instruments were used, and hence the likely extent of passive literacy, she shows that it was not confined to Romance speakers, and that the crucial variables were whether the region in question had been part of the Roman Empire, or strongly influenced by it, and how long Christianity had been established there.[44] The earliest foyers of popular heresy – Aquitaine and the Auvergne, the Rhineland and the Low Countries – score high on both tests.

The rapidly rising level, use, and prestige of literacy in the eleventh- and twelfth-century West benefited those who commanded it in all the expected ways, including that of defining their status and extending their power through the elaboration of a concept of heresy and the means of enforcing it both intellectually and practically. But as its uses became increasingly general, and the habits of mind it stimulated spread to those who were not themselves literate, literacy also began to empower those over whom its power was exercised. The reading and translation of the confession at Arras provides a direct insight into the connection between passive literacy and the creation of textual communities by the formally illiterate. It may even suggest that if active literacy was a condition of the making of heresy,

---

[41] *Acta synodi Atrebatensis*, PL 142, col. 1312.
[42] Clanchy, *From Memory*, pp. 159–66, 202–14, 246–7.
[43] In McKitterick, *Carolingians*, p. 269.
[44] In ibid., p. 270.

understood as the creation among the elite of a conception of enforced orthodoxy, so-called passive literacy was equally a condition of popular receptivity to the active dissemination of heretical teaching.

However, literacy was not new in the eleventh century, and nor was its association with power. On the other hand, neither the fear nor the reality of popular heresy seems to have been a significant presence in the Carolingian world. Accusations were occasionally exchanged among scholars and ecclesiastical politicians, arising from much the same mixture of intellectual ferment and personal intrigue that characterized academic disputes in the eleventh and twelfth centuries, or the twentieth. There is little to suggest that they were turned outwards from such circles before the eleventh century, to be used as a means of asserting social distance or direct power over the *pauperes*, or conversely that frustrated, disillusioned, or rebellious groups among the *pauperes* expressed their grievances or aspirations through the medium of religious dissent.

It is clearly hard to think of heresy or dissent as in any simple sense a consequence of the spread of literacy, active or passive, if one was new in the eleventh century and the other was not. The case of England will make the point. There is neither space nor need to reopen here the old (and logically unanswerable) question why there was no popular heresy in early medieval England. The solution probably lies largely in the firmness of secular administrative control exerted over that much-governed country throughout the relevant period. Additionally, many of the functions which might have been served by religious dissent in the most critical decades, the later eleventh and first half of the twelfth centuries, were catered for by English-speaking hermits who were allowed to exercise a good deal of influence by the conquerors in a mutually convenient accommodation which it would have suited neither side to jeopardize by excessive zeal in matters of doctrine.[45]

The English hermits do not falsify the thesis that active literacy assisted the promulgation of heresy as an instrument for the fortification and aggrandizement of the large community, while passive literacy made possible the articulation of dissent in the small. They simply remind us that neither did so exclusively. Just as the imputation of heresy was only one of many through which the clerks of the twelfth century asserted themselves, along with Judaism, leprosy, sodomy, and others,[46] the articulation of dissent was only one of the ways in which the *pauperes* could attempt to proclaim their solidarity, or to establish the means of mutual support, the expression of shared values and the pursuit of common goals.

If literacy helped indispensably to sharpen and define the frontier between the "great" and the "little" communities after the millennium, it also represented a vehicle by which that frontier might be crossed – or breached. In that ambiguity lies the dilemma of the literate. However necessary it may be to insist on the harshness with which the new social order was ordained and imposed, no Catholic prelate could turn his back on the spiritual condition of the *pauperes* without making a nonsense of his office and faith. Nor did most of them do so. We need not make heavy weather of the elementary assertion that the western Church throughout our period was an evangelical Church, and took its pastoral responsibilities seriously. However patchy and imperfect the results, its commitment to the principle that its teachings and services should be available in good condition to the whole people was the chief engine of both the Carolingian and the Gregorian reforms. The problem of mediation

[45] Henry Mayr-Harting, "Functions of a twelfth-century recluse," *History* 60 (1975): 337–52.
[46] R. I. Moore, *The Formation of a Persecuting Society: Power and Deviance in Western Europe, 950–1250* (Oxford, 1987).

between the great and little communities could not be left to historians. It was a central preoccupation of ecclesiastical policy.

The solution which proved successful turned out to be one which in some ways resembled the heretic and his following, and was most directly in competition with him – the parish. On the face of it this may seem paradoxical. A great deal of what Henry of Lausanne opposed (and in this he was untypical only in the coherence of his thought) was directly, though neither exclusively nor necessarily, associated with the dissemination of the parish system – the payment of tithe and for church buildings, the sacramental view of marriage, insistence on infant baptism and on confession to priests, and so on. To that extent the growth of popular heresy in the twelfth century and beyond was increasingly a reaction against the success of reform.[47] But it had not been so from the outset. There is a good deal to suggest that at an earlier period the parish had often been seen as the expression of the community itself, rather than of the bishop's authority over it. The early dissemination of the parish system in much of northern and western Europe was closely associated with the extension of cultivation and the formation of new communities that went with it.[48] The reformers of the eleventh century and the middling and humble people who on so many occasions supported them indispensably had a common enemy in the system of proprietorship which converted the Church, its priests and its services into sources of seigneurial revenue. The canons of the Peace Councils are more than sufficient witness that popular enthusiasm was readily avail- able to secure the improvement of the services offered by local churches, including the maintenance of fabric and the support of the priest, on what was seen as the necessary condition of independence from lay control.[49] What was obnoxious about paying for the services of the priest, now and later, was not necessarily the payments themselves – after all, the priest had to live – so much as their appropriation by the lord, which not only increased the burden but, like clerical marriage, diminished the quality of the service. There are indications that an early effect of the success of the reform movements, and probably still more of the extension of cultivation in areas where those who could supply the labour found themselves to a degree in a sellers' market, was to give parishioners a good deal of freedom in the management of parochial affairs, and the parish itself a correspondingly high degree of identification with its community.[50]

The period of liberty (or anarchy, as it is more usually described in the context, to which it belongs, of Georges Duby's characterization of this period as an age of disorder between two ages of order) was, of course, short-lived. The control which had once been exercised by unreformed laymen was slowly but (on the whole) surely reasserted by reformed bishops. Once again, the parish priest might find himself caught in the middle, in danger of wander- ing into heresy as a result of identifying too closely with his flock. Albero of Mercke, near Cologne, lost his benefice in the 1160s for denying the validity of the mass of tainted priests, yet the implication of his position also was to reject what his bishop maintained, the

[47] Moore, *Origins*, pp. 73–81, 89–90.
[48] Robert Fossier, *Enfance de l'Europe, Xe–XIIe siècles* (Paris, 1982), pp. 345–58, 499–500; Leopold Génicot, *Rural Communities in the Medieval West* (Baltimore, 1990), pp. 90–107.
[49] R. I. Moore, "Family, community and cult on the eve of the Gregorian reform," *Transactions of the Royal Historical Society* 5/30 (1980): 49–70.
[50] Robert Fossier, *Chartes de coutume en Picardie (XIe–XIIe siècles)* (Paris, 1974), pp. 67–154; P. Duparc, "Les cimetières, séjours des vivants (XIe–XIIe siècles)," *Bulletin philologique et historique* (Paris, 1969): 483–504; Susan Reynolds, *Kingdoms and Communities in Western Europe 900–1300* (Oxford, 1984), pp. 77–100.

authority and ascendancy of the great community over the little.[51] Lambert le Bègue's criticism of the laxity of his fellow priests in the diocese of Liège in the 1160s led to his dismissal and imprisonment on charges of heresy, yet it is quite clear that the real cause of his troubles was too close an identification with his parishioners – including, to return to the question of literacy, making a vernacular translation of the Acts for use at private prayer meetings. It is notable that one of the accusations against Lambert, though he vehemently denied it, was that the most devout of his followers absented themselves from mass.[52]

Another indication that there was more in common than has always been noticed between the priest and the heretic, and between the parish and the sect, is the similarity of treatment accorded to them in the following century, under the provisions of Lateran IV. The determination of an Eudes of Rouen or a Robert Grosseteste to eradicate ignorance and corruption among his parish priests was not much more different in spirit than were the inquests they conducted in method from those which a Peter Martyr or a Jacques Fournier brought to the pursuit of heresy. One aspect of it is that, just as in the eleventh century literacy in the wrong places was *ipso facto* ground for suspicion, so in the thirteenth the priest's fitness to represent the great community to the little was seen to require that he should be literate. It was necessarily so, for the parish too was in its way a textual community, and in that capacity its institutionalization under regular auspices represented, among other things, acceptance that a society with the high level of "passive" literacy which we have identified as a condition for the successful dissemination of popular heresy required religious services appropriate to its skills and expectations. That, after all, was what the heretics had set out to offer.

---

[51] Moore, *Origins*, pp. 187–9.
[52] Paul Fredericq, *Corpus documentorum inquisitionis haereticae pravitatis Neerlandicae* (Ghent, 1890), II, 9, 36, trans. in part Moore, *Birth*, pp. 101–11. For discussion, J. B. Russell, *Dissent and Reform in the Early Middle Ages* (Berkeley, 1965), pp. 90–6; Moore, *Origins*, pp. 191–4.

22 Religion, Folklore, and Society in the Medieval West

Jean-Claude Schmitt

Choosing eleven articles written over the past ten years for a single volume obliges one to consider one's own reflections with a certain detachment in order to extract their common thread. Moreover, it leads to an understanding of how continuity in research is to a large extent implicit, undergirding those writings already published. These writings are merely isolated reference points until the time when the historian, reexamining his or her own work, deliberately attempts to establish a link and demonstrate coherency among them.

Paradoxically, a close examination of specific aspects of one's work also means understanding in a concrete way, and also with some apprehension, that the writing of history belongs to the era in which the historian lives and to the intellectual and social environment in which it is forged. Today we are far from the positivist illusion prevalent a century ago when historians thought it possible to disappear behind their texts, which could speak for themselves and tell "what really happened." Today we must specify the "place" we are coming from.

As for me, I belong to that generation of historians who, at the end of the 1960s, became aware of the importance of a few new factors in the study of societies past and present.

First of all we realized the importance of limits, what ethnologists have called the "margins" (after A. Van Gennep), or "liminality" (after Victor Turner). Societies always view themselves in terms of the Other, a figure that is necessarily fictitious in its discourse no matter what the objective reality is. Contrary to what was believed for a long time, margins, similar to the margins on a white page, the marches of a state, the frame of a picture, or the marginal figures in history, do not play a merely passive role of closure.[1] Instead, an otherness that resists imposes itself when least expected and puts the ball back into the center; it may be a dynamic principle in the social game.

Images of otherness are multiple and changeable according to the era and society. I began by concentrating on one aspect of "otherness" found in the ideology and society of the Late Middle Ages: that of the Beguine or the Begard, who were mendicants, although fit to work, and who lived in the manner of the religious but were wholly lay. What is the purpose of the

---

[1] As a starting point, I would suggest my article "L'historie des marginaux," in J. Le Goff, R. Chartier, and J. Revel, *La Nouvelle Histoire* (Paris: Rets-CEPL, 1978), pp. 344–68. On the approach of otherness in historical discourse also see F. Hartog, *Le miroir d'Hérodote. Essai sur la représentation de l'autre* (Paris: Gallimard, 1980).

"margin" in this case? It served to formulate, by means of accusations of heresy and societal parasitism (which incidentally were not well founded), a social order and a work ethic.[2]

Gradually I became interested in issues that were related yet at the same time dissimilar: those which arose in feudal society due to the presence of a folkloric culture that was distinct from the erudite culture of the Church. I will explain later what I mean by this. For the moment I would like to acknowledge my debt to Jacques Le Goff who, 20 years ago, was one of the first to highlight the importance of folkloric culture in medieval Christianity. Le Goff's work led to a different conception of the whole field of medieval culture and religion. It led to a reevaluation of texts as representing an exclusively clerical point of view, showing how some of these were products of an encounter between different cultural logics, products of daily compromises as well as, at times, true and real conflicts.

Secondly, historians in those years began to recognize the importance of the "symbolic" in the working of societies. This is not completely new: for example, it is impossible even today not to admire Marc Bloch's book on thaumaturgic kings published in 1924. Yet the very way in which this book remained isolated from the other works of this great historian and then was rediscovered tells us much about the evolution of historians' interests.[3] Obviously this evolution is linked to the major changes in intellectual life that have occurred over the last 20 or 30 years: the challenge to the more rigid outlines of Marxism (the intangible distinction between material infrastructure and ideological or institutional superstructure, the evolutionary and linear pattern of historical development) has coincided with the affirmation, as an effect of structuralism, of a logic proper to thought. I myself do not believe that a healthy criticism of Marxism destroys its pertinence or that an analysis of structures exhausts their historical significance.

By turning attention to margins and considering the symbolic, in both cases history, no matter what specific direction it took, encountered neighboring disciplines, in particular anthropology. Most likely the term "historical anthropology," by now a little worn, often hides the languid continuation of traditional historical practices. Nonetheless, it is necessary to go back 20 years in order to understand the novelty that this approach represented. On the other hand, the approach has not been imposed on historians alone: anthropologists have likewise seen their "terrain" taken up into the flow of history, which suddenly reared up in the era of colonization. European ethnology itself, abandoning its traditional identification of "folklore" with peasant culture, discovered the vivacity of a new popular culture, either working–class or suburban.

These changes have not left the historian indifferent. A new "territory" has opened up to their curiosity: that of popular cultures of the past. Beginning in the 1960s, one of the most noteworthy innovations of historical studies related to that which for convenience sake can be called "popular culture." The impact of this field is seen not only in the number of articles and books published but also in the breadth, the frequency, and the intensity of debate that these works caused in the academic world and by the resonance that the same studies had in the population at large. Why did this new topic appear among historians and why was it so popular?

Obviously the popularity of "popular culture" is not solely the result of the interests of historians as a group, or of the orientation of the social sciences in general. It is a topic that

---

[2] J.-Cl. Schmitt, *Mort d'une hérésie. L'Eglise et les clercs face aux béguines et aux béghards du Rhin supérieur du XIVe au XVe siècle* (Paris: Mouton/EHESS, 1978).
[3] The volume *Les rois thaumaturges* has been republished recently by Gallimard (Paris, 1983), with an introduction by J. Le Goff.

interests society as a whole and it is directly related to the most important changes that have taken place since the last world war, accelerated urbanization and triumphant industrialization, often destructive of the environment. Both of these phenomena have led to a fear in European societies that their rural and ancestral roots are being lost and that the natural balances are being broken. Did not the "paradise lost" of rural life have a sufficient attraction for the generation of lost illusions, which at the end of the 1960s, led a "return to the land" that had little future?

At the same time, becoming aware of the invasion of "mass culture," that is, of an apparent homogenization of culture owing to the effect of the mass media, has reawakened in some people ambiguous feelings of nostalgia for regional and traditional particularism as well as a hostility toward and contempt for a new culture denounced as "empty." Nonetheless, certain historians and sociologists have paid attention to the new wealth of sounds and images (from pop music to advertising), to the diverse social modes of consumption, and to the appropriation of new cultural objects, such as cinema and television.[4]

Alongside these changes the period has also undergone a vast de-Christianization in places where traditional religion had for centuries been an obligatory frame of reference giving meaning and temporal rhythm to human activity. Here, also, can be seen contrasting attitudes exhibited both by Christians and above all by churches: on the one hand there is the propensity to exalt a "popular religion" that clerics in past centuries had continually denounced, and on the other hand there is a more forward-looking view, found in the numerous postconciliar reactions, which has tended to accelerate the demolition of religious conformity in the name of a transparency and an authenticity that, it is said, reconcile Christians with their God.

Nothing here could be considered as outside the trends found in the history of "popular culture" or of "popular religion." What has happened here is the same that has happened for the history of death, as Philippe Ariès and others after him have shown. When our contemporaries, and among them historians, suddenly discovered the emptiness that "the concealment of death" had created around and before them, they turned to the past in order to understand how we had arrived at this and why today death no longer gives a sense to life.

The same holds true for the history that here interests us, but with a difference nonetheless: historians in this case seem much more divided, less unanimous in defining their methods and in evaluating the results. The history of death has also known debates, but the stakes paradoxically have seemed less "existential" to the historians concerned.[5] Debates on popular culture and above all "popular religion" have been more lively and the positions more insuperable because they have translated specific ideological preconceptions and positions found in the intellectual and religious environment of today. Has there not been a great continuity from the ancient Church to the modern university? And how can one not see that history, for those who today write it and make a profession of it, is like a mirror in which they hope to see a flattering reflection of what they think they are, but in which they discover instead a cruel image of what they really are?

I have no intention of returning here to a detailed discussion of all that recent historiography has had to offer on this subject. The articles that follow [i.e., in Schmitt's book] speak of that, the first one in particular [entitled "Folkloric Traditions in Medieval Culture"]. Rather I would like, in light of the most recent studies, to summarize the broad orientations of research on the subject and to set out my own personal positions.

[4] R. Hoggart, *The Uses of Literacy* (Harmondsworth: Penguin, 1957).
[5] Particularly between the historians Michel Vovelle and Philippe Ariès.

"Popular"?

All recent research has attempted to escape two opposing obstacles, the first of which is unanimity. This consists in describing Christianity as a perfect unity and defining the expression "Christian people" as nothing other than the community of the faithful in which each individual participates in a "common religion." In a broad and polemical article, the American historian John Van Engen has recently sought to rehabilitate such a vision of *christianitas* [Christianity].[6] He begins with a broad outline of studies carried out on the "Christian Middle Ages," noting that this notion was first strongly contested by Catholic historians, such as Gabriel Le Bras, Jean Delumeau, and others, for whom the countryside in particular was "Christianized" only after the Council of Trent. He then goes on to express his displeasure with the influence that sociology and anthropology have had on some historians, particularly Jacques Le Goff and myself, which had led to the idea of a folkloric culture "totally distinct" from the culture of literate clerics. Van Engen insists instead on a common religion, on its "customary" side, contending that within a parish context everyone participated in the major sacraments and in a common faith. According to Van Engen, we must study the documents that tell us about "ordinary" religious life and stop privileging "extraordinary" facts, such as the beliefs of Cathar peasants in Montaillou, studied by E. Le Roy Ladurie, or the myth of the holy greyhound Guinefort, which I myself have examined.[7]

I am willing to agree with many of these propositions. I believe, for example, along with my critic, that the parish was the essential element not only of religious life but also of society as a whole. However, I am in profound disagreement with other assertions he makes.

An *a priori* rejection of the methods and issues of other social sciences (sociology, anthropology, psychoanalysis, etc.) prevents the historian from correctly analyzing concepts such as rituals, myths, spatial and temporal structures, and the production of the imaginary, including visions and dreams. Interdisciplinary studies on these topics are more necessary now than ever, in the same way that comparative studies are, which alone allow us to understand the specificity of each singular historical experience. Any retreat into a "field" or a narrowly defined discipline is always regression.

According to Van Engen, the solidly learned, ecclesiastical, and Latin character of the documentation impedes the study of "popular religion," which by definition is lacking in written sources, proof that it is a secondary issue. The amount of documentation would permit us in some way to measure the importance of historical issues. The obstacle is certainly real, but this position confuses norms, which ecclesiastical texts hoped to impose on the "Christian population," with reality, above all the reality of the Christian population. It means ignoring everything that does not pass through the written and that does not go from "high" to "low" in the social body. It means ignoring what are diverse cultural objects (oral traditions, rituals, fables, legends, etc.) and above all cultural "logics," which are extraneous to the biblical-Roman foundations of the clerical culture but which can

---

[6] John Van Engen, "The Christian Middle Ages as an Historiographical Problem," *American Historical Review* 91 (1986): 519–22.
[7] E. Le Roy Ladurie, *Montaillou, village occitan de 1294 à 1324* (Paris, 1975) [published in English as *Montaillou: The Promised Land of Error* (New York: G. Braziller, 1978)]. J.-Cl. Schmitt, *Le saint lévrier. Guinefort guérisseur d'enfants depuis le XIIIᵉ siècle* (Paris, 1979) [published in English as *The Holy Greyhound: Guinefort, Healer of Children since the Thirteenth Century* (New York: Cambridge University Press, 1983)].

nonetheless, as shown by the cults of saints, absorb popularized aspects of the literary culture.[8]

The fact remains that Van Engen has also very conveniently highlighted the second stumbling block, that which Peter Brown has correctly referred to as the "two-tiered model."[9] I am well aware of the fact that certain formulations that are perhaps a bit too rigid or purposely provocative have led people to believe that I defend the idea of two cultures, a "learned" one and a "folkloric" one.[10] I believe that the following articles [i.e. in Schmitt's book] will show that things are, in my view, more complex than that. Nonetheless the strongly literary quality of the documentation cannot be used for arguing in favor of a "humanistic" thesis, but rather it reveals the extraordinary power of writing in a society that was almost completely illiterate. Moreover, it draws attention to a powerful form of control and thus also to possible points of contention and resistance, different realities of which the texts speak only in the moment in which they are suppressed. Thus it is not a matter of negating the essential unity of every society and culture, but the accent should also be placed on internal variations instead of being satisfied with a reconciliatory, customary, and mellifluous image that poorly masks the ideological preconceptions of certain authors.

An analysis of the vocabulary in Latin texts often leads to a "conflictual" reading of medieval culture. I know well how necessary it is to distrust expressions that, like *vulgus* [the people, the masses, the crowd], do not necessarily go at the same pace as the penetration of a folkoric tradition into learned documents. Even *superstitio* generally denotes "superfluous" and sinful behavior, even on the part of clerics, and not necessarily beliefs and "superstitious" practices in the sense used by Jean-Baptiste Thiers at the end of the seventeenth century, and other folklorists after him. Yet at the same time historians of *exempla* [stories that bear moral lessons for use in sermons] are well aware of the fact that using *dicitur* (it is said) at the beginning of a story does not necessarily indicate that the story was actually heard in confidence by a preacher in the oral tradition. It can in fact mean that he read it in the same manner as other stories that more properly begin with *legitur* [it is read (in the sense of it is written)]. Even supposing that he had actually heard the story, it was another priest who transmitted it to him. The same prudence must be used with the word *rusticitas* [rusticity]. Peter Brown has shown that in Late Antiquity the term did not necessarily refer to "peasant superstitions" but that rather it stigmatized the attempts of the Roman aristocracy to appropriate saints' tombs: for the aristocracy the funerary cults pertained to the private sphere, while bishops were trying to establish a public cult for these "very special dead people," who were saints. The bishops used this term to condemn the lack of *reverentia* [respect, reverence] owed to the saints and not in reference to "pagan survivals' in the Christian cult of the dead.

The fact remains that historians must pay attention to all these words, since in one way or another they reveal, in addition to open conflicts, the differences and fractures that prevent a unanimous vision (a vision that I believe must be transcended). The attitude of a historian

---

[8] A good example is found in the detailed study of F. Delpech, "De Marthe à Marta ou les mutations d'une entité transculturelle," in Y. R. Gornquerne and A. Esteban, eds, *Cultures populaires. Diferencias, divergencias, conflictos* (Madrid: Casa de Velásquez, Universidad Complutense, 1986), pp. 54–92.
[9] Peter Brown, *The Cult of the Saints. Its Rise and Function in Latin Christianity* (Chicago: University of Chicago Press, 1981). On this book and more generally on the current history of medieval holiness see J.-Cl. Schmitt, "La Fabrique des saints," *Annales ESC* 39 (1984) 286–300.
[10] See in particular my first critical article, which I will not discuss in detail here since it has already appeared in Italian: J.-Cl. Schmitt, "Religion populaire et culture folklorique," *Annales ESC* 31 (1976): 941–53.

such as Van Engen is very revealing to me. Calling into question the ethnohistorical studies that Le Goff and I have been able to make, and more generally our recourse to structural anthropology – and he cites what to me is the fundamental study by the literary historian R. Howard Bloch,[11] Van Engen finds nothing to place in opposition to these new approaches except the *summa* [thorough theological discussion] of the theological historian Dieter Harmening, which I consider useful in its content but no less contestable in its "theses."[12] Harmening's book studies the notion of *superstitio* in the ecclesiastical literature of the Middle Ages, and I cannot praise enough the remarkable erudition of the author. But after demonstrating how most penitentials, conciliar canons, and canonical summaries repeat, sometimes in their precise formulae, the accusations that Caesar of Arles made against "superstitions" in the sixth century (here meaning in the sense of deviations from the faith and from Christian rites), Harmening concludes that these texts do not help us to study popular traditions since the authors were content to transmit, with the sole virtue of literary genre, an empty form. Certainly it is true that medieval culture was largely based on the idea of compilation. In fact it is in this that medieval culture succeeded in manifesting its innovative genius through selecting, omitting, and transforming the cultural heredity trans-mitted from the past. However, the idea of passive repetition was not part of this, and hence it is possible that differences existed between the formulae and the "superstitions" that they presumed to condemn. Are we really so sure, by the way, that they reproduced without modification a more ancient text, for example that of Caesar of Arles? Even small changes can be highly significant, and Harmening himself does not fail to notice them in abundance. How is it possible not to be struck, for example, by the originality of the *Decretum* of Burchard of Worms in the eleventh century? The novelty of a large part of his content would have been unthinkable without the pressure of a specific situation, both in time (with respect to the tradition of penitentials in the Early Middle Ages) and in space (showing the meaning-fulness of Germanic traditions in the Rhine culture of this period). Here I am in complete agreement with the criticism formulated contemporaneously by the Soviet historian Aron Gurevich.[13]

I claim my vision of medieval culture to be complex. It certainly places in the foreground a fundamental opposition between a culture that is learned, literary, written, Latin, and clerical (the social realities indicated by these terms coincide only in part), and one that is folkloric. In this I mean an opposition both in terms of their content and in the logic of how they functioned. Why do I highlight this contrast? First of all, because medieval society belongs to the type of society anthropologists call "complex," in contrast to "primitive" societies, which lack both a written language and a state. Secondly, because the possession and use of written language in such a society represents an extraordinarily powerful tool of control, which was held above all by the Church (and even exclusively so insofar as the Church was the sole guardian of the interpretation and diffusion of the Scriptures, the sacred book), but then, beginning in the eleventh and twelfth centuries, claimed by others, includ-ing royal chancellors and then officials of other lords and by poets and authors of romances who created a vernacular literary language. The Roman Church remained up through the

---

[11] R. H. Bloch, *Etymologies and Genealogies. A Literary Anthropology of the French Middle Ages* (Chicago: University of Chicago Press, 1983).
[12] D. Harmening, *Superstitio. Uberlieferungs- und theoriegeschichtliche Untersuchungen zur kirchlich-theologischen Aberglaubensliteratur des Mittelalters* (Berlin: E. Schmidt, 1979).
[13] Aron Gurevich, *Contadini e santi. Problemi della cultura popolare nel Medioevo* (Turin: Einaudi, 1986), pp. 360–3.

later Middle Ages the principal bureaucracy, which better than all other administrations secured the triumphal combination of the written and the state.

There are multiple advantages for me to contrast this with the term "folklore." First of all, it allows historians to become familiar with the numerous and indispensable works of the "folklorists" and ethnologists. Secondly, it makes historians aware of cultural logics that were distinct from those of official Christianity, which have so profoundly influenced our culture. Finally, it allows me to avoid other expressions, such as "popular religion," which are much more loaded with historiographical and ideological prejudice.

The situation for me is even more complex. My vision of medieval culture is multipolar (and not dual), interactional (and not subordinate to univocal currents), and attentive to both mediations and mediators. Such "cultural intermediaries" (a general form of which the "organic intellectuals" of Antonio Gramsci [Italian Marxist social and political theoretician] are merely an example) played an essential role in the dynamic of the system. Put simply, I intend to accent relationships rather than stereotyped positions and "cultural levels" that could be established once and for all.

These relationships are not limited to the primary opposition of Church/populace. It is necessary to keep in mind the specific positions (in that which Pierre Bourdieu calls the "religious field") of the urban and rural clergy, the *ordinario* (the hierarchy of secular clerics), and the monks and friars, as well as the strategic positions of the parish priests and of the various social classes that formed the core of the laity.[14] This allows us to imagine far more complex relationships among distinct and multiple poles.

These relationships are not necessarily direct, but rather pass through intermediaries. I believe a very important contribution of the work of Gurevich has been his insistence on the role of a "middle culture" located between the oral culture of the laity and the learned and Latin culture of the clerical intellectual elite. Middle culture is defined by the work of those cultural intermediaries who were preachers or compilers, and those who wrote encyclopedias, bestiaries, liturgical and canonical summaries, and collections of miracles and *mirabilia* [marvels] for other clerics. Gurevich closely analyzed the case of one of them from the twelfth century, Honorius of Autun. We know only his name; we do not even know where he lived – this is also an indication of his social position and his role. Nonetheless his work, the *Elucidarium* (this name in itself [*Clarification*] is a whole program) was widely spread, first in Latin and then in the vernacular tradition of the *Lucidari*.[15] After the Middle Ages other cultural intermediaries appeared, this time also in the lay world. Do I need to remind anyone of the other prime example, the miller Menocchio studied by Carlo Ginzburg?[16]

These relationships did not work in one direction only, and they were not stigmatized as a "vulgarization" of cultural models or as a "descent" from high to low on the sociocultural ladder. Such a model was important both to society as a whole as well as to its parts, for example, the lay aristocracy.[17] It is also necessary to keep in mind the inverse phenomenon of the "folklorization" of learned culture: the whole field of narrative literature (*visiones*

---

[14]   P. Bourdieu, "Genèse et structure du champ religieux," *Revue française de sociologie*, 12 (1971): 295–334.

[15]   Gurevich, *Contadini e santi*, pp. 243–76.

[16]   C. Ginzburg, *Il formaggio e i vermi. Il cosmo di un mugnaio del '500* (Turin: Einaudi, 1976) [published in English as *The Cheese and the Worms* (Harmondsworth: Penguin, 1982)].

[17]   Georges Duby has been attracting attention for some time on this point. See "La vulgarisation des modèles culturels dans la société féodale," in his *Hommes et structures du Moyen Age* (Paris and The Hague: Mouton, 1973), pp. 299–308.

[visions], *miracula* [miracles], *mirabilia, exempla* [exemplary tales]) witnesses this amply and I will provide a number of specific examples later on.

The point at which all these currents met, which was also the site of the strongest tensions in the core of medieval culture, was consequently found in the center of this, within the circle of "shared culture," where objects and reason were exchanged and where thought, clerical and lay alike, functioned according to analogous rules, those of "mythical thought." This can be seen clearly in legends and folkloric tales, but also, at a more complex level of literary elaboration, in court romances, and finally in a large number of the texts and acts of the clergy itself. It is seen in the devotional literature of visions and voyages to the afterlife as well as in the network of symbols woven by liturgy in sacred space and in calendar time. Historically it was also in this "middle" yet essential part of clerical culture that the first cracks were found under the effect of "rationalistic" interventions by the most learned poles of clerical culture. There was a tendency here for the traditional symbolism of liturgy, which articulated the materiality of the substances (holy oil, the wood of the cross, the bread and blood of the sacrifice, etc.) as the powerful evocator of names and the form of objects and gestures, to be substituted by a spiritual *allegoria* [allegory] that was even more concerned with relating each of these elements to the major aspects of Revelation. It spelt the end to the polyvalent richness of the great Cluniac liturgy: in the thirteenth century with William Durand, theology (and more generally university science) created an opposition between the logic of contradiction and the logic of ambivalence, which was characteristic of symbolic ways of thinking and acting. In my opinion the historical role of medieval theology has thus been considerable. In fact it was here where western modernity was born by means of the internal criticism of the traditional religious language. It is in this "discourse on God" that God began to die. Moreover, for the issue that interests us, the emergence of this new pole in the dominant position within legitimate culture also had considerable importance for the formation of those persons (preachers, inquisitors, and the like) who were called upon to deal with the mass of the laity.

In effect it was clerical culture itself that first rejected "mythical thought," a process that began in the twelfth century, and that asserted itself at the end of the Middle Ages, in particular starting with the Council of Trent [1545–63]. Clerics above all were the ones who encountered this "mythical thought" and judged it with increasing severity in the great mass of the Christian population, in the folkloric culture fed by its local roots, whether in some village, or small town, or urban neighborhood. Thus the divorce had already begun in this period; however, it did not yet impede still numerous exchanges, which constitute a fortune for historians, because their documentation depends on them. Nonetheless, this divorce signals the beginning of a long process of marginalization, which led to the establishment of folklore as it existed in the eighteenth and nineteenth centuries.

"Religion"?

If I prefer to use the term "culture," it is naturally out of concern for inclusiveness and, once again, to make specific reference to the anthropological approach. I also choose it because when dealing with the Middle Ages, I mistrust the term "religion." The use of this latter term comes spontaneously, appearing particularly apt for the "age of faith" that the Middle Ages was. However, it also means forgetting the significance that this word has taken on during the last century, when it began to indicate a particular sector of human activity and thought, a specific category that was becoming isolated at the same time as were such others as economy and politics. The nineteenth century in particular relegated our notion of "religion" to "private life," which was simultaneously establishing itself in middle-class society. Religion, which continued to be ritualized and collective in many of its aspects, became an individual affair linked to the indefeasible right of the individual and considered to be secret from the public power of the lay state. From this derives the imbalance appearing in this era in the notion of religion that privileged content alone: belief and faith over collective rites. All of this, if applied without discernment to the Middle Ages, is deeply anachronistic. We have a good illustration once again in the article of John Van Engen, who does not hesitate to write that "in medieval Christianity religious culture rested ultimately on 'faith' or 'belief,' meaning professed assent to certain propositions as well as inner conviction."[18] That this was the ambition of certain clerics, or in any case of certain theologians, is probable. But the "religion" of the Middle Ages was above all participation in rituals and even more generally participation in an entire social organization and in the sum of symbolic practices and of relationships of meaning among men, between men and nature, and between men and the divine. All of this transcends to a large extent what we generally call "religion," and thus it would be necessary at least to speak about "the religious." Once again vocabulary teaches the historian: we will see later on how the Latin term *fides*, far from indicating only what we call "the faith," designates a whole social organization (*fides christiana*); or again, how the *credo* [creed, or official statement of orthodox belief], considered by Van Engen to be the pillar of *christianitas*, could be a formula valid for all uses.

Thus it would not be appropriate in this instance to make arbitrary cuts: in the Middle Ages religion was not an entity distinct from "culture," neither in the general nor in the anthropological sense of the word. In fact for the period I work on, I do not really see how to make room for a profane culture, meaning a culture that could do without constant reference to the sacred or to the world beyond death.

I do not even think it legitimate to analyze the traditional categories of "religion" and "magic" as two distinct realities. Just because they were distinguished and utilized as such by the Church does not mean that they are pertinent instruments of analysis for the historian, as we will see later on [Schmitt is referring to the collection of his own essays]. Their use in medieval texts is no less useful for informing us about different approaches to the sacred and, above all, about the relationship between ecclesiastical and folkloric culture. Keith Thomas has shown that the terms "magic" and "religion" do not have value *per se* but that they must be situated within their historical context of conflict in which the Church itself was a "magical agency" endowed, however, with the power to identify and condemn the magic of others: "in general, the ceremonies of which it disapproved were 'superstitious'; those which it accepted were not." Keith Thomas thus accepts notions of "magic" and "religion" but, like Peter Brown, he does so in order to show that they were instruments of a social conflict and of a politics based on language.[19]

Perhaps it is necessary to be even more daring and, like Richard C. Trexler, refuse categorically a type of terminology that creates constant confusion between the language of the analyst and that of the historical documents. "Religion," "belief," "spirituality," and even more so "popular religion" block the necessary delimitation of the object (in the case of Trexler, Florentine public life in the later Middle Ages and the Renaissance), which was instead based on the key notion of "ritual." For Trexler, this notion comprises public ceremonies, including interpersonal relationships and individual behavior, and it transcends or renders empty the notion of religion:

[18] Van Engen, "The Christian Middle Ages," p. 545.
[19] K. Thomas, *Religion and the Decline of Magic* (Harmondsworth: Penguin, 1978), pp. 53, 55.

Ritual is at the base of religion, after all. Our ancestors were right when they defined religion as a common behavior, and we deceive ourselves to think of it as a community of belief. A religion is a system of reverential behavior shared by a sworn community, and group authority is rooted in the normative replication of that decorum.

Starting with this notion, Trexler shows how the Florentine community created itself by means of a ritual that put people into relationship with one another and with the divine, all of which goes beyond the common meaning of "religion." Ritual is at the same time a staging of and agent for diversity, which cannot be ascribed *a priori* but which is the product of a permanent readjustment of classes in the city's public life: between non-noble patricians (*optimates*), artisans, Ciompi workers [day-laborers in the woolen cloth industry, who staged a rebellion in 1378], youths (*fanciulli*), women, and others. They are modifications on the relationships among these groups and classes that make up the plot of Florentine history, from the Republic to the establishment of the Medici family through Savonarola. Even in the extreme positions taken by the author, this study shows clearly the type of systematic criticism to which historians must first submit their vocabulary, shows how risky it is to delimit the object *a priori*, and shows, finally, to what extent the opening up of traditional history to an anthropology of historical societies can be satisfying.[20]

Clearly I am not advocating a separation between "religion" and "folklore" as the great Italian medievalist Raoul Manselli did. A historian of "popular religion," he defined "folklore" as a combination of beliefs which, coming into contact with popular religion, can either influence religion ("folklorization") or itself be influenced ("Christianization of folklore"), but is extraneous to religion due to its non-Christian origin. For Manselli it was a matter of "pagan survivals." He stated that folklore does not even have to be within the competence of the historian of "popular religion," who should limit himself to the "religious sphere." This would be the case of "a magic formula, an act, a story," that would have "no influence on religious life" and that, after having been "assimilated into the world of popular religion," would become once again "simply a popular tradition without any spiritual component."[21] Here we clearly see all the preconceptions of an approach that mutilates itself by cutting into the living tissue of social realities and symbolic practices in order to establish subdivisions and, above all, hierarchies that are completely subjective and exclusions that cannot be justified.

I believe it opportune to take into consideration three lessons:

1. In the first place, there is no such thing as an innocent and risk-free cut into the social tissue observed by the historian. It is necessary to conduct a global analysis of a society that has been fragmented by the compounded efforts of generations of historians (from the eighteenth century onward), who have divided the field into skills and "fields" with respect to duration (periodization), space, and object (distinction between economic, social, and religious history based on an erroneous conception of different "levels" of social reality). In the footsteps of Marcel Mauss [French anthropologist, 1872–1950], Louis Dumont, in defense of what he calls "methodological holism," has recently asked, rightly so, why on earth, when constructing a history of our society, historians have rejected that which is obligatory in the approach of the anthropologist when conducting an "ethnology of the other."[22]

[20] R. C. Trexler, *Public Life in Renaissance Florence* (New York: Academic Press, 1980), p. xviii.

[21] R. Manselli, *La religione popolare del Medioevo (secc. VI–XII)* (Turin: Giappichelli, 1974).

[22] L. Dumont, *Essaies sur l'individualism. Une perspective anthropologique sur l'idéologie moderne* (Paris: Seuil, 1983).

2. Without isolating in a rigid way various cultural levels, it is necessary to consider the dynamics of cultural exchanges among different poles that can be identified by their ways of thinking, their cultural objects, and the position of the participants in the social field, whose number and relative situations cannot be determined beforehand.
3. Thirdly, this approach noticeably modifies the issue of chronology, which is crucial for historians. From the moment when historians agree to speak in terms of structures and relationships, I believe that for them, as for anthropologists and linguists, synchrony [analysis of similarities apart from time] will come first, rather than diachrony [analysis of change through time]. It is only after having conceptualized the system of relationships that make up an object that it is possible to search for a comprehension of its evolutions and duration, or rather its intertwining durations, just as Fernand Braudel demonstrated some time ago.

The position I am defending here does not mean in any way that historians must abandon the requirements of their discipline, and I do not see how history could have suffered from a debate with structuralism. History as a discipline has come out strengthened, and I repeat my conviction that explanations of social phenomena in the final analysis cannot be anything other than historical.

It amazes me even more when I read John Van Engen saying that the recourse of certain medievalists to trifunctional Indo-European schema is witness to their ahistorical conception of folkloric culture, since the learned culture is the only one capable of providing a grip on the movement of history.[23] In Jacques Le Goff's works on Mélusine, and more generally on his trifunctional outline of medieval society, we are obviously dealing with something completely different.[24] These works demonstrate the formation of a specific economic and social system that managed to express itself at a precise moment and within a particular ideological framework. In addition it shows the distinctive medieval version of the model (how, for example, the medieval king incarnated the three Indo-European functions simultaneously and how in his role as sovereign judge he vied with the Church for control over the first function.)

The criticism surprises me even more because we have never failed to caution against searching for such extended continuities, more often than not badly supported by the documents, as to become mere postulates. One example of what should not be done is found in a recent book by the American art historian Pamela Berger.[25] Her attention was drawn to a particular aspect of certain iconographic images of the Flight into Egypt, beginning in the thirteenth century and becoming very frequent afterward until the sixteenth century: in addition to the holy family and Herod's soldiers sent after them, there appear a wheat field and harvesters. This scene evokes the "grain miracle," also found in the mysteries of the same period, but which is never mentioned in the Gospels or even in the Apocrypha. This legend tells how Mary, to flee her pursuers, asked a peasant who was planting grain (evidently in February) to tell the soldiers that he had not seen her pass since sowing time. As soon as she finished speaking, the wheat crop grew miraculously, hiding the holy family from

[23] Van Engen, "The Christian Middle Ages," p. 531.
[24] J. Le Goff, "Mélusine maternelle et défricheuse," in his *Pour un autre Moyen Age. Temps, travail et culture en Occident: 18 essais* (Paris: Gallimard, 1977), pp. 307–31, and "Les trois fonctions indoeuropéennes, l'histoire et l'Europe féodale," *Annales ESC* 34 (1979): 1187–1215.
[25] P. Berger, *The Goddess Obscured: Transformation of the Grain Protectress from Goddess to Saint* (Boston: Beacon Press, 1985).

the enemies' view. From sower the peasant became harvester, and the response that he gave to the soldiers persuaded them to abandon their chase.

According to Berger, this story, before it was applied to the Virgin, had already been introduced into the hagiographical legends of various female saints who had lived in the Early Middle Ages. It seems certain that these saints, because of other symbolic aspects of their legends as well as the fact that most of their feast days were in February, were associated with the protection of sowing. Yet historians cannot help noticing that the grain miracle does not appear in texts or images before the fourteenth century (in the case of St Radegund) and in other cases (Valpurga, Milburga) only in the folklore of that same century. No antecedents to the legend of the Virgin have been found and it is probable that the legendary life of the Virgin itself influenced the others. As a result the legends surely cannot be considered as intermediary reference points between an old mythical, prehistoric source, either ancient or Germanic, which the author attempts to delineate, and the medieval cult of the Virgin. In fact for the author the Virgin is merely the last incarnation of the same and "single magico-religious idea," that of Mother-Earth, attested to, according to her, in ancient civilizations (Anatolia, Crete, Egypt) and in ancient Celtic, German, Greek, and Roman paganism (Demeter, Ceres, Cybele, etc.).[26] Her arbitrary hypothesis of linear time and reductive vision of history, which abolishes all diversity, stand in opposition to a synchronic reconstruction of specific cultural systems, a first step in comparing them and eventually putting them into relationship with one another in a historical continuity. It is no less surprising to notice how far the old theories of Mother-Earth (and matriarchy), revived by a certain type of feminism, can still be taken seriously today.[27] In the case under consideration, it is regrettable how the author sacrifices the central thesis of her book to an obsession: the legend of the grain miracle. She forgets to ask questions about essential aspects of the legend, such as the reasons for accelerated time and for the inversion of time (the peasant harvesting in February), as well as, with reference to the words that the peasant must pronounce, the reason for the strategy, which was to allow the peasant to avoid telling a lie.

Furthermore, nothing allows us to state that folkloric traditions are immutable: quite the contrary. For me there is no doubt that the story of the grain miracle was formulated between the thirteenth and fourteenth centuries in a precise agricultural and social context, whatever prior elements became part of this unique legend. The real problem is to figure out how the tale was formulated and how it entered into hagiography and folkloric tradition. Only the historian, one who is sensitive to transformations of social structure and who sees these over the "long haul," can solve such a problem.[28]

[26] Ibid., p. 1.
[27] See the pertinent criticism of Beat Wagner, *Zwischen Mythos und Realität. Die Frau in der frühgriechischen Gesellschaft* (Frankfurt: Haag-Herchen Verlag, 1982).
[28] J. Le Goff, *L'Imaginaire médiévale. Essais* (Paris: Gallimard, 1985), preface, pp. xii–xiii.

Index of Persons and Places

Medieval History from Blackwell Publishers

ENGLAND AND ITS RULERS: 1066-1272
Second Edition
M. T. Clanchy
0-631-20556-X hardcover
0-631-20557-8 paperback

ABELARD - A Medieval Life
M. T. Clanchy
0-631-20502-0 hardcover

THE CATHARS
Malcolm Lambert
0-631-14343-2 hardcover
0-631-20959-X paperback
"*The Cathars* is to be welcomed as the most comprehensive and up-to-date treatment of the subject now available in English." *Alexander Murray, University College, London.*

THE CLOSING OF THE MIDDLE AGES?
England, 1471-1529
Richard Britnell
0-631-16598-3 hardcover
0-631-20540-3 paperback

ELEANOR OF PROVENCE. Queenship in Thirteenth-century England
Margaret Howell
0-631-17286-6 hardcover

ELEANOR OF AQUITAINE. Queen and Legend
D. D. R. Owen
0-631-20101-7 paperback

TO ORDER CALL :
1-800-216-2522 (N. America orders only) or
24-hour freephone on 0500 008205
(UK orders only)

BLACKWELL
Publishers

VISIT US ON THE WEB : http://www.blackwellpublishers.co.uk